BERKSHIRE
ENCYCLOPEDIA OF SUSTAINABILITY

VOLUME 7

CHINA, INDIA, AND EAST AND SOUTHEAST ASIA: ASSESSING SUSTAINABILITY

Editors Sam Geall, *chinadialogue;* Jingjing Liu, *Vermont Law School;* Sony Pellissery, *Institute of Rural Management, Anand*

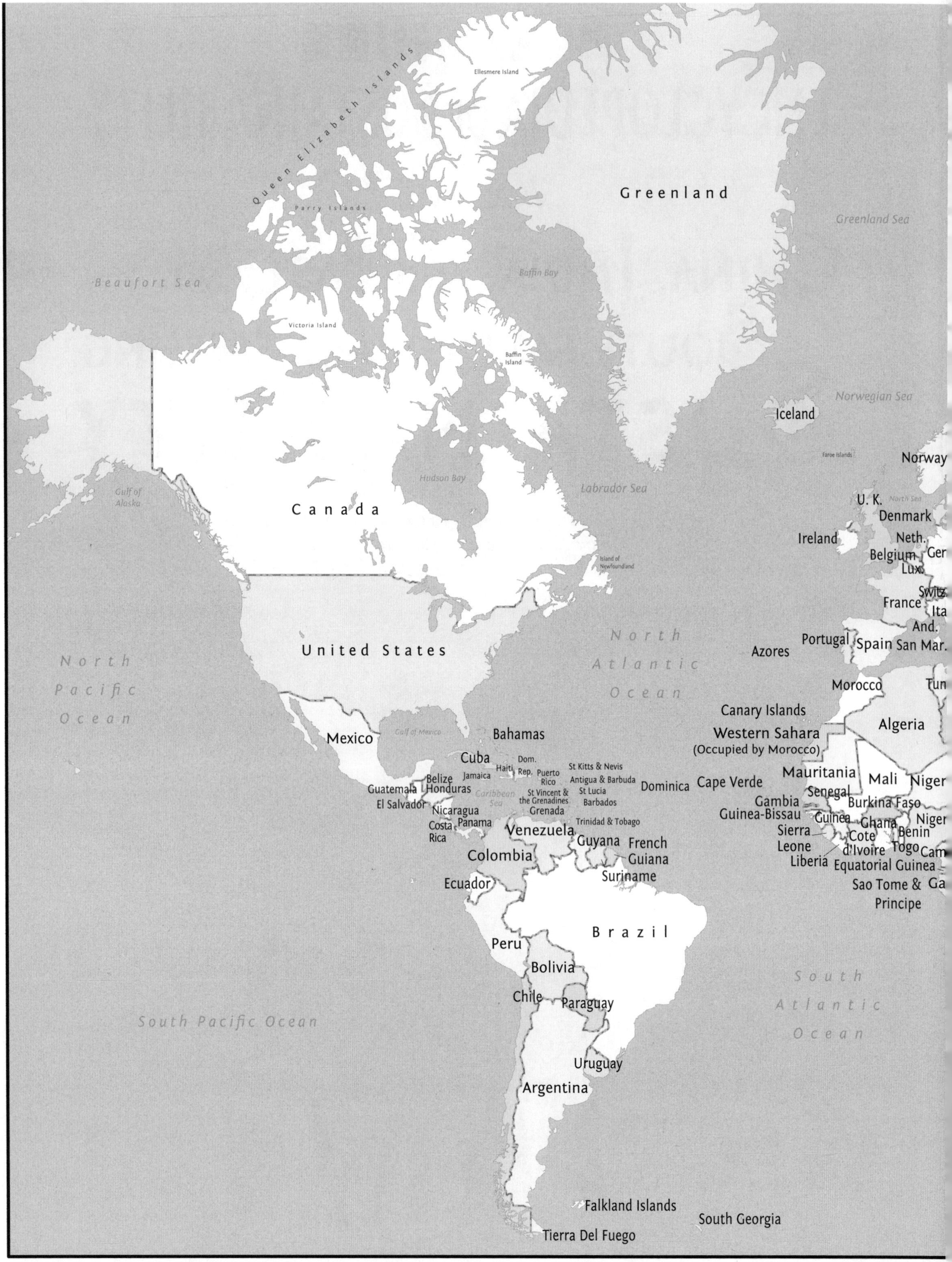
Queen Elizabeth Islands
Ellesmere Island
Parry Islands
Greenland
Greenland Sea
Beaufort Sea
Baffin Bay
Victoria Island
Baffin Island
Norwegian Sea
Iceland
Faroe Islands
Norway
Hudson Bay
Gulf of Alaska
Labrador Sea
Canada
U. K.
North Sea
Denmark
Ireland
Neth.
Belgium
Ger
Lux.
Island of Newfoundland
Switz
France
Ita
And.
North Atlantic Ocean
Portugal
Spain
San Mar.
Azores
United States
North Pacific Ocean
Morocco
Tun
Canary Islands
Algeria
Mexico
Gulf of Mexico
Bahamas
Western Sahara
(Occupied by Morocco)
Cuba
Dom. Rep.
Haiti
Jamaica
Puerto Rico
St Kitts & Nevis
Antigua & Barbuda
Mauritania
Mali
Niger
Belize
Guatemala
Honduras
Caribbean Sea
St Vincent & the Grenadines
St Lucia
Dominica
Cape Verde
Senegal
El Salvador
Barbados
Gambia
Burkina Faso
Nicaragua
Grenada
Guinea-Bissau
Guinea
Ghana
Niger
Costa Rica
Panama
Trinidad & Tobago
Sierra Leone
Benin
Venezuela
Guyana
French Guiana
Cote d'Ivoire
Togo
Cam
Colombia
Liberia
Equatorial Guinea
Suriname
Ga
Ecuador
Sao Tome & Principe
Brazil
Peru
Bolivia
South Atlantic Ocean
Chile
Paraguay
South Pacific Ocean
Uruguay
Argentina
Falkland Islands
South Georgia
Tierra Del Fuego

The darkened areas on this map indicate regions covered in this volume.

© 2012 by Berkshire Publishing Group LLC

All rights reserved. Permission to copy articles for internal or personal noncommercial use is hereby granted on the condition that appropriate fees are paid to the Copyright Clearance Center, 222 Rosewood Drive, Danvers, MA 01923, USA, telephone +1 978 750 8400, fax +1 978 646 8600, e-mail info@copyright.com. Teachers at institutions that own a print copy or license a digital edition of *China, India, and East and Southeast Asia: Assessing Sustainability* may use at no charge up to ten copies of no more than two articles (per course or program).

Digital editions

The *Berkshire Encyclopedia of Sustainability* is available through most major e-book and database services (please check with them for pricing). Special print/digital bundle pricing is also available in cooperation with Credo Reference; contact Berkshire Publishing (info@berkshirepublishing.com) for details.

For information, contact:
Berkshire Publishing Group LLC
122 Castle Street
Great Barrington, Massachusetts 01230-1506 USA
info@berkshirepublishing.com
Tel +1 413 528 0206
Fax +1 413 541 0076

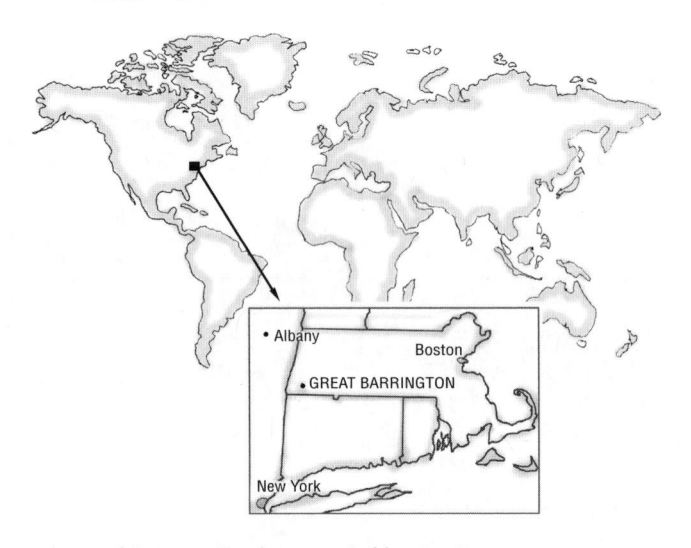

Library of Congress Cataloging-in-Publication Data

Berkshire encyclopedia of sustainability: / China, India, and East and Southeast Asia: Assessing sustainability, edited by Sam Geall, Jingjing Liu, and Sony Pellissery.
    v. cm.
  Includes bibliographical references and index.
  Contents: vol. 7. China, India, and East and Southeast Asia: Assessing sustainability —
  ISBN 978-1-933782-69-0 (vol. 7 print : alk. paper)
    1. Environmental quality—Encyclopedias. 2. Environmental protection—Encyclopedias. 3. Sustainable development—Encyclopedias. I. Geall, Sam. II. Liu, Jingjing. III. Pellissery, Sony.

Berkshire encyclopedia of sustainability (10 volumes) / edited by Ray Anderson et al.
    10 v. cm.
  Includes bibliographical references and index.
  ISBN 978-1-933782-01-0 (10 volumes : alk. paper) — 978-1-933782-00-3 (10 volumes e-book) — ISBN 978-1-933782-15-7 (vol. 1 print : alk. paper) — ISBN 978-1-933782-57-7 (vol. 1 e-book) — ISBN 978-1-933782-13-3 (vol. 2 print : alk. paper) — ISBN 978-1-933782-55-3 (vol. 2 e-book) — ISBN 978-1-933782-14-0 (vol. 3 print : alk. paper) — ISBN 978-1-933782-56-0 (vol. 3 e-book) — ISBN 978-1-933782-12-6 (vol. 4 print : alk. paper) — ISBN 978-1-933782-54-6 (vol. 4 e-book) — ISBN 978-1-933782-16-4 (vol. 5 print : alk. paper) — ISBN 978-1-933782-09-6 (vol. 5 e-book) — ISBN 978-1-933782-40-9 (vol. 6 print : alk. paper) — ISBN 978-0-9770159-0-0 (vol. 6 e-book) — ISBN 978-1-933782-69-0 (vol. 7 print : alk. paper) — ISBN 978-1-933782-72-0 (vol. 7 e-book) — ISBN 978-1-933782-18-8 (vol. 8 print : alk. paper) — ISBN 978-1-933782-73-7 (vol. 8 e-book) — ISBN 978-1-933782-19-5 (vol. 9 print : alk. paper) — ISBN 978-1-933782-74-4 (vol. 9 e-book) — ISBN 978-1-933782-63-8 (vol. 10 print : alk. paper) — ISBN 978-1-933782-75-1 (vol. 10 e-book)
    1. Environmental quality—Encyclopedias. 2. Environmental protection—Encyclopedias. 3. Sustainable development—Encyclopedias. I. Anderson, Ray, et al.
    HC79.E5B4576   2010
    338.9'2703—dc22
                                      2009035114

Editors

Editors
Sam Geall
chinadialogue

Jingjing Liu
Vermont Law School

Sony Pellissery
Institute of Rural Management, Anand

Associate Editors
E. N. Anderson
University of California, Riverside

Joel Campbell
Troy University

Joanna I. Lewis
Georgetown University

Muhammad Aurang Zeb Mughal
Durham University

Mark Wilson
Northumbria University

Advisory Board
Ray C. Anderson, *Interface, Inc.*; Lester R. Brown, *Earth Policy Institute*; Eric Freyfogle, *University of Illinois, Urbana-Champaign*; Luis Gomez-Echeverri, *United Nations Development Programme*; Daniel M. Kammen, *University of California, Berkeley*; Ashok Khosla, *International Union for Conservation of Nature*; Christine Loh, *Civic Exchange, Hong Kong*; Sunita Narain, *Center for Science and Environment*; Cheryl Oakes, *Duke University*

Production Staff

Publisher
Karen Christensen

Project Coordinator
Bill Siever

Copyeditors
Mary Bagg
Kathy Brock
Elaine Coveney
Cindy Crumrine
Carolyn Haley
Elma Sanders
Stephanie Schwartz Driver
Vali Tamm

Editorial Assistants
Ellie Johnston
Ginger Nielsen-Reed
Amanda Prigge

Design
Anna Myers

Information Management
Trevor Young

Composition and Indexing
Aptara, Inc.

Printer
Thomson-Shore, Inc.

Image Credits

The illustrations used in this volume come from many sources. There are photographs provided by Berkshire Publishing's staff and friends, by authors, and from archival sources. All known sources and copyright holders have been credited. We welcome further information from readers and will be glad to provide additional acknowledgement based on new information.

Front cover photo by Carl Kurtz.

Inset cover photo is of the Tianshan range, with Tianchi (Heavenly Lake) in the foreground. Photo by Joan Lebold Cohen.

The image for the volume introduction and index, titled "Grand Panorama of the Kowloon Walled City," is a schematic diagram of the Kowloon section of Hong Kong, as recorded by a Japanese team shortly before the demolition of the walled city. Retrieved from the Zoohaus website at http://zoohaus.net/WP/?p=4872.

Engraving illustrations of plants and insects by Maria Sibylla Merian (1647–1717).

Photos used at the beginning of each section:

A. *Agricultural fields, China.* Photo by Thomas Christensen.

B. *Bird in Beijing park, China.* Photo by Berkshire Publishing.

C. *Glaciers in the Himalaya.* Photo by Dan Miller.

D. *Forest view in Delhi, India.* Photo by Liz Wilkes.

E. *Cherry trees (sakura) in bloom during the Hanami festival, Fukui City, Japan.* Photo by Amanda Prigge.

F. *Forest and mountains, Japan.* Photo by Amanda Prigge.

G. *Antelope in Delhi, India.* Photo by Liz Wilkes.

H. *The Himalaya, Nepal, as seen from the Mercury-Atlas 9 (MA-9) spaceflight.* Photo courtesy of the National Archives.

I. *Road in Mysore, India.* Photo by Liz Wilkes.

J. *Sea lily, Indonesia.* Photo courtesy of NOAA Okeanos Explorer Program, INDEX-SATAL 2010.

continued on next page

K. *Petronas Towers, Kuala Lumpur, Malaysia.* Photo by Ameenullah, www.morguefile.com.

L. *Rock formation, China.* Photo by Berkshire Publishing.

M. *Construction in Mumbai, India.* Photo by Liz Wilkes.

N. Salmonella *bacteria in a Petri dish.* Photo by Jean Guard-Petter, United States Department of Agriculture.

O. *Coastline, Mikuni Town, Tōjinbō, Sakai City, Fukui Prefecture, Japan.* Photo by Amanda Prigge.

P. *Public park in Beijing, China.* Photo by Berkshire Publishing.

R. *Forest shrine, Eiheiji, Japan.* Photo by Amanda Prigge.

S. *Koi fish in pond, Nishiyama Park in Fukui Prefecture, Japan.* Photo by Amanda Prigge.

T. Panax quinquefolius *(American ginseng).* Photo courtesy of the United States Fish and Wildlife Services.

U. *Still image of Bangkok, Thailand, from video taken by the crew of Expedition 29 onboard the International Space Station.* Image courtesy of the Image Science & Analysis Laboratory, NASA Johnson Space Center. Still number ISS029-E-37074.

W. *People with camel on the Yamuna River by the Taj Mahal.* Photo by Liz Wilkes.

Y. *Yangzi (Chang) River, China.* Photo by Joan Lebold Cohen.

Contents

Map of the World   ii–iii

List of Entries   viii–x

Reader's Guide   xi–xiv

List of Contributors   xv–xxi

Series List: The Encyclopedia of Sustainability   xxii

Introduction   xxiii–xxviii

"Activism, Judicial" through "Yangzi (Chang) River"   1–402

Index   403–409

List of Entries

A

Activism, Judicial

Agriculture (China and Southeast Asia)

Agriculture (South Asia)

Association of Southeast Asian Nations (ASEAN)

Automobiles and Personal Transportation

B

Beijing, China

Biodiversity Conservation Legislation (China)

Biosafety Legislation (China)

C

Chennai, India

China

Cities—Overview

Climate Change Migration (India)

Climate Change Mitigation Initiatives (China)

Consumerism

Corporate Accountability (China)

D

Delhi, India

Dhaka, Bangladesh

E

E-Waste

Ecotourism

Education, Environmental (China)

Education, Environmental (India)

Education, Environmental (Japan)

Education, Female

Endangered Species

Energy Industries—Nuclear

Energy Industries—Renewables (China)

Energy Industries—Renewables (India)

Energy Security (East Asia)

F

Fisheries (China)

Five-Year Plans

G

Gandhism

Ganges River

Gender Equality

Genetic Resources

Great Green Wall (China)

Green Collar Jobs

Guangzhou, China

H

The Himalaya

Huang (Yellow) River

I

India

Indigenous Peoples

Information and Communication Technologies (ICT)

J

Jakarta, Indonesia

Japan

K

Korean Peninsula

Kuala Lumpur, Malaysia

L

Labor

M

Media Coverage of the Environment

Mekong-Lancang River

Microfinance

Mumbai, India

N

Nanotechnology

National Pollution Survey (China)

Nongovernmental Organizations (NGOs)

O

One-Child Policy

Outsourcing and Offshoring

P

Parks and Preserves

Pearl River Delta

Property Rights (China)

Public Health

Public–Private Partnerships

Public Transportation

R

Reforestation and Afforestation (Southeast Asia)

Religions

Rule of Law

Rural Development

Rural Livelihoods

S

Shanghai, China

Singapore

South–North Water Diversion

Southeast Asia

Steel Industry

T

Three Gorges Dam

Tibetan Plateau

Tokyo, Japan

Traditional Chinese Medicine (TCM)

Traditional Knowledge (China)

Traditional Knowledge (India)

Transboundary Water Issues

U

Utilities Regulation and Energy Efficiency

W

Water Security

Water Use and Rights (India)

White Revolution of India

Y

Yangzi (Chang) River

Reader's Guide: Articles by Category

Note: most articles appear in more than one category

BUSINESS AND ECONOMICS

Automobiles and Personal Transportation

Consumerism

Corporate Accountability (China)

Ecotourism

Five-Year Plans

Green Collar Jobs

Labor

Microfinance

Outsourcing and Offshoring

Public-Private Partnerships

Steel Industry

ENVIRONMENTAL HISTORY

China

Ganges River

Himalaya, The

Huang (Yellow) River

India

Indigenous Peoples

Japan

Korean Peninsula

Mekong-Lancang River

Parks and Preserves

Pearl River Delta

Southeast Asia

Tibetan Plateau

Traditional Knowledge (China)

Traditional Knowledge (India)

White Revolution of India

Yangzi (Chang) River

HUMAN AND PHYSICAL GEOGRAPHY

Beijing, China

Chennai, India

Cities—Overview

Climate Change Migration (India)

Climate Change Mitigation Initiatives (China)

Delhi, India

Dhaka, Bangladesh

Ganges River

Guangzhou, China

Himalaya, The

Huang (Yellow) River

Indigenous Peoples

Jakarta, Indonesia

Kuala Lumpur, Malaysia

Mekong-Lancang River

Mumbai, India

One-Child Policy

Parks and Preserves

Pearl River Delta

Property Rights (China)

Rural Development

Rural Livelihoods

Shanghai, China

Singapore

Tibetan Plateau

Tokyo, Japan

Water Security

Yangzi (Chang) River

Industry and Manufacturing

Automobiles and Personal Transportation

Beijing, China

Consumerism

Energy Industries—Nuclear

Energy Industries—Renewables (China)

Energy Industries—Renewables (India)

E-Waste

Green Collar Jobs

Information and Communication Technologies (ICT)

Labor

Nanotechnology

Outsourcing and Offshoring

Shanghai, China

Steel Industry

Utilities Regulation and Energy Efficiency

Tokyo, Japan

Natural Resources

Agriculture (China and Southeast Asia)

Agriculture (South Asia)

Ecotourism

Endangered Species

Fisheries (China)

Huang (Yellow) River

Ganges River

Genetic Resources

Mekong-Lancang River

Parks and Preserves

Pearl River Delta

Reforestation and Afforestation (Southeast Asia)

Rural Livelihoods

South–North Water Diversion

Traditional Chinese Medicine (TCM)

Transboundary Water Issues

Water Security

Water Use and Rights (India)

Yangzi (Chang) River

Politics, Law, and Government

Activism, Judicial

Association of Southeast Asian Nations (ASEAN)

Biodiversity Conservation Legislation (China)

Biosafety Legislation (China)

Five-Year Plans

Gandhism

One-Child Policy

Property Rights (China)

Rule of Law

Transboundary Water Issues

Utilities Regulation and Energy Efficiency

Water Security

Water Use and Rights (India)

Science, Technology, and Medicine

Automobiles (India and China)

Biosafety Legislation (China)

Energy Industries—Nuclear

Energy Industries—Renewables (China)

Energy Industries—Renewables (India)

Energy Security (East Asia)

E-Waste

Genetic Resources

Great Green Wall (China)

Green Collar Jobs

Information and Communication Technologies (ICT)

Nanotechnology

South–North Water Diversion

Three Gorges Dam

Traditional Chinese Medicine (TCM)

Utilities Regulation and Energy Efficiency

Society and Social Welfare

Agriculture (China and Southeast Asia)

Agriculture (South Asia)

Climate Change Migration (India)

Consumerism

Ecotourism

Education, Environmental (China)

Education, Environmental (India)

Education, Environmental (Japan)

Education, Female

E-Waste

Fisheries (China)

Gandhism

Gender Equality

Indigenous Peoples

Labor

Media Coverage of the Environment

Microfinance

National Pollution Survey (China)

Nongovernmental Organizations (NGOs)

One-Child Policy

Public Health

Public Transportation

Religions

Rural Development

Rural Livelihoods

Traditional Chinese Medicine (TCM)

Traditional Knowledge (China)

Traditional Knowledge (India)

Water Security

Water Use and Rights (India)

White Revolution of India

List of Contributors

Abe, Osamu
Rikkyo University
Education, Environmental (Japan)

Abedin, Jakerul
Macquarie University
Transboundary Water Issues

Adnan, Md. Sarfaraz Gani
Chittagong University of Engineering and Technology (CUET)
Dhaka, Bangladesh (co-author: Carolyn Roberts)

Albright, Scott M.
University of Hawaii at Hilo
Jakarta, Indonesia

Allison, Elizabeth
California Institute of Integral Studies
Himalaya, The

Arora, Aanchal
TERI University, New Delhi
Automobiles and Personal Transportation (co-author: Kaushik Ranjan Bandyopadhyay)

Bai, Xuemei
The Australian National University
Cities—Overview

Bandyopadhyay, Kaushik Ranjan
TERI University, New Delhi
Automobiles and Personal Transportation (co-author: Aanchal Arora)

Banerjee, Tirtho
Journalist, Lucknow, India
Ganges River

Bastakoti, Ram Chandra
Asian Institute of Technology, Klong Luang, Pathumthani, Thailand
Mekong-Lancang River (co-authors: Joyeeta Gupta and Hao Li)

Bhandari, Vivek
Independent scholar, Jaipur, India
Education, Environmental (India) (co-author: Rahul Ghai)

Bharucha, Zareen Pervez
University of Essex
Agriculture (South Asia)
Water Security

Bharvirkar, Ranjit
Itron Inc.
Utilities Regulation and Energy Efficiency (co-authors: Chris Greacen, Chuenchom Sangarasri Greacen, Fredrich Kahrl, Mahesh Patankar, Priya Sreedharan, and James H. Williams)

Bhushan Sharan, Awadhendra
Centre for the Study of Developing
  Societies, Delhi
Delhi, India

Boas, Ingrid
University of Kent
Climate Change Migration (India)

Briones, Ruth P.
Greenergy Solutions Inc., Quezon City,
  The Philippines
Public-Private Partnerships

Buckley, Ralf
Griffith University, Australia
Ecotourism

Chapple, Christopher Key
Loyola Marymount University
Religions

Cheng, Gong
Minzu University of China
Traditional Chinese Medicine (TCM)

Cui Can
Beijing Institute of Technology Law School
National Pollution Survey (China)
  (co-author: Gong Xiangqian)

Cullet, Philippe
University of London
Water Use and Rights (India)

Cumo, Christopher M.
Independent scholar, Canton, Ohio, USA
Agriculture (China and Southeast Asia)

Cybriwsky, Roman Adrian
Temple University
Tokyo, Japan

Dodgen, Randall
Sonoma State University
Huang (Yellow) River

Dummer, Trevor J. B.
Dalhousie University
Public Health

Eiselen, Sieg
University of South Africa
E-Waste

Eisen, Joel Barry
University of Richmond
Energy Industries—Renewables (China)

Erasga, Dennis S.
De La Salle University–Manila
Indigenous Peoples

Forbes, William
Stephen F. Austin State University
Korean Peninsula

Geall, Sam
chinadialogue
Five-Year Plans (co-author:
  Sony Pellissery)
Media Coverage of the Environment

Gerth, Karl
University of Oxford
Consumerism

Ghai, Rahul
Independent development practitioner, Western Rajasthan
Education, Environmental (India) (co-author: Vivek Bhandari)

Gong Xiangqian
Beijing Institute of Technology Law School
National Pollution Survey (China) (co-author: Cui Can)

Greacen, Chris
Palang Thai
Utilities Regulation and Energy Efficiency (co-authors: Ranjit Bharvirkar, Chuenchom Sangarasri Greacen, Fredrich Kahrl, Mahesh Patankar, Priya Sreedharan, and James H. Williams)

Greacen, Chuenchom Sangarasri
Palang Thai
Utilities Regulation and Energy Efficiency (co-authors: Ranjit Bharvirkar, Chris Greacen, Fredrich Kahrl, Mahesh Patankar, Priya Sreedharan, and James H. Williams)

Green, Gary P.
University of Wisconsin, Madison
Green Collar Jobs (co-author: Yifei Li)

Gu, Dejin
Sun Yat-sen University Law School
Activism, Judicial (co-author: Jingjing Liu)

Guo, Xiumei
Curtin University
One-Child Policy (co-author: Dora Marinova)

Gupta, Joyeeta
UNESCO-IHE Institute for Water Education, Delft, The Netherlands
Mekong-Lancang River (co-authors: Ram Chandra Bastakoti and Hao Li)

Halim, Sadeka
University of Dhaka
Gender Equality (co-author: Muhammad Zakir Hossin)

Hayes, Peter
Nautilus Institute at Global Studies, RMIT University
Energy Security (East Asia) (co-authors: Fredrich Kahrl, David F. von Hippel, and James H. Williams)

Hilger, Tim
National University of Singapore
Nanotechnology (co-author: Darryl S. L. Jarvis)

Horgan, John C.
Concordia University–Wisconsin
Shanghai, China

Hossin, Muhammad Zakir
ASA University Bangladesh (ASAUB)
Gender Equality (co-author: Sadeka Halim)

Jain, Vaneesha
Luthra and Luthra Law Offices
Traditional Knowledge (India)

Jarvis, Darryl S. L.
National University of Singapore
Nanotechnology (co-author: Tim Hilger)

Jhunjhunwala, Ashok
Indian Institute of Technology (IIT) Madras
Information and Communication Technologies (ICT) (co-author: Janani Rangarajan)

Ji, Xia
University of Regina
Education, Environmental (China)

Jiang, Hong
University of Hawaii at Manoa
Great Green Wall (China)

Kahrl, Fredrich
Energy and Environmental Economics, Inc.
Energy Security (East Asia) (co-authors: Peter Hayes, David F. von Hippel, and James H. Williams)
Utilities Regulation and Energy Efficiency (co-authors: Ranjit Bharvirkar, Chris Greacen, Chuenchom Sangarasri Greacen, Mahesh Patankar, Priya Sreedharan, and James H. Williams)

Lal, Sanjay
Clayton State University
Gandhism

Lewis, Joanna I.
Georgetown University
Climate Change Mitigation Initiatives (China)

Li, Hao
Chanjiang River Scientific Research Institute, Wuhan, China
Mekong-Lancang River (co-authors: Ram Chandra Bastakoti and Joyeeta Gupta)

Li, Pansy Hon-ying
The Hong Kong Polytechnic University
Guangzhou, China (co-author: Carlos Wing-Hung Lo)

Li, Yifei
University of Wisconsin, Madison
Green Collar Jobs (co-author: Gary P. Green)

Lide, James
History Associates Incorporated
Yangzi (Chang) River

Liu, Jingjing
Vermont Law School
Activism, Judicial (co-author: Dejin Gu)

Lo, Carlos Wing-Hung
The Hong Kong Polytechnic University
Guangzhou, China (co-author: Pansy Hon-ying Li)

Magee, Darrin
Hobart and William Smith Colleges
South-North Water Diversion

Marinova, Dora
Curtin University
One-Child Policy (co-author: Xiumei Guo)

Mathew, Leemamol
Institute of Rural Management
Education, Female (co-author: Fengping Zhao)

McNeely, Jeffrey A.
International Union for Conservation of Nature (IUCN)
Endangered Species

Mitra, Arup
Institute for Economic Growth, Delhi
Labor

Mondal, Pinki
Columbia University
Parks and Preserves (co-author: Harini Nagendra)

Montgomery, Heather A.
International Christian University
Microfinance

Nadarajah, Yasothara
Royal Melbourne Institute of Technology (RMIT)
Kuala Lumpur, Malaysia

Nagendra, Harini
Ashoka Trust for Research in Ecology and the Environment
Parks and Preserves (co-author: Pinki Mondal)

Nardi, Dominic J., Jr.
University of Michigan
Association of Southeast Asian Nations (ASEAN)

Neidel, J. David
National University of Singapore
Reforestation and Afforestation (Southeast Asia)

Nesamani, K. S.
Ford Foundation International Fellowship Program
Public Transportation

Nijman, Jan
University of Amsterdam
Mumbai, India

Oldenski, Lindsay
Georgetown University
Outsourcing and Offshoring

Padovani, Florence
Paris 1 Sorbonne University
Three Gorges Dam

Patankar, Mahesh
Customized Energy Solutions
Utilities Regulation and Energy Efficiency (co-authors: Ranjit Bharvirkar, Chris Greacen, Chuenchom Sangarasri Greacen, Fredrich Kahrl, Priya Sreedharan, and James H. Williams)

Patel, Amrita
National Dairy Development Board, India
White Revolution of India

Pellissery, Sony
Institute of Rural Management, Anand
Energy Industries—Renewables (India) (co-author: Badrinarayanan Seetharaman)
Five-Year Plans (co-author: Sam Geall)
Rural Development (co-author: Li Sun)
Rural Livelihoods

Rangarajan, Janani
IIT Madras's Rural Technology and Business Incubator (RTBI)
Information and Communication Technologies (ICT) (co-author: Ashok Jhunjhunwala)

Rangarajan, Mahesh
University of Delhi
India

Ricci, Kenneth N.
Scientech: A Curtiss-Wright Flow Control Company
Energy Industries—Nuclear

Roberts, Carolyn
University of Oxford
Dhaka, Bangladesh (co-author: Md. Sarfaraz Gani Adnan)

Rock, Melissa Y.
Dartmouth College
Beijing, China

Savage, Victor R.
National University of Singapore
Singapore

Seetharaman, Badrinarayanan
National Law School of India University
Energy Industries—Renewables (India) (co-author: Sony Pellissery)

Silveira, André F. Reynolds Castel-Branco da
University of Cambridge
Pearl River Delta

Sonnenfeld, David A.
State University of New York College of Environmental Science and Forestry
Rule of Law

Sreedharan, Priya
Energy and Environmental Economics, Inc.
Utilities Regulation and Energy Efficiency (co-authors: Ranjit Bharvirkar, Chris Greacen, Chuenchom Sangarasri Greacen, Fredrich Kahrl, Mahesh Patankar, and James H. Williams)

Stewart, Michelle O.
University of Colorado at Boulder
Tibetan Plateau

Sun, Jinong
Fayetteville State University
Steel Industry (co-author: Wenxian Zhang)

Sun, Li
Bielefeld University
Rural Development (co-author: Sony Pellissery)

Surendra, Lawrence
University of Mysore
Chennai, India

Takano Takenaka Kohei
Research Institute for Humanity and Nature
Genetic Resources

Telesetsky, Anastasia
University of Idaho College of Law
Fisheries (China)

Thompson, Kirill Ole
National Taiwan University
Traditional Knowledge (China)

Totman, Conrad
Yale University, Emeritus
Japan

Vermeer, Eduard B.
International Institute for Asian Studies, Leiden
China

von Hippel, David F.
Nautilus Institute for Security and Sustainability
Energy Security (East Asia) (co-authors: Peter Hayes, Fredrich Kahrl, and James H. Williams)

Wells-Dang, Andrew
Independent scholar, Hoi An, Vietnam
Nongovernmental Organizations (NGOs)

Williams, James H.
Monterey Institute of International Studies
Energy Security (East Asia) (co-authors: Peter Hayes, Fredrich Kahrl, and David F. von Hippel)
Utilities Regulation and Energy Efficiency (co-authors: Ranjit Bharvirkar, Fredrich Kahrl, Chris Greacen, Chuenchom Sangarasri Greacen, Mahesh Patankar, and Priya Sreedharan)

Wilson, Mark
Northumbria University
Southeast Asia

Yu Wenxuan
China University of Political Science and Law
Biodiversity Conservation Legislation (China)
Biosafety Legislation (China)

Zhang, Dongyong
Henan Agricultural University
Corporate Accountability (China)

Zhang, Wenxian
Rollins College
Steel Industry (co-author: Jinong Sun)

Zhao, Fengping
Zhengzhou University
Education, Female (co-author: Leemamol Mathew)

Zhu, Jieming
National University of Singapore; Tongji University
Property Rights (China)

Berkshire Encyclopedia of Sustainability

- Volume 1: *The Spirit of Sustainability*
- Volume 2: *The Business of Sustainability*
- Volume 3: *The Law and Politics of Sustainability*
- Volume 4: *Natural Resources and Sustainability*
- Volume 5: *Ecosystem Management and Sustainability*
- Volume 6: *Measurements, Indicators, and Research Methods for Sustainability*
- Volume 7: *China, India, and East and Southeast Asia: Assessing Sustainability*
- Volume 8: *The Americas and Oceania: Assessing Sustainability*
- Volume 9: *Afro-Eurasia: Assessing Sustainability*
- Volume 10: *The Future of Sustainability*

green press INITIATIVE

Berkshire Publishing is committed to preserving ancient forests and natural resources. We elected to print this title on 30% postconsumer recycled paper, processed chlorine-free. As a result, we have saved:

13 Trees (40' tall and 6-8" diameter)
5 Million BTUs of Total Energy
1,302 Pounds of Greenhouse Gases
5,868 Gallons of Wastewater
372 Pounds of Solid Waste

Berkshire Publishing made this paper choice because our printer, Thomson-Shore, Inc., is a member of Green Press Initiative, a nonprofit program dedicated to supporting authors, publishers, and suppliers in their efforts to reduce their use of fiber obtained from endangered forests.

For more information, visit www.greenpressinitiative.org

Environmental impact estimates were made using the Environmental Defense Paper Calculator. For more information visit: www.edf.org/papercalculator

Introduction to China, India, and East and Southeast Asia: Assessing Sustainability

This volume—*China, India, and East and Southeast Asia: Assessing Sustainability*—is the first of three *Encyclopedia of Sustainability* volumes to be devoted to a particular region. This volume covers a huge region in terms of both population and geographical size, a region that embodies many of the Earth's superlatives—pick up any newspaper on any given day and it is clear that there are a lot of things afoot. Even sticking to environmental matters, the mind reels at the sheer amount of activity: new cities sprouting like mushrooms in China; countrywide coal shortages in India; renewable energy projects taking shape, being argued over, sold, and traded; Chinese mining and other corporate interests investing in seemingly every country on Earth; solar-powered (and rainwater-collecting and shade-providing) "Supertrees" being built in Singapore's Gardens by the Bay; and consumerism and a desire for Western living standards taking hold in various places, in ways that would have seemed unimaginable two decades ago.

With all that's going on in the region, it may seem preposterous to attempt to produce a volume in an encyclopedia—which is by definition stuck in time—dedicated to the subject. Any book that tries to cover both China *and* India (not to mention their neighbors) will have difficulties. In China's case, the fact that it has experienced a quick (and ongoing) transition to a market economy, while still being governed by a one-party system, defies easy description. Meanwhile, India's status as the world's largest democracy comes with fairly predictable results.

The value of an encyclopedia, however, is its ability to present a comprehensive view of how things stand at one point in time. It forces us to slow down, to look in depth at what's happening in many fields, in many countries, across river systems and mountains, forests, factories, laboratories, gigantic cities, rural villages, and everywhere in between. The vast panoply of the region is preserved in time.

Encyclopedias are also wonderful for their ability to present a vast array of facts and figures to the curious reader. To pick but a few superlatives, the parts of Asia covered in this volume include the following (although it should be noted that not all of these facts appear in this book; sources appear below the Acknowledgements section):

- The Earth's **highest point**: Mt. Everest, on the China-Nepal border, at 8,848 meters high.
- The Earth's **lowest point**: the Mariana Trench, off the coasts of Japan and the Philippines, at 11,033 meters deep.
- The first, second, and fourth **most populous nations**: China (1.34 billion people), India (1.2 billion people), and Indonesia (248.2 million people), respectively.
- The **most crowded place**: purported to be Hong Kong's Mongkok (or Mong Kok) neighborhood (meaning *busy place* or *busy corner* in Cantonese). The previous record holder, Kowloon Walled City—pictured in the image above in a schematic map drawn up by a Japanese firm before the city was torn down by order of the Chinese government in 1993—was also in Hong Kong and is thought to have been the most crowded place of all time before its destruction.
- The **largest casino**: Macao, China.
- The **largest film industry**: Bollywood (the informal name for the film industry in Mumbai, India) produces more films each year than does Hollywood. The name comes from Mumbai's former name, Bombay, combined with Hollywood.
- The **largest conurbation** (i.e., megacity): Tokyo has over 35 million residents in four prefectures.

XXIII

- The **largest rare-earth metal refinery:** under construction in Malaysia as of 2012; the refinery owners (the Australian company Lynas) hope to overcome China's overwhelming monopoly on the substances, which are vital to the manufacture of smart phones and other electronics. The owners claim to be improving on China's dismal environmental record regarding rare-earth metal refineries. (See the article "Rare Earth Metals" in Volume 4 of this series, *Natural Resources and Sustainability,* for more on this subject.)
- The **largest mega-region:** according to the 2010–2011 UN-Habitat biannual report *The State of the World's Cities,* Hong Kong-Shenzhen-Dongguan-Guangzhou in southern China had a combined estimated total of 120 million residents in 2011.
- The **largest generator of electricity:** the controversial Three Gorges Dam in China's Hubei Province generates an estimated 20 times the electricity-generating power of the Hoover Dam in the United States. Roughly 1,000 towns and villages were relocated to make room for the dam's massive reservoir.
- The **most (and fastest) Internet users:** China had an estimated 420 million Internet users in 2010, representing roughly 23 percent of the world's Internet users. South Korea has the fastest Internet connections of any country on the planet.
- The **worst air:** according to the 2011 Environmental Performance Index (EPI), South Asia in general, and India in particular, placed last in the world for air quality. India was at the bottom of the list (number 132), followed by Nepal (131), Bangladesh (130), Pakistan (129), and China (128).
- The lowest **per capita emissions:** many of the countries at the bottom of the list for air quality are also the least polluting, per capita. In 2008, India was ranked number 122 in the world, with 1.5 metric tons of carbon dioxide emitted per capita; Nepal was ranked number 188, Bangladesh was 161, Pakistan was 137, and China was 66. South Korea ranked number 22, the highest per capita emitting country under consideration in this volume. (The top ten countries in the world are mainly in the Middle East, with the United States coming in at number 10, with 18 metric tons of carbon dioxide emitted per capita.)
- The first and second **deadliest floods** of all time: the Yangzi (Chang) River in 1931 and the Huang (Yellow) River in 1887, respectively—both in China. Proponents of the Three Gorges Dam say that the new dam potentially will save the lives of millions of people on the flood-prone Yangzi; opponents say the new dam may do that now but will make the flooding worse in the future.
- The first and second **busiest ports** in the world: Shanghai and Singapore, respectively.
- The world's **largest democracy:** India (as mentioned previously).
- The **rainiest year** in recorded history: Cherrapunji, India, had 26.4 meters of rain in 1861 (the fairly rainy city of New York, in comparison, typically sees 1.14 meters of rain in a given year).
- The **world's largest encyclopedia:** China was home to what the *New York Times* called "the most colossal literary work ever carried out by man" before it tragically was lost to humanity in a fire in 1900. The *Yongle Dadian,* or *Great Compendium of the Yongle Reign,* was an enormous literary encyclopedia that was completed in 1408 and had 22,877 chapters in 11,095 volumes; the table of contents alone spanned 60 volumes.

The list could go on.

Clearly, Asia is a singular place, and one that can't easily be covered in a single book, let alone on a topic that's as intriguing (and slippery to define) as sustainability. While we would aspire to have the reach of the *Yongle Dadian,* and would love to be able to call this series the *Great Compendium of Sustainability,* we must, of necessity in this modern age, set our goals somewhat more realistically.

What the reader will find in this volume of the *Encyclopedia of Sustainability* is a fascinating patchwork of material, including a general overview of cities in Asia, as well as a selection of cities, including Dhaka, Chennai, Singapore, Beijing, Mumbai, Shanghai, Jakarta, and Tokyo. There are articles on the environmental histories of China, India, Southeast Asia, Japan, and the Korean peninsula, as well as the Tibetan Plateau, the Himalaya, and a selection of key rivers such as the Mekong-Lancang, Ganges, Yangzi, and Huang. There are articles on the steel, automobile, nanotechnology, and information and communication technology (ICT), industries; articles on energy (renewable and otherwise), energy projects (after all, Asia has witnessed in recent years the creation of the aforementioned Three Gorges Dam and the devastating earthquake and tsunami that crippled Japan's Fukushima nuclear power plant in March of 2011—possibly taking with it the future of the entire industry, at least in Japan, although it may be too soon to judge), and energy security; articles on the traditional knowledge of China and India, both of which have huge implications for the modern nations of today; and general articles on public health, public transportation, microfinance, water security, rural development and livelihoods, consumption, and the influence of religions on current (and past and future) sustainability thought.

Other articles cover country-specific topics such as China's One-Child Policy and India's "white revolution," during which the country was transformed into the world's largest producer of milk, providing, according to author Amrita Patel, sustainable livelihoods to more than 70 million smallholder dairy farmers. Sustainability is not possible without considering the livelihoods of the people involved, be they urbanites or rural dwellers, rich or poor.

Sustainability in the Asian Context

Sustainability as a word may be somewhat new; the term emerged in various places in the early 1970s to describe the idea of preserving resources in such a way that future generations will be able to benefit from them without the economy collapsing in the process. The *idea* of sustainability, however, is certainly not a new one, despite the increasing use of the word to describe seemingly everything remotely ecologically oriented on the planet. In his article "Traditional Knowledge (China)," Kirill Ole Thompson of National Taiwan University points to the *Classic of Changes*—the *I Ching* (*Yijing*)—and its suggestion that there is a continuity between humanity and nature; to go against this is to risk going against the natural harmony of the world. On the other hand, he goes on to write, "the philosopher Mozi (flourished 479–438 BCE) believed that the Confucian rituals diverted resources needed by society as a whole and were wasteful. His principle of 'impartial regard' stressed fairness, and preached economy in expenditures and conservation in the use of natural resources. His pragmatic approach, however, was so human-centered that it justified exploitation of nature for human uses."

Perhaps the culmination of this human-centered exploitation of resources was Mao Zedong's well-known and disastrous campaigns against the environment. One of the more infamous of these was his Wipe Out the Four Pests campaign, a synchronized mass strategy to eliminate China's rats, mosquitoes, flies, and sparrows, which ate grain seeds and were therefore considered enemies of the state. The result: because the birds, which were driven close to extinction, ate insects, infestations of locusts and other insects spread, ruining a large portion of the crop. Millions starved as a result. This is an extreme example of a tragic lack of sustainability in more ways than one. (Another of Mao's schemes was the idea to launch China into the industrial age by forcing villagers across the country to start small-scale iron smelteries in their backyards, with similarly disastrous results.)

Mohandas Gandhi, on the other end of the spectrum, was a leader who took a different approach to nature, one that would later be closely identified with sustainability. Sanjay Lal writes in his article "Gandhism,"

> Fully adopting Gandhian nonviolence means taking no more from nature than is truly necessary. This means that human practices will be sustainable, as the resources provided by the environment are sufficient for all people to obtain what they need. When, for example, we desire warmth and convenience in travel to the extent that we endanger the world's oil supply, we accept violence as a legitimate means for preserving our lifestyle.

There are countless instances in the region of the perils of not living in harmony with nature, whether by design or not. Bangladesh is a well-known example of people living in harm's way, due to poverty or otherwise; its 161 million citizens are famous for their resilience in the face of frequent—and frequently cataclysmic—monsoonal flooding. The huge nation (huge in population, that is: the entire country would fit inside the US state of Illinois, with 12.5 times the population) faces equally huge challenges in the years ahead, as most climate change models point to rising sea levels; the big question is how *much* the seas could rise. Any rise will cause problems for a country where the majority of the population lives mere meters above sea level.

Some environmental disasters develop slowly, over the course of decades: there are cycles of flooding, drought, and desertification, and the famine and associated human miseries that go with them. Other disasters happen in a matter of hours. The most infamous chemical disaster of all time took place in Bhopal, India, in 1984, when the Union Carbide plant there leaked methyl isocyanate into the surrounding city, killing an estimated 3,800 people outright in a few short hours, and leading to an estimated 20,000–30,000 subsequent deaths. (This topic, discussed briefly by Sam Geall in "Media Coverage of the Environment" in this volume, is covered in more depth in "Bhopal Disaster" in Volume 3 of this series, *The Law and Politics of Sustainability*.) With any disaster, the hope is that people learn from their mistakes—in this case, lax international (and domestic) environmental laws governing the actions of multinational corporations. The cataclysmic tsunamis that hit South Asia in December of 2004 and Japan in March of 2011 show the perils of large populations living close to tsunami-prone coastlines. The extreme fertility of volcanic soils—and the generally beautiful surroundings where volcanoes tend to be found, for various geological reasons—means that populations in volcano-riddled Indonesia and the Philippines, to name but two nations, face existential dangers of another variety.

But it is not all bad, which is the point of this book. A book only about our helplessness in the face of nature would be depressing indeed—and it would tell only half the story. In his article "Reforestation and Afforestation (Southeast Asia)," for instance, J. David Neidel outlines some of the many strategies currently underway to bring forest cover back to denuded areas in Southeast Asia. Many readers will be familiar with television images of masked inhabitants of cities such as Jakarta, Indonesia, their atmosphere choked with smoke from the innumerable fires started to clear land for crops and other uses. These innovative strategies take many forms, depending on local circumstances. In the Philippines, for instance, a reforestation approach known as *rainforestation* (or *rainforestation farming*) has been developed to mix economically and ecologically important species. This approach, which allows for local communities to gain multiple economic benefits while restoring forest cover to the land, is necessary in the Philippines where the rural population density is very high. The practice of rainforestation is now being promoted widely in Cambodia, Vietnam, Sri Lanka, and southern China, as well as in the Philippines.

Sustainability happens on all levels, from people making individual choices to governments of huge nations passing laws (whether initiated from the "ground up" or from on high, as is generally the case in China, although even that is changing). The well-known Chipko movement (discussed by George Alfred James in Volume 1 of this series, *The Spirit of Sustainability*) was a successful Gandhian-inspired grassroots movement for forest sustainability that flourished in what is now the Indian state of Uttarakhand in the western Himalaya between 1973 and 1981. (The name of the movement is derived from the resolution of the local people to embrace—*chipko*—the trees in order to prevent the ax from doing its work.) The Chipko movement was one of the first so-called tree-hugging movements.

Our hope is that readers of all sorts will be inspired by the material found in this book to find new ways to make daily living a more sustainable thing: not simply a buzzword but a real, tangible thing.

The Editors

Acknowledgements

Berkshire Publishing would like to thank the following people for their help and advice in various matters. In a project of this scope there are many to acknowledge, of course, but these people deserve our special thanks:

Hanling Yang, *Environmental Defense Fund*.

Mark Elvin, *Australian National University*.

Will Galloway, *frontofficetokyo and Waseda University*.

Jennifer Turner, *Wilson Center*.

Dominic Nardi, *Jr., University of Michigan*.

Ibon Galarraga, *Basque Centre for Climate Change (BC3)*.

Ralf Buckley, *Griffith University*.

Terje Oestigaard, *The Nordic Africa Institute*.

Frederick R. Steiner, *the University of Texas at Austin*.

Kenneth Ricci, *Scientec, Redwood City, California*.

Makarand Dehejia, *Alliance for Sustainable Energy & Industry*.

Elizabeth Allison, *California Institute of Integral Studies*.

Peter Whitehouse, *Case Western Reserve University.*

Nazim Muradov, *Florida Solar Energy Center.*

Frank Rosillo-Calle, *Imperial College London.*

Molly Anderson, *College of the Atlantic.*

Yu Wenxuan, *China University of Political Science and Law and Visiting Scholar, Vermont Law School.*

Martin Price, *Perth College, University of the Highlands and Islands.*

Maureen G. Reed, *University of Saskatchewan.*

Adam Minter, *independent writer, Shanghai.*

Christopher Key Chapple, *Loyola Marymount University.*

Fredrich Kahrl, *Energy and Resources Group, University of California, Berkeley.*

Eduard B. Vermeer, *International Institute for Asian Studies (IIAS), Leiden.*

Gregory Fulkerson, *State University of New York, Oneonta.*

Mary Evelyn Tucker, *Yale University.*

Darrin Magee, *Hobart and William Smith Colleges.*

Zareen P. Bharucha, *University of Essex.*

Bed Mani Dahal, *Kathmandu University.*

Robert Brook, *University of Wales.*

Heather Chappells, *Saint Mary's University and Dalhousie University.*

Shen Lei, *Chinese Academy of Sciences.*

Ian Pattison, *University of Southampton.*

Robert Engelman, *Worldwatch Institute.*

Evan Ward, *Brigham Young University.*

Alvin Lin, *China Climate and Energy Policy Director, Natural Resources Defense Council.*

Basireddy Sudhakara Reddy, *Indira Gandhi Institute of Development Research (IGIDR).*

William Loxley, *Asian Development Bank, The Philippines.*

Jiang Lu, *Shanxi University Law School.*

Gareth Price, *Chatham House, United Kingdom.*

Kerry Brown, *Chatham House, United Kingdom.*

James D. Sellmann, *University of Guam.*

Steven Morse, *University of Surrey.*

Carolyn Roberts, *University of Oxford.*

J. David Neidel, *National University of Singapore.*

Arnold Zeitlin, *Editorial Research & Reporting Associates (ERRA); Visiting Professor, Guangdong University of Foreign Studies.*

Peter Adriaens, *University of Michigan.*

Irene Dameron Hager, *Ohio State University.*

Steven C. Hackett, *Humboldt State University.*

Donald G. Hodges, *University of Tennessee.*

Karen Hussey, *The Australian National University.*

Gordon Irons, *McMaster University.*

Uma Lele, *independent scholar.*

Robin Lewis, *Hobart and William Smith Colleges.*

Stephen Morse, *University of Surrey.*

Carmen Revenga, *The Nature Conservancy.*

Ian Spellerberg, *Lincoln University.*

Michelle O. Stewart, *University of Colorado at Boulder.*

Our profound thanks to you all for your generous help and advice.

Sources

The following sources are listed roughly in order of appearance in the introduction.

Population: United States Central Intelligence Agency (US CIA). (2012). *The world factbook*. Retrieved May 14, 2012, from https://www.cia.gov/library/publications/the-world-factbook/index.html

Mega-region population: United Nations Human Settlements Programme (UN-HABITAT). (2011). *The state of the world's cities 2010/2011: Bridging the urban divide.* Retrieved May 14, 2012, from http://www.unhabitat.org/content.asp?cid=8051&catid=7&typeid=46

Most crowded place: New Tang Dynasty (NTD) Television. (2011). Life in Mong Kok, the world's most crowded place. Retrieved May 14, 2012, from http://english.ntdtv.com/ntdtv_en/ns_life/2011-10-26/life-in-mong-kok-the-world-s-most-crowded-place.html

Kowloon Walled City: Zoohaus. (2010). Documento Kowloon que quita el sentío! [Kowloon document that takes the breath away!]. Retrieved May 21, 2012, from http://zoohaus.net/WP/?p=4872

Tokyo's population: Cox, Wendell. (2011, May 10). Japan's 2010 census: Moving to Tokyo. *NewGeography*. Retrieved April 5, 2012, from http://www.newgeography.com/content/002227-japan%E2%80%99s-2010-census-moving-tokyo

Film industry: Lubin, Gus. (2011, November 21). The largest film industry in the world has banned smoking in movies. *Business Insider*. Retrieved May 14, 2012, from http://articles.businessinsider.com/2011-11-21/news/30424373_1_tobacco-advertising-smoking-scenes-advertising-ban

Air pollution: *Los Angeles Times*. (2012, February 2). The worst air pollution in the world. Retrieved May 14, 2012, from http://latimesblogs.latimes.com/world_now/2012/02/worst-air-pollution-in-the-world.html

Per capita carbon dioxide emissions: World Bank. (2012). CO_2 emissions (metric tons per capita) [Database]. Retrieved May 14, 2012, from http://data.worldbank.org/indicator/EN.ATM.CO2E.PC/countries

Three Gorges Dam: China's Three Gorges Dam [Website, Mount Holyoke College, World Politics 116]. (2007). Benefits: Flood control, hydroelectric power, and navigation. Retrieved May 14, 2012, from http://www.mtholyoke.edu/~vanti20m/classweb/website/benefits.html; Handwerk, Brian. (2006). China's Three Gorges Dam, by the numbers. *National Geographic*. Retrieved May 14, 2012, from http://news.nationalgeographic.com/news/2006/06/060609-gorges-dam_2.html

Rare earth metals refinery: Burgess, James. (2012, February 2). World's largest rare earth metal refinery to open in Malaysia. *OilPrice*. Retrieved May 14, 2012, from http://oilprice.com/Latest-Energy-News/World-News/Worlds-Largest-Rare-Earth-Metal-Refinery-to-Open-in-Malaysia.html

Internet users in China: Internet World Stats. (2010). China: Internet usage stats and population report. Retrieved May 14, 2012, from http://www.internetworldstats.com/asia/cn.htm

Internet speed in South Korea: Sutter, John D. (2010, March 31). Why internet connections are fastest in South Korea. CNN. Retrieved May 14, 2012, from http://articles.cnn.com/2010-03-31/tech/broadband.south.korea_1_broadband-plan-south-korea-broadband-internet?_s=PM:TECH

Busy ports: *Economic Times*. (2011, December 24). Retrieved May 14, 2012, from http://articles.economictimes.indiatimes.com/2011-12-24/news/30554773_1_container-traffic-teus-port-operator

A

Activism, Judicial

Judicial branches in many Southeast Asian countries, such as the Philippines, have taken an activist approach to addressing environmental issues in recent years. Despite encouraging legislative achievements, lawmakers in China and India both face enormous challenges to enforcing existing laws effectively and significantly improving environmental quality. China, India, and the Philippines ranked 121st, 123rd, and 50th, respectively, in the 2010 Environmental Performance Index's rankings of 163 countries on 25 environmental performance indicators.

As the two largest developing countries in the world, China and India have experienced enormous environmental challenges as a result of rapid economic development and urbanization. In order to reduce pollution and remediate the damage to natural resources, both countries began building their respective environmental legislative infrastructure in the 1970s, and have since developed a relatively comprehensive set of environmental laws and regulations. Since 1979, around thirty environmental statutes have been enacted in China, addressing issues such as pollution control, natural resources conservation, desertification prevention, energy conservation, and clean production. China is also in the process of drafting a comprehensive law for climate change. In India, major environmental statutes such as the Water Prevention and Control of Pollution Act, the Air Prevention and Control of Pollution Act, and the Environmental Protection Act have been passed since 1974, serving as the legislative foundation of India's environmental protection efforts (Karanjia 2009, 50, 51).

Despite these encouraging legislative achievements, enormous challenges face both countries as they attempt to enforce existing laws effectively and thus significantly improve environmental quality. The 2010 Environmental Performance Index ranks 163 countries on 25 performance indicators to measure how close these countries are to established environmental policy goals. China and India ranked at 121 and 123, respectively, while the Philippines and the United States were placed at 50 and 61, respectively (Environmental Performance Index 2010). In China, several major barriers, including prioritization of economic development, weak regulatory infrastructure, lack of financial and human resources, limited role of civil society, and a relatively weak judiciary, have led to inadequate enforcement of environmental laws (Liu and Moser 2011, 222). In India, as the environmental engineer Vinod K. Sharma has pointed out, some major environmental statutes have inherent deficiencies such as overlapping authorities and lack of public participation. In addition, existing environmental laws have not been efficiently implemented and enforced. These concerns pressed the Indian judiciary to play a more active role in environmental governance (Cha 2005, 205). Besides China and India, judicial branches in some Southeast Asian countries have taken certain degrees of an activist approach to address environmental issues. The Philippine judiciary is an example in this regard. This article thus will focus specifically on judicial activism in China, India, and the Philippines.

Judicial activism is a highly controversial term subject to different interpretations. While the law professor Lino A. Graglia viewed it specifically as "the practice by judges of disallowing policy choices by other governmental officials or institutions that the Constitution does not clearly prohibit" (Graglia 1996, 296), it can also be interpreted to include such judicial practices as ignoring precedent, making legislations, departing from accepted interpretive methodology, and conducting result-oriented judging (Kmiec 2004, 1463–1476). Given the substantial differences in legal system and political tradition as well as cultural heritage among countries, activism in one country may be considered standard practice in another. In the context of this article, judicial activism can be understood as a means by the courts to go beyond existing laws to improve environmental enforcement and ensure the public's pursuit of a clean and healthy environment. How to achieve this goal depends on the judicial branch's own capacity and its relationship with the other branches of government. The Rio Declaration on Environment and Development (1992) also emphasized the government's role to facilitate and encourage public awareness and participation by making information widely available, and stressed as well as the importance of ensuring effective access to judicial redress and remedy (the Rio Declaration on Environment and Development 1992, Principle 10). Given the different legal, economic, political, social, historical, and cultural contexts in China, India, and the Philippines, judicial activism has taken a different path in each country.

China

In China, the idea of judicial activism started to develop when Shengjun Wang assumed the position as the chief justice of the Supreme People's Court (SPC), which administers the entire Chinese judiciary, issues judicial interpretations, and plays an important role in the legislative process as the country's highest judicial organ. Wang stressed the importance of public opinion and upholding party leadership (Cohen 2008), which further undermines the independence of the Chinese judiciary. He also promoted judicial activism as a means to better address social conflicts, in particular encouraging the use of mediation to resolve disputes (Wang 2010). Although the emphasis on mediation invited questions on the danger of diluting the judiciary's efforts in adjudicating cases, Chinese courts have made innovative progress in addressing the country's widespread environmental problems under Chief Justice Wang's leadership, especially in attempts to overcome obstacles plaguing administrative enforcement, ensure public participation in environmental protection, and establish a system to have the polluter pay for pollution cleanup costs.

Chinese environmental laws impose a variety of responsibilities upon polluters. Noncompliance is blatant, however, due to environmental agencies' weak commitment and lack of capacity. Failure to comply is particularly severe in transboundary pollution across multiple jurisdictions, because environmental agencies located in areas where pollution initiates may neglect their enforcement duties, while agencies in areas where the environmental harm actually occurs have no jurisdiction over the polluter (Gu 2005). Judicial activism can effectively address this dilemma. In *Two Lakes and One Reservoir Administration v. Tianfeng Chemical Plant*, heard in 2007 by the Environmental Tribunal of Qingzhen People's Court, the first specialized environmental tribunal in China, the plaintiff was a water environment enforcement agency directly affiliated with Guiyang Municipal Government, and the defendant was located in Anshun, which borders Guiyang. The defendant did not build a proper wastewater treatment facility for its chemical residue, which caused severe pollution to Hongfeng Lake, the primary drinking-water source for 4 million residents of Guiyang. The court supported the plaintiff's claim and ordered the defendant to stop polluting and take effective measures to eliminate imminent danger to the environment. Under existing Chinese law, the plaintiff of a civil case must have a direct interest with the case, so lawsuits brought on behalf of the public interest are technically not permitted. In this case the court was able to expand the standing so that the plaintiff could bring the first environmental public interest case in Guizhou Province, and to do so against a polluter outside its own administrative jurisdiction.

In other occasions the judiciary went beyond existing substantive and procedural laws to ensure citizens' rights to participate in environmental protection. The 2008 case of *Hongming Liu v. Shanghai Songjiang District Environmental Protection Bureau* is such an example. The plaintiff in this case alleged that the defendant's approval of a factory's environmental impact assessment report violated relevant laws and regulations both substantively and procedurally, and requested the court rescind the approval. The trial court ruled against the plaintiff, and its decision was affirmed by the appeals court. Although the plaintiff did not prevail, this case had important ramifications regarding citizens' rights to participate in environmental protection. Improper or inadequate enforcement by environmental agencies is one of the major contributors to China's extensive environmental problems, and for a long time government actions have not been sufficiently reviewed and restrained by the judiciary. In this case, the court initiated judicial oversight of government actions by reviewing issues related to the agency's alleged violation. This kind of judicial review is crucial to preventing dysfunction in environmental enforcement. For instance, the plaintiff was not permitted to bring this lawsuit to court according to existing Chinese Administrative Litigation Law. But the court noted that the plaintiff enjoyed the right to live in a pollution- and damage-free environment and therefore *was* entitled to file the lawsuit. In this case the court not only permitted the plaintiff to file this lawsuit against a government agency, but also acknowledged an environmental right that is not recognized by the Chinese constitution or existing environmental statutes. The court's willingness to go beyond substantive and procedural laws positively impacts citizens' rights to participate in environmental protection, and helps pave the way for environmental public interest litigation that may be brought against government agencies in future.

Judicial activism in China also enables the establishment of a system that requires the polluter to pay for pollution cleanup costs. In addition to infringing upon personal and property safety, pollution can cause severe damage to the environment itself. Under existing laws, only when there are damages to the marine ecological environment, oceanic fishing resources, or marine protection zones can government agencies responsible for overseeing and administering marine environment bring litigation as trustees of such natural resources against polluters for compensation, but no legal remedy is provided under current legislation to compensate environmental damages caused by pollution occurring on the land. In the 2008 case of *Guangzhou Municipality Haizhu District Procuratorate v. Zhongmin Chen*, the defendant was the owner of a small laundry facility that illegally discharged wastewater into a local river. Guangzhou Maritime Court supported the plaintiff's claims and ordered the defendant to pay over 110,000 yuan (approximately $18,000) to compensate for damages to the environment, and the fund would be used exclusively for cleaning up the pollution. This was the first environmental public interest case brought by public prosecutors in Guangdong Province (Liu forthcoming 2012). The court not only expanded the standing requirement to allow public prosecutors to bring this lawsuit on behalf of public interest, but also addressed the legislative loophole by granting remedy to damages upon the environment itself by land-originated pollution.

The practice of judicial activism has emerged in China with several dozens of environmental tribunals established at different court levels across the country since 2004. These green tribunals absorb experience from the worldwide trend for specialized courts, tribunals, and green judges to adjudicate environmental cases, and they aim to address local governments' concerns regarding the increasing high-profile environmental accidents. These green tribunals help streamline the process of hearing environmental cases, allow cases to be heard by judges with enhanced technical expertise, and expand standing requirements to encourage environmental public interest litigation that general courts commonly do not accept under existing Chinese law (Liu and Moser 2011, 222).

India

The most powerful statement on the environment in India is a constitutional amendment: the 42nd Amendment to Article 48A, which includes a provision on environmental protection and states that it is now a fundamental duty to ensure a clean and healthy environment (Karanjia 2009, 51–52). Article 21 of the Indian constitution is the key fundamental rights provision, which states "no person shall be deprived of his life or personal liberty except according to procedure established by law." The Indian judiciary has expanded fundamental rights to include the right to a clean and healthy environment (Karanjia 2009, 52–53). In efforts to accommodate and facilitate environmental public interest litigation, Indian courts exhibit sincere willingness to promote environmental protection by liberalizing the traditionally strict standing requirements and improving access to justice (Cha 2005, 200). Such expanded standing allows any public-minded Indian citizen to file environmental lawsuits on behalf of the public interest all the way to the Indian Supreme Court (Cha 2005, 203). The judiciary's devotion to environmental protection has to some degree raised the environmental awareness of the citizens (Karanjia 2009, 61) and led to better governance, delivery of public services, and accountability of officials (Rajamani 2007, 319).

One of the most high profile environmental cases ever to come before the Supreme Court, *M. C. Mehta v. Union of India* (the *Delhi Vehicular Pollution Case*), involved an extensive effort from various sectors to reduce vehicular emissions and improve ambient air quality in the highly urbanized and populous city of Delhi. Years of litigation led to the Supreme Court's influential decision to order conversion of the entire city's bus fleet to compressed natural gas (CNG), aiming to reduce vehicular emissions. The decision was followed by years of compliance efforts and several deadline extensions; finally at the end of 2002, all city buses previously burning diesel had converted to CNG. This case provides an example of Indian citizens' attitude toward environmental protection and what they are willing to tolerate for a clean and healthy environment (Rajamani 2007, 298–301, 316). When it comes to sustainable development, the Indian judiciary has also tried to strike a balance between development and environmental protection. The Supreme Court applied the doctrine of sustainable development for the first time in a landmark case, *Vellore Citizen Welfare Forum v. Union of India*, in 1996 (AIR n.d.). The court wrote in this case that the traditional belief that development and ecology are opposed to each other is no longer acceptable, and sustainable development is the answer.

Although the Supreme Court of India has exercised its judicial power as a way of redressing the executive branch's failure to adequately enforce environmental laws, this activist approach has invited extensive debate and criticism. One concern is that liberalizing standing rules runs the risk of an explosion in litigation that can overburden the courts and induce delay in the judicial process (Cha 2005, 210). In addition, the activist judiciary has sometimes overstepped its judicial authority and taken on a legislative role that should be reserved for democratically elected individuals, while the judgments issued by the courts suffer the same degree of difficulty in enforcement as the existing laws (Cha 2005, 206, 212). The courts' activist stance was also blamed for restricting the development of a responsible and independent government and placing an enormous burden on the limited resources of the executive branch (Rajamani 2007, 315). The courts even went so far to publicly criticize the government, leading to increased tensions between the two branches (Cha 2005, 218).

Philippines

In response to various environmental issues, Philippine lawmakers have passed over one hundred bills, but sufficient enforcement of these laws is lacking (Halagueña 2011, 2–3). Although Article II of the Philippine constitution refers to the right to a balanced and healthful ecology, this only serves as a guideline for legislation, not a self-executing provision that can be judicially enforced (Gatmaytan-Magno 2010, 26). In the landmark case of *Juan Antonio Oposa and Others v. the Honorable Fulgencio S. Factoran and another*, however, a group of Filipino minors brought a lawsuit on behalf of themselves (as well as generations yet unborn) to seek cancellation of all existing timber license agreements in this country as a way of preventing unsustainable damages to its natural forest resources. The Supreme Court held that the petitioners can represent the succeeding generations to sue since "every generation has a responsibility to the next to preserve that rhythm and harmony for the full enjoyment of a balanced and healthful ecology." Despite comments on *Oposa*'s limited actual value (Gatmaytan-Magno 2010, 3), the expanded standing and recognition of intergenerational equity in this case invited widespread attention and high praise from the international environmental community. In the 2008 *Metropolitan Manila Development Authority v. Concerned Residents of Manila Bay*, the Supreme Court issued the Philippines' first writ of continuing mandamus, which compels relevant government agencies to perform their mandated duties to preserve, rehabilitate, and protect Manila Bay, and enables the court to enjoy jurisdiction over this case for as long as relevant government agencies fail to do so; the court also required relevant agencies to submit quarterly reports on the cleanup progress (Halagueña 2011, 2–3). The court's order to grant itself jurisdiction over this case for as long as relevant government agencies fail to perform their duties with relation to Manila Bay triggered vibrant discussions internationally, including in China. In addition, over one hundred green courts were established in 2008, and the Rules of Procedure on Environmental Cases was promulgated in 2010 to help promote efficient and effective judicial enforcement of environmental law (Halagueña 2011, 3–4).

Comparisons

Judicial activism exhibits different characteristics in China, India, and the Philippines as a result of the unique legal background and social dynamics of each country. In China, there is not yet a right to a clean environment under the constitution, and even if there was one, the Chinese constitution is not directly enforceable. Chinese courts do not have the authority to interpret the constitution, and consistent with the civil law tradition, judges have a much more limited role in "making" law. This is very different from Indian judiciary's practice of expanding fundamental rights under the constitution to include a judicially enforceable right to a clean and healthy environment. In addition, as mentioned above, expanded standing allows any public-minded citizens or groups to file environmental public interest lawsuits all the way to the Indian Supreme Court. In the four-level court system in China, most cases are adjudicated at the lowest two levels of courts, and China's SPC hardly hears any case in the first instance trial, or in the second instance trial for that matter. Another notable difference lies in the fact that the Indian Supreme Court and higher-level courts are taking the lead to promote stronger environmental governance in a more top-down approach, while the green court/tribunal movement in China started at the local level by initiating various experiments to develop a more effective adjudication model for environmental cases. Some of the experiments have over time been acknowledged by the SPC, and therefore show more of a bottom-up development mode. Overall, today in India few areas in the environmental governance arena are not within judicial oversight (Rajamani 2007, 295). But the judiciary in China depends upon local governments for financial resources and personnel advancement opportunities and, therefore, plays quite a restricted role in reining in government power. Indian judiciary's open criticism of the executive branch would be unthinkable to Chinese judges. Instead, Chinese courts have adopted a more cooperative and pragmatic approach to involving environmental agencies and public prosecutors, as well as the police, to work together on promoting environmental public interest litigation.

When comparing judicial activism in the Philippine Supreme Court with that of the Indian Supreme Court, the Filipino law professor Dante Gatmaytan-Magno claims that while the Indian judiciary takes on legislative and executive functions in addition to its original duties, its Philippine counterpart "has resisted the temptation to act outside the boundaries of its constitutional duties" despite the executive branch's failure to forcefully enforce environmental law (Gatmaytan-Magno 2010, 25). Furthermore, the case of *Metropolitan Manila Development Authority v. Concerned Residents of Manila Bay* illustrates that judicial activism may not be necessary if existing environmental laws provide clear and complete mandates of government agencies (Gatmaytan-Magno 2010, 22). This is equally true for the case of *Two Lakes and One Reservoir Administration v. Tianfeng Chemical Plant* in China, if the laws prescribe rational approaches to address enforcement challenges in transboundary pollution. China could also learn from the Philippines' experience of promoting special procedural rules so as to ensure adequate and efficient disposal of environmental cases. In all three countries, judicial activism has facilitated civil society development by providing a platform for nongovernmental organizations (NGOs) to explore useful solutions and shape environmental policy through public interest litigation. For example, Friends of Nature and Chongqing Green Volunteers Union brought China's first environmental public interest case filed by grassroots NGOs against two chemical plants over chromium pollution at a specialized environmental tribunal in Yunnan Province, which allows courts within its jurisdiction to accept public interest cases brought by environmental NGOs.

Implications

Environmental lawsuits are inherently complex and technical, and they demand a unique set of expertise, so it will be very helpful for judiciaries from different countries to share their experience on best practices in environmental adjudication. Some peer-to-peer learning opportunities have already proved to be valuable in this regard. Ultimately, a competent and independent judiciary with the power to exercise meaningful checks on government actions is indispensable to a country's path to good environmental governance and long-term sustainable development.

Jingjing LIU
Vermont Law School

Dejin GU
Sun Yat-sen University Law School

See also Biodiversity Conservation Legislation (China); Biosafety Legislation (China); China; Five-Year Plans; India; Indigenous Peoples; Media Coverage of the Environment; Nongovernmental Organizations (NGOs); Public-Private Partnerships; Rule of Law; Southeast Asia

Further Reading

All Indian Reporter (AIR) PVT, Ltd. (n.d.). Environmental protection in India: Judicial activism and beyond. Retrieved December 1, 2011, from http://www.airwebworld.com/articles/index.php?article=1421#sdendnote20sym

Cha, J. Mijin. (2005). A critical examination of the environmental jurisprudence of the courts of India. *Albany Law Environmental Outlook Journal, 10*(2), 197.

Cohen, Jerome A. (2008, October 18). Body blow for the judiciary. *South China Morning Post*. Retrieved March 28, 2012, from http://lawprofessors.typepad.com/china_law_prof_blog/2008/10/jerome-cohen--1.html

Environmental Performance Index 2010. (n.d.). Retrieved March 28, 2012, from http://www.epi2010.yale.edu/

Gatmaytan-Magno, Dante. (2010). Judicial restraint and the enforcement of environmental rights in the Philippines. *Oregon Review of International Law, 12*(1), 1–30.

Graglia, Lino A. (1996). It's not constitutionalism, it's judicial activism. *Harvard Journal of Law and Public Policy, 19*, 293.

Gu, Dejin. (2005). Balance of regional environmental interest. *Research on Law and Commerce, 4*.

Halagueña, Risa. (2011). Developments in Philippine: Access to environmental justice. *The Effectius Newsletter, 11*. Retrieved December 1, 2011, from http://www.effectius.com/yahoo_site_admin/assets/docs/Risa_Halague%C3%B1a_Newsletter11.5424002.pdf

Karanjia, Vahbiz P. (2009). Why India matters: The confluence of a booming economy, an activist supreme court, and a thirst for energy. *Villanova Environmental Law Journal, 20*(1), 49.

Kmiec, Keenan D. (2004). The origin and current meanings of "judicial activism." *California Law Review, 92*, 1441–1477.

Liu, Jingjing. (forthcoming 2012). China's procuratorate in environmental civil enforcement: Practice, challenges and implications for China's environmental governance. *Vermont Journal of Environmental Law, 12*.

Liu, Jingjing, & Moser, Adam. (2011). Environmental law—China. In Klaus Bosselmann, Daniel Fogel, & J. B. Ruhl (Eds.), *The Encyclopedia of Sustainability: Vol. 3. The Law and Politics of Sustainability* (pp. 220–223). Great Barrington, MA: Berkshire Publishing.

Peerenboom, Randall. (2002). *China's long march to the rule of law*. Cambridge, UK: Cambridge University Press.

Rajamani, Lavanya. (2007). Public interest environmental litigation in India: Exploring issues of access, participation, equity, effectiveness and sustainability. *Journal of Environmental Law, 19*(3), 293–321.

The Rio Declaration on Environment and Development. (1992). Retrieved April 1, 2012, from http://www.unesco.org/education/information/nfsunesco/pdf/RIO_E.PDF

Wang, Alex. (2007). The role of law in environmental protection in China: Recent developments. *Vermont Journal of Environmental Law, 8*, 195–224.

Wang, Shengjun. (2010, May 6). Grasp judicial principles, adhere to judicial activism, and promote the scientific development of the work of the People's Courts: Letter to the Forum on judicial activism of People's Courts. Retrieved December 1, 2011, from http://www.court.gov.cn/xwzx/yw/201005/t20100506_4813.htm

Wolfe, Christopher. (1997). *Judicial activism: Bulwark of freedom or precarious security?* (Rev. ed.). Lanham, MD: Rowman & Littlefield Publishers.

Agriculture (China and Southeast Asia)

The success of intensive agriculture and the Green Revolution has blessed China and Southeast Asia with abundant food but has harmed the environment. The misuse of agrochemicals has polluted soil, water, and air and threatened biodiversity. China and Southeast Asia have made strides toward sustainable agriculture by conserving soil, practicing no-tillage and minimum tillage, adopting integrated pest management, planting legumes, and returning marginal land to forest and pasture.

Environmentally sustainable agriculture may mean different things to soil scientists, agronomists, plant breeders, rural economists, and entomologists. Without doubt, farmers also have their own understanding. In 1987 the Brundtland Commission, set up by the United Nations, defined sustainable development as "development which meets the needs of the current generation without compromising the ability of future generations to meet their own needs" (Research Center for Regional Resources, Indonesian Institute of Sciences 2003, 3). In the context of agriculture, sustainable development must include the preservation of the productive capacity of soil, water, and air. A special controversy surrounds the last of these—air, or the Earth's atmosphere. Some scientists believe that the increase in carbon dioxide in the air, causing climate change, may endanger the sustainability of agriculture. Others believe that, because plants use carbon dioxide, an increase in carbon dioxide in the air may increase yields and so advance sustainability.

Farmers in China and Southeast Asia have practiced sustainable agriculture for millennia. For some nine thousand years these regions have grown rice with little degradation of the soil. Traditional rice culture aimed to produce a constant if modest yield over many years rather than the maximum yield in the short term at the peril of future harvests. Farmers laid rice straw on the field after the harvest to increase the amount of organic matter in the soil. In traditional agriculture, farmers flooded their rice paddies to suppress the growth of weeds. This floodwater sustained the growth of nitrogen fixing microbes in the soil. Bunds protected soil from erosion. The fact that these methods have sustained ever-larger populations over millennia suggests that they have been sustainable. Were the case otherwise, populations in China and Southeast Asia could not have expanded.

Advent of Unsustainable Practices

Since the European Enlightenment period in the eighteenth century, science has attracted attention for the good it can do. Scientists have underscored the utilitarian value of their work in order to secure funding from governments and the private sector. Agricultural science, arising during the Enlightenment and expanding in the nineteenth, twentieth, and twenty-first centuries, promised evermore abundant harvests. The success of scientific agriculture in the West did not immediately affect farming in China and Southeast Asia, where traditional practices proved difficult to dislodge. Communism, arising in China and parts of Southeast Asia in the twentieth century, coexisted uneasily with the capitalist West. Under the regime of Mao Zedong (1893–1976), attempts to reform agriculture in China caused dislocations in the countryside, resulting in famine that killed millions of Chinese in the 1950s and 1960s.

In famine's aftermath, governments in China and Southeast Asia were eager to increase the production of staples, especially rice. The high-yielding varieties of rice, corn, and wheat of the Green Revolution demanded large applications of fertilizer to yield maximum grain. Farmers and scientists, who should have known better, assumed that if a small amount of fertilizer yielded modest gains, larger and larger quantities would yield record harvests. The result was that farmers overused fertilizer. In addition, they applied large amounts of herbicide and pesticide to their crops. All these agrochemicals penetrated groundwater, making it unsafe to drink, and moved into rivers, streams, and lakes, contaminating them as well.

In the heady days of the Green Revolution during the 1960s and 1970s, growers in China and Southeast Asia double and triple cropped their land, a practice with deep historical roots, but one now pursued with less foresight than in the past. In their haste to prepare their field for a second or third crop, farmers burned the rice straw they had once used to enrich the soil. The results were both air pollution and a decline in the soil's content of organic matter. Since the 1960s the trend in China and Southeast Asia has been to substitute inorganic fertilizer for manure with the consequence being a decrease in the content of organic matter in the soil and degradation of soil structure. Intensive farming degraded the soil's capacity to supply nitrogen to a crop, and the promiscuous use of water threatened its quantity and quality. Up to half the freshwater in China and Southeast Asia goes to rice paddies (Spoor, Heerink, and Qu 2007, 267). So much water is used that rivers diminish during the dry season to the extent that saltwater from the ocean flows into their mouths. This brine endangers rich collections of flora and fauna. In addition, groundwater used for irrigation may be high in calcium and magnesium, which reduces the availability of potassium, one of the three main plant nutrients, needed for absorption by roots.

A dearth of labor contributes to environmentally unsustainable agriculture. The youth, who in bygone generations grew up to farm as their parents had, in the twentieth and twenty-first centuries increasingly left home for a job in the city. In Bali, Indonesia, for example, the young are drawn to find work in the hotels and restaurants that support tourism. Bereft of labor, farmers turn to chemicals. Rather than transplant rice seedlings in the field and flood or weed by hand—laborious processes—farmers seed the field directly and so are unable to flood it at the outset of the growing season to control weeds. Instead they rely on herbicides to prevent the germination of new weeds and to kill established ones. The trend toward using agrochemicals thus is facilitated by the fact that herbicides are cheaper and more available than hand labor.

China

China's productivity is exceptional. With just half the farmland per person that the rest of the world has, China feeds 20 percent of the global population (Spoor, Heerink, and Qu 2007, 409). This productivity is sustainable in the long term only if agriculture does not degrade the environment and its natural resources. In the short term, however, the environment has buckled under the weight of agriculture. Of China's three chief grains—rice, corn, and wheat—rice demands the most water (corn the least), and, because rice is China's principal grain, demands on the nation's water resources are great. In the northern semiarid lands, farmers irrigate corn and wheat with water from the Huang (Yellow) River. So great was the demand for irrigation in 1972 that the Huang River dried up before reaching the ocean (Managi and Kaneko 2009, 146). Climate change has exacerbated this problem. As rainfall has decreased and temperatures increased, farmers have had access to less water from the Huang River for irrigation.

There is evidence, too, that fertilizer use is excessive. Since 1962 China has increased its use of fertilizers fiftyfold on its crops in general (Spoor, Heerink, and Qu 2007, 293). Since 1980 fertilizer use has doubled, so that China applies 30 percent of the world's nitrogenous fertilizer (Spoor, Heerink, and Qu 2007, 293). Rice paddies, harboring excess nitrogen from the application of too much fertilizer to the soil, emit nitrogen gas, which warms the planet. Some Chinese farmers apply 50 percent more fertilizer than necessary. China applies three times more fertilizer per hectare than the world average, more per hectare than all but the Netherlands, South Korea, and Japan. Fertilizer runoff imperils China. Half the nation's drinking water has too many nitrates. China's groundwater has as much as three-and-a-half times the allowable healthy limit of nitrates (Spoor, Heerink, and Qu 2007, 293). Because of fertilizer pollution, water from Lake Taihu on the border of Zhejiang and Jiangsu provinces, for example, is no longer safe to drink. Nutrients from fertilizer support algae growth in summer and the emission of an unpleasant odor. The degradation of the lake led neighboring Punjiang County in 2002 to mandate a decrease of one-third in the use of agrochemicals by 2005 (Spoor, Heerink, and Qu 2007, 294). Yet fertilizer use has increased as rice growers diversify by cultivating vegetables, fertilizing greenhouse vegetables at the highest rate: 2,388 kilograms per hectare in Shandong, China (Spoor, Heerink, and Qu 2007, 299). No less worrisome is the fact that since 1980 herbicide use has tripled in China. Pesticide use is also high, particularly on cotton, tomatoes, and apples. Agrochemicals are the leading pollutants of water in China. China's increasing population is a burden, compelling farmers to convert marginal land to crops. Some of the results of all these trends are deforestation, salinization, desertification, and a decrease in the amount of groundwater.

Yet there are reasons for optimism. Even given the intensification of agriculture during the Green Revolution,

Chinese growers have held onto the diversity of their past by planting traditional varieties of rice along with the new high-yielding hybrids. Chinese farmers protect the habitat of the Chinese forest frog, which can eat thousands of insects per year, reducing the need for insecticides. Syngenta China, a subsidiary of a Swiss firm, works with farmers to conserve soil in orchards and on slopes. It promotes no-tillage and minimum-tillage practices—planting with little or no plowing to help reduce erosion and nutrient loss—for wheat, canola, rice, and corn. Since 2006 Syngenta China has awarded scholarships to students at undergraduate and graduate levels whose research focuses on sustainable agriculture.

Persuading China's farmers to adopt sustainable practices is challenging because the majority of these people are ill educated, poor, and have little land. Despite this challenge, however, some farmers in Sichuan Province practice no-tillage on land planted to wheat and canola, even though the growth of weeds on no- and minimum-till land is troublesome; accordingly, these farmers do find the need to use the herbicide Gramoxone to kill weeds. Because these farmers do not plow their land they save sixty to ninety person days of labor per hectare. Because the soil is not broken it is less likely to erode and dry out, protecting crops against drought. Chinese growers who practice no-tillage report higher yields of wheat and rape, though as a rule no-till agriculture is not as productive as conventional intensive agriculture. Along the Yangzi (Chang) River farmers practice no-tillage on land planted to cotton, rice, wheat, and canola. These farmers double crop their land, growing wheat and canola in winter and cotton and rice in summer. No-till farming is prevalent in Anhui, Jiangsu, Hubei, and Hunan provinces.

In western China, farmers are using no-till practices for corn crops, and many of those who had once polluted the air by burning rice straw have returned to the ecologically sound practice of incorporating it into the soil. The farmer who uses rice straw as mulch needs less herbicide to control weeds. Some farmers combine rice culture with integrated pest management (IPM), which is a strategy of reducing the population of pests through environmentally sustainable biological, chemical, physical, and mechanical means. The farmer who relies on biological controls, by protecting the Chinese forest frog for example, need apply less pesticide to a crop. Citrus growers in Zhejiang Province and growers of tea and peaches in Sichuan practice soil conservation. In the 1980s China's government promoted sustainable agriculture by returning marginal and hilly land to forest and pasture to reduce erosion. A poor population tends to exploit land and other natural resources because their need is dire; rising rural incomes in China may undergird a desire to manage natural resources without exploiting them.

Southeast Asia

In Southeast Asia as in China, the technology and chemicals that make agriculture more productive threaten natural resources. Some observers maintain that agriculture in Southeast Asia degrades natural resources more than do factories, cars, and airplanes. Soil erosion is a serious problem; perhaps the most serious problem, however, is the overuse of fertilizer, pesticide, and herbicide, which damage soil, water, and air. The conversion of arable land to cities and roads is another barrier to sustainable agriculture in Southeast Asia. In addition, many farmers do not practice sustainable agriculture, sacrificing sustainability for the prospect of rapid growth in the production of crops in the short term. Southeast Asia's intensive rice cultivation and livestock raising, on its current path, may not be sustainable.

Indonesia

Although Indonesia is primarily Muslim, some Hindus reside on the Indonesian island of Bali. Because these Hindus regard rice as a sacred plant, its cultivation must be sustainable and in harmony with natural resources. The peasant tradition in Bali underscores the management of farmland for the long term rather than for maximum yields in the short term. Yet certain forces are undermining this tradition. Tourism has brought with it an ethos of exploitation in which land is a commodity, not something worthy of conservation. The young who leave the family farm for a job in a hotel or restaurant lose respect for the land and other natural resources. The drift toward the free market fosters a focus on short-term gain without regard to sustainability. These threats to sustainability may already have harmed Bali: once a rice exporter, Bali must now import rice from Java and Lombok.

In the Indonesian province of East Kalimantan, some farmers fallow land to restore fertility and avoid overcropping. In one village peasants fallow land for as long as thirty years. In other areas the fallow lasts four to six years. The practice of fallowing land requires the use of more land than intensive agriculture. This extensive agriculture may undermine sustainability. Farmers are eager to possess as much land as possible and cut down forest to secure more land for agriculture, which leads to deforestation. The farmers who practice extensive agriculture raise few pigs and chickens and so do not have manure to enrich the soil.

Other, more sedentary farmers practice a more sustainable two-year rotation, double cropping the first year. That year they first plant rice, corn, spinach, and cucumbers, crops that deplete the soil of nutrients. The second cropping that year is peanuts, soybeans, and beans:

legumes that fix nitrogen in the soil, contributing to its fertility. Farmers may fertilize the soil with manure at this stage, if they have it. Some farmers raise chickens and livestock for this purpose as well as for meat. In year two of the rotation, farmers triple crop the land, first planting cacao seedlings and vegetables. The second cropping is rice, corn, and spinach. The third, again, is peanuts, soybeans, and beans.

In Java the four chief crops are rice, corn, peanuts, and soybeans. Between 1993 and 2002 the area planted to peanuts in Java increased 1.3 percent, but that planted to soybeans fell 4.4 percent, making an assessment of the sustainability of Javanese agriculture difficult (Research Center for Regional Resources, Indonesian Institute of Sciences 2003, 82). In the twenty-first century, new varieties of peanuts and soybeans have the potential to expand acreage because their yield and other desirable traits should coax farmers to plant them and so improve the soil by fixing nitrogen in it. Even with the capacity of legumes to fix nitrogen in the soil, Java's farmers still fertilize the land with nitrogen-rich urea. In addition to fertilizers, Java's farmers use pesticides. Because the government subsidizes the cost of pesticides, farmers often overuse them, making them progressively ineffective and damaging natural resources. Indonesian scientists have modeled IPM as a way of reducing the dependence on pesticides. Between 1991 and 1999, Indonesian farmers reduced pesticide use 56 percent and increased yields 10 percent (Resosudarmo 2001, 1).

Malaysia, Vietnam, and Myanmar (Burma)

In the nineteenth century, the cultivation of pepper and gambier in Malaysia depleted the soil within fifteen years. Worse, cassava depleted the soil in just five years. Soil exhaustion led farmers to exploit new lands with little regard for rehabilitating land that was no longer productive. In the twentieth century, farmers cleared mangrove and freshwater swamps for sugarcane at the expense of biodiversity. Coffee trees dotted hills, subjecting them to erosion. In the early twentieth century, the rubber plant and later oil palm emerged as important crops. Rubber was favored on land that cassava had depleted. At first growers interplanted rubber with coffee, but as rubber grew in profitability large planters transitioned to rubber plant monoculture. Between 1905 and 1907 the hectares of land planted to rubber in Malaysia more than tripled, following a rise in prices on the European market (Dove, Sajise, and Doolittle 2011, 65). When the elite planters grew rubber in monoculture, soil eroded. Without the dense network of roots that had existed in the once prevalent forest, rubber monoculture left the soil unable to absorb large quantities of water. Rainwater that passed through the soil took nutrients from it. Between 1902 and 1939 rubber plantations in Malaysia lost a small fraction of a metric ton of topsoil per year (Dove, Sajise, and Doolittle 2011, 69); in 1940 alone Malaysia lost 1.1 billion metric tons of soil to erosion.

Rubber has been also a crop of the small farmer, not just of the large plantations. Grown in orchards with fruit trees, rubber has been part of a biodiverse peasant holding. Because leaf litter has enriched the soil, smallholder rubber has depleted few nutrients from the soil. In the late 1920s smallholders and elites alike began to interplant rubber and legumes. In the 1970s Malaysia's government, alert to the depletion of natural resources, sought to prevent the planting of rubber and oil palm on slopes subject to erosion, but problems remained.

Factories that processed rubber and palm oil have discharged waste that contained E. coli bacteria into rivers. The use of herbicides and pesticides has decreased the diversity of aquatic life in Malaysia's lakes, rivers, and streams. The cultivation of rubber and oil palm and the processing of their products has generated more than one-third of Malaysia's pollution (Dove, Sajise, and Doolittle 2011, 83).

Since 1989 the yield of rice has increased faster than the population in Vietnam, a prospect that might have surprised the British economist T. Robert Malthus, who in the early nineteenth century theorized that population growth would always outpace food production. Vietnam produces a surplus of rice but to the detriment of the environment because fertilizer and pesticide use is intensive. The increase in the use of pesticides coincided with the introduction of high-yielding varieties of rice in the 1980s and 1990s. Herbicide use is also problematic. More than 95 percent of rice growers in Vietnam apply a pre-emergent herbicide to prevent weeds from germinating early in the growing season (Spoor, Heerink, and Qu 2007, 242). The remaining growers, perhaps more environmentally conscious, flood their fields at the beginning of the growing season to prevent the germination of weeds and then must transplant rice seedlings in the field—a laborious process. Agrochemicals have polluted water in Vietnam. To lessen the reliance on pesticides scientists have promoted IPM. Between 1996 and 2000 pesticide use decreased 25 percent because Vietnamese farmers transitioned to IPM (Spoor, Heerink, and Qu 2007, 243). By 2001, 70 percent of farmers in Vietnam practiced IPM (Spoor, Heerink, and Qu 2007, 241).

Myanmar (Burma) is among Asia's leading rice growers and consumers. The problems of excessive use of fertilizers, herbicides, and pesticides have—as in China, Indonesia, Malaysia, and Vietnam—degraded natural resources. The diversion of freshwater to irrigation threatens the quantity and quality of water for other uses. Among Myanmar's environmental problems are soil erosion, salinization, deforestation, depletion of soil nutrients, reduction in soil structure and the activity of soil microbes, and soil acidification. Soil erosion is serious in the hills and on flat terrain, but the worst effect is on the dry farming regions. Erosion might be countered by terracing hills and plowing in contoured strips. Myanmar is among the countries that rely least on fertilizers and other chemicals. Although the avoidance of chemicals doubtless reduces yields, it saves land from the problems of the overuse of agrochemicals. In recent years, however, bean farmers have begun to use insecticides, whose residues are not always absent from the legumes.

Toward Sustainability

The Green Revolution gave China and Southeast Asia the chemicals and crops to increase food production. The fact that these regions can feed more people now than before underscores the success of the Green Revolution. Yet the Green Revolution, in its reliance on agrochemicals, harmed natural resources. Perhaps China and Southeast Asia need a second Green Revolution, one that allows farmers to produce food without degrading natural resources. The components of this Green Revolution need to be practiced on a large scale to overcome harm done by the first revolution. IPM has the potential to diminish the region's reliance on pesticides, as the example of Vietnam has illustrated. The planting of legumes on a large scale might reduce China and Southeast Asia's dependence on nitrogenous fertilizer. The return of marginal land to forest, made possible by an increase in yield per hectare, might reduce erosion, a serious problem in Malaysia and Myanmar. Minimum-till and no-till practices might have difficulty producing yields sufficient to keep pace with population growth. Their widespread adoption might, however, lessen erosion in China and Southeast Asia and also reduce the emission of greenhouse gases as farmers would not need to use tractors to plow land.

Christopher CUMO
Independent scholar, Canton, Ohio, USA

See also Agriculture (South Asia); Consumerism; Education, Environmental (*several articles*); Huang (Yellow) River; Nongovernmental Organizations (NGOs); Reforestation and Afforestation (Southeast Asia); Rural Livelihoods; Traditional Knowledge (China)

FURTHER READING

Altieri, Miguel A. (Ed.). (1987). *Agro-ecology: The scientific basis of alternative agriculture.* Boulder, Colorado: Westview Press.

Brown, Colin G.; Waldron, Scott A.; & Longworth, John W. (Eds.). (2008). *Sustainable development in western China: Managing people, livestock and grasslands in pastoral areas.* Cheltenham, UK: Edward Elgar.

Colman, David, & Vink, Nick. (Eds.). (2005). *Reshaping agriculture's contributions to society: Proceedings of the twenty-fifth international conference of agricultural economists.* Malden, MA: Blackwell Publishing.

Dove, Michael R.; Sajise, Percy E.; & Doolittle, Amity A. (2011). *Beyond the sacred forest: Complicating conservation in Southeast Asia.* Durham, NC: Duke University Press.

Lansing, Stephan J. (1983). *The three worlds of Bali.* New York: Praeger.

Managi, Shunsuke, & Kaneko, Shinji. (2009). *Chinese economic development and the environment.* Cheltenham, UK: Edward Elgar.

Organisation for Economic Co-Operation and Development (OECD). (2006). *Environment, water resources and agricultural policies: Lessons from China and OECD countries.* Paris: OECD.

Pinstrup-Anderson, Per. (1999). Food policy research for developing countries: Emerging issues and unfinished business (IFPRI Annual Report 1999). Washington, DC: International Food Policy Research Institute. Retrieved March 3, 2012. from http://www.ifpri.org/sites/default/files/publications/10-19e1.pdf

Research Center for Regional Resources, Indonesian Institute of Sciences (PSDR-LIPI). (2003). *Sustainable agricultural development in Southeast Asia.* Jakarta, Indonesia: PSDR-LIPI.

Resosudarmo, Budy P. (2001). Impact of the integrated pest management program on the Indonesian economy. Retrieved March 3, 2012, from http://een.anu.edu.au/download_files/een0102.pdf

Shi, Tian. (2010). *Sustainable ecological agriculture in China: Bridging the gap between theory and practice.* Amherst, NY: Cambria Press.

Spoor, Max; Heerink, Nico; & Qu, Futian. (2007). *Dragons with clay feet? Transition, sustainable land use, and rural environment in China and Vietnam.* New York: Lexington Books.

Tuck-Po, Lye; de Jong, Wil; & Ken-ichi, Abe. (2003). *The political ecology of tropical forests in Southeast Asia: Historical perspectives.* Kyoto, Japan: Kyoto University Press.

Wilson, Trevor. (Ed.). (2006). *Myanmar's long road to national reconciliation.* Singapore: Institute of Southeast Asian Studies.

Wood, Adrian, & van Halsema, Gerardo E. (2008). *Scoping agriculture—wetland interactions: Towards a sustainable multiple-response strategy.* Rome: Food and Agriculture Organization of the United Nations.

Agriculture (South Asia)

Domestic agriculture has historically been the primary source of food, fodder, raw materials, and income in South Asia, and has provided the basis for the varied economic, social, political, and cultural arrangements of the region. This continues to be the case. With over 90 percent of South Asian cropland dedicated to growing food, maintaining sustainable, resilient, and economically viable agricultural systems in the region remains critically important.

In accordance with the great diversity of climate, terrain, and resource endowments, agriculture in South Asia varies greatly in type and scale. The Millennium Ecosystem Assessment (MA 2005)—a formal assessment of the state of the world's ecosystems and their contribution to human well-being—cites the 2001 review *Farming Systems and Poverty* (Dixon, Gulliver, and Gibbon 2001) as the most "comprehensive approach to date [of classifying] the farming systems of the developing world" (MA 2005, 750). This review describes eleven key farming systems of importance in South Asia. These include rice farming, various types of dryland cultivation systems, pastoral and agro-pastoral systems, tree-crop systems, and urban agriculture.

The Green Revolution

The Green Revolution was a set of research and technology-transfer initiatives initiated in the 1960s in underdeveloped nations to increase crop yield through the use of high-yielding crop strains, fertilizers, pesticides, and better-controlled water supplies. It introduced pivotal and long-standing changes in agricultural policy, practice, and outcomes in the region and therefore occupies an important place in the history of agriculture. Over the course of a few decades, starting during the 1960s in India, it aimed to industrialize agriculture in order to boost production, especially of food. The key innovation was the introduction of modified, high-yielding varieties of wheat, supported by the spread of irrigation, the application of inorganic fertilizers and pesticides, and increased mechanization. These methods supported remarkable agricultural growth and, by extension, partially ameliorated hunger and poverty. In South Asia, 80 percent of the growth in agricultural output between 1961 and 1999 resulted from yield increases (Dixon, Gulliver, and Gibbon 2001). In India, the Green Revolution was credited with averting catastrophic famine, making the country self-sufficient in food production, and enabling the maintenance of buffer stocks of grain.

Across the region, the spread of technologies and inputs pioneered within the Green Revolution transformed traditional agriculture. The Indian researcher Gopal Bhatta and German professor Werner Doppler, for example, describe how "the adopted use of agrochemicals rapidly changed Nepalese [farming practices] from [being] indigenous knowledge–based integrated farming practices to more market-oriented, intensive, and monoculture practices" (Bhatta and Dopler 2011, 165). While it is recognized that these transformations saved millions from hunger and malnutrition, Green Revolution technologies have not maintained their momentum, and their sustainability implications have been criticized on a number of fronts. Key concerns include the uneven spread of benefits, resource depletion, and land degradation.

The Green Revolution technologies targeted farmers with relatively favorable endowments of land and water. In India for example, farmers in the Punjab, who had relatively large amounts of land and were located in favorable areas (with fertile soils and access to irrigation and transport infrastructure) were able to capitalize on Green Revolution technology. By contrast, smallholders in dryland regions in the rest of the country continue to face significant challenges, and it is these farmers who will play an important role in future food security.

Intensive irrigation and the application of inorganic inputs, such as fertilizers, have been implicated in severe resource degradation. An emphasis on high-yielding varieties has been associated with monocultural production and reduced reliance on diverse traditional varieties, leading to increased incidence and severity of pest infestations and nutrient loss.

Despite the gains of the Green Revolution, the prevalence of hunger and undernutrition in South Asia remains high. Rural population density is also high, placing great pressure on the resource base in settled areas. The future of South Asian agriculture will depend on being able to maintain or improve this resource base while increasing yields, diversifying farmers' livelihoods, and providing stable markets.

Sustainability Challenges

Agriculture in the region faces a variety of challenges, some of them caused by unsustainable land and water management practices and exacerbated by the demands of population growth and industrial development.

Heavy water use, driven in part by the Green Revolution and partly from historic overuse of centralized irrigation projects, has resulted in depleted rivers and groundwater levels, and in large tracts of land becoming degraded. In irrigated regions, overirrigation causes severe and often irredeemable degradation from waterlogging and salinization. An estimated 6.3 million hectares in Pakistan's Indus River basin are affected, and about half of these rely on irrigated agriculture for subsistence (Qureshi et al. 2007). The Indian professor and researcher Ajay Singh and colleagues describe how over-irrigation in the heavily irrigated Indian state of Haryana has been a significant driver of waterlogging over some 500,000 hectares of land that are no longer arable (Singh et al. 2012).

In many places, further expansion of irrigation potential is difficult, as most readily accessible freshwater sources have already been tapped. The construction and use of large, centralized irrigation systems is associated with profound social, cultural, and environmental impacts, as detailed in a seminal review by the World Commission on Dams (2000) titled *Dams and Development*.

Other Sources of Nutrients and Energy

Similarly to farming communities around the world, farmers in South Asia depend not only upon their crops for their livelihoods, but also on wild or partially cultivated species found on or around their farms. These wild species provide nutrients and energy to communities most vulnerable to hunger and malnutrition (Bharucha and Pretty 2010). Studies of individual communities in Bangladesh, Nepal, and India have attempted to collate the number of wild species used for food on which farming communities depend. (See table 1 below.)

TABLE 1. Number of wild food species used by farming communities in selected countries of South Asia

Country	Type of System	Number of Wild Species
Bangladesh	Floodplain rice farming	102
India	Agro-pastoral systems; deciduous forest	73
India	Transhumance and rain-fed agriculture; temperate forest	21
India	Mornaula Reserve Forest in western Himalaya	114
India	Sikkimese Himalaya	190
India	Rain-fed agricultural community of Deccan Plateau; 79 species of plants used, plus hunting of monitor lizards, wild pigs, rabbits, and fish	79
Nepal	Chepang community; shifting cultivation	85

Source: Adapted from Bharucha and Pretty (2010).

South Asian farmers, then, are also important stewards of the region's biodiverse landscapes. The transition toward industrialized, monocultural production and changing land use (e.g. through unplanned or poorly regulated urbanization and industrialization) threatens the wild species on which these farmers depend and their role as biodiversity stewards protecting important ecosystem goods and services.

Future Prospects

The availability of sufficient, and timely, water, from either rainfall or irrigation infrastructure, has been a historic concern and is likely to become more pressing due to climate change, the deterioration of irrigation infrastructure, the cultivation of water-intensive crops, and the demands made by a rising population, increasing urbanization, and industrialization. In the future, rainfed regions will have to supply the increasing demands associated with increased agricultural productivity. In these situations, the overextraction of groundwater to compensate for inadequate or untimely rainfall is an increasingly pressing concern.

The extent of productive agricultural land in South Asia is also increasingly threatened by the processes associated with urbanization and industrialization, which render it subject to the impacts of salinization, waterlogging, nutrient loss, and erosion. Sustainable intensification—increasing the agricultural productivity of a given tract of land, while reducing the environmental impacts associated with the increased production—rather than the expansion of farmland, is likely to be the most practical strategy for the foreseeable future (Royal Society 2009). Agricultural practices that conserve or improve upon the resource base (adding soil fertility, using less water, and improving biodiversity) are likely to result in sustainable yield increases (Pretty et al. 2006).

Biophysical challenges include the impacts of climate change, which will affect different countries and regions in different ways. Overall, climate change is expected to result in a 10–40 percent decrease in crop production in the region by the end of the century (Aggarwal and Sivakumar 2011).

Climate change will also overlap with other stressors, such as those generated by globalization. One study has already described the combined effects of climate change and globalization on agriculture in India (O'Brien et al. 2004). As countries industrialize and globalize, population increases and changing dietary preferences (usually in the form of consumption of greater amounts of food as well as in transitions from pulses—edible crop seeds, such as peas and beans—to cereals, and increases in the consumption of meat) put demands on growth. Industrialization also implies that South Asian farmers will have to produce ever greater amounts of raw materials for industry. As demands for alternative sources of energy escalate, agricultural land will also have to grow biofuel. Equally deep challenges are presented by the fact that hunger stems not just from a lack of adequate food production, but also from lack of *access* to sufficient quantities of food. Ensuring that these needs are met sustainably will be critical to ensuring that they will continue to be met in the future.

With the recognition that the Green Revolution and later modernizations have led to various unsustainable outcomes, there has been a resurgence of interest in the broad group of agricultural practices that produce sustainable intensification (Godfray et al. 2010; Royal Society 2009). In contrast to the Green Revolution model of top-down, expert-led innovation and extension, the new emphasis on resource-conserving agriculture seems to broadly recognize the importance of *local* knowledge, participation, and context-specific innovations.

Zareen Pervez BHARUCHA
University of Essex

Agricultural Challenges in Bangladesh

Bangladesh has a long history of dealing with natural disasters such as floods and cyclones. Many in Bangladesh face unparalleled agricultural challenges as a result. A subset of the population lives on ephemeral islands called chars. These islands, often no larger than a square kilometer, disappear as soon as they appear, brought into and out of existence by the changing tides, the rise and fall of the rivers, the seasons, and rainfall; effects that will be exacerbated as climate change affects weather patterns. Farmers and their families often must pack their belongings (including their house) and relocate quickly, find a new char, and set up their house and a new garden immediately. National Geographic has compared this existence to "winning an Olympic medal in adaptation" (Belt 2011).

As climate change affects weather patterns and sea levels, farmers in Bangladesh have implemented the use of climate change–resistant crops such as a variety of rice called BINA Dhan–7, also known as paijam. This variety of rice, developed by the Bangladesh Institute of Nuclear Agriculture (BINA), withstands floods, drought, and pest attacks, and matures faster with a higher yield than traditional varieties. Another variety cultivated by the Bangladesh Rice Research Institute (BRRI) known as BRRI–47 tolerates higher levels of salinization and waterlogging. The cultivation of these and other climate change–resistant crops such as tomatoes, sweet potatoes, onions, and especially cereals, has given the region hope for a source of sustainable agriculture as previously lost arable land can be reclaimed for food production (Haq 2012).

Still other farmers have adapted by changing to cultivation of different crops altogether. Rice paddies once stretched across the land. Now, as a result of longer summers, and disrupted precipitation patterns, the salinity of the sea creeps in, turning rivers and groundwater salty, even fifty kilometers inland. With the land too salty to grow rice, the farmers have begun raising shrimps or crabs in the brackish ponds (Belt 2011).

There are still challenges, however, of a rising population in an already densely populated nation. Bangladesh is vulnerable to rising sea levels, and as at-risk groups such as dense coastal populations are forced to relocate, the number of climate change refugees is predicted to increase to 250 million by 2050. The people of Bangladesh have cultivated an attitude of adaptation in the face of adversity, however, giving them a head start on preparations for climate change in the coming decades (Belt 2011).

See also Agriculture (China and Southeast Asia); Education, Environmental (*several articles*); India; Rural Development; Rural Livelihoods; Traditional Knowledge (India); Water Security; Water Use and Rights (India); White Revolution of India

Further Reading

Aggarwal, Pramod K., & Sivakumar, Mannava V. K. (2011). Global climate change and food security in South Asia: An adaptation and mitigation framework. In Rattan Lal, Mannava V. K. Sivakumar, Syed Mohammad Abul Faiz, A. H. M. Mustafizur Rahman & Khandakar R. Islam (Eds.), *Climate change and food security in South Asia* (pp. 253–275). Dordrecht, The Netherlands: Springer. Retrieved April 3, 2012, from http://www.springerlink.com/content/978-90-481-9515-2/#section=796392&page=1&locus=14

Belt, Don. (2011). The coming storm. Retrieved April 13, 2012, from http://ngm.nationalgeographic.com/2011/05/bangladesh/belt-text

Bharucha, Zareen, & Pretty, Jules. (2010). The role and use of wild foods in agricultural systems. *Philosophical Transactions of the Royal Society B, 365*(1554), 2913–2926.

Bhatta, Gopal Datt, & Doppler, Werner. (2011). Smallholder peri-urban organic farming in Nepal: A comparative analysis of farming systems. *Journal of Agriculture, Food Systems, and Community Development, 1*(3), 163–180.

Dixon, John; Gulliver, Aidan; & Gibbon, David. (2001). *Farming systems and poverty: Improving farmers' livelihoods in a changing world*. Rome: FAO and World Bank.

Foley, Jonathan A., et al. (2011). Solutions for a cultivated planet. *Nature, 478*(7369), 337.

Godfray, Charles, et al. (2010). Food security: The challenge of feeding 9 billion people. *Science, 327*, 812–818.

Haq, Naimul. (2012, January 5). Farmers bet on climate-proof crops. Retrieved April 13, 2012, from http://ipsnews.net/news.asp?idnews=106370

Millennium Ecosystem Assessment (MA). (2005). Drivers for change in ecosystem condition and services. *Millennium Ecosystem Assessment: Scenarios*. Washington, DC: Island Press.

O'Brien, Karen, et al. (2004). Mapping vulnerability to multiple stressors: Climate change and globalization in India. *Global Environmental Change, 14*(2004), 303–313.

Pretty, Jules N., et al. (2006). Resource conserving agriculture increases yields in developing countries. *Environmental Science and Technology, 40*(4), 1114–1119.

Qureshi, Asad S.; McCornick, Peter G.; Qadir, Manzoor; & Aslam, Z. (2007). Managing salinity and waterlogging in the Indus Basin of Pakistan. *Agricultural Water Management, 95*(1), 1–10.

Royal Society. (2009). *Reaping the benefits: Science and the sustainable intensification of global agriculture.* Retrieved May 20, 2010, from http://royalsociety.org/Reapingthebenefits/

Singh, Ajay; Panda, Sudhindra Nath; Flügel, Wolfgang-Albert; & Krause, Peter. (2012). Waterlogging and farmland salinisation: Causes and remedial measures in an irrigated semi-arid region of India. *Irrigation and Drainage.* doi: 10.1002/ird.651. Retrieved April 3, 2012, from http://www.geoinf.uni-jena.de/fileadmin/Geoinformatik/c5wafl/papers/Waterlogging_and_Salinisation_2012.pdf

World Commission on Dams (WCD). (2000). *Dams and development: A new framework for decision-making.* London: Earthscan. Retrieved April, 4, 2012, from http://www.unep.org/dams/WCD/

Association of Southeast Asian Nations (ASEAN)

The Association of Southeast Asian Nations (ASEAN) responded rapidly to regional haze and wildlife trafficking but has not collectively addressed the threat of dams to its major rivers. While ASEAN promulgates environmental guidelines and action plans to address these challenges, it has only agreed upon a single legally binding law. Moreover, ASEAN currently possesses no mechanism to enforce environmental laws.

On 8 August 1967, Indonesia, Malaysia, the Philippines, Singapore, and Thailand formed the Association of Southeast Asian Nations (ASEAN) in order to promote peace and stability in the region. Given the ongoing Vietnam War and Indonesia's history of confrontation with its neighbors, the countries agreed that they would not interfere in each other's domestic affairs. Brunei Darussalam joined the association in 1984 upon gaining independence from Britain. When the Cold War ended, ASEAN admitted Cambodia, Laos, Myanmar (Burma), and Vietnam. East Timor, which seceded from Indonesia in 2001, has also indicated its willingness to join. In December 2008, the ASEAN Charter came into force, conferring legal personhood on the organization and delineating the rights and responsibilities of ASEAN states.

As of 2010, Southeast Asia's population exceeded 600 million, with Indonesia by far the largest country, with 245 million people. Unlike the European Union, ASEAN is characterized by considerable political, economic, ethnic, and cultural diversity. Governments in the region range from democratic Philippines and Indonesia to moderately authoritarian Singapore and Malaysia to Communist Vietnam. Economic conditions vary drastically, from Singapore, which has a per capita gross domestic product (GDP) higher than Great Britain's, to Cambodia and Myanmar, two of the poorest countries in the world. The majority of Southeast Asians still work in agriculture and live in rural areas, but increasingly many have moved to booming metropolises in search of manufacturing jobs.

Some scholars estimate that environmental degradation costs Southeast Asia between 3 and 8 percent of GDP per year (Barkenbus 2001). In 1978, ASEAN placed environmental issues on its formal agenda. It has since passed more than 170 environmental laws, programs, and guidelines. In 1997, ASEAN adopted the Vision 2020 statement, which proclaimed its goal of "a clean and green ASEAN with fully established mechanisms for sustainable development to ensure the protection of the region's environment, [and] the sustainability of its natural resources. . . ." (ASEAN 1997). Subsequently, ASEAN agreed upon the Hanoi Plan of Action (1999–2004) and the Vientiane Action Program (2004–2010) to implement Vision 2020. Most of these documents are only guiding principles, however, and do not have any binding force.

ASEAN also facilitates discussion and cooperation between national environmental officials through the ASEAN Ministerial Meeting on the Environment (AMME) and the ASEAN Senior Officials on the Environment (ASEON). The AMME meets formally once every three years and informally once a year in order to adopt guiding objectives and principles for environmental management, as well as strategic plans of action on the environment. In addition, ASEAN has issued several resolutions urging members to honor multilateral environmental agreements.

Ecosystem and Biodiversity Protection

United Nations (UN) agencies and environmental nongovernmental organizations (NGOs) consider Southeast Asia crucial for the protection of biodiversity hotspots.

The region contains more than two hundred mammalian, two hundred avian, and thirty reptile and amphibian species currently considered threatened or endangered. Because of its rapid economic growth over the past few decades, Southeast Asia risks losing much of its biodiversity. According to the UN Food and Agriculture Organization, from 2000 to 2005, the average annual deforestation rate in Southeast Asia was 1.35 percent, compared to the global average of 0.18 percent. Several ASEAN countries, particularly Indonesia and Vietnam, have become key source and transit hubs in the illegal wildlife trade. More ominously, China and India have both begun to exploit Southeast Asia's natural resources in order to fuel their own economic growth.

In 1985, ASEAN members signed the Agreement on the Conservation of Nature and Natural Resources—the first of only two legally binding intergovernmental environmental treaties ever produced through ASEAN. The treaty would have imposed fairly rigorous obligations on ASEAN members to create protected areas and prohibit exploitation of endangered species. It would also have required members to conduct environmental impact assessments for projects that might significantly affect the natural environment. As of mid-2011, however, only Indonesia, the Philippines, and Thailand had ratified the treaty (notably, the newer ASEAN members have not even signed it).

ASEAN's more recent efforts to protect biodiversity have focused on coordination and capacity building among its member states. In October 2000, ASEAN agriculture and forestry ministers adopted regional criteria and indicators for sustainable management of natural tropical forests. In 2005, ASEAN launched the ASEAN Regional Centre for Biodiversity Conservation to strengthen biodiversity management capacity and to prepare to meet the UN Millennium Development Goals. Later that year, in partnership with the United States Agency for International Development, it launched the ASEAN Wildlife Enforcement Network (ASEAN-WEN) to allow members to share information and best practices. From July to September 2010 alone, ASEAN-WEN members conducted 110 major law enforcement actions, recovered 11,390 live animals, and arrested 57 individuals (ASEAN-WEN 2011).

Marine and Water Resources

Southeast Asia has some 173,000 kilometers of coastline and several major river systems, and ASEAN countries have increasingly resorted to hydropower as a solution to their energy needs. While the Mekong was once known as the world's last great wild river, today several countries are building dams along it. Laos has already begun construction on the Nam Theun II dam with assistance from the World Bank, while China plans more dams farther upriver. In June 2011, a minor war between the government of Myanmar and the Kachin Independence Army erupted over the construction of the Myitsone Dam on the Irrawaddy River.

The ASEAN region is home to 34 percent of the world's coral reefs, as well as one hundred threatened or endangered fish species. The fishing industry provides both employment and food in Southeast Asia's rural areas. For example, Cambodia relies upon Mekong River fish for about 80 percent of its animal protein. Illegal fishing has undermined national efforts to regulate the fishing industry, however. In 2003, illegal fishing cost Indonesia an estimated $103.3 million (Palma and Tsamenyi 2008). Illegal fishers often employ destructive practices such as blast fishing, which has destroyed many of the coral reefs around the Philippines.

In October 2005, ASEAN produced a strategic plan of action on water resources and management, which focuses primarily on improving access to clean drinking water and sanitation services. ASEAN has also worked to integrate member state efforts on coastal management. ASEAN has not yet taken a position on the Mekong dams, however, partly because its own members are deeply divided. For example, the Nam Theun II would bring Laos much-needed foreign exchange and provide Thailand with a clean source of energy, but it could potentially deprive Cambodia and Vietnam of much of their fisheries and freshwater resources. Laos, Thailand, Cambodia, and Vietnam established the Mekong River Commission in 1995 to conduct research and manage the river's resources, but notably neither China nor Myanmar has joined.

Pollution, Haze, and Climate Change

Climate change could pose a significant threat to ASEAN members. In 2002, the ASEAN secretariat estimated that a doubling of carbon dioxide (CO_2) levels could cost ASEAN members 2.1–8.6 percent of their GDP. Many Southeast Asians fear that climate change will lead to more extreme weather events, such as the Indian Ocean tsunami in 2004, which killed an estimated 167,000 Indonesians and 8,200 Thais, and cyclone Nargis in 2008, which killed more than 140,000 Burmese. At the same time, Southeast Asia is both a victim and a major producer of greenhouse gases (GHG). Between 1990 and 2000, the region's GHG emissions grew by 27 percent, much higher than the global average. Largely due to extensive forest fires, Indonesia is now the third-largest contributor of GHG, behind only the

United States and China. Some estimates predict that CO_2 emissions from the region will rise fourfold from 2002 to 2030 (Asian Development Bank 2009).

Southeast Asia has become a crucial player in global climate change negotiations. Cambodia, Indonesia, Malaysia, Myanmar, the Philippines, Singapore, Thailand, and Vietnam all ratified the Kyoto Protocol. In December 2007, Indonesia chaired a key meeting of Kyoto Protocol parties on the island of Bali. Moreover, Indonesia has vocally advocated for the Reducing Emissions from Deforestation and Forest Degradation in Developing Countries (REDD) program. ASEAN, however, does not negotiate or implement treaty obligations on behalf of its members. Shortly before the Bali summit, ASEAN did issue a declaration laying out its members' key negotiating positions, reaffirming its support for the clean development mechanism (CDM) in the Kyoto Protocol, and urging Annex I parties to the protocol to confront their "historic responsibility" by taking the lead in emissions reductions.

ASEAN's report to the 2002 Johannesburg World Summit on Sustainable Development called regional haze "the most serious problem in the region." In 1997 and 1998, slash-and-burn agriculture in Indonesian Borneo (Kalimantan) spread calamitous amounts of smoke over much of neighboring Brunei, Malaysia, and Singapore. While estimates vary, that single event might have cost the region as much as $6.3–$9 billion in lost tourism, agriculture, and biodiversity benefits and affected 20 to 70 million people in five countries (Tay 2008, 199). The haze has recurred in subsequent years, most notably in 2006—ironically, just months after Indonesian president Susilo Bambang Yudhoyono announced, "Let us declare a war against haze." Indonesian officials blame illegal loggers, particularly Malaysian firms, for setting the fires, although much of the haze seems to come from legal plantations.

The severity of the problem convinced ASEAN to adopt the Regional Haze Action Plan, but it did not provide for effective implementing institutions—a key concern given Indonesia's chronic inability to quell the forest fires. In June 2002, ASEAN members signed the Agreement on Transboundary Haze Pollution (ATHP), ASEAN's second environmental treaty, and the only one that has received sufficient signatures to enter into force. The ATHP goes beyond ASEAN's usual approach of noninterference in two key ways. First, the treaty requires states to prevent activities within their jurisdictions from harming other members. Second, the treaty adopts the principle of "common and differential responsibility," acknowledging that the burden of resolving the problem might not fall upon all member states equally. The treaty also establishes the ASEAN Coordinating Center for Transboundary Pollution Control and the ASEAN Transboundary Haze Pollution Control Fund.

Despite the relatively ambitious aims of the ATHP, Indonesia, the source of the haze, refused to ratify the treaty, citing its inability to prevent the fires. While the government has cooperated with efforts to confront the haze, most notably allowing provincial officials in Jambi and Riau to cooperate with colleagues from Singapore and Malaysia, some politicians warned that acceding to the treaty would compromise Indonesia's sovereignty. At the eleventh meeting of the Sub-Regional Ministerial Steering Committee on Transboundary Haze Pollution in March 2011, Indonesia announced that it planned to finally ratify the ATHP. Even if Indonesia were to join, however, the ATHP possesses neither enforcement mechanisms to sanction noncompliance nor benchmarks to measure progress.

Challenges of Enforcement

ASEAN has created an incipient legal framework, but its actual ability to improve the region's environment remains unclear. As noted above, ASEAN has produced only one legally binding environmental treaty. The ASEAN Charter incorporates Vision 2020 (Article 1(9)), but it is not clear whether this provision is legally binding or merely aspirational. More importantly, ASEAN has no body like the European Union Court of Justice to resolve environmental disputes. Article 22(2) of the ASEAN Charter does promise to establish a dispute settlement mechanism, but it is not yet clear whether the body would have the power to impose sanctions, or even whether environmental disputes would fall under its jurisdiction.

ASEAN seems most effective when serving as a coordinating mechanism among its members. ASEAN provides a forum in which environmental officials can share information and coordinate actions, such as with ASEAN-WEN. ASEAN can also pool resources to establish regional centers for research and policy analysis. This is an especially constructive role given Southeast Asia's cultural and linguistic diversity, which might otherwise impede regional cooperation. Given the transboundary impacts of dams, the AMME and ASEON should include dams on their agenda and develop a forum to resolve riverine disputes.

Another challenge for ASEAN is to find innovative ways to engage nonstate and subnational actors. While many Southeast Asian countries have active environmental NGOs, few of them operate across borders or at the ASEAN level. In many countries, natural resource management falls under the jurisdiction of state and local governments. In fact, working at the subnational level and with NGOs might allow ASEAN to address environmental challenges even when national governments lack the will or means to do so.

Dominic J. NARDI Jr.
University of Michigan

See also Activism, Judicial; Biodiversity Conservation Legislation (China); Biosafety Legislation (China); Climate Change Mitigation Initiatives (China); Corporate Accountability (China); Nongovernmental Organizations (NGOs); Parks and Preserves; Rule of Law; Transboundary Water Issues

FURTHER READING

Asian Development Bank. (2009). *The economics of climate change in Southeast Asia: A regional overview*. Retrieved January 30, 2012, from http://www.adb.org/Documents/Books/Economics-Climate-Change-SEA/PDF/Economics-Climate-Change.pdf

Asian Environmental Compliance and Enforcement Network (AECEN). (2011). Homepage. Retrieved July 30, 2011, from http://www.aecen.org/

Association of Southeast Asian Nations (ASEAN). (1997). ASEAN vision 2020. Retrieved February 18, 2012, from http://www.aseansec.org/1814.htm

Association of Southeast Asian Nations (ASEAN). (2011). Environment homepage. Retrieved July 30, 2011, from http://environment.asean.org/

Association of Southeast Asian Nations-Wildlife Enforcement Network (ASEAN-WEN). (2011). ASEAN-WEN action update (July–September 2010). Retrieved August 1, 2011, from http://www.asean-wen.org/index.php?option=com_docman&task=doc_download&gid=45&Itemid=96

Barkenbus, Jack. (2001). APEC and the environment: Civil society in an age of globalization (Asia Pacific Issues No. 51). Honolulu, Hawaii: East West Center.

Craig, Donna G., & Robinson, Nicholas A. (Eds.). (2004). *Capacity building for environmental law in the Asian and Pacific Region: Approaches and resources*. Manila, Philippines: Asian Development Bank.

Koh, Kheng Lian (Ed.). (2009). *ASEAN environmental law, policy and governance: Selected documents* (Vols. I & II). Singapore: World Scientific Publishing Co.

Letchumanan, Raman. (2010). Is there an ASEAN policy on climate change? In *Climate change: Is Southeast Asia up to the challenge?* (SR004, pp. 50–62). London: London School of Economics. Retrieved August 1, 2011, from http://www2.lse.ac.uk/IDEAS/publications/reports/SR004.aspx

Nguitragool, Paruedee. (2010). *Environmental cooperation in Southeast Asia: ASEAN's regime for trans-boundary haze pollution*. London: Routledge.

Palma, Mary Ann, & Tsamenyi, Martin. (2008). *Case study on the impacts of illegal, unreported and unregulated (IUU) fishing in the Sulawesi Sea*. Asia-Pacific Economic Cooperation Fisheries Working Group. Retrieved from http://www.illegal-fishing.info/uploads/APEC08fwgIUUfishing.pdf

Tay, Simon. (2008). Haze. In Donald K. Emmerson (Ed.), *Hard choices: Security, democracy, and regionalism in Southeast Asia* (pp. 219–240). Palo Alto, CA: Walter H. Shorenstein Asia-Pacific Research Center, Stanford University.

Share the *Encyclopedia of Sustainability*: Teachers are welcome to make up to ten (10) copies of no more than two (2) articles for distribution in a single course or program. For further permissions, please visit www.copyright.com or contact: info@berkshirepublishing.com

Automobiles and Personal Transportation

The automobile industry is an important and growing economic sector in Asian countries, particularly in India and China. The increasingly widespread adoption of liquid petroleum–fueled personal transportation vehicles has been accompanied by higher consumption of petroleum (often imported) and an increase in greenhouse gas emissions and atmospheric pollution. Electric vehicles may represent a better way to support the inevitable growth in personal modes of transportation, but they may come with their own costs.

The automobile industry plays a major role in the economic scenario of a country. In the initial stages of evolution of the automotive industry, motoring was considered a sport rather than a means of transportation. The history of automobiles started with the invention of the first transport medium running on the roads in early 1769. It took over a century from the creation of this first self-propelled road vehicle for motorcars to generate enough demand for widespread production. Both road and railroad vehicles originally were designed with steam engines, but these added so much weight that they were a poor choice for road vehicles—although steam engines were used successfully in locomotives. Vehicles with electric engines were invented between 1832 and 1839; even though electricity turned out to be effective for running streetcars, electric cars were heavy, slow, and expensive, and they needed to stop for recharging frequently. In the late nineteenth century the first gasoline-powered cars were built in Europe, and by 1900 both steam and electric road vehicles were abandoned in favor of those powered by gas.

The primary fuels now used in automobiles, namely gasoline and diesel, are essentially derived from crude oil. But over time alternative fuels have evolved, including methanol, ethanol, compressed natural gas (CNG), liquefied petroleum gas (LPG), biodiesel, and hydrogen. These alternative fuels were intended primarily to (1) reduce dependence on imported petroleum, a nonrenewable resource concentrated in a handful of countries located mainly in the Middle East; (2) improve energy security and diversity; and (3) reduce the harmful tailpipe emissions associated with the combustion of gasoline and diesel.

In fact, a large number of buses and trucks in many urban areas of Asia and Europe already operate on alternative fuels like CNG and LPG. The trend for expanding the use of these clean-burning gaseous fuels for private automobiles, however, has not been very encouraging. Converting to these alternative fuels faces three main barriers: (1) their low energy-storage density—that is, total possible miles that can be driven on one tank of fuel, (2) the relatively low price of petroleum-based products like gasoline and diesel due to price controls and subsidies, and (3) engineering challenges in adapting current internal combustion engines to use of these alternative fuels.

A large number of Asian countries currently are investigating using biofuels (ethanol and biodiesel) to run automobiles, either by blending them with liquid petroleum fuels or in an unblended form. Due to inadequate availability of nonagricultural feedstocks and waste, however, coupled with a dearth of adequate wastelands, especially in Asia, production and usage of these fuels would inherently lead to a trade-off, diverting feedstocks that are otherwise used as food or animal feed to biofuel production. Even for nonagricultural feedstocks, the trade-off and loss of biodiversity may arise because of inadequate wastelands. Furthermore, a number of life cycle–based research studies question whether biofuel production is really harmless to the environment and if the savings in water and energy consumption is at the level claimed. Finally, biofuels are more expensive than gasoline and diesel and currently are not viable without government support.

Switching from liquid petroleum fuels to gaseous fuels (like hydrogen) will be just as difficult. Transitioning to gaseous fuels will require additional infrastructure (such as fueling stations), necessitating a careful analysis of its design, construction, and environmental safety, while current gasoline and diesel filling stations obviously do not require this additional research.

India

The first car in India was driven on the streets of Mumbai (Bombay), and until the end of the 1940s, automobiles either were imported already assembled or built from imported parts. The dawn of vehicle-manufacturing activity in India occurred when Hindustan Motors (in 1942) and Premier Auto (in 1944) established their own manufacturing plants with imported know-how from General Motors and Fiat, respectively. In its early stages of development, the automobile industry was not accorded much importance by the government. During the post-liberalization era after 1991, however, India initiated a number of reform measures (fiscal measures, tax reforms, and reforms in equity regulations and foreign exchange) that turned out to be particularly beneficial for the automobile industry, leading to a significant growth spurt. The liberalization, coupled with the increasing globalization of the Indian automobile industry, also offered a plethora of opportunities for Indian auto-parts manufacturers. This wave of liberalization and globalization, along with increased urbanization, led to a rapid increase in the number of vehicles and the distance traveled by people, resulting not only in higher energy consumption but also associated harmful tailpipe emissions and atmospheric pollution.

There are essentially eleven kinds of vehicles on Indian roads: the scooters, motorcycles, and mopeds included in the two-wheeled segment; the passenger-carrying and load-carrying vehicles that comprise the three-wheeler category; and the passenger cars (including taxis), multi-utility vehicles, light commercial vehicles, buses, trucks, and tractors that constitute the four- and six-wheeler segments. There are a number of manufacturing firms in each category that produce different models of vehicles of varying sizes and capacities. Automobiles in India are powered largely by liquid petroleum fuel, and as domestic production of crude dwindles and dependence on imported crude oil increases, the transportation sector is becoming more vulnerable to the increasing volatility of international oil prices.

Although the automotive industry is a crucial driver of the Indian economy, the rapid growth in the number of automobiles since 1991 has also led to negative social and environmental spillovers. Air quality has been deteriorating in India, as it has in many developing countries, and most cities exceed the National Ambient Air Quality Standards (NAAQS) set by the US Environmental Protection Agency. This, along with the fact that sixty out of sixty-two Indian metropolitan areas have exceeded World Health Organization (WHO) standards on particulate matter, is a major concern in Indian cities (Nesamani 2010). To make matters worse, the price differential between diesel and gasoline is growing wider (a disparity that has been maintained consistently) at the same time that diesel is being promoted as a more environmentally friendly option, creating perverse incentives for the rapid growth in the number of diesel cars on Indian roads.

The number of registered motor vehicles in India increased from 21 million in 1991 to more than 105 million in 2008 (MORTH 2011). Two- and three-wheelers represent the largest share of the vehicle population and constitute around 80 percent of the current fleet (MORTH 2011). Since the late 1990s automobile manufacturers have been focusing on improving energy efficiency, and as a result the fuel consumption per vehicle-kilometer has been decreasing progressively, accompanied by a decline in air pollution.

China

In China the development of the automobile industry can be divided into four phases, which correspond to the stages of industrialization in the country: the central control and planning era (1947–1997), the growth phase (1979–1994), the consolidation period (1994–2004), and the current stage (since 2004). Most research on the automobile sector in China has noted its complexity, since it is characterized by joint ventures between domestic and foreign manufacturers. At the same time, the lack of technological research and development (R&D) capability has meant that China's automobile industry has been reduced to contracting manufacturing outfits that produce designs brought in from abroad.

In China, accelerated economic growth and consumer demand for goods has resulted in a rapid expansion in the number of vehicles, which increased from 5.5 million in 1990 to 90 million in 2005. Two-wheelers account for nearly 61 percent of the current vehicle fleet, but that share is expected to decline to 52 percent by 2025, as the most significant increase has been in the number of cars and sport-utility vehicles (SUVs) (ADB 2006). These changes can be explained by growth in income and the availability of cheap domestic cars. The expansion in the number of vehicles has increased the demand for fuel substantially and caused congestion and pollution concerns. The study carried out by the Asian Development Bank (ADB) predicts that the growing number of passenger and freight vehicles in India and China will increase demand for oil, and that India's fuel consumption for road transportation will quadruple from 2005 levels by 2025, while China's will triple in the same time period (ADB 2006).

Vehicles and Greenhouse Gases

For several years now, *World Economic Outlook* (*WEO*)—the flagship publication of the International Energy Agency (IEA)—has been emphasizing that the transportation sector (driven primarily by the rapid pace of urbanization) will constitute an increasing share of future energy consumption and accompanying flows of greenhouse gas (GHG) emissions, especially carbon dioxide (CO_2); as of 2007, nearly 23 percent of the world's energy-related CO_2 emissions came from the transportation sector (IEA 2009a). Data from the IEA also indicate that the increase in transportation-related CO_2 emissions has been the highest over the past three decades. It is clear that growth in the transportation sector and its future pattern of energy consumption will have a very significant role to play in global attempts to mitigate GHG emissions. Given the potential for rapid expansion in the Indian and Chinese automobile sectors in the future, aggressive efforts will be required to reduce vehicular emissions in both countries by identifying alternative fuels.

Road-based mobility in India presents two major concerns. First, India imports more than 75 percent of the crude petroleum used in meeting its energy requirements, primarily to cater to the demands of the transportation sector. Second, although India has a low overall vehicle density, personal modes of transportation (two-wheelers and cars) accounted for more than four-fifths of the country's motor vehicles in 2009, as compared to their share of a little over three-fifths in 1951 (MORTH 2011). The ownership of these personal modes, especially cars, is skewed toward urban areas. It's obvious that as India shifts to a higher growth trajectory and more of its people become urbanized, the ownership of these personal vehicles (again, especially cars) will grow rapidly due to increases in per capita income and the accompanying growing aspirations of the middle class, which represents a very large segment of Indian metropolitan areas. The problem may be compounded by an increasing consumer preference for larger personal vehicles with features that consume more energy (such as power steering, air-conditioning, etc.), leading to higher energy consumption and accompanying higher GHG emissions. The biggest challenge related to road-based mobility in India, therefore, lies in decoupling the inevitable growth in personal modes of transportation from an analogous growth in oil consumption and associated GHG emissions (especially CO_2) (Bandyopadhyay 2010a).

The automobile industry in China has been experiencing rapid development since 2000. A strong consumer base with sufficient levels of purchasing power, coupled with a modern, upgraded road system, has helped China become a leader in the global automobile industry. If one adds to this cheap labor and a favorable geographical location, China naturally stands out as one of the most attractive destinations for the major global players in the automobile market (RNCOS 2012).

One of the key drivers of the automobile industry's rapid growth in China is the proactive role of the government. Recognizing the need to free the economy—especially the automobile sector—from its dependence on oil imports, in late 2008 China conducted alternative-energy vehicle demonstration projects in eleven cities. In December 2008 the national government also began offering a subsidy of about $7,300 on the purchase of electric-drive vehicles. Both industry and the government have set ambitious goals to increase the number of electric vehicles for the near future. In 2009 the ten largest Chinese automotive companies formally established the Electric Vehicle Industry Alliance, which is working to create electric-vehicle standards, including standards for key vehicle parts. Meanwhile, the Chinese government has set a number of goals for the next few years to increase the use of electric-drive vehicles, although none of these targets are compulsory (IEA 2009b).

Toward Electric Vehicles

It is estimated that more than 20 million electric vehicles are on Chinese roads, mostly in the form of two-wheeled electric bikes (e-bikes) and scooters (IEA 2009b). Government policies have promoted e-bikes by eliminating competition and banning gasoline-powered two-wheeled vehicles in several provinces. In August 2009, the Ministry of Industry and Information Technology (MIIT) published a directory of new-energy vehicles that listed five four-wheeled electric-vehicle models, of which two—the ZhongTai 2008EV (a small SUV) and the Build Your Dreams (BYD) F3DM (a sedan)—are considered to be mass-market models. Production capacity and sales volume of electric vehicles are both likely to increase in the future, as demonstrated by the entry of new players in China's automobile industry. The Renault-Nissan Alliance has formed a partnership with MIIT to bring electric vehicles to China, and Chinese automaker Chery recently introduced the all-electric S18 model.

In India, although the manufacture of electric vehicles in the form of two-wheeled bikes and scooters has reached mass-production levels in India, four-wheeled vehicles—especially light-duty vehicles (LDVs), which include passenger cars, SUVs, pick-up trucks, and so on—have yet to catch up. In the two-wheeled segment, YObykes (manufactured by Electrotherm, a Gujarat-based company) offers two scooterette and four bike models with horsepower that ranges from 200 to 250 watts. These light vehicles can operate at a top speed of 25 kilometers per hour and have a range of up to 75 kilometers on a full charge of six to eight hours. YObykes's plant has a production capacity of 250,000 units per year (IEA 2009b). The company has also introduced high-speed and high-powered electric two-wheelers in order to compete with conventional scooters, and is planning to roll out the first electric motorcycle operated on battery power. Other major producers of electric two-wheelers include EKO Vehicles in Bangalore and ACE Motors based in Pune. EKO Vehicles launched the world's first hybrid motorcycle in 2009, with two models called Strike and ET. These new bikes were developed in collaboration with companies in the United States and the United Kingdom, and they run on a combination of battery power and gasoline, doubling the mileage from every liter of gas. The e-bike industry sector also includes regional companies, such as Scooters India, Atlas Cycles, and Avon Cycles.

The Reva Electric Car Company, a joint venture between Maini Group India and AEV California, was the pioneer in popularizing electric cars in India. The company was founded in 1994 in Bangalore and launched the first two-seater electric car—known as the REVA*i*—soon after in India. The green-car revolution that Reva started is now being carried forward by the country's other major carmakers, such as Tata Motors: at the 2010 Delhi Auto Expo the company showcased its Tata Indica Vista Electric model, and it featured an electric version of the Tata Nano at the Geneva Motor Show the same year.

Future Outlook

Most Indian cities are characterized by congested city roads, low vehicular speeds, and short driving distances. These characteristics make India a good market for the current fleet of electric-run vehicles, whose features are ideally suited for these conditions. India is also uniquely and favorably positioned as a manufacturing center for these vehicles primarily because of the availability of spare parts and hardware required for automobiles and low manufacturing costs. The country's other notable advantages include low labor costs; low production start-up costs; availability of R&D facilities in the electrical, electronics, and auto-component industries; and a potentially huge urban domestic market (Maini 2003).

Electric vehicles have lower maintenance requirements than gas-powered vehicles, since they lack oil filters, air filters, spark plugs, and radiators. In India, moreover, low-speed electric vehicles with less than

250 watts of power and maximum speeds under 25 kilometers per hour are exempt from registration, and hence do not come under the purview of the Central Motor Vehicle Acts and Rules. Despite these aforementioned advantages, and the environmental benefits of electric vehicles (such as reduced fossil-fuel consumption, lower GHG and non-GHG emissions, augmented fuel economy, and reduced noise pollution), these vehicles have remained nonstarters and have yet to realize the sales that Indian driving conditions would seem to warrant.

A number of recent studies have singled out key constraints (some technical and some functional) to the adoption of electric vehicles. These include high prices; limited driving range; a lack of infrastructure for charging vehicles; a slow pace of improvement in technology, especially as it relates to motors and performance; durability and cost of batteries; a dearth of holistic government support; and regulatory challenges. In addition to these factors, there is some question about whether electric vehicles are really environmentally benign, since the electricity used is generated from coal-fueled thermal power plants (Bandyopadhyay 2010b).

Kaushik Ranjan BANDYOPADHYAY and
Aanchal ARORA
TERI University, New Delhi

See also China; Cities—Overview; Consumerism; E-Waste; Energy Industries—Nuclear; Energy Industries—Renewables (China); Energy Industries—Renewables (India); Energy Security (East Asia); Five-Year Plans; Green Collar Jobs; India; Public Transportation; Utilities Regulation and Energy Efficiency

FURTHER READING

Asian Development Bank (ADB). (2006). *Energy efficiency and climate change considerations for on-road transport in Asia*. Manila, The Philippines: ADB.

Bandyopadhyay, Kaushik Ranjan. (2010a). Reconciling economic growth with low carbon mobility in India. In 3iNetwork & Infrastructure Development Finance Company (Eds.), *India Infrastructure Report, 2010: Infrastructure development in a low carbon economy* (pp. 237–257). New Delhi: Oxford University Press.

Bandyopadhyay, Kaushik Ranjan. (2010b). Potential and challenges of electricity driven vehicles in India. *Energy Security Insights*, 5(2), 7–12.

Holweg, Matthias; Luo Jianxi; & Oliver, Nick. (2005). The past, present and future of China's automobile industry: A value chain perspective (Working paper). Cambridge, MA: Centre for Competitiveness and Innovation, Cambridge-MIT Institute.

International Energy Agency (IEA). (2009a). CO_2 *emissions from fuel combustion*. Paris: IEA.

International Energy Agency (IEA). (2009b). *Technology roadmap: Electric and plug-in hybrid electric vehicles*. Paris: IEA.

Maini, Chetan. (2003). Electric vehicles: Paving the path of Indian future. Retrieved April 20, 2012, from www.foindia.org/Archive/News/ElectricVehiclesinIndia.pdf

Ministry of Road Transport, and Highways (MORTH), Government of India. (2011). *Road transport yearbook 2007–09*. New Delhi: MORTH.

Nag, Biswajit; Banerjee, Saikat; & Chatterjee, Rittwik. (2007). Changing features of the automobile industry in Asia: Comparison of production, trade and market structure in selected countries (Working paper series, no. 37). Bangkok, Thailand: Asia-Pacific Research and Training Network on Trade, UNESCAP.

Nesamani, K. S. (2010). Estimation of automobile emissions and control strategies in India. *Science of the Total Environment*, 408, 1800–1811.

Orsato, Renato J., & Wells, Peter. (2007). U-turn: The rise and demise of the automobile industry. *Journal of Cleaner Production*, 15(11–12), 994–1006.

Piplai, Tapas. (2001). Automobile industry: Shifting strategic focus. *Economic and Political Weekly*, 36(30), 2892–2897.

RNCOS. (2012, February). *China automobile sector analysis*. Noida, India: RNCOS industry research solutions.

Berkshire's authors and editors welcome questions, comments, and corrections. Send your emails about the *Berkshire Encyclopedia of Sustainability* in general or this volume in particular to: sustainability.updates@berkshirepublishing.com

B

Beijing, China

19.6 million est. pop. 2010

The city of Beijing, in preparation for hosting the 2008 Olympic Games, addressed numerous environmental problems, taking steps to improve air quality, address the depletion of ground- and surface water, build sewage treatment facilities, and raise environmental awareness throughout the city. Since then, however, continued fast-paced urbanization and economic development in subsequent years have impeded progress toward creating a greener, cleaner, healthier, and environmentally sustainable city.

The dynamic city of Beijing is situated as the political and cultural capital of the People's Republic of China (PRC). Strategically located in eastern China at the northerly tip of the North China Plain, this thriving metropolis, also officially a province, is one of four municipalities under direct control of the central government. According to the Beijing Municipal Bureau of Statistics, the 2010 national census reported that China's capital city population grew to 19.6 million: an increase of over 6 million residents from its last census in 2000, amounting to an average annual growth rate of 3.8 percent. Beijing's growth over that decade exceeded sixfold the national average annual growth rate of 0.57 percent (Xinhua 2011).

The municipality encompasses 16,801 square kilometers and is surrounded primarily by Hubei Province, with the exception of the Tianjin Municipality to the southeast. The most densely populated areas are located within the two center city districts of Dongcheng and Xicheng, where population density exceeds 22,000 and 26,000 persons per square kilometer, respectively. Six concentric ring roads encircle the city to create ever larger and more extensive beltways, facilitating the horizontal development of the city to its rural periphery. The innermost Second Ring Road contains both Dongcheng and Xicheng districts within it. The recently completed Sixth Ring Road is the most remote, situated approximately 15 to 20 kilometers from the center city; it consists of 130 kilometers of expressway connecting the newly developing and sprawling high-rise and suburban areas along Beijing's urban fringe.

Much urban redevelopment was both justified and expedited in order to prepare for hosting the 2008 Summer Olympic Games (Brady 2009). Large-scale modernization and construction efforts dramatically changed the physical and social landscape in both positive and negative ways: many center-city *hutong* (alleyway) neighborhoods were demolished and replaced by modern commercial and high-rise buildings; highway and subway construction facilitated both the outward growth of the city and the increased purchase and use of private cars; round-the-clock construction adversely impacted air quality and contributed to noise pollution; and increased demand for water and electricity resources, in concert with population growth due in part to the influx of rural construction laborers. All this created new tensions as the city and central governments sought to create a "New Beijing, Great

Olympics" to impress domestic and international onlookers alike.

Hosting the 2008 Olympic Games

The Beijing Olympic Committee worked hard to brand the 2008 games as the "Green Olympics," alongside promotion of it being the "People's Olympics" and the "High-Tech Olympics" (BOCOG 2008a). These three concepts were adopted in an effort to display both China's progress toward modernity and its commitment to sustainable growth and development aided by technological intervention and achievement.

Indeed, officials established an ambitious series of measures to aid their attainment of a Green Olympics supported by a heavy investment equivalent to nearly US$17 billion. A large portion of these funds was used to subsidize the installation of cleaner technologies for nearby industries, to pass and enforce legislation regulating noncompliant and polluting factories, and to build enhanced public transport systems, waste treatment systems, and green Olympic venues (UNEP 2009). During the summer of 2008, more than two months before the opening ceremonies on 8 August, construction projects were halted, and heavily polluting industries such as steel mills, coke plants, and refineries in and around the capital were either closed or required to reduce production in an effort to reduce particulate matter in the air. Further, coal-burning power plants were charged to reduce their emissions by 30 percent throughout the summer (Jacobs 2008). Additional green initiatives included education campaigns encouraging citizens to adopt water- and energy-saving practices and the implementation of restrictions that assigned alternating driving days depending upon even- or odd-numbered license plates. In addition, the Beijing government resorted to its rather common practice of "seeding the sky" with silver iodide in order to induce rainfall in the city as a means to reduce remaining air pollution in preparation for hosting the games.

A February 2009 United Nations Environment Programme (UNEP) report highlighted both Beijing's achievements and its shortcomings in its quest for a green Olympics. Overall, the report explained that "the 2008 Games marked a step forward in terms of an eco-friendly mass spectator sporting event" (UNEP 2009). While the report does assert that Beijing could have done more to engage with nongovernmental organizations and to reduce the carbon footprint of both the Olympic and Para-Olympic Games, it concludes that the games did raise the environmental bar and created a lasting legacy for the city, particularly for Beijing residents and businesses.

Transportation and Traffic Congestion

With more than 4.9 million cars on Beijing streets in 2011—a number that is expected to double by 2015—traffic congestion and its associated air pollution continue to be problems for China's capital city into the foreseeable future (Penkowski 2011; Xu 2011). Although heavily polluting cars have been taken off the city streets (particularly within Beijing's Fifth Ring Road, and owing to stringent standards implemented prior to the Olympic Games), the newer cars purchased by a growing middle class have more than replaced the older, heavily polluting vehicles. The Beijing government has attempted to implement measures to literally curb the growing desire for personal car ownership, including restricting car purchases, introducing toll charges on certain roads, increasing parking fees, introducing a lottery system to limit new car registrations, encouraging purchases of alternative energy cars, and expanding its subway system. Such measures are proving to be somewhat effective at combating traffic congestion and its associated air pollution. When the government eases traffic restrictions and measures, however, large-scale gridlock seizes traffic throughout the city, as was the case in September 2010 prior to the October national holiday, when a record-breaking 140 traffic jams were reported on a Friday night (*Global Times* 2010).

Citywide efforts are underway to ease congestion problems. From the 1980s through 2000, Beijing had only two subway lines. After winning the bid to host the 2008 Olympic Games, the local and national governments committed to greatly expanding the subway system. By the time of the 2008 Olympics a total of eight lines were functioning. As of early 2012 that number had expanded to fifteen lines delivering over 2.18 billion rides in 2011. Eight additional lines currently under construction are due to be completed by 2017 at a cost equaling approximately US$30 billion. The intent is that the expanded subway system and its affordable fares will entice increases in ridership and decreases in automobile-associated air pollution. Crowded subways and long commutes, however, continue to frustrate many current and potential riders.

Air Pollution

Accolades were given to Beijing just after the successful hosting of a "green" Olympics for its valiant efforts to mitigate air pollution. As time has passed, however, the temporary reprieve from excessive air pollutants owing to the reduced or halted factory production and stringent rules around private car use in 2008 have faltered, as factories have picked up production, city construction continues unabated, and private car purchases and use remain high.

In January 2012, the Beijing environmental authorities, responding to a public outcry at a lack of air quality transparency, agreed to release more detailed data on the presence of smaller particulate matter that more accurately reflects the current state of the city's air quality. Previously, authorities only released data on particulate matter at least 10 microns in diameter (PM_{10}). Particulate matter at least 2.5 microns in diameter ($PM_{2.5}$), which makes up much of the pollution in the city, had only been monitored by a rooftop station at the US Embassy in Beijing. Despite the Beijing government's concession to release their own $PM_{2.5}$ data from various locales around the city, there remains some dispute about the accuracy of the readings owing to stark differences between the Beijing's governmental readings and those by the US Embassy, with the former providing relatively optimistic readings of $PM_{2.5}$ (*USA Today* 2012). The discrepancy in data findings is only one point of contention. A related concern is disagreement on what constitute acceptable levels of fine particulates in the air. China's proposed guidelines would allow fine particulate ($PM_{2.5}$) levels up to three-and-a-half times higher than WHO guidelines to still be rated excellent (Andrews 2011). Further, government projections of increased numbers in Beijing's "blue sky days" (days that meet air quality standards) do not accurately reflect the state of Beijing's air quality, as irregularities in monitoring and reporting of air quality as well as relocation of monitoring stations to the urban periphery (outside the Sixth Ring Road) call into question claims of reduced air pollution.

Coal consumption—in addition to automotive exhaust, construction, and factory emissions—is a notable contributor to Beijing's air pollution problems. In 2010, Beijing's coal consumption was 24 million tonnes, which accounted for 30 percent of the city's energy production. In an effort to reduce pollutants associated with coal, Beijing's development and reform commission reduced its cap for coal consumption to 13.6 million tonnes a year by 2015. In order to achieve this target, four of the city's major coal-burning power plants are to be replaced by ones utilizing natural gas. Further, the local government has contributed the equivalent of US$1.9 billion since 2010 to convert coal-fired residential heating systems to electric systems (UPI 2012). The cost of sustained air pollution can be assessed not only in rising health concerns for local residents (as long-term exposure can lead to substantially increased risk of developing cardiovascular disease) but also in its significant disruption of air and ground traffic due to poor visibility (Shan and Wang 2011).

Water Supply and Sewage Treatment

Currently more than two-thirds of Beijing's water supply comes from groundwater sources that are being drained faster than they can be replenished, while the remaining third comes from much-depleted reservoirs and rivers. Per capita water availability in Beijing has decreased drastically over the past sixty years, declining from 1,000 cubic meters in 1949 to less than 230 cubic meters in 2007. The total water use in 2007 was reported at 3.25 billion cubic meters, and the estimated supply deficit was approximately 400 million cubic meters. Domestic water consumption accounts for 39 percent of the total, whereas agriculture, industry, and urban consumption account for 38, 20, and 3 percent, respectively (Probe International 2008).

Ninety percent of Beijing's surface water comes from rivers and streams that lie in nearby Hebei Province, Shanxi Province, and Inner Mongolia (Probe International 2008). Within the municipality there are five rivers and over two hundred streams, most of which are completely dried up. The average annual precipitation for Beijing is 590 millimeters and has been declining for the past few decades owing to frequent periods of drought. In addition, with the expansion of the urban landscape, water runoff is unable to penetrate concrete and pavement, further complicating efforts to replenish groundwater reserves. Drought and population pressures, however, are not the sole causes of Beijing's water situation. Probe International, a Canadian public interest research group, asserted in their report titled *Beijing's Water Crisis* that the current conundrum "stems more from decades of short-sighted policies that have degraded its watershed and a political fixation on large-scale and environmentally damaging engineering projects to keep the taps flowing at little or no charge to consumers" (Probe International 2008, 26). Unfortunately, Beijing authorities have not yet shifted their water policy focus to decreasing demand and extraction of water resources as a means to avert the crisis. Instead, they have sought to meet demand through further extraction of water resources outside of the Beijing municipality, increased runoff from upstream areas (such as Shanxi and Hebei provinces) into Beijing's water reservoirs, and strategically exploiting and protecting municipal groundwater through restrictions on extraction by nearby provinces and the introduction of a water licensing system to limit the use of water for growing vegetables (Probe International 2008).

A Beijing Olympic Action Plan devised measures to construct sewage treatment and recycling systems in an effort to address the water-related challenges. According to the Action Plan, by 2008 over 90 percent of the sewage in the Beijing urban area should be treated and half of the treated sewage recycled. The UNEP Beijing Olympic Games Environmental Review reported that by 2006 Beijing had already reached the 90 percent sewage treatment target and the amount of reclaimed water use surpassed 10 percent of total city use.

Land Use and Population Growth

Contemporary economic development and rapid urbanization have dramatically altered Beijing's land use and growth trajectory. In particular, increasing suburbanization, expansion of the city's outward-oriented concentric ring road system, and urban planning based on a multi-nucleated approach have led to city sprawl via the expropriation of surrounding rural lands, which has contributed to the subsequent loss of cropland, forests, and grasslands (Xie 2007). At the same time, urban redevelopment and revitalization initiatives in Beijing's urban core, in "Old City" Beijing (within the Second Ring Road), have further pushed longtime local residents toward the expanding urban periphery. This intracity migration alongside a massive influx of migrants from other provinces into Beijing and additional Chinese cities has contributed to the rise of urban villages and increased urban expansion to meet the needs of a growing urban population. In 2000, nearly 18.9 percent of Beijing residents had migrated from other provinces. By 2010, the percentage of migrants living in Beijing had increased to 35.9 percent of the total urban population (Xinhua 2011). While these numbers show significant population growth owing to the large and growing migrant communities moving to Beijing, these numbers may underestimate the true size of Beijing's urban migrant population as many unauthorized migrants, the "floating population," evade enumeration (Haub 2010). The dual pressures of urban development and expansion combined with increasing population growth pose particular challenges for Beijing's long-term urban planning and environmental sustainability.

Outlook

Hosting the 2008 Olympic Games galvanized momentum toward making Beijing a green city. Impressive efforts were made, in time for the opening of the games, to ensure cleaner air, improved transportation infrastructure, and completion of citywide sewage treatment plants, and to educate local residents on the benefits of green practices that reduce water and energy consumption. These notable achievements were short-lived, however, as numerous environmental problems continue to hinder the city's progress toward sustainable living. Transparency in the reporting of pollutants, further education for both local residents and industry on ways to curb polluting practices, and the implementation of policy to promote sustainable use and reuse of natural resources and minimize wasteful commercial consumption are among some of the steps necessary to move Beijing toward becoming a greener, cleaner, and healthier city in which to live and work.

Melissa Y. ROCK
Dartmouth College

See also Automobiles and Personal Vehicles; China; Cities—Overview; Education, Environmental (China); Green Collar Jobs; Guangzhou, China; Pearl River Delta; Public Transportation; Shanghai, China; South-North Water Diversion

FURTHER READING

Andrews, Stephen Q. (2011, December 5). Beijing's hazardous blue sky. *chinadialogue*. Retrieved March 8, 2012, from http://www.chinadialogue.net/article/show/single/en/4661-Beijing-s-hazardous-blue-sky

BBC News Asia-Pacific. (2011, September 2). Beijing "plan congestion charge" to ease traffic woes. Retrieved March 8, 2012, from http://www.bbc.co.uk/news/world-asia-pacific-14761711

Beijing Organizing Committee for the Games of the XXIX Olympiad (BOCOG). (2008a, August 8–24). Three concepts. Retrieved March 8, 2012, from http://en.beijing2008.cn/bocog/concepts/

Beijing Organizing Committee for the Games of the XXIX Olympiad (BOCOG). (2008b, August 8–24). Green Olympics: Progress v challenge. Retrieved March 8, 2012, from http://en.beijing2008.cn/12/12/greenolympics.shtml

Brady, Anne-Marie. (2009). The Beijing Olympics as a campaign of mass distraction. *The China Quarterly, 197*, 1–24.

China Daily. (2010, June 30). Beijing records less "blue sky" days this year. Retrieved March 8, 2012, from http://www.chinadaily.com.cn/china/2010-06/30/content_10042397.htm

Fallows, James. (2011, December 5). China air-quality catastrophe: It's back. *The Atlantic*. Retrieved March 8, 2012, from http://www.theatlantic.com/international/archive/2011/12/china-air-quality-catastrophe-its-back/249479/

Global Times. (2010, September 20). Record-breaking gridlock heralds holidays. Retrieved March 8, 2012, from http://www.globaltimes.cn/metro-beijing/highlights/photo/2010-09/575411.html

Hancock, Tom. (2011, November 2). Beijing's subway system growing rapidly, but unevenly. *SmartPlanet*. Retrieved March 8, 2012, from http://www.smartplanet.com/blog/global-observer/beijings-subway-system-growing-rapidly-but-unevenly/378

Haub, Carl. (2010, November 1). 37 percent of the world population now being counted. *Behind the Numbers: The PRB blog on population, health, and the environment*. Retrieved March 27, 2012, from http://prbblog.org/index.php/2010/11/01/37-percent-of-world-population-now-being-counted/

Jacobs, Andrew. (2008, April 14). Beijing details its plans for a green Games. *The New York Times*. Retrieved March 8, 2012, from http://www.nytimes.com/2008/04/14/world/asia/14iht-beijing.4.11978516.html

Littlefield, Amy. (2009, June 19). Beijing Olympics were smoggier than we thought. *Los Angeles Times*. Retrieved March 8, 2012, from http://latimesblogs.latimes.com/greenspace/2009/06/olympics-pollution-beijing.html

Perkowski, Jack. (2011, October 21). Traffic congestion in Beijing. *Forbes*. Retrieved March 8, 2012, from http://www.forbes.com/sites/jackperkowski/2011/10/21/traffic-congestion-in-beijing/

Probe International Beijing Group. (2008). *Beijing's water crisis: 1949–2008 Olympics*. Retrieved March 8, 2012, from http://www.chinaheritagequarterly.org/016/_docs/BeijingWaterCrisis1949-2008.pdf

Shan, Juan, & Wang Qian. (2011). Exposure to smog is severe hazard. *China Daily*. December 6, 2011. Retrieved March 8, 2012, from http://www.chinadaily.com.cn/china/2011-12/06/content_14216428.htm

United Nations Environment Programme (UNEP). (2007). Beijing 2008 Olympic Games: An environmental review. 8.3: Wastewater management. Retrieved March 8, 2012, from http://www.unep.org/publications/ebooks/beijing-report/Default.aspx?bid=ID0E1WCI#ID0ERADI

United Nations Environment Programme (UNEP). (2009, February 18). Beijing Olympics get big green tick: UNEP report spotlights achievements and highlights some shortcomings of 2008 games. Retrieved March 8, 2012, from http://www.unep.org/documents.multilingual/default.asp?documentid=562&articleid=6086&l=en

United Nations Volunteers. (2007, November 21). Chinese volunteers launch environmental awareness campaign. Retrieved

March 8, 2012, from http://www.unv.org/en/what-we-do/thematic-areas/culture-sports/doc/chinese-volunteers-launch-environmental.html

United Press International (UPI). (2012, March 5). Beijing aims for coal reductions. Retrieved March 8, 2012, from http://www.upi.com/Business_News/Energy-Resources/2012/03/05/Beijing-aims-for-coal-reductions/UPI-56701330965451/

USA Today. (2012, January 21). Beijing releases key air pollution data. Retrieved March 8, 2012, from http://www.usatoday.com/news/world/story/2012-01-21/beijing-air-pollution/52712794/1

US Embassy, Beijing. (n.d.). Beijing air quality index (measurement of PM2.5). Retrieved March 8, 2012, from http://iphone.bjair.info/

Xie, Yichun, et al. (2007). Tempo-spatial patterns of land use changes and urban development in globalizing China: A study of Beijing. *Sensors, 7*, 2881–2906.

Xinhua News. (2011, May 5). Beijing's population tops 19.6 million, migration key contributor to growth. Retrieved March 27, 2012, from http://news.xinhuanet.com/english2010/china/2011-05/05/c_13860069.htm

Xu, Jia. (2011, April 4). Beijing traffic congestion eases. *China Daily*. Retrieved March 8, 2012, from http://www.chinadaily.com.cn/2011-04/18/content_12345368.htm

chat — Berkshire's authors and editors welcome questions, comments, and corrections. Send your emails about the *Berkshire Encyclopedia of Sustainability* in general or this volume in particular to: sustainability.updates@berkshirepublishing.com

Biodiversity Conservation Legislation (China)

China's biodiversity legal system consists of constitutional provisions, laws, regulations, rules, and normative documents. The main areas of focus include ecosystem protection and conservation; natural reserves management; wild animal and plant protection; management of domestic animal germplasm resources, crop germplasm resources, and traditional Chinese medicine species; new variety management; and quarantine. Subsequent legislation ideally would address effective protection, sustainable utilization, and promotion of social and economic development.

According to Article 2 of the Convention on Biological Diversity, *biodiversity* refers to "the variability among living organisms from all sources including, inter alia, terrestrial, marine and other aquatic ecosystems and the ecological complexes of which they are part; this includes diversity within species, between species and of ecosystems." China has a wealth of biodiversity. The country is home to more than 30,000 types of higher plants and more than 6,300 species of vertebrates—accounting for 10 percent and 14 percent of the world's total, respectively—and it also has about 600 types of terrestrial ecosystems (Biodiversity Clearing-House Mechanism of China 2004). But biodiversity loss is serious in China. Ecosystem and species diversity is threatened by environmental degradation; river and lake sedimentation has become increasingly serious; lake levels have decreased, as have groundwater levels; oasis and vegetation loss in arid areas is more common; natural forests are being cut; reclamation and destruction of grasslands continues; red tide is damaging the marine ecosystem; beach erosion and seawater encroachment is getting worse; wildlife populations are decreasing; and many rare plant and animal species are in danger of extinction (SEPA 1999, 10).

Meanwhile, invasive species pose a serious threat to biological genetic resources and biological system safety. The most important reason for biodiversity loss in China is ineffective legal measures on biodiversity development and utilization. The weak enforcement of some existing laws, regulations, and rules is also contributing to biodiversity loss in China.

Legal System

In China, the biodiversity legal system consists of constitutional provisions, laws, regulations, rules, and normative documents. Articles 9 and 26 of the Constitution provide that the state protects rational utilization of natural resources and rare animals and plants, and forbids organizations and individuals from embezzling or damaging natural resources. These are the highest-level provisions for biodiversity conservation and sustainable utilization in China.

Laws make up the next level of the Chinese legal hierarchy and provide a general framework for biodiversity management. Relevant laws include, but are not limited to, the Environmental Protection Law (1989), Forest Law (1998), Marine Environmental Protection Law (1999), Agriculture Law (2002), Water Law (2002), Land Administration Law (2004), Law on Protection of Wild Animals (2004), Fisheries Law (2004), Seed Law (2004), Patent Law (2000), Law on Prevention and Control of Desertification (2001), Law on Animal Epidemic Prevention (2007), Grassland Law (2008), Law on the Entry and Exit Animal and Plant Quarantine (2009 amended), and the Law on Water and Soil Conservation (2010).

China's biodiversity-related regulations, rules, and normative documents focus on the conservation and protection of ecosystems, species resources, and genetic resources. The purpose of many of the regulations is to administratively implement the above-mentioned environmental laws. Some of the measures do not directly target biodiversity conservation but nevertheless play an important role in it.

Areas of Focus

China's main areas of focus in biodiversity conservation law include ecosystem protection and conservation, natural reserves management, wild animal and plant protection, management of domestic animal germplasm resources, management of crop germplasm resources, management of traditional Chinese medicine species, new variety management, and quarantine. (A germplasm is a collection of genetic material for an organism.)

Ecosystem Protection and Conservation

Ecological function protection zones are classified as headwaters conservation, soil conservation, wind prevention and sand fixation areas, biodiversity conservation, and flood accommodation (MEP and CSA 2008). Living environment conservation for wild animals and wild plants includes the establishment of natural reserves in the zones and waters where the key protected organisms are living and propagating. Legislation also provides for the conservation of forests, grasslands, aquatic ecosystems, water and soil, and marine ecosystems.

Natural Reserves Management

China classifies natural reserves into four levels, namely national, provincial, municipal, and county level, and categorizes the reserves into three categories: key, buffer, and experiment area. Each reserve is managed according to its level and category. Specific conservation measures include prohibitions on lumbering, herding, hunting, fishing, medicine collecting, cultivation, grass burning on wastelands, mine exploitation, stone pitting, sand excavating, and so on.

Wild Animal and Plant Protection

Although the state has ownership over wild animal resources, institutions and individuals enjoy rights to use these resources. Based on the catalog of key protected wild animals, China protects rare and endangered wild animals and categorizes them into state- and local-level, and class-I and class-II species. Different measures are adopted accordingly for each species. China categorizes key protected wild plants into state-level and local-level, and the state-level plants are further distinguished as class-I and class-II. Different measures are adopted accordingly for each level and class. The management measures include collecting permits, limited selling and buying, import and export management, resource surveys and filing, and so on.

Domestic Animal Germplasm Resource Management

China conserves germplasm resources of domestic animals based on a classification system. Governments at the county level and above give support to the survey, evaluation, conservation, breeding, and utilization of domestic animal and poultry germplasm resources. The import and export, breeding and farming, and management of these resources are also subject to administrative regulation.

Crop Germplasm Resource Management

The state has ownership over crop germplasm resources. Any institutions and individuals who provide germplasm resources to foreign countries must get prior approval from competent agricultural or forest authorities under the State Council. Institutions and individuals are not allowed to collect or cut natural germplasm that the state protects. When it is necessary to cut or collect for special purposes like scientific research, individuals and institutions must seek approval from competent agricultural or forest authorities under the State Council and provincial governments.

Traditional Chinese Medicine Species Management

China classifies wild medicine materials into three grades. Anyone who collects materials of grades II or III must get a permit for medicine collection. The key protected traditional Chinese medicine species are listed in the national medicine standards. Species can be protected if they have been identified by hygiene authorities under the State Council as being in compliance with provincial, autonomous region, and municipal city standards.

New Variety Management

In China, new plant species apply for a so-called species right in accordance with the regulations on new plant species conservation. Microorganisms are not regarded as animals or plants and can thus be protected under the patent law. The nonbiological production method of animals and plants can be conferred with patent rights.

Quarantine

The following articles are not allowed to enter China: pathogens, pests and other harmful organisms, animals and plants from epidemic-stricken countries and regions, corpses of animals and plants, and soil. When entry of these articles is necessary, a request must be submitted to competent authorities responsible for animal and plant quarantine.

Room for Improvement

These legal measures play important roles in biodiversity conservation in China, but many experts believe existing legislation focuses more on economic value rather than biodiversity itself (Yang 2003; Liu, Xie, and Wu 2006). Without statutes that specifically deal with biodiversity, conservation efforts can be thwarted. For example, according to a report for *Southern Weekday* by Pang Ruifeng (2001), in 2000 Monsanto submitted sixty-four patent applications for soybeans with the marker gene related to high productivity; the company illegally obtained these soybean varieties from China. China had no special legislation dealing with biopiracy at that time and could not take effective measures to prevent Monsanto's theft. It can also be argued that protection for the rights of the state, as well as for the rights of indigenous people and local communities, need to be improved. Biodiversity conservation depends on public participation, incentive measures, and environmental impact assessments; it would also benefit from clarification of liabilities and penalties in laws and regulations. Accordingly, changes could be made in the following ways.

Objectives

The objectives of biodiversity legislation ideally comprise three elements: effective protection, sustainable utilization, and promotion of social and economic development. *Effective protection* means providing sufficient legal basis for the protection of the three aspects of biodiversity (species diversity, genetic diversity, and ecosystem diversity); such legislation considers protection as a primary objective when it conflicts with biodiversity use. *Sustainable utilization* means a pattern of biodiversity use that meets human needs while preserving biodiversity so that these needs can be met not only in the present but also for generations to come. *Promoting social and economic development* means providing ecological basis for social and economic progress based on the effective protection and sustainable use of biodiversity.

Possible Next Steps

A sound biodiversity legal system should thus include comprehensive legislation (in the form of specific laws) and regulations or rules to protect the three elements of biodiversity.

Comprehensive legislation would benefit biodiversity conservation by emphasizing measures that protect the ecological system as a whole, its genetic resources, and related traditional knowledge, including in situ conservation and ex situ conservation (e.g., the relocation of species habitat). Biodiversity use thus should be sustainable, ensuring a reasonable quality and quantity of biodiversity. Public participation can be encouraged in supporting this legislation, providing incentive measures for the whole society to engage in biodiversity conservation.

Special regulations would be aimed at implementing the national statutes. Biological genetic resource legislation might focus on access and benefit sharing of genetic resources, and traditional knowledge related to genetic resources could also be included in the regulations. Biosafety regulations ideally would include stipulations on contained research, environmental release, commercialization, transboundary movement, emergency, legal liability, and so on (Yu 2009, 277–294).

Some existing legislation ideally could be amended to achieve conservation goals. Genetic resource conservation could be added to existing regulations on the protection of wild plants, and access to wild plant genetic resources and relevant traditional knowledge could be prohibited without approval. Existing forest, grassland, and water laws could be amended to better focus on species protection from the perspective of biodiversity conservation, which means protecting ecological functions instead of economic functions.

Further legislation could put more emphasis on individual rights to use and conserve biodiversity. The rights to genetic resources could be more clearly defined and include access and benefit sharing and rights on traditional knowledge related to these genetic recourses. Legislation might stipulate the subjects who can access and share the benefits of genetic resources, the application and approval process, monetary and nonmonetary benefits, and so on.

Public participation is helpful in addressing biodiversity issues. In the Asia-Pacific region, some local communities (for example, in the Philippines) have been directly responsible for protecting existing resources and even maintaining delicate ecosystems and their flora and fauna (Tolentino 1998). China's subsequent biodiversity legislation ideally would make stipulations on the approaches and procedures for public participation; for example, laws could require public hearings for important decisions and policies that may affect biodiversity. This may encourage environmental nongovernmental organizations (NGOs) to participate in biodiversity conservation and may promote public participation in the legislative process.

China's biodiversity conservation mainly depends on government financing and international funds, which some researchers see as insufficient for resolving problems of biodiversity loss (Xia 2006). There are not enough incentive measures in existing legislation, which discourages participation and makes it difficult to engage the whole of society on desertification prevention (GEF/UNDP 2006, 141). Certain incentive measures could raise more funds for biodiversity conservation. For instance, projects related to biodiversity conservation could be given an income tax reduction during a certain period, say three years from when the project is established. The government might also provide subsidies for the biodiversity protection activities of NGOs.

In addition, stipulations on biodiversity loss could be included in China's criminal law, and an environmental damage compensation law might improve the enforceability of biodiversity violations. Such a law could address neglect in biodiversity management and accessing genetic resources without approval as well as other issues.

YU Wenxuan
China University of Political Science and Law

See also Biosafety Legislation (China); China; Corporate Accountability (China); Education, Environmental (China); Endangered Species; Genetic Resources; Great Green Wall (China); Nongovernmental Organizations (NGOs); Parks and Preserves; Reforestation and Afforestation (Southeast Asia); Rural Livelihoods; Traditional Chinese Medicine (TCM); Traditional Knowledge (China)

FURTHER READING

Biodiversity Clearing-House Mechanism of China. (2004, February 26). General situation of biodiversity in China. Retrieved April 11, 2011, from http://www.biodiv.gov.cn/dyxxz/200402/t20040226_88574.htm

GEF/UNDP China National Environment Convention Performance Capability Self-assessment Office. (2006). Report on self-assessment of China's capability of performing international environment convention. Beijing: China Environmental Science Press.

Liu Xaiochun, Xie Qingxia, & Wu Xiaojun. (2006). Research on the status and perfection of wetland conservation law of China. *Science Mosaic, 12.*

Ministry of Environmental Protection (MEP) & China Science Academy (CSA). (2008). *National ecological function districts* (White Book). Beijing: MEP & CSA.

Pang Ruifeng. (2001, October 25). Is it an infringement of Monsanto's rights to plant Chinese soybeans? *Southern Weekday.*

State Environmental Protection Administration (SEPA). (1999). Report on ecological issues in China. Beijing: China Environmental Science Press.

Tolentino, Lourdes E. (1998). Public participation in Philippine biodiversity conservation. Retrieved September 14, 2011, from http://enviroscope.iges.or.jp/modules/envirolib/upload/1504/attach/ir98-2-5.pdf

Xia Yingzhe. (2006, October). China-GEF: National plan and international cooperation on biodiversity (paper, Sino-EU Biodiversity Strategy Seminar).

Yang Yuan. (2003). On the perfecting of the system of the animal protection law in China. *Territory & Natural Resources Study, 2003*(1).

Yu Wenxuan. (2009). On biosafety legislation. Beijing: Tsinghua University Press.

Berkshire's authors and editors welcome questions, comments, and corrections. Send your emails about the *Berkshire Encyclopedia of Sustainability* in general or this volume in particular to: sustainability.updates@berkshirepublishing.com

Biosafety Legislation (China)

The basic environmental protection law, special biosafety legislation, and laws relevant to biosafety management provide the legal basis for biosafety management in China. The major legal institutions include evaluations, safety measures, labeling, reporting, licensing, supervision, and inspection. The existing legislation should be improved in administration and the legal system. New legislation could provide additional research safety measures and improve consumer safety and legal rights.

Despite bringing new opportunities for agriculture worldwide, genetically modified organisms (GMOs) pose potential risks and have negatively affected ecosystems (Levin and Strauss 1991, 297–318) and food safety (Ho and Lim 2004, 20). These risks and effects influence society's healthy social and economic development. These consequences are called the *biosafety problem*. China is paying more and more attention to GMO biosafety by enacting and implementing key pieces of legislation, but China still faces unresolved challenges in biosafety legislation.

Existing Legislation

China has established and implemented special biosafety legislation. Four laws make up the main parts of the current biosafety legal system. The government issued regulations on GMO biosafety management in 2001. Management measures on GMO biosafety evaluation, GMO labeling, and the safety of GMO imports were issued in 2002 and revised in 2004. Related laws, regulations, and rules make up the rest of the legislative framework.

The state runs a classification-based administration and evaluation institution for GMO biosafety. The institution evaluates research, experiments, production, processing, and business operations as well as the import and export of GMOs. It evaluates the risks or potential risks posed by GMOs to human beings, animals and plants, microorganisms, and the ecological environment.

Organizations involved in GMO research must be equipped with appropriate safety facilities and measures. GMO biosafety teams ensure the safety of GMO research experiments within their own institutions. Risk control measures are in place for organizations and individuals who transport and store GMOs.

The Ministry of Agriculture examines, supervises, and manages GMO labeling. Departments of agriculture of local people's governments above the county level supervise and manage GMO labeling within their own administrative regions. The departments under the central government supervise the local level and handle cases of significant influences. The General Administration of Quality Supervision, Inspection, and Quarantine inspects, tests, and verifies GMO labeling at ports. Organizations and individuals label the GMOs listed in the GMO directory so that the labels bear the name of the main materials that contain the genetically modified ingredients.

Researchers of levels III and IV GMOs report data to State Council administrative departments prior to initiating their research. Level III research poses medium risks to human health and ecosystems, and level IV research presents high risks. Researchers submit reports on production, processing, safety management, and product trace lists at regular intervals to agricultural administrative departments of county-level governments.

Supervising administrative departments monitor inspected institutions and individuals, stakeholders (people who have a stake in an enterprise), and authenticators. These departments ask for certificates or other documents related to GMO biosafety. Licenses for GMOs include certificates of GMO biosafety and non-genetically modified agricultural produce, temporary certificates and approval documents of imported GMOs, permits for transboundary movement of genetically modified products, documents for inspection and approval of GMO labeling, and permits for GMO processing.

Researchers and institutions must provide research or copy related files, accounting certificates, and other documents. Administrative departments require related organizations and individuals to be clear about the specific issues of GMO biosafety and to stop illegal activities. In case of an emergency, the departments will seal or seize GMOs.

Legislation for the Future

China has always paid serious attention to GMO biosafety management. Since the turn of the twenty-first century, China has reinforced supervision and management of GMO biosafety, instituted a technical support system of GMO safety, and promoted healthy development of the GMO industry. China has actively participated and cooperated internationally on GMO biosafety, playing an increasingly important role in international affairs on this issue (Chinese Ministry of Agriculture 2010). Despite these achievements, many aspects of GMO safety need improvement. Perfecting the biosafety legal system requires comprehensive legislation.

This legislation ideally should consist of the following provisions:

- general principles that include objectives, scope, objects, basic policies, basic principles, basic institutions, scientific research, education and training, governmental responsibilities, rights and obligations, and rewards
- supervision and management, requiring national and local authorities to coordinate the management of GMOs, conduct spot supervision and inspection, qualify risk assessment organizations, outline risk levels, conduct hearings, engage in dispute resolution, and manage GMO products
- contained research including risk assessment, filing, examination and approval, risk management, and international cooperation in research
- approving environmental release and commercialization, assessing risk control, meeting the environmental protection obligations, recording and managing files, labeling, and other risk control measures
- transboundary movement guidelines establishing basic principles, applications for import, risk assessment of imports, approval of imports, import permits, notification, transboundary transportation management, examination and approval of exports, and transboundary movement of special genetic resources

Legislation ideally includes laws on safety—safety of crop production, forestry, genetically modified microorganisms, genetically modified food, poultry and livestock genes, and wildlife genes. To enforce these laws, increase coordination, reduce risk, and strengthen enforcement, the subsequent legislation should improve legal institutions that manage GMOs.

Risk assessment is an important aspect of GMO legislation. A certified organization would require institutions and individuals researching GMOs to conduct risk assessments of the donor, the carrier, and the host; determine the biological characteristics of the involved GMOs; and determine the risk level of the GMOs.

The relevant administrative departments of the State Council would require research institutions' staff undertaking level I GMO research to file records. Researchers working on GMO levels II, III, and IV would submit applications to an administrative department of the State Council corresponding to their affiliation and could begin researching only after their applications are approved. Researchers conducting interim experiments would obtain licenses to continue their research.

A certified organization would conduct a risk assessment on institutions researching GMOs and draft a report on their findings. After this report was combined with a preliminary opinion of examination, a related administrative department would sign it. The Management Office of National Biosafety, after receiving the report, would organize experts from the Consulting Committee of National Biosafety to evaluate the report and issue a recommendation, which would be submitted to the administrative department of environmental protection of the State Council for approval.

Labeling should cover both primary and processed GMO products. When distributors place GMO products on the market for the first time, the distributor must clearly label the GMO's ingredients (Yu 2009, 284–285). Because the public has the right to biosafety information, both the public and environmental nongovernmental organizations should be able to file lawsuits for failure to label. Producers and distributors of GMO products would disclose potential risks to ecosystems and public health. The administrative authorities would clearly stipulate the approaches and procedures on how to exercise the public's right to know, legal consequences of infringement, and the procedures for redress.

Outlook

With improvement in the aforementioned aspects of the legal system and administrative and legal institutions, biosafety legislation will provide more sufficient and effective support for biosafety management and consumer rights protection.

YU Wenxuan
China University of Political Science and Law

See also Agriculture (China and Southeast Asia); Agriculture (South and East Asia); Biodiversity Conservation Legislation (China); Genetic Resources; Public Health; Rule of Law

FURTHER READING

Chinese Ministry of Agriculture. (2010, March 15). Q&A: Agro-GM technology and biosafety. *Science and Technology Daily*.

Ho Mae-Wan, & Ching, Lim Li. (2004). *A GM-free sustainable world*. Penang, Malaysia: Third World Network.

Levin, Morris A., & Strauss, Harlee S. (Eds.). (1991). *Risk assessment in genetic engineering: Environmental release of organisms*. New York: McGraw-Hill.

Yu Wenxuan. (2009). *On biosafety legislation*. Beijing: Tsinghua University Press.

C

Chennai, India

4.6 million est. pop. 2011

Chennai, located on India's southeastern coast, is the capital of the state of Tamil Nadu. It is known for its beautiful (though threatened) beaches and its popular film industry (known as Kollywood). Although it is one of the most industrially advanced cities in India, Chennai's division into a poor and working class north and an affluent south affects the relative quality of public sanitation, health, and transportation.

Chennai (formerly known as Madras) is situated at the eastern end of the southern Indian peninsula lying in the northern part of the eastern coastal plains. The total area of the district is 178 square kilometers; Chennai is the fourth largest city in India after Delhi, Mumbai (Bombay), and Kolkata (Calcutta). The 2011 census reported the population of the city of Chennai itself as around 4.6 million (Government of India 2011); the surrounding regions make the population much higher than that. According to the 2001 census, its population was around 4.3 million, with a growth rate of 17 percent between 1981 and 1991, which went down to just under 10 percent between 1991 and 2001. It has the fourth largest slum population among Indian cities, with about 820,000 people, close to 18 percent of the population, living in slum conditions. Although the city faces issues of land, water, and waste management, overall Chennai has received favorable rankings compared to other cities in worldwide quality of life surveys done by organizations such as Mercer.

Chennai is in a low-lying area, with a land surface that is very flat. The elevation gradually increases farther inland, but the average elevation is roughly 6 meters above sea level, making drainage a serious problem. Chennai was once known for its pleasant scenery and was said to be a town open to the sky and full of gardens with mango, coconut, guava, and orange trees. Most of the roads were flanked by groves of palm and other trees, and a number of houses had gardens displaying fine trees with lush canopies and creeping vines. Today, in the congested city, gardens and groves are less common, but Chennai can still be proud of the well-maintained green belts found in several public parks. Stretches of casuarina plantations on the sea coast beyond the mouth of the Adyar River in the south, and the coastal suburban region of Tondiarpet in the north, supply firewood to the city. Due to water shortages and a lack of space, even house gardening is not very common anymore (Chennai District n.d.). At the same time, Chennai is also one of the few cities in the world that possesses a national wildlife park in the heart of the city. Guindy National Park, 2.7 square kilometers, conserves one of the world's rarest vegetation types—the tropical dry evergreen forest. Guindy National Park prides itself on its biodiversity, being home to black bucks, spotted deer, jackals, a variety of snakes, geckos, tortoises, and over a hundred species of birds and sixty species each of butterflies and spiders—all free-ranging fauna living with minimal interference from human beings. The park boasts over 350 species of plants and is a great boon for both the amateur and professional botanist. The Madras Naturalists Society, founded in 1978, has produced ecologists and naturalists of renown (Surendra 2010, Baskaran 2010).

Business and Industry

Chennai prospers in a wide variety of industrial and commercial areas. It has one of the largest software parks in India. It is considered the health capital of India, with 45 percent of foreign health tourists to India and 30 to 40 percent of domestic tourists heading to Chennai for advanced health interventions. Chennai is a leading manufacturing hub for automotive, electronic, and hardware products and has long been a major manufacturing center, including in the large-scale machinery sector such as textiles, petrochemicals, and apparel. Chennai enjoys an eminent position in the country's film industry and has a number of studios in Kodambakkam. (Chennai's film industry is known as Kollywood, a portmanteau of the Kodambakkam district and Hollywood. The more familiar [to Westerners] Bollywood is in Mumbai; the name comes from the city's former name, Bombay.) The city is also emerging as a center for the aerospace industry.

The port of Chennai is one of the most active ports of India; is the second largest port after Mumbai; and is the third oldest among the twelve major ports of India.

Sustainability

For Chennai as for other cities, sustainability is related to the city's original natural endowments, the manner in which the built environment has enhanced or reduced these natural endowments, and the new loads on the carrying capacity of the city. The extent to which carrying capacity is strained also affects livability, another index for measurement of sustainability in social, economic, cultural, ecological, and environmental terms. Important issues for sustainability and livability include assured energy supply, transport infrastructure (especially public transport), public housing, planned aspects of the city, civic amenities, and essential services such as provision of clean water, sanitation, and disposal of solid wastes.

Transport

Chennai, and Tamil Nadu in general, from the 1970s have emphasized improving transport connectivity and public transport. In the early 1970s, a World Bank Report ranked Tamil Nadu high among developing regions of the world with good urban transport services. Over the years, while rural transport connectivity has vastly improved, urban public transportation has not kept up with growing demand. Chennai is served by an extensive though inadequate bus transportation system, a rail network that connects the southern parts of the city to the northern port areas, and an urban rail transport system that cuts across the city and also serves inner city areas. Because Chennai had been one of the major port cities since British colonial times (along with Mumbai and Kolkata) and one of the three presidencies under British rule, rail connectivity from Chennai to the rest of the country has always been good and has improved over the years. Chennai airport, though bursting at its seams and not well managed, is still a major airport hub to the rest of India and other parts of the world.

Environmental Troubles on the Beach

Chennai is known for its beaches, which run along the coastline from just north of Madras Port, to the south as far as beyond Mahabalipuram to Kalpakkam, where a nuclear power plant is located. Within the city, the two famous stretches of beach are the Marina Beach, a popular visiting place for Chennai's citizens including early morning joggers, and Elliots Beach, farther south, once a quiet beach whose tranquility as of 2012 was being threatened by new city planning. Plans of urban beach development have met great local resistance; as the Indian architect and urban designer Pushpa Arabindoo has stated, "the conceptualization of public spaces in India [is] a problematic one, arising from a difference between the Western and indigenous perception of open spaces" (Arabindoo 2011, 381).

There is a long history of the more prosperous population trying to mold parts of the beach into exclusive recreation locales that would exclude the (often poor) local public. Wanting to change the image of Marina Beach from "the second longest public toilet in the world" (quoted in Arabindoo 2011, 388, from an advertisement in *The Hindu*) to a globally known beach resort, city planners launched the Marina Beautification Plan in January 2003. Although the plan was supported by public groups such as Citizens Rights Action Group (CRAG), it created conflict with many other groups, such as the fisher communities that would be relocated as a result of the project. Environmental nongovernmental organizations (NGOs) have allied themselves with the fisher communities to defend the communities' rights to their traditional ways of life and use of the beach, which the government relocation mandates fail to take into account. These mandates threaten to make such public spaces less accessible, especially to the city's less well-to-do people who have traditionally used the beaches for leisure, relaxation, and survival (Arabindoo 2011).

The issue of sand mining is also controversial in relation to the beaches. The public works department (PWD) made temporary roads to facilitate removing sand from sandbars at the mouth of the river and relocating it to the Ennore thermal power plant to build up ground levels and prevent water stagnation in low-lying areas. Activists from several groups have opposed this action, claiming the removal of the sandbars will affect water table levels and erosion patterns along the beach. They also say the act of building roads, even temporary roads, and mining the sand are in direct violation of the Coastal Regulation Zone (CRZ) laws that prevent development within 200 meters of the high tide line. While PWD workers claim their orders came from a government mandate, activists point out that "the State government is responsible for enforcing the [CRZ] law. It is ironic that the enforcer itself is violating the law" (Sreevatsan 2011).

Water Resources and Sanitation

The city's social demography has a largely poor and working class northern area and an affluent south, with most bureaucrats and wealthier folk living in the southern parts of the city. Their social and economic positions ensure better delivery of civic services in these more affluent parts of the inner city. Large numbers of settlements have grown up in the city's peripheries in the south, west, and north, bringing massive problems of urban management. Solid waste disposal has become a major problem over the years and has contributed off and on to the city's image as a "dirty city" (Dahiya 2005).

Chennai's water resources are derived both from rains and from the groundwater that is recharged by floodwater flows, since the rivers and floodwaters of the southern peninsula flow in a southeasterly direction into the Bay of Bengal. This underscores the uniqueness of the Chennai wetlands compared to the overall geology and ecology of Tamil Nadu. It is against this geological and ecological historical background that we should understand the network of wetlands and man-made tanks, including temple tanks, which are part of an extensive natural and man-made system in and around Chennai. They store the flows and act as a vast catchment network for the water, especially close to the coast. These wetlands and tanks not only store the surface water flows during the monsoons but also serve to charge the groundwater aquifers and serve as flood control mechanisms.

It is reported that Chennai used to have about 150 small and large water bodies in and around it. As of 2012, however, the number has fallen to twenty-seven. In the 1990s, Chennai's prominent public interest group, the Citizen-Consumer and Civic Action Group (CAG), tried to stop massive housing projects of the Tamil Nadu Housing Board in the low-lying areas and lakebeds of Velachery, Ambattur, Nolambur, Chitlapakkam, and Kakkalur through public interest litigations. These projects had received financial approval from the World Bank and HUDCO.

In the wake of the recent flooding disasters in China (June–September 2011) and Bangkok, Thailand (July–December 2011), it is clear that wetlands, swamps, and water bodies—especially within urban or mega-urban regions—must be responsibly managed. Viewing them as sites for dumping debris and creating new marketable land is multiplying the possibilities of floods and related disasters, thus enhancing the risks of making cities not only ecologically unsustainable but also gradually affecting economic sustainability and reducing the livability of urban regions.

Chennai's annual rainfall is 120 centimeters, but increasingly this rainfall, partly as a result of global climate changes, is happening over a shorter duration and is more intensive. This has resulted in flash floods and increased the frequency and extent of floods. News of vast areas in Chennai being inundated after the rains is becoming a regular annual feature during the monsoons, and economic loss caused by flooding is becoming a regular occurrence.

Chennai is also a city known for its problem with water security, which has been met by concerted efforts to promote rainwater harvesting through both legislation and massive public education campaigns. According to the State of Asian Cities published by the United Nations Economic and Social Commission for Asia and the Pacific (UN-ESCAP) and the United Nations Human Settlements Programme (UN-HABITAT), in most Asian cities today the problem has less to do with the *access to* than with the *quality of* potable water. In Chennai and Mumbai, for instance, it was found that coverage was 100 percent and 97 percent, respectively, but water was available for only four or five hours a day. These findings point to a serious concern—namely, that water resources currently available to Asian cities are becoming severely depleted (UN-HABITAT 2011).

Waste Management and Citizen Action

Solid waste is a problem on its own in managing the sustainability of cities, but it also has impacts on air and groundwater pollution. As elsewhere in the Asia-Pacific region, most of Chennai's waterways and river systems are heavily polluted by the dumping of urban, domestic, and industrial solid waste. Groundwater aquifers in low-lying areas of the city are also becoming increasingly contaminated with domestic and industrial waste, heavy metals, and other industrial pollutants.

In the world as a whole, solid waste dumping contributes to 3 percent of greenhouse gas emissions. On the other hand, more than 72 percent of total greenhouse gas emissions occurring under anaerobic conditions could be avoided by altering disposal methods, such as incineration, that aerosolize particles into the air (Bogner et al. 2007). Chennai and its surrounding municipalities have been struggling with managing the solid waste generated in its communities.

Given that centralized and privatized solid waste collection and disposal systems have not been fully effectual, a number of women's associations and resident welfare associations have been tackling the problem of collecting and managing solid waste themselves. In the mid-1990s, when a municipality near Chennai suspended waste collection services, a local women's group stepped in to fill the gap and eventually persuaded officials to support their revolutionary program, demonstrating in the process how grassroots groups can have a positive effect on urban governance. Similar efforts have sprung up across the peri-urban areas surrounding Chennai. It is through such community efforts that the livability index of cities like Chennai is sought to be enhanced.

Lawrence SURENDRA
University of Mysore

See also Cities—Overview; Delhi, India; Dhaka, Bangladesh; India; Media Coverage of the Environment; Mumbai, India; Information and Communication Technologies (ICT); Nongovernmental Organizations (NGOs); Public Health; Public Transportation; Public-Private Partnerships; Water Security; Water Use and Rights (India)

FURTHER READING

Arabindoo, Pushpa. (2011). City of sand: Stately re-imagination of Marina Beach in Chennai. *International Journal of Urban and Regional Research, 35*(2), 379–401. Retrieved March 29, 2012, from http://graduateinstitute.ch/webdav/site/cies/shared/events/Brown_Bags/city%20of%20sand%20marina%20beach.pdf

Baskaran, Theodore S. (2006). Madras to Chennai: Review of "Chennai not Madras: Perspectives on the city" by A. R. Venkatachlapathy (Ed.). *Frontline Magazine, 23*(25). Retrieved March 29, 2012, from http://www.frontlineonnet.com/fl2325/stories/20061229000507800.htm

Baskaran, Theodore S. (Ed.). (2010). *The Sprint of the Blackbuck*. New Delhi: Penguin.

Bogner, Jean, et al. (2007). Waste management. In Bert Metz, Ogunlade R. Davidson, Peter R. Bosch, Rutu Dave, & Leo A. Meyer (Eds.), *Climate change 2007: Mitigation, Contribution of Working Group III to the Fourth Assessment Report of the Intergovernmental Panel on Climate Change* (pp. 585–618). Cambridge, UK: Cambridge University Press.

Chennai District. (n.d.) District profile. Retrieved March 19, 2012, from http://www.chennai.tn.nic.in/chndistprof.htm#geog

Chennai Metropolitan Development Authority. (2008). Seminar on second master plan for Chennai Metropolitan Area, 2026: Avenues and opportunities. Proceedings and recommendations. Chennai, India: Government of Tamil Nadu. Retrieved March 13, 2012, from http://www.cmdachennai.gov.in/SMPS/B_Proceedings.pdf

Citizen Consumer and Civic Action Group (CAG). (n.d.). Homepage. Retrieved March 13, 2012, from http://www.cag.org.in/home.php

Dahiya, Bharat. (2003a). Hard struggle and soft gains: Environmental management, civil society and governance in Pammal, South India. *Environment & Urbanization, 15*(1), 91–100.

Dahiya, Bharat. (2003b). Peri-urban environments and community driven development: Chennai, India, cities. *The International Journal of Urban Policy and Planning, 20*(5), 341–352.

Dahiya, Bharat. (2005). Understanding local politics, democracy and civil society: Environmental governance in urban India. In Crispin Bates & Subho Basu (Eds.), *Rethinking Indian political institutions* (pp. 107–124). London: Anthem Press.

Dahiya, Bharat, & Pugh, Cedric. (2000). The localisation of Agenda 21 and the Sustainable Cities Programme. In Cedric Pugh (Ed.), *Sustainable cities in developing countries: Theory and practice at the millennium* (pp. 152–184). London: Earthscan.

Ellis, Rowan. (2010). Who participates? Rethinking civil society in the context of competing definitions of urban sustainability. Washington, DC: World Bank. Retrieved March 13, 2012, from http://siteresources.worldbank.org/INTURBANDEVELOPMENT/Resources/336387-1272506514747/Ellis.pdf

Government of India, Ministry of Home Affairs. (2011). Cities having population 1 lakh [one hundred thousand] and above, Census 2011. Retrieved April 5, 2012, from http://www.censusindia.gov.in/2011-prov-results/paper2/data_files/India2/Table_2_PR_Cities_1Lakh_and_Above.pdf

Nair, Santha Sheela. (2011). Sustainable water and sanitation: Two Indian cases. In Esther Charlesworth & Rob Adams (Eds.), *The EcoEdge: Urgent design challenges in building sustainable cities*. London: Routledge.

Nair, Santha Sheela. (n.d.). Meeting the challenge in sustainable water supply and sanitation. Retrieved March 13, 2012, from http://www.cityedge.org.au/images/download/presentations/nair.pdf

Sreevatsan, Ajai. (2011, February 8). Concern over sand mining. Retrieved March 29, 2012, from http://www.thehindu.com/todays-paper/tp-national/article1166302.ece

Surendra, Lawrence. (2010). Inspiring essays: Review of "Sprint of the blackbuck." *Frontline Magazine, 27*(20). Retrieved March 29, 2012, from http://www.frontlineonnet.com/fl2720/stories/20101008272007600.htm

United Nations Human Settlements Programme (UN-HABITAT). (2011). The state of Asian cities 2010/2011. Retrieved March 13, 2012, from http://www.unhabitat.org/content.asp?cid=8891&catid=643&typeid=46&AllContent=1

Vaidyanathan, A. (Ed.). (2001). Tanks of South India. New Delhi: Centre for Science and Environment.

Berkshire's authors and editors welcome questions, comments, and corrections. Send your emails about the *Berkshire Encyclopedia of Sustainability* in general or this volume in particular to: sustainability.updates@berkshirepublishing.com

China

1.34 billion est. pop. 2012

China is one of the world's largest countries and has the world's largest population, most of whom live in the alluvial plains in the east and south. With this size come environmental problems. Although twenty-first-century legislation has been strong on pollution controls, policing these controls and enforcement has been weak. China is the world's largest consumer of coal but in recent years has invested tremendous amounts of money in renewable energy.

China's land size is slightly smaller than the United States but with more than four times the population: 1.34 billion people as of 2011 (US CIA 2012). The East China Sea, the Yellow Sea, and the South China Sea border China on the east and south. Mountains and deserts separate China from Afghanistan, Bhutan, India, Kazakhstan, North Korea, Kyrgyzstan, Laos, Mongolia, Myanmar (Burma), Nepal, Pakistan, Russia, Tajikistan, and Vietnam. Its huge variety of people reflects this geographical diversity. The majority of the people—more than 90 percent—are Han, the people the world traditionally thinks of as "the Chinese." The country is generally dry in the north, where wheat is the preferred staple, and wet in the south, where rice is dominant. Although people have been working the land for millennia (agriculture first emerged in north and south China with the domestication of millet and rice around 7000 BCE or earlier), this article picks up with the rule of the Manchus, who doubled the size of the Chinese empire during the Qīng dynasty (1644–1911/12).

The Manchus

Under the rule of the Manchus, the size and geographical and cultural diversity of the empire were unlike those of any other country. In the northern and western regions, camels passed through the inner Asian desert oases in Xinjiang, yaks filled the stables of Buddhist monasteries on the plateau of Tibet, sheep grazed the pastures of Mongolia, and horses and deer roamed the plains and forests of Manchuria. In the southwestern and southern regions, indigenous peoples fought losing battles against the invasions of Han-Chinese colonists, miners, traders, and soldiers who came to exploit the riches of the tropical rain forests, the timber, the copper, iron, and tin mines, and eventually their farming soils. Concentrated in the fertile river valleys and plains in the eastern half of China, the Han-Chinese population had grown from about 150 million in 1700 to maybe 350 million in 1800 and 450 million in 1900 (Guo 1985), creating an enormous demand for metals, timber, cotton, wool, fuel, pork, and many other products. Spurred on by the new American crops such as maize, potatoes, and tobacco, and a growing demand for tea, many farmers went on to exploit the hills and mountains of central and south China, and millions even went overseas. Economic growth was uneven, and so were its environmental effects on different regions, but population pressures on natural resources increased wherever people could move.

Landscape Made by Human Hand

From the eighteenth century, loggers felled forests with increasing speed, and farmers reclaimed the land for growing maize or tubers. Farmers and other settlers ruthlessly exploited the shrinking natural vegetation and other resources of the hills and upstream areas. Many mountain soils could not sustain a long period of farming; they rapidly eroded and became too thin and stony to support agriculture. China never officially registered land, which makes it difficult to estimate the speed of the agricultural reclamation process. On gentler slopes and along river valleys, farmers built terraces to conserve water, soil, and nutritional elements. They reclaimed lakes and low-lying land in river floodplains for irrigated agriculture. The resulting anthropogenic soils became stable and produced high yields of rice. Much of China's landscape thus was created by human hand. Land and people became vulnerable to floods and droughts, however, as riverbeds were raised and natural vegetation and flood retention capacities reduced. Along the coast the silt-laden rivers deposited a great deal of sediment, and farmers reclaimed land from the sea on a large scale, not only at the mouth of the Huang (Yellow) River; but also near those of the Yangzi (Chang) and other rivers.

Dry and Irrigated Farming

Water is in short supply in northern China but ample in southern China. The monsoon climate brings an uneven distribution of rainfall, with spring droughts and summer floods. Surface water traditionally irrigated some land along the rivers of northern China and near mountains, but most farming was dry. Shallow wells supplied water for vegetables and drinking. Wheat, millet, sorghum, and maize were dominant crops. Diets were poor and particularly lacking in animal protein. Constrained by poverty and difficult transport, only some farmers could afford to grow cotton, tobacco, peanuts, and other cash crops or to keep pigs for manure and pork. Most people lived in walled rectangular villages spread evenly across the North China Plain. In contrast, in the Yangzi River basin in central and southern China, water was abundant and, where necessary, farmers caught it in tanks and reservoirs in the hills and subsequently stored it in paddy fields. Rice yields were high, transport was convenient, and silk production, tea growing, weaving, and other industries supplemented people's income. The population was dense, crowding the cities, market towns, and villages that stretched along rivers, roads, and canals.

Factors of Change

In the final years of the Manchu dynasty, four new elements began to change China's traditional environment.

First came modern transport. The government gave Chinese and foreign railway companies concessions to build railroads. These companies began to develop land and to exploit mines and forests, and new cities sprang up. Because of improved railway transport, millions of colonists moved into Manchuria and other outlying regions. Famines were much reduced. Great droughts in northern China during 1876–1878 and in northwestern China during 1899–1900 and 1929–1930 cost millions of lives, but in 1922 the North China Plain was saved by its railways. China had more than 20,000 kilometers of railways during the 1930s. Modern tar roads and rubber-tired carts and trucks greatly reduced short-distance transport costs. Companies tore down old city walls to make way for new development. Political strife between warlords continued to tear China apart, however. Modern development—other than mining—remained concentrated in the coastal areas, particularly in Japan-controlled Manchuria and Taiwan and in a few cities.

Second, after 1870 modern mining and other industries developed, such as the Pingyuan coal mines near Beijing, the Hanye ironworks in Hubei Province, the Shuikoushan lead mines in Hunan Province, and the Dongchuan copper mines in Yunnan Province. Most iron and copper mines and kilns for porcelain and bricks traditionally relied on wood fuel in their immediate surroundings and would move elsewhere once they depleted the timber resources. The new, large-scale mines used coal, and the railways soon served them. After 1895 foreign industries developed in the western treaty ports. Under foreign protection Shanghai, Tianjin, Guangzhou (Canton), and other cities rapidly developed into industrial and commercial centers. The 1933 industrial survey reported 3,800 mostly urban, modern factories. Textiles, coal mining, iron smelting, oil pressing, and flour milling all adopted new large-scale technologies. Industry introduced new products, and cigarettes, matches, electricity, and machinery changed people's lives. The urban population expanded rapidly, leading to crowded housing, crime (Shanghai became associated with kidnapping and vice), and unsanitary conditions. Even so, city life was more secure than life in the countryside. The economic crisis of the 1930s, World War II, and subsequent civil war retarded China's modern industrial development, and in 1949 only some coastal cities and Manchuria had modern industry.

Third, Chinese entrepreneurs living overseas, Western missionaries, and (mainly) US agricultural scientists brought new crops, animal breeds, and cultivation techniques into China. US cotton, Italian wheat, British pigs, Swiss goats, and Russian and Dutch dairy cattle gave higher returns than most local varieties. Many local varieties eventually disappeared, although some qualities were maintained in crossbreeds. Chinese cotton and soybean growers began to produce for the Japanese market and native factories. Through increasing commercialization, the rural standard of living improved slightly in most regions.

Fourth, China's government became more economically exploitative and socially invasive. Legal arrangements replaced traditional property regimes, allowing fuller exploitation of land and other natural resources. The state revoked traditional Mongolian land rights, for instance, and sold them to Japanese, Russian, and Chinese chartered companies. Improved communications, modern arms, and new bureaucracies strengthened the reach of the state. Nationalism and other ideologies demanded China should be strong and its people be lifted from poverty. Rising expectations led to revolutionary movements and civil wars, in which warring parties mobilized available natural and human resources on an unprecedented scale.

Rural Misery

In spite of such modernization efforts, the image of China as a country plagued by bandits, soldiers, opium, and natural disasters remained a valid one. The 1931 and 1935 floods of the Yangzi River and the deliberate dike breaks in Shandong to force the Huang River into a southern course in 1938 destroyed millions of lives, cattle, and homes. The Japanese invasion and atrocities such as the mass murders in Nanking sent millions fleeing to the interior, from where the government of Free China (i.e., the areas not under control of the Japanese army) continued its struggle. Less dramatic but ever present were stark poverty, high infant and child mortality, and many epidemic diseases. About 1 million Chinese, mostly urban young adults working indoors, died of tuberculosis every year. Cholera and malaria were common. Most farmers, working barefoot in the paddy fields, spreading night soil (human excrement) over their vegetables, living with their pigs, and drinking unsanitary water, were infested with parasites and affected by viruses and died before the age of sixty. Families split up early, and few managed to attain the Confucian ideal of three generations living under one roof.

Forests and Vegetation Cover

By 1800 loggers had felled most of China's original forest, with some stands remaining in the northeast and southwest. China's forest cover decreased more rapidly because railroads made commercial exploitation feasible and also because farmers reclaimed land for agricultural use. Official data (909 million hectares of forest in 1934 and 841 million hectares with 6 billion cubic meters of timber in 1947) are highly questionable (Xiong 1989, 18). By 1940 Manchuria's forest cover and timber stocks had been halved, and by 1985, halved again. In the Yangzi River upper basin, forest cover shrank from 50 percent to less than 20 percent (Li 1985, 19–23). In particular historians have blamed the Great Leap Forward of 1958–1961 for large-scale wanton felling of forests to acquire building material and fuel for new rural industries. Commercial logging, agricultural land reclamation, household fuel use, and desiccation all had great impact. The consequent changes in river regimes caused greater vulnerability to floods and droughts.

Under communism and the communes established in 1958, afforestation campaigns were organized on a massive scale. Villages were obliged to plant a hundred trees per inhabitant, mostly along roads but also on waste hills to provide fuel and to combat erosion. Often done without sustained follow-up, tree planting failed more than it succeeded. Along the northern deserts where the government had reclaimed pastures to create farmland, for instance, they created a giant shelterbelt of trees to reduce wind velocity and protect the new farmland against desertification—an almost hopeless effort.

The forest area (land with a canopy density of at least 20 percent) grew to 125 million hectares with 11 billion cubic meters of live timber in 1988 and 175 million hectares with 14 billion cubic meters of timber by 2008 (National Bureau of Statistics of China 2009). Most forests are young and low in quality. In 1988 the government raised the price of timber, severely restricted its use for building purposes and sleepers (wooden pieces upon which floorboards are attached), and began importing pulp and paper. Reserving land for forest growth (by now 1 million square kilometers) and selling long-term leases of local forest, pastures, and wasteland to individual farmers have been adopted as solutions for collective squandering of resources and failing common property regimes, but with mixed success. After 2000, the government gave farmers sizable subsidies for taking erosion-prone farmland on steep slopes out of grain cultivation and converting it to forest, tree crops, or grassland. Low grain prices and rising agricultural labor costs contributed to the great success of this Grain for Green program. The government ended the program in 2006 because of high budgetary costs and rising grain prices. In response to growing demand, the area devoted to growing fruit increased during the 1980s and has doubled since 1990 to 12 million hectares, mostly on wasteland in the hills but also on formerly cultivated land. Although the government has actively promoted tree planting for combating water and soil erosion, clearing secondary vegetation for fruit orchards does not necessarily have positive effects.

Socialist Planning in Agriculture

Central socialist planning is known for its great successes and even greater failures. Mao Zedong's megalomaniacal Great Leap Forward was different in that it combined central targets for production and supply with local autarchy and mass campaigns. Results were disastrous. In 1958, large people's communes organized farming along military lines and started a mass campaign to produce iron in 600,000 small furnaces. The urban population jumped from 90 million in 1957 to 130 million in

1960. The cities could not sustain this influx, and food shortages followed. The idea to open up new land, clear forests, terrace hills, and build reservoirs everywhere proved counterproductive and environmentally destructive. Distribution networks broke down, grain output dropped, and the resulting famine of 1960–1961 cost 20 to 25 million lives. There were long-lasting effects on natural resources; for instance, the decimated fish population of China's largest lake, Qinghai, has not recovered since then. It also created an obsession with local self-reliance in foodgrain.

The large fields that collective farming created, although more efficient in the use of oxen, machinery, irrigation, fertilizers, and pesticides, were vulnerable to erosion and salinization. Since 1958, more than 35 million hectares (a third of China's original farm acreage) have been lost or diverted to other uses (Vermeer 1986, 143). The government reclaimed almost twice as much land for agriculture, but these were mostly areas with poor soils, remote areas, or steep hill slopes. The state settled Chinese citizens in border regions, from the Sanjiang Plains' marshes in the extreme north to the tropical forests of the island-province of Hainan and the deserts of Xinjiang Uygur Autonomous Region. Their irrigated agriculture destroyed the pastures and livelihood of native people. By the 1970s, land reclamation, overgrazing, and reduced precipitation—another consequence of deforestation—had turned a half-million square kilometers of northern prairies into deserts and reduced grass by one-third to one-half on remaining prairies. One-sixth of China suffered from serious soil erosion. One-quarter of China's reservoir capacity had silted up, and because of land reclamation and siltation, natural lakes such as the Dongting Hu had lost most of their flood retention capacity (Vermeer 1986; Ma 2004). Flood dangers increased as people settled along riverbeds, and buildings and bridges restricted the rivers' flood channels.

At the command of village cadres, peasants built roads, terraces, reservoirs, polders (low-lying land reclaimed from a body of water), electricity lines, and schools and other social services, but they had no freedom and only a very small increase in income. The general dissatisfaction led the government to abolish collective production in the early 1980s. The resulting loss of village control led again to (now individual) wanton felling of trees and indiscriminate exploitation of land and other resources. Higher prices and greater trading opportunities stimulated investments in tree crops and animal husbandry, however, and land improvement and property rights became more secure. Before the end of the 1980s, family farming and secure land tenure had become the norm again.

Diversification

A continuous growth of the village population in hilly and mountainous areas under the collective system pushed the expansion of farmland. In the 1980s, higher agricultural prices, improved transport, and free trade contributed to further expansion. Once the government allowed villagers to migrate and find employment in factories in the cities of eastern and southern China, however, farming became less attractive, and the population pressure on mountain land eased as people left their unsustainable farms. Central and provincial government budgets financed successive poverty alleviation programs. These programs raised average rural incomes in poor counties and villages well above subsistence levels and provided almost universal education, health care and other services, and access to electricity and roads. The programs moved several million farmers out of inaccessible areas and relocated them in concentrated villages. By 2007, 15 million rural people, half of whom lived in minority areas, were officially designated as still living in absolute poverty, but many more (42 million rural and 25 million urban people) received some sort of living allowances (State Ethnic Affairs Commission 2009, 24–27; National Bureau of Statistics of China 2008, 893). Safe drinking water has remained a major concern for many villages.

Worries that China could not feed its population have been (and still are) unfounded because the output of grain continued to rise considerably faster than the population, and diets improved with more pork, vegetables, fruits, fish, and dairy products. By 2000, urban people spent less than 40 percent of their income on food, much of which was on meat, fish, and fruit. Not quantity but quality and safety of food became a major concern, because of serious scandals with tainted and dangerous food products, such as the addition of melamine to baby formula powder. The one-child policy (restricting married urban couples to one child per family) accelerated demographic transition, and annual population growth slowed to below 0.6 percent after 2000. Because of rural migration (the 2010 census counted 221 million migrants) and economic growth, the urban population kept increasing and rose from 36 percent of the total population in 2000 to 50 percent in 2010 (National Bureau of Statistics of China 2011). Improved crop varieties, expanded irrigation, and (starting in the late 1960s) ever-increasing application of chemical fertilizers and electric pumping spurred continuous increases in grain yield. Chemical fertilizer use doubled between 1980 and 1990 to 24 million tonnes, and had doubled again by 2009. Around 2000, higher prices, proper incentives, and (at least partially) continued foodgrain sowing requirements caused an overproduction of cereals, and for some years, the government reduced the sowing acreage by about 10 percent. The area sown to rice shrank considerably because, pressed by a shortage of labor, many farmers in central and south China reverted to single-harvest rice. From 2003, the state promoted regional commercial specialization in farm products. Between 1997 and 2009, total farmland area was reduced by 9 million hectares to 122 million hectares, while fruit orchards and tea plantations expanded from 9 to 13 million hectares (National Bureau of Statistics of China 2010a). The reduction would have been considerably greater if urban governments requisitioning farmland for construction had not been obliged to open up compensatory farmland in outlying regions.

Farmers as of 2012 sow about 90 million hectares to cereals each year, yielding more than 172 million tonnes of rice, more than 100 million tonnes of wheat, and more than 145 million tonnes of maize, enough to produce 650 million pigs and 45 million cattle a year—50 and 75 percent, respectively, more than around 1995 (figures from National Bureau of Statistics of China's *Statistical Yearbook*, various years). Most are held in stables and fed with grain, and livestock feed needs have spurred most of the growth in grain demand. Although imports and exports of grain remain very limited, China has imported soybeans in ever-greater quantities, rising to 50 million tonnes in 2010. These imports have had sizable effects on land use in Brazil and other exporting countries.

China's very high levels of fertilizer application, needed to sustain high yields, and intensive animal husbandry have come at substantial environmental costs. The serious nitrification of surface waters and eutrophication (aquatic plant life growth that depletes oxygen in the water) of all major lakes goes unchecked. Red tides (algal bloom) have become a regular occurrence along the Bohai Sea and southern coast. Chinese leaders always have been committed politically to support cheap fertilizer and higher farm incomes. The government started national surveys of soil pollution and agricultural pollution sources in 2007, which may indicate some attitudinal shift. The government has played a positive role in reducing and improving the use of pesticides. It has promoted bioengineering in the twenty-first century, and genetically modifies most of its cotton and much of its soybeans and maize, primarily to increase resistance against pests and pesticides. Apart from cost reductions, reduction of pesticide use has enhanced cotton growers' health. China imports large amounts of high-quality cotton for its manufacture and export of textiles. If a similar readiness to accept imports of products with which China has no comparative advantage would be extended to food crops, there may be more wheat and rice imports in the future. Only then will further nitrification of China's surface waters be halted.

Global Warming

Global warming has intensified droughts in the north and floods in the south of China. Regional effects are uneven. Since the early 1980s, average temperatures increased only slightly in east China (and dropped in northeast China), but rose by 1.5°C–2°C in western China. Pastures and irrigated farmland in semidesert areas have suffered most, but higher temperatures have lengthened the growing season in western mountain areas. Since 1990 the area under irrigation has been expanded by 11 million hectares, but water shortages severely limit future agricultural growth. During the 1990s, on average, 5–15 million hectares were seriously stricken by flood every year, and 2–3 million hectares by drought (China Environment Yearbook Society 1990–2010). After 2005, droughts became much more serious. It was extremely dry in 2009, extremely wet in 2010. Central and local governments stepped up state investments in reservoirs and dikes and undertook to widen the Yangzi River's flood channel after the devastating 1998 floods, reducing annual damages from floods.

Between 2000 and 2009 China's available surface water decreased by 10 percent to 238 billion cubic meters, and groundwater decreased even more (National Bureau of Statistics of China 2010a, 5). Dwindling water resources and increased industrial and residential water use have aggravated problems with water quality, particularly in northern China where about 60 percent of the Sungari, Liao, Hai, and Huai rivers are seriously polluted, class 4—unfit for human or animal use—or worse. Water pollution is the main reason why the planned transfer of water from the Yangzi River through the Grand Canal to supplement Beijing and Tienjin has failed. A giant project now under construction that will supply Beijing with water from the Hanshui (a tributary of the Yangzi River) at Danjiangkou may run into similar problems, even if experts consider its environmental effects.

Industrial Planning, Growth, and Improvement

Fearing foreign invasion, China set up many heavy industries in remote mountain areas after 1965. In socialism, big was beautiful, but all provinces and cities tried to, or had to, become self-reliant. Socialist planning invited local governments and factories to maximize output and distribute according to plan, regardless of efficiency or cost. Resources such as land, water, and ores had no value in their own right, but only from invested labor. This led to hoarding raw materials, wasteful use of energy and land, and blind production. Because China was isolated and without access to foreign technology, most industries continued to copy or adapt the Soviet technology of the 1950s. When China finally woke up to the demands of the market in the 1980s, it found that large parts of its industrial apparatus were mislocated and that almost all were outdated. Traditional state-owned industries could not compete with the new industries' foreign technology (and, increasingly, foreign capital) established in the coastal regions. They often could not compete with small rural industries either. In the 1990s, the government consolidated, privatized, or closed many state-owned industries. Efficiencies in the use of energy, materials, capital, and labor improved greatly.

Tens of millions of the young rural poor migrated to cities and coastal areas owing to increasing regional differentials. Average rural income in poor interior provinces was only one-tenth that in Shanghai and Guangzhou. Village collective provisions, supported by state subsidies and antipoverty programs, proved effective in providing a minimal sustenance of life, primary education (obligatory since 1986), and health care. Employment in agriculture was unrewarding, however, and many small rural industries lost their competitive advantage. As direct state involvement in the economy declined, the central government concentrated on planning and building a new infrastructure, producing and supplying energy, and building large factories in selected industries. Its largest single project may have been the multipurpose Three Gorges dam and reservoir, designed to supply electricity, regulate floods, and improve shipping on the Yangzi River—but eventually requiring resettlement of more than a million people. Around 1995, the state still directed planning at employment creation in small towns. When peasants voted with their feet, authorities eventually accepted the inevitability, and positive socioeconomic benefits, of rapid urbanization. Urban housing, drinking water, sanitation, and general adoption of gas instead of coal for cooking purposes became political priorities. Since 1990 urban population has increased by 3.6 percent per year, and by 2010, half of China's population was urban.

In the new century, political worries about the socially destabilizing effects of increasing differentials led to a grand program to develop the physical and social infrastructure of a dozen poor provinces in western China. The state built new railroads, highways, and factories to integrate their industries with the advanced coastal regions and more fully exploit the mining resources of the western regions. China's 2008–2009 economic stimulus program accelerated investments even more, and the central government relaxed or decentralized its planning and environmental standards. Now coal-fired and hydropower stations send their electricity east along three ultrahigh voltage (UHV) lines, pipelines transport oil and gas from Xinjiang and Shaanxi provinces to Shanghai and Beijing, and the state has drawn Tibet into the national economy with the world's highest railroad to Qinghai Province. Reducing the negative environmental effects of this forced rapid development has been a major challenge, because local governments are insufficiently equipped (or interested) in doing environmental impact assessments or monitoring project construction. Traditional lifestyles of minority peoples are disappearing, even if some have been reenacted and cultural monuments restored to serve the interests of a rapidly growing number of Han-Chinese tourists.

Rising incomes and expectations have made involuntary resettlement from construction areas more difficult. New farmland is hard to create and unrewarding, and many farmers are unfit for urban jobs. Compensation standards for people who lose their land to reservoirs, highways, or other construction were raised in 1991 and again in 1998 in response to popular protests. Since 2006 regulations require that their living standards should remain at least equal, but that is easier said than done.

Industrial Pollution and Remedial Measures

In 1972 pollution accidents affected the fish supply to Beijing from the Guanting Reservoir and the shellfish of Dalian Bay. The government disclosed that mercury and other heavy metals dumped in the Sungari and Nenni rivers were poisoning fish and people. Such disclosure reflected a beginning awareness of the need to check pollution and prepared China for participation in the 1972 Stockholm conference on the environment (the United Nations Conference on the Human Environment) and adoption of its first environmental regulations. A 1977 survey of sea pollution found high industrial discharges of heavy metals and serious oil spills; 560 square kilometers of oil covered the Bohai Bay, a traditional provider of shrimp and fish to the banquets of China's ruling elite (Hua 1989).

Early remedial policies focused on management of river systems, waste-release standards for new or expanding large industries, cleanup of major cities, reduction in pesticide use, food safety inspection, and research and monitoring. After 1979 scientists screened industrial expansion plans for their discharge standards. Regulators first focused on the metallurgy, oil, textile, paper, food, building materials, and machinery industries. Compliance was very uneven, however, depending on the development level and financial resources of the responsible local governments.

A trial environmental law was passed in 1979. It focused on prevention and the "polluter pays" principle. The government introduced surface-water-quality standards in 1983 and 1986 and made local governments responsible for monitoring water quality and preventing further degradation. The laws set three standards of ambient air quality for different types of areas. The government charged polluting enterprises for above-standard emissions. It passed laws for conservation of forests, grassland, fisheries, and wild animals during the mid-1980s. By 2000, more than 1,200 nature reserves occupied 10 percent of China's territory, half of which were in Tibet and Xinjiang. The government introduced environmental laws for the marine environment (1982), water pollution (1984), air pollution (1987), solid waste (1995), and noise (1996). A growing number of construction projects required environmental impact assessments. In 2000, the state introduced a total emission control permit system for certain areas, whereby emission quotas are distributed or traded.

The 1980s were a period of rapid, visible, and cost-effective early advances in pollution prevention and treatment efforts. In 1982 the State Council ruled that 6 or 7 percent of investments in capital construction and renovation projects should go to pollution prevention and treatment. A tax on urban construction created an important financial source for local government. Environmental protection became a standard part of the government's five-year plans. In the 1990s, politicians and administrators became better educated, younger, and more receptive to urban public pressure for improvement of the quality of their environment. By 1987, 0.8 percent of gross domestic product (GDP) was spent on environmental protection, and its proponents demanded that this should rise to 1.5–2 percent eventually. This percentage subsequently fell, however, and only at the end of the 1990s did it increase to around 1 percent, and in the twenty-first century it rose to 1.3–1.5 percent of GDP (calculated from National Bureau of Statistics of China, various years). Its official term, *environmental pollution treatment*, is a misnomer, because a growing and substantial part (in 2008 almost one-half, in 2009 one-third) represents those investments in new construction projects that are required to comply with environmental regulations.

Weak Enforcement of Rules

Why was follow-up of early advances so difficult? In practice, sanctions on polluting behavior of enterprises were weak. Because pollution costs were lower than treatment costs, it paid to pollute. State-owned enterprises saw pollution charges (which remained very low) as just one more state tax. Management was lax, inspections were few and sloppy, and treatment installations might have been turned off to save costs. As in other socialist countries, in China local governments were the owners of the enterprise, monitors of its environmental performance, and judges at the same time. They feared that investments in the environment might come at the expense of employment and profits. The state increased local environmental protection bureaus to 130,000 workers by 2000, but their hands were tied. Bureaucracies made the decisions; they were not imposed by law or demanded by public opinion. The diversity in technological levels and scale within many industrial branches in China further complicated an imposition of uniform standards. China set ambitious targets for reduction of emissions by its industries, but monitoring has been uneven, and rural industries and farmers are hardly covered.

Industrial pollution has been spreading. By the mid 1990s one-half of China's industrial production came from township and village enterprises, largely outside of the control of local environmental protection bureaus. It took time, considerable political effort, and concentrated action to close down the worst-polluting industries in the most affected eastern areas of China. Prompted by unacceptable levels of water pollution and drinking-water disasters, China began cleanup programs for major cities, Taihu Lake, and medium-size river basins. By 2000, 82 percent of industrial wastewater discharged by urban industries was up to standard, compared with 50 percent in 1990. These changes drove polluting industries to interior provinces and rural areas, where they became harder to control. In spite of greater energy efficiency and coal washing, rapid industrial growth pushed China's total sulfur dioxide and soot emissions to 18 and 10 billion tonnes, respectively, in 2000. Only after 2005, because of flue gas desulfurization requirements, did sulfur dioxide emissions drop below 25 million tonnes (National Bureau of Statistics of China 2001 and 2010). The volume of dangerous solid waste increased continuously, and heavy-metal pollution contaminated soils and drinking water. The authorities often failed to notice pollution of factory terrains for a long time, until crops and people in the surrounding areas started to suffer from its effect on groundwater. Scientists have detected alarmingly high levels of lead and mercury poisoning in many places in China.

The deteriorating trend was mitigated when industries were consolidated and upgraded. More realistic pricing of energy and resources, state-of-the-art foreign factories, pressure from a more affluent and environmentally aware public, and government planning all played a role. Popular protests against polluting factories became very common, and (if nonviolent) the authorities increasingly accepted them as useful to government actions against illegal polluters. Under a new law, environmental impact assessment of new projects required soliciting the opinion of affected people. The government's 2001–2005 environmental plan recognized that ecological deterioration had run out of control, set ambitious targets, and used the need for conservation and prevention of pollution as a means to impose a restructuring of industries. Since 2003, however, the unexpectedly high rate of growth in heavy industries such as steel, aluminum, glass, and cement, fueled by extremely high rates of investment, cheap land and capital, large demand for urban housing and transportation, and exports, have made China's economy more energy intensive than before. Industrial output rose by 15 percent or more annually.

Between 2000 and 2009, energy production and consumption doubled, and in spite of rising oil imports, 70 percent of it remained based on coal. Energy savings and a change in energy mix became public policy. In 2007 China set a target of 15 percent of electricity generation from renewable sources for 2020, most of which will come from hydropower, possibly 3 to 4 percent from wind, and less than 1 percent from solar and biofuel (China Electric Power Press 2009, 19–28). China's windmills operate less than two thousand hours a year on average, however, and require large investment subsidies in pumped-storage stations and power lines. As long as cogeneration technologies are immature, biofuel remains costly as well. At the Copenhagen Climate Conference in 2009, China committed itself to double the current share of noncarbon final energy to 15 percent by 2020. Now China has become the world's largest investor in and producer of renewable energy installations, such as windmills, solar heating, and photovoltaic installations, and also the largest builder of nuclear power stations (at present, twenty-eight units), but the 2011 Fukushima, Japan, earthquake disaster at the nuclear power plant there has called the recent target of 86 gigawatts by 2020 (generating maybe 5 percent of China's total electricity by then) into question.

The need for power from coal will continue to grow. In 2010, China produced 45 percent of the world's output of raw coal (3.2 billion cubic meters) and net imports added another 146 million. Fifty-four percent of its oil demand had to be imported, and gas was still underdeveloped. On the positive side, by 2010 almost all thermopower stations were equipped with desulfurization installations, and most small stations had been closed. Industry reduced the release of carbon dioxide in paper, chemicals, and other industries by one-half and more. Because of stricter application of release standards, investments in water treatment, desulfurization and dust and soot removal installations, and the phasing out of less efficient and wasteful production technologies, industry greatly reduced per unit product energy use, emissions of waste gas, and release of wastewater. As a result, with the exception of carbon dioxide, total industrial emissions stabilized and decreased after 2005. In contrast, in spite of more treatment facilities, emissions from residential use increased, partly because of increased statistical coverage. Between 2005 and 2010, the share of industry in China's carbon dioxide release dropped to one-third of the total and of sulfur dioxide to one-quarter (and in absolute terms, by 12 and 14 percent). Private cars (1 million in 1990, 6 million in 2000, 46 million in 2009) rather than factories became the cities' worst air polluters (calculated from National Bureau of Statistics of China, various years).

Eventually, rather than legislation or punitive sanctions, China's fast economic growth, improvements in education, foreign investment, technological innovation, and increased environmental awareness (leading to greater political pressure on city mayors to clean up their cities) were the more important contributors to the improved efficiency and cleaner production of China's industries. Shortages in energy (in particular electricity and oil) and water since the 1980s has led to more economic resource use and a shift to more efficient technology. Efficiency gains can only partly offset the environmental consequences of rapid urbanization and annual industrial growth rates of more than 10 percent, however. For reasons of employment and in some cases national security, China has shown no inclination to increase imports of energy-intensive products. Its choice to become the world's largest manufacturing base for heavy industrial products such as steel and cars continues to burden its environment.

International Cooperation

Foreign countries and organizations have lent considerable support to China's environmental efforts. That goes both for institutional support, such as in legislation and training programs, and for investment projects. China demanded, and got, the creation of the Multilateral Fund as a condition for ratifying the 1987 Montreal Protocol on Substances That Deplete the Ozone Layer. Others mainly financed the phasing-out of chlorofluorocarbon coolants in its refrigerator industry. In 1998 it signed the Kyoto Protocol and subsequently became the largest recipient by far of clean development mechanism (CDM) project subsidies. China adopted a national climate change program in 2007 and committed in Copenhagen to reduce emissions of greenhouse gases per unit GDP by 40–45 percent by 2020. As a developing nation (the International Energy Agency predicted its emissions would increase from 19 percent of the world total in 2005 to 27 percent in 2030), however, China could not accept any emission quota.

Outlook

China's principles in global environmental issues were laid down in 1990: the environment should remain linked to the needs for economic development; developed countries are mainly responsible for present pollution; the interests of developing countries should not be hurt by "green" demands; the world economic order should promote participation of developing countries in solving global problems; and by reducing its own environmental problems China, as a large country, will contribute to the global situation.

China's international stand is a clever combination of global concerns and self-interest in continued economic growth, which invites Western countries and companies to actively contribute to and participate in environmental improvements in China—and thereby reduce global problems. Meanwhile, consumers in Western countries should be aware that most of the environmental costs of their imported products, their ecological footprint, are borne by China's people, water, air, and soils.

Eduard B. VERMEER
International Institute of Asian Studies, Leiden

See also Agriculture (China and Southeast Asia); Beijing, China; Cities—Overview; Climate Change Mitigation Initiatives (China); Education, Environmental (China); Energy Industries—Renewables (China); Fisheries (China); Five-Year Plans; Great Green Wall (China); Guangzhou, China; The Himalaya; Huang (Yellow) River; Indigenous Peoples; Mekong-Lancang River; National Pollution Survey (China); Pearl River Delta; Shanghai, China; South-North Water Diversion; Three Gorges Dam; Tibetan Plateau; Water Security; Yangzi (Chang) River

FURTHER READING

Berrah, Nourredine, et al. (2007). *Sustainable energy in China: The closing window of opportunity.* Washington, DC: The World Bank.

Bing, Fengshan. (Ed.) (2008). *Zhongguo kezaisheng nengyuan fazhan zhanlüe yanjiu zongshu* [Compendium of studies on the development strategies of renewable energy] (5 vols.). Beijing: Zhongguo dianli chubanshe.

China Electric Power Press. (2009). *China electric power yearbook.* Beijing: China Electric Power Press. (in Chinese)

China Environment Yearbook Society. (1990–2010). *Zhongguo huanjing nianjian* [China environment yearbook] (annual series). Beijing: China Environment Yearbook Press.

Day, Kristen A. (Ed.) (2005). *China's environment and the challenge of sustainable development.* Armonk, NY: M. E. Sharpe.

Economy, Elizabeth. (2004). *The river runs black: The environmental challenge in China's future.* Ithaca, NY: Cornell University Press.

Edmonds, Richard. (Ed.). (1998). *Managing the Chinese environment.* Oxford, UK: Oxford University Press.

Elvin, Mark, & Liu, Tsui-jung. (1998). *Sediments of time: Environment and society in Chinese history.* Cambridge, UK: Cambridge University Press.

Energy Research Institute, National Development and Reform Commission. (2010). Study on China biomass energy technology development roadmap. Retrieved January 13, 2012, from http://www.efchina.org/FReports.do?act=detail&id=302

Guo Songyi. (1985). Population increase and migration during the Qing period. *Qingshi luncong* [Articles on Qing history], *5*, 113–138. (in Chinese)

Hua, Z. (1989). Red tide in China Coast and its countermeasure. *Haiyang Tongbao* [Ocean Bulletin], pp. 1–5.

Li Ting. (Ed.). (1985). *Dangdai Zhongguodi linye* [Contemporary forestry of China]. Beijing: China Social Sciences Press.

Ma Jun. (2004). *China's water crisis* (Nancy Yang Liu & Lawrence R. Sullivan, Trans.). Norwalk, CT: EastBridge.

Ma, Xiaoying, & Ortolano, Leonard. (2000). *Environmental regulation in China: Institutions, enforcement, and compliance.* Lanham, MD: Rowman and Littlefield.

Managi, Shunsuke, & Kaneko, Shinji. (2010). *Chinese economic development and the environment.* Cheltenham, UK: Edward Elgar.

Marks, Robert. (1997). *Tigers, rice, silk, and silt: Environment and economy in late imperial south China.* Cambridge, UK: Cambridge University Press.

National Bureau of Statistics of China. (2001, 2008–2010a). *China statistical yearbook* (annual series). Beijing: China Statistics Press.

National Bureau of Statistics of China. (2010b). *Zhongguo tongji zhaiyao 2010* [China statistical abstract]. Beijing: China Statistics Press.

National Bureau of Statistics of China. (2011). *China statistical yearbook 2011.* Beijing: China Statistics Press. Retrieved March 12, 2012, from http://www.stats.gov.cn/english/publications/

Office of the Leading Group on Promotion of Sustainable Development Strategy, P. R. China (2008). Review of sustainable development in China: Agriculture, rural development, land, drought and desertification (document submitted to the 16th Session of the Commission on Sustainable Development of the United Nations, May 5–6, 2008). Retrieved March 14, 2012, from http://www.un.org/esa/agenda21/natlinfo/countr/china/2007_fullreport.pdf

Shapiro, Judith. (2001). *Mao's war against nature: Politics and the environment in revolutionary China.* New York: Cambridge University Press.

Sinopec. (2011). Environment & society: Social responsibility. Retrieved August 22, 2011, from http://english.sinopec.com/environment_society

Smil, Vaclav. (2004). *China's past, China's future: Energy, food, environment.* New York: RoutledgeCurzon.

State Ethnic Affairs Commission. (2009). *Proceedings of the Sino-Australian Workshop on Poverty Alleviation and Human Rights Development in the Minority Regions.* Beijing: China Agricultural Science and Technology Press.

United States Central Intelligence Agency (US CIA). (2012). The world factbook: China. Retrieved January 27, 2012, from https://www.cia.gov/library/publications/the-world-factbook/geos/ch.html

Vermeer, Eduard B. (1986). Agriculture and ecology in China. In Birthe Arendrup et al. (Eds.), *China in the 1980s: And beyond* (pp. 143–164). London: Curzon Press.

Vermeer, Eduard B. (1998). Industrial pollution in China and remedial policies. *The China Quarterly* (Special Issue: China's Environment), *156*, 952–985. doi:10.1017/S0305741000051419

Vermeer, Eduard B. (2011). The benefits and costs of China's hydropower: Development or slowdown? *China Information*, *25*(1), 3–32.

Wang, Yingzhong. (2010). *Zhongguo shuili shuidian gongcheng yimin wenti yanjiu* [Research into the problem of resettlees from water conservancy and hydropower projects in China]. Beijing: Zhongguo shuili shuidian chubanshe.

World Bank. (1997). *Clear water, blue skies: China's environment in the new century.* Washington, DC: World Bank Press.

Xiong Datong. (Ed.). (1989). *Zhongguo jindai linyeshi* [A modern history of forestry in China]. Beijing: China Forestry Press.

Zheng Yisheng. (Ed.). (2005). *Kexue fazhan guan yu jianghe kaifa* [Scientific valley development]. Beijing: Huaxia chubanshe.

Ziran zhi you [Friends of Nature]. (Eds.). (2010). *Zhongguo huanjing fazhan baogao (2010)* [Annual report on environment development in China, 2010]. Beijing: Shehui kexue wenjian chubanshe. (Also available in English by E. J. Brill, Leiden, The Netherlands)

Cities—Overview

Cities in Asia, some of the largest and fastest growing in the world, also have the largest urban populations globally. Cities in this region are highly diverse in terms of social, economic, and environmental performance, and many serve as growth engines for their nations. Asian cities face significant social and environmental challenges, but their rapidly changing nature presents an opportunity for them to become sustainable cities, in turn contributing to sustainability of the region and the world.

Although Asia's rate of urbanization is lower than the world's average, it has the largest urban population and the largest anticipated future growth. The level of urbanization varies widely among countries within the region, however. In very highly urbanized nations, such as South Korea (where 81 percent of the population lives in urban areas) and Japan (where 66 percent of its people are urbanized), urbanization started much earlier, and currently there is a high urbanization ratio. China is an example of a rapidly urbanizing nation; it entered the rapid-urbanization era after the 1980s and has a current urbanization ratio of around 50 percent. In the least urbanized nations—such as India (29 percent), Bangladesh (27 percent), and Cambodia (22 percent)—urbanization either occurred steadily or rather slowly, and current urbanization ratios are below 30 percent (US CIA 2012).

According to the United Nations (UN) Population Bureau, Southeast Asia and East Asia are a couple of the regions that have the fastest urban population growth rates in the world: for Southeast Asia, the average annual rate was 3.1 percent between 1990 and 2008 (UNESCAP 2010). In China, the proportion of the population living in urban areas was only 17 percent in 1980—far below the world average of around 40 percent at the time—but by the end of 2011 (only three years after the world average crossed the 50 percent threshold) it had reached 51 percent (Li and Chen 2012; UN 2007). While it is difficult to forecast city growth, and the UN projection of urban population growth has shown a large percentage of error (Montgomery 2008), this trend of rapid urbanization is expected to continue, and it is anticipated that several hundred million people will be added to the populations of cities in China and India alone over the next couple of decades. In fact, China already has the world's largest "megaregion": Hong Kong-Shenzhen-Dongguan-Guangzhou in southern China. According to the 2010–2011 UN-Habitat biannual report *State of World Cities*, this megaregion had 120 million residents in 2011.

Urban growth is manifested both in terms of the growing number of cities and the expansion of existing cities. According to the UN, ten out of nineteen of the world's "megacities" (those with populations over 10 million) are in East and Southeast Asia, and six of the world's ten largest megacities are in this region: Tokyo, Mumbai (Bombay), New Delhi, Shanghai, Kolkata (Calcutta), and Dhaka (UN 2007). At the same time, many new cities are emerging. There were only about 193 cities in China in 1978, but this number had reached 654 by 2009 (National Bureau of Statistics of China 2010). One of the most extreme examples of emerging cities in China is Shenzhen City (part of the Hong Kong-Shenzhen-Dongguan-Guangzhou megaregion), which over a period of about thirty years (1978–2005) has grown from a cluster of small villages into a modern megacity with a population of more than 10 million (Hang 2006, 32, 38).

There are three factors contributing to the growth of cities in East and Southeast Asia: migration from rural to urban areas, the natural growth of population in cities, and administrative upgrades or reconfigurations that incorporate larger areas into cities. There are both push and pull factors underlying rural-to-urban migration. Some of the major pull factors are access to better education, job opportunities, and aspirations for a better, modern life; conversely, poverty, labor surpluses, and lack of job and other opportunities in rural areas push people out of their villages. The degree to which natural growth contributes to overall growth in urban populations varies from country to country. In China, the contribution is minimal—or even negative—due to the strict implementation of the one-child policy in cities, while in countries with high population growth, such as India, it plays a larger role. Chongqing, China, is an extreme example of a case in which reconfiguration of administrative boundaries contributed to urban growth. The city was carved out of Sichuan Province in 1997 in order to handle the ecological, economic, and social challenges of the construction of the Three Gorges Dam, and it is now the largest city in China, with 32 million people in 2009 and 82,401 square kilometers in administrative area (Chongqing Municipal Government 2011).

Government policies in Asia have attempted to either encourage or discourage urbanization. Across countries, there is a strong positive correlation between urbanization level and income, and although it is still under debate whether such cross-country relationships necessarily mean urbanization will bring about increased income (Bloom, Canning, and Fink 2008), some national governments promote urbanization based on this relationship. In China, urbanization and industrialization now are viewed as the "two wheels that carry the vehicle of economic growth" in the country, but this was not the view prior to the 1978 implementation of the reform and opening-up policy; until then there was a strong historical bias in China against urbanization.

Urban growth is manifested not only in population concentration, but also in the expansion of urban land use. Recent studies show that as urban land expands, urban economies grow, and this economic growth spills over into the surrounding region. Consequently, there is a strong economic incentive for cities to expand (Bai, Chen, and Shi 2011). Such expansion can be problematic in terms of impact on agriculture and food security, however, as the lands converted into urban land use are often the most fertile agricultural land.

This kind of rapid urban land expansion is often achieved at the expense of farmers and other rural residents. The number of protests and disputes over insufficient compensation for land transfers and forced evictions has increased and become a serious social issue in China. It also is questionable whether urbanized land is being utilized efficiently, since some of the rapid urban land expansion and conversion is driven by high real estate prices fueled by speculation. Many newly built apartment buildings are purchased for investment purposes rather than as primary residences. This has resulted in low occupancy rates and near empty buildings and even towns: Kangbashi, for example, is a new town that was built to host a population of 300,000, but it currently has only 30,000 residents (*Daily Mail* 2010). Some well-designed, well-constructed towns are almost entirely empty, and are referred to as "ghost towns" or "ghost cities." (See figure 1 on the next page.) To some, this is reminiscent of real estate bubbles in Japan during 1980s and more recently in Hong Kong, and the risk of economic crash associated with them.

Role in National Economy and Urban Poverty

For many countries in the region—and for Japan, South Korea, and China in particular—urbanization has been concurrent with industrialization. Most industrial enterprises (and therefore financial and other related service industries) are located in or near cities, which attract and absorb increasing numbers of people and act as a growth engines for these nations. In other countries, the informal sector constitutes a large portion of the economy: for example, in India much of the urban population works in the service sector (largely informally), which makes up 61 percent of the economy (US CIA 2012). The collective contribution of cities to a country's economy greatly exceeds their share of its population. Shanghai, for instance, represents 2 percent of China's population but contributes some 17 percent of the gross domestic product (GDP). The populations of Bangkok, Thailand, and Ho Chi Min City, Vietnam, represent less than 10 percent of nationwide totals, but these cities contribute up to half of the GDP of their respective countries. According to the UN Economic and Social Commission for Asia and the Pacific (UNESCAP), eastern and northeastern Asia have a 47 percent urban population share, while the urban share of GDP is 85.5 percent. The numbers in southern and eastern

Figure 1. The Ghost City of Chenggong, China

Source: Imagery from Spot Image, DigitalGlobe, and GeoEye. Map data from MapABC and Google.

Chenggong is a newly built town in Yunnan Province in southwestern China, near the city of Kunming. This example of a ghost city features 100,000 new apartments, brand new office skyscrapers, and grand boulevards, all built since 2003—and empty of people. Chenggong reflects how the dramatic pace of urban development in China sometimes exceeds demand, or beyond the economic capacity of ordinary citizens, leaving vast urban landscapes devoid of inhabitants.

Asia are similar, representing 46.5 percent and 80.5 percent, respectively (UN-Habitat 2011).

Cities typically enjoy higher average income levels than rural areas, and in fact, China has one of the highest disparities between urban and rural incomes in the world, with a ratio of 3.23 to 1 (Pan and Wei 2011). The difference in income between urban and rural areas has contributed in part to the perception that poverty is largely a rural, rather than an urban, issue. Focusing on statistical averages, however, it masks the significant poverty and inequality issues within many cities. In some cities, such as Mumbai, up to 50 percent of urban residents are slum dwellers living without basic urban infrastructure (access to water, sanitation, etc.), working in informal sectors with very little income, and often facing the threat of eviction from the city government (Nijman 2008). Even in rapidly industrializing cities that enjoy high economic growth rates, the fruit of development does not always reach the poor and other vulnerable groups. In China, it's estimated that there are up to 167 million migrant workers in cities (Ruan 2010). These migrant workers are at the core of the economic prosperity of coastal cities, but they are significantly more disadvantaged than the permanent residents of these cities due to the lack of proper social security and health care, and are often discriminated against in terms of access to education for their children and other welfare services.

There seems to be no silver bullet to the problem of urban poverty, which continues to present a significant threat to residents' health and well-being, and a significant challenge to the ability of cities to manage and govern. National and international aid agencies tend not to address urban poverty issues sufficiently through their programs, since usually the average standard of living is higher in cities than in their surrounding regions, with the result that urban poverty is not seen as a pressing problem. Slum-upgrading projects that attempt to encourage slum dwellers to move out of slums by providing alternative housing have been unsuccessful due to a lack of jobs that are sustainable—and in some cases due to the involvement of organized crime in real estate speculation. Researchers and nongovernmental organizations (NGOs) have advocated for recognizing the rights of slum dwellers as urban residents, and are calling for more focus, political will, and civic engagement in addressing these issues (Satterthwaite 2001).

Environment

Urbanization in Asia results in environmental costs. The environmental impacts of cities include *upstream impacts* through resource demand from other regions, *inner-city impacts* such as changing urban environmental quality, and *downstream impacts* through pollution discharged beyond cities.

Cities are open systems that require large amounts of input—including water, energy, food, and other materials—to grow and to support their functions. Researchers estimate that in the long run, demand for construction materials in China (including cement, wood, and steel) will exceed supply (Fernández 2007; Shen et al. 2005). In water-scarce regions such as northern China, cities compete with agriculture for limited water resources, with the latter often ending up using untreated wastewater discharged from cities for irrigation. In both India and China higher incomes and globalized diets have resulted in a demand in cities for diversified food that includes an increase in animal protein consumption. This in turn has resulted in changing food production systems in rural areas, producing an increase in nutrient flows, such as phosphorus, through the urban systems (Li et al. 2011; Pingali and Khawaja 2004).

According to the World Bank, in 2006 sixteen out of the twenty most polluted cities in the world were in China (Walsh 2007). As demonstrated by the frequent incidence of heavy smog and the recent public outcry over the concern of its health impact in Beijing, air pollution has been and still is one of the top environmental concerns for large cities in the region. Major sources of pollution include industrial discharge, a high proportion of coal in the country's energy mix, and private car transportation, with the share of transportation-related pollution increasing in most cases. Despite controls on the number of cars that can be registered each year in China's major cities, private car ownership has increased sharply. Air pollution in cities is blamed for the large increase in pulmonary cancer and other respiratory diseases in China.

While probably less visible to the public than air pollution, water pollution from urban-based industries and municipal sewage discharge is severe. In China, the majority of the river sections flowing through large cities are polluted, and water pollution has further exacerbated the water shortage problems confronting up to two-thirds of Chinese cities (CNS 2012). Water pollution historically has been linked to some of the most serious diseases caused by environmental contamination, such as Minamata disease in Japan and Onsan disease in South Korea (neurological diseases caused by mercury and cadmium, respectively), and it is now linked to the high incidence of cancer in many parts of China. Strengthening the monitoring of pollution in conjunction with implementing existing environmental regulation effectively is key for industrial water-pollution control, while installing urban sewage-treatment infrastructure and ensuring proper operation of existing treatment plants are essential for reducing municipal wastewater pollution.

Across Asia, the issues that dominate urban environmental issues vary among cities and are determined largely by income level. In relatively low-income cities, the substandard living conditions of urban slum dwellers are the reason for a high incidence of waterborne infectious diseases, such as diarrhea. A lack of infrastructure to provide water means that slum dwellers often have to pay more than other urban residents for potable water. In rapidly industrializing countries like China, air and water pollution from industrial production is often the dominant issue. In high-income countries like Japan and South Korea, cities have experienced phases of heavy pollution in the past, but conventional pollution problems now are largely under control. Lifestyle-related environmental issues, however, show little sign of declining, as per capita resource consumption and carbon dioxide (CO_2) emissions in these cities are much higher than in others, and they continue to grow.

The spatial extent of environmental effects from cities can be local, regional, or even global (Grimm et al. 2008), depending on the type of impacts. Environmental issues related to poverty, such as those caused by limited access to safe water and sanitation, usually are confined to a locality. In contrast, environmental problems caused by industrial production tend to be both local and regional, and the effects related to consumption and lifestyle frequently have global impacts (Bai 2003; McGranahan et al. 2005).

The link between cities and climate change has become a hot topic both in research and in practice. On the one hand, since cities contribute up to 78 percent of total CO_2 emissions globally, climate mitigation actions must take place in cities (Grimm et al. 2008). Cities in Asia generally have lower per capita CO_2 emissions as compared to Western megacities, but many exhibit a rapidly increasing trend. On the other hand, most major cities with dense populations in the region are located in low-lying coastal areas, and this, together with relatively weak financial and human capital compared to their Western counterparts, makes them among the cities most vulnerable to impacts from climate change in the world. The effect of sea-level rise is likely to exacerbate other local factors, such as the land subsidence (sinking) that has been observed in some of the largest coastal cities. Tokyo, Shanghai, and Osaka have all subsided several meters due to excessive groundwater extraction, a trend that has been duplicated in megacities like Jakarta and Bangkok (Nicholls and Cazenave 2010). Despite the potential severity of risks from climate change, most cities in the region seem to be underprepared for upcoming climate-change adaptation challenges (Fuchs, Conran, and Louis 2011). Furthermore, recent research shows that in some cities climate change likely will impact the availability of water and food security (McDonald et al. 2011).

Toward Sustainable Cities

It has been observed that the battle for sustainability will be won or lost in cities. This is particularly true in Asia. Urbanization shows no sign of slowing down, let alone reversing its course, and cities will most likely keep emerging and growing in this region. The significance of cities and urban life in the region was highlighted at the Shanghai World Expo 2010, whose theme was "Better City, Better Life." While understanding the challenges accompanying urbanization, it is important to recognize the opportunities cities present in terms of enhancing human well-being and sustainability.

Sustainability has been a hot topic in many cities in the region, and a large number of good practices are documented. For example, a recent book published by the Asian Development Bank (ADB) entitled *Urbanization and Sustainability in Asia: Good Practice Approaches to Urban Region Development* (ADB 2006) contains thirty-seven case studies of "good practice" urban development projects presented from twelve countries in Asia (Bangladesh, Cambodia, China, India, Indonesia, Laos, Malaysia, Pakistan, the Philippines, Sri Lanka, Singapore, Thailand, and Vietnam). The case studies include examples of infrastructure, as well as environmental, housing, social, and governance projects and programs of different size and complexity. Other innovative practices and experiments include the successful proliferation of solar water heaters in Rizhao, China; the introduction of bus rapid-transit systems in Guangzhou, China; and the establishment of eco-industrial parks in Kitakyushu, Japan.

These innovative practices suggest that "positive changes are within reach," as noted in the recent *State of Asian Cities Report 2010/2011* (UN-Habitat 2011). These individual good practices are often isolated bright spots, however, which need to be coordinated and scaled up in order to achieve widespread sustainability. There are clear gaps in both systematically analyzing these innovative practices and in transferring knowledge, and it's important to examine how innovative practices were initiated and set in motion, who the key actors were, what kind of linkage network these actors supported, what the key barriers were in implementation, and what the eventual pathway of the practices was (Bai, Roberts, and Chen 2010). It is essential that the information gleaned from such systematic analyses be taken up and shared across cities.

As Asian countries, particularly China and India, gain more economic power and their citizens grow increasingly aware of the importance of habitat sustainability, we hope cities will acquire more capacity to address the current and upcoming sustainability challenges they face. Good urban governance and processes will be essential in harnessing these positive potentials and directing cities toward sustainability.

Xuemei BAI
Australian National University

See also Beijing, China; Chennai, India; Delhi, India; Dhaka, Bangladesh; Guangzhou, China; Jakarta, Indonesia; Kuala Lumpur, Malaysia; Mumbai, India; One-Child Policy; Pearl River Delta; Public Health; Public Transportation; Shanghai, China; Singapore; Three Gorges Dam; Water Security

FURTHER READING

Asian Development Bank (ADB). (2006). *Urbanization and sustainability in Asia: Good practice approaches to urban region development*. Mandaluyong City, Philippines: ADB.

Bai, Xuemei. (2003). The process and mechanism of urban environmental change: An evolutionary view. *International Journal of Environment and Pollution, 19*(5), 528–541.

Bai, Xuemei; Roberts, Brian; & Chen Jing. (2010). Urban sustainability experiments in Asia: Patterns and pathways. *Environmental Science & Policy, 13*(4), 312–325.

Bai, Xuemei; Chen Jing; & Shi Peijun. (2011). Landscape urbanization and economic growth in China: Positive feedbacks and sustainability dilemmas. *Environmental Science & Technology, 46*(1), 132–139.

Bloom, David E.; Canning, David; & Fink, Günther. (2008). Urbanization and the wealth of nations. *Science, 319*(5864), 772–775.

China News Service (CNS). (2012). China per capita water resource only 28% of world average, 2/3 of cities facing water shortage. Retrieved April 20, 2012, from http://finance.chinanews.com/ny/2012/02-16/3673445.shtml [in Chinese]

Chongqing Municipal Government. (2011). About Chongqing. Retrieved April 20, 2012, from http://en.cq.gov.cn/AboutChongqing/

Daily Mail. (2010). The ghost towns of China: Amazing satellite images show cities meant to be home to millions lying deserted. Retrieved April 20, 2012, from http://www.dailymail.co.uk/news/article-1339536/Ghost-towns-China-Satellite-images-cities-lying-completely-deserted.html

Fernández, John E. (2007). Resource consumption of new urban construction in China. *Journal of Industrial Ecology, 11*(2), 99–115.

Fuchs, Roland; Conran, Mary; & Louis, Elizabeth. (2011). Climate change and Asia's coastal urban cities. *Environment and Urbanization Asia, 2*(1), 13–28.

Grimm, Nancy B., et al. (2008). Global change and the ecology of cities. *Science, 319*(5864), 756–760.

Hang Ma. (2006). *"Villages" in Shenzhen: Persistence and transformation of an old social system in an emerging mega city* (Doctoral dissertation, Bauhaus-Universität Weimar, 2006). Retrieved April 20, 2012, from http://e-pub.uni-weimar.de/opus4/frontdoor/index/index/year/2006/docId/771

Li Gui-Lin; Bai, Xuemei; Yu Shen; Zhang Hua; & Zhu Yong-Guan. (2011). Urban phosphorus metabolism through food consumption. *Journal of Industrial Ecology*. doi: 10.1111/j.1530-9290.2011.00402.x

Li Peilin, & Chen G. (2012). Urbanization leads China's new development stage. In Ru Xin, Lu Xueyi & Li Peilin (Eds.), *Blue book of China's society: Society of China analysis and forecast* (pp. 1–16). Beijing: China Social Sciences Press.

McDonald, Robert I., et al. (2011). Urban growth, climate change, and freshwater availability. *Proceedings of the National Academy of Sciences, 108*(15), 6312–6317.

McGranahan, Gordon, et al. (2005). Urban systems. In Rashid Hassan, Robert Scholes, & Neville Ash (Eds.), *Ecosystems and human well-being: Volume 1. Current state and trends*. Washington, DC: Island Press.

Montgomery, Mark R. (2008). The urban transformation of the developing world. *Science, 319*(5864), 761–764.

Nicholls, Robert J., & Cazenave, Anny. (2010). Sea-level rise and its impact on coastal zones. *Science, 328*(5985), 1517–1520.

Nijman, Jan. (2008). Against the odds: Slum rehabilitation in neoliberal Mumbai. *Cities, 25*(2), 73–85.

Pan Jiahua, & Wei Houkai. (2011). *Blue book of cities in China: Annual report on urban development of China no. 4*. Beijing: China Social Sciences Press. [in Chinese]

Pingali, Prabhu, & Khawaja, Yasmeen. (2004, February 5–7). Globalisation of Indian diets and the transformation of food supply systems (inaugural keynote address to the 17th Annual Conference of the Indian Society of Agricultural Marketing). Hyderabad, India.

Roberts, Brian, & Cohen, Michael. (2002). Enhancing sustainable development by triple value adding to the core business of government. *Economic Development Quarterly, 16*(2), 127–137.

Ruan Yulin. (2010, March 30). 167 million peasant workers in China integrated into urbanization statistics. Retrieved April 20, 2012, from http://www.sei.gov.cn/ShowArticle2008.asp?ArticleID=196950

Satterthwaite, David. (2001). Reducing urban poverty: Constraints on the effectiveness of aid agencies and development banks and some suggestions for change. *Environment and Urbanization, 13*(1), 137–157.

Shen Lei; Cheng Shengkui; Gunson, Aaron J.; & Wan Hui. (2005). Urbanization, sustainability and the utilization of energy and mineral resources in China. *Cities, 22*(4), 287–302.

United Nations (UN). (2007). *World urbanization prospects: The 2007 revision*. New York: UN Department of Economic and Social Affairs/Population Division.

United Nations Economic and Social Commission for Asia and the Pacific (UNESCAP). (2010). *Statistical yearbook for Asia and the Pacific 2009*. Bangkok, Thailand: UNESCAP.

United Nations Human Settlements Programme (UN-Habitat). (2011). *State of Asian cities*. Fukuoka, Japan: UN-Habitat.

United States Central Intelligence Agency (US CIA). (2012). The world factbook: India. Retrieved April 18, 2012, from https://www.cia.gov/library/publications/the-world-factbook/geos/in.html

Walsh, Bryan. (2007). The world's most polluted places: Linfen, China. Retrieved April 20, 2012, from http://www.time.com/time/specials/2007/article/0,28804,1661031_1661028_1661016,00.html

Share the *Encyclopedia of Sustainability*: Teachers are welcome to make up to ten (10) copies of no more than two (2) articles for distribution in a single course or program. For further permissions, please visit www.copyright.com or contact: info@berkshirepublishing.com

Climate Change Migration (India)

India is vulnerable to climate change because of global warming and may therefore experience climate change migration, or people migrating because of climate-induced phenomena such as natural disasters. Climate migration is not high on India's policy agenda because it does not resonate with India's more pressing challenges for sustainability. India is more likely to take up climate migration policies discussed in the context of sustainable development, disaster management, and urbanization.

Scientists expect one of the main humanitarian consequences of climate change to be climate change–induced migration, or climate migration. People migrate because of climate-induced events such as natural disasters, droughts, rising sea levels, lack of sufficient rainfall for agriculture, and the like. Evidence, however, remains inconclusive about the extent of the phenomenon. Experts estimate that between 50 million and 250 million or even 1 billion people may migrate by the year 2050 (Christian Aid 2007; Myers 2002; UNFCCC Executive Secretary 2007). Estimates differ depending on the definitions researchers use and the methods they employ.

Despite this lack of clear evidence, the international community is increasingly aware that climate migration is an issue for concern. The parties to the United Nations Framework Convention on Climate Change (UNFCCC) adopted in 2010 a paragraph under the Cancún Adaptation Framework that commits parties to undertake "measures to enhance and improve understanding, coordination and cooperation with regard to climate change induced displacement, migration and planned relocation, where appropriate, at national, regional and international levels" (UNFCCC 2010). No global governance system to address climate migration exists, however, and national programs to address climate migration still require much development.

India is highly vulnerable to climate change impacts such as drought, glacier melt, and sea-level rise. As argued by Jairam Ramesh, the former Indian minister of state for environment and forests (MoEF), "No country in the world is as vulnerable, on so many dimensions, to climate change as India" (MoEF 2010). While based on inconclusive evidence, India is often discussed in the light of potential cross-border climate migration from Bangladesh (Beckett 2006; Rajan 2008; Gautam 2009). As a consequence, one could expect that the government of India is concerned about climate migration. Both on an international and domestic level, however, India's policy development and political activities pay little attention to climate migration. Its National Action Plan on Climate Change (NAPCC) of 2008, for example, does not cover the issue of climate migration or displacement. The summary of the Mission on Strategic Knowledge within the NAPCC mentions climate migration briefly, yet the full report on this particular mission, released in 2010, does not once refer to the matter.

India's primary challenge is to reconcile the pursuit of economic growth and its objective of becoming a global power with domestic and civil society concerns over poverty, environmental degradation, disaster management, democratic legitimacy, and urbanization. India does not take up the issue of climate migration because the worldwide debate on climate migration has not taken into account India's position in this sustainability challenge. Nevertheless, some alternative approaches to climate migration are emerging that may resonate with India's point of view.

Challenges for Sustainability

The larger debate on climate security has submerged international discussions on climate migration. During the debate on climate change and security in the United Nations (UN) Security Council held in July 2011, the UN secretary-general stated that "environmental refugees" will be "reshaping the human geography of the planet" (UN Secretary-General 2011). Proponents of these debates, including many industrialized countries and small island developing states, hope to increase action to combat climate change by raising climate security concerns.

This narrative of climate change as a threat to national and international security, however, does not resonate with India's policy makers. The simplest explanation for India's negative stance in this debate is that it fears climate-change action will become the UN Security Council's responsibility. A select number of powerful countries control the decision making in this scenario (see also Sindico 2007).

Moreover, India perceives talk of mass climate migration as another of the West's scare tactics to push India to commit itself to binding mitigation measures in the name of climate security. India argues that the West is historically responsible for climate change; India cannot permit itself any actions that could harm its economic growth because these actions may interfere with its domestic goals for sustainable development and poverty alleviation. Although this argument is only partly valid, because the poor may not appropriately benefit from economic growth, this line of thinking prevails. India thus does not feel obligated to commit itself to binding carbon emission targets to combat climate change.

India's third concern about the climate security narrative is that it labels developing nations as vulnerable because they are considered to be most susceptible to climate security impacts, such as migration or resource conflict. India envisions a different profile for itself. It wants the international community to perceive it as an important global player, an emerging world power; it does not want the West to label it a victim.

India's government officials who lead on climate change do not enthusiastically discuss climate migration when it is raised in the context of climate security. Moreover, climate change itself is a highly politicized topic. The current discourse on climate change places the debate into two camps—the developing world versus the developed world—which obstructs discussion opportunities for partnerships and solutions.

Vocabulary that resonates well with India's current policy objectives and civil society concerns revolves around concepts of economic growth, sustainable development, distribution, equity, resilience, and disaster management—all questions of sustainability. An increasingly active debate takes place in India on reconciling socioeconomic issues with the aim to maintain and increase its economic growth. Protests and political debate arise over issues such as forced human displacement resulting from development projects, for instance, in the debate over a 2011 draft bill called the National Land Acquisition and Rehabilitation & Resettlement Bill, proposed by the Ministry of Rural Development. In light of these activities, Navroz K. Dubash, a senior researcher at the Centre of Policy Research in Delhi, states that rather than separating environmental or climate migration as new issues that India needs to address, it would be more effective to place these issues within these current debates on sustainable development, poverty alleviation, and economic growth and their consequences for forced displacement. Dubash argued, "We should be having better disaster management anyway, we need to think about movement of our population anyway, we need to think about processes of urbanization anyway; we should think about this independent of climate change. It actually gets in the way if you want to address these matters for climate change reasons" (personal interview with author, 23 August 2011).

The question remains why, independent of international debates, India itself has not identified internal climate migration as a concern within its NAPCC. Certain regions, such as the low-lying Sundarbans delta, are highly vulnerable to climate change impacts such as sea-level rise and disasters (Danda et al. 2011). According to S. C. Acharyya, the joint project director of the Sunderban Development Board (under the aegis of the government of West Bengal, Kolkata [Calcutta]), no policies are in place or under development to address or manage climate migration in the Sundarbans on a structural basis (personal interview with author, 27 August 2011).

Critics in the government of India argue that projections about climate migration are too far in the future and refer to a lack of convincing evidence that climate migration will indeed take place. They contend that India needs to focus on scientific climate change trends, such as rainfall patterns, rather than on specific socioeconomic matters. They say that climate change adaptation would make climate migration policies unnecessary. Moreover, India has issues of more immediate concern, such as poverty, sustainable development, population growth, and urbanization. Because India cannot tend to all these challenges at once, it must prioritize its plans on climate change. As a consequence, climate migration is not high on the agenda.

Other urgent issues include agriculture, water, and disaster management. India created a National Disaster Management Authority in 2005. Climate migration could potentially play a role in this context; disaster displacement and disaster management are areas where policy makers increasingly take into account climate change factors. The National Institute for Disaster Management, for instance, tries to raise awareness of long-term disaster displacement within policies on relief and rehabilitation for affected communities.

A Way Forward

Research indicates that climate migration may become an increasing concern in the coming decades. Natural disasters are already displacing people in the twenty-first century (Yonetani 2011). If no set of effective mechanisms is put in place, scientists expect these displacements to increase. In order to create such mechanisms, however, government and society must support them. In the Indian context, policy makers are unlikely to take action on climate migration if the topic continues to be raised primarily in debates on climate security or even climate change. The discussion on climate migration must be embedded within the context of the sustainability challenges India faces. They can thus draw connections between, for instance, climate migration and rural development, disaster management, community resilience, forced displacement, and preventive adaptation.

Several researchers have already adopted such a strategy. They emphasize matters of resilience, livelihoods, development, and adaptation (see, e.g., Stojanov et al. 2008). Groups such as the International Organization for Migration (IOM) mainstream climate migration concerns within disaster risk reduction, adaptation, and general migration activities (IOM 2010a and 2010b).

Certain governmental programs in India can be supported to increase action on climate migration. Gujarat is a leading state on disaster management. It developed a reconstruction and rehabilitation policy in response to a 2001 earthquake. This policy dealt with the "provision of housing, social amenities, infrastructure, and livelihood support" (GSDMA 2001). The Gujarat State Disaster Management Authority (GSDMA) also includes a more general reconstruction and rehabilitation plan within its overarching Gujarat State Disaster Management Policy. Nonetheless, there is much more to do in India to make long-term recovery, rehabilitation, and resettlement processes more effective.

India's Mahatma Gandhi National Rural Employment Guarantee Act is useful in the context of climate-related migration. The act guarantees every rural household one hundred days of work per year through labor programs that improve communities' livelihood security. Programs like this reduce the pressure on people to migrate in periods of distress, such as during a drought.

If the international community wants India to seriously consider climate-related migration, they need to discuss the issue through lenses of disaster response, livelihood resilience, development, or urbanization. This discussion may lead to the Indian government's higher appreciation of the issue—essential if the international community wants to protect the rights of current and future climate migrants.

Ingrid BOAS
University of Kent

Author's note: This research is based on interviews conducted by the author in India with the government, nongovernmental organizations, scientists, and think tanks in August 2011, and through telephone interviews in the period June–November 2011. Special thanks to Navroz Dubash, whose interview with the author was very constructive in the development of the author's argument.

See also Climate Change Mitigation Initiatives (China); Education, Environmental (India); India; Indigenous Peoples; Rule of Law; Rural Livelihoods

Further Reading

Balchand, K. (2011, October 18). Jairam wants Land Acquisition Bill passed during winter session. Retrieved October 30, 2011, from http://www.thehindu.com/news/national/article2549500.ece

Beckett, Margaret. (2006, October 24). Beckett: Berlin speech on climate and security. Retrieved February 15, 2012, from http://ukingermany.fco.gov.uk/en/news/?view=Speech&id=4616005

Bierman, Frank, & Boas, Ingrid. (2010). Preparing for a warmer world: Towards a global governance system to protect climate refugees. *Global Environmental Politics, 10*(1), 60–88.

Black, Richard. (2001). *Environmental refugees: Myth or reality?* (New Issues in Refugee Research, Working Paper No. 34). Geneva: United Nations High Commissioner for Refugees.

Black, Richard, et al. (2011). *Foresight: Migration and global environmental change: Future challenges and opportunities* (Final Project Report). London: The Government Office for Science.

British Broadcasting Corporation (BBC) News South Asia. (2011, May 9). India: Uttar Pradesh farmers protest spreads. Retrieved October 30, 2011, from http://www.bbc.co.uk/news/world-south-asia-13330343

Castles, Stephen. (2002). *Environmental change and forced migration: Making sense of the debate* (New Issues in Refugee Research, Working Paper No. 70). Geneva: United Nations High Commissioner for Refugees.

Christian Aid. (2007). *Human tide: The real migration crisis*. London: Christian Aid.

Danda, Anamitra Anurag, et al. (2011). *Indian Sundarbans delta: A vision*. New Delhi: World Wide Fund for Nature-India. Retrieved February 15, 2012, from http://awsassets.wwfindia.org/downloads/indian_sundarbans_delta__a_vision.pdf

Gautam, P. K. (2009). Climate change and migration. In Institute for Defence Studies and Analyses Working Group Report 2009 (Ed.), *Security implications of climate change for India* (chap. 4). New Delhi: Academic Foundation.

German Advisory Council on Global Change (WBGU). (2007). *World in transition: Climate change as a security risk*. Berlin: WBGU.

Gujarat State Disaster Management Authority (GSDMA). (2001). Gujarat earthquake reconstruction and rehabilitation policy. Gandhinagar, India: GSDMA. Retrieved January 24, 2012, from http://www.gsdma.org/pdf/Earthquake%20Rehabilitation%20Policy.pdf

Gujarat State Disaster Management Authority (GSDMA). (n.d.). Gujarat State disaster management policy. Gandhinagar, India: GSDMA. Retrieved 24 January, 2012, from http://www.gsdma.org/pdf/GSDMPolicy%20_revised%20on%2025th%20October_.pdf

International Organization for Migration (IOM). (2010a). Disaster risk reduction, climate change adaptation and environmental migration: A policy perspective. Geneva: IOM. Retrieved October 30, 2011, from http://publications.iom.int/bookstore/free/DDR_CCA_report.pdf

International Organization for Migration (IOM). (2010b). *Migration, Climate Change and the Environment: Operational Activities*. Retrieved October 30, 2011, from http://www.iom.int/jahia/Jahia/operational-activities

Martin, Susan F. (2010). *Climate change, migration and adaptation. Study team on climate-induced migration*. Washington, DC: German Marshall Fund of the United States. Retrieved October 30, 2011, from http://www.gmfus.org/galleries/default-file/SMartin Adaptation_V3.pdf

Ministry of Environment and Forests (MoEF), Government of India. (2010). Climate change and India: A 4x4 assessment. Delhi: MoEF. Retrieved October 30, 2011, from http://moef.nic.in/downloads/public-information/fin-rpt-incca.pdf

Ministry of Home Affairs (MHA), Government of India. (2011). *Disaster management in India*. Delhi: MHA.

Ministry of Rural Development. (2011, July 27). *The draft national land acquisition and rehabilitation and resettlement bill, 2011* (for discussion purposes only). New Delhi, India: Ministry of Rural Development. Retrieved October 30, 2011, from http://www.thehindu.com/multimedia/archive/00738/The_Draft_National__738172a.pdf

Ministry of Rural Development. (2008). *The National Rural Employment Guarantee Act 2005 (NREGA). Operational Guidelines 2008* (3rd ed.). New Delhi: Ministry of Rural Development. Retrieved January 24, 2012, from http://rural.nic.in/sites/downloads/programmes-schemes/Nrega_guidelinesEng.pdf

Ministry of Science and Technology, Government of India. (2010) *National mission on strategic knowledge for climate change: Under National Action Plan on climate change*. Delhi: Government of India.

Myers, Norman. (2002). Environmental refugees: A growing phenomenon of the 21st century. *Philosophical Transactions: Biological Sciences, 357*(1420), 609–613.

Myers, Norman, & Kent, Jennifer. (1995). *Environmental exodus: An emergent crisis in the global arena*. Washington, DC: Climate Institute.

Nicholls, Robert. (2004). Coastal flooding and wetland loss in the 21st century: Changes under the SRES climate and socio-economic scenarios. *Global Environmental Change, 14*(1), 69–86.

Patkar up in arms against new draft bill on land acquisition. (2011, August 1). *The Times of India*. Retrieved October 30, 2011, from http://articles.timesofindia.indiatimes.com/2011-08-01/mumbai/29837705_1_land-acquisition-definition-of-public-purpose-medha-patkar

Prime Minister's Council on Climate Change, Government of India. (2008). National action plan on climate change. Retrieved October 30, 2011, from http://pmindia.nic.in/climate_change.html

Rajan, Sudhir Chella. (2008). *Blue alert: Climate migrants in South Asia: Estimates and solutions*. Bangalore, India: Greenpeace.

Sindico, Francesco. (2007). Climate change: A security (council) issue? *Climate Change Law Review, 1*, 29–34.

Stojanov, Robert, et al. (2008). *Development, environment and migration: Analysis of linkages and consequences*. Olomouc, Czech Republic: Palacky University.

United Nations Framework Convention on Climate Change (UNFCCC) Executive Secretary. (2007, April 6). UNFCCC Executive Secretary says significant funds needed to adapt to climate change impacts (press release of the Secretariat of the United Nations Framework Convention on Climate Change). Retrieved February 15, 2012, from http://unfccc.int/files/press/news_room/press_releases_and_advisories/application/pdf/070406_pressrel_english.pdf

United Nations Framework Convention on Climate Change (UNFCCC). (2010). Cancún Adaptation Framework: Outcome of the work of the Ad Hoc Working Group on long-term cooperative action under the convention. Retrieved October 30, 2011, from http://www.glogov.org/images/doc/cop16_lca.pdf

United Nations (UN) Secretary-General. (2011, July 20). With environmental refugees reshaping human geography, Security Council has unique duty to mobilize action to confront climate change threat, says Secretary-General (speech at UNSC debate on Maintenance of Peace and International Security). New York: Department of Public Information, News and Media Division. Retrieved October 30, 2011, from http://www.un.org/News/Press/docs/2011/sgsm13712.doc.htm

United Nations (UN) Security Council. (2007, April 17). Security Council holds first-ever debate on impact of climate change on peace, security, hearing over 50 speakers (5,663rd Meeting). New York: United Nations Department of Public Information News and Media Division.

United Nations (UN) Security Council. (2011, July 20). Security Council, in statement, says "Contextual information" on possible security implications of climate change important when climate impacts drive conflict. New York: Department of Public Information, News and Media Division. Retrieved October 30, 2011, from http://www.un.org/News/Press/docs/2011/sc10332.doc.htm

Warner, Koko; Afifi, Tamer; Dun, Olivia; Stal, Marc; & Schmidl, Sophia. (2008). *Human security, climate change and environmentally induced migration*. Bonn, Germany: United Nations University Institute for Environment and Human Security.

Warren, Rachel, et al. (2006). Understanding the regional impacts of climate change (research report prepared for the Stern Review on the Economics of Climate Change, Working Paper 90). Norwich, UK: Tyndall Centre for Climate Change Research.

Yonetani, Michelle. (2011). *Displacement due to natural hazard-induced disasters: Global estimates for 2009 and 2010*. Geneva: Internal Displacement Monitor Centre. Retrieved November 25, 2011, from http://www.internal-displacement.org/8025708F004BE3B1/(httpInfoFiles)/15D7ACEC7ED1836EC12578A7002B9B8A/$file/IDMC_natural-disasters_2009-2010.pdf

Climate Change Mitigation Initiatives (China)

By 2012, China had become the world's largest emitter of greenhouse gases. At the core of the climate change challenge is China's energy sector. Despite a reliance on coal-based energy to fuel its rapidly growing economy, China has made major achievements in promoting energy efficiency and low carbon energy technologies. Many new mitigation efforts are underway, including China's first ever carbon target and carbon emissions trading programs.

Continued growth in the prosperity of the population is viewed as fundamental to maintaining political stability in China, and progress to date in this regard has been impressive. Although China roughly quadrupled its gross domestic product (GDP) between 1980 and 2000, it did so while merely doubling the amount of energy it consumed over that period, marking a dramatic achievement in energy intensity (ratio of energy consumption to GDP) gains not paralleled in any other country at a similar stage of industrialization. This allowed China's energy intensity and, consequently, the emissions intensity (ratio of carbon dioxide–equivalent emissions to GDP) of its economy to decline. Without this reduction in the energy intensity of the economy, China would have used more than three times the energy that it did during this period. The energy savings over this time period meant less reliance on imported energy resources, and less carbon dioxide emissions.

China's Mitigation Challenge

Between 2002 and 2005, however, this trend reversed, and growth in energy consumption surpassed economic growth for the first time in decades. As China's energy demand has boomed, its emissions have soared. Looking ahead, most projections put China's emissions in 2030 at a level close to 500 percent higher than its 1990 levels (EIA 2011). Globally, this translates to China's emissions accounting for almost 50 percent of all new energy-related carbon dioxide (CO_2) emissions by 2030. If China's emissions continue to grow at the rate of 8 percent per year (the average annual growth rate between 2005 and 2010), by the year 2030 it could be emitting as much CO_2 as the entire world is today. In contrast, US emissions are only expected to increase by 22 percent above 1990 levels by 2030 (EIA 2011). In historical terms, the United States is by far the largest contributor to the greenhouse gases now in the atmosphere. It is responsible for 27 percent of energy-related CO_2 emissions since 1900, while China accounts for only about 10 percent of these cumulative emissions. China's per capita greenhouse gas (GHG) emissions are below the world average and approximately one-third those of the United States. (See figure 1 on the next page.)

China's increase in energy-related emissions in recent years has been driven primarily by industrial energy use, fueled by an increased percentage of coal in the overall fuel mix. Industry consumes about 70 percent of China's energy, and China's industrial base supplies much of the world. In 2010, for example, China produced about 66 percent of the world's aluminum and 44 percent of its steel (International Aluminum Institute 2012; World Steel Association 2012). Studies have estimated the CO_2 emissions embedded in China's domestic production of goods for export represent about 30 percent of the country's total annual CO_2 emissions (Xu et al. 2011).

China relies on coal for more than two-thirds of its energy needs, including approximately 80 percent of its electricity needs. China's power sector is the largest source of CO_2 emissions in the country, responsible for about one-half of energy-related CO_2 emissions. Within

Figure 1

Share of Annual Global CO2 Emissions

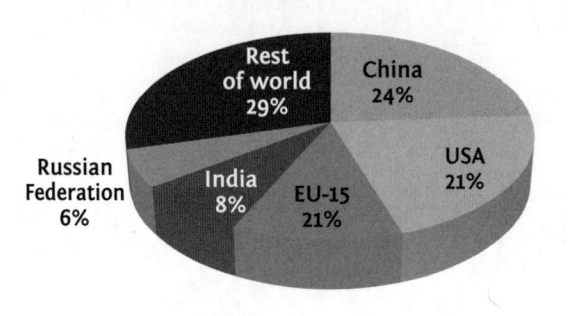

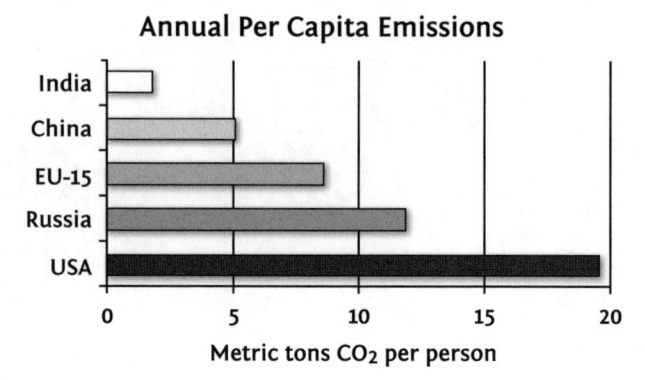

- Rest of world 29%
- China 24%
- USA 21%
- EU-15 21%
- India 8%
- Russian Federation 6%

Annual Per Capita Emissions (Metric tons CO2 per person)

- India: ~2
- China: ~5
- EU-15: ~8
- Russia: ~12
- USA: ~20

Notes: Data are for 2010 and include CO_2 emissions from fossil fuels only.
ROW = Rest of World.

Sources: CDIAC (2011); World Bank (2011).

In historical terms, the United States is by far the largest contributor (27 percent) to the greenhouse gases now in the atmosphere; China accounts for only about 10 percent of these cumulative emissions. China's per capita greenhouse gas (GHG) emissions (on the right in this figure) are below the world average and approximately one-third those of the United States. As China's energy demand has boomed in recent years, however, its emissions have soared.

the power sector, about 98 percent of China's CO_2 emissions comes from coal use (IEA 2007). Currently, more coal power plants are installed in China than in the United States and India combined. China's coal power use is expected to more than double by 2030, representing an additional carbon commitment of about 86 billion tons (IEA 2007). Although China is also expanding its utilization of nuclear power and non-hydroelectric renewables, these sources comprise 2 percent and 0.7 percent of China's electricity generation, respectively, whereas hydroelectricity contributes about 16 percent (National Bureau of Statistics 2007; REN 21 2006 and 2010). Given China's substantial domestic coal reserves and its heavy investment in coal-fired power plants over the past few decades, coal will likely remain an inescapable foundation of its economy for years to come. Rendering coal a climate-friendly energy source, however, will require significant advances and sustained investment in new technologies that burn it more efficiently and capture and sequester the resulting greenhouse gas emissions.

China's Mitigation Actions

China has begun to implement many national policies and programs to address its increasing greenhouse gas emissions and reliance on fossil fuels. Nuclear power and hydropower are key elements of China's low-carbon energy development strategy, and the country is planning to expand the use of conventional and nonconventional natural gas, which, if used to displace coal, could help to decarbonize the power sector. Several demonstration projects are underway in China using high-efficiency coal gasification and even carbon capture and sequestration technologies, but for the time being these technologies are considered too costly to be deployed at full scale. Perhaps the most impressive achievements since 2005 have been in the areas of energy efficiency and renewable energy. In addition, China surprised much of the world by announcing a national carbon target prior to the 2009 UN climate negotiations in Copenhagen, and by disclosing the development of a domestic cap and trade program (a system designed to limit the aggregate emissions of sources through the assignment of allowances that are surrendered following the release of emissions) for carbon emissions in 2011.

Energy Efficiency Programs and Intensity Targets

A suite of energy efficiency and industrial restructuring programs has aimed to drive down China's energy intensity. One of the core elements of China's Eleventh Five-Year Plan period, spanning from 2006 to 2010, was to lower national energy intensity by 20 percent. China's Top 1,000 Program has helped to cut energy use among its biggest energy-consuming enterprises (accounting for 33 percent of its overall energy consumption, 47 percent of industrial energy consumption, and 43 percent of its CO_2 emissions) (Price and Wang 2007). The Ten Key Projects Program (first launched in 2004) provides financial support to companies that implement energy-efficient technology. In addition, many inefficient power and industrial plants have been targeted for closure, which helped contribute to the decline in energy intensity experienced during the Eleventh Five-Year Plan period, with a reported 72.1 gigawatts (GW) of thermal capacity shut down between 2006 and 2010—equivalent to 16 percent of the total capacity added over that period (Wen 2011). Elsewhere in the world, it is very unusual, if not unprecedented, to shut down such a large number of power plants in the name of efficiency (Gallagher and Lewis 2012).

The government has also strengthened local accountability for meeting the Eleventh Five-Year Plan targets by intensifying oversight and inspection. Each province and province-level city was required to help meet China's goal to cut energy intensity by 20 percent, and was assigned its own target ranging from 12 to 30 percent (Ohshita, Price, and Tian 2011). Governors and mayors were held accountable for meeting their targets, and experts from Beijing conducted annual site visits to facilities in each province to assess their progress (*China Daily* 2006).

Programs included in the Twelfth Five-Year Plan (2011–2015) build directly on the Eleventh Five-Year Plan energy intensity target and its associated programs, including a new target to reduce energy intensity by an additional 16 percent by 2015 (*China Daily* 2011). While this may seem less ambitious than the 20 percent reduction targeted in the Eleventh Five-Year Plan, it likely represents a much more substantial challenge. The largest and least efficient enterprises have already undertaken efficiency improvements, leaving smaller, more efficient plants to be targeted in this second round. Also under preparation is a new Top 10,000 program, which is modeled after the Top 1,000 Program, but it adds an order of magnitude of companies to the mix. But as the number of plants grows, so do the challenges of collecting accurate data and enforcing targets. Even though the country likely fell just short of meeting its Eleventh Five-Year Plan energy intensity target of 20 percent (the government reported a 19.1 percent decline was achieved), there is no doubt that much was learned through efforts to improve efficiency nationwide.

Carbon Management Programs

While estimates have been made of the potential carbon emissions savings that could accompany the Eleventh Five-Year Plan's target of reducing energy intensity by 20 percent (Lin et al. 2007), China never put forth any targets that explicitly quantified its carbon emissions until late 2009. Leading up to the Copenhagen climate negotiations, the Chinese government pledged a 40–45 percent reduction in national carbon intensity (the ratio of carbon emissions to GDP) from 2005 levels by 2020 (Government of the PRC 2009). To achieve this 2020 target, the Twelfth Five-Year Plan set an interim target of reducing carbon intensity by 17 percent, relative to 2010 levels, by 2015.

Historically, China has been consistent in its position in the international climate negotiations that, as a developing country, it will not take on any binding international commitments to reduce its GHG emissions. At the December 2011 climate negotiations in Durban, South Africa, China expressed a willingness for the first time to adopt legally binding commitments (rather than just voluntary commitments) as part of a future climate change agreement. There is no question that China's announcement of its first carbon target represents a monumental change in its approach to global climate change. It is also important to recognize, however, that even with this target in place, growth in absolute emissions could continue to increase rapidly. A meaningful reduction of emissions encouraged by a carbon intensity target hinges upon future economic growth rates and the evolving structure of the Chinese economy, as well as on the types of energy resources utilized and the deployment rates of various technologies, among other factors. Carbon intensity, like energy intensity, has declined substantially over the past two decades. Between 1990 and 2005, China reduced its carbon intensity by 44 percent. It is also projected to reduce its carbon intensity by 46 percent, from 2005 levels, before 2020, while still growing its emissions by 73 percent during this same period (EIA 2009). This has sparked much debate over whether such a domestic policy target is sufficient based on China's role in the global climate challenge.

If implemented effectively, a carbon intensity target will not only accelerate the energy efficiency improvements already taking place in response to the energy intensity target, but will also further promote the development of low-carbon energy sources like nuclear, hydropower, and renewables. In addition, implementing a carbon policy through a domestic carbon trading program, or through other financial incentives like a carbon tax, would be a significant step toward implementing a comprehensive climate policy in China, complementing ongoing efforts to improve energy efficiency and promote low-carbon energy sources. An October 2011 National Development and Reform Commission (NDRC) notice announced that seven provinces had been selected to pilot cap and trade programs for CO_2, including Guangdong, Hubei, Beijing, Tianjin, Shanghai, Chongqing, and Shenzhen; these programs are currently under development (NDRC 2011).

Renewable and Non-Fossil Energy Targets

The Twelfth Five-Year Plan includes a target to increase non-fossil energy sources (including hydro, nuclear, and renewable energy) to 11.4 percent of total energy use (up from 8.3 percent in 2010) (Government of the PRC 2011; Zhang 2011). While not formally enshrined in the Twelfth Five-Year Plan, another recent notable announcement is a cap on total energy consumption of 4 billion tons of coal equivalent (tce) in 2015 (Fellman 2010). To meet the cap on energy consumption, annual energy growth would need to slow to an average of 4.24 percent per year, down from 5.9 percent between 2009 and 2010.

The Twelfth Five-Year Plan also includes many new industrial policies to support clean energy industries and related technologies. Industries targeted include the nuclear, solar, wind, and biomass energy technology industries, as well as hybrid and electric vehicles, and energy savings and environmental protection technology industries (Government of the PRC 2010). During the Eleventh Five-Year Plan period, an estimated 15.3 percent of government stimulus funding was directed toward innovation, energy conservation, ecological improvements, and industrial restructuring (HSBC 2010).

One key element of China's energy strategy, as well as its low-carbon development strategy, is the promotion of renewable energy technologies. This effort was kick-started with the passage of the Renewable Energy Law of the People's Republic of China that became effective on 1 January 2006 (NPC 2005). The Renewable Energy Law created a framework for regulating and promoting renewable energy in China. It established a national renewable energy target; a mandatory connection and purchase policy; a feed-in tariff system (a monetary incentive system designed to encourage the use of renewable energy); and a cost-sharing mechanism, including a special fund for renewable energy development. In December 2009 amendments to the Renewable Energy Law were passed, further strengthening the process through which renewable-electricity projects are connected to the grid and dispatched efficiently. Additional policies to promote renewable energy include mandates and incentives to support the development of domestic technologies and industries. China invested $50 billion in 2010 in renewable-energy development, far more than any other country in the world (Renewable Energy World 2011). China now leads the world in wind power deployment and is rapidly becoming a global leader in both the manufacturing and deployment of most key renewable energy technologies.

Looking Ahead

China's mitigation challenge is considerable, due to the scale of its emissions, its energy sector, its economic growth, and its population. The achievements China has already made, however, in promoting energy efficiency and the use of clean energy technologies are also considerable. As China takes additional measures to mitigate the CO_2 emissions that are contributing to global climate change, the rest of the world may be able to learn from both its challenges and its achievements.

Joanna I. LEWIS
Georgetown University

See also Automobiles and Personal Vehicles; Climate Change Migration (India); Consumerism; Corporate Accountability (China); Education, Environmental (China); Energy Industries—Nuclear; Energy Industries—Renewables (China); Energy Security (East Asia); Five-Year Plans; Great Green Wall (China); Green Collar Jobs; National Pollution Survey (China); Reforestation and Afforestation (Southeast Asia); Steel Industry; Utilities Regulation and Efficiency

FURTHER READING

Carbon Dioxide Information Analysis Center (CDIAC). (2011). Fossil fuel CO_2 emissions. Retrieved December 19, 2011, from http://cdiac.ornl.gov/trends/emis/meth_reg.html

China Daily. (2006, July 27). Officials made accountable for energy saving. Retrieved December 19, 2011, from http://www.china.org.cn/english/BAT/175957.htm

China Daily. (2011, March 5). Key targets of China's 12th five-year plan. Retrieved December 19, 2011, from http://www.chinadaily.com.cn/china/2011npc/2011-03/05/content_12120283.htm

Energy Information Administration (EIA). (2009 and 2011). *International energy outlook*. Washington, DC: US Department of Energy.

Fellman, Joshua. (2010, October 20). China to hold primary energy use to 4.2 billion tons in 2015, Xinhua says. *Bloomberg*. Retrieved December 19, 2011, from http://www.bloomberg.com/news/2010-10-30/china-to-hold-primary-energy-use-to-4-2-billion-tons-in-2015-xinhua-says.html

Gallagher, Kelly Sims, & Lewis, Joanna I. (2012). China's quest for a green economy. In Norman J. Vig & Michael E. Kraft (Eds.), *Environmental policy: New directions for the twenty-first century* (8th ed.). Washington: CQ Press.

Government of the People's Republic of China (PRC). (2009). *Guowuyuan changwuhui yanjiu jueding woguo kongzhi wenshiqiti paifang mubiao* [Standing Committee of China State Council to study the decision to control greenhouse gas emissions targets]. Retrieved December 19, 2011, from http://www.gov.cn/ldhd/2009-11/26/content_1474016.htm

Government of the People's Republic of China (PRC). (2010, September 8). *Guowuyuan tongguo jiakuai peiyu he fazhan zhanluexing xinxing chanye de jueding* [State Council's decision on speeding up the cultivation and development of emerging strategic industries]. Retrieved December 19, 2011, from http://www.gov.cn/ldhd/2010-09/08/content_1698604.htm

Government of the People's Republic of China (PRC). (2011, March 16). *Zhonghua renmin gongheguo guomin jingji he shehui fazhan di shier ge wunian guihua gangyao* [The People's Republic of China's 12th Five Year Plan for economic and social development]. Retrieved December 19, 2011, from http://news.xinhuanet.com/politics/2011-03/16/c_121193916.htm

The Hong Kong and Shanghai Banking Corporation Ltd. (HSBC). (2010, October). *China's next 5-year plan: What it means for equity markets*. Hong Kong: HSBC.

International Aluminum Institute. (2012). Current and alternative source statistics. Retrieved December 19, 2011, from http://www.world-aluminium.org/Statistics/Current+statistics

International Energy Agency (IEA). (2007). *World energy outlook 2007*. Paris: IEA & OECD.

Lin, Jiang; Zhou, Nan; Levine, Mark; & Fridley, David. (2007). Taking out one billion tons of CO_2: The magic of China's 11th Five-Year Plan? Berkeley, CA: Lawrence Berkeley National Laboratory.

National Bureau of Statistics. (2007). *China energy statistical yearbook 2006*. Beijing: China Statistics Press.

National People's Congress (NPC). (2005). The Renewable Energy Law of the People's Republic of China. Beijing: NPC.

National Development and Reform Commission (NDRC). (2011, October). *Guojia fazhan gaige wei bangongting guanyu kaizhan tan paifangquan jiaoyi shidian gongzuo de tongzhi* [NDRC notice on launching pilot trading programs for the development of carbon emissions rights], Notice 2601. Retrieved December 19, 2011, from http://www.ndrc.gov.cn/zcfb/zcfbtz/2011tz/t20120113_456506.htm

Ohshita, Stephanie; Price, Lynn; & Tian, Zhiyu. (2011). Target allocation methodology for provinces in China: Energy intensity in the 12th Five-Year Plan. Berkeley, CA: Lawrence Berkeley National Laboratory.

People's Daily Online. (2011, January 6). *Zhang Guobao: Shi'er wu mo lizheng feihuashi nengyuan zhan yici nengyuan bizhong 11.4%* [Zhang Guobao: Working hard to make non-fossil energy account for 11.4 percent of primary energy at the end of the Twelfth Five Year Plan]. Retrieved December 19, 2011, from http://energy.people.com.cn/GB/13670716.html

Price, Lynn, & Wang, Xuejun. (2007). Constraining energy consumption of China's largest industrial enterprises through top-1000 energy-consuming enterprise program. Berkeley, CA: Lawrence Berkeley National Laboratory.

Renewable Energy Policy Network for the 21st century (REN 21). (2006 and 2010). *Renewables global status report*. Paris: REN 21 Secretariat.

Renewable Energy World. (2011, January 11). 2010 Clean energy investment hits a new record. Retrieved December 19, 2011, from http://www.renewableenergyworld.com/rea/news/article/2011/01/2010-clean-energy-investment-hits-a-new-record

Wen Jiabao. (2011, March 5). Report on the work of the government, delivered at the fourth session of the Eleventh National People's Congress. Retrieved December 19, 2011, from http://news.xinhuanet.com/english2010/china/2011-03/15/c_13779521.htm

World Bank. (2011). Population data. Retrieved December 19, 2011, from http://data.worldbank.org/indicator/SP.POP.TOTL

World Steel Association. (2012). Statistics archive. Retrieved December 19, 2011, from http://www.worldsteel.org/statistics/statistics-archive.html

Xu, Ming; Li, Ran; Crittenden, John C.; & Chen, Yongsheng. (2011). CO_2 emissions embodied in China's exports from 2002 to 2008: A structural decomposition analysis. *Energy Policy, 39*(11), 7381–7388.

Consumerism

Nowhere is the tension between growing mass consumerism and accelerating environmental degradation more pronounced than in contemporary China. Consumerism in China is not a new development; for hundreds of years Chinese have used material goods to convey status and identity. But mass consumerism is a relatively new phenomenon that has both advantages for those who can afford the new lifestyles and profoundly destructive consequences for the Chinese and global environments.

The development of modern mass consumerism in China and subsequent transformation of most aspects of life has been both beneficial and detrimental to the Chinese. Hundreds of millions of people have been lifted from poverty and have the opportunity to enjoy products and services previously unavailable or unaffordable. In the past few decades, China has become the world's largest consumer of a number of products, including everything from meat to mobile phones. The lives of tens and even hundreds of millions of consumers in urban China increasingly resemble their US, Japanese, and European counterparts. At the same time, China's rapid increase in per capita consumption threatens its environment, as well as the world's.

Chinese elites have used luxury goods as a way to create identity and communicate status for hundreds of years. As late as 1800, the wealthiest part of China in the lower Yangzi Valley surrounding Shanghai may have been as wealthy as the richest part of Western Europe. And local elite circles created social capital by exchanging rare gifts, assembling expensive dowries, collecting art objects, and hosting lavish weddings and funerals. Textiles, teas, opium, books, and other commodities were consumed well beyond the regions where they were produced. Consumption habits gradually spread down the social hierarchy and luxuries such as sugar and tea became more widely consumed.

But "modern consumerism," which refers to the consumption of branded, mass-produced goods and services, and the orientation of social life and rhetoric around consumption, is a more recent phenomenon. The bleak material conditions in China during World War II through the civil war (1945–1949) and throughout the Maoist era (1949–1976) misleadingly suggest that modern Chinese consumerism arrived only after the death of Mao and Maoism. But China has had elements of modern consumerism since the late nineteenth and early twentieth century. Urban China, particularly the key treaty ports of Guangzhou and Tianjin, and, even more particularly, Shanghai, encouraged consumerism through modern retailing, exhibition halls, and advertising. Varying modes of transportation, such as rickshaws, automobiles, and bicycles, established more integrated markets, and new public environments within modern schools and workplaces were used to showcase new products. In addition, urban China supplied the energy sources to power the new consumer products and lifestyles. During this time, Chinese people, especially (but not exclusively) urban elites, introduced new objects into their homes and leisure activities. A growing number of Chinese altered their appearance from head (Western-style hats) to toe (leather shoes and cotton socks).

Understanding the impact of these commodities is challenging, particularly with regard to the way people used and thought about all the products and services they consumed. Unlike people living in the United States and Western Europe, the Chinese did not leave detailed probate records revealing exactly what their households owned, but the memoirs of foreign travelers readily show that Chinese adapted imports for local and even individual purposes. For instance, fashionable urban women in the early twentieth century confidently mixed and matched traditional and imported clothing articles to invent their own original styles. This adaptation was also common for those Chinese citizens who were least likely to have access to information about (or contact with) foreigners and the way they used their material artifacts. The Chinese were seldom encumbered by the knowledge of a product's intended use. Urban slum dwellers, for example, built shacks out of discarded iron Standard Oil cans.

Despite these consumptive behaviors, Chinese consumers were not always free to purchase whatever they could afford, nor could they determine the social significance of the items they bought. In China, modern consumerism has always been connected with imperialism. During the nineteenth century, European, US, and eventually Japanese businesses and consumers demanded access to Chinese markets. Through the First Opium War (1839–1842), the British, and subsequently many others, achieved access to Chinese markets at a time when the relative superiority of Chinese material culture had declined markedly. That is, the products of the industrializing imperialist powers were appealing, and the Chinese learned to desire imports. In the nineteenth century, the most prominent of these imports were opium and Western military hardware, but by 1900 the desire for imports extended to a vast array of consumer goods including silk, considered to be the symbolic heart of China. Japanese silk displaced Chinese silk in foreign markets and increasingly penetrated the domestic market. From concepts of male and female beauty, to forms of sport and entertainment, to styles of architecture and personal appearance, Chinese associated the foreign and Western with a better and more fashionable lifestyle.

During the first half of the twentieth century, the rapid increase in imports and the desires they stimulated threatened powerful domestic interest groups. Chinese politicians worried about trade deficits and the new consumer lifestyles. Educated elites, who had begun to read works on Western political economy, feared the loss of sovereignty implicit in the growing foreign dominance of the economy, and manufacturers struggled to produce products to compete against new imports. These concerns ultimately produced a multifaceted "Buy Chinese" campaign conducted in cities across the country. Advocates developed countless ways to exhort fellow Chinese to consume China-made goods, including skillfully co-opting foreign commodity spectacles like product exhibitions. Also, as the outbreak of frequent anti-imperialist boycotts demonstrates, they forced consumers to buy Chinese. Nevertheless, in the absence of a powerful state to enforce the nationalistic consumption of Chinese products through tariffs, such efforts had limited success.

The establishment of the People's Republic of China in 1949 soon ended the ease with which consumers embraced consumerism for four reasons: Mao Zedong's well-known anti-urban biases; the initial decision to emulate the Soviet Union's economic model with its emphasis on state-owned heavy industry and neglect of consumer goods; the elimination of private enterprise; and the appeal of autarkic (self-sufficient) economic growth after a century of imperialism. The Communists gradually forced foreign multinational companies to leave China and eliminated most foreign brands from the marketplace by imposing higher tariffs and outright bans. After some initial hesitation, which allowed consumer lifestyles to persist into the mid-1950s, the state appropriated all private enterprises, eliminating the trend-setting consumer class of urban capitalists.

"Consumerism" is not usually associated with Mao's China because, under Mao, China radically reshaped consumerism. But Mao's influence never fully eliminated it from Chinese life. China continued to mass-produce a limited number of branded goods, and consumer goods and services remained objects of everyday discussion and important building blocks for personal and collective identity. The Communists worked tirelessly to eliminate all traces of consumerism, particularly following the shift to ideological over material incentives during the Great Leap Forward (1958–1960) and the Cultural Revolution (1966–1976), but even the most extreme attempts to eliminate consumerism may have had the unintended consequence of heightening a form of consumer consciousness.

The spread of consumerism in East Asia since World War II now culminates in China. In 1978, Deng Xiaoping began depoliticizing daily life and launched economic reforms that led to growth rates equal to Japan's earlier record levels. Since then, the Chinese state has staked its political legitimacy on economic growth and encouraged citizens to consume, a shift in attitudes and policies toward consumerism embodied in the popular Communist Party slogan of the 1980s: "To get rich is glorious!"

The market reforms of the late 1970s and 1980s introduced tremendous uncertainty for consumers. Fixed prices shifted to market prices, creating new consumer issues, including resentment of unfair pricing, the sales of imitations through deceptive packaging, food adulteration, false advertising claims, product liability, and warranty issues. Chinese consumerism was fraught with media scandals, consumer panics, and rumors surrounding products and services. For instance, in the summer of 1985, a scandal erupted over the sale of supposedly dirty imported used clothing that was sold as new. Furthermore, a Beijing textile and clothing association report concluded that the clothing was not just used but came from people with diseases. That winter at least twenty cities and counties participated in efforts to find and destroy the offending clothing.

This unstable environment led to a consumer movement that assumed academic, bureaucratic, and social dimensions. In 1983, the Chinese government sponsored the creation of the Chinese Consumers' Association, the country's central consumer protection association. By 2001, the association had over 3,000 local branches across China and had received over 6 million consumer complaints. The 1980s also saw the beginnings of the academic study of consumerism and the publication of consumer magazines and newspapers to protect "consumer rights," as they became known. Finally, the Chinese Communist Party recast itself as a protector of consumers. The party-state established regulatory agencies such as the National Administration of Industry and Commerce, which regulates trademarks and advertisements, and the Commodity Inspection Bureau, which requires companies to add product warnings.

Since the beginning of this millennium, but especially after the global financial crisis of 2008, Chinese and world political and business leaders have pinned their hopes for domestic and global economic growth on Chinese consumers. In other words, Chinese must save less and consume more. In 2008, rising political star Li Keqiang voiced the conventional wisdom among top policy makers, that "Boosting domestic demand is essential for propping up growth," (China's vice premier . . . 2008) especially in the face of global economic weakness.

Chinese leaders have implemented policies designed to address the anxieties that lead Chinese to save as much as they can rather than spend. To counter rising costs of living, Chinese leaders have permitted the establishment of private lending companies, have accelerated urbanization, and have instituted extended holidays around the lunar New Year, National Day (1 October), and, until 2007, Labor Day (1 May). They have also deregulated the financial sector to facilitate consumer borrowing through mortgages, credit cards, and car loans.

The consumer boom is on and consumerism is becoming as entrenched a part of social and economic life in urban China as it is in other developed economies, bringing the same set of trade-offs. For example, growing prosperity allows the Chinese to consume more meat, a source of protein once considered a luxury. Indeed, the purpose of the thousands of KFC's, McDonald's, and other fast-food restaurants now spread out across urban China is to make money by convincing Chinese to eat more pork, chicken, and beef. It is working. Fifty years after a famine (1959–1961) killed 30 million Chinese, they now consume quadruple the amount of calories from animals than they did in 1985 (Gerth 2010). This transition from famines to feasts has its downsides, however. In addition to such obvious consequences as the increase in childhood obesity, the new Chinese diet also produces 2.7 billion tons of animal manure, most of which is left untreated (Gerth 2010). Also, ever increasing numbers of cattle, goats, and sheep graze on ecologically fragile hills and steppes, consuming vast swaths of grassland and loosening topsoil that is more readily taken up in the form of massive sandstorms. Beijing alone is inundated with a half million tons of sand every year. Deserts have already swallowed up thousands of villages, and entire cities have had to be built to house the displaced. The country has become the leading exporter of dust, as tens of millions of tons of China's dust and coal pollution enter jet streams and reach Korea, Japan, and as far as the west coast of the United States (Gerth 2010).

Cement is particularly noteworthy as an example of how links between consumption and environmental problems build on one another. Contemporary China is unimaginable without cement, the binding agent critical to the production of concrete. Without cement and concrete, the burgeoning forest of buildings at the center of the more than one hundred cities with over a million residents, and at the center of thousands of smaller towns, would not exist. Neither would there be the vast network of highways and roads that are appearing at record rates, connecting these cities and towns. Cement production requires energy, and to produce this energy, China burns more coal. As late as the mid-1980s, Shanghai had only a handful of tall buildings; twenty years later it had four thousand—nearly twice as many as New York. Across the country, many more are on the way: in the second decade of the twenty-first century, Beijing is *adding* the equivalent of three Manhattans of office and residential space. The same growth rates are true of highways and local roads, which also use vast amounts of cement. Even outside the cities, national and local governments see road building as a way to employ migrant workers during the post-2008 economic crisis and as part of a long-standing program to reduce rural poverty by providing isolated farmers better access to markets and nonfarm jobs. While no recent traveler to China would be surprised to learn that the country produces and uses nearly half the world's cement, they probably are not aware that the chemical reaction at the center of making cement creates vast quantities of carbon dioxide. In fact, cement production accounts for 5 percent of all the world's carbon dioxide emissions and a fifth of China's (Gerth 2010). China also plans to accelerate its urbanization by encouraging hundreds of millions more farmers to relocate to new satellite cities. The result is an alarming amount of cement. Duplicating this same relationship between consumption and environmental impacts on countless other categories brings to the fore the scale and the scope of the problem.

While some politicians and scholars anxiously wonder whether Chinese will consume enough to rescue the global economy, others speculate the opposite. The rise of Chinese consumerism, with its reliance on a rapidly escalating use of nonrenewable resources, has created urgent questions about the sustainability of modern consumerism in China and elsewhere. The scale and scope of environmental problems directly related to the production of consumer goods for China and for the world cannot be overstated. Acid rain already falls on a third of the country, and 300 to 600 million Chinese lack access to clean drinking water. With sixteen of the world's twenty most polluted cities, a third of all urban residents breathe polluted air, and over 400,000 people a year are dying prematurely from asthma, emphysema, and lung cancer. What will happen as Chinese consumers, further urged by their government and the world, to "catch up" with the global North in per capita consumption of energy and other goods and services? Likewise, what's the responsibility and culpability of the rest of the world for creating this dire situation?

There are signs of hope. China has seen the rise of a grassroots environmental movement that is trying to change the practices and thinking of Chinese consumers themselves. Environmental advocacy is also changing manufacturing practices. Even before a national ban on certain types of disposable items was announced, hundreds of small companies in China were already manufacturing more sustainable alternatives, including biodegradable disposable articles such as chopsticks made from yam starch and tableware made from rice husks, starch, and cardboard. Likewise, reports in the media about the dangers of Styrofoam boxes have helped dampen consumer demand for white garbage (the name given by the Chinese to disposable Styrofoam tableware), despite the weak enforcement of the earlier bans (Gerth 2010)

But reshaping consumer practices by showing the link between comfortable new lifestyles and their environmental impacts is not easy. Even in the industrialized world, where environmental movements have been in place for much longer, it is an uphill battle. It remains difficult to get individuals who think of themselves primarily as self-interested "consumers" to even consider—not to mention pay more for—such intangibles as a patriotic duty to buy more expensive domestic products, let alone a concern for the environment. If the tension between the desire for consumer-led economic growth, on the one hand, and environmental sustainability, on the other, cannot be resolved in contemporary China, then it will not be resolved in India, Indonesia, Vietnam, or any other country that follows (and is pushed) down the same developmental path of favoring short-term economic growth over long-term environmental sustainability.

Karl GERTH
University of Oxford

See also Automobiles and Personal Vehicles; Beijing, China; China; Corporate Accountability (China); E-Waste; Ecotourism; Education, Environmental (China); Gandhism; Green Collar Jobs; Guangzhou, China; Information and Communication Technologies (ICT); Labor; Media Coverage of the Environment; Microfinance; One-Child Policy; Outsourcing and Offshoring; Religions; Shanghai, China

FURTHER READING

China's vice premier urges demand boost to sustain growth: State media. (2008, August 20). *AFP*. Retrieved March 22, 2012, from http://www.channelnewsasia.com/stories/afp_asiapacific_business/view/369941/1/.html

Croll, Elisabeth. (2006). *China's new consumers: Social development and domestic demand*. New York: Routledge.

Davis, Deborah S. (Ed.). (2000). *The consumer revolution in urban China*. Berkeley: University of California Press.

Gerth, Karl. (2010). *As China goes, so goes the world: How Chinese consumers are transforming everything*. New York: Hill & Wang.

Gerth, Karl. (2003). *China made: Consumer culture and the creation of the nation*. Cambridge, MA: Harvard University Press.

Pomeranz, Kenneth. (2000). *The great divergence: China, Europe and the making of the modern world economy*. Princeton, NJ: Princeton University Press.

Corporate Accountability (China)

Although the term corporate accountability *originated in the West, the idea has deep roots in Chinese history and has been increasingly embraced by both corporations and policy-making agencies of the state. With unique cultural background and economic development, China's adoption of corporate accountability has become the center of discussion worldwide, and its successful implementation will have great significance for global sustainability.*

Corporate accountability is essential to sustainability. It requires a company to be economically, socially, and environmentally accountable to all its stakeholders (the people who have a stake in an enterprise), including the shareholders, suppliers, customers, and employees, and the local community in which the company operates. Corporate accountability goes beyond being just a voluntary initiative to emphasize the legal obligation of a company to improve its social and environmental performance. China's expanding global economic influence, with one-fifth of the world's population, has made it a vital player in a global sustainable future.

In practice, corporate accountability in China has always been the "ideological and political work" of the administrative departments (Jensen 2006, 13). The Chinese government has frequently used awareness campaigns to promote corporate accountability, for example, by holding meetings and displaying slogans such as "serve the people" and "socialist spiritual civilization." "Harmonious society" is one recent slogan that was introduced in 2004 at the Fourth Plenum of the Chinese Communist Party (CCP), sixteenth plenary meeting.

Origins

Although the term *corporate accountability* in its current form in China is relatively new, unsurprisingly (given the country's institutional history and transition) the underlying principles of sustainability have a long and interesting history. The earliest ideas related to sustainability in China were recorded during the Xià dynasty (2100–1766 BCE) in the Huang (Yellow) River area (the "cradle of the civilization of China") in the form of religious beliefs. At this time, people respected the mountains and rivers in the same way they did their spiritual icons (Yu 1999). The basic idea of accountability is also reflected in Chinese Confucianism, which appeared 2,500 years ago, and in the classic text *Chunqiu*. The Confucian virtue *yi* represents righteousness—following correct principles or norms when obtaining and distributing benefits. In contrast to *yi* is *li*, the narrow view that emphasizes benefits and profits without wider consideration of impacts. The relationship between *yi* and *li* can be described by the Confucian view that a person of noble character understands *yi*, while a person of low standing knows only *li*. A businessman with a *li* character pursues just short-term profit and self-interest, while one with a *yi* character considers longer-term and broader gains. At the same time, the ancient philosophy also requires people to respect the given social hierarchy, for example, the son obeys the father, the wife obeys the husband, the inferior obeys the superior. So in the Chinese context, corporate accountability is also linked to "traditional Chinese paternalistic notions of the superior bestowing approval, protection and favor upon his inferiors," and "the Chinese tradition of leaders educating the people by performing as role models for righteousness" (Jensen 2006, 19).

The Modern Context

The evolution of corporate accountability in modern China is linked to economic reform and can be divided into two periods: the socialist planned-economy period

(1950–1978) and the transitional period (after 1978) when China launched its transformation from a socialist planned economy to a socialist market economy.

In the planned economy, the notion of sustainability had an important place. In 1955, Chairman Mao Zedong called for green policies because they would benefit agriculture, industry, and other aspects of society (Li 2010). Equality and social justice were also among China's objectives during the Mao era (Li and Fan 2006). The slogan "serve the people," introduced by Mao when the People's Republic of China was first established, called for state organizations to be socially responsible. As the representatives of the state, the state-owned enterprises (SOE) were to serve the people from cradle to grave, employing people for life and providing employees and their families with comprehensive welfare such as free accommodation, education, and medical services; other free public facilities; discounted food; and so on. Workers' rights were central, and during this period, corporate accountability in both urban and rural areas was very high. (In rural areas, peasants were well looked after by their communes.) During this period, corporate accountability was strongly politicized due to the socialist nature of the enterprises, and obeying state orders and serving the employees were central concerns for socialist enterprises. Corporate accountability was a political responsibility.

Economic reform began to affect SOEs around 1984 (Wu 2003), and corporate accountability at first followed the planned economy pattern. According to the 1999 *China Statistical Yearbook*, seventeen thousand schools in China in 1998 (30 percent of the total) were state run. These schools taught more than 7 million students and employed 626,000 staff. Apart from investment in school infrastructure, SOEs spent 6.4 billion yuan ($773 million) annually to keep the schools running. In the same year, one-third of the medical services in China (approximately ninety-one-thousand institutions) were state run, and the total yearly expenditure was 3.1 billion yuan ($37 million). From 1985 to 1992, the government tried various measures to reform the SOEs without eliminating state ownership, but these reforms failed.

Learning from the previous experiences, the CCP fourteenth plenary meeting in 1992 called for ownership reform. The traditional socialist practice of state-owned enterprises was discarded, and the state started to downsize and withdraw from direct economic management. Private firms were allowed to exist and grow, and SOEs were permitted to pursue their own interests. Profitability became the primary goal of firms. A survey of 210 SOEs in China reported on corporate objectives. Of these, 45.7 percent chose high profits as their first objective, 24.7 percent chose growth, and 9.8 percent chose increasing market share, while only 2.6 percent regarded increasing employees' income as their first objective (Ma 1992).

Changes in the role of the state and to the objectives of the firms have resulted in large changes in corporate accountability. The most significant of these was the elimination of the cradle-to-grave welfare provision enjoyed by workers at SOEs. Health and education services largely shifted from a state-payer to a user-payer principle, and this resulted in inequality of access. Indeed, in many remote rural areas, people cannot afford medical services or education. In 1997, following the state policy of "invigorating large firms while relaxing control over the small ones" (*zhuda fangxiao*), many small SOEs went bankrupt. According to the 2001 *China Statistical Yearbook*, from 1998 to 2000, 21.4 million people were laid off by SOEs. These workers became the new urban poor who struggled to find jobs in the increasingly market-oriented environment, and this caused widespread social unrest. Labor protests have increased sharply in frequency and severity. The state has been attempting to address these issues through a variety of social security programs, but this effort has only partly alleviated the situation due to the limited access to and the misuse of the social security fund, attributed to inadequate laws, lack of transparency, and inadequate public supervision (Xinhua News Agency 2010).

Poor labor practices have been another problem related to corporate accountability. A report on child labor in Chinese firms that produced licensed goods for the 2008 Beijing Olympic Games helped bring China's poor labor practices into the spotlight (Taylor 2007). It was reported that children as young as twelve were hired to produce Olympic merchandise by firms in China's Guangdong Province. Undercover researchers working in the firms reported that adult workers were paid half the legal minimum wage, and that children doing the same jobs were paid even less. Both children and adults worked up to fifteen hours a day, seven days a week. It was also reported that workers were instructed to lie to inspectors about their wages, health, and safety conditions, and that anyone who told the truth was fired.

Researchers have uncovered poor labor practices at many Chinese suppliers to international corporations, and even Apple Corporation has admitted that some of its Chinese suppliers use child labor. At Foxconn, one of Apple's long-term contractors, high stress and long working hours contributed to the suicides of thirteen workers (Reuters 2010). According to the *Nike Corporate Social Responsibility Report FY 07 08 09*, more than 20 percent of Nike's original equipment manufacturers have asked their employees to work sixty hours or more per week (Nike n.d.). The National Labor Committee (NLC) in the United States claimed that Dongguan Kunying Computer Goods Company, a Chinese supplier for Microsoft, employed hundreds of child laborers and asked them to work long hours; one worker was found to work a thirty-four-hour shift at the pay rate of sixty-five cents per hour. According to the NLC, Dongguan Kunying forbids its workers to talk to each other, to listen to music, or even to use the toilet during working hours. A management consulting company listed seventeen poor labor practices on their website, including child labor, illegal restriction of personal freedom by taking workers' ID documents, enforced overtime, low wages, bad accommodation, and poor workplace health and safety conditions (Wohua Consulting 2012). Some Chinese companies continue to use toxic substances without adequate safety measures. Cadmium, for example, is strictly regulated in Western countries but still widely used in China (*Shanghai Daily* 2008).

Chinese labor laws give workers the right to form unions, and by law all companies that have more than one hundred employees are required to have unions, but it is estimated that only a little over 60 percent of companies in China do have such unions (Hays 2008). Even those unions that do exist are arms of the state controlled by the CCP. The unions do not negotiate contracts and do little in the way of the traditional union activities seen in Western countries, such as lobbying for better wages and better working conditions.

Consumer product quality problems revealed in recent years are another concern related to corporate accountability. Some food companies, for example, have taken advantage of weak enforcement of regulations by blending fake ingredients into products, signing contracts agreeing to produce one product only to switch the raw material to something cheaper later on, and coloring food to make old and stale food look more appetizing. In 2008, around three thousand children were sickened and at least six died from drinking tainted milk, and this scandal led to a worldwide recall of Chinese dairy products. Lessons were not learned from this event, however, and in 2011 the Chinese government quality watchdog found that some products of Mengniu, China's biggest dairy firm, contained aflatoxin, a substance produced by a food fungus that can cause severe liver damage, including liver cancer.

Weak enforcement of regulations has also led to extreme abuse of intellectual property rights, and virtually any product can be copied. China is the origin of many counterfeit products and other forms of stolen intellectual property rights.

From an environmental perspective, China's high economic growth rate in recent years has been at the expense of massive energy consumption and extensive resource and capital investment. China is the world's second largest energy consumer after the United States (Fredriksen 2006). In 1980, China consumed approximately 1.8 million barrels of oil per day, and this rose to approximately 6.4 million barrels per day in 2004—an increase of more than 250 percent. In aggregate terms, China is the world's number-one emitter of carbon dioxide (CO_2), one of the most abundant greenhouse gases, so China's environmental issues are not just a domestic concern (Auffhammer and Carson 2008). While some progress in improving energy efficiency and reducing CO_2 emissions has been made, 75 percent of China's energy production is still dependent on coal. Meanwhile, demand for automobiles is growing quickly, and respiratory illness and heart disease related to air pollution are the leading causes of death in China. Various studies estimate that pollution costs China about 7 to 10 percent of gross domestic product (GDP) a year (Korth and Cleveland 2004). To mitigate environmental degradation, the Chinese state has put in place several environmental laws and policies, but because of lack of enforcement, these actions have not improved the situation significantly.

All these issues reflect low corporate ethical values in China in general, and high profit seems to be the motivation of many firms. Although the situation can be explained by China's unique culture and stage of development, the country has been criticized for its lack of corporate accountability and is under increasing pressure to improve.

Current Trends and Future Perspectives

Several emerging initiatives suggest that corporate accountability will be more important in China's future.

Emergence of International Nongovernmental Organizations

The Chinese government itself has established a few public charitable organizations, such as the Chinese Children and Teenagers' Fund (1981), Project Hope

(1989), the Poverty Alleviation Foundation (1989), and the China Charity Federation (1994). Although some researchers see these organizations as fund-raising mechanisms for the government (Young 2002), the charities have secured substantial private funding. Since 2000, some independent nongovernmental organizations (NGOs) have emerged, such as Amity Foundation, the Chinese Christian Service Organization, and the YMCA (Young Men's Christian Association). According to China Development Brief (2012), there were more than two hundred international NGOs operating in China as of 2011. In the past, these nonpublic NGOs had been discouraged by the government organizations who were supposed to be responsible for the relevant areas, but gradually hostility decreased, partly because the NGOs have provided services effectively and efficiently.

Charitable Donations and Trust

Statistics from the Ministry of Civil Affairs showed that in 2005 the total charitable donations in China made up less than 1 percent of gross national product (China's gross national product, or GNP, in 2005 was $1,529 billion) (Mackey 2005). In contrast, in 2006, Americans donated $295 billion (Thomas 2007), which accounted for 2.6 percent of its GNP. Less than 1 percent of China's 10 million firms made any charitable donations at all (Mackey 2005). Recent scandals have inhibited charitable donations in China; in one well-known incident, a young woman named Guo Meimei, who claimed online that she was the general manager of a charity organization, posted pictures of herself with a luxury car and leather bags. According to a media report citing the Ministry of Civil Affairs, donations fell by 80 percent immediately after this and other scandals were publicized (Moore 2011).

Policy Initiatives

The CCP fifteenth plenary meeting called for a "new industrialization path," the core aim of which is to increase industrialization by way of developing new technology and improving efficiency. The slogan "harmonious society" was introduced in 2004, and it was followed in 2007 by President Hu Jintao's call at the CCP seventeenth plenary meeting for Chinese firms to take social responsibility, indicating official support for the concept of corporate accountability by China's politicians and hence by the Chinese business community. Since 2008, all publicly listed companies in China have been required to publish corporate social responsibility reports along with their annual reports. Related laws and regulations in the areas of corporate governance, labor, and environmental protection have been strengthened. Chinese consumers, like their counterparts elsewhere in the world, have become more aware of their rights and are increasingly calling for businesses to act responsibly. Chinese media and other organizations have begun to challenge the business practices of companies. Such an atmosphere has fostered an optimistic outlook for China's sustainability. For many Chinese companies, corporate accountability offers an opportunity to change and hence to raise their visibility, profile, and brand recognition internationally. Moreover, corporate accountability will improve business practice standards, benefitting employees, consumers, and the international business community.

Dongyong ZHANG
Henan Agricultural University

See also Activism, Judicial; Automobiles and Personal Transportation; Climate Change Mitigation Initiatives (China); Consumerism; Five-Year Plans; Labor; National Pollution Survey (China); Nongovernmental Organizations (NGOs); Traditional Knowledge (China)

FURTHER READING

Auffhammer, Maximilian, & Carson, Richard T. (2008). Forecasting the path of China's CO_2 emissions using province-level information. *Journal of Environmental Economics and Management, 55*(3), 229–247.

China Development Brief. (2012). Directory of international NGOs. Retrieved December 28, 2012, from http://www.chinadevelopmentbrief.com/dingo/

Fredriksen, Katharine A. (2006). China's role in the world: Is China a responsible stakeholder? Statement before U.S.-China economic and security review commission. Retrieved January 22, 2012, from http://www.uscc.gov/hearings/2006hearings/transcripts/aug_3_4/testimony_kathy_fredriksen.pdf

Hays, Jeffrey. (2008). Chinese labor rights: Laws, trade unions and lawsuits. Facts and Details. Retrieved January 17, 2012, from http://factsanddetails.com/china.php?itemid=363&catid=9&subcatid=60

Jensen, Mads Holst. (2006, March 10–11). Serve the people! Corporate social responsibility (CSR) in China (Copenhagen Discussion Paper 2006-6). Frederiksberg, Denmark: Asia Research Centre, Copenhagen Business School.

Korth, Kim, & Cleveland, John. (2004). The China factor: mystery, myth or magic? CTMA roundtable. Retrieved January 17, 2012, from http://ctma.com/wp-content/uploads/CTMAChinaPresentationbyIRN-Feb2604.pdf

Li, H. (2010). *Zhongguo kechixu fazhan sixiang yanjin yanjiu* [Research on the Chinese evolving idea of sustainable development]. *Economics and Law, 12*, 396–397.

Li Xiu-fang & Fan Jian-zheng. (2006). An analysis of Mao Ze-dong's thought on equality. *Journal of Xuchang College, 1*, 96–99.

Ma, J. (1992). *Woguo guoyou qiye xingwei mubiao de shizheng fenxi* [An empirical study of the corporate objectives of Chinese SOEs]. *Economic Research, 7*, 19–25.

Mackey, Michael. (2005, May 14). The new Chinese philanthropy. *Asia Times Online.* Retrieved November 15, 2011, from http://www.atimes.com/atimes/China/GE14Ad06.html

Moore, Malcolm. (2011, December 8). Chinese charity donations fall 80 per cent. *The Telegraph*. Retrieved January 28, 2011, from http://www.telegraph.co.uk/news/worldnews/asia/china/8943224/Chinese-charity-donations-fall-80-per-cent.html

National Bureau of Statistics of China. (1999). *China statistical yearbook*. Beijing: China Statistics Press.

National Bureau of Statistics of China. (2001). *China statistical yearbook*. Beijing: China Statistics Press.

Nike, Inc. (n.d.). *Corporate responsibility report FY 07 08 09*. Retrieved January 23, 2012, from http://www.nikebiz.com/crreport/content/pdf/documents/en-US/full-report.pdf

Reuters. (2010). Foxconn worker plunges to death at China plant: Report. Retrieved January 19, 2012, from http://www.reuters.com/article/2010/11/05/us-china-foxconn-death-idUSTRE6A41M920101105

Shanghai Daily. (2008, January 3). Call for crackdown on deadly cadmium poison. Retrieved January 28, 2012, from http://www.china.org.cn/english/health/237983.htm

Taylor, Andrew. (2007). China: Child labor caution for China Olympics. Retrieved November 15, 2011, from http://www.corpwatch.org/article.php?id=14513

Thomas, Jeffrey. (2007, June 26). Charitable donations by Americans reach record high. Retrieved November 20, 2011, from http://www.america.gov/st/washfile-english/2007/June/200706261522251CJsamohT0.8012354.html

Wickerham, Joshua, & Zadek, Simon. (2009, March). Fortune China: AccountAbility managerial survey on corporate responsibility: China's corporate social responsibility change maker. Retrieved November 9, 2011, from http://csrtoday.org/sites/default/files/AccountAbility_Wickerham%20Zadek_Fortune%20China_CSR%20Managerial%20Survey_2009_March.pdf

Wohua Consulting. (2012). *Zhongguo qiye dangqian bijiao tuchu de laogong wenti huizong* [Summary of poor labor practices in Chinese firms]. Retrieved January 29, 2012, from http://www.21mcc.org/gziso900085.html

Wong, Loong. (2009). Corporate social responsibility in China: Between the market and the search for a sustainable growth development. *Asian Business & Management, 8*(2), 129–148.

Wu, J. (2003). *Economic reform in temporary China*. Shanghai: Yuandong Publishing House.

Xinhua News Agency. (2010). Draft law to prevent misuse of social security funds. Retrieved November 14, 2011, from http://www.chinadaily.com.cn/business/2010-10/25/content_11455336.htm

Xu, Shangkun, & Yang, Rudai. (2009). Indigenous characteristics of Chinese corporate social responsibility conceptual paradigm. *Journal of Business Ethics, 93*, 321–333.

Young, Nick. (2002, January–February). Corporate citizenship, three "C"s: Civil society, corporate social responsibility and China. *China Business Review, 29*(1), 34–39.

Yu, H. (1999). *Shijing* [The Book of Songs]. Shanxi, China: *Shanxi Guji Chubanshe* [Shanxi Ancient Books Publishing House].

D

Delhi, India

18 million est. pop. 2010

Delhi, the capital of India, is an ancient city faced with the challenges of a large, rapidly growing population, too little urban infrastructure, and industrial pollution. Despite attempts to create a master plan for the city, problems persist. Policy makers and courts are intervening to attempt to improve the quality of life in the city.

In 1911, the capital of British India was built adjacent to the medieval city of Shahjahanabad/Dilli. New Delhi, with its wide streets and neat bungalows, epitomized planned modernity in a colonial context. Delhi, by contrast, became increasingly referred to as Old Delhi and as the site of a dark and blighted modernity. Already densely populated, the city became overcrowded, with the significant number of clerks and laborers who resided in the old city but worked in adjacent New Delhi. Overcrowding and its associated issues emerged as a serious environmental challenge, and the government sought relief through programs of slum eradication, housing and services improvement, and urban expansion (Legg 2007). Unfortunately, these efforts often benefited some parts of the city more than others. For example, clean, piped water replaced water from wells and cisterns, but the geography of pipes remained uneven, with superior services being provided to the colonial and native elite (Hosagrahar 2005). The extent to which the flow of wastewater posed a risk, either to the residents of Delhi themselves or to communities downstream, was not perceived to be a major issue in this period, and as a result, governmental efforts did not address it. The resulting contamination of the Yamuna River persists to the present time.

Postcolonial Delhi

India obtained its independence from Britain in 1947. The country was simultaneously partitioned into two states—India and Pakistan—largely on the basis of the religious beliefs of the residents. Neighbors and communities turned upon each other, and millions of refugees fled, Muslims to Pakistan and Hindus to India. Delhi became an important migration destination at this time. Its population swelled by 90 percent between 1941 and 1951, and the urban density increased by more than 100 percent (Datta 1986). Military construction during World War II and the sudden appearance of small household units also left their mark on the unplanned, rapid growth of the city. Most of the industrial activity was established in "obsolete and obsolescent" structures, often in residential areas in the old city. Faced with creating order, providing appropriate housing in a relatively poor postcolonial city, safely locating its industries, and ensuring that the air and the water of the city were polluted as little as possible, the Indian government invited American experts to help draw up a master plan for the city. The master plan recommended zoning and the appropriate location of residence and industries. It also recommended that large and polluting industries be located on the margins of the city or beyond it. Smaller and less intrusive industries were to be relocated in designated industrial areas within the urban boundaries of Delhi. Low-cost housing, selective urban renewal, and limited slum demolition and reconstruction were key measures proposed in the master plan.

Contemporary Delhi

The master plan failed through the 1970s and 1980s. Small-scale and household industries in traditional craft sectors and modern electronic ones, operating through a range of legal, semi-legal, and illegal arrangements, mushroomed all over the city. The master plan's optimal population estimate for 1981 was 4.5 million, but in fact the city grew to 6.2 million. Since then, the numbers have increased even further, reaching 13.8 million by 2001 (Planning Commission 2009, Annex A-1.1, 72). Much of this growth is on account of migration, with the net migration projected to increase from 1.7 million in 2001 to 2.4 million in 2021, by which time the total population is expected to reach 23 million (Department of Environment and Forests 2010, 2–6; Planning Commission 2009, 93). The explosion of industrial enterprise and population growth—there are roughly 129,000 industrial units estimated to be operating in Delhi currently, and the city's population is close to 18 million—create massive challenges for the residents of Delhi.

Increased population growth will exacerbate an already difficult situation with regard to urban basic services. According to estimates from 2012, only about 75 percent of the urban population has piped water, only half are connected to sewers, and over 50 percent of the city's population reside in slum housing, squatter settlements, and unauthorized colonies (Planning Commission 2009, 93 and 181–183). Environmental pollution is also likely to add to the health burdens. Local groundwater is overexploited, which affects both its quality and long-term sustainability. The flows of industrial wastewater and untreated sewage have made the segment of the Yamuna River that traverses the city a dead zone. Waterborne diseases are common. Delhi also ranks among the world's most severely air-polluted cities, a result of vehicular pollution, industrial pollution, and emissions from power plants.

Twenty-First-Century Urban Challenge

Historical environmental issues thus continue to impact Delhi in the new century. One response to these challenges might be a renewal of the commitment to planning norms to achieve sustainable and orderly urban development. Another option is a more radical alternative: replacing an essentially Western model of urban planning with an Asian form of urbanism, with mixed, rather than zoned, spatial arrangements and with more decentralized management. The Indian Supreme Court is taking a leading role in establishing a context for the development and environmental debate. From the early 1990s, it recognized the right to clean air and water as basic human rights, and in 1998, it mandated the complete switch from diesel to compressed natural gas (CNG) for public transportation in Delhi (Divan and Rosencranz 2001, 49–51 and 274–279). The courts and policy makers increasingly recognize that the environmental challenges facing cities are complex and technical, that there is often a lack of data, that controversies surround assessments of health and environmental impacts, and that there is difficulty in reaching consensus.

Awadhendra BHUSHAN SHARAN
Centre for the Study of Developing Societies, Delhi

See also Agriculture (South and East Asia); Automobiles and Personal Vehicles; Chennai, India; Climate Change Migration (India); Dhaka, Bangladesh; Education, Environmental (India); Energy Industries—Renewables (India); Gandhism; Ganges River; India; Microfinance; Mumbai, India; Public Health; Utilities Regulation and Efficiency; Water Use and Rights (India); White Revolution of India

FURTHER READINGS

Bharat, Lal Seth, & Suresh Baba, S. V. (2007). *Sewage canal: How to clean the Yamuna*. New Delhi: Centre for Science and Environment.
Datta, V. N. (1986). Punjabi refugees and Greater Delhi. In Robert E. Frykenberg (Ed.), *Delhi through the ages: Essays in urban history, culture and society* (pp. 442–462). Delhi: Oxford University Press.
Department of Environment and Forests, Government of Delhi. (2010). *State of environment report for Delhi, 2010*.
Divan, Shyam, & Rosencranz, Armin. (2001). *Environmental law and policy in India: Cases, materials and statutes* (2nd ed.). Delhi: Oxford University Press.
Hosagrahar, Jyoti. (2005). *Indigenous modernities: Negotiating architecture and urbanism*. London: Routledge.
Legg, Stephen. (2007). *Spaces of colonialism: Delhi's urban governmentalities*. Hoboken, NJ: Wiley-Blackwell.
Menon, A. G. Krishna. (1997). Imagining the Indian city. *Economic and Political Weekly, 32*(46), 2932–2936.
Planning Commission, Government of India. (2009). *Delhi development report*. New Delhi: Academic Foundation and Planning Commission, Government of India.
Sen, Jai. (2001, April). The unintended city. *Seminar, 500*, pp. 39–47). Retrieved March 2, 2012, from http://www.india-seminar.com/2001/500/500%20jai%20sen.htm (Originally published April 1976)
Sundaram, Ravi. (2011). *Pirate modernity: Delhi's media urbanism*. London: Routledge.
Verma, Geeta Dewan. (2002). *Slumming India: Of slums and their saviours*. Delhi: Penguin.

Dhaka, Bangladesh

16 million est. pop. 2008

Dhaka has seen many rulers: a succession of Buddhist and Hindu groups, followed by Muslim Mughals and the British; it became the administrative center of East Pakistan after the partition of India in 1947 and capital of the new country of Bangladesh in 1971. Urban growth has accelerated, and cheap labor has made the city an international center for textiles and mass-market goods. Although poverty, flooding, air and water pollution, and unplanned development pose problems, literacy standards are increasing, and there is a growing, aspirational middle class.

Dhaka City is centrally located in Bangladesh, in the southern part of the district of Dhaka, about 200 kilometers north of the Bay of Bengal. It is surrounded by distributaries of the Ganges (Padma, in Bangladesh) and Brahmaputra rivers: the Buriganga River in the south, the Balu and the Shitalakhya rivers in the east, Tongi Khal in the north, and the Turag River in the west. The inner areas of the city lie on a Quaternary river terrace, marginally above the contemporary floodplains of the major rivers, and hundreds of detached backwater lakes of all sizes dot the surrounding developed area. In addition, as a result of the accelerated rate of urbanization (Hossain 2008), a substantial portion of the adjacent lower-lying deltaic land is now also occupied, putting Dhaka residents at severe risk of seasonal flooding from the Himalayan rivers in the monsoon season.

History

The known archaeological heritage of Dhaka begins in the seventh century CE, when a small city-state was located on the river banks of the Buriganga. Historically, Dhaka's origins appear to be centered around the present "old town" (of pre-Mughal period), with the city expanding westward and northward under the later Mughal and British administrations. During the brief period when East and West Pakistan were parts of one country (following partition from India in 1947 and prior to independence in 1971), urban development extended farther north. The city has subsequently expanded rapidly in an unplanned way and now has a total population in excess of 16 million (Bangladesh Bureau of Statistics 2008). Already classified as a megacity, at currently projected growth rates it could be the home of 25 million people by 2025 (Davis 2006).

Pre-Mughal (before 1608) and Mughal (1608–1764) Periods

A succession of Buddhist and Hindu groups controlled the region before the Mughals came to Dhaka in 1606; Islam Khan made Dhaka his permanent capital, and the expansion of the present old town to Sadar Ghat took place then (GOB 1993). His successor, Ibrahim Khan (reigned 1617–1624), promoted construction of a 22-kilometer south–north road from Buriganga to Tongi, and an east–west road from Dolaikhal to Babupura, allowing the establishment of many industries and factories, particularly for textile production (GOB 1993). Alongside the progressive control of the river channels for international shipping, these new transport routes allowed Dhaka to emerge as one of the most significant centers of trade in South Asia, despite the local absence of valuable raw materials. In 1717 the capital was shifted away from Dhaka, to Rajamahal (Murshidabad), which resulted in a temporary check to population growth and urban development in Dhaka City (Mamun 1994).

British Period (1764–1947)

Toward the beginning of the British colonial period, in the eighteenth century, Dhaka experienced a further dramatic decrease in population as a result of famines, floods, disease epidemics, and loss of trade and business. Population growth nevertheless re-established relatively quickly, and the built-up area began to expand again with construction of new housing, transport and utility services, and health and educational facilities. Notable developments in the educational sector included the establishment of Dhaka College in 1835, Jagannath College in 1858, Eden College in 1880, the Teachers' Training College in 1909, and Dhaka University in 1921 (Mamun 1994).

Pakistan Period (1947–1971)

After the partition of India in 1947, during which the subcontinent was divided on broadly religious grounds into the new nation of India (with a majority Hindu population) and the much less populous Pakistan (where Muslims predominated), the mass movement of communities prompted civil unrest and many deaths, continuing a tradition of violent political upheaval that persisted throughout the twentieth century. Dhaka was identified as the administrative center of East Pakistan, but the province was separated from the larger and more powerful West Pakistan region by 1,800 kilometers of Indian territory, as well as by linguistic and cultural differences. Local administrators faced many challenges, though these did not seriously check Dhaka's population growth nor the explosive development of housing, industry, government offices, and infrastructure. Rapid development took place particularly in the outlying areas of Mohammedpur, Mirpur, Tejagaon, Ramna, Purana Palton, and Segun Bagicha, many of which were recognized after 1956 by the Dhaka Improvement Trust for development and effectively incorporated into the city (Alam and Huq 2003).

Bangladesh Period (since 1971)

Political disagreements between East and West Pakistan, combined with anger over the perceived mismanagement of the relief efforts following the devastating cyclone Bhola in 1970, created a climate for a bloody civil war. The resultant popular uprising led to the emergence of the new nation of Bangladesh in 1971, and Dhaka was reinstated as its capital city.

The significant influx of immigrants from rural areas and the natural growth of population after the cessation of hostilities rapidly made Dhaka one of the most densely populated cities in the world. Informal settlements (slums, squatters, and pavement communities) emerged in the central areas, and many of the major problems faced by the city during the last fifty years are associated with this unplanned development. Extreme traffic congestion, air and water pollution, and lack of access to green space are endemic, and the environmental and health standards experienced by many residents are shocking to Western visitors. A substantial proportion of Dhaka's housing has no piped water or sewerage systems, and waste disposal systems are inadequate; despite substantial aid to this sector from Japan, much domestic refuse is thrown into local watercourses and lakes. The lack of progress with infrastructural development is fostered by widespread corruption among badly paid public officials.

Despite these challenges, there is nevertheless a rapidly growing Dhakaite middle class that is aspirational and entrepreneurial. Interest in Bangla culture and music is strong. There is a keen sense of history and a lively and generally free press. Alongside modern shopping malls there are small parks and open spaces surrounding national historic sites and monuments. Education is valued, as indicated by the huge rise in attendance at schools and in private as well as public universities. The literacy rate in Dhaka is increasing fairly quickly. Estimated at 62 percent in 2001, by 2010 it had climbed to almost 73 percent, significantly higher than the national average of 56 percent (Banglapedia 2006). This combination of extreme social and environmental problems and progress driven by high ambitions makes Dhaka a city of fascinating contrasts.

Demographics

The population of Dhaka is currently growing at an estimated 4 percent per year, one of the highest rates among Asian cities (McGee 2006). The continuing growth reflects ongoing migration from rural areas to the Dhaka urban region, which accounted for 60 percent of the city's growth in the 1960s and 1970s. The city's population has also grown with expansion of the city boundaries, a process that added more than a million people to the city in the 1980s alone (McGee 2006).

Economy

The ready availability of cheap labor has allowed Dhaka to emerge as an international center for the textiles and ready-made garment industries, leatherworking, and factories producing mass-market consumer goods. The presence of these facilities throughout the city adds to the traffic congestion, with supply and distribution trucks weaving their way among almost half a million cycle rickshaws and huge numbers of cars. Heavy industries such as ship-breaking yards and the hundreds of smoke-producing brickworks along the river frontages add to the acute local pollution problems.

The annual per capita income of Dhaka is estimated at US$1,350, with 34 percent of households living below the poverty line (Cities Alliance 2000), including a large segment of the population who come from villages in search of employment (Lawson 2002). For these people, life in Dhaka is a struggle to feed, clothe, and educate themselves and their children, and unemployment rates are high. By contrast, Dhaka's burgeoning middle classes drive a market for imported modern consumer and luxury goods (Banglapedia 2007; Lawson 2002). At present Dhaka has three traditional business districts, namely Motijheel, Kawran Bazar, and Mirpur, whereas the wealthier areas of Dhanmondi, Gulshan, and Bashundhara-Baridhara support a growing information technology sector, multinational corporation offices, larger shopping malls, and universities. Interspersed among the many commercial organizations and aid agencies, there are also social enterprise initiatives, including the Nobel award–winning Grameen Bank, which advances microcredit to entrepreneurs.

Perceived Opportunities in Dhaka

For millions of the rural poor in Bangladesh, Dhaka remains an attractive destination. Compared to other places in the country, it offers the best chance of economic opportunity, and this promotes their migration. Foreign investors select Dhaka because of the macroeconomic stabilization in Bangladesh over the years, the relatively inexpensive land, and the recent improvements in the transportation and shipping systems. Other factors that make Dhaka attractive to investors include the large and growing pool of cheap and generally compliant labor, especially of migrant women; its rich and active cultural environment; the general freedom from racial, religious, or ethnic violence, unusual in metropolitan areas internationally; and the broadly democratic and secular governmental system. Political awareness is strong, and memories of the war of independence from Pakistan still relatively fresh, but the occasional *hartals* or strikes tend not to escalate into major confrontations. It is alleged that traditional moral values and kinship networks in the city help keep Dhaka society comparatively free from many modern urban vices, though prostitution and child abuse are nevertheless widely prevalent.

Md. Sarfaraz Gani ADNAN
Chittagong University of Engineering and Technology (CUET)

Carolyn ROBERTS
University of Oxford

See also Agriculture (South Asia); Consumerism; Ganges River; Labor; Public Transportation; Religions; Urbanization

FURTHER READING

Alam, Mozaharul, & Huq, Saleemul. (2003). Flood management and vulnerability of Dhaka City. In Alcira Kreimer, Margaret Arnold & Anne Carlin (Eds.), *Building safer cities: The future of disaster risk* (pp. 121–135). Washington, DC: World Bank.

Bangladesh Bureau of Statistics. (2008). Statistical pocket book. Retrieved April 5, 2012, from http://www.bbs.gov.bd/PageWebMenuContent.aspx?MenuKey=117

Banglapedia: National Encyclopedia of Bangladesh. (2006). Dhaka division. Retrieved April 5, 2012, from http://www.banglapedia.org/httpdocs/HT/D_0157.HTM

Banglapedia: National Encyclopedia of Bangladesh. (2007). Chowdhury, Abdul Matin. Retrieved April 5, 2012, from http://www.banglapedia.org/httpdocs/HT/C_0237.HTM

Cities Alliance. (2000). Asian city development strategies: Fukuoka Conference 2000; Dhaka. Retrieved April 5, 2012, from http://web.archive.org/web/20040909085826/http://www.citiesalliance.org/fukuoka.nsf/Attachments/CP_Dhaka/$File/CPF_Dhaka.PDF

Davis, Mike. (2006). *Planet of slums*. London: Verso.

Government of Bangladesh (GOB). (1993). *Bangladesh District Gazetteer: Greater Dhaka*. Dhaka, Bangladesh: Ministry of Establishment.

Hossain, Shahadat. (2008). Rapid urban growth and poverty in Dhaka City. *Bangladesh e-Journal of Sociology*, 5(1), 12–56. Retrieved April 5, 2012, from http://www.bangladeshsociology.org/BEJS%205.1%20Rapid%20Urban%20Growth%20and%20Poverty%20final.pdf

Islam, Nazrul. (1999). Dhaka City: Some general concerns. In Naved Hamid & Saleemul Huq (Eds.), *Reforming Dhaka City management: Asian cities in the 21st century* (Vol. 3, pp. 71–82). Mandaluyong City, Philippines: Asian Development Bank.

Lawson, Alastair. (2002). Good times for bourgeois Bangladeshis. BBC News. Retrieved April 5, 2012, from http://news.bbc.co.uk/2/hi/south_asia/2018535.stm

Mamun, Muntasir. (1994). *Dhaka: Smriti bismritir nagari* [Dhaka: The city of memoirs and forgetfulness]. Dhaka, Bangladesh: University Press Limited.

McGee, Terry. (2006). Urbanization takes on new dimensions in Asia's population giants. Washington, DC: Population Reference Bureau. Retrieved April 5, 2012, from http://www.prb.org/Articles/2001/UrbanizationTakesonNewDimensionsinAsiasPopulationGiants.aspx

Rizwanul, Islam, & Muqtada, M. (Eds.). (1986). *Bangladesh: Selected issues in employment and development*. Oslo Blindern, Norway: Unipub.

e

E-Waste

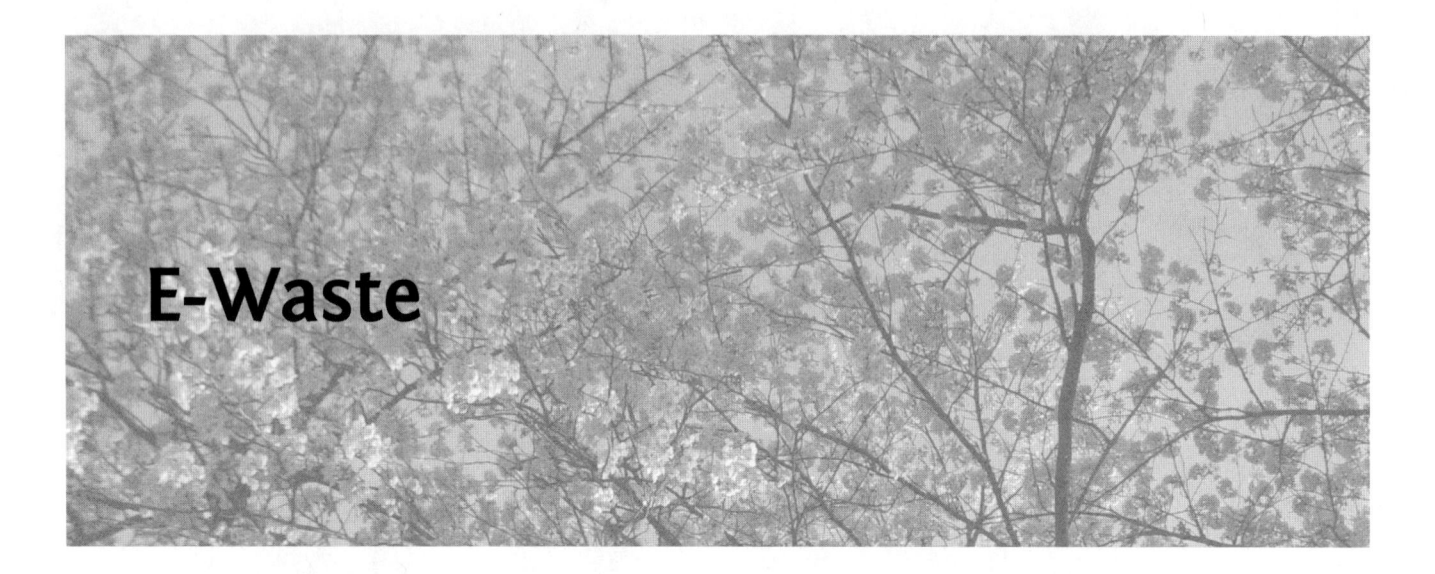

The waste from discarded electronic products, known as e-waste, has become a problem of huge proportion in Asia, especially in China and India where hazardous e-waste from developed countries is often dumped or recycled in adverse conditions. The highly toxic substances of e-waste necessitate special handling to prevent health hazards and environmental damage. International conventions and national legislation now attempt to regulate the disposal and recycling of toxic waste, as well as the recycling of valuable nonrenewable resources in electronics.

E-waste refers to redundant electronic products ranging from calculators, cell phones, and computers to television monitors, microwave ovens, and refrigerators. Most of these products have a relatively short lifespan of between three and five years because constant technological innovation renders older products obsolete very quickly. E-waste is the fastest growing stream of waste in developed countries, placing greater strain by sheer volume on already overburdened waste disposal systems and sites.

In Asia the problem of e-waste is twofold. First, in developed countries such as Japan and Korea, and also in developing countries such as China and India, the production and distribution of electronic products has grown exponentially in the past thirty years. In the developing countries the growth is set to increase much quicker than in the developed countries. Second, some of the countries in the region, like China and India, have become dumping grounds for hazardous e-waste from developed nations such as the United States, Germany, and the United Kingdom. The e-waste is either dumped without treatment or recycled without adequate, regulated supervision.

E-waste contains a number of highly toxic substances, such as lead, mercury, and cadmium, all of which have the potential to cause serious harm to the environment and human health. This hazard requires that electronic products be dealt with separately from normal household waste in order to prevent the harmful chemicals and heavy metals from contaminating the landfills, water sources, and air. The cost of recycling e-waste has led to developed countries exporting their e-waste to developing countries that often do not have the capability to properly treat e-waste. In Asia, China and India have become the prime dumping grounds.

E-waste also contains a number of very valuable resources such as gold, silver, copper, and palladium. As of 2012, 90 percent of these valuable nonrenewable resources go to waste because e-waste is not being recycled. The focus of e-waste treatment has steadily shifted to recycling of these resources. The United Nations Environment Programme (UNEP) has played an important part in this process.

The Nature of E-Waste

E-waste includes a wide range of domestic devices ranging from refrigerators, washing machines, and television sets to mobile phones, personal computers, fax machines, printers, and electronic toys. Apart from their role in normal households, these products also figure in the health, education, communication, security, and entertainment industries, and in businesses in general. The steady growth in e-waste is set to continue as emerging markets are catching up to the markets in the developed world (UNEP 2009a, 1–2).

It is estimated, depending on inclusions and exclusions of products, that between 20 and 50 million tonnes of electronic waste are generated each year (ETBC 2012b). These huge volumes of waste decay much slower than household waste and take up space in waste dumps already stretched toward their limit with other forms of household waste (Hull 2010, 5–6).

E-waste consists of a wide range of components. Some are bulky: the steel and aluminum in refrigerators and washing machines, the plastic compounds in television, computer and printer housings and keyboards, and glass in television sets. Some are minor parts of e-waste bulkwise, but contain significant amounts of valuable or toxic materials. Modern electronics can contain up to sixty different elements. Printed wiring boards and mobile phones contain the most complex mix of substances and are major sources of base metals such as copper and tin, many precious metals such as gold, silver, palladium, and special metals such as cobalt, indium, and antimony. A tonne of mobile phones without batteries contains 130 kilograms of copper, 3.5 kilograms of silver, 340 grams of gold, and 140 grams of palladium. The lithium-ion (Li-ion) batteries add another 3.5 kilograms of cobalt (UNEP 2009b, 7–8).

Besides the e-waste that is highly toxic because of metals such as lead, mercury, cadmium, hexavalent chromium, beryllium, barium, and nickel, e-waste made from plastic poses risks. Many plastic compounds, as well as the brominated flame retardants used in computer and television housings, cables, and printed circuit boards, cause toxic fumes on incineration, creating health hazards for workers in informal recycling processes (Templeton 2009, 766–768).

An investigation by the Basel Action Network and Greenpeace in 2002 into the recycling operations in Guiyu, a rural Chinese community in Guangdong Province, illustrates the dangers of e-waste (BAN 2004). Within five years of becoming a recycling center, the groundwater of the town was contaminated to such an extent that water had to be brought in for the community from a source 30 kilometers away. Despite the dangers, the community was still using local surface water for their everyday needs such as cooking and washing. Guiyu remains a major recycling center in China.

Similarly, India has become a popular dumping ground for hazardous waste. India has numerous waste recycling centers, some legal but many illegal (Quadri 2010, 468–469). The workers in many of these centers work fourteen-hour shifts, seven days a week, in dangerous conditions and often without protective clothing or gear. Regulations, if any, often remain unimplemented (Quadri 2010, 473–474).

Recycling Minerals vs. Mining

The UNEP states that "e-waste is usually regarded as a waste problem, which can cause environmental damage if not dealt with in an appropriate way. However, the enormous resource impact of electrical and electronic equipment (EEE) is widely overlooked" (UNEP 2009a, 6). There is a need to simply reduce the amount of waste as with other recyclable products such as glass and paper and to avoid the toxic elements from polluting the environment or creating health hazards, but there is also a need to recycle valuable minerals that are not a renewable resource. It requires significantly lower amounts of energy to recycle these metals than to mine them, resulting in much less carbon emission. It is still much more expensive, however, to recycle these materials than to mine them.

The Asian electronics industry is a major consumer of base metals, precious, and special metals that are mined at great environmental cost by primary producers in places such as Canada, Australia, Russia, China, and South Africa. The use of special minerals, called rare earth elements (REE), in the production of electronic products has become contentious as 95 percent of these minerals are mined in China and exported to the rest of the world (Hurst 2010). Although significant new deposits have been found in South Africa (Yahoo! Finance 2011), Greenland (Greenland Minerals and Energy 2012a and 2012b) and in the seabed near Hawaii (Arthur 2011), and will be developed by countries including Korea and Japan, the current shortage of REE and the dependence on China will remain for a number of years; REE are likely to be in short supply until these sources are exploited (Humphries 2011, 3–4).

The electronics industry alone consumes the following estimated amounts of metals produced annually: gold, 3 percent; silver, 3 percent; palladium, 13 percent; cobalt, 15 percent; indium, 80 percent; ruthenium, 80 percent, and antimony, 50 percent (UNEP 2009a, 7–8). Potentially more than 40 million tonnes of base and precious metals can be recycled annually, based on 2009 volumes.

Whereas mining for base metals (such as iron and copper) and precious metals is quite widespread, the current mining of REE is located primarily in China. In 2010 China upset world markets when it suspended export to Japan due to a diplomatic dispute (Folger 2012). Since 2010 China has also been reducing its exports to protect its own electronics industries as its current known deposits are only sufficient for twenty years at current production levels (Folger 2012). Most of the mining of REE takes place in the Bayan Obo district of Inner Mongolia in China and comes at a heavy environmental cost. The pollution of the air and water is widespread in the immediate vicinity, contaminating the Huang (Yellow) River and the water sources of many villages. Soils around the mines are dangerously polluted with toxic or radioactive heavy metals (Hurst 2012).

The Steps of Recycling

The recycling of e-waste consists of collecting, dismantling, processing, and end processing. The collection of e-waste is dependent on consumer awareness and cooperation in sorting waste and disposing of e-waste separately. This is done either by consumers using special containers for collections of e-waste by authorities curbside, or the provision of special dumpsites and collection containers by sellers or producers. In Japan consumers can return e-waste either to manufacturers or the post office (Chung and Murakami-Suzuki 2008, 128–129). It is a crucial part of the recycling chain. Dismantling and preprocessing consists of sorting e-waste into different components, removing valuable items such as chips and processors that can be reused as well as hazardous materials, and shredding and crushing of bulk materials. This can be a very labor-intensive process. End-processing usually requires expensive high-tech equipment relying on big volumes to be economically viable. Regionalization of such facilities therefore makes economic sense. Low-tech informal end-processing often leads to the kind of environmental damage and health risks illustrated by the Chinese Guiyu example.

As responsible recycling is expensive, there is a lucrative illegal trade in e-waste where primary producers responsible for recycling simply export their e-waste to developing countries to be dumped or recycled. Recycling costs in these countries, for example China, India, and Pakistan, are much lower due to lower labor costs and far fewer, if any, regulations imposed on recycling operations (Templeton 2009, 763–764). The restrictions of international and national regulations aimed at preventing the cross-border export of hazardous waste has led to a lucrative illegal trade in e-waste that is hard to contain.

The market for recycling e-waste is enormous. For example, it is estimated that the treatment of e-waste produced in the United States alone is worth in excess of $5 billion annually (Majmudar 2011). This estimate provides a strong indication of the size of the e-waste recycling market as a whole and will increase as the price of REE rises. Stricter controls and decreasing costs of recycling may lead to the development of viable recycling industries in the developed nations and a decrease in the illegal trade and dumping of e-waste.

International Agencies and E-Waste

A number of international agencies or organizations promote responsible recycling of e-waste. UNEP was established in 1972 by the United Nations to advocate global environmental protection. The responsible recycling of e-waste has become an important part of UNEP's focus. As part of their Solving the E-Waste Problem (StEP) initiative, in 2009 UNEP published a report *Recycling: From E-waste to Resources,* which was a major contribution to the debate and knowledge about the responsible treatment of e-waste.

The Basel Action Network (BAN) is a nongovernmental environmental action group based in the United States but focused on confronting the global environmental injustice and economic inefficiency of toxic trade (toxic wastes, products, and technologies) and its devastating impacts. BAN first raised awareness about the plight of the Guiyu residents. It has reported on similar situations elsewhere.

These and many other organizations play an important role in raising the awareness of the responsible treatment of e-waste and confronting the illegal dumping of e-waste in developing countries.

Regulatory Landscape

There are a number of international, regional, and national regulations that are relevant for the management of e-waste. Examining some of these compulsory instruments can determine the extent to which e-waste is regulated and how effective these instruments have been to date.

On the International Front

No international convention specifically targets e-waste. Instead a number of conventions deal with the cross-border transportation of toxic waste in general. E-waste is a fairly new phenomenon that can be considered within the scope of the broader definition of toxic waste contained in international conventions. The problem has not been a lack of regulation, but a lack of proper implementation. The European Union's 2009 Waste Electrical and Electronic Equipment (WEEE) Directive is one such initiative to ensure proper implementation and compliance with its obligations under the Basel Convention of 1989.

As of 2012 numerous countries have national legislation specifically addressing e-waste management, including the exportation of e-waste. In the Asian region, Japan, South Korea, Taiwan, and India have introduced legislation specifically aimed at e-waste management (Chung and Murakami-Suzuki 2008, 126 ff).

Basel Convention 1989 The Basel Convention on the Transboundary Movement of Hazardous Waste is the most important multilateral convention for controlling the movement of hazardous waste across international boundaries. It entered into operation in 1992 (Pratt 2011, 156 ff). Its main objective is to ensure that the export of hazardous waste between countries is done in a way that is environmentally responsible. There are 179 parties to the convention, but three original signatories—Afghanistan, Haiti, and the United States—have not ratified it. A 1995 amendment to the convention, the Basel Ban Amendment, aims at a ban of all export of hazardous waste between developed and developing countries. Due to its controversial nature, which in part concerns the lack of regulations about what constitutes recycling, it had not entered in to force by the end of 2011.

The Basel Convention has not yet been successful in eliminating the large-scale exportation of e-waste, partly because the United States has not ratified the convention and partly due to strategies circumventing the convention, such as exporting e-waste under the guise of equipment destined for reuse in the importing country. E-waste continues to be dumped in India despite its ratification of the convention (Quadri 2010, 468–469).

Bamako Convention

1991 African nations were not satisfied with the Basel Convention because it did not contain a total ban on the export of toxic waste. They believed that the recycling exception created a loophole that would be exploited by unscrupulous parties in developed countries (Tladi 2000, 213). The Bamako Convention of 1991, Convention on the Ban of Import into Africa and the Control of Transboundary Movement and Management of Hazardous Wastes within Africa, mirrors the Basel Convention in many respects, but contains an all-out ban on the importation of toxic waste into Africa. The convention entered into force in 1998 and has been ratified by twenty-four African nations. Due to poor implementation, the convention has also not yet achieved the desired objectives.

The European WEEE Directive 2002/96/EC

Although the European WEEE Directive is only applicable within the European Union, it has had a beneficial influence on the regulatory provisions and on changes in policy in South Korea. The principle of extended producer responsibility (EPR) was adopted by South Korea under this influence. This principle requires the producers of electronic products to take greater responsibility to collect and properly dispose of e-waste.

Domestic Asian Regulation of E-Waste

India, like China, is a country in which there has been a great deal of low-tech e-waste recycling in poor and hazardous conditions for workers (Manasvini and Kulshrestha 2008, 71–72). Mumbai is an important area where this kind of recycling is conducted. Under pressure from a campaign led by several environmental groups (RSC 2011), India has introduced E-Waste (Management and Handling) Rules 2010, which will come into effect in May 2012. The measures include the principle of EPR for recycling, reducing levels of toxic materials in electronic products, and establishing collection centers. It does not, however, address the importation of e-waste.

Japan has two laws dealing with e-waste, the Law for the Promotion of Effective Utilization of Resources (Resources Law) and the law for the Recycling of Specified Kinds of Home Appliances (Recycling Law). The Resources Law encourages manufacturers to enhance measures for the recycling of goods and the reduction of waste and is applicable to personal computers and some small-size batteries. The Recycling Law places compulsory obligations on manufacturers and applies to television sets, refrigerators, washing machines and air conditioners. Manufacturers of home computers have been involved in the recycling of their products since 2003. The recycling cost is fee based and is included in the price of new computers.

South Korea introduced recycling measures for electronic products in 1992 with the Law for the Promotion of Resources Saving and Reutilization to address the problems of overflowing landfills and scarce resources. The system was initially based on an advance deposit that had to be paid by manufacturers to the Ministry of Environment to cover future recycling costs. Deposits were returned in proportion to the amount of e-waste that was collected and recycled properly. But the deposits were too small, and there was insufficient incentive for manufacturers to effectively recycle. In 2003 a new system was introduced known as the producer recycling system. This system extended the responsibilities of producers to recycle and has been more successful.

Outlook

There is a growing awareness of the problems that e-waste poses to waste management in general, the management of toxic waste, and the export to and dumping of e-waste in developing countries that do not have the capacity to properly deal with such waste. There is a need for better enforcement of the existing international and national regulations that restrict the dumping of e-waste. Consumer awareness will play a key role in the more effective collection and recycling of e-waste. Organizations like UNEP will play an important role in this regard. There are indications that the United States, one of the largest producers of e-waste, will exercise stricter control over the dumping of e-waste in developing nations. This will have a similar beneficial effect to the stricter measures that have been imposed by the members of the European Union.

Sieg EISELEN
University of South Africa

See also China; Consumerism; Green Collar Jobs; Information and Communication Technologies (ICT); Japan; Korean Peninsula; Nanotechnology; Outsourcing and Offshoring; Public Health; Southeast Asia; Steel Industry

Further Reading

Arthur, Charles. (2011, July 4). Japan discovers "rare earth" minerals used for iPads. *The Guardian*. Retrieved February 13, 2012, from http://www.guardian.co.uk/technology/2011/jul/04/japan-ipads-rare-earth

Basel Action Network (BAN). (2003). China serves as dump site for computers. Retrieved March 28, 2012, from http://www.ban.org/ban_news/china_serves.html

Basel Action Network (BAN). (2004). Dante's digital junkyard. Retrieved March 28, 2012, from http://www.ban.org/ban_news/dantes_digital_040406.html

Boon, Joel. (2006, Spring). Stemming the tide of patchwork policies: The case of e-waste. *Transnational Law and Contemporary Problems, 15*(2), 731–757.

Chung Soo-Wu, & Murakami-Suzuki Rie. (2008). A comparative study of e-waste recycling systems in Japan, South Korea and Taiwan from the EPR perspective: Implications for developing countries. In Kojima Michikazu (Ed.), *Promoting 3Rs in developing countries: Lessons from the Japanese experience* (pp. 125–145). Chiba, Japan: Institute of Developing Economies (IDE).

Courtney, Rob. (2006, July). Evolving hazardous waste policy for the digital era. *Stanford Environmental Law Journal, 25*, 199–227.

Dittke, Mark. (2009, August). A review of South African environmental and general legislation governing e-waste. Retrieved December 14, 2011, from http://www.ewasa.org/downloads/files/ewasa%20legal%20review.pdf

Drayton, Heather L. (2007, Fall). Economics of electronic waste disposal regulations. *Hofstra Law Review, 36*(1), 149–183.

Electronics TakeBack Coalition (ETBC). (2012a). Brief comparison of state laws on electronic recycling. Retrieved March 28, 2012, from http://www.electronicstakeback.com/wp-content/uploads/Compare_state_laws_chart.pdf

Electronics TakeBack Coalition (ETBC). (2012b). E-waste facts and figures. Retrieved March 28, 2012, from http://www.electronicstakeback.com/wp-content/uploads/Facts_and_Figures_on_EWaste_and_Recycling.pdf

E-waste hazardous to human life. (2010, February). *ReSource, 12*(1), 37–39, 41.

Ezroj, Aaron. (2010). How the European Union's WEEE & RoHS Directives can help the United States develop a successful national e-waste strategy. *Virginia Environmental Law Journal, 28*, 45–72.

Fehm, Sarah. (2011, Fall). From iPod to e-waste: Building a successful framework for extended producer responsibility in the United States. *Public Contract Law Journal, 41*(1), 173–192.

Folger, Tim. (2012, April). Rare earth elements. *National Geographic*. Retrieved March 28, 2012, from http://ngm.nationalgeographic.com/2011/06/rare-earth-elements/folger-text

Greenland Minerals and Energy Ltd. (2012a). Rare earth elements at Kvanefjeld. Retrieved February 13, 2012, from http://www.ggg.gl/rare-earth-elements/rare-earth-elements-at-kvanefjeld/

Greenland Minerals and Energy Ltd. (2012b). Kvanefjeld: REEs, uranium, zinc. Retrieved February 13, 2012, from http://www.ggg.gl/projects/kvanefjeld-rees-uranium-zinc/

Hull, Eric V. (2010). Poisoning the poor for profit: The injustice of exporting electronic waste to developing countries. *Duke Environmental Law and Policy Forum, 21*(1), 1–48.

Humphries, Marc. (2011, September 6). Rare earth elements: The global supply chain (Congressional Research Service Report). Retrieved February 13, 2012 from http://www.fas.org/sgp/crs/natsec/R41347.pdf

Hurst, Cindy. (2010, November 15). The rare earth dilemma: China's rare earth environmental and safety nightmare. *The Cutting Edge*. Retrieved February 13, 2012, from http://www.thecuttingedgenews.com/index.php?article=21777

International Business Times. (2010, November 3). China's dream for rare earths rests on grim costs. Retrieved February 13, 2011, from http://www.ibtimes.com/articles/78461/20101103/rare-earth-china.htm

International ICT Policies and Strategies. (2011, June 25). E-waste law and regulatory framework in India. Retrieved February 13, 2012, from http://ictps.blogspot.com/2011/06/e-waste-law-and-regulatory-framework-in.html

INTERPOL Pollution Crime Working Group. (2009, May). Electronic waste and organized crime: Assessing the links. Lyon, France: INTERPOL.

Kellner, Rod. (2009). Integrated approach to e-waste recycling. In Ronald E. Hester & Roy M. Harrison (Eds.), *Issues in environmental science and technology: Vol. 27. Electronic waste management*. London: Royal Society of Chemistry.

Knee, Jeremy. (2009, Fall). Guidance for the awkward: Outgrowing the adolescence of state electronic waste laws. *Environs Environmental Law and Policy Journal, 33*(2), 157–187.

Kutz, Jennifer. (2006). You've got waste: The exponentially escalating problem of hazardous e-waste. *Villanova Environmental Law Journal, 17*, 307–329.

Lee, Soo-cheol, & Na, Sung-in. (2010). E-waste recycling systems and sound circulative economies in East Asia: A comparative analysis of systems in Japan, South Korea, China and Taiwan. *Sustainability, 2*(6), 1632–1644.

Luther, Linda. (2007, September 10). Managing electronic waste: An analysis of state e-waste legislation (CRS Report for Congress). Washington, DC: Congressional Research Service.

Majmudar, Nishad. (2011, September 18). E-waste: Recyclers, scrap haulers vie to keep US computer trash home. *Washington Post.* Retrieved March 29, 2012, from http://www.washingtonpost.com/business/economy/e-waste-recyclers-scrap-haulers-vie-to-keep-us-computer-trash-home/2011/09/15/gIQAJi7EdK_story.html

Manasvini. Krishna, & Kulshrestha, Pratiksha. (2008). The toxic belt: Perspectives on e-waste dumping in developing nations. *U.C. Davis Journal of International Law and Policy, 15*(1), 71–93.

McCrea, Hannah. (2011, Summer). Germany's take-back approach to waste management: Is there a legal basis for adoption in the United States? *Georgetown International Environmental Law Review, 23*(4), 513–529.

National Environmental Management Authority (NEMA). (2010). *Guidelines for management of e-waste in Kenya.* Nairobi, Kenya: NEMA. Retrieved February 13, 2012, from http://gesci.org/assets/files/Knowledge%20Centre/E-Waste%20Guidelines_Kenya2011.pdf

Pratt, Laura A. W. (2011, Winter). Decreasing dirty dumping? A re-evaluation of toxic waste colonialism and the global management of transboundary hazardous waste. *Texas Environmental Law Journal, 35*(2), 147–178.

Proactiveinvestors Australia. (2009, June 18). Greenland Minerals and Energy confirms huge rare earth resource in Greenland. Retrieved February 13, 2012 from http://www.proactiveinvestors.com.au/companies/news/1767/greenland-minerals-and-energy-confirms-huge-rare-earth-resource-in-greenland-1767.html

Quadri, Shaza. (2010). An analysis of the effects and reasons for hazardous waste importation in India and its implementation of the Basel Convention. *Florida Journal of International Law, 22*(3), 468–493.

Royal Society of Chemistry (RSC). (2011, July 13). Manufacturers targeted by India's e-waste laws. Retrieved December 14, 2011, from www.rsc.org/chemistryworld/News/2011/July/13071101.asp

Templeton, Nicola J. (2009, Spring/Summer). The dark side of recycling and reusing electronics: Is Washington's e-cycle program adequate? *Seattle Journal for Social Justice, 7*(2), 763–797.

Tladi, Dire. (2000). The quest to ban hazardous waste import into Africa: First Bamako and now Basel. *Comparative and International Law Journal of South Africa, 33*(2), 210–222.

United Nations Environment Programme (UNEP). (2009a, January 28). Solving the e-waste problem (StEP) white paper: E-waste take-back system design and policy approaches. Retrieved December 14, 2011, from http://www.step-initiative.org/pdf/white-papers/StEP_TF1_WPTakeBackSystems.pdf

United Nations Environment Programme (UNEP). (2009b, July). *Recycling: From e-waste to resources.* Retrieved December 14, 2011, from http://www.unep.org/PDF/PressReleases/E-Waste_publication_screen_FINALVERSION-sml.pdf

Widawsky, Lisa. In my backyard: How enabling hazardous waste trade to developing nations can improve the Basel Convention's ability to achieve environmental justice. *Environmental Law, 38*(2), 577–626.

Yahoo! Finance. (2011, December 5). Frontier Rare Earths and Korea Resources Corporation sign definitive strategic partnership agreement. Retrieved February 13, 2011, from http://finance.yahoo.com/news/Frontier-Rare-Earths-Korea-cnw-1531259259.html

Yoon, Hyunmyung, & Jang, Yong-Chul. (2006, May 8–11). The practice and challenges of electronic waste recycling in Korea with emphasis on extended producer responsibility (EPR) In *Proceedings of the 2006 IEEE International Symposium on Electronics and the Environment, 2006* (pp. 326–330). Scottsdale, AZ: IEEE.

Share the *Encyclopedia of Sustainability*: Teachers are welcome to make up to ten (10) copies of no more than two (2) articles for distribution in a single course or program. For further permissions, please visit www.copyright.com or contact: info@berkshirepublishing.com

Ecotourism

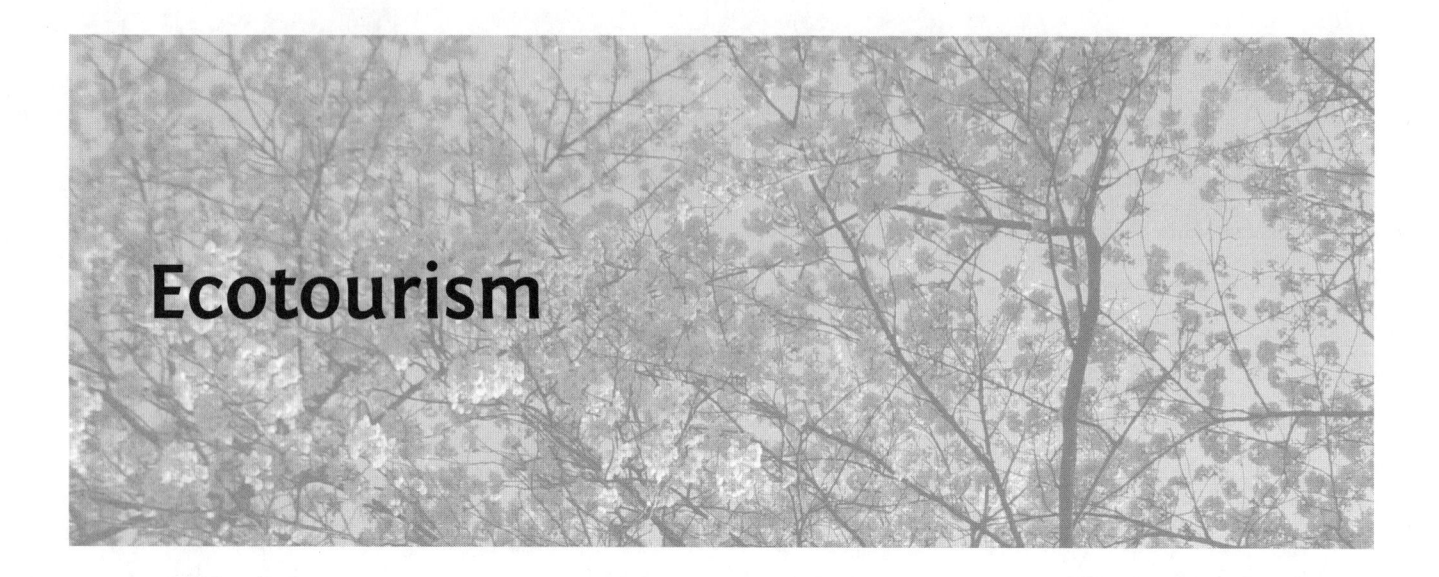

With the enormous environmental and cultural diversity to be found in the countries of Asia, both international and domestic tourism have turned toward forms of ecotourism. In the Asian context this may be seen as tourism that relies on nature and culture as attractions, and which contributes to protecting them by minimizing impacts, educating tourists, and changing land-use practices.

Ecotourism is generally defined as a form of tourism that: relies on nature-based products, settings, destinations and attractions; is managed to minimize impacts; includes education and interpretation components; and contributes to conservation, through financial or political mechanisms (Buckley, 2009a, 2009b, 2010a). In many cases this may extend to include local and traditional cultures and cultural landscapes in addition to natural environments.

The underlying concept of ecotourism is that, unlike other industry sectors, commercial tourism can make a positive net contribution to conservation of the natural environment by creating financial and political capital and incentives that outweigh its own direct negative impacts. This is a concept with long historical antecedents in many cultures. It includes the Western model of national parks and wilderness areas, not only as reservoirs of biodiversity, but also as places that can provide opportunities for visitors to appreciate nature.

The term *ecotour* was first used in the 1960s, with the first formal definitions appearing in the 1980s. During the 1990s, government tourism-planning documents began to mention ecotourism with increasing frequency, and ecolabeling programs proliferated in tourism as in other sectors (Font and Buckley 2001). It was also during this decade that commercial tourism operations began to claim themselves as ecotourism, albeit often on tenuous grounds (Buckley 2003). The United Nations International Year of Ecotourism in 2002 provided mainstream intergovernmental recognition. In the subsequent decades, both the practical examples and the political influence of ecotourism continued to expand; and while much of this activity is greenwash (i.e., rhetorical claims of green benefits made merely for marketing purposes), there has also been significant growth in commercial tourism operations that do indeed contribute to conservation (Buckley 2009c, 2010a, 2010b).

As of 2012, a number of parallel and related terms have come into common use. Terms such as *nature-based tourism, adventure tourism* (Buckley 2006, 2010c), and *outdoor recreation* refer only to the product dimension. Terms such as *sustainable tourism* and *responsible tourism* (Saarinen et al. 2009) refer only to management of impacts on natural and social environments. The term *conservation tourism* (Buckley 2010a) is a more strictly defined subsector of ecotourism, where tourism generates a demonstrable net gain for conservation.

Plans produced by government and financial donor agencies refer routinely to ecotourism, but principally as a potential mechanism to provide economic and political opportunities for impoverished peoples in developing nations. The term is much less used in developed Western nations. It is used in Japan, however (Maita and Kaizu 1998), and has been adopted widely in China, through the term *shengtai luyou*, ecology tourism (Buckley et al. 2008). This includes cultural and health-related components not generally attributed to Western definitions of ecotourism.

Significance for Sustainability

No matter how sustainability is defined in a tourism context (Buckley 2012), conservation of the natural environment is a key component. In its most fundamental and meaningful sense, namely the continuing ability of the planet to support populations and societies of humans as well as other species, there are two key components to sustainability. The first is to stabilize and reduce both the size of the global human population, and per capita consumption and pollution of natural resources and environment. The second is to maintain biological diversity and ecosystem services and functions, including the fundamentals of edible food, drinkable water, breathable air, and stable climate (Buckley 2012).

Currently, conservation of biodiversity is under particularly severe stress in many parts of the world, with species extinctions continuing despite international efforts to prevent them. Many individual species are under threat from a wide range of human activities and related disturbances. Two particularly severe types of threats are the large-scale logging and clearance of native vegetation for industrialized agriculture in developing nations with high biodiversity and the targeted poaching of individual rare species for the illegal international trade in animal parts. Both these activities are driven ultimately by networks of wealthy, powerful, and unscrupulous individuals, with local residents either coerced or co-opted to allow such activities to continue.

Ecotourism can, in some instances at least, help to counteract these threats to sustainability by providing a local source of income that depends on intact natural ecosystems and biodiversity, and thus providing both means and incentives to protect them. The means may include financial capital that can fund lawsuits, and political capital generated both by regional economic activity and by international publicity from tour operators and their clients. Worldwide, there are as yet relatively few private tourism companies that make a demonstrable net contribution to conservation of threatened species and ecosystems and hence to this key aspect of sustainability (Buckley 2010a, 2010b, 2011, 2012). There are, however, a number of public national park systems that now rely heavily on revenue from individual park visitors (Buckley 2009c). There are also many private companies that claim to use minimal-impact practices or to contribute to human social welfare, but whose net overall effect on sustainability is nonetheless negative (Buckley 2009a, 2009b, 2011).

Regional Patterns and Dynamics

Because of differences in history, culture, environment, economics, and modern politics, ecotourism has evolved in different ways in different countries, producing regional signatures that are recognizable at continental scale (Buckley 2003). Within the Asian region, there are also distinct differences between individual countries in the types of product available, the principal markets to whom they are offered, and the ways in which they are regulated and promoted by governments. Most discussion of this information, however, is available only in the languages of the countries concerned and has not percolated into the English-language academic literature. There is only limited interchange between China and the West, for example, regarding government, industry, and academic understandings of ecotourism-(Buckley et al. 2008). Similar situations exist for Japan (Maita and Kaizu 1998) and Russia (Chizhova 2004). Individual case studies of successful ecotourism ventures have been reported for countries throughout the Asian region (Buckley 2003, 2010a), but these are isolated instances that do not convey a full picture of ecotourism policies and practices in the countries concerned.

Across most of the Asian region, increasing wealth coupled in some cases with greater political freedom has led to enormous expansion in domestic tourism markets. Initially, the largest components of these new markets were in travel to visit friends and relatives and in urban tourism. As of 2012, there have recently been large expansions in the nature-based, wildlife, adventure, and ecotourism markets. It seems that international tourism, both inbound and outbound, has helped to catalyze domestic outdoor tourism in these countries.

In China, the national government, many provincial governments, and a number of local governments have all adopted policies to promote various forms of ecotourism. Most of the main attractions are scenic, commonly with associated historical connotations. Nationally known icon destinations, such as Jiuzhaigou National Park and World Heritage Area, attract up to 20 million visitors per year, which has created significant impacts and management issues (Buckley 2010a). The giant panda remains the icon of Chinese wildlife tourism, and panda reserves such as Wolong are correspondingly popular, even though most of the panda-watching opportunities are at captive breeding areas that act as large zoos. The western Chinese provinces of Yunnan and Sichuan, and increasingly also Tibet, are major domestic tourism destinations for residents of the eastern seaboard cities, supplementing longstanding destinations such as the karst landscapes of Guilin and Kunming.

A number of the minority peoples of western China and adjacent nations hold cultural festivals of various types, and some of these have become tourist events. Particularly well known is the Naadam Festival of the Mongolian peoples, which showcases the Mongolian cultural landscape (Buckley, Ollenburg, and Zhong 2008). In western Yunnan Province, one local government area has renamed itself Shangri-La in order to attract tourists (Buckley 2010a). Most recently, China's national government tourism portfolio has established a national ecotourism certification program. The approach taken is rather different from tourism ecocertification programs in other countries: instead of certifying tour operators, products, or guides, it certifies destinations as worthy of an ecotourism designation (Zhong, Buckley, and Xie 2007). This is likely to become a significant feature of domestic tourism marketing within China.

Ecotourism in India also has a strong focus on national parks and icon wildlife species, most notably the tiger. Indian national parks rely principally on government funding at both central and state levels, with less than 10 percent of revenue coming from visitor fees. In general, there is no tourism development within the parks themselves, but there are growing agglomerations of tourist accommodations in the gateway areas of the better-known parks. There is now a substantial, though as yet relatively unsophisticated, self-drive domestic wildlife tourism market (i.e., traveling in one's own vehicle), within the large and wealthy Indian middle class. Inbound international ecotour operators commonly offer packages that include scenic, cultural, and architectural as well as wildlife-watching components.

One interesting recent development is the construction of upmarket ecolodges adjacent to some of the national parks in Madhya Pradesh, modeled on the highly successful game lodges of eastern and southern Africa. These have been built by a joint venture between the African operator & Beyond and the Taj Hotel Group from India. The initial clientele for these Taj Safari Lodges consisted principally of international wildlife and bird-watching tourists. For at least some of these lodges, however, the majority of the market is now domestic (Buckley 2010a). In the lowland Terai region where Nepal borders India to the north, upmarket wildlife-watching lodges have a long history. Tiger Tops and its associated lodges at Chitwan and Bardia national parks are particularly well known and currently emphasize minimal-impact management measures. For historical reasons, a small number of lodges in Nepal are inside the boundaries of these national parks. The majority, however, are in gateway areas, as is the case in India.

Outdoor tourism in the Himalayas focuses principally on scenery and adventure activities, though there are also growing community-based, wildlife, and bird-watching components. This region includes most of Nepal, Bhutan, much of Tibet and adjacent provinces of western China, and the Indian states of Himachal Pradesh in the northwest and Arunachal Pradesh in the northeast. It also includes the mountainous areas of Afghanistan and northern Pakistan, which historically supported thriving tourist industries but are now largely off limits because of severe security concerns, including military actions. Both international and domestic tour operators in the Himalayan nations offer a range of mountaineering, trekking, and whitewater rafting tours (Buckley 2006, 2010c), some of which qualify as ecotourism.

There is also a growing adventure tourism market, with a largely domestic clientele, in the Sayan Mountains of southern Siberia, though many of these also involve hunting and fishing and would probably not be considered ecotourism. The Lake Baikal region, however, is visited by international natural history tours, especially for bird watching. Similarly, the Kamchatka Peninsula on Russia's eastern seaboard is known for its volcanoes, grizzly bears, and salmon fishing, all of which attract both domestic and international tourists (Buckley 2006). In Mongolia and the adjacent Chinese province of Inner Mongolia, nature-based tourism relies principally on the desert landscapes of the Gobi and the high-altitude grasslands used by the nomadic horsemen of central Asia (Buckley, Ollenburg, and Zhong 2008).

Southeast Asia is a much smaller region than the countries considered above, but it has a rapidly developing ecotourism sector. Nature-based attractions include, for example: opportunities to see orangutans in Malaysia and Indonesia; the limestone islands of Ha Long Bay in Vietnam and Phang Nga Bay in Thailand; both lowland and montane rain forest national parks throughout the region; and a wide range of cultural, archaeological, and historical features. There is also a significant adventure tourism sector, with a growing domestic component. Many of the world's most famous surfing destinations, for example, are on the southwestern coastline and islands of Indonesia (Buckley 2010c). Cultural aspects, as well as nature and adventure, form an important component of inbound international tourism to Indonesia, and also to Papua New Guinea and Pacific Island nations such as Fiji, Tonga, and Samoa. Examples of individual ecotourism enterprises in each of these countries have been compiled by Ralf Buckley (2003, 2010a) and Heather Zeppel (2006).

Asia is a vast region, stretching from the permanently frozen Russian Arctic and the tundra of northern Siberia to the tropical and equatorial rain forest of Southeast Asia; from the high peaks and plateaus of Tibet and the Himalayas to small Pacific Island nations barely above sea level; and from the hyperarid deserts of the Taklamakan to the permanently humid rain forests and the mangrove forests of Southeast Asia and the Sundarbans. There is an equivalent diversity in human cultures, with the modern civilizations of countries such as India, China, Nepal, and Thailand reflecting a continuous history of several millennia. Throughout these regions there are also tribal peoples with relatively small populations, some of which promote their traditional cultural practices as tourist attractions. Both human and natural environments are thus so highly diverse in the Asian region that there is no single signature style for

Asian ecotourism products or enterprises. In addition, the pace of domestic economic, social, and political change in many Asian nations is particularly rapid, and the scale of little-studied domestic tourism far exceeds that of better-known international tourism. The Asian region is already highly significant for global ecotourism, and current indications are that this significance will continue to increase.

Organizations and People

Ecotourism in Asia is influenced by organizations of the same types as on other continents. Most influential are the tourism ministries and agencies in the national governments of individual countries and their counterpart industry associations. State and provincial government agencies are also very influential in some countries, particularly India and China. It is these government agencies that fund tourism infrastructure and that determine what particular areas and aspects will be featured in their tourism marketing campaigns. In addition, if there are national certification programs, whether for ecotourism or for tourism quality standards more broadly, these are likely to be far more influential than voluntary private-sector programs, even if the latter are international.

Multilateral agencies of the United Nations, such as the World Tourism Organization (UNWTO), Environment Programme. (UNEP), Educational, Scientific and Cultural Organization (UNESCO), and Development Programme (UNDP), are active throughout the Asian region, and so also are international nongovernmental organizations (NGOs) such as Conservation International, the Nature Conservancy and the World Wide Fund for Nature. All of these have interests in ecotourism, and this also applies for a number of domestic NGOs. There are cross-border consultative organizations of various types (e.g., in the Mekong River basin) but the individual countries concerned generally seem to act in their own interests with little consideration of their neighbors. In ecotourism as in other sectors, in Asia as worldwide, each country tends to pursue its own initiatives, more in competition than cooperation.

Outlook

There is every reason to suppose that outdoor nature-based and adventure tourism will continue to grow throughout the Asian region, driven largely by the rapidly increasing wealth and political freedom of the enormous domestic populations within the Asian region itself. How much of this growth will adopt principles and practices of ecotourism (Buckley 2009a, 2011) is much more difficult to predict. Currently, concerns over conservation, minimal-impact management, and environmental education are generally stronger among international inbound tourists than within the domestic markets. There are instances throughout the region, however, where both public organizations such as national parks agencies, and individual private tourism enterprises have successfully used tourism to contribute to conservation and local communities. To date, these have relied largely on international visitors. As in other parts of the world, there are cultural, socioeconomic, and legal factors that determine how fast and how far these approaches will spread into the much larger domestic market.

Key legal factors relate, for example, to the regulation of tourism in protected areas, but also to the regulation of large-scale high-impact developments in competing sectors such as forestry, mining, and hydropower. Economic growth boosts domestic tourism but also increases demand from these competing sectors. The social role and significance of tourism, and of nature-based and ecotourism specifically, are very strongly affected by cultural factors. Culture also provides the context for attitudes toward conservation and the welfare of individual animals; opinions about large-scale development in different industrial sectors and the degree to which its environmental impacts should be controlled; and relationships between individuals, enterprises, and governments.

Many cultures associated with eastern Asian ethnicities, such as those of China, Japan, and Korea, for example, have much more limited concern about suffering by individual animals than cultures associated with Caucasian ethnicities. Buddhist cultures, in contrast, generally have much more stringent rules than the West against causing harm to other creatures. There is a strong commercial demand within China for the body parts of various rare animal species, and this drives wildlife poaching industries throughout Asia and indeed worldwide, notably including tigers in India. Tiger tourism can help to fund anti-poaching patrols in Indian national parks, and there is now a large and growing Indian domestic market for self-drive visits to national parks in search of tigers. Low-impact wildlife watching relies, however, on vehicles following an orderly protocol to approach animals slowly, indirectly, and in turn. Self-drive tourists can cause considerable disturbance even to habituated tigers.

While it has been suggested (Cater 2006) that ecotourism is a Western construct, in reality it seems to have transboundary parallels and antecedents worldwide, including in Asia. As ecotourism develops in different parts of the world, it blends local and international approaches and cultural contexts, and in consequence, both policies and products differ between countries. As noted earlier, the Asian region has enormous cultural as well as environmental diversity, and we can expect that many different models of ecotourism will evolve throughout the region.

Ralf BUCKLEY
Griffith University, Australia

See also Biodiversity Conservation Legislation (China); Consumerism; Education, Environmental (*several articles*); Endangered Species; Genetic Resources; Indigenous Peoples; Media Coverage of the Environment; Microfinance; Nongovernmental Organizations (NGOs); Parks and Preserves; Rural Development; Rural Livelihoods; Traditional Knowledge (China); Traditional Knowledge (India)

FURTHER READING

Buckley, Ralf C. (2003). *Case studies in ecotourism*. Wallingford, UK: CAB International.

Buckley, Ralf C. (2006). *Adventure tourism*. Wallingford, UK: CAB International.

Buckley, Ralf C. (2009a). *Ecotourism: Principles and practices*. Wallingford, UK: CAB International.

Buckley, Ralf C. (2009b). Evaluating the net effects of ecotourism on the environment: A framework, first assessment and future research. *Journal of Sustainable Tourism 17(6):* 643–672.

Buckley, Ralf C. (2009c). Parks and tourism. *Public Library of Science Biology, 7*(6), e1000143.

Buckley, Ralf C. (2010a). *Conservation tourism*. Wallingford, UK: CAB International.

Buckley, Ralf C. (2010b). Safaris can help conservation. *Nature, 467*(7319), 1047.

Buckley, Ralf C. (2010c). *Adventure tourism management*. London: Elsevier.

Buckley, Ralf C. (2011). Tourism and environment. *Annual Review of Environment and Resources 36*, 397–416.

Buckley, Ralf C. (2012). Sustainable tourism: research and reality. *Annals of Tourism Research*. doi: 10.1016/j.annals.2012.02.003

Buckley, Ralf C.; Cater, Carl; Zhong, Linsheng; & Chen, Tian. (2008). Shengtai luyou: Cross-cultural comparison in ecotourism. *Annals of Tourism Research, 35*(4), 945–968.

Buckley, Ralf C.; Ollenburg, Claudia; & Zhong, Linsheng. (2008). Cultural landscape in Mongolian tourism. *Annals of Tourism Research, 35*(1), 47–61.

Cater, Erlet. (2006). Ecotourism as a Western construct. *Journal of Ecotourism, 5*(1–2), 23–39.

Chizhova, Vera P. (2004). Impacts and management of hikers in Kavkazsky State Biosphere Reserve, Russia. In Ralf C. Buckley (Ed.), *Environmental impacts of ecotourism* (pp. 377–381). Wallingford, UK: CAB International.

Font, Xavier, & Buckley, Ralf C. (Eds.). (2001). *Tourism ecolabelling: Certification and promotion of sustainable management*. Wallingford, UK: CAB International.

Maita, A., & Kaizu, Y. (Eds.). (1998). *Entering the ecotourism age*. Shuppan, Tokyo: Makino. (in Japanese).

Saarinen, Jarkko; Becker, Fritz; Manwa, Haretsebe; & Wilson, Deon. (Eds.). (2009). *Sustainable tourism in southern Africa: Local communities and natural resources in transition*. Bristol, UK: Channel View Publications.

Zeppel, Heather D. (2006). *Indigenous ecotourism: Sustainable development and management*. Wallingford, UK: CAB International.

Zhong, Linsheng; Buckley, Ralf C.; & Xie, Ting. (2007). Chinese perspectives on tourism eco-certification. *Annals of Tourism Research, 34*(3), 808–811.

Education, Environmental (China)

As a global giant in size, resources, and population, China will be a key player in upcoming decades as the world addresses global environmental issues. As it deals with its internal challenges, the country is implementing environmental education on all societal and governmental levels as it experiences industrial, economic, and consumer growth.

The good news about the environment in China is that the Chinese people and various Chinese governmental agencies are becoming more and more aware of the bad news: long-term environmental abuse creating a bleak reality and promising a dire future. World Watch Institute president emeritus Christopher Flavin once said:

> During the course of this century, Asia in general and China in particular will stand ever-closer to the center of the global economy and environment.... China has become central to the challenge of environmentally sustainable development. Rapid economic growth is propelling many of China's 1.3 billion people into the consumer society, increasing the pressures on its own resources as well as those of other nations. (Flavin 2004, 1)

He further elaborated that the decisions China makes regarding its environment will "have a major bearing on the future health of humanity and the planet due to its large population size, growing economic power, and wide cultural influence" (Flavin 2004, 1–2). China is a huge country with diverse natural and cultural features. This article provides an overview of environmental education in mainland China only, as the complexities of EE in the two Special Administrative Regions—Hong Kong and Macao—and in Taiwan warrant articles of their own.

Nationwide, a grassroots-based environmental movement is gradually taking hold. This bottom-up activism focuses on public education and voluntarism around issues such as water and air pollution, waste management, energy conservation, biodiversity preservation, enforcement of environmental laws and regulations, and even on civic engagement and democratic governance. Concern for environmental problems and ecological degradation in China has now become the public domain. Many Chinese communities have become aware of the importance of environmental sustainability in achieving sustainable development and an ecological civilization. The number of individuals and communities committed to addressing environment-related problems has increased steadily since the late 1970s, with exponential growth of environment-related nongovernmental organizations (NGOs) since the late 1990s and the "green school" movement at the turn of twenty-first century.

Major approaches to environmental education in China include formal education (undertaken by K–12 schools and postsecondary education institutions), nonformal education (including programs and activities made available by environmental NGOs, museums, and parks), and informal education (such as the media, newspapers, books and magazines, and community poster boards). These various agencies for environmental education often collaborate among themselves, as illustrated by the Environmental Educators' Initiative program described later in this article.

The Global Context

Several international conferences organized by the United Nations and the agreements reached at these conferences have shaped the development of environmental education (EE) in the global context. According to the report on the first Intergovernmental Conference on Environmental Education in Tbilisi, Georgia, USSR, in 1977, EE is a process aimed at developing "a world population that is aware of, and concerned about, the total environment and its associated problems, and which has the knowledge, skills, attitudes, motivation, and commitment to work individually and collectively toward solutions of current problems and the prevention of new ones." The former Canadian Research Chair in Environmental Education Lucie Sauvé wrote that EE is basically "education about our relationship with the environment." This relationship can be broken into categories. Environment is "considered as nature (to be appreciated, respected, and preserved); as a resource (to be managed and shared); as a problem (to be avoided or to be solved); as a system (to understand so as to improve decision-making); as a place to live (to get to know and improve); as the biosphere (in which all live together over the long term); and as a community project (in which one is to become actively involved)" (Sauvé 2002, 1).

Since the late 1980s, education for sustainable development (ESD)—which was promoted by the World Commission on Environment and Development's Brundtland Report, also known as *Our Common Future* (1987), later endorsed by the 1992 Earth Summit in Rio de Janeiro, and adopted by United Nations Agenda 21—has been gaining popularity worldwide. The debate about the relationship between EE and ESD, however, continues to the present day. Agenda 21 is a historical document that has guided the international discourse in EE since the early 1990s, calling for reorienting education toward sustainable development; that is, education for the kind of "development that meets the needs of the present without compromising the ability of future generations to meet their own needs" (WCED 1987, 41). The United Nations Decade of ESD (2005–2014) is a global initiative to meet ESD challenges. Over 100 Regional Centers of Expertise (RCE) in ESD have been created worldwide under the leadership of the United Nations University Institute of Advanced Studies (UNU-IAS). Higher education institutions such as universities, colleges, and technical institutes are lead organizations in this REC-ESD initiative to respond to the ESD decade challenge.

Development of EE in China

Environmental education in China has been mainly following international development in EE, while maintaining its own unique characteristics. Starting in the 1970s, both the content and methodology of environmental education in China, as well as the people engaged in EE work, have broadened and diversified.

As stated in the academic journal *Chinese Education and Society*, Premier Zhou Enlai of China was regarded as the first person to bring environmental protection into the limelight in China (Editorial Department 2004, 40). He arranged the First National Environmental Protection Workshop during the Cultural Revolution in 1973, the same year that EE was formally established in China via a broad legislative mandate that provided for environmental protection. The mandate, titled Regulations about Protecting and Improving the Environment, included a section focusing specifically on EE. Ever since, EE in China has grown steadily in sophistication (Kwan and Lidston 1997, 88).

In China's seventh Five-Year Plan (1986–1990), the director of the Centre for Environmental Education and Communications of the State Environmental Protection Agency (SEPA) stressed three main objectives for environmental protection: "First, SEPA sought to raise the environmental awareness of all Chinese citizens. Second, it hoped to raise the political, professional, and managerial capabilities of those engaged in environmental protection. Third, it set out to increase the number of environmental protection specialists throughout all segments of Chinese society" (Kwan and Lidston, 1997, 88). The SEPA document emphasized the importance of developing professional leaders to promote EE in schools and workplaces.

In 1992, the State Education Commission and SEPA jointly held the First National Environmental Education Workshop. The principle that "education is the foundation of environmental protection" was presented at the meeting, and the importance of EE in basic education was affirmed. That meeting propelled EE into a new phase in China (Editorial Department 2004, 41).

In March 2003, the Ministry of Education of China issued a memo on the publication of the "Outline for Environmental Education in Elementary and Middle Schools," which is seen as "new assurance to the sustainable development strategy" in China. The release and implementation of this document indicates that the national education system is "undergoing a major overhaul" (Editorial Department 2004, 40).

EE in the Formal Education System

Environmental education entered formal schooling in China at the tertiary level (Lin and Ross 2004, 5). Beijing Normal University became the first higher-education institution in China to offer a graduate degree program in EE in 1993. Since then, the EE academic community has become actively involved with EE scholars and activists from outside of China, and they have launched a series of training sessions in EE. Environmental education used to be integrated into existing subjects of study, and is now offered as stand-alone courses, especially at the tertiary education level. Integrating EE materials in various courses and curricularization of EE can form a new and mutually complementary education framework.

The Green School Movement

The "green schools" promoted by the Center for Environmental Education and Communication (CEEC) of the Ministry of Environmental Protection of China has played a key role in developing EE for elementary and middle school administrators, teachers, and students. The criteria for green schools vary from province to province. In general they include structural guarantees (including an EE leadership team headed by the school principal, EE plan for the school, and funding allocation for EE); the physical aspect of the school (water and energy conservation, school-grounds greening, waste management, environmental management and pollution control); and the human dimensions of the school (infusion of environmental protection knowledge, practice, and regulations into school curriculum and instruction; EE-themed extra-curricular activities and school- and community-wide public campaigns; EE-related displays; environmental awareness and practices of students, teachers, and administrative personnel; and teaching and learning achievements). Green schools have become a significant development in Chinese education, with more than 4,000 schools registered as green schools nationwide by 2003; by 2004, there were more than 17,200 green schools in China (Lin and Ross 2004, 7). There is, however, a tendency to pursue quantity at the cost of quality. According to the educator Zhang Yuanzeng (2004), "a 'green school' is an open school. . . . [It] breaks down the psychological and cultural barrier that separates itself from the outside world, and becomes a part of the social environment (e.g., the local community)." Authentic EE is envisioned much as "quality education" across the curriculum; that is, it requires holistic thinking and the ability to explore, reflect, and act from both teachers and students (Lin and Ross 2004, 8). In reality and in practice, fewer schools than are claimed can truly be considered green schools.

The Environmental Educators' Initiative Program

In 1997, realizing the importance of high-quality environmental educators to the success of environmental education, China joined with international efforts to develop professional environmental educators for the country. The Environmental Educators' Initiative (EEI) project was initiated by the World Wide Fund for Nature (WWF) China Office, funded by British Petroleum (BP), and jointly managed by the Ministry of Education of China, WWF, and BP. The overall objectives of EEI included capacity building for environmental educators, integration of EE into the basic education curriculum, and sustainability of EE. The initiative introduced student-centered and inquiry-based learning, which complemented the developing Chinese curriculum. With the program deeply rooted in the formal education system, the EEI hopes that EE will eventually reach 100 percent of the 197 million school students in China. The EEI project and the basic education reform in China, as a historical coincidence, focused on similar objectives and promoted similar educational practices. The potential impact of EEI on Chinese education and society is believed to be tremendous, but it remains to be studied further.

Nonformal and Informal Environmental Education

Environmental education has gone beyond the formal education system. It is now "taught to tourists in recreational spots, farmers in rural areas, media operators, administrators who plan courses and edit teaching materials at the national and regional level, and decision-makers in the government" (Tian 2004, 36).

The 1992 United Nations Conference on Environment and Development, known as the Rio Earth Summit, and the adoption of Agenda 21 have made the Chinese public aware of environmental problems facing industrialized and developing nations. The public in China began to learn about global ecological and environmental issues from the media coverage of this international event. The Chinese government gradually began to pay more attention to environmental issues. This kind of government action prompted the public to become "more cognizant about environment related issues" (Tian 2004, 37).

Environmental NGOs have been carrying out a large number of activities to promote EE in China. Friends of Nature, established in 1994, was the first environmental NGO registered in China, with the aim to "promote environmental education, nature protection, public participation, build and diffuse green culture with China's own characteristics" (Hong, Guo, and Marinova 2006, 328). The agenda of Friends of Nature goes beyond the purely green concerns about the natural environment into the broader arena of sustainability, which includes issues about social justice, equity, and intergenerational rights (Hong, Guo, and Marinova 2006, 329). Since then, environmental NGOs and environment-related clubs or associations in universities have grown in both numbers and in their impact on Chinese government and society. Chinese NGOs are different from NGOs in the West, in that Chinese NGOs usually must be affiliated with or "sponsored" by state-authorized agencies. Despite the tight state control on NGOs, environmental NGOs in China have been able to operate with a share of autonomy and have managed to "push the envelope" in their interactions with governmental organizations. The issues taken on by these environmental NGOs have also shifted from localized environmental issues to issues of global concern, such as climate change.

Environmental NGOs have also had significant influence on EE in schools. They connect their environmental activities with the schools' educational system and increase the students' participation in environmental activities. They have facilitated the establishment of EE centers and green schools. The EEI program is a good example of such collaboration between the formal education system and nonformal organizations in EE. Environmental NGOs, such as Friends of Nature, Green Earth Volunteers, Global Village, and Green Rivers, have played a special and important role in disseminating knowledge and promoting environmental protection in China. These NGOs in general elicit wide participation from both society and schoolchildren due to their focus on ordinary people's interests. They also enjoy trust from a wide range of professionals including university professors, journalists, lawyers, and celebrities, all of whom ensure a sound base of support. For instance, according to one report, since its establishment in 1996, membership in Friends of Nature has grown to more than eight thousand, including more than three thousand active participants and over thirty groups, and it has won numerous national and international awards (Hong, Guo, and Marinova 2006, 326). It is argued in the same article that irrespective of the wide range of achievements made by environmental NGOs in China, "their capacity for activities is not strong enough to overturn China's ever-increasing environmental problems. There is also not much cooperation between the various NGOs and . . . there is no law in China related to environmental NGOs" to ensure that NGOs have a lawful position and rights (Hong, Guo, and Marinova 2006, 300). All in all, environmental NGOs in China "have become quite influential in policy making and environmental education, and are the key to understanding China's environmental movement and education" (Hong, Guo, and Marinova 2006, 324).

In the informal education sector, Chinese government (especially at the national level) has embarked on massive public campaigns through the media (television, newspapers, radios, the Internet) to raise public awareness and understanding of environmental problems. For example, China's Environmental Watch media campaign was jointly initiated in 1993 by the Committee on Environment and Resources Protection of the National People's Congress (NPC), the Propaganda Department of the Central Committee of the Chinese Communist Party, the Ministry of Radio and Television, and the National Environmental Protection Agency to facilitate China's Agenda 21. It is aimed at educating the public about current environmental problems and how everyone can contribute to minimizing such problems (Chen 1999). The scope of governmental involvement in public education about the environment is unique in global terms and is a crucial element in understanding the environmental movement in China.

Characteristics of EE in China

Environmental education in China, as a kind of state-supported public good, is mostly equated with education about environmental protection and environmental awareness, and it is often treated as environmental science and technology education (Ji 2007). It aims at serving sustainable development goals as well as part of the larger goals of achieving quality education in China.

Environmental education in China operates primarily from the point of view that the environment is seen as a group of problems to be solved and avoided as well as resources to be sustainably managed and used. This perception is only starting to broaden to include views of the environment as nature to be appreciated and respected, and with its own intrinsic value; as a system or places to live; and as a community project to be actively involved in. Mark Elvin, author of the book *The Retreat of the Elephants: An Environmental History of China*, wrote that the "classical Chinese culture was as hostile to forests as it was fond of individual trees" (Elvin 2004, xvii). This paradox in the Chinese psyche is reflected in EE in China as the mechanistic and technocentric scientism blends with the pursuit of spiritual development and an ecological civilization.

Environmental education in China is anthropocentric—that is, a human-centered view of the world. The majority of people are concerned with human health, safety, and welfare issues. "The human-centered resource management mentality" of state-supported EE in China can only go so far in achieving real harmony between humans and the rest of nature (Ji 2007).

The major constraint of EE in China is the examination-oriented formal education system, which keeps most, if not all, teachers from trying to integrate EE topics and methods into their teaching practices. Exam pressures inhibit teaching innovation and embrace a too-narrow definition of school learning (Lin and Ross 2004, 8). Schools in general, and high schools in particular, lack positive attitudes toward and a commitment to carrying out EE. To further EE in formal education, the teaching system needs to transition from an emphasis on exams to an emphasis on quality education. Preparing teachers (both preservice and in-service) to take on the challenges and opportunities in EE is a pressing task not only for China but also the world.

EE in China has been summarized as "(1) a response to environmental degradation and the practical needs of society; (2) a knowledge-focused area of scientific learning in the national interest; (3) a field of study with Chinese characteristics; (4) a political tool and an element in national propaganda; (5) an administratively led and centrally controlled innovation; and (6) a field of study in conflict with mainstream education" (Stimpson and Kwan 2001).

Outlook for the Future

As long as a high-stakes, examination-oriented ideology dominates the formal education system in China, environmental education at the basic education level will remain a neglected subject or a "just for show" area of study. In higher education, the outlook for EE is brighter, as highly demanded EE- and ESD-related courses are being offered at more and more universities.

In the domains of nonformal and informal EE, hundreds of environmental NGOs have played and will continue to play an essential role, as will the mass media. Diverse individuals and NGOs are involved in EE, where there is much room for multilateral collaboration and collective consciousness-raising.

The maturity and environmental activism displayed by environmental NGOs has not yet appeared in China's formal education system. This is not surprising considering that the political function of formal schooling is a means to enforce conformity among subjects of the state, rather than cultivating well-informed and active citizens. Bottom-up environmentalism and EE will continue to play an essential role in the revitalization and development of a civil society in China.

Much of the EE in China is focused on environmental protection knowledge, skills, and values, heavily leaning on the scientific and technical aspects (the empirical). What is needed to balance and to achieve breakthrough in EE work in China lies in the ethical and aesthetical domains. There is much potential for progress in both the theoretical and practical aspects of EE by learning from Chinese literature and from traditional Chinese philosophies such as Daoism, Confucianism, and Buddhism.

Readers interested in gaining an in-depth understanding of any particular aspect of EE in China should consult the following resources as well as those listed in the Further Reading section. The journal *International Research in Geographical and Environmental Education* (vol. 4, issue no. 2, 1995) devoted a forum to environmental education in China. Two issues of the 2004 journal *Chinese Education and Society* (vol. 37, issue nos. 3 and 4) were dedicated to the EE, ESD, and green school movements in China. *Schooling for Sustainable Development in Chinese Communities*, edited by John Chi-Kin Lee and Michael Williams (2009), gives details to the focus of this article, especially regarding EE in Hong Kong as well as in Taiwan and Macao. *Environmental Education* magazine, published in the Chinese language, also provides a platform for environmental educators and activists to share and exercise ideas.

The environmental education initiatives at various levels and by different institutions in China are complex and evolving. Ignoring China and its associated environmental and social issues is not an option for any country. Education has a crucial role to play, and a long way to go.

Xia JI
University of Regina

See also Activism, Judicial; China; Consumerism; Corporate Accountability (China); Education, Environmental (India); Education, Environmental (Japan); Education, Female; Five-Year Plans; Green Collar Jobs; India; Information and Communication Technologies (ICT); Japan; Korean Peninsula; Media Coverage of the Environment; Nongovernmental Organizations (NGOs); Southeast Asia

FURTHER READING

Chen, Yuxiang. (1999). China's environmental watch: A media campaign. Retrieved March 12, 2012, from http://www.unescap.org/drpad/vc/conference/bg_cn_16_cew.htm

Economy, Elizabeth C. (2005). *The river runs black: The environmental challenge to China's future.* Ithaca, NY: Cornell University Press.

Editorial Department. (2004). The environmental education outline and the environmental education magazine. *Chinese Education and Society, 37*(3), 39–45.

Elvin, Mark. (2004). *The retreat of the elephants: An environmental history of China.* New Haven, CT: Yale University Press.

Flavin, Christopher. (2004). Hearing on Asia's environmental challenges: Testimony of Christopher Flavin. Worldwatch Institute. Retrieved July 5, 2005, from http://www.worldwatch.org/node/1796

Hong, Jin.; Guo, Xiumei.; & Marinova, Dora. (2006). NGOs and environmental education in China. In Sandra Wooltorton & Dora Marinova (Eds.), *Sharing wisdom for our future. Environmental education in action: Proceedings of the 2006 Conference of the Australian Association of Environmental Education* (pp. 324–332). Retrieved July 10, 2010, from http://www.aaee.org.au/docs/2006%20conference/35_Hong_Guo_Marinova.pdf

Jacoby, Jill B., & Ji, Xia. (2010). *Artists as transformative leaders for sustainability.* In Benjamin W. Redekop (Ed.), *Leadership for environmental sustainability* (pp. 133–144). New York: Routledge Studies in Business Ethics.

Ji, Xia. (2001). Teachers' perceptions of citizen characteristics and environmental concerns: A comparative study of teachers in Minnesota, Hong Kong, and Guang Dong. Unpublished research report for the United States Information Agency's College and University Affiliations Program (USIA-CUAP) international project.

Ji, Xia. (2007). Teacher educators' significant life experiences: Stories and reflections from the environmental educators' initiative (EEI) in China. (Dissertation, University of Minnesota, 2007). *Dissertation Abstracts International-A,* 68/08, 3350 (UMI No. 3279680).

Jiao, Zhiyan; Zen, Hongying; & Song, Xuhong. (2004). An overview of "green school" development in China in 2001. *Chinese Education and Society, 37*(3), 49–54.

Knapp, Doug. (2000). The Thessaloniki declaration: A wake-up call for environmental education. *Journal of Environmental Education, 31*(3), 32–39.

Kwan, Tammy, & Lidston, John. (1997). Environmental education in China: National policy interpreted on local level. *Environmental Education Research, 4*(1), 87–98.

Lai, On-Kwok. (1998). The perplexity of sponsored environment education: A critical view on Hong Kong and its future. *Environmental Education Research, 4*(3), 269–284.

Lin, Jing, & Ross, Heidi. (2004). Guest editors' introduction: Context and history of the rise of environmental education in China and the "green schools." *Chinese Education and Society, 37*(3), 5–9.

Lu, Hongyan. (2003). Bamboo sprouts after the rain: The history of university student environmental associations in China. *China Environment Series (Woodrow Wilson International Center for Scholars), 6,* 55–66. Retrieved June 6, 2010, from http://wilsoncenter.net/topics/pubs/5-feature_4.pdf

McBeach, Jerry, & McBeach, Jennifer. (2009). Environmental education in China: A preliminary comparative assessment. Retrieved June 6, 2010, from http://www.ccny.cuny.edu/aacs/Conference_Paper_2009/Jerry_and_Jenifer_McBeath.doc

Ministry of Education of China. (2003). *Zhōng xiǎoxuéshēng huánjìng jiàoyù zhuāntí jiàoyù dàgāng* [Outline for environmental education in elementary and middle schools]. Retrieved June 6, 2010, from http://d.wanfangdata.com.cn/Periodical_hjjy200304001.aspx

Palmer, Joy A. (1998). *Environmental education in the 21st century: Theory, practice, progress and promise.* London: Routledge.

Palmer, Joy A., & Neal, Philip. (1994). *The handbook of environmental education.* London: Routledge.

Sauvé, Lucie. (2002). Environmental education: Possibilities and constraints. *Connect: UNESCO International Science, Technology & Environmental Education Newsletter, 27*(1–2), 1–4. Retrieved July 10, 2010, from http://unesdoc.unesco.org/images/0014/001462/146295e.pdf

Stimpson, Philip G. (1997). Environmental challenge and curricular responses in Hong Kong. *Environmental Education Research, 3*(3), 345–357.

Stimpson, Philip G., & Kwan, Francis Wong Bing. (2001). Environmental education in Guangzhou in the People's Republic of China: Global theme, politically determined. *Environmental Education Research, 7*(4), 397–412.

Taiwan Embassy. (2010, May 27). Taiwan passes Environmental Education Act. Retrieved June 16, 2010, from http://www.taiwanembassy.org/ct.asp?xItem=143313&ctNode=2237&mp=1&nowPage=1&pagesize=50

Taiwan Today. (2010, May 19). Environmental Education Act passed in legislature. Retrieved June 16, 2010, from http://www.taiwantoday.tw/ct.asp?xItem=103733&CtNode=436

Tian, Qing. (2004). Historical review of environmental education in China. *Chinese Education and Society, 37*(3), 34–38.

Tsang, Eric Po Keung. (2003). Heading towards environmental citizenship: The case of the green school initiative. In Peter Hills & Man Chi-sum (Eds.), *New directions in environmental education for Hong Kong* (pp. 33–42). Hong Kong: University of Hong Kong Press.

United Nations Conference on Environment and Development (UNCED) & United Nations Environment Programme (UNEP). (1992). Agenda 21. Retrieved March 8, 2012, from http://www.unep.org/Documents.Multilingual/Default.asp?documentid=52

United Nations Educational, Scientific and Cultural Organization (UNESCO). (1978). The Tbilisi declaration. Retrieved June 6,

2010, from http://www.cnr.uidaho.edu/css487/The_Tbilisi_Declaration.pdf

United Nations Educational, Scientific and Cultural Organization (UNESCO). (2011). Education for sustainable development. Retrieved March 13, 2012, from http://www.unesco.org/new/en/education/themes/leading-the-international-agenda/education-for-sustainable-development/

United Nations Educational, Scientific and Cultural Organization, Education and Information for Human Development (UNESCO-EPD). (1997). Declaration of Thessaloniki. Retrieved July 10, 2010, from http://unesdoc.unesco.org/images/0011/001177/117772eo.pdf

United Nations University Institute of Advanced Studies (UNU-IAS). (2011). Regional centers of expertise in education for sustainable development (RCE-ESD). Retrieved July 5, 2010, from http://www.ias.unu.edu/sub_page.aspx?catID=108&ddlID=183

World Commission on Environment and Development (WCED). (1987). Report of the World Commission on Environment and Development: Our common future. Retrieved March 8, 2012, from http://upload.wikimedia.org/wikisource/en/d/d7/Our-common-future.pdf

Wu, Fengshi. (2009). Environmental activism in China: Fifteen years in review, 1994–2008 (Harvard-Yenching Institute Working Paper Series). Retrieved July 3, 2010, from http://www.harvard-yenching.org/sites/harvard-yenching.org/files/WU%20Fengshi_Environmental%20Civil%20Society%20in%20China2.pdf

Xu, Hui. (1995). Some considerations on school environmental education in China. *International Research in Geographical and Environmental Education*, *4*(2), 90–91.

Zhu, Huaixin. (1995). Education and examinations: A major constraint hindering environmental education in the People's Republic of China. *International Research in Geographical and Environmental Education*, *4*(2), 106–107.

Education, Environmental (India)

India's ecological diversity poses formidable challenges for its environmental education initiatives, which have been gaining momentum since the 1980s. An active civil society, a multitude of grassroots movements, and the government are shaping environmental awareness and education. As India's economy continues to expand rapidly, both formal and informal institutions are actively transforming initiatives for environmental education in the country. Many challenges remain, especially those associated with India's "demographic dividend."

The character of environmental education initiatives in any society has to be understood as an outcome of its historical and sociocultural conditions. India is the world's largest democracy, and ecologically it is a land of tremendous diversity. Culturally it is varied as well, with close to thirty officially recognized languages, twenty-two thousand distinct dialects, many ethnic groups, and a large tribal population. India also has the world's second largest population and is inhabited by more than a billion people, many of whom continue to subsist on agricultural and forest products. Finally, it is the home of most major religions in the world, all of which have shaped each other over time and many of which espouse their own distinct beliefs on the nature, meaning, and management of the environment.

For these reasons, discussions of environmental awareness and education in India must be built around an appreciation of the interplay among the economic, cultural, and political forces that are shaping the region both formally and informally. India's diversity means that environmental issues often provoke conflicting reactions from different social groups, which adds to the difficulty of discussing environmental education. For instance, debates over the need for big dams, nuclear power, or genetically modified crops are often shaped by the competing viewpoints that come from the differing beliefs people hold about their relationship with the natural environment. On these issues, the country's vibrant democracy facilitates a culture of healthy public debate. Environmental education in India continues to be shaped by the ways in which these debates are conducted, and it is a fertile zone for disagreement and compromise in the country today.

Historical Background

Since attaining independence in 1947, India's leaders have faced the challenging task of advancing a shared understanding of how to manage a large population living in an ecologically diverse subcontinental landmass. After the departure of the British, India emerged as a democratic republic with a federal structure, which provided the framework for its people to manage their state, their ecology, and their economy. Under the leadership of its first prime minister, Jawaharlal Nehru—a socialist leader with an abiding commitment to environmental conservation—India's challenge was to balance strengthening the weak postcolonial economy (reliant largely on agriculture) with the imperative of keeping India democratic and free.

India inherited a rich and diverse body of environmental learning when it became independent, and its multicultural character has ensured that it has served as a crucible for the production of knowledge pertinent to environmental conservation. This is because groups living in different agroclimatic regions have developed a variety of environmentally sensitive practices that have been refined over centuries and have stood the test of time. For instance, the historical water conservation methods of Rajasthan's nomadic tribal communities continue to shape current water management policies in this desert region. The same is true of coastal communities and their relationship with marine ecosystems. Both populations rely on premodern practices of sustainability and pass this knowledge on through locally embedded systems of environmental education.

Environmental education practices in contemporary India, therefore, result from the interplay between traditional and modern forms of knowledge—between communally embedded ideas about conservation on the one hand, and more recent governmental attempts at national assets management on the other. As India's movement for independence from British rule gained momentum at the beginning of the twentieth century, men like Mohandas Karamchand Gandhi and Rabindranath Tagore articulated a conception of environmental protection that sought harmony between premodern and modern concepts of ecology. To varying degrees, their views on sustainability, environmental protection, and ecological harmony have shaped the dominant currents of environmental education in independent India. Indeed, it would be fair to say that many varieties of environmentalism in India today continue to build on the legacy of these thinkers.

Since the 1970s, environmental education has been sustained by new energies unleashed from the state, civic organizations, and (more informally) a plethora of environmental movements in different parts of the country. From this period on, the sense of urgency accorded to the need for environmental education has been largely a response to the mounting concern for environmental protection in a maturing nation. In the late 1980s environmental education began to be impacted by the global environmental movement as well, as a result of India's growing awareness of it during the previous decades. The adoption of neoliberal economic reforms by the Indian government in 1991 gave India's environmental engagement with the world a further boost, a momentum that was sustained by a boom in communications technology and the growth of India's mobile transnational workforce. All of these forces built on the intellectual foundations that had been laid during India's movement for national independence, and provided the fertile ground in which India's environmental education initiatives continue to take root.

Government Initiatives

In 1972, the first United Nations Conference on the Human Environment was held in Stockholm, Sweden. The Indian prime minister, Indira Gandhi—the only head of state to attend—highlighted the link between poverty and the environment:

> Unless we are in a position to provide employment and purchasing power for the daily necessities of the tribal people and those who live in or around our jungles, we cannot prevent them from combing the forests for food and livelihood; from poaching and from despoiling the vegetation. . . . How can we speak to those who live in villages and slums about keeping the oceans, the rivers, and the air clean when their own lives are contaminated at the source? The environment cannot be improved in conditions of poverty. (Gandhi 1996, 15)

The Indian government's efforts with respect to environmental education grew out of conference deliberations, and were formally initiated around the time of the United Nations Educational, Scientific and Cultural Organization's (UNESCO) Intergovernmental Conference on Environmental Education in Tbilisi, USSR, in 1977. The recommendations that emerged from that conference recognized the pressing need for increasing awareness of environmental problems and understanding the interrelationships between human beings and the environment.

The 1970s and 1980s were a period of concerted planning and institution building for environmental education. The government-funded Department of Science and Technology (DST) and Council for Scientific and Industrial Research (CSIR) had both supported environmental research over the years, creating momentum for other institutions to build upon. Two notable institutions were established in New Delhi—the School of Environmental Sciences at

Jawaharlal Nehru University in 1974, and the Centre for Energy Studies at the Indian Institute of Technology Delhi in 1976—creating a framework for the growth of higher education in environmental studies. By using a multidisciplinary approach that integrated environmental studies into geology, chemistry, physics, and biology, these institutions laid the foundation for a comprehensive environmental education curriculum in schools and colleges. The rich experience and perspectives gained in these institutions motivated many young minds to respond to issues of modern industrial growth and its impact on the environment and ecosystems. It was at this time that popular-science movements initiated through citizen forums on science and mass campaigns like Bharat Gyan Vigyan Samiti actively dedicated themselves to deepening environmental education with a focus on environmental protection.

In 1980 Indira Gandhi's government created the Department of Environment. The Ministry of Human Resource Development (MHRD), and more particularly the Ministry of Environment and Forests that was created in 1985, have been largely responsible for the dissemination of environmental education in India. In this period, an institutional framework was laid out for systematically promoting environmental education. "Centres of Excellence," such as the Centre for Environment Education (CEE) in Ahmedabad and the C. P. Ramaswami Environmental Education Centre in Chennai, have been carrying out a range of interventions for integrating environmental education into the learning environment for children in both urban and rural India. Other programs, like the National Green Corps and the National Environment Awareness Campaign, are supplemented by outreach and funding for environmental education initiatives. The Environmental Orientation to School Education program (supported by the MHRD) is based on the idea that a compact area with a distinct ecosystem should be the basic unit for designing education programs. The program provides assistance to relevant voluntary organizations for developing location-specific teaching materials and innovative programs that relate student activities to local environmental concerns. Finally, the 1986 National Policy on Education states clearly that environmental education must form an integral part of the curriculum at all educational levels to ensure that students appreciate the importance of protecting the environment.

Civic Engagement and Nongovernmental Organizations

By the mid-1980s India's institutional framework for environmental education was taking shape—but how successful were the government's attempts at incorporating environmental education into the real lives of India's people? This question remains unanswered, in part because the quality of instruction varies widely from school to school, and also because there are serious questions about whether teachers are as prepared as they need to be to provide this quality instruction.

Having said this, it is clear that environmental awareness has increased over the past few decades. The scale of civic engagement with environmental politics grew dramatically in the 1980s, and it is highly likely that the formalization of environmental education and the increase in environmental civic activism fed off each other. The realization of the promise of environmental education, as envisioned in the state's multipronged framework, owes as much to the conscious environmental activism of citizens and the active role played by the judiciary in India in the 1990s as it does to government initiatives. The noted lawyer M. C. Mehta filed petitions in 1991 and 2004 urging India's Supreme Court to direct the National Council for Education and Training (NCERT) and University Grants Commission to introduce environmental education as a mandatory subject in schools and colleges all over India. Nongovernmental organizations (NGOs) like the Uttrakhand Seva Nidhi and the Kerala Sastra Sahitya Parishad have conducted key experiments in grounding environmental education in the lives of individual communities to allow them to manage their ecologies in a planned and considered manner. These initiatives have linked environmental education with community action for environmental protection successfully. Other NGOs actively committed to promoting environmental education are Eklavya, Kalpvriksha, the World Wide Fund for Nature, and the Foundation for Ecological Security.

The founding of the Centre for Science and Environment (CSE) by Anil Aggarwal and Sunita Narain, Development Alternatives by Ashok Khosla, the Research Foundation for Science Technology and Ecology, and Navdanya by Vandana Shiva needs to be considered in the context of this increasing popular awareness about the environment and the growth of citizen-led initiatives. Each of these organizations has in its own way advocated for a radical version of environmentalism that assumes an intimate link between the natural resources and livelihoods of small and marginal communities. Their outreach activities have brought a political edge to environmental education by stressing the relevance of issues of justice and equity in the environmental debate, and their magazines—such as CSE's *Down to Earth* for adults and *Gobar Times* for children—have played a crucial role in disseminating information about the importance of environmental conservation and in documenting key environmental issues in India.

By reaffirming that a stable ecology forms the backbone of environment as a human-centered domain, these NGOs have enriched environmental education in India. They have demonstrated that as India's reliance on natural resources grows in conjunction with its rapidly expanding economy, environmental problems are best addressed by balancing the findings of hard science with sociopolitical mobilizations that are often local, grounded, and concerned with the immediacy of everyday life. Questions regarding the management of land, water, and air are central to many policy discussions in India today, and are hotly debated in India's democratic spaces. Experiments in environmental education engage with these discussions, and are expanding their reach and impact.

The Question of Our Times

In 2007 the Fourth International Conference on Environmental Education was held at the CEE. Participants adopted the Ahmedabad Declaration, which noted (among other things) the increasing income disparity in India, the challenges of managing climate change, the loss of India's biodiversity, and the increasing popularity of ecologically destructive, unsustainable lifestyles and consumption patterns among the young. The declaration received wide circulation even as India's economy continued to grow, and is a sobering reminder of the challenges confronting environmental education in this fast-changing country.

Often it has been observed that in the coming decades India will benefit a great deal from its "demographic dividend"—the fact that the majority of Indians are below the age of twenty-five. While this demographic attribute is indeed likely to benefit India's economy—since a large proportion of the population will remain a part of the country's workforce for many decades to come—the challenge for those committed to environmental education is the following: to what degree is India's predominantly young population educated about the need to embrace a sustainable future? India has made rapid progress in its environmental policy framework over the past three decades, but how enthusiastically those constituting the country's demographic dividend will embrace ecologically responsible practices remains to be seen. For environmental education to realize its fullest potential in India, the government, civic organizations, and the private sector will have to pool their resources and creativity in the service of environmental sustainability for many years to come.

Vivek BHANDARI and
Independent scholar, Jaipur, India

Rahul GHAI
*Independent development practitioner,
Western Rajasthan*

See also Activism, Judicial; Education, Environmental (China); Education, Environmental (Japan); Education, Female; Gandhism; India; Nongovernmental Organizations (NGOs); Rule of Law

FURTHER READING

Bharucha, Erach. (2004). *Textbook for environmental studies for undergraduate courses of all branches of higher education*. New Delhi: University Grants Commission.

Bharucha, Rustam. (2003). *Rajasthan: An oral history*. Delhi: Penguin.

C. P. Ramaswami Environmental Education Centre (CPREEC). (n.d.). Homepage. Retrieved March 28, 2012, from http://www.cpreec.org/

Centre for Energy Studies (CES). (n.d.). Homepage. Retrieved March 30, 2012, from http://ces.iitd.ac.in/

Centre for Environment Education (CEE). (n.d.a). About CEE. Retrieved March 28, 2012, from http://www.ceeindia.org/cee/index.htm

Centre for Environment Education (CEE). (n.d.b). Education for children. Retrieved March 28, 2012, from http://www.ceeindia.org/cee/educationfor_children.html

Centre for Science and Environment (CSE). (2012). Homepage. Retrieved March 28, 2012, from http://www.cseindia.org/

Development Alternatives. (2011). Homepage. Retrieved March 29, 2012, from http://www.devalt.org/

Down to Earth. (n.d.). Homepage. Retrieved March 28, 2012, from http://www.downtoearth.org.in/

Foundation for Ecological Security (FES). (2012). Homepage. Retrieved March 31, 2012, from http://fes.org.in/

Fourth International Conference on Environmental Education (ICEE). (2007, November 24–28). The Ahmedabad Declaration 2007: A call to action. Ahmedabad, India.

Gadgil, Madhav, & Guha, Ramachandra. (1998). Towards a perspective on environmental movements in India. *Indian Journal of Social Work, 59*(1), 449–472.

Gandhi, Indira. (1996). *Safeguarding environment.* New Delhi: New Age International Publishers. (Original work published 1984)

Gobar Times. (2012). Homepage. Retrieved March 28, 2012, from http://www.gobartimes.org/

Gopal, Brij. (2005). Issues in ecological research and environmental management. *Bulletin of the National Institute of Ecology, 15,* 277–286.

Green Teacher. (2012). Homepage. Retrieved April 2, 2012, from http://www.greenteacher.org/

M. C. Mehta v. Union of India, Supplementary Affidavit on Behalf of NCERT, Writ Petition (Civil) No. 800, Supreme Court of India (1991).

Ministry of Environment and Forests, Government of India. (n.d.a). Homepage. Retrieved March 28, 2012, from http://moef.nic.in/index.php

Ministry of Environment and Forests, Government of India. (n.d.b). About the Ministry: Centre for Environment Education. Retrieved March 28, 2012, from http://moef.nic.in/modules/about-the-ministry/centres-of-excellence/?f=environmental-education&l=l1

Navdanya. (2009). Homepage. Retrieved March 30, 2012, from http://www.navdanya.org/

Panigrahi, Srikanta K. (2004). Environment education: Need of the hour. *Yojana, 48*(6), 13–22.

Rangarajan, Mahesh, & Sivaramakrishnan, Kalavathi. (2012). *India's environmental history* (2 vols.). Ranikhet, India: Permanent Black.

Sarabhai, Kartikeya V.; Raghunathan, Meena; & Jain, Shivani. (2002). Environmental education: Some experiences from India. In Bishnu B. Bhandari & Institute for Global Environmental Strategies (IGES) (Eds.), *The path to success: Some pioneering examples of environmental education.* Hayama, Japan: IGES.

School of Environmental Sciences, Jawaharlal Nehru University. (n.d.). Homepage. Retrieved April 5, 2012, from http://www.jnu.ac.in/main.asp?sendval=SchoolOfEnvironmentalSciences

Sonowal, C. J. (2009). Environmental education in schools: The Indian scenario. *Journal of Human Ecology, 28*(1), 15–36.

Berkshire's authors and editors welcome questions, comments, and corrections. Send your emails about the *Berkshire Encyclopedia of Sustainability* in general or this volume in particular to: sustainability.updates@berkshirepublishing.com

Education, Environmental (Japan)

Environmental education in Japan has been implemented systematically since the latter half of the 1980s. The 1990s, however, saw a shift from the narrow definition of environmental education, which focused on environmental conservation, to the broader definition of education for a sustainable society, involving other perspectives and including social justice. Education for sustainable development has begun to move beyond Japanese schools to nongovernmental organizations, corporations, and local communities.

Environmental education holds promise of playing a significant role as a means to build a sustainable society. At the 2002 World Summit on Sustainable Development (Johannesburg Summit), the Japanese government, in conjunction with Japanese nongovernmental organizations (NGOs), proposed the United Nations Decade of Education for Sustainable Development (2005–2014, hereinafter called the Decade of Education). With this as a backdrop, environmental education has been spreading rapidly, as revealed by the Act on Enhancing Motivation on Environmental Conservation and Promoting of Environmental Education enacted in 2003.

International issues, including the environment, are inextricably associated with one another and are increasingly deepening into an unsustainable situation in parallel with accelerated globalism. Breaking through such unsustainability and actualizing a sustainable society is an urgent task, and environmental education from the viewpoint of education for sustainable development is crucial to achieving this goal.

Beginnings

Environmental education in Japan dates back to pollution and nature protection education in the 1960s. The latter half of the 1950s in Japan witnessed health hazards brought on by pollution, which threatened not only adults' but also children's health. Consequently, pollution education was initiated as an educational activity to protect children from environmental destruction and conserve communities from the standpoint of ensuring quality of life. In 1971, the primary and junior high school curriculum guidelines in social studies were altered to incorporate pollution education. Accordingly, the Ministry of Education, Science, Sports and Culture initiated pollution education, and entities such as the prefectural boards of education created and distributed their "Guide to Pollution Education Teaching."

The destruction of nature was an unfortunate consequence of the rapid economic growth of the 1960s, and numerous active nature protection campaigns appeared throughout Japan. The Nature Conservation Society of Japan was established in 1951 and utilized nature observation tours as part of nature protection education.

Japan thus started pollution and nature protection education in the first half of the 1970s. The two types of education, however, did not lead to wider activities at that time due to resistance to antipollution and nature protection campaigns from the public and private sectors.

Integration and Dissemination

The term *environmental education* was first widely introduced to Japan around 1972. It was not until the latter half of the 1980s, however, that environmental education encompassing pollution and nature protection education was initiated systematically. In 1987, the term was not yet common, but schools, individuals, and NGOs were beginning to consider and develop environmental activities. At this time the Nature Conservation Society of Japan started to cultivate nature observation instructors, which was Japan's first attempt at training teachers in the field of environmental education. During the same period, there was a movement to set up an academic society that would engage in environmental education; this led to the establishment of the Japanese Society of Environmental Education in 1990.

While environmental education efforts took shape at the grassroots level, the Environment Agency (later renamed as the Ministry of the Environment) produced environmental education guidelines entitled "In Search of 'a Better Environment Created by All'" in 1988. These are considered to be the first environmental education plan by a governmental institution in Japan and a clear acknowledgement of the necessity to position environmental education as part of environmental policy. At the same time, the prefectural governments and major cities began to create guidelines for environmental education that referred to the roles of each sector and partnerships in promoting environmental education, by situating it as part of an environmental administration. In this way, environmental education efforts by the environmental administration began expanding rapidly beginning in the latter half of the 1980s. (See figures 1 below and 2 on the next page.)

In 1990, the Ministry of Education, Science, Sports and Culture (later renamed the Ministry of Education, Culture, Sports, Science and Technology) set out to create the "Guide to Environmental Education Teaching." It can be said that this marked the introduction and institutionalization of environmental education into schools by the government. In addition, Article 25 of the 1993 Basic Environmental Law, entitled Education and Learning on Environmental Conservation, incorporated environmental education into Japanese law for the first time; this was triggered by global environmental issues that emerged in the 1980s and also via the 1992 Earth Summit in Rio de Janeiro, Brazil. In 1991, the Central Environmental Council of the Ministry of the Environment

Figure 1. Environmental Education Activities in Japan Prior to the Latter Half of the 1990s

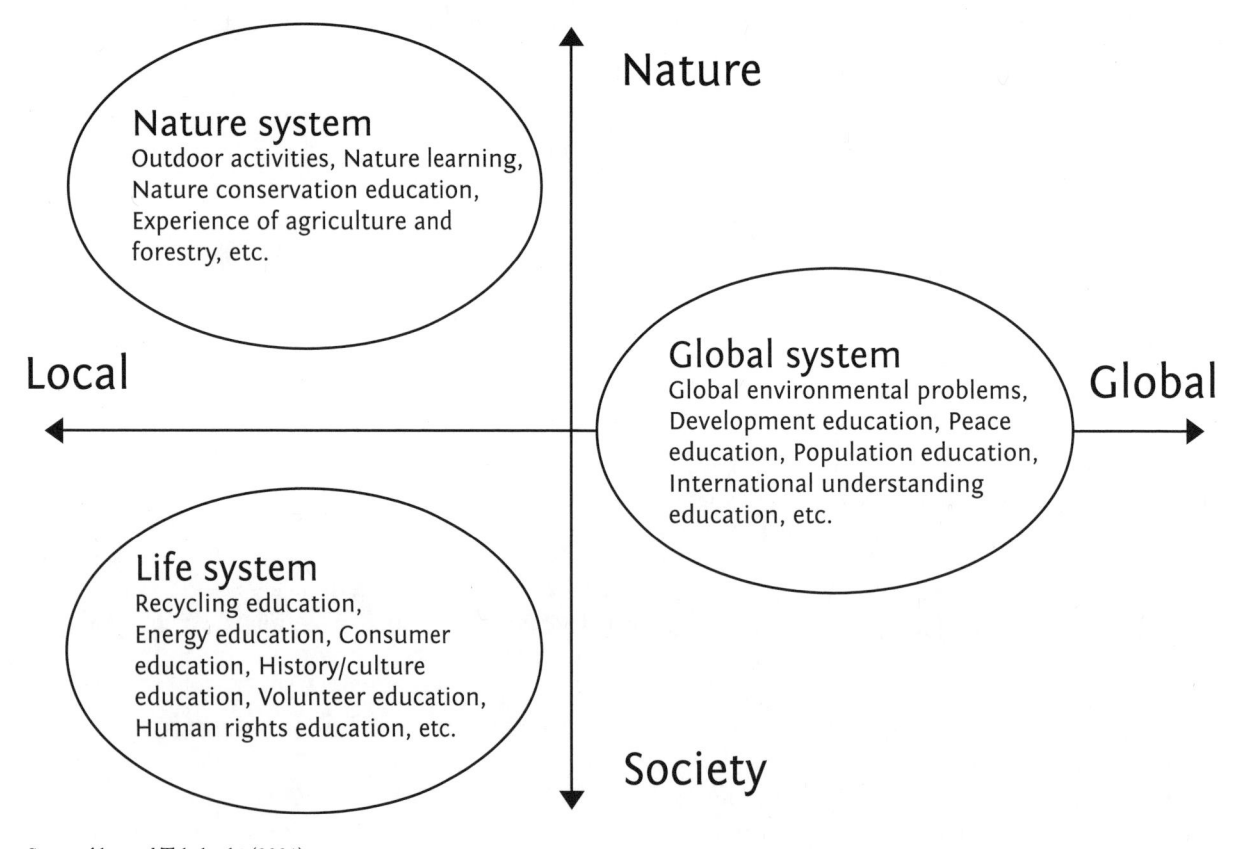

Nature system
Outdoor activities, Nature learning, Nature conservation education, Experience of agriculture and forestry, etc.

Global system
Global environmental problems, Development education, Peace education, Population education, International understanding education, etc.

Life system
Recycling education, Energy education, Consumer education, History/culture education, Volunteer education, Human rights education, etc.

Axes: Nature — Society (vertical); Local — Global (horizontal)

Source: Abe and Takahashi (2001).

Early activities were conducted separately in the nature, life, and global systems. Compare figure 2.

Figure 2. Environmental Education Activities in Japan Beginning in the Latter Half of the 1990s

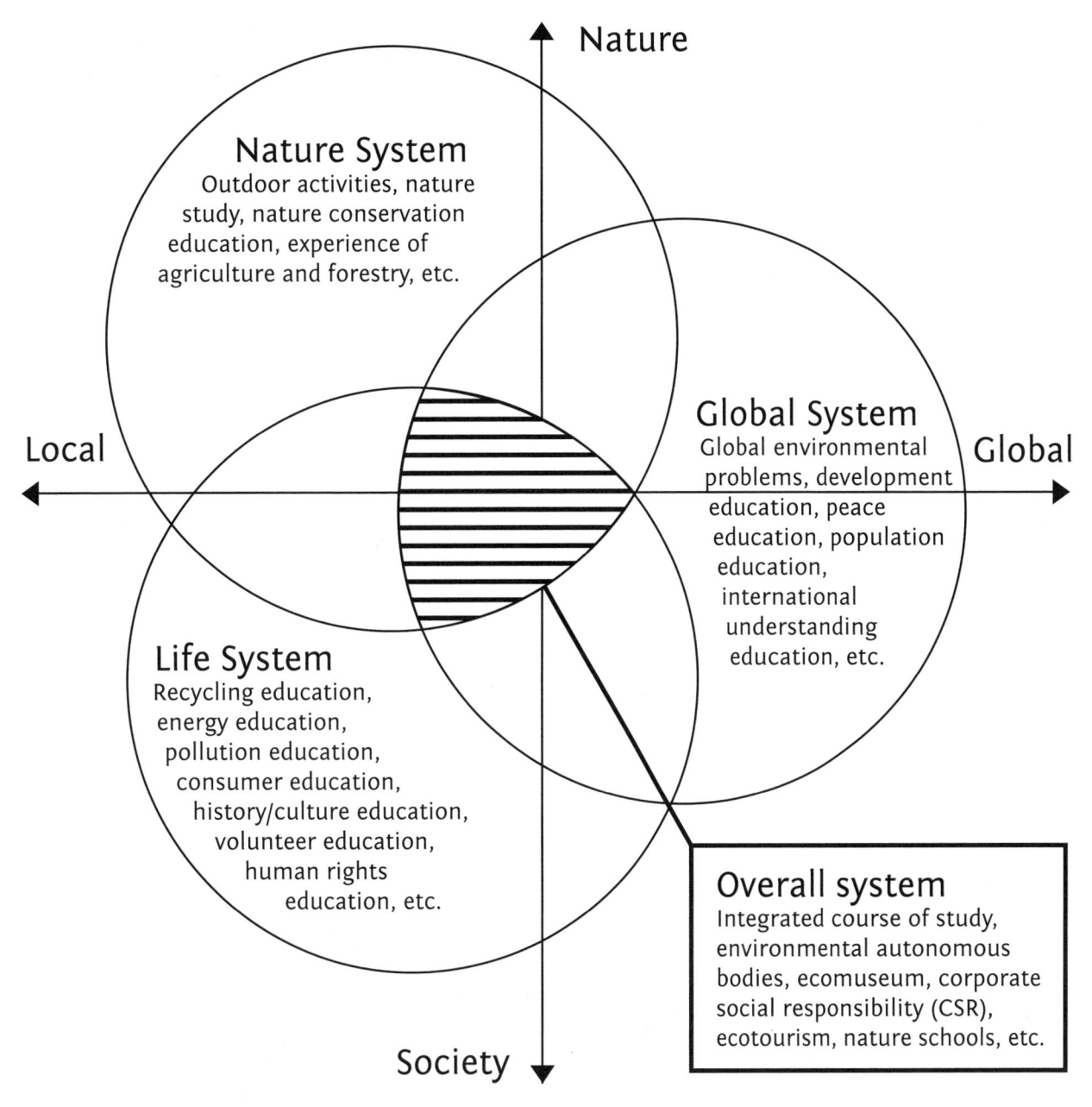

Nature System: Outdoor activities, nature study, nature conservation education, experience of agriculture and forestry, etc.

Global System: Global environmental problems, development education, peace education, population education, international understanding education, etc.

Life System: Recycling education, energy education, pollution education, consumer education, history/culture education, volunteer education, human rights education, etc.

Overall system: Integrated course of study, environmental autonomous bodies, ecomuseum, corporate social responsibility (CSR), ecotourism, nature schools, etc.

Axes: Nature / Society, Local / Global

Source: Abe and Takahashi (2001).

Since the latter half of the 1990s, activities have been conducted in the overall system, or at the intersection of the nature, life, and global systems. Compare figure 1.

announced guidelines for environmental education entitled "Environmental Education/Environment Awareness in the Future." This report was pivotal in that it pointed out the significance of shifting from the narrow definition of environmental education, in which mainly environmental conservation is pursued, to the broader definition of environmental education as encompassing other perspectives including social justice (or education for a sustainable society). Concurrent with these processes was the global trend of moving from environmental education to education for sustainable development (ESD) after the 1992 Earth Summit. The report presented concrete policies that aimed to realize a sustainable society by connecting various entities, measures, places, human beings, and nature—with the key word being "connecting."

In response to Japan's proposal of the Decade of Education at the 2002 Johannesburg Summit came the Act on Enhancing Motivation on Environmental Conservation and Promoting of Environmental Education, commonly known as the Act on Promoting of Environmental Conservation Activities and Environmental Education. This was initiated by lawmakers and was enacted in 2003 as an individual law of Articles 25 and 26 of Japan's Basic Environmental Law. (The act was revised in 2011.) The 2004 basic guidelines, formulated on the act, included concrete measures to promote environmental education. As many as five ministries—the Ministry of the Environment; Ministry of Education, Culture, Sports, Science and Technology; Ministry of Agriculture, Forestry and Fisheries; Ministry of Economy, Trade and Industry; and Ministry of Land, Infrastructure, Transport and Tourism—have jurisdiction over the law, expanding the range of environmental education.

NGOs, the other entity involved in proposing the Decade of Education, set up the Japan Council on the UN Decade of Education for Sustainable Development (ESD-J) in 2003 as a network organization that promotes the Decade of Education both at home and abroad. In the ESD-J, organizations and individuals working on ESD in wide-ranging areas concerning not only nature protection but also development, human rights, peace, and youth education engage in policy recommendations and ESD activities.

At the end of the 1990s, hands-on activities through environmental education started to be laid out in both public and private sectors. In particular, the Council on Lifelong Learning indicated in its 1999 recommendation that children were severely lacking in nature and life experiences, which led the Ministry of Education, Science, Sports and Culture to initiate the promotion of nature experiences for children as part of lifelong learning. Subsequently, the promotion of nature experience activities was incorporated into the Social Education Act and the School Education Act when they were revised in 2002. This encouraged youth centers as well as NGOs to promote nature experience activities for children.

Pertaining to the cultivation of instructors, the Council for Outdoor and Nature Experiences (CONE), a network of Japan's major NGOs engaged in nature experience activities, was established in 2000 and embarked on the promotion of these activities and training instructors. The number of registered instructors, as of 2011, already exceeded 25,000. Furthermore, nature schools providing primarily nature experience activities were founded in the 1980s, and, as of 2011, there were more than 3,500 of them nationwide. These nature schools have been set up by NGOs, the public sector, and corporations and are in most cases located in farming and mountain villages. Currently, they even play the role of centers for building sustainable communities.

As the environmental administration placed more emphasis on education, various types of centers were built as facilities for learning and for collecting and communicating information about environmental education. Since the 1990s, Japan has seen the unique development of, in particular, urban environmental education facilities engaging in life environmental issues (e.g., Tokyo Gas Wonder Ship House established in Yokohama in1998), information- and interaction-oriented environmental education facilities stimulating partnerships among different sectors (e.g., Global Environmental Outreach Centre [GEOC] established in Tokyo in 1996), and large-scale museums whose main pillar is environmental education (e.g., Ibaraki Nature Museum established in Ibaraki in 1994). Most of these facilities are geared toward participatory and experiential exhibitions and programs.

At School

In the 1990s, the Ministry of Education, Science, Sports and Culture began actively pushing environmental education. The Fifteenth Central Education Council of 1996 positioned "the period of integrated study" (hereinafter called "integrated study") as a required subject from the third grade to high school. Integrated study includes hours for voluntary, cross-sectional, and comprehensive learning by students and has been implemented at all public primary, secondary, and high schools since the fiscal year 2002. Integrated study deals with a variety of interconnected topics such as the environment, social welfare, health, and international understanding. Based particularly on environmental education, integrated study provides comprehensive learning activities by paying attention to diverse connections in terms of generation, urban city and agricultural village, social welfare, health, and culture. The integrated study course is expected to play an essential role in cultivating the practical ability to work on the environment, which is most central to environmental education.

In the early 2000s, results from the Organisation for Economic Co-operation and Development (OECD) Program for International Student Assessment (PISA), which evaluates education systems worldwide, were not good; as a result, Japanese school education shifted its focus to the cognitive domain in response to pressure from the business community. Because of this, environmental education efforts and integrated study have not been as prevalent in spite of the need. On the other hand, when the Fundamental Law of Education was amended in 2006, the phrase "to foster an attitude to respect life, care for nature, and contribute to the conservation of the environment" was incorporated into Article 2, with the intention of promoting environmental education. With this mandate in place, along with the 2011 revision of the Act on Enhancing Motivation on Environmental Conservation and Promoting of Environmental Education, a system to promote environmental education has been instituted.

By Corporations and Communities

Since the 1990s, corporate environmental education efforts have been developed through environmental reports, social philanthropy (such as various subsidized activities related to the environment), and the environmental standards (known as ISO 14001) of the International Organization for Standardization (ISO), the world's largest developer and publisher of international standards. Since the latter half of the 1990s, the number of corporations engaging in environmental education as an aspect of corporate social responsibility (CSR) specifically has been on the rise. Moreover, since the onset of the Decade of Education, there have been widespread ESD efforts as part of sustainable community building. One representative example is learning-based local revitalization in Minamata City, Kumamoto Prefecture. The city, which was devastated by the mercury pollution–caused illness labeled Minamata disease beginning in the 1950s, has re-evaluated all the areas in the city and has been evolving ESD-based community building, targeting all residents. As Japanese provincial cities face serious problems of aging, depopulation, and destruction of nature, it can be said that ESD will play a vital role in building sustainable communities.

Japan's environmental education has been expanding its network not only domestically but also internationally. For example, the Japan Overseas Cooperation Volunteers, a project of the Japan International Cooperation Agency, has been dispatching approximately thirty volunteers every year to facilitate environmental education overseas. Also, the Japanese, South Korean, and Chinese governments erected the Tripartite Environmental Education Network (TEEN) in 2002 as part of the framework of the Tripartite Environmental Ministers Meeting (TEMM) for purposes including the sharing of experiences by each entity and jointly developing curricula. This sort of international cooperation is an important area to address for the future of environmental education.

Outlook: Toward a Sustainable Society

Japan's environmental education originated in pollution and nature protection education and has been growing by incorporating advanced cases from Western countries such as experience-based environmental education programs, nature trails, and nature centers. It has developed, however, into education for sustainable development and is implemented not only in each school subject but also in the integrated study curriculum. Since the 2000s when ESD was introduced, various stakeholders (i.e., those people who have a stake in an enterprise) have been able to collaborate with one another and proceed with their efforts as part of sustainable society building. In particular, collaboration between schools and communities through sustainable community building and comprehensive environmental education efforts are unique to Japan.

Although laws for promoting environmental education have been formulated, their legal force is not strong, and it is hard to say that they are having a significant effect. In addition, pressure on schools from the business and education communities to develop students' abilities in traditional academic subjects has weakened environmental education efforts. Meanwhile, the Decade of Education has had a great impact on the further promotion of Japan's environmental education and its institutionalization toward a sustainable society through close ties with other educational initiatives. It is now necessary to build a system to promote environmental education, to cultivate leaders in the field, and to connect a wide range of sustainability-related efforts and places from the viewpoint of ESD.

Osamu ABE
Rikkyo University

See also Education, Environmental (China); Education, Environmental (India); Education, Female; Japan; Media Coverage of the Environment; Nongovernmental Organizations (NGOs); Public Health; Public-Private Partnerships; Tokyo, Japan

FURTHER READING

Abe, Osamu, & Takahashi, Masahiro. (2001). *Kankyō-kyōiku to media* [Environmental education and media]. In Institute for Global Environmental Strategies (Ed.), *Kankyō-media ron* [Theory of environmental media] (pp. 44–59). Tokyo: Chuohoki.

Abe, Osamu. (2010). Movement and challenges of education for sustainable development in Japan. *Journal of Developments in Sustainable Agriculture, 6*(1), 1–7.

Elias, Derek, & Sachathep, Karampreet. (2009). *ESD currents: Changing perspectives for the Asia-Pacific.* Bangkok, Thailand: UNESCO Bangkok.

Japan Environmental Education Forum. (2009). *Kankyô-kyôiku no chie* [The wisdom of Japan's environmental education]. Tokyo: Shogakukan.

Nomura Ko & Abe Osamu. (2009). The education for sustainable development movement in Japan: A political perspective. *Environmental Education Research, 15*(4), 483–496.

Nomura, Ko, & Abe, Osamu. (2010). Higher education for sustainable development in Japan: Policy and progress. *International Journal of Sustainability in Higher Education, 11*(2), 120–129.

Nomura, Ko; Yoshihiro, Natori; & Abe, Osamu. (2010). Region-wide education for sustainable development networks of universities in the Asia-Pacific. In Robin Sakamoto & David W. Chapman (Eds.), *Cross-border partnerships in higher education: Strategies and issues* (pp. 209–227). New York: Routledge.

Ryan, Alexandra; Tilbury, Daniella; Corcoran, Peter B.; Abe, Osamu; & Nomura, Ko. (2010). Sustainability in higher education in the Asia-Pacific: Developments, challenges, and prospects. *International Journal of Sustainability in Higher Education, 11*(2), 106–119.

Ubukata, Hidenori; Kanda, Fusayuki; & Omori, Susumu. (Eds.). (2010). *ESD (jizoku-kanô-na-kaihatsu no tameno kyôiku) wo tsukuru* [Creating ESD (Education for Sustainable Development)]. Kyoto, Japan: Minerva Shobo.

United Nations (UN). (2006). *Wagakuni ni okeru "kokuren jizoku-kanô-na-kaihatsu no tameno kyôiku no jûnen" jisshi keikaku (ESD jisshi keikaku)* [United Nations Decade of Education for Sustainable Development implementation plan in our country (ESD implementation plan)]. Retrieved March 3, 2012, from http://www.env.go.jp/policy/edu/desd/esd_keikaku.pdf

United Nations Department of Economic and Social Affairs. (1992). Agenda 21. Retrieved March 3, 2012, from http://www.un.org/esa/dsd/agenda21/?utm_source=OldRedirect&utm_medium=redirect&utm_content=dsd&utm_campaign=OldRedirect

United Nations Educational, Scientific and Cultural Organization (UNESCO). (1997). Declaration of Thessaloniki. Retrieved March 3, 2012, from http://unesdoc.unesco.org/images/0011/001177/117772eo.pdf

Share the *Encyclopedia of Sustainability*: Teachers are welcome to make up to ten (10) copies of no more than two (2) articles for distribution in a single course or program. For further permissions, please visit www.copyright.com or contact: info@berkshirepublishing.com

Education, Female

Education of women provides important social benefits in areas such as improved health, nutrition, hygiene, family planning, household management, and conservation of natural resources. Government interventions have played a crucial role in the improvement of female education in India and China. The prevailing rate of female illiteracy still stands, however, as a challenge to sustainable development.

Female education is one of the basic foundations for sustainable development. Educating women is essential to reduce fertility rates, increase child health and maternal health, reduce maternal morbidity, increase nutritional intake of the family, make use of good sanitation and hygiene, and to increase the decision-making capacity of women in the household. Therefore, the rate of female illiteracy in the two most populous countries, India and China, is a central issue to address in the movement toward sustainability.

In traditional societies like that of India and China, however, often women's potential to control resources through the exercise of independent decision making is limited. For instance, patriarchal structure could deny property rights to women. Education has an important role to relieve both men and women from these clutches of binding structures.

India

A country with 1.21 billion people, 17 percent of the world's population, India is home to 586.5 million women. Among them, 35 percent above the age of seven are illiterate, as shown by the provisional census data of 2011 (Census of India 2011). This indicates that India is lagging behind acceptable standards of female education.

The struggle to improve education for women started in India even before independence from British rule in 1947. Mohandas Gandhi (1869–1948), the father of the nation, was one of the prominent figures to lay the foundation for women's education and participation in development and sustainability. He said, "Educate one man, you educate one person, but educate a woman and you educate a whole civilization." Many visionaries promoted this spirit and worked for women's empowerment and education; hence female education underwent far-reaching changes in independent India. The government of India ensured the education of women through plans, policies, and programs launched over the years. In 1958 the government formed the National Committee on Women's Education to determine the obstacles in the way of girls' education and make recommendations to bring education for girls to an equal level with that for boys. The committee gave high priority to the expansion of girls' education at the elementary stage, as well as a campaign against the traditional prejudices toward the education of girls, appointment of women teachers, and special central assistance to states until 80 percent of girls six to eleven years of age are enrolled in school. The National Policies on Education (1968, 1986) stated the need for educating women in order to accelerate social transformation. The focus of the modified National Policy on Education (1992) was to use education as an agent to bring changes to the status of women and to reduce the gender inequality prevailing in the education system.

The National Policy for the Empowerment of Women (2001) is especially significant from the point of view of sustainability. Some of the training programs for women include agriculture-related activities like horticulture, raising livestock and poultry, managing fisheries, soil conservation, social forestry, and dairy development, leading to knowledge and skills that help protect natural resources. The Right to Education Act, which came into force on 1 April 2010, ensures enrollment and elementary education for all female children through its legislation that every child between six and fourteen years of age has the right to free and compulsory education.

When the country introduced planned development through five-year plans in 1952, improvement of women's education was one focus in the overall development of the country. From the very first plan (1952–1957) to the eleventh plan (2007–2012), empowerment of women has been given pivotal attention. The sixth plan (1980–1985) included a special chapter on women and development that adopted a multidisciplinary approach with health, education, and employment for women. The educational aspect of five-year plans focuses on reducing student dropout rate; increasing enrollment; reducing the gender gap in literacy rate; increasing the number of women teachers, especially in rural areas; promoting greater enrollment of women in professional courses; and expansion of functional literacy programs, especially in areas having low female literacy. The five-year plans recognize that educating and empowering women is important to alleviate poverty, protect health, improve nutrition, reduce mortality rate, encourage population control, and increase women's access to natural and social resources—all benefits to help keep the country healthy and lively.

The aforementioned policies and plans for women's education had a great impact on the country from the sustainability perspective, including the benefits of literacy for informed family planning to reduce burdens on an overpopulated environment. The female literacy rate improved from less than 9 percent in 1951 to 65 percent in 2011. Female education has brought substantial changes in the fertility rate, family-planning methods to control population, and infant mortality rate. According to the National Family Health Survey (NFHS I 1992–1993, NFHS II 1998–1999, and NFHS III 2005–2006), the fertility rate decreased from 3.4 percent in NFHS I to 2.7 percent in NFHS III (NFHS 2009). Though fertility has declined in all educational groups, the largest decrease (1.9 percent) was among literate women. The use of contraceptives increased with education (57 percent for literates and 43 percent for illiterates), which is a positive step toward sustainable population levels. Overall infant mortality rate declined sharply with increasing education of mothers, from a high of 87 deaths per 1,000 live births for illiterate mothers to a low of 33 deaths per 1,000 live births for mothers who have at least completed a high school education (NFHS II). NFHS III records that 51 percent of pregnant women sought medical help during pregnancy, of which 85 percent were literates and 30 percent were illiterates. The above figures show that education plays a crucial role in women's health practices. Still, however, a large percentage of women and of the Indian population as a whole is illiterate. Between the law and its practice is a gap that needs to be bridged in order to progress toward sustainability.

China

Female education in China only started at the end of the nineteenth century, under the influence of Western missionaries who opened all-girl schools and with the efforts of the Reformists, headed by Kang You-Wei and Liang Qi-Chao. In 1906 there were 8,005 female students attending secondary school and 164,719 female students in primary schools (Dong Guang-Chuan 1930, 133).

Supported by a series of regulations and policies that aimed to establish a unified educational system with genuine equality between women and men, female education during the period of Republican China (1911/12–1949) had made substantial progress, although its percentage was very small, and the continuous wars seriously hindered the development of women's education. According to statistics published by the national government, there were 1.36 million female graduates from primary schools during 1931–1935, and 6.48 million during 1937–1945. As for secondary education, there were only 3,249 girl students studying in secondary schools in 1922, which accounted for 3 percent of the total; this number dramatically increased to 33,073 in 1929, and to 56,851 in 1931, a jump to 15 percent of the total (Huang Xin-Xian 1992, 106–107). Two years before the 1949 revolution, the proportion of female students among graduates, undergraduates, and junior college students were 14, 18, and 18 percent respectively (Wei Yu 1995, 14).

In 1949, when the People's Republic of China (PRC) was founded, the rate of female illiteracy was over 90 percent. To raise the cultural level of the entire population, the first constitution of the PRC (1954) expressly granted women equal rights to access to education, and the Chinese government launched three comprehensive nationwide campaigns against illiteracy in 1952, 1956, and 1958. The number of female illiterates decreased by 16 million in 1958 (State Council Information Office 1994, 8 and 9), and the illiteracy rate of women aged fifteen years and over in 1982 was 49 percent (Zhang Ping 1995, 35). Meanwhile, the proportion of women enrolled in basic education also greatly increased: the proportion of girls among primary school pupils was only 28 percent in 1951; it increased to 39 percent in 1965 and to 44 percent in 1980 (Gu Ning 2005, 57). In higher education, this proportion increased from 18 percent in 1947 to 23 percent in 1951 and to 27 percent in 1965 (Gu Ning 2005, 58).

Since 1978 female education in China has entered a new era. Firstly, the promulgation of a number of laws and policies has provided a better environment for the development of female education. Written into the 1982 constitution was the commitment to "making primary education compulsory and universal, developing secondary, vocational and higher education." Also, the rights and opportunities of women to have access to education have been clearly defined in a series of laws related to all levels of education. Secondly, the State Council issued the National Program of Women's Development in 1995, 2000, and 2011 (the 1995–2000, 2001–2010, and 2011–2020 programs), in which specific targets and related policies and measures in different periods have been put forward. In addition, the Hope Project, the Spring Buds Program, the Red Phoenix Project, and the Women's Illiteracy Eradication Campaign were launched one after another beginning in 1989, especially to help girls attend school and provide women with access to basic education.

In 1982, the illiteracy rate of women ages fifteen and over was 45 percent; it fell rapidly to 32 percent in 1990, to 14 percent in 2000, and 10 percent in 2009. The ratio of primary school attendance for girls in 2010 reached 99.58 percent, which was higher than for boys, and the ratio of junior school attendance was 95 percent, almost the same as for boys. In senior school education, this rate reached 48 percent of total enrollment in 2009. The most remarkable achievement in female education lies in higher education institutions, in which the proportion of females has increased from 23 percent in 1980 to 34 percent in 1990, 41 percent in 2000, and 50 percent in 2009 (National Bureau of Statistics of China 2009).

Female education in China has been improving steadily, in particular over the last decades of the twentieth and the beginning of the twenty-first centuries; in addition to the increase of women's participation in all levels of education, the percentage of women students at college and higher level institutions has grown faster than other levels. This has had significant impact on women's gender equality and social development, especially on their employment and political participation.

Future Perspectives

Although the economies of China and India are among the fastest developing in the world, the rates of female illiteracy and rural poverty are still major issues. The data from India and China show that educating women is an essential element for sustainable development, since education provides them with quality information on health care, sanitation, population control, decision making, and conservation of natural resources. Growing population is a severe threat to sustainability, and a strong positive relationship between female education and declining fertility rate gives hope for a population decline in the next seventy to one hundred years, provided there continues to be increased educational opportunities for women in highly populated countries. A reduced population is a crucial step toward poverty reduction, better health, protection of natural resources, and sustainable development; the best method to achieve this will be through educating more women. Where access to education for women has been limited, the emphasis on developing and promoting female education is a key factor for sustainable development.

Leemamol MATHEW
Institute of Rural Management

Fengping ZHAO
Zhengzhou University

See also Education, Environmental (*several articles*); Five-Year Plans; Gandhism; Gender Equality; Microfinance; One-Child Policy; Property Rights (China); Public Health; White Revolution of India

Further Reading

Brown, Phillip H., & Park, Albert. (2002) Education and poverty in rural China. *Economics of Education Review, 21*(6), 523–541.

Census of India. (2011). *Census 2011*. Delhi: Government of India.

Dong Guang-Chuan. (1930). A brief history of female education in China. *Quarterly Review of Humanities and Arts College of Henan University* (Vol. 2). (in Chinese)

Gu Ning. (2005). Achievements, problems and suggested measures in women's education since the foundation of new China. *Contemporary China History Studies, 12*(6), 56–64. (in Chinese)

Huang Xin-Xian. (1992). *Female education in recent China*. Fujian, China: Fujian Education Publishing House. (in Chinese)

Liu Ju-Cai. (1990). *History of women's movement in recent China*. Beijing: China Women Publishing House. (in Chinese)

Mukherjee, Deepa. (2007). Women's education in India: Trends, interlinkages and policy issues. In J. B. G. Tilak (Ed.), *Women's education and development*. New Delhi: Gyan Publishers. Retrieved March 3, 2012, from http://mpra.ub.uni-muenchen.de/4871/1/MPRA_paper_4871.pdf

National Bureau of Statistics of China. (2009). *Official statistics: China*. Beijing: National Bureau of Statistics China.

National Family Health Survey (NFHS). (2009). NFHS I, II & III. Mumbai, India: International Institute of Population Sciences. Retrieved March 26, 2012, from http://www.nfhsindia.org/

Singh, Andrea M., & Burra, Neera. (1993). *Women and Wasteland Development in India*. New Delhi: Sage Publications.

State Council Information Office. (1994). *Official statistics: China*. Beijing: Sate Council Information Office.

Wei Yu. (1995). *Female education in China*. Hangzhou, China: Zhejiang Education Publishing House. (in Chinese)

Zhang Ping. (1995). *The current situation of Chinese women*. Beijing: Hong-Qi Press. (in Chinese)

Endangered Species

The magnificent species richness of Asia, from elephants to orchids, shares the continent with about half the world's people. Human habitat conversion and poaching have threatened many species with extinction. Increasing numbers of protected areas, better research, and growing public awareness have enabled Asia to bring its fair share of species back from the edge of extinction.

Asia is the richest continent in the world in terms of numbers of species of mammals, birds, reptiles, amphibians, and plants. With the world's highest mountains, vast areas of forests, tens of thousands of islands, a long coastline with abundant coral reefs, and a wide range of ecosystem types, Asia has long been a center of evolution for both plants and animals. The continent also supports about half of the world's human population. The conflict between humans and the species who share Asia's forests, grasslands, deserts, wetlands, and marine habitats has threatened many species with extinction. Such species are more formally known as *endangered*.

Extinction is nothing new, as indicated by the loss of the dinosaurs. Once the dinosaurs became extinct about 65 million years ago, mammals and birds flourished in Asia, including spectacular genera like *Paraceratherium*, part of the rhinoceros family whose species stood over 7 meters high and may have weighed as much as 18 tonnes. They survived until about 23 million years ago as part of a suite of large mammals occupying the lush river valleys and plains of those ancient times. Over the past million years or so, dozens of species of large Asian mammals have become extinct, including the largest primate that has ever existed (known as *Giganotpithecus blacki*), the woolly mammoth (*Mammuthus primigenius*), the woolly rhinoceros (*Coelodonta antiquitatus*), and numerous ancestral relatives of today's elephants, hippos, deer, hyenas, and wild cattle. Many species of human ancestors were also lost, ranging from *Homo erectus*, who ranged from China to Java from about 500,000 years ago, to the diminutive Flores Man (*Homo floresiensis*), who apparently lasted until about 15,000 years ago.

These extinctions were part of the natural process of evolution linked to natural causes, especially climate change as ice ages ebbed and flowed over hundreds of thousands of years. Ice sheets during the ice age connected the Indonesian islands of Java, Sumatra, and Borneo to the mainland, and then separated them again as the great ice sheets withdrew for the last time about 18,000 years ago. Early humans hunting also may have played an increasing role as their technology and hunting methods became more sophisticated, a precursor of problems to come.

Categories of Threat

Humans today primarily drive the extinction process as Asia's growing population claims more of its resources. The authoritative global list of threatened species is the International Union for Conservation of Nature's (IUCN) Red List, which is constantly updated and as of 2011 includes more than 60,000 species (IUCN 2011). The Red List divides the assessed species into categories based on their risk of extinction. Those that are already gone are classified as *extinct* (although some species, often called *Lazarus species*, that have not been seen for over one hundred years still reappear from time to time). Those that remain only in captivity are called *extinct in the wild*, although wildlife rehabilitators may return some of these species to their natural habitat after some time in captivity; a good case in Asia is Père David's deer, or milu (*Elaphus davidianus*). The duke of Bedford moved the last few individuals to England in the late 1800s, where he and his descendants nurtured them in captivity until they returned many of the deer to China in the 1980s. Following further captive breeding, wildlife rehabilitators have returned herds to several protected areas, including Tian'ezhou Wetland Reserve in Hubei province and Dafeng Reserve in Jiangsu province, both in China.

Species on the verge of extinction are *critically endangered*, highly likely to be lost unless urgent action is taken. The IUCN lists some 68 mammals and 60 birds in Asia as such, including both the Javan (*Rhinoceros sondaicus*) and Sumatran rhinoceros (*Dicerorhinus sumatrensis*). Species considered endangered also require conservation action but with somewhat lower urgency; 167 Asian mammals and 95 birds fall into this category (such as tigers, *Panthera tigris*, and the Sarus crane, *Grus antigone*). Together, these categories list the species generally considered as endangered in a general sense.

The Red List assigns species that are not yet endangered to categories ranging from *vulnerable* to *near threatened*, *least concern*, *data deficient*, or *not evaluated* (the last including most plants and the vast majority of invertebrates). They are not yet endangered, although some may become so, even while some endangered species join one of these less threatened categories.

Many countries have their own lists of endangered species and give them a designation under national legislation. IUCN considers Asian elephants (*Elephas maximus*) endangered on a global basis, for example, but critically endangered in China, where only a few survive in the southern edge of Yunnan Province. Many other species are found only in a single country; the Red List labels them *country endemic species*. The status their countries give them nationally is typically the same as their global status, provided the country assigns the status based on the scientifically rigorous IUCN criteria. Indonesia, China, and the Philippines are especially rich in national endemic species of both plants and animals, either because of their large size and multiple types of ecosystems or because they have many islands where species evolved in the absence of crossbreeding with their nearest relatives.

Threats

Human activities bring most of the threats to endangered species. The most serious threat is habitat conversion. A species-rich tropical forest in Borneo that landowners have converted to an oil palm plantation or rice fields, for example, can no longer support many species of plants, much less large mammals like orangutans. Considerable evidence has shown convincingly that the smaller the area of habitat, the fewer the number of species that will be able to occupy the habitat. Asia has lost the majority of its most species-rich habitats, including 70 percent of its wetlands, at least 20 percent of its coral reefs, and about 60 percent of its tropical forests (Sadhi et al. 2004; Wilkenson 2008). These trends show no sign of slowing as human demand continues to grow for land to cultivate crops (including for biofuels) and for fish (which leads to overfishing and destructive fishing methods such as using explosives on coral reefs).

Overexploitation is another leading cause of species loss. Hunters exterminated Thailand's Schomburgk's deer (*Rucervus schomburgki*) by the 1930s, when a hunter shot the last individual in a Buddhist temple in 1938. Schomburgk's was a swamp deer with perhaps the most magnificent antlers of any species. Hunting became easier as farmers converted the deer's swamp habitat to rice fields to meet the accelerating foreign demand for rice; exports from Bangkok increased from 87,000 tonnes of rice in 1860 to 880,000 tonnes in 1910 (Owen 1971). No government agency worried much about what happened to the deer that occupied the former swampy grasslands that were now earning significant foreign exchange. The kouprey (*Bos sauveli*), a unique species of wild cattle whose last retreat was Cambodia, disappeared in the late 1990s or early 2000s, again due to overhunting, perhaps by soldiers whose hunger for meat was far stronger than any government conservation measures at that unstable time in the country's history.

Some overhunting may have been at least somewhat inadvertent, such as the loss of the Yangzi (Chang) River dolphin, or Baiji (*Lipotes vexillifer*), the only species of its family. The Chinese once venerated this dolphin as a "river princess." China denounced this status during the Great Leap Forward, and the species became fair game for fishers. By the 1950s, only 6,000 individuals remained; declaring the species protected was ineffective against the pressure of entanglement in fishing gear, the use of illegal electric fishing methods, and collisions with riverboat traffic. No one has seen the Baiji since 2007 (Turvey et al. 2007). The IUCN has declared it functionally extinct, the first known human-caused extinction of a cetacean (the order that includes whales and dolphins).

An earlier tragic case is Steller's sea cow (*Hydrodamalis gigas*), which once grazed on sea grasses from California to Japan. The local people who lived along the coastline harvested it for meat, skins for making boats, and fat for eating and burning in lamps. When the German naturalist Georg Steller first described the species for science in 1741, its population was already declining even in its redoubt (protected barrier) off the coast of Kamchatka, Russia. European sailors on their way to Alaska to hunt seals and other species found this massive source of meat, 8 meters long and weighing some 9 tonnes, a welcome sight. They hunted the defenseless giant to extinction within twenty-seven years, a remarkably rapid road to extinction. No conservation laws were in place, and even had there been such laws, the capacity to enforce them was sorely lacking.

Pollution and the spread of non-native species have also posed significant threats to species in Asia. The invasion of new predators such as rats decimated the population of flightless birds. When the Polynesians first settled the Pacific Islands, they carried Asian rats (*Rattus exulans*) aboard their ships. The combination of hungry people, hungry rats, and flightless birds led to the extinction of some 2,000 species, about 20 percent of the total number of bird species on the planet at that time (Steadman 1995). But the major threat looming on the horizon today is climate change. Just as at the end of the latest ice age some 18,000 years ago (when north Asian species such as the woolly mammoth, the woolly rhinoceros, and many others disappeared as the glaciers retreated), climate change today is changing the distribution of habitats and therefore the distribution of species that depend on those habitats. Although the precise impacts of climate change on the range of species remain somewhat unpredictable, it is safe to say that changing climates are further threatening many endangered species. Detailed projections suggest that climate change that alters rainfall patterns and raises temperatures threatens at least 15 percent and perhaps as many as 37 percent of species (Thomas et al. 2004). Lizards, amphibians, and insects, along with many plants, are especially vulnerable.

Conservation

Scientists are discovering many species in Asia, including some that are quite remarkable. Since the end of the Indo-Chinese wars in 1975, field biologists have discovered numerous new species, including some from parts of the country that were heavily bombed or defoliated. These include large mammals such as the Vu Quang ox, or saola (*Pseudoryx nghetinhensis*), the giant muntjac (*Megamuntiacus vuquangensis*), and the pygmy muntjac (*Muntiacus truongsonensis*)—the latter two being, respectively, the largest and smallest of their genus of deer. Scientists discovered an entire new family of bats roosting in limestone caves in Thailand in 1975, finding some individuals just 50 meters from the notorious "death railway" the Japanese built to link Thailand with Burma during World War II. The Thai naturalist Kitti Thonglongya discovered the "bumblebee bat" (*Craseonycteris thonglongyai*), possibly the world's smallest mammal. Naturalists discovered a new rodent in 2005 that was so distinctive that it now has its own genus: *Laonastes*. Vendors sold *Laonastes aenigmamus*, known as the Laotian rock rat, for food in a Lao market town. Scientists continue to discover primates, too, including a new species of macaque from northeastern India (*Macaca munzala*, 2004) and the Burmese snub-nosed monkey (*Rhinopithecus strykeri*, 2010). Field biologists have discovered numerous birds, amphibians, reptiles, and plants. These scientists continue to fill out the list of Asian species. Such discoveries warrant a note of concern, however: most of these species have escaped discovery because they are rare and their populations are probably declining, which makes them candidates for being listed as endangered once biologists better understand their status.

Another encouraging step forward for conservation in Asia is a growing level of government and public support for conservation of threatened species. All Asian countries have established protected areas; all are parties to the Convention on Biological Diversity; all have laws in place to protect endangered species; and many have nongovernmental conservation organizations. The Convention on International Trade in Endangered Species (CITES), to which all Asian countries are party, controls the international illegal trade in endangered species. Although habitat loss, poaching, and illegal trade continue, millions of people visit Asia's many protected areas and, by so doing, demonstrate popular support for the conservation of natural ecosystems and their components. International support for conservation from both governments and international conservation organizations that have established branch offices in many Asian countries is also contributing to species conservation in Asia.

Species conservation successes are becoming more common, often beginning with a crisis but ending with at least the hope of eventual restoration. Hunters shot the last wild Arabian oryx (*Oryx leucoryx*), an antelope unique to the Arabian peninsula that some have thought gave rise to the myth of the unicorn, in 1972, but captive breeding has returned more than 1,000 individuals of the species to wild or semiwild habitats ranging from Oman to Abu Dhabi. The efforts to save the giant panda (*Ailuropoda melanoleuca*) followed decades when the species was a popular target for hunters, including Kermit Roosevelt and Theodore Roosevelt Jr., who were the first Westerners known to have shot a panda. The growing human population in China fragments the panda's habitat, which usually includes several species of bamboo that form 99 percent of the panda's diet. Driven by famines and foreign demand for panda skins, hunters pushed the panda population below 1,000 individuals by the 1960s, and the species seemed well on its way to extinction. But in the 1980s, a new government policy promoted field studies and more effective management of protected areas for pandas with more than forty such reserves now supporting as many as 3,000 giant pandas. International support has also helped, including the United Nations Educational, Scientific and Cultural Organization's

(UNESCO) listing of the Sichuan Giant Panda Sanctuaries as a World Heritage Site. At least for now, the panda population seems to be secure and growing.

Outlook

With solid research, sufficient funding, law enforcement, removal of the major threats, appropriate technology, and perseverance, no endangered species need ever become extinct at the hands of humans. Many could return to play their historical role as part of the complex natural ecosystems that have enriched Asia's cultures.

Jeffrey A. McNEELY
International Union for Conservation of Nature

See also Association of Southeast Asian Nations (ASEAN); Biodiversity Conservation Legislation (China); Climate Change Mitigation Initiatives (China); Ecotourism; Education, Environmental (*several articles*); Fisheries (China); Genetic Resources; Media Coverage of the Environment; Nongovernmental Organizations (NGOs); Parks and Preserves; Traditional Chinese Medicine (TCM); Yangzi (Chang) River

FURTHER READING

Baillie, Jonathan; Hilton-Taylor, Craig; & Stuart, Simon. (Eds.). (2004). *A global species assessment: 2004 IUCN red list of threatened species*. Gland, Switzerland: International Union for Conservation of Nature.

Birdlife International. (2001). *Threatened birds of Asia*. Cambridge, UK: Birdlife International.

Goodall, Jane. (2009). *Hope for animals and their world: How endangered species are being rescued from the brink*. New York: Grand Central Publishing.

Hoffman, Michael, et al. (2010). The impact of conservation on the status of the world's vertebrates. *Science, 330*(6010), 1503–1509.

International Union for Conservation of Nature (IUCN). (2011). IUCN red list of threatened species. Retrieved February 1, 2012, from www.iucnredlist.org

International Union for Conservation of Nature (IUCN), Species Survival Commission. (2001). IUCN red list categories and criteria version 3.1. Gland, Switzerland: IUCN.

MacArthur, Robert H., & Wilson, Edward O. (1967). *The theory of island biogeography*. Princeton, NJ: Princeton University Press.

Martin, Paul. (Ed.). (1984). *Quaternary extinctions: A prehistoric revolution*. Phoenix: University of Arizona Press.

Owen, Norman G. (1971). The rice industry of mainland Southeast Asia, 1850–1914. *Journal of the Siam Society, 59*(2), 75–143.

Sadhi, N.S., et al. (2004). Southeast Asian Biodiversity: An impending disaster. *Trends in Ecology and Evolution, 19*(12), 654-659.

Schaller, George B. (1993). *The last panda*. Chicago: University of Chicago Press.

Stanley Price, Mark. (2010). *Animal reintroductions: The Arabian oryx in Oman*. Cambridge, UK: Cambridge University Press.

Steadman, David W. (1995). Prehistoric extinctions of Pacific island birds: Biodiversity meets zooarcheology. *Science, 267*(5201), 1123–1131.

Thomas, Chris D., et al. (2004). Extinction risk from climate change. *Nature, 427*, 145–148.

Turvey, Samuel T., et al. (2007). First human-caused extinction of a cetacean species? *Biology Letters, 3*(5), 537–540.

Wilkenson, Clive. (Ed.). (2008). *Status of coral reefs of the world*. Townsville, Australia: Global Coral Reef Monitoring Network and Reef and Rainforest Research Center.

Berkshire's authors and editors welcome questions, comments, and corrections. Send your emails about the *Berkshire Encyclopedia of Sustainability* in general or this volume in particular to: sustainability.updates@berkshirepublishing.com

Energy Industries—Nuclear

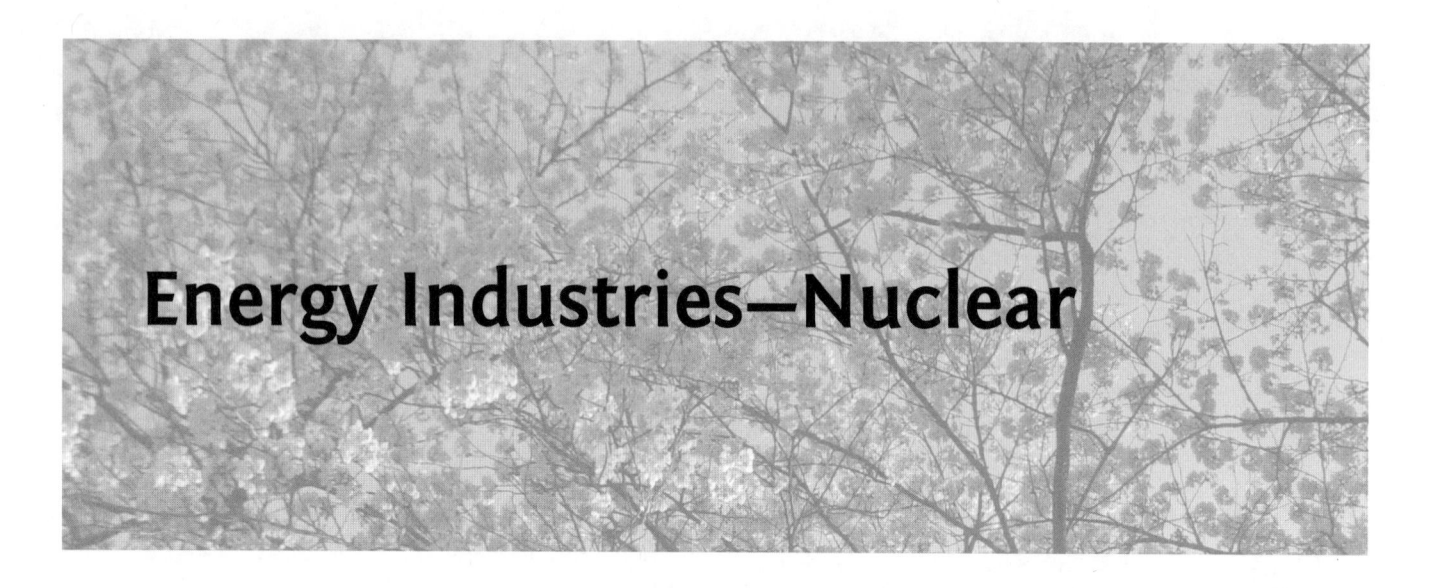

While environmentalists, nuclear security experts, and the citizen populations of East Asian nations are concerned about nuclear waste, nuclear weapons proliferation, and reactor safety, Asian government leaders and economic analysts are promoting nuclear fission as one of the few practical alternatives to coal-powered electricity in a world where fossil fuels are causing increasingly serious problems. Long-term sustainability of nuclear-powered energy resources remains an open issue.

Nuclear energy comes from the splitting (fission) or combining (fusion) of atomic nuclei. Nearly all energy used by humanity is indirect nuclear energy. Most of it comes from the nuclear fusion of the sun, which provides light for solar energy and the heat that drives global wind and water circulation, and has also provided the sunlight that has created our coal, petroleum, and natural gas reserves through plant photosynthesis over the past 400 million years. When we speak of the nuclear energy industry in the twentieth and early twenty-first centuries, however, we are referring to the artificial fission reactors, fueled mainly by the heavy metal uranium, that were invented in the 1940s and that by 2008 provided 14 percent of the world's electricity. It is this industry that is at issue when both benefits and risks of nuclear-powered energy resources are weighed in the sustainability balance.

Fundamentals of Nuclear Energy

Nuclear fuel is made from the elements uranium and thorium. Uranium ores contain a mixture of 0.7 percent isotope uranium-235 (U-235), the only naturally available fissile isotope (an isotope that can sustain a fission chain reaction to release energy), and 99.3 percent isotope uranium-238 (U-238), which is not fissile. Thorium is about three times more abundant in the Earth's crust than uranium, but its only isotope, thorium-232 (Th-232), is not fissile. Neutrons from a nuclear reaction can transmute U-238 to fissile plutonium-239 (Pu-239), and transmute Th-232 to fissile uranium-233 (U-233). While less than 0.2 percent of the world's potential nuclear fuel can readily be used for energy, the other 99.8 percent could be converted into a fissile form in breeder reactors—fission reactors specialized to use neutrons to transmute uranium and thorium as efficiently as possible. Although many experimental breeder reactors have been built, nearly all of today's nuclear energy comes from conventional reactors that consume mainly U-235, and breed only small amounts of Pu-239, while producing heat. In most cases, the nuclear fuel is enriched uranium where the fraction of U-235 has been boosted artificially from the natural abundance 0.7 percent up to a concentration between 3 and 5 percent relative to the U-238 in the fuel. Most of the U-238 in a conventional reactor is not transmuted, and it ends up unused in the nuclear fuel waste unless the waste is reprocessed.

In a nuclear power plant, the heat from fission in U-233, U-235, or Pu-239 boils water. Energy in the boiling water (steam) turns a turbine and a dynamo to generate electricity. The turbine-dynamo part of a nuclear power plant is similar to the turbine-dynamo systems in coal, petroleum, and natural gas power plants. The main differences between a nuclear power plant and a conventional power plant are related to the behavior of the fuel. Coal, natural gas, and petroleum react with oxygen in combustion to release chemical energy and carbon dioxide as products. Fissile isotopes react with neutrons to release nuclear energy, more neutrons, and fission products (split nuclei). The other major distinction is the difference in magnitude between the two types of reaction. Burning 100 grams of coal or petroleum can boil about 1 liter of water. Fissioning 100 grams of a fissile isotope can boil about 3 million liters of water. Clearly, the energy concentrated in a small amount of nuclear material is far greater than anything in ordinary human experience. This great concentration of energy results in both the great potential and the significant concerns and fears about nuclear energy.

History

The possibility of a fission chain reaction in U-235 was first recognized in 1939, on the eve of World War II. Concerned that such a reaction might be used for military purposes, Britain, Germany, and the United States began secret nuclear research programs. In 1942 the United States created the first sustained artificial nuclear chain reaction. In less than three years, the United States built three nuclear weapons, using two of them in August 1945 to destroy the Japanese cities of Hiroshima and Nagasaki at the end of World War II. Early nuclear energy development thus was inextricably linked with weapons development. Immediately after the war, the Soviet Union began its own nuclear program, producing nuclear weapons by 1949. Britain followed in 1952, France in 1960, and China in 1964.

Work on peaceful applications of nuclear energy followed soon after weapons development, with the first demonstration of a nuclear-powered electric generator in the United States in 1951, the connection of a nuclear plant to the power grid in the Soviet Union in 1954, and the first commercial nuclear power plant in Britain in 1956. By 1960 nuclear power plants operated in four nations, including France, together producing over 700 megawatts of electricity. For the next two decades the nuclear energy industry grew rapidly, expanding into the world's industrialized nations including most of Europe and Canada, Argentina, Japan (1963), India (1969), Pakistan (1971), South Korea (1978), and Taiwan (1978). By 1980 there were over two hundred nuclear reactors worldwide producing over 70,000 megawatts of electricity.

Orders for new nuclear power plants slowed in the 1980s in Europe and North America in response to concerns raised by the environmental movement and citizen's groups, which opposed nuclear power plants based on evidence that radioactive contamination from nuclear waste and nuclear accidents can be bad for the environment and people's health and safety. New regulations resulting from environmentalist pressures, and from the Three Mile Island nuclear reactor accident near Harrisburg, Pennsylvania, in 1979, made nuclear power costs less competitive with other power plants and contributed to financial losses for most companies completing nuclear plants in the 1980s. The more disastrous Chernobyl reactor accident in Ukraine in 1986 increased opposition to nuclear energy in Europe, including the Soviet states, which previously had no strong antinuclear movement. In 1991 China began operating its first nuclear power plant.

Since the Chernobyl accident, there have been few new nuclear reactor projects in North America and western Europe, while growth in nuclear energy continues mainly in China, Russia, India, South Korea, and Japan. The Fukushima Daiichi reactor incident, caused by a massive tsunami in Japan in March 2011, increased concern about nuclear safety in Japan and other Asian nations, delaying many nuclear power plant projects and triggering an energy crisis in Japan.

Japan, South Korea, and Taiwan

Economic studies have compared the costs of electricity generated by various energy sources. Since sources like solar and wind power require no fuel but have high construction costs per unit of power produced, a fair comparison must average in the cost of construction, operation and maintenance, interest charges on loans, and fuel costs per megawatt-hour (Mwh) of electricity generated over the lifetime of the power plant. This is called the *levelized electricity cost* or LEC. The LEC for coal-generated electricity in India is approximately $50/Mwh (cost figures are in year-2010 US dollars). Historically, the LEC for electricity generation using natural gas, petroleum, and nuclear power have been higher than coal power costs in most places. For example, the LEC for nuclear power in Japan has historically been about $130/Mwh, while the LEC for natural gas power plants in Japan has varied with the price of natural gas from $60 to $130/Mwh. Companies that design large-scale solar energy systems estimated the LEC for solar power in 2010 at $200 to $400/Mwh, depending on location and weather. The LEC for large-scale wind generators in 2010 was estimated at $70 to $140/Mwh depending on location and prevailing winds.

In choosing their energy infrastructure, nations consider the LEC and also the variability of fuel prices and weather. For example, solar and wind power are not affected by fuel prices, but they vary widely from day to day. As a result, nations like Denmark that have maximized their wind power have chosen not to exceed 20 percent electricity generation from wind because their generation and distribution system cannot compensate for daily wind fluctuations larger than that. Historically, less than 10 percent of the cost of nuclear power has been nuclear fuel; the cost of construction and financing make up most of the LEC for nuclear energy. In contrast, the cost of coal and its transportation accounts for about 30 percent of the LEC for coal-powered electricity; and the cost of petroleum and gas fluctuate due to market volatility, contributing between 40 and 80 percent of the LEC for those electricity sources.

Japan, Korea, and Taiwan import between 60 and 90 percent of the energy resources they use for electricity. (See table 1 below.) This makes them economically vulnerable to petroleum and natural gas price fluctuations. In the wake of the disruptions caused by the 1973–1974 oil embargo imposed by the Arab members of the Organization of Petroleum Exporting Countries (OPEC), all three of these nations made the strategic decision to begin generating a large fraction of their electricity from nuclear power plants. Since the price of uranium represents only a small fraction of the LEC for nuclear power, large fluctuations in the uranium market price in recent years have not had a significant effect on the cost of nuclear energy. Therefore one major economic impact of nuclear power in East Asia has been to stabilize the cost of

TABLE 1. Percentage of Electricity Generated by Nuclear Power for East Asian Nations in 2009

Country	Operating Reactors	Nuclear-Generated Electricity	Percent of Total	Uranium Reserves	Other Electricity Resources Source	Percent	Reserves
Japan	58*	280 MMwh	29%	6,600 T	Coal	25%	Imported
					Natural gas	29%	Imported
					Hydroelectric	8%	
					Petroleum	7%	Imported
					Renewables	1%	
China	13	60 MMwh	2%	170,000 T	Coal	79%	115 BT
					Natural gas	1%	3000 BCM
					Hydroelectric	17%	20 BB
					Petroleum	1%	
South Korea	21	150 MMwh	33%	25,000 T	Coal	47%	Imported
					Natural gas	15%	Imported
					Hydroelectric	1%	
					Petroleum	3%	Imported
					Renewables	1%	
India	20	16 MMwh	3%	170,000 T	Coal	68%	61 BT
					Natural gas	8%	1,100 BCM
					Hydroelectric	15%	
					Petroleum	4%	6 BB
					Renewables	2%	
Taiwan	6	41 MMwh	17%	None	Coal	47%	Imported
					Natural gas	20%	Imported
					Hydroelectric	6%	
					Petroleum	6%	Imported
					Renewables	4%	
Pakistan	3	1.6 MMwh	2%	None	Natural gas	33%	840 BT
					Hydroelectric	31%	
					Petroleum	35%	0.4 BB

Notes: *Prior to the Fukushima nuclear plant disaster in March 2011.

MMwh = million megawatt-hours of electricity generated by nuclear power during 2009.
T = metric tonnes uranium. Twenty-five tonnes of uranium can produce 1 MMwh of electricity in a light water reactor.
BT = billion metric tonnes of coal.
BCM = billion cubic meters of natural gas.
BB = billion barrels of petroleum.

Sources: ENS (2012); IAEA (2007); US CIA (2012); US EIA (2011); and WNA (2010a).

electricity in Japan, South Korea, and Taiwan. Continuing this trend, as of 2012 there are currently five new nuclear reactors under construction in South Korea and two in Taiwan (ENS 2012). Due to the disaster in Fukushima, four of Japan's reactors were permanently shut down, all but two of Japan's nuclear reactors have been taken offline as of early 2012 (Fackler 2012), and work on new plants that were under construction will likely halt.

India and Pakistan

Nuclear power provides only a small percentage of the electricity produced in India and Pakistan. (See table 1 on previous page.) This is partly because India and Pakistan are at earlier stages of economic development than Japan and South Korea, and nuclear power plants require a larger capital investment up front than other types of power plants. It is also partly caused by the nuclear weapons Non-Proliferation Treaty (NPT) of 1970, which tried to prevent nuclear weapons proliferation by threatening nuclear technology sanctions against any nation developing nuclear weapons outside of the United States, the Soviet Union, France, Britain, and China.

Recognizing the potential of India's large thorium deposits as a nuclear fuel, in the 1950s nuclear scientist Homi Bhabha proposed a three-stage strategy for developing nuclear energy in India. In stage one, India would use its limited uranium resources to start up heavy water reactors, a type of relatively low-cost reactor that can produce electricity while breeding nonfissile U-238 into fissile Pu-239. In stage two, the Pu-239 would start up fast breeder reactors, designed to produce more electricity while breeding more Pu-239 and also breeding nonfissile thorium into fissile U-233. In stage three, the U-233 would start up thorium breeder reactors designed to use India's large thorium reserves, converting thorium to U-233 while producing still more electricity. While this ambitious program would make best use of India's limited uranium resources, it required the development of new nuclear reactor systems beyond the light water reactors that became the standard for power generation in most Western nations. Stage one of India's nuclear program began when Canada and the United States assisted India in building the Canada India Research Utility Services (CIRUS) heavy water research reactor between 1956 and 1960, the first Indian reactor of sufficient size to breed significant quantities of plutonium. Plutonium from the CIRUS reactor was used to create India's first nuclear detonation in 1974. For violating the terms of the NPT, India was subjected to an embargo of nuclear fuel and technology for the next thirty-four years. This embargo substantially slowed the progress of India's three-stage plan.

International cooperation resumed in 2008 with the US-India Civil Nuclear Agreement. As of 2012, with renewed access to nuclear fuel and technology from Russia and France, India is now expanding its nuclear power industry as rapidly as it believes is economically prudent. Nine new nuclear reactors are under construction, mostly of the Indian heavy water reactor design. New findings of large uranium deposits in the southeastern state of Andhra Pradesh have increased India's reserves from less than 80,000 metric tonnes in 2008 to over 170,000 metric tonnes of uranium metal in 2011. India continues its stage three program toward the eventual aim of using thorium breeder reactors to provide much of the nation's energy. If India succeeds, there is enough thorium in the country to provide all the electricity India would need for thousands of years.

Pakistan began separating plutonium from its reactor called PARR-1 (Pakistan Atomic Research Reactor) in 1972 and began purifying and enriching uranium in 1976. In 1998 Pakistan performed a series of nuclear weapons tests. As a result, nuclear sanctions were imposed on the country in 1998, slowing their nuclear energy industry; however, the nuclear fuel and technology embargo against Pakistan has not been completely enforced. China continues to supply reactor fuel for two of Pakistan's three nuclear power reactors and is assisting with the construction of two new reactors.

China

In the 1980s, Chinese leadership began to promote nuclear energy as an alternative to coal and hydroelectric power. Coal has become an economic concern for China in part because, as industrialization expands to areas that are farther from the main coalfields in northeast China, the cost of coal transportation increases the cost of electricity significantly. For nuclear fuel, containing energy a million times denser than coal, the transportation distance matters much less. China is also increasingly concerned about the pollution effects of coal; a 2007 World Bank report produced in collaboration with the Chinese government implied that hundreds of thousands of people die prematurely each year in China from illnesses caused by coal-related air and water pollution. The report estimates current losses from coal pollution may cost China up to 4 percent of its gross domestic product (GDP). By 2012, China had surpassed the United States as the largest global emitter of the carbon dioxide gas that is accelerating the rate of climate change, and almost half of that is produced by coal-burning power plants to generate electricity. China and other nations are increasingly motivated to curb carbon dioxide emissions before climate change accelerates to rates that could cause more severe economic and environmental disruption. At current rates of consumption, China has forty years of known reserves of natural gas and coal; however, with the country's economic growth averaging 8 percent for the past twenty years, China's fossil fuel horizon may be closer.

For all of these reasons, China is maintaining a vigorous nuclear energy development program. As of 2012, it has thirteen operating reactors producing nuclear power and another twenty-seven new reactors under construction, with a planned total generation capacity of 27,000 megawatts to be added in the next five years. The country also has active research programs in new nuclear fission technologies: high-temperature gas-cooled reactors, a possible future source of hydrogen fuels to replace petroleum; breeder reactors to produce fissile fuel from U-238 and Th-232 when nuclear fuel supplies become more expensive; and heavy water reactors, which are useful for exploiting a wider variety of nuclear fuel systems. All of these research programs show that China, like India, is making major long-term strategic commitments to nuclear fission. Currently China is the world leader in nuclear energy growth. In comparison, the United States leads the world in total number of reactors, with 104 light water reactors producing 810 million megawatt-hours (MMwh) of electricity per year, while France leads in percentage among large nations, generating 80 percent of its electricity from 58 nuclear reactors.

Sustainability

Later in this century, the projected world population of 9–12 billion people will be pursuing an acceptable standard of living in equilibrium with Earth's environment. This will require a shift in global energy use away from fossil fuels, which are adding carbon dioxide to the atmosphere and accelerating climate change. Currently the only non-carbon-intensive sources that provide more than 1 percent of the world's energy are nuclear fission and hydroelectric power for electricity, and biomass for heating and cooking. Since the world's river systems are insufficient to increase hydroelectric much further, other options will be pursued. In places where land is inexpensive and steady winds are available, wind energy is now cost-competitive with natural gas and nuclear fission; however, without grid-scale energy storage, the variability of winds limits this source to no more than 20 percent of electricity grid supply. Solar energy is currently an option in relatively wealthy regions, like California, where the cost of electricity is a small fraction of the overall economy. The LEC for solar-generated electricity is too expensive to supply a major portion of the grid electricity for developing nations like China and India, but these costs may decrease over several decades. As with wind power, the variability of weather will limit the usefulness of solar power, even when LEC decreases, to no more than 20 percent of electricity grid supply until grid-scale energy storage is available.

For developing nations in East Asia, there may be an alternative to grid electricity: where the economy is primarily agricultural, for example in large parts of China and India, locally generated renewable electricity could provide a much larger fraction of the electricity requirements than 20 percent, even if wind and solar energy are intermittent. Many of the energy-intensive activities in an agricultural economy, such as pumping water, do not require 100 percent availability. When there is excess wind and solar power, irrigation pumps can run at maximum capacity, and when there is less wind or solar power, irrigation and other non-time-critical equipment can be idled to conserve electricity for communications, lighting, and other high-demand uses. Limited, intermittent electricity supply of this sort may not meet current Western expectations of carefree convenience, but may serve well enough to enhance quality of life and economic development if properly managed by the community.

In an optimistic scenario, by mid-century electricity generation will come from 10 percent hydroelectric, 20 percent solar, and 20 percent wind power, with the remaining half of the world's electricity continuing to come mostly from coal and nuclear fission, in part because global prices of natural gas and petroleum are expected to rise much faster than coal. Technologies such as grid-scale energy storage, enhanced geothermal systems, biomass electricity generation, and nuclear fusion are in their infancy, and there is no certainty that these energy sources can scale up to meet demand, or how many decades it might take for them to do so. Therefore for the first half of the twenty-first century, the growing economies of East Asia will continue to build more coal and nuclear power plants. Coal is less expensive in the short term if the environmental, pollution, and climate factors are ignored. Nuclear fission is likely to remain the most economical and practical alternative to coal for base-load (nonfluctuating) electricity supply.

Critics of nuclear fission have questioned its sustainability partly because if the consumption of uranium doubles worldwide, the available U-235 resources could be consumed in less than fifty years. That appeared to be true in the 1990s; however, increased uranium prices since 2000 led to increased mineral exploration, and known uranium reserves have more than doubled. According to the International Atomic Energy Agency (IAEA) and the Nuclear Energy Agency (NEA), uranium reserves now provide enough fuel for today's nuclear reactors for 230 years at current consumption rates. Even if the price of uranium doubled, it would be cost-effective to reprocess the uranium fuel currently in use and to increase the enrichment work done on mined uranium, yielding another doubling of available fissile material for nuclear power—without appreciably increasing the cost of nuclear power, since the price of fuel, as noted above, is a small fraction of the LEC for nuclear energy. Therefore even if the world doubled its nuclear fission capacity, there would still be enough uranium to last over two hundred years. Proponents of nuclear power note that breeder reactors could use Th-232 and U-238, increasing the usable nuclear fuel by over a factor of a hundred, thus providing energy for thousands of years.

Safety and Environmental Impact

Nuclear power plants produce far less air pollution, water pollution, and carbon dioxide emission than coal power plants. Nuclear energy remains controversial, however, because the reactor failures at Three Mile Island, Chernobyl, and Fukushima Daiichi have reduced public confidence in reactor safety and in the companies that operate nuclear reactors. Critics of nuclear energy, including the Green Party in Germany, the Union of Concerned Scientists in the United States, and Greenpeace International, describe the worst-case scenario reactor failure as an unacceptable risk: a damaged reactor core may release radioactive contamination into a highly populated area, resulting in thousands of cases of cancer and premature deaths. These critics also warn that the accumulation of nuclear waste is a toxic legacy of radioactive isotopes that remain dangerous to the environment for thousands of years—longer than any engineered container can be proven to last. Finally, global security experts warn that the spread of nuclear energy to more nations will inevitably increase the risk of nuclear weapons proliferation and may increase the risk of nuclear terrorism.

Nuclear energy organizations including IAEA, the American Nuclear Society, and the World Nuclear Association point to energy, injury, and fatality statistics from independent health, economic, and safety organizations such as the US Occupational Safety and Health Administration (OSHA), World Health Organization (WHO), the *Lancet* medical journal, and the ExternE (External costs of Energy, a research project of the European Commission) economic studies. These data show that, of the major energy sources, nuclear energy has caused the fewest casualties per unit of electricity produced in the last half century. Worldwide deaths including industry workers and members of the general population due to occupational accidents and pollution from the coal industry have been estimated at 25 deaths per MMwh compared to 0.07 deaths per MMwh of nuclear energy, even including 4,000 estimated cancer deaths from the Chernobyl disaster. In between these two extremes, natural gas is estimated at 4 deaths per MMwh, wind power at 0.2 deaths per MMwh, and hydroelectric power at 0.1 deaths per MMwh (IEA 2002).

Nuclear reactors built today are Generation II or Generation III designs, and most include a steel-reinforced concrete containment shell to inhibit radiation release in severe accidents. Nuclear safety analysts contend that the fatalities from Chernobyl were due to flawed Generation I reactor design, poor government communication with its people, and the lack of a containment shell; whereas Generation II reactors with containment shells such as Three Mile Island and Fukushima, or the even safer Generation III reactors, have extremely small probability of releasing enough radiation to cause major losses of life. Other energy industries, particularly hydroelectric dams, have had failures that caused far greater loss of life (for example, the devastating Banqiao Dam failure in China's Henan Province in 1975) than the Chernobyl disaster.

Nuclear power proponents contend that the nuclear waste issue can be managed with fuel reprocessing technologies currently being developed in France: long-lived radioactive isotopes can be recycled back into the reactor core in the form of mixed-oxide (MOX) fuel, while shorter-lived radioisotopes can be chemically separated from the waste and used for medical, research, and industrial applications. Without breeder reactors, however, to convert most of the unused U-238 to fissile material, the current fuel cycle in France consumes mainly U-235 while producing an ever-growing inventory of U-238, plutonium, and spent fuel. Breeder reactors are needed to achieve the closed fuel cycle that nuclear waste management experts recommend. Large-scale breeder reactors were operated in Russia and France in the 1980s and 1990s, but the French fast breeder reactor called the Superphénix suffered from technical problems and was shut down in 1998. The Russian BN-600 fast breeder reactor had similar technical problems, though it is still operating.

Without breeder reactors, light water reactor fuel waste will eventually be buried in geological repositories, a significant concern to many environmental groups. Widespread nuclear fuel reprocessing may also increase the risk of weapons proliferation in nations that refuse to comply with IAEA safeguards. Nuclear security experts warn that proliferation and nuclear terrorism must be prevented by keeping strong safeguards on all fissile material and operating nuclear reactors. Although this has not yet been completely achieved, significant progress has been made on strengthening worldwide safeguards on fissile material. In the long term, a switch from mainly uranium-based nuclear reactors to mainly thorium breeder reactors could reduce the risk of weapons proliferation: thorium breeder nuclear fuel and thorium nuclear waste can be made proliferation resistant (much harder to use for nuclear weapons), due to the isotopic mixture produced in thorium breeder reactors.

Near-Term Future in East Asia

Responses to the 2011 Fukushima incident have varied widely. The governments of China, Pakistan, and Russia have initiated safety reviews based on lessons learned at Fukushima, but they have stated their intention to continue their current rate of nuclear energy development. Similarly, the government of Vietnam stated its intention to go ahead with the construction of its first two nuclear reactors. The government of India stated that nuclear energy is still a major part of its electricity development plan in the twenty-first century, while acknowledging that there will be delays in implementing nuclear power plans because the general population of India is now much less enthusiastic about nuclear energy. In Japan, while economic analysts and energy officials continue to describe nuclear energy as Japan's best energy option, citizens have abruptly turned against nuclear energy to such an extent that most of Japan's fifty-four undamaged nuclear power plants have been idled in the months since the March 2011 tsunami, causing an energy crisis (Fackler 2012). Public dissatisfaction with the government after the tsunami and Fukushima nuclear power plant disaster ended the administration of the prime minister, Naoto Kan, in August 2011, one of many signs that the Japanese people's faith in the government's nuclear energy policy has been severely damaged (*The Economist* 2012). In most other nations of East Asia, including South Korea and Taiwan, governments and energy officials continue to describe nuclear energy as a practical low-carbon energy solution, while their general populations are ambivalent or opposed because of safety concerns.

Kenneth N. RICCI
Scientech: A Curtiss-Wright Flow Control Company

With thanks to Makarand Dehejia
for editorial advice.

See also China; Energy Industries—Renewables (China); Energy Industries—Renewables (India); Energy Security (East Asia); Five-Year Plans; Green Collar Jobs; India; Japan; Korean Peninsula; Media Coverage of the Environment; Public Health; Southeast Asia; Utilities Regulation and Efficiency

FURTHER READING

Barton, Charles. (2008, April 15). Thorium fuel cycle development in India. Retrieved August 22, 2011, from http://energyfromthorium.com/2008/04/15/thorium-fuel-cycle-development-in-india/

The Economist. (2012, March 10). Japan after the 3/11 disaster: The death of trust. Retrieved March 26, 2012, from http://www.economist.com/node/21549917

Engbarth, Dennis. (2011, March 17). Public demands safety review of new reactor. Retrieved August 22, 2011, from http://www.oceanconserve.org/shared/reader/welcome.aspx?linkid=213278&keybold=ocean%20AND%20%20energy%20AND%20%20waves

European Nuclear Society (ENS). (2012). Nuclear power plants, worldwide. Retrieved March 26, 2012, from http://www.euronuclear.org/info/encyclopedia/n/nuclear-power-plant-world-wide.htm

Fackler, Martin. (2012, March 8). Japan's nuclear energy industry nears shutdown, at least for now. *New York Times*. Retrieved March 26, 2012, from http://www.nytimes.com/2012/03/09/world/asia/japan-shutting-down-its-nuclear-power-industry.html?_r=1

Fetter, Steve. (2009, January 26). How long will the world's uranium supplies last? *Scientific American*. Retrieved August 22, 2011, from http://www.scientificamerican.com/article.cfm?id=how-long-will-global-uranium-deposits-last

GlobalSecurity.org. (2003). Pakistan nuclear weapons. Retrieved August 22, 2011, from http://www.globalsecurity.org/wmd/world/pakistan/nuke.htm

International Atomic Energy Agency (IAEA). (2007). Country nuclear power profiles, 2007 edition. Retrieved April 2, 2012, from http://www-pub.iaea.org/MTCD/publications/PDF/cnpp2007/pages/countryprofiles.htm

International Energy Agency (IEA). (2002). Environmental and health impacts of electricity generation: A comparison of the environmental impacts of hydropower with those of other generation technologies. Retrieved August 22, 2011, from http://www.ieahydro.org/reports/ST3-020613b.pdf

Massachusetts Institute of Technology (MIT). (2010). The future of the nuclear fuel cycle: An interdisciplinary MIT study. Retrieved August 22, 2011, from http://web.mit.edu/mitei/docs/spotlights/nuclear-fuel-cycle.pdf

Schneider, Mycle, & Marignac, Yves. (2008). Spent nuclear fuel reprocessing in France. Retrieved August 28, 2011 from http://www.psr.org/nuclear-bailout/resources/spent-nuclear-fuel.pdf

Taipei Times. (2011, March 29). South Korea reaffirms commitment to expanding nuclear power generation. Retrieved August 22, 2011, from http://www.taipeitimes.com/News/biz/archives/2011/03/29/2003499358

Tolley, George S., & Jones, Donald W. (2004). The economic future of nuclear power: A study conducted at the University of Chicago. Retrieved August 22, 2011, from http://www.ne.doe.gov/np2010/reports/NuclIndustryStudy-Summary.pdf

United States Central Intelligence Agency (US CIA). (2012). World factbook. Retrieved April 2, 2012, from https://www.cia.gov/library/publications/the-world-factbook/

United States Energy Information Administration (US EIA). (2011). Levelized cost of new generation resources in the Annual Energy Outlook 2011. Retrieved April 2, 2012, from http://www.eia.gov/oiaf/aeo/electricity_generation.html

World Bank. (2007). Cost of pollution in China. Retrieved August 22, 2011, from http://siteresources.worldbank.org/INTEAPREGTOPENVIRONMENT/Resources/China_Cost_of_Pollution.pdf

World Nuclear Association (WNA). (2010a.) Asia's nuclear energy growth. Retrieved April 2, 2012, from http://webcache.googleusercontent.com/search?q=cache:http://www.world-nuclear.org/info/inf47.html

World Nuclear Association. (2010b). The nuclear fuel cycle. Retrieved August 22, 2011, from http://www.world-nuclear.org/info/inf03.html

World Nuclear Association. (2010c). Outline history of nuclear energy. Retrieved August 22, 2011, from http://www.world-nuclear.org/info/inf54.html

World Nuclear Association. (2011a). Nuclear power in China. Retrieved August 22, 2011, from http://www.world-nuclear.org/info/inf63.html

World Nuclear Association. (2011b). Nuclear power in India. Retrieved August 22, 2011, from http://www.world-nuclear.org/info/inf53.html

World Nuclear Association. (2011c). Nuclear power in Japan. Retrieved August 22, 2011, from http://www.world-nuclear.org/info/inf79.html

World Nuclear Association. (2011d). Nuclear power in South Korea. Retrieved August 22, 2011, from http://www.world-nuclear.org/info/inf81.html

Share the *Encyclopedia of Sustainability*: Teachers are welcome to make up to ten (10) copies of no more than two (2) articles for distribution in a single course or program. For further permissions, please visit www.copyright.com or contact: info@berkshirepublishing.com

Energy Industries—Renewables (China)

China has become a world leader in the development, manufacturing, and deployment of solar, wind, and hydropower technologies in an amazingly short time. China has added substantial new electric generation capacity from renewable sources, and has developed robust renewables manufacturing industries. Although industry progress and deployment of new capacity have been exceptionally strong, the nation must address substantial challenges to further growth and project deployments.

In China, as in other nations around the world, renewable energy sources can reduce demand for polluting electricity sources and decrease emissions of greenhouse gases (GHGs) (IPCC 2011). China has embarked on an aggressive effort to develop renewable energy, including solar, wind, hydropower, and biomass, and has become a world leader in developing, manufacturing, and deploying renewable energy technologies (China Greentech Initiative 2011).

China's push to develop renewables has yielded impressive results in recent years. In 2010, renewable power sources accounted for 8 percent of final energy and 17 percent of electricity in China. The total installed capacity of 246 gigawatts (GW) of renewables in 2010 was one-fourth of all electric power generation capacity (China Electricity Council 2011). There is enormous potential for future deployment of renewables in China. According to a government forecast, for example, wind power has an estimated potential capacity of 253 GW (Liu and Kokko 2010; McElroy et al. 2009). There are numerous challenges to successful deployment of renewables, however, including governmental policies that require continuing refinement to promote renewable energy (Kahrl et al. 2011).

Since its Renewable Energy Law went into effect in 2005, China has implemented numerous laws and programs designed to promote renewables as part of its strategy to meet its growing demand for electricity, address domestic air pollution, and slow or reverse the nation's increasing rate of GHG emissions. The need to take action to promote renewables in China is readily apparent. China continues to experience poor air quality, and in 2007 it overtook the United States to become the world's largest emitter of GHGs (Zhou et al. 2011; United States Department of Energy 2010). Although comprehensive strategies are necessary to address GHG emissions in all sectors of China's economy, the electric power sector is a focus of governmental attention because it produces 30 percent of China's GHG emissions (McKinsey and Co. 2009)., China has taken measures in the electric power sector to address emissions from conventional power plants, such as shutting down inefficient coal-fired plants (China Electricity Council 2011). Deployment of renewable energy is important to help China transition to a lower-carbon electricity system (Kahrl et al. 2011). By diversifying the overall portfolio of plants used to generate electricity, fewer outages will take place and the system can be more effectively balanced. China still needs to improve its electric grid to reap these benefits (Kahrl et al. 2011).

Without rapid deployment of renewables, China's increasing energy demand and huge spending on new fossil fuel generation plants would overwhelm the global effort to address climate change (McKinsey and Co. 2009; Wang and Watson 2009). China is behind the United States and Europe in per capita energy demand, but the increasing appetite of many of its 1.3 billion people for a better standard of living has resulted in swift increases in demand, suggesting large increases ahead (China Greentech Initiative 2011;

Zhou et al. 2011). Demand for electricity in China doubled between 2000 and 2006 (Martinot and Junfeng 2010). Experts estimate that it will triple again between 2008 and 2035, although a recent study claims demand will level off or decrease after then (EIA 2010; Zhou et al. 2011). The central government has taken a number of steps to curb demand for energy, including new energy intensity targets under the current Five-Year Plan (NDRC 2011a), regulations that require electric grid companies to meet specific demand reduction targets (NDRC 2010), and a proposal for a national system that would set targets for energy use (Juan 2012).

By one estimate, China will build more new electric generation capacity by 2025 than currently exists in the United States (China Greentech Initiative 2011). Coal-fired plants account for 74 percent of electric generation capacity (China Electricity Council 2011). China has added 200 GW of coal-fired plants in the last five years, or as much as one-fifth of the United States' total capacity (China Greentech Initiative 2011). China therefore must continue to pay attention to cutting pollution from its fossil fuel plants, but renewable energy sources are important as well. According to a study of China's energy and carbon emissions outlook to 2050, aggressive renewables deployment and other measures such as greater use of supercritical coal generation (using extremely high steam pressure) and carbon capture and sequestration, as well as increased nuclear power use and accelerated energy efficiency programs, could cut the nation's share of coal-fired electric generation capacity to 47 percent (assuming a wind, solar, and biomass total capacity of 535 GW) or even as low as 30 percent by 2050 (assuming 608 GW) (Zhou et al. 2011).

Deployment

In 2010, China obtained a larger share of its electricity from renewable energy sources than did the United States (17 percent versus 8.8 percent) (China Electricity Council 2011; Eisen 2011). The 17 percent figure trailed that of European leader Denmark (29 percent), but was on par with Germany's 16 percent of electricity generated from renewables (Commission of the European Communities 2010). As is true elsewhere, the vast majority of China's total comes from hydropower, with 216 GW of hydro capacity (22 percent of total generating capacity) installed in 2010, including up to 22.5 GW of electricity from the Three Gorges Dam, the world's largest hydropower station (China Electricity Council 2011). China added 22 GW of new hydropower capacity in 2009, and set a target to add 120 GW more under the Twelfth Five-Year Plan (China Greentech Initiative 2011). The next largest source, wind power, accounted for 3 percent of 2010 generating capacity (China Electricity Council 2011).

Although installed wind power capacity is far behind hydropower capacity, it is growing rapidly. Wind skyrocketed from a mere 400 kilowatts (KW) in 2001 to 44.7 GW of installed capacity in 2010 (China Wind Energy Association 2011; Li; Hubacek, and Siu 2011). This increase put China above the United States at the top position in world installed capacity. Many wind turbines in China face challenges connecting to the electric grid, however, so there is disagreement about the significance of this achievement. China installed the first 5.2 GW stage of capacity in their largest wind farm, a project in Gansu province nicknamed Three Gorges on the Land, which will total an estimated 10 GW when complete, in late 2010, with 1.2 GW connected to the electric grid (China Greentech Initiative 2011). Under China's Twelfth Five-Year Plan, they will deploy an astonishing 100 GW more of wind capacity by 2016.

In contrast to the United States, where the Cape Wind project in Nantucket Sound off Massachusetts faced numerous delays (Bosselman et al. 2010), offshore wind is off to a fast start in China. The 102 megawatts (MW) Shanghai Donghaiqiao project began full operation in 2010 (Yu and Zheng 2011). By some estimates, offshore wind may provide 30 GW installed capacity by 2020 (China Greentech Initiative 2011).

Solar power deployment has grown, but not as rapidly. In 2005, total installed capacity of solar photovoltaic (PV) power in China was a mere 70 MW, most of which supplied power to rural areas (NDRC 2007). A modification of pricing policies added more than 500 MW of capacity in 2010, which surpassed the total of all previous years combined (REN21 2011). Solar has made dramatic inroads in hot water heaters: 10 percent of Chinese households have them, or sixty times the US share, and the total of 40 million installed units was nearly two-thirds of the world total. China plans for 30 percent of households to have solar hot water by 2020 (Wong and Light 2009).

Biomass in China consists of crop stalks, firewood, and other organic sources (Peidong et al. 2009). Development of generation from biomass, with 3.2 GW of installed capacity in 2010, has lagged behind other renewables because of challenges in obtaining sufficient feedstock supplies (China Greentech Initiative 2011).

Governmental Support

China's commitment to renewable energy includes a strong Renewable Energy Law, government plans, regulations, and aggressive mandates (Eisen 2010).

Governmental Entities

China's National Development and Reform Commission (NDRC) develops national macroeconomic plans and sets energy prices (Kahrl et al. 2011). The National Energy Administration and newly created National Energy Commission also have energy policy responsibilities (Ma 2011). Other ministries promoting development and deployment of renewables include the Ministry of Science and Technology, the Ministry of Housing and Rural Development (formerly the Ministry of Construction), the Ministry of Finance, which administers the Renewable Energy Development Fund, and the Ministry of Agriculture, which is jointly responsible with the NDRC for rural biomass development (China Greentech Initiative 2011).

China's state-owned energy companies are also important in renewables policy (Kahrl et al. 2011), purchasing and transmitting electricity generated from renewables under governmental mandates. The five generating companies are state controlled. One grid company, the State Grid Corporation, is state owned, and the other, the Southern Power Grid Company, is privately owned. The State Electricity Regulatory Commission (SERC) regulates the electricity grid (SERC 2011). Because the NDRC has planning and pricing responsibilities, however, the SERC's regulatory powers are not as broad as those of the Federal Energy Regulatory Commission in the United States (Williams and Kahrl 2008).

China's provinces play a significant role in promoting renewables, although individual provinces vary in their commitment to renewables. Some provincial governments, such as those in Jiangsu, Zhejiang, and Shandong provinces, have specific policies promoting renewables, including preferential pricing for solar PV installations that provincial budgets fund (China Greentech Initiative 2011).

Pre-2005 Programs

Before 2006, China had relatively small programs for renewable energy deployment and no unified legal framework (Eisen 2010). Programs focused on bringing power to the millions of rural residents without access to electricity, including the 1985 Plan for Rural Electrification and the Brightness Program, which deployed thousands of small-scale wind and solar PV systems in remote areas and brought 1.3 million people access to electricity (China Greentech Initiative 2011). The China Township Electrification Program targeted 1,065 townships in twelve provinces and deployed village-level hydropower, PV, and PV/wind hybrid systems (National Renewable Energy Laboratory 2004). A low-interest loan fund for rural energy systems began in 1987 (Peidong et al. 2009). As a result of these programs and others, only 8 percent of Chinese residents today lack access to electricity (China Greentech Initiative 2011).

The central government State Council's 1994 "White Paper on Population, Environment, and Development in the 21st Century" identified a "medium- to long-term objective for the economic and social development of renewable energy," and a Ride the Wind Program aimed at developing a domestic wind turbine industry (Ru et al. 2012; State Council 1994). Barriers remained to scaling up deployment, however, including the lack of renewable portfolio standards (policies that require energy to come from renewable sources), feed-in tariffs (to encourage the use of renewable resources), and other market-pricing mechanisms designed to spur deployment of renewable energy projects (Fan, Sun, and Rem 2005).

Post-2005 Commitment

Several landmark documents established China's national commitment to renewables:

- the Renewable Energy Law of 2005 (and plans and regulations developed to implement it) (State Council 2009)
- NDRC's 2007 Medium- to Long-Term Renewable Energy Development Plan for Renewable Energy (National Development and Reform Commission 2007)
- the Eleventh and Twelfth national Five-Year Plans for economic and social development (NDRC 2006a and 2011a)

In 2005, the Renewable Energy Law (REL) created a national policy for renewable energy development, capacity targets for individual renewable energy sources, mandates for electric power companies to purchase electricity generated from renewables, and a pricing strategy. The REL is a brief framework, with specifics found in agency plans and regulations. Article 2 defined hydropower, wind power, solar, geothermal, and marine energy as eligible renewable energy sources, but not nuclear power (which is promoted separately). Article 4 made construction of renewable energy facilities a national "priority area for development" and article 8 called for a national renewable energy plan, including capacity targets, with provinces to develop specific implementation plans.

Under article 14, China's electricity grid corporations must interconnect with and purchase all the electricity generated by approved renewable energy facilities located in their service areas. Article 19 called for the central government to set purchase prices for power generated from renewables and to adjust them periodically as necessary. The REL also created a national fund to foster renewable energy development and other economic incentives.

NDRC and SERC regulations implemented article 14, mandating interconnection (physical connection of renewable power producers to the electric grid) and requiring grid companies to purchase electricity generated by renewable power producers (NDRC 2006; SERC 2007). The NDRC required utilities to purchase *all* electricity generated from renewable sources in their grid areas and mandated utilities to provide grid connection services and technical support.

There has been some resistance to this purchase mandate, especially because local officials lack performance benchmarks tied to power purchases from renewable energy projects (McElwee 2008). The state designed a 2009 REL amendment to secure enhanced compliance, entitling renewable power producers kept off the grid to damages of up to twice their economic loss (State Council 2009). Other amendments called for more national oversight of renewable energy projects, a requirement to develop a regulation to force electric companies to purchase specific amounts of electricity, and changes to the national research and development fund.

The NDRC's 2007 Medium and Long-Term Development Plan for Renewable Energy in China (2007 Plan) contained policy guidance and set a national goal to satisfy 15 percent of total primary energy consumption by 2020 from non–fossil fuel sources (NDRC 2007). The 2007 plan set targets for individual renewable energy technologies (NDRC 2007). China surpassed both the solar and wind targets and has revised both targets upward several times. The initial solar target of 1.8 GW by 2020 has been revised upward to 15 GW by 2015. The initial wind target of 5 GW has been revised upward to 100 GW by 2015 (NDRC 2011a).

China's Five-Year Plans, which guide the nation's economic development, have set national goals to promote renewables. The Eleventh Five-Year Plan (2006–2010) stressed environmental and climate change objectives. The Twelfth Five-Year Plan (2011–2015) has gone further, putting renewables development and other environmental objectives at the top of China's economic and social development program. Experts consider this plan the impetus for a "green revolution" in China (*chinadialogue* 2011). Among other goals, it calls for renewables and nuclear energy to account for 11.4 percent of the energy mix (up from 8 percent) within five years as part of a goal of reducing the carbon intensity (carbon dioxide emissions per unit of GDP) of China's economy by 40–45 percent by 2020 from 2005 levels (NDRC 2011a).

The Twelfth Five-Year Plan increased the solar, wind, and hydropower targets, as noted above (NDRC 2011a). The Twelfth Five-Year Plan also terms "new energy" one of three Strategic Emerging Industries that will receive targeted investments of 5 trillion RMB ($761 billion) over the next ten years, and make up 8 percent of GDP by 2015 and 15 percent by 2020 (*chinadialogue* 2011).

Grid-Connected Electricity

Under the REL, China has adopted different pricing arrangements for different renewable resources and is working toward creating a more stable investment climate for renewable energy generators. Until recently, much pricing was through a competitive tender (bidding) system, with the government administering bidding for contracts for specified amounts of electricity generated from renewables (Liu and Kokko 2010). The lowest bidder wins each contract and supplies the power, assuming it meets other requirements. In solar, wind, and biomass power, China has moved to fixed pricing comparable to European-style feed-in tariffs (FITs), which offers generators guaranteed prices and has proven to be successful in stimulating industry development in Europe and elsewhere (Liu and Kokko 2010; Bosselman et al. 2010).

A 2006 NDRC regulation established fixed pricing for biomass generation (NDRC 2006b). This pricing differed from a European FIT because the prices paid to generators were not designed to yield a specific rate of return (Bosselman et al. 2010). The regulation fixed the prices instead at the price of electricity generated from desulfurized coal, plus a subsidy that increased in 2010 to 0.35 RMB ($0.05) per kilowatt hour (kWh) (Martinot and Junfeng 2010).

China priced wind power with a tender system for projects greater than 50 MW, with provincial governments approving and pricing smaller projects (Liu and Kokko 2010). Unlike European-style FITs set for long terms, ad hoc prices send inconsistent signals to investors in wind projects. In numerous provinces, state-owned power companies, which have no responsibility to make profits, submitted winning bids below the cost of generating electricity, further hampering wind power development (Liu and Kokko 2010). Foreign companies also criticized the bidding process for a lack of transparency.

The NDRC replaced the bidding system in 2009 with a new feed-in tariff that creates four different regions, with prices lower in regions such as Inner Mongolia with substantial wind power capacity online than in regions with less wind power development (NDRC 2009). Critics have praised this system as setting a more favorable and stable investment climate for wind power, leading to rapid increases in capacity (China Greentech Initiative 2011). The new tariff system does not apply to offshore wind projects, however, for which tariffs have not been set (Martinot and Junfeng 2010).

Until 2011, China retained the project-specific bidding process for solar power projects. China's state-owned power companies undercut all other companies in every bidding round through 2010, which led to criticism of the pricing process and calls to set national feed-in tariff rates (China Greentech Initiative 2011). The feed-in tariff sets the rate for purchases of power generated from solar at 1–1.15 yuan, depending on the location and date of project approval (NDRC 2011b). As noted above, this spurred more solar development in 2010 than in all previous years combined, although total installed capacity was still less than 1 GW at the end of 2010 (REN21 2011).

Financing

China overtook the United States by 2009 in annual non–research and development spending on renewables, spending $34.6 billion versus the United States' $18.6 billion (Pew Charitable Trusts 2010). In 2010, China spent 354 billion RMB ($54.4 billion) in all on clean energy, including renewable energy, energy efficiency, and transmission infrastructure improvements (China Greentech Initiative 2011).

The state-owned China Development Bank made $43.6 billion in loans to solar and wind power companies in 2010 (China Greentech Initiative 2011). Most users of electricity pay a small surcharge on their electric bills into a fund that has supported wind and biomass energy projects (Peidong et al. 2009). Other financial incentives include the Ministry of Finance's Special Fund for Wind Manufacturing and the China Export-Import Bank's tax credits (China Greentech Initiative 2011).

The Golden Sun program provides subsidies for utility-scale solar installations of 300 KW and higher, up to a cap of 680 MW, or 20 MW for each of China's thirty-four provinces and autonomous regions (Ministry of Finance, Ministry of Science and National Energy Board 2009). As of 2010, projects totaling 624 MW have applied for the subsidies (China Renewable Energy Industries Association 2012). China has also subsidized end users' installations of renewable energy equipment. The Ministry of Finance and Ministry of Housing and Urban-Rural Development began a subsidy program in 2009 for rooftop and building-integrated PV (BIPV) installations (Ministry of Finance and Ministry of Housing and Urban-Rural Development 2010). Subsidy levels for 2010 were 13 RMB per watt ($1.90/watt) for grid-connected PV and 17 RMB per watt ($2.50/watt) for BIPV (Martinot and Junfeng 2010).

On the international level, the Clean Development Mechanism (CDM) under article 12 of the Kyoto Protocol supports GHG emissions reductions projects (United Nations Framework Convention on Climate Change 2012; Lewis 2010). Under the CDM, nations with specific reduction targets undertake projects in other nations not obligated to reduce emissions and gain Certified Emissions Reductions (CERs) credits toward their reduction targets. China has the most CDM projects in the world. Many of these projects involve renewables, particularly wind power, although other types of projects generate more CERs (Lewis 2010; Peidong et al. 2009). A European study of China and the CDM notes that CERs are important to project profitability, even with governmental subsidies (EU-China CDM Facilitation Project 2009). Some scholars dispute this, however, claiming that investment in renewable energy projects is front-loaded and that at most the availability of CERs may tip the balance in favor of proceeding with a project (Lewis 2010).

Industries

The 2007 Plan encouraged development of domestic renewable energy industries. Since then, Chinese companies have rapidly increased their share of the domestic market for renewable energy technologies, displacing foreign firms that once dominated. China's domestic wind turbine industry rose from virtual nonexistence to prominence within five years, and now has three of the world's largest manufacturers (Ru et al. 2012). Chinese manufacturers' MW-size turbines are now deployed in most domestic installations (Ru et al. 2012; Martinot and Junfeng 2010). In solar, China is now the largest manufacturer of PV cells and modules, supplying almost 40 percent of all solar PV worldwide in 2009, with most output exported (China Greentech Initiative 2011).

Official governmental policies, including the tax and subsidy programs described above, promote renewables manufacturing. China's policies follow a commitment to "indigenous innovation" that supports domestic manufacturers (Ru et al. 2012). Government financing of state-owned energy companies and procurement laws of state-owned companies that favor domestic suppliers promote domestic firms (China Greentech Initiative 2011).

Given the growth of domestic companies and their support from the government, the outlook for foreign firms is changing rapidly. The Chinese government officially encourages foreign renewable energy investments. In 2009, the Chinese government removed import duties and included polysilicon and wind turbines over 2 MW in a Catalogue of Technology and Products Encouraged to Import (Ministry of Commerce 2011). Until 2010, a regulation required domestic production of 70 percent of the value of materials and components in wind turbines installed in China, but in 2010 the government eliminated this requirement (Martinot and Junfeng 2010). The reality, however, is that foreign firms have found it increasingly difficult to get their technology adopted in Chinese projects. State-owned companies and other Chinese energy companies typically win bidding to develop utility-scale solar and wind facilities (China Greentech Initiative 2011). The US International Trade Commission and Department of Commerce commenced investigations in 2011, responding to petitions from American solar manufacturers that Chinese government regulations and subsidies amounted to unfair promotion of Chinese firms that allowed them to sell their products at below-market prices overseas (United States International Trade Administration 2011).

Challenges

While industry growth and deployment of new capacity has been impressive, continued expansion of renewable energy in China faces a host of challenges. Investment in new transmission lines and updated grid management is important for continued development of renewables (Lin 2010; McKinsey 2009). China's windiest sites are often located far from dense urban areas and the power grid, as is also the case in the United States (McElroy et al. 2009). The task of integrating power generated from renewables into the grid is challenging, because the grid was not designed to handle renewable energy facilities that generate power on an intermittent basis and provincial grid companies that vary in their management capabilities run the system (Williams and Kahrl 2008). As recently as 2009, nearly one-fourth of all installed wind turbines were not connected to the nation's electric grid (Kahrl et al. 2011). China needs to address considerable technical challenges, including the need for improved grid infrastructure to handle electricity from large wind farms (Li, Hubacek, and Siu 2011).

Transmission bottlenecks remain, and China is building major high-voltage lines to transmit large amounts of electricity across the country and support renewables integration into the grid under the State Grid Corporation's Strong and Smart Grid plan (Zhou et al., 2011). The state plans to spend as much as $44 billion by 2020 on power lines to connect remote provinces to eastern cities (Lin 2010; Wong and Light 2009). This plan stands in marked contrast to the United States' difficulties in overcoming a myriad of obstacles to building new transmission lines (Bosselman et al. 2010).

Challenges remain. Because it has lagged behind the West in technological innovation in the renewables sector, China needs more skilled engineers and continued research and development efforts in renewables technologies (China Greentech Initiative 2011). The lack of uniform pricing for renewables sends inconsistent signals to the industry, and further policy developments in this area will be an important factor in the industries' further growth and more deployment of renewables capacity (Kahrl et al. 2011). China's utilities need to do more work to integrate renewables into their grids, particularly by making long-range forecasts and plans for meeting demand that include renewables (Kahrl et al. 2011). There is a lack of uniform technical standards for interconnection and a lack of data (and follow-up policies) on how effectively renewable power is integrated into the grid (Lin 2010). Although the Twelfth Five-Year Plan emphasizes renewables and other environmental objectives, it also continues to promote growth and development, which will often lead local officials to strive for the latter at the expense of the former (China Greentech Initiative, 2011).

Given all these challenges, however, it is still likely that China's exponential growth in renewables will continue as the nation intends to become greener in its electric generation mix to address electricity needs, air quality, and climate change goals.

Joel Barry EISEN
University of Richmond

See also Automobiles and Personal Vehicles; Climate Change Mitigation Initiatives (China); Energy Industries—Nuclear; Energy Industries—Renewables (India); Energy Security (East Asia); Five-Year Plans; Green Collar Jobs; Information and Communication Technologies (ICT); Microfinance; Outsourcing and Offshoring; South-North Water Diversion; Steel Industry; Three Gorges Dam; Transboundary Water Issues; Water Security; Water Use and Rights (China)

Further Reading

Bosselman, Fred; Eisen, Joel B.; Rossi, Jim; Spence, David B.; & Weaver, Jacqueline. (2010). *Energy, economics, and the environment*. New York: Foundation Press.

China Clean Energy Database. (2011). Homepage. Retrieved May 9, 2011, from http://www.chinacleanenergydb.com

chinadialogue. (2011). China's green revolution: Energy, environment and the 12th five-year plan. Retrieved May 9, 2011, from http://www.chinadialogue.net/

China Electricity Council. (2011). (in Chinese). China's power industry annual development report 2011. Retrieved March 5, 2012, from http://tj.cec.org.cn/niandufazhanbaogao/2011-06-27/58873.html

China Greentech Initiative. (2011). The China greentech report 2011. Retrieved April 27, 2011, from http://cgtr.china-greentech.com/CGTI-ChinaGreentechReport2011.pdf

China Renewable Energy Industries Association. (2012). (in Chinese). Subsidy standards of the Golden Sun program. Retrieved March 5, 2012, from http://www.creia.net/?Topic/detail/t/9/id/1395.html

China Wind Energy Association. (2011). (in Chinese). 2010 China wind power installed capacity statistics. Retrieved March 5, 2012, from http://www.cwea.org.cn/

Commission of the European Communities, Eurostat. (2010). Energy, transport and environment indicators. Retrieved May 9, 2011, from http://epp.eurostat.ec.europa.eu/cache/ITY_OFFPUB/KS-DK-10-001/EN/KS-DK-10-001-EN.PDF

Davidson, Michael. (2011). Clean energy standard: How China does long-term targets. *Switchboard*. Retrieved May 9, 2011, from http://switchboard.nrdc.org/blogs/mdavidson/clean_energy_standard_how_chin.html

Downs, Erica S. (2008, Nov.–Dec.). China's "new" energy administration. *China Business Review*, 42–45. Retrieved May 9, 2011, from http://www.brookings.edu/articles/2008/11_china_energy_downs.aspx

Eisen, Joel B. (2010). China's renewable energy law: A platform for green leadership? *William and Mary Environmental Law and Policy Review, 35*(1), 1–52.

Eisen, Joel B. (2011). The new energy geopolitics? China, renewable energy, and the "greentech race." *Chicago-Kent Law Review, 86*(1), 9–58.

EU-China CDM Facilitation Project. (2009). The Pre-2012 CDM market in China: Policy context and current developments. Retrieved May 24, 2010, from http://www.euchina-cdm.org/media/docs/CDM_Project_The_Pre_2012_CDM_Market_in_China_2009_07_20_EN.pdf

Fan, J.; Sun, W.; & Rem, D-M. (2005). Renewables portfolio standard and regional energy structure optimisation in China. *Energy Policy, 33*, 279–287.

Intergovernmental Panel on Climate Change (IPCC). (2011). Special report on renewable energy sources and climate change mitigation. Retrieved May 9, 2011, from http://srren.ipcc-wg3.de/

International Energy Agency (IEA). (2010). World energy outlook 2010. Retrieved May 2, 2011, from www.iea.org/weo/

Juan, Du. (2012). Energy use to be regulated by central system. *Xinhua*. Retrieved March 5, 2012, from http://news.xinhuanet.com/english/china/2012-01/11/c_131354068.htm

Kahrl, Fredrich, et al. (2011). Challenges to China's transition to a low carbon electricity system. *Energy Policy, 39*, 4032–4041.

Lewis, Joanna I. (2010). The evolving role of carbon finance in promoting renewable energy development in China. *Energy Policy, 38*, 2875–2886.

Li, Xin; Hubacek, Klaus; & Siu, Yim Ling. (2011). Wind power in China—Dream or reality? *Energy Policy, 37*, 51–60.

Lin, Alvin. (2010). China's renewable energy legal framework and emissions reductions potential from "strong, smart grid." Retrieved May 9, 2011, from http://china.nrdc.org/files/china_nrdc_org

Liu, Feng-Chao; Simon, Denis Fred; Sun, Yu-tao; and Cao, Cong. (2011). China's innovation policies: Evolution, institutional structure, and trajectory. *Research Policy, 40*, 917–931.

Liu, Yingqi, & Kokko, Ari. (2010). Wind power in China: Policy and development challenges. *Energy Policy, 38*, 5520–5529.

Ma, Jinlong. (2011). On-grid electricity tariffs in China: Development, reform and prospects. *Energy Policy, 39*, 2633–2645.

Martinot, Eric, & Junfeng, Li. (2010). China's latest leap: An update on renewables policy. *Renewable Energy World, 13*(4), 51–57.

McElroy, Michael B; Lu, Xi; Nielsen, Chris P.; & Wang, Yuxuan. (2009). Potential for wind-generated electricity in China. *Science, 325*, 1378.

McElwee, Charles. (2008). China's renewable energy law. Retrieved May 24, 2010, from http://www.chinaenvironmentallaw.com/2008/03/27/china%E2%80%99s-renewable-energy-law/

McKinsey & Company. (2009). China's green revolution: Prioritizing technologies to achieve energy and environmental sustainability. Retrieved May 24, 2010, from http://www.mckinsey.com/locations/greaterchina/mckonchina/reports/china_green_revolution_report.pdf

Ministry of Commerce, People's Republic of China. (2011). (in Chinese). To encourage imports of technologies and products catalog (2011 edition). Retrieved March 5, 2012, from http://cys.mofcom.gov.cn/aarticle/af/201104/20110407502723.html?2305308655=823392802

Ministry of Finance & Ministry of Housing & Urban-Rural Development, People's Republic of China. (2010). (in Chinese). Notice of the organization of the applications for 2010 BIPV demonstration projects. Retrieved March 5, 2012, from http://www.mof.gov.cn

Ministry of Finance, Ministry of Science & National Energy Board, People's Republic of China. (2009). (in Chinese). Notice on the implementation of the Golden Sun Demonstration Project. Retrieved March 5, 2012, from http://www.mof.gov.cn/zhengwuxinxi/caizhengwengao/2009niancaizhengbuwengao/caizhengwengao200907/200911/t20091118_233416.html

National Development & Reform Commission (NDRC), People's Republic of China. (2006a). 11th five-year plan for national economic & social development of the People's Republic of China. Retrieved May 20, 2010, from http://en.ndrc.gov.cn/hot/t20060529_71334.htm

National Development & Reform Commission (NDRC), People's Republic of China. (2006b). Provisional administrative measures on pricing and cost sharing for renewable energy power generation. (English translation, unofficial). Retrieved May 24, 2010, from http://www.chinacleanenergydb.com/renewable-energy/regulations

National Development & Reform Commission (NDRC), People's Republic of China. (2006c). Regulation on the administration of power generation from renewable energy. (English translation, unofficial). Retrieved May 24, 2010, from www.martinot.info/China_RE_Law_Guidelines_2_NonAuth.pdf

National Development & Reform Commission (NDRC), People's Republic of China. (2007). Medium and long-term development plan for renewable energy in China. (English translation, unofficial). Retrieved May 24, 2010, from http://en.chinagate.cn/reports/2007-09/13/content_8872839.htm

National Development & Reform Commission (NDRC), People's Republic of China. (2009). (in Chinese). Notice on policy to improve grid-connected power pricing for wind power. Retrieved March 5, 2012, from http://www.sdpc.gov.cn/zcfb/zcfbtz/2009tz/t20090727_292827.htm

National Development & Reform Commission (NDRC), People's Republic of China. (2010). (in Chinese). Notice on demand side management measures. Retrieved March 5, 2012, from http://zfxxgk.ndrc.gov.cn/PublicItemView.aspx?ItemID=%7B4e15ff26-455e-44ad-b0fa-141cabf851b2%7D

National Development & Reform Commission (NDRC), People's Republic of China. (2011a). 12th five-year plan for national economic & social development of the People's Republic of China. Retrieved May 9, 2011, from http://en.ndrc.gov.cn

National Development & Reform Commission (NDRC), People's Republic of China. (2011b). Solar PV tariff policy notice. Retrieved March 5, 2012, from http://www.ndrc.gov.cn/zcfb/zcfbtz/2011tz/t20110801_426501.htm

National Renewable Energy Laboratory. (2004). Renewable energy in China: Township Electrification Program. Retrieved March 5, 2012, from http://www.nrel.gov/docs/fy04osti/35788.pdf

Peidong, Zhang, et al. (2009). Opportunities and challenges for renewable energy policy in China. *Renewable and Sustainable Energy Reviews*, 13, 439–449. Retrieved May 9, 2011, from http://english.qibebt.cas.cn/rh/as/200907/P020090709511239637331.pdf

Pew Charitable Trusts. (2010). Who's winning the clean energy race? Growth, competition and opportunity in the world's largest economies. Retrieved May 24, 2010, from www.pewtrusts.org/uploadedFiles/wwwpewtrustsorg/Reports/Global_warming/G-20%20Report.pdf

Renewable Energy Policy Network for the 21st Century (REN21). (2009). Recommendations for improving the effectiveness of renewable energy policies in China. Retrieved March 5, 2012, from http://www.ren21.net/REN21Activities/Publications/RegionalStatusReports/ChineseRenewablesReport/tabid/5441/Default.aspx

Renewable Energy Policy Network for the 21st Century (REN21). (2011). Renewables 2011 global status report. Retrieved March 5, 2012, from http://www.ren21.net/Portals/97/documents/GSR/REN21_GSR2011.pdf

Ru, Peng, et al. (2012). Behind the development of technology: The transition of innovation modes in China's wind turbine manufacturing industry. *Energy Policy*, 43, 58–69.

State Council, People's Republic of China. (1994). White Paper on China's Population, Environment, and Development in the 21st Century. Retrieved March 5, 2012, from http://www.unescap.org/esid/psis/population/database/poplaws/law_china/ch_record014.htm

State Council, People's Republic of China. (2010) (in Chinese). Notice of the establishment of a National Energy Commission. Retrieved March 5, 2012, from http://www.gov.cn/zwgk/2010-01/27/content_1520724.htm

State Council, People's Republic of China, Legislative Affairs Office. (2009). (in Chinese). Renewable Energy Law of the People's Republic of China (with 2009 amendment). Retrieved March 5, 2012, from http://www.chinalaw.gov.cn/article/xwzx/fzxw/200912/20091200176803.shtml

State Electricity Regulatory Commission (SERC), People's Republic of China. (2007). Measures on supervision and administration of grid enterprises in the purchase of renewable energy power. English translation (unofficial). Retrieved May 9, 2011, from China Clean Energy Database, http://www.chinacleanenergydb.com

State Electricity Regulatory Commission (SERC), People's Republic of China. (2011). Homepage. Retrieved May 20, 2010, from http://www.serc.gov.cn/english/index.htm

United Nations Framework Convention on Climate Change. (2012). Clean Development Mechanism. Homepage. Retrieved March 5, 2012, from http://cdm.unfccc.int/

United States Department of Energy, Energy Information Administration (DOE EIA). (2010). Independent statistics and analysis: Country analysis briefs: China. Retrieved April 29, 2010, from http://www.eia.doe.gov/countries/country-data.cfm?fips=CH

United States International Trade Administration. (2011). Commerce initiates antidumping duty (AD) and countervailing duty (CVD) investigations of crystalline silicon photovoltaic cells, whether or not assembled into modules (solar cells) from the People's Republic of China (China). Retrieved March 5, 2012, from http://ia.ita.doc.gov/download/factsheets/factsheet_prc-solar-cells-ad-cvd-init.pdf

Wang, Tao, & Watson, Jim. (2009). China's energy transition: Pathways for low carbon development. Retrieved April 29, 2010, from http://www.sussex.ac.uk/sussexenergygroup/documents/china_report_forweb.pdf

Williams, James H., & Kahrl, Fredrich. (2008). Electricity reform and sustainable development in China. *Environmental Research Letters*, 3(4), 1–15. Retrieved April 29, 2010, from http://iopscience.iop.org/1748-9326/3/4/044009/fulltext

Wong, Julian, & Light, Andrew. (2009). China begins its transition to a clean-energy economy. *Center for American Progress*. Retrieved May 18, 2010, from http://www.americanprogress.org/issues/2009/06/china_energy_numbers.html

Yu, James, & Zheng, Jie. (2011). Offshore wind development in China and its future with the existing renewable policy. *Energy Policy*, 39, 7917–7921.

Zhou, Nan, et al. (2011). China's energy and carbon emissions outlook to 2050. *China Energy Group*. Retrieved May 9, 2011, from http://china.lbl.gov/publications/2050-outlook

---

chat   Berkshire's authors and editors welcome questions, comments, and corrections. Send your emails about the *Berkshire Encyclopedia of Sustainability* in general or this volume in particular to: sustainability.updates@berkshirepublishing.com

Energy Industries—Renewables (India)

Access to energy is extremely unequal in India: centers of economic growth require an ever-increasing supply, while large sections of the rural population have minimal amounts for even lighting and cooking. Renewable energy sources offer a potential solution to this situation. Programs like renewable purchase obligations (RPOs) and renewable energy certificates (RECs) are helping to stimulate the use and growth of renewable energy.

India's rapid growth has placed an immense strain on its energy resources. The country has depended primarily on coal reserves for its electricity generation, and 80 percent of its oil is imported. In recent times large hydropower projects and nuclear-power generation projects have run into problems. Renewable energy (particularly solar and wind) has huge potential in India given this situation, but at present it is underutilized—in 2011 it constituted just about 4 percent of the electricity mix (MNRE 2011, 9). It is estimated that a multifold increase in real per capita gross domestic product (GDP) by 2030 will be accompanied by a fivefold increase in the demand for power to fuel large infrastructure projects, transportation, manufacturing, and households. A steady supply of environmentally sound, efficient, and affordable energy is the need of the hour.

Institutional Framework

Following the great global oil shocks of the 1970s, India set up the Commission for Additional Sources of Energy (CASE) in 1981 under the aegis of the Department of Science & Technology, Ministry of Human Resource Development, to demonstrate and develop renewable energy technologies. The following year the Ministry of Power created the Department of Non-conventional Energy Sources (DNES), subsuming CASE. The first half of the 1980s was consumed by technology demonstrations and development, and in 1987 the Indian Renewable Energy Development Agency (IREDA) was established to overcome barriers to developing new technologies, such as entry costs and risk perception. This public-sector nonbanking financial institution was to provide term loans at rates lower than market interest rates for projects supporting renewable energy and energy efficiency (Rao 2004). In 1992 DNES was upgraded to the Ministry of Non-conventional Energy Sources (MNES).

In 1993 the MNES created a ten-year plan for procuring power from renewable energy sources, whose guidelines were intended to help state utilities in setting purchase prices for power from renewable energy sources (IPPAI Legal Summit and Vipradas n.d.). The guidelines also provided for buyback on the usage of renewable energy, banking concessions, wheeling and third-party sales, along with financial incentives, such as fully accelerated depreciation for renewable energy projects. The policy did not address commercial parameters such as renewable energy technology development and project costs, however. Through the Akshay Urja program, special shops providing sales and service support to users of renewable energy devices were set up. Improvements in the energy sector during the 1990s also came through the privatization of government-controlled utilities and the establishment of statutory bodies to coordinate the work of the MNES, such as the Central Electricity Regulatory

Commission (CERC) and State Electricity Regulatory Commissions (SERCs) that were created in 1998, and the State Nodal Agencies for specific sectors of renewable energy.

In 2006 the MNES was renamed the Ministry for New and Renewable Energy (MNRE), with the stated objective of ushering in an era of energy security by increasing the proportion of clean power sources and improving the affordability of and access to renewable energy. As a nodal ministry, extension programs are largely implemented through state renewable energy development agencies. The MNRE also coordinates research through specialized technical institutions such as the Solar Energy Centre, Centre for Wind Energy Technology, Sardar Swaran Singh National Institute of Renewable Energy (whose speciality is bioenergy research and development), and the Alternate Hydro Energy Centre.

Laws and Policies

Most of the policies concerning renewable energy were formulated at the turn of the twenty-first century. Until 2003, the Indian Electricity Act of 1910, the Electricity (Supply) Act of 1948, and the Electricity Regulatory Commission Act of 1998 governed the power sector. The Electricity Act of 2003 was ratified in June of the same year to unify and coordinate these pieces of legislation and to introduce reforms. The Electricity Act authorizes CERC to set preferential tariffs for electricity that is generated and cogenerated from renewable sources, and mandates that state authorities establish minimum renewable power purchases (called renewable purchase obligations or RPOs) and promote the generation of electricity from renewable sources (Ministry of Law and Justice 2003).

Pursuant to its commitment under the act, the government ratified the National Electricity Policy (NEP) in 2005. The policy affirms the urgent need to promote renewable sources of energy by promoting competition in these projects and reducing capital costs. The NEP reinforces the RPO obligations of SERCs, who also bear responsibility for progressively raising the share of electricity generated from renewable energy sources and who have the option of implementing differential pricing to promote nonconventional energy sources. It also obligates SERCs to provide grid connectivity for renewable sources (Ministry of Power 2005). In 2006 the Ministry of Power ratified the National Tariff Policy (NTP), mandating that SERCs set RPO levels by April 2006, with purchases by distribution companies to be made through a competitive process (Ministry of Power 2006). In recognition of the special potential of solar energy in India, the NTP was subsequently amended to include solar-specific RPOs (Nag and Maheshwari 2012).

As of 2012 RPOs have been ratified for twenty-one states, some of which have chosen a source-based obligation over and above the solar-specific RPOs suggested by the NTP. The Forum of Regulators (the apex policy-formulating body under the Ministry of Power), however, has recommended that regulatory policies be coordinated to promote the interstate exchange of renewable power in order to compensate for the varying availability of resources and different levels of development of those resources across states (Renewable Energy Certificates in India n.d.a). In response, CERC issued a notification of regulations in 2010 that introduced renewable energy certificates (RECs) as a way to address this imbalance. Distribution companies issue RECs to generating companies for electricity, which the distribution companies sell at their average purchase price. The RECs can be traded with distribution companies across the country, and renewable purchase obligations are then met by producing the adequate number of RECs (one REC is issued for the production of one megawatt hour of power). This program gives generators the tradable option of either selling electricity at a preferential tariff, or selling electricity generated separately from environmental benefits. A SERC is responsible for enforcement (Renewable Energy Certificates in India n.d.b).

In 2006 India's prime minister directed the Planning Commission to convene a committee of experts to make recommendations with respect to energy policy. The committee's Integrated Energy Policy was circulated that year, proposing an overhaul of the country's approach to energy policy and suggesting that incentives must be linked to energy generated, as opposed to capacity created. The document also called for mandatory feed-in laws, which are designed to speed up investment in renewable energy technology through the use of long-term contracts for renewable energy producers (Press Information Bureau 2008), a position that India's National Action Policy on Climate Change (NAPCC) reinforced in 2008. In 2009, CERC introduced a system of feed-in tariffs for the production of wind, solar, small hydro, and biomass energy designed to increase electricity generation from these sources over the next ten years.

The Central Electricity Regulatory Commission also issued the Indian Electricity Grid Code in 2010, which included special provisions for scheduling wind- and solar-energy generation in the sale of electricity across states (when the capacities of the plants are greater than 10 megawatts and 5 megawatts, respectively, and when they are connected to 33 kilovolt–connection plants). Furthermore, a September 2010 CERC notification grants connectivity and open access to the interstate transmission of renewable-energy generation projects larger than 50 megawatts, on the condition that only the lead generator undertake operational and commercial responsibilities on behalf of all of them (CERC 2010). The requirement for dedicated transmission lines to the receiving distributor have been eliminated for projects generating in excess of 250 megawatts.

The NAPCC also established eight missions focused on combating climate change; of these, the National Solar Mission and, more broadly, the National Mission on Enhanced Energy Efficiency address renewable energy (National Portal of India 2010). The NAPCC has set targets for renewable energy purchases as well, at 5 percent of total grid purchases, which are to be increased by 1 percent every year for ten years. To improve accountability, it recommends that central and state governments set up verification mechanisms to ensure that renewable energy is actually produced. In order to limit noncompliance, it has underscored its power to levy penalties when utilities fall short of renewable-source portfolio standards (IREDA and ABPS 2009).

The Eleventh Five Year Plan (2007–2012) established a target of 10 percent power-generation capacity, a goal that has already been reached. Meanwhile, India's goal for its 2012–2017 plan period is to add 17 gigawatts of renewable energy-based power generation, and CERC has set a green-energy target of 15 percent power generation from renewable energy by 2020 (IREDA and ABPS 2009).

Other incentives have been introduced at the federal level. The report of the Thirteenth Finance Commission introduced three performance-oriented grants of 50 billion rupees each, which will be given to states as incentives to increase the share of electricity generated from renewable sources for the periods 2010–2011 and 2013–2014 (Thirteenth Finance Commission 2009). The 2010–2011 Union Budget levied a *cess* (tax) on coal consumption for the first time, which will be paid into a National Clean Energy Fund (D&B 2011). (The 2012 Union Budget has not made any specific announcement on the utilization of 38.6 billion rupees that has been collected so far.) The government expects to collect nearly 100 billion rupees by 2015. Among other things, the central government also has provided for accelerated tax depreciation, tax holidays, reduced customs duty, excise duty exemptions, and generation-based incentives for investments in the renewable energy sector.

As part of its rural electrification project, the Rajiv Gandhi Grameen Vidyutikaran Yojana (RGGVY) project provides that all rural and below-poverty line households are eligible for a 90 percent subsidy of capital-equipment costs for renewable and nonrenewable energy systems (*Economic Times* 2008). The MNRE's Strategic Plan for New and Renewable Energy Sector 2011–2017, however, notes that implementation of the RGGVY has been hampered by continuing supply constraints, but it points out that biomass and solar photovoltaic–based solutions are possible substitutes. The ministry's goal is to supply power to ten thousand villages using biomass-based systems, and over one thousand using solar power, by 2022 (MNRE 2011).

Capacity and Generation

With its bountiful natural resources and geographical features conducive to generating renewable energy, India is uniquely positioned to meet the challenges of energy security. As of 2011, its installed renewable-energy capacity is approximately 11 percent of total generation capacity, but the real contribution to energy generation is closer to 4 percent, excluding large (i.e., generating more than 25 megawatts) hydropower projects. If these projects are included, total renewable energy capacity is closer to 33 percent, with actual consumption close to 18 percent (MNRE 2011, 9).

Currently rural energy requirements are met predominantly through unsustainable traditional sources, such as kerosene, fuel wood, crop residue, and waste. Some of the areas that have potential for renewable-source energy generation are biogas, solar, and wind energy. Biogas as an off-grid system requires particular consideration, since India is the biggest producer of milk in the world, much of which comes from animals on small farms (one or two milking animals). The Ministry of Environment and Forests livestock census shows that about 300 million tons of dung are produced every year in India, of which only a very negligible fraction is converted into biogas (MoEF 2010). The MNRE aims to expand the number of family-size biogas plants to 2 million by 2022, which would support cooking needs in rural areas. Other biomass substances such as rice husks and municipal solid waste also offer good potential.

India is underutilizing solar power in comparison to other renewable energy sources. (See table 1.) The use of solar water heaters is expanding rapidly, however, which has the potential to reduce demand from conventional energy sources in urban areas. Similarly, the introduction of solar-cooking equipment and lighting devices are projected to outstrip the use of kerosene in the future.

Future Challenges

One of the funding mechanisms for developing renewable-energy technologies is the National Clean Energy Fund, which was created by levying a cess on each ton of coal extracted. Apart from this model, however, the challenge facing the renewable energy sector is creating scalable entrepreneurship models that not only can take care of the financial elements involved, but also can increase the acceptability of devices (for example, cooking stoves) among traditional populations, such as those living in rural agrarian communities.

Badrinarayanan SEETHARAMAN
National Law School of India University

Sony PELLISSERY
Institute of Rural Management, Anand

TABLE 1. 2010 Energy Use from Renewable Sources in Megawatts

	Grid Interactive Renewable Power	Off-grid/ Distributed Renewable Power
Biomass power	865.60	232.17
Biomass gasification	–	122.14
Wind power	11,807.00	–
Small hydropower	2,735.42	–
Bagasse cogeneration	1,334.03	–
Waste to energy	64.96	46.72
Solar power	10.28	2.46
Aerogenerators*	–	1.07
Total	15,691.41	404.56

* Note: an "aerogenerator" is a new design for an offshore wind turbine that is V-shaped and has been described as being in the shape of a sycamore seed.

Source: MNRE (2011).

India currently relies most heavily on wind power among renewable energy sources. Solar power is still underutilized, but its use to power water heaters, cooking equipment, and lighting is growing rapidly.

See also Education, Environmental (India); Energy Industries—Nuclear; Energy Industries—Renewables (China); Energy Security (East Asia); India; Five-Year Plans; Gandhism; Ganges River; Green Collar Jobs; Utilities Regulation and Energy Efficiency

Further Reading

Central Electrical Regulatory Commission (CERC) Notification, No. No-L-1/(3)/2009-CERC (2010). Retrieved April 5, 2012, from http://www.cercind.gov.in/Regulations/Amendment_to_connectivity_regulations.pdf

Dun and Bradstreet Information Services India (D&B). (2011). *Union budget 2010–11: Impact analysis*. Retrieved April 5, 2012, from http://contents.dnb.co.in/Special_Reports/D&B_Union_Budget_Impact_Analysis_2010-11.pdf

Economic Times. (2008, December 14). Electricity for all by 2012: Power minister. Retrieved April 5, 2012, from http://articles.economictimes.indiatimes.com/2008-12-14/news/27723999_1_rggvy-cent-subsidy-power-connections

Independent Power Producers Association of India (IPPAI) Legal Summit & Vipradas, Mahesh. (n.d.). Renewable energy obligations and tariff in India. Retrieved April 5, 2012, from http://www.ippai.org/articles.aspx?a_id=17

Indian Renewable Energy Development Agency (IREDA) & ABPS Infrastructure Advisory Private Limited (ABPS). (2009). Roadmap for implementation of renewable energy certificate mechanism for India. Retrieved April 5, 2012, from http://toolkits.reeep.org/file_upload/107010543_1.pdf

Ministry of Environment and Forest (MoEF), Government of India. (2010). *India: Greenhouse gas emissions 2007*. Retrieved April 16, 2012, from http://moef.nic.in/downloads/public-information/Report_INCCA.pdf

Ministry of Law and Justice, Government of India. (2003). The electricity act, 2003. Retrieved April 5, 2012, from http://www.powermin.nic.in/acts_notification/electricity_act2003/pdf/The%20Electricity%20Act_2003.pdf

Ministry of New and Renewable Energy (MNRE), Government of India. (2011). Strategic plan for new and renewable energy sector for the period 2011–2017. Retrieved April 5, 2012, from http://mnre.gov.in/file-manager/UserFiles/strategic_plan_mnre_2011_17.pdf

Ministry of Power, Government of India. (2005). National electricity policy. Retrieved April 5, 2012, from http://www.powermin.nic.in/whats_new/national_electricity_policy.htm

Ministry of Power, Government of India. (2006). Tariff policy. Retrieved April 5, 2012, from http://www.mahadiscom.in/consumer/national%20tariff%20policy.pdf

Nag, Avirup, & Maheshwari, Amit. (2012). The viewpoint: Is India's solar policy framework "investment grade?" Retrieved April 5, 2012, from http://barandbench.com/brief/1/2105/the-viewpoint-is-indias-solar-policy-framework-investment-grade

National Portal of India, Government of India. (2010). Document details for: National Action Plan for Climate Change (NAPCC): Documents. Retrieved April 16, 2012, from http://india.gov.in/innerwin20.php?id=15651

Press Information Bureau, Government of India. (2008). Integrated energy policy. Retrieved April 5, 2012, from http://www.pib.nic.in/newsite/erelease.aspx?relid=46172

Rao, B. Venkateswara. (2004). Financing of renewable energy and options for technology transfer. Retrieved April 5, 2012, from http://www.resourcesaver.com/file/toolmanager/O105UF1342.pdf

Renewable Energy Certificates in India. (n.d.a). Bottlenecks in implementing REC mechanism in India. Retrieved April 5, 2012, from http://rec.indscanblog.com/bottlenecks-in-implementing-rec-mechanism-in-india/

Renewable Energy Certificates in India. (n.d.b). Renewable energy trading to start from Mar 30. Retrieved April 5, 2012, from http://rec.indscanblog.com/renewable energy-trading-to-start-from-mar-30/

Thirteenth Finance Commission. (2009). *Thirteenth Finance Commission 2010–2015: Volume 1*. Retrieved April 5, 2012, from http://fincomindia.nic.in/writereaddata/html_en_files/tfc/13fcreng.pdf

Energy Security (East Asia)

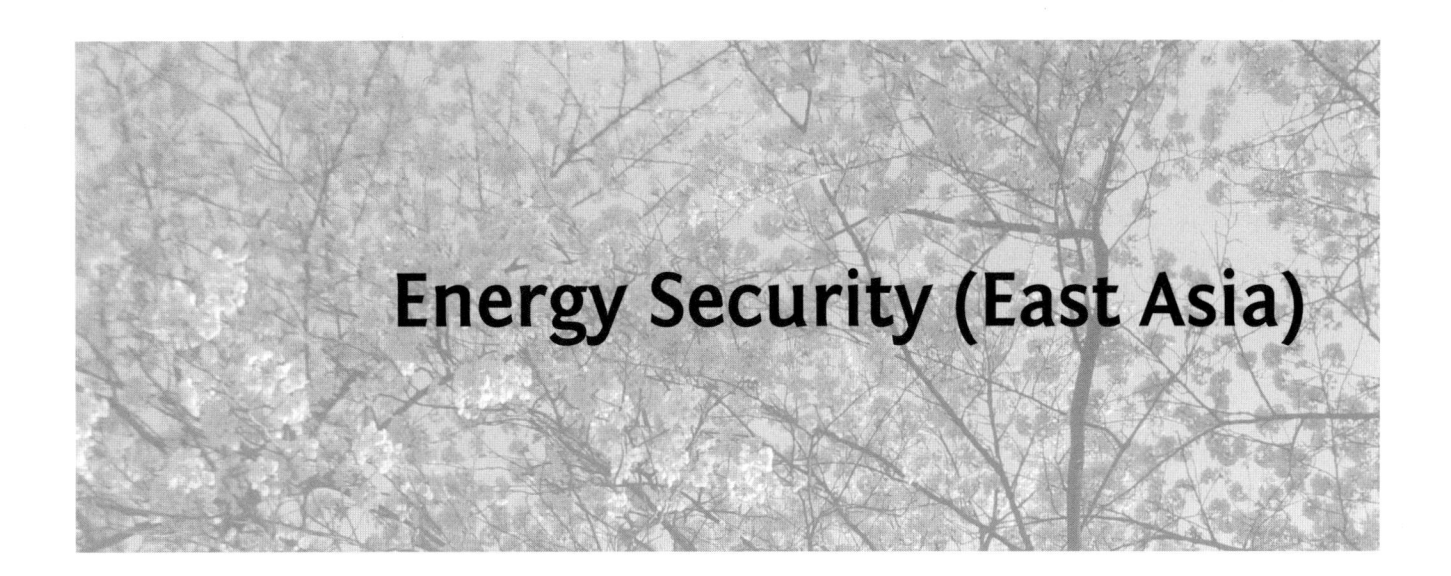

The term energy security *has typically meant little more than securing access to sufficient quantities of fossil fuels at reasonable prices. A broader concept of energy security is needed to adequately consider the full costs and benefits of potential energy policies to cope with challenges ranging from climate change to the social, political, and radiological fallout of Japan's Fukushima nuclear power plant accident in 2011.*

For policy makers in East Asia and globally, the term *energy security* has been interpreted mostly to mean assuring access to fuel oil, coal, and natural gas. This concept is occasionally broadened to consider the benefits of other types of home-grown energy supplies such as renewable energy and nuclear power, though the latter's status as a "domestic" resource may be arguable. This conventional energy security concept, however, has become less salient to policy formation due to increasingly global, diverse energy markets combined with emerging energy-related local, regional, national, and transnational issues, including climate change, local air pollution, acid rain, and water quantity and quality issues. The nuclear disaster at the Fukushima Daiichi plant in Japan, initiated by the March 2011 Sendai earthquake and tsunami, was underlain by a complex set of energy security–related policy decisions dating back decades, and provides only one example of why a broader view of energy security is in order. Japan made a choice in the 1970s to focus on nuclear energy as a key to reducing its dependence on foreign oil and other fuels, as well as its exposure to the volatility of the oil market. This energy security policy, together with its subsequent nuclear energy technology and siting choices and the close relationship between regulators and the regulated in the nuclear industry, all helped to set the stage for the unfortunate combination of natural disaster and technological/institutional failure. With the March 2011 accident as a riveting cautionary example, policy makers around northeast Asia and beyond—including in China—are realizing that there are multiple facets to energy security that must be considered. In order to be of use today, a policy-oriented rationale for energy security must encompass not only energy supply and cost but also environmental, economic, technological, social, and national and international security considerations. As a consequence, a more comprehensive operating definition of energy security is needed, along with a practical framework for analysis of which future energy plans, paths, or scenarios are likely to yield greater energy security in that broader sense.

Work done in the late 1990s as a part of the Nautilus Institute's Pacific Asia Regional Energy Security (PARES) project began the development of a broader definition of energy security and described an analytical framework designed to help compare the energy security characteristics—both positive and negative—of different quantitative energy paths as developed using various software tools. This analytical framework has been elaborated and adapted for use in subsequent Nautilus Institute projects. Additional details of the PARES project's achievements can be found in the report *A Framework for Energy Security Analysis and Application to a Case Study of Japan*, available from Nautilus Institute (Suzuki et al. 1998). The present article draws from PARES project documents, as well as from summaries of the energy security analysis approach that has evolved from the project and were published earlier (for example, von Hippel 2004), and developed in related articles (Hayes and von Hippel 2006), as well as articles published in the November 2011 Asian Energy Security Special Section of the journal *Energy Policy* (von Hippel et al. 2011a; von

Hippel, Savage, and Hayes 2011), and a chapter in *The Routledge Handbook of Energy Security* (von Hippel et al. 2011b). Along with a summary of conventional approaches to defining energy security, descriptions of key elements of the broader energy security definition are provided below, along with a brief investigation into trends in implementing a more comprehensive view of energy security specifically in Chinese energy planning. As it is impossible to cover every aspect of this broad and varied topic in an article of this length, the focus here is on providing a summary of an approach to evaluation of energy security costs and benefits, along with a few specific examples of the consideration of energy security in energy planning.

Conventional and Broader Definitions

Many of the existing definitions of energy security begin, and end, with a focus on maintaining energy supplies and particularly supplies of fuel oil (see, for example, Clawson 1997). This supply-based focus has several goals as its nominal cornerstones: reducing vulnerability to foreign threats or pressure, preventing a supply crisis (including from restrictions in physical supply or an abrupt and significant increase in energy prices), and minimizing the economic and military impact of a supply crisis if it occurs (see, for example, Samuels 1997). Current national and international energy policies, however, have been facing many new challenges—with the figurative fallout from the Fukushima accident just the newest and thus currently most imperative of these—and as such need to have their effectiveness judged by additional criteria. This broader array of criteria needs to be considered among key components of new energy security concepts.

Why has oil been the primary focus of energy security policy? There are good reasons behind this particular focus. First, oil is still the dominant fuel, amounting to about 34 percent of global primary energy supply as of 2011 (BP 2011). Second, the Middle East, where the largest oil reserves exist, is still one of the most politically unstable areas in the world, and it is still unclear whether or not the numerous uprisings that began in late 2010 across the Middle East and North Africa, termed the "Arab Spring," and other geopolitical shifts will help to stabilize the region over the longer term. Third, and related to the second reason, oil supply and prices are often influenced by political decisions of oil suppliers and buyers. Fourth, world economic conditions are vulnerable to oil price volatility, since there are certain key sectors that are heavily dependent on oil (transportation, petrochemical industries, agriculture, military equipment, and others) with limited short-term alternatives for substitution.

Fifth, the key words here are *volatility* and *instability*; although globalization has improved the transparency of the oil market, oil prices remain to some extent at the mercy of speculators (Harris 2008; Singleton 2011), as well as being affected by fluctuations in currency values, subject to manipulation by oil suppliers and, of course, sensitive to the forces of market supply and demand. This was dramatically shown when oil prices roughly doubled between mid-2007 and mid-2008, followed by a 75 percent decline in price by early 2009, followed by a return to fall 2007 price levels (near $80 per barrel) by early 2010, with prices rising to $115 per barrel in 2011 before falling back to $80 by the fall of 2011 (Reuters 2008a and 2008b; USDOE EIA 2011).

Only a few studies have made serious attempts to clarify the concept of energy security. One was that of the Working Group on Asian Energy and Security at the Massachusetts Institute of Technology (MIT) Center for International Studies. The MIT Working Group defined the three distinct goals of energy security mentioned above: reducing vulnerability to foreign threats or pressure, preventing a supply crisis from occurring, and minimizing the economic and military impact of a supply crisis once it has occurred (Samuels 1997). These goals implicitly assume that an oil supply crisis is the central focus of energy security policy, and the central concerns are the reduction of threats to oil supply and crisis management. This view has had wide currency among key energy policy makers in both the East and West. Though the major energy consuming/importing countries have largely shared the above view of conventional energy security thinking, there are critical differences in how they have pursued energy security policy. Important factors include natural and geopolitical conditions. One country might have abundant natural resources (for example, Russia) and another might not (for example, Japan or the Republic of Korea). Some consuming countries are located close to energy-producing countries, and some are distant or are separated by daunting geographical or political barriers (such as the seas, difficult terrain, sensitive ecosystems, and North Korean borders separating the Russian Far East from its potential fuel customers in the Republic of Korea, China, and Japan), and thus need to transport fuel over long or difficult distances. Those conditional differences can lead to basic differences in energy security perceptions.

In sum, there are three major attributes that define the differences in energy security thinking between countries. First is the degree to which a country is rich or poor in energy resources. Second is the degree to which market forces are allowed to operate, as compared to the use of government intervention to set prices and select resources to address energy security concerns—for example, the degree to which countries are willing to trust that international markets will supply fuels in the event of a crisis. Third is the degree to which long-term versus short-term planning is employed. (See von Hippel et al. 2011a, for a comprehensive discussion of these attributes.) Despite these differences in thinking, however, energy policies in both resource-poor countries and resource-rich countries are arguably converging, as both types of countries confront the need to face a new paradigm in energy policy.

Issues and Concerns

National energy policies must address issues and needs on multiple fronts and must incorporate these considerations into a new concept of energy security.

Environment

If environmental problems are to be solved, energy policies will have to be reformulated. International environmental problems such as acid rain and global climate change present arguably the greatest impetus for changes in definitions of what it means to be energy secure. Some of these problems have relatively straightforward (though often expensive) technical solutions, including flue gas desulfurization devices to reduce the emissions of acid rain precursors. Other problems, such as greenhouse gas emissions and related climate change and long-term radioactive waste management, require solutions that consider a much longer time perspective and that demand much more national and international coordination than businesses and governments currently practice.

Technology

Risks associated with development and deployment of advanced technologies have been understated by conventional energy policy thinking, which tends to see them as short-term, not long-term. The clearest examples of risks associated with advanced technologies include nuclear accidents such as those at Three Mile Island in the United States (1979), Chernobyl in the former Soviet Union (1986), and Fukushima (2011). Natural disasters also affect complex energy infrastructure, such as Hurricane Katrina's impacts on oil and gas production in the Gulf of Mexico (2005) and the impact of the July 2007 earthquake near Niigata, Japan, on the seven-unit Kashiwazaki-Kariwa nuclear plant. Advanced fossil fuel systems also carry risks, with examples being major spills during oil transport and the April 2010 Deepwater Horizon oil rig fire and spill in the Gulf of Mexico.

Another class of issues related to advanced technologies includes the failure of research and development (R&D) efforts to perform as expected, such as the US programs during the 1970s and 1980s that attempted to develop synthetic fuels, a fast breeder reactor, and solar thermal resources. Risks from dependence on advanced technologies can be transnational; the accident at Chernobyl spread a radioactive cloud across much of Europe, and the impact of the Fukushima crisis, while not severe for other nations in the radiological sense, is having reverberating and profound impacts on energy policy not just in Japan but around the world (Schneider 2011; Takubo 2011). Also, markets for advanced technologies are becoming global, and as a result technological risks can be exported. Nuclear technology, for example, is being exported to a number of developing countries, most notably China and India, but also Vietnam (Bloomberg News 2011) and potentially Indonesia, Thailand, Pakistan, and Malaysia (IAEA 2007), as well as Middle Eastern nations including the United Arab Emirates (World Nuclear Association 2010). As the world moves rapidly toward more technology-intensive energy systems, a new energy security concept must address the various domestic and international risks associated with reliance on advanced and sometimes unproven technologies, as well as the risk-reduction benefits that such technologies may bring.

Demand-Side Management

Until the mid-1980s, conventional energy policy almost always sought to assure energy supply while assuming that demand was a given—and often assuming also that demand would continue to grow, sometimes exponentially. This notion has been changing since the mid-1980s, when the concept of demand-side management (DSM)—balancing demand and supply of energy by making energy use more efficient or changing its timing—was first incorporated into energy planning. Now, management of energy demand is almost on an equal footing with management of supply. New technologies such as distributed generation and smart grids in fact blur the distinction between demand and supply, in that the distributed generation can serve both on-site demand and demand on the electrical grid, and in that control and data gathering equipment used in smart grids can be used to manage both distributed electricity supply equipment and electricity demand. In addition, DSM is recognized as a key tool in the achievement of climate change mitigation and other environmental goals. Making effective use of DSM for energy policy development requires a shift from the conventional supply-side-oriented paradigm. There are risks associated with DSM technologies and policies, just as there are with energy supply options. Risks stem from, for example, DSM measures or programs not performing as expected, though these risks are more often related to social and economic factors than to technical considerations. Often risks of DSM underperformance can be reduced by the large number of small, independent applications of energy efficiency and related technologies that are typical in DSM implementation.

Social and Cultural Factors

Not in my backyard (NIMBY) stances and environmental justice concerns are becoming global phenomena, making it increasingly difficult, time-consuming, and costly in many countries, including in northeast Asia, to find sites for what are considered "nuisance facilities," such as large power plants, waste treatment and disposal facilities, oil refineries, or liquefied natural gas terminals. There are enviro-economic concerns as well, such as matching risk to host communities with compensation, but even in cases where the parties bearing the risk receive payment, circumstances can change that cause, for example, host communities to reconsider whether the economic compensation they are receiving, or indeed any amount, suffices to offset the risk. The social impact of the Fukushima accident is again a prime example, as nuclear reactor host communities throughout Japan are, as of late 2011, carefully considering whether or not to allow the restarting of reactors taken off-line for inspection, even though reactors produce huge revenues for the communities. Public confidence is also a key social factor influencing energy policy. Once lost, public confidence is hard to recover. Cultural factors can include the loss of homelands and ancestral sites through, for example, inundation by new reservoirs for large dams—as with the Three Gorges Dam in China, completed in 2006—or through destruction of landscapes by coal mining operations. Accounting for social and cultural factors and the role of public confidence in energy choices are therefore central components of a new concept of energy security.

International Relations and the Military

New dimensions in international relations and new military risks are challenging traditional energy policy making. The end of the Cold War has brought in its wake a new level of uncertainty in international politics. Although the risk of a world war is drastically reduced, the threat of regional clashes has increased, as demonstrated by ongoing conflicts in the Middle East, the Balkans, and the former Soviet states of the Caucasus, to name just a few. The international politics of plutonium fuel cycle development, with its associated risks of nuclear terrorism and proliferation, is an area where energy security and military security issues meet. Political factors can further complicate these risks, as, for example, in North Korea in the leadership transfer following the death of ruler Kim Jong-il in December 2011. The brave new world of post–Cold War international relations must be accounted for in a new concept of energy security.

Comprehensive Concept

The above five key components—environment, technology, demand-side management, social and cultural factors, and post–Cold War international relations—are central additions to the traditional supply-side point of view in a more comprehensive energy security concept.

A nation-state is energy secure to the degree that fuel and energy services are available to ensure (a) survival of the nation, (b) protection of national welfare, and (c) minimization of risks associated with supply and use of fuel and energy services. The six dimensions of energy security include energy supply, economic, technological, environmental, social and cultural, and military/security dimensions. Energy policies must address the domestic and international (regional and global) implications of each of these dimensions.

What distinguishes this definition of energy security is its emphasis on the imperative to consider both the national and extraterritorial implications of the provision of energy and energy services, while recognizing the potentially complex impacts of national energy security policies on the different dimensions of energy security, as well as the complexities, uncertainties, and subjective judgments inherent in measuring national energy security. The definition takes into consideration emerging concepts of environmental security, which include the effects of the state of the environment on human security and military security, and the effects of security institutions on the environment and on prospects for international environmental cooperation (Matthew 1995).

Evaluating and Measuring

Given the multiple dimensions of energy security identified above, and the linkages and overlaps between energy security dimensions and the dimensions of sustainability and sustainable development, a framework for evaluating and measuring—or at least comparing—the relative attributes of different approaches to energy sector development is needed. Such a framework should be designed to help identify the relative costs and benefits of different possible energy futures—essentially, future scenarios driven by suites of energy and other social policies. The discussion below identifies some of the policy issues associated with the dimensions of energy policy noted above, and presents a framework for evaluating energy security, as broadly defined.

Conceptual Framework

The dimensions of energy security as broadly defined above are provided in table 1, along with a sampling of

TABLE 1. Energy Security Conceptual Framework

Dimension of Risk or Uncertainty	Policy Issues	Examples of Management Strategies — For Routine Risk	Examples of Management Strategies — For Radical Uncertainty
Energy Supply	• Domestic vs. imported • Absolute scarcity • Technology/energy intensity • Incremental, market-friendly, fast, cheap, sustainable?	• Substitute technology for energy use • Put efficiency first • Diversify of import sources and types of fuel	• Detect potential and analyze technological breakthroughs • Explore to develop new reserves
Economic	• Price volatility • Cost-benefit ratio • Risk-benefit ratio • Social cost of supply disruption • Local manufacturing of equipment • Labor • Financing aspects • Benefits of "no regrets" strategies	• Compare costs/benefits of insurance strategies to reduce loss-of-supply disruption • Invest to create supplier-consumer interdependence via shared infrastructure • Insure by fuel stockpiling (uranium reactor fuel, oil, gas, coal), global (IEA) or regional quotas (energy charters)	• Export energy-intensive industries • Focus on information-intensive industries • Export energy or energy technologies
Technological	• R&D failure • Technological monoculture vs. diversification • New-materials dependency in technological substitution strategies • Catastrophic failure • Adoption/diffusion or commercialization failure	• Invest in renewables • Improve resilience and optimize scope of energy supply, demand, and distribution systems • Consider nuclear fuel cycle (recycling vs. once-through, alternative uranium resources)	• Develop permanent nuclear waste storage/disposal strategies
Environmental	• Local externalities • Regional externalities both atmospheric and maritime • Global externalities • Pursue precautionary principle	• Risk-benefit analysis and local pollution control • Pursue treaties • Emissions mitigation • Technology transfer	• Work to understand thresholds for radical shifts of state such as sea level rise and polar ice melt rate
Social-Cultural	• Managing consensus and conflict in domestic or foreign policy making among different actors • Institutional capacities to address problems • Siting and downwind distributional impacts • Populist resistance to or rejection of technocratic strategies • Existing perceptions and lessons from history with regard to different energy systems	• Transparency • Participation • Accountability • Side payments and compensation • Education • Training	

(*continued*)

TABLE 1. *Continued*

Dimension of Risk or Uncertainty	Policy Issues	Examples of Management Strategies	
		For Routine Risk	For Radical Uncertainty
International-Military	• International management of plutonium • Proliferation potential • Sea lanes and energy shipping • Geopolitics of oil and gas supplies	• Nonproliferation treaty/security guarantees (NPT/SG) regime • Security and physical protection of energy facilities against terrorism • Creation of security alliances • Naval power projection • Transparency and confidence building	• Disposition and disposal of excess nuclear warhead fissile materials • Military options for resolving energy-related conflicts, securing infrastructure • Combating terrorism

Source: authors.

policy issues with which each dimension of energy security is associated, plus examples that might be used to address the types of both routine and radical risk and uncertainty that are faced in the planning, construction, and operation of energy systems. It should be noted that while table 1 provides what is intended to be an extensive, but by no means complete, list of policy issues, even the categories shown are not necessarily independent. Certain energy technologies will be affected by climate change (for example, hydroelectric power and inland nuclear power plants may be affected by changes in water availability), and there are many other examples of interdependence that need to be carefully thought through in a full consideration of the energy security impacts of candidate energy policies.

Testing Different Energy Scenarios

Evaluation of energy security impacts of different policy approaches will include such tasks as deciding on manageable but useful level of detail, incorporation of uncertainty, consideration of risks, evaluating tangible and intangible costs and benefits, comparing impacts across different spatial levels and time scales, and balancing analytical comprehensiveness and transparency. With these factors in mind, a framework was devised by the authors that is based on a variety of tools, including diversity indices and multiple-attribute (trade-off) analyses, as described below. A prime example of a tool for evaluation of alternative energy and environmental paths or scenarios for a nation or a region is the Long-range Energy Alternatives Planning (LEAP) software system, developed and distributed by the Stockholm Environment Institute (SEI–US) and used in the Asian Energy Security project (COMMEND 2012). Central to the application of the framework is its application to the search for robust solutions—sets of policies that meet multiple energy security and other objectives at the same time.

The framework for the analysis of energy security (broadly defined) includes the following steps:

1. Define objective and subjective measures of energy (and environmental) security to be evaluated. (Within the overall categories presented in table 1, these measures could vary significantly between different analyses.)
2. Collect data and develop candidate energy paths/scenarios that yield roughly consistent energy services but use assumptions different enough to illuminate the policy approaches being explored.
3. Test the relative performance of paths/scenarios for each energy security measure included in the analysis.
4. Incorporate elements of risk.
5. Compare path and scenario results.
6. Eliminate paths that lead to clearly suboptimal or unacceptable results and iterate the analysis as necessary to reach clear conclusions.

The possible dimensions of energy security, and potential measures and attributes of those dimensions, range from the routinely quantified—such as total direct costs, capital costs, greenhouse gas emissions, or fraction of fuels sourced from abroad—to essentially unquantifiable—such as risk of social or cultural conflict (see von Hippel et al. 2011a and 2011b, for additional examples). It should be noted that many of these dimensions and measures can and do interact, and a solution to one problem may exacerbate another. It is therefore incumbent on the analyst evaluating energy security policy choices and on policy makers reviewing analytical results to take a comprehensive approach to reviewing the options available, making sure to consider different points of view.

There is often a temptation, in step 5 of the procedure above, to attempt to put the attributes of energy security into a common metric, for example, an index of relative energy security calculated through a ranking and weighting system. Such systems almost invariably, however, involve procedures that amplify small differences between paths/scenarios, play down large differences, hide necessarily subjective analytical choices, and give an illusion of objectivity to weighting choices that are by their nature quite subjective. More reliable is the laying out of each of the energy security attributes of each path/scenario side by side, which allows reviewers, stakeholders (i.e., those people who have a stake in an enterprise), and decision makers to see the differences and similarities between different energy futures for themselves and to apply their own perspectives and knowledge, in consultation with each other, to determine what is most important in making energy policy choices. Also not explicitly included in steps 5 or 6 are mathematical tools for optimizing energy security results over a set of paths or scenarios. Optimization can be attractive, as it appears to identify one "best" path for moving forward. Optimization models can in some cases offer useful insights, provided that the underlying assumptions and algorithms in the analysis are well understood by the users of the results. Optimization, however, like weighting and ranking, involves subjective choices that may appear objective, especially when applied across a range of different energy security attributes, and as such should be employed only with caution and with a thorough understanding of its limitations in a given application.

Toward a Comprehensive Approach: China

Although energy planning worldwide continues, arguably dominated by traditional energy security considerations (securing adequate supplies at a reasonable price), a more comprehensive type of energy security analysis is beginning to be used in a number of nations and contexts. In the United States in the 1980s and 1990s, elements of the comprehensive energy planning framework described above were required in some states under the rubric of least-cost or integrated resource planning (see, for example, Swisher, Jannuzzi, and Redlinger 1997). With climate and environment increasingly becoming issues that impinge on energy planning, particularly in the post-Fukushima world, energy planners are more frequently called upon to meet multiple objectives in development of energy policies. This is increasingly the case in China.

The context for energy planning in China has changed markedly. As a result of the economic downturn that followed the Asian financial crisis of 1997–1998, and a major restructuring of state-owned industries, China had an energy surplus in the late 1990s and early 2000s. Over the course of the early 2000s, with the gross domestic product growing in excess of 10 percent per year, this surplus dramatically turned to deficit, and by the end of the first decade of the twenty-first century China had become the world's second-largest crude oil importer and a net importer of coal, its most abundant domestic energy resource.

Increased reliance on oil and coal imports was an important factor driving changes in energy planning in China, but not the only one. Four other developments contributed to a broadening of the scope of energy security considerations, even if not always explicitly labeled as such. First, energy prices in general, and coal prices in particular, rose dramatically, raising fears of inflation and its impact on social and political stability. Second, China's leadership determined that the environmental impacts of uncontrolled fossil fuel combustion, once seen as a necessary cost of development, were no longer acceptable. Third, the corporatization of China's state-owned enterprises created a new political economy of monopoly power in the energy industries, to which the government's long-term solution, given its limited regulatory powers, is competition and diversification. Fourth, rapidly rising energy imports and the need to secure energy supplies has made energy an important, and costly, dimension of China's foreign policy.

All of these factors led to a concerted effort by China's leadership to diversify energy sources, focusing on domestic resources but also on reducing the share of coal in the country's energy mix. In the early twenty-first century, the National Development and Reform Commission (NDRC), China's chief planning agency, developed plans to massively increase use of energy from biofuels, hydropower, nuclear, solar, and wind, making China a global leader in alternative energy.

These efforts have had mixed success, however. China, as of 2012, is now more dependent on coal than it was a decade ago because its economy and energy demand grew faster than the expansion of noncoal energy resources. Additionally, development obstacles for alternative energy are emerging, and expansion plans have been scaled down. Biofuel plans, for instance, ran aground on conflicts with food and land security and have been significantly reduced or abandoned. With greater attention in China to the environmental and social impacts of large dams, hydropower development is increasingly subject to scrutiny, with some domestic hydropower projects postponed and a high profile cross-border project with Myanmar (Burma) cancelled. As a result of the Fukushima disaster, the NDRC's nuclear plans have been similarly scaled back, with new plant applications put on hold and the broader future of nuclear expansion in China uncertain. Wind development is also uncertain, as integrating large amounts of wind into China's inflexible, coal-dominated power system has proved difficult.

The collision of broad energy security concerns with a realization of the uncertainties and limits of new energy resources has created a new dimension to China's energy security discourse —moderating energy demand growth. End-use energy efficiency has been a core part of China's energy strategy since the 2000s, but energy efficiency is now also seen to be a finite resource. With limited options for expanding energy services, China's Twelfth Five-Year Plan (2011–2015) set more moderate targets (6–7 percent per year) for national gross domestic product growth. Importantly, these national targets are much lower than those set by provincial officials, setting the stage for a conflict in priorities between the central and provincial governments. China, perhaps more than any other nation, has recognized the links between the pace of economic growth and the severity of emerging energy security concerns across a wide spectrum of issues—trade, macroeconomic, environmental, political, and foreign policy. China's leaders will undoubtedly continue efforts to diversify energy sources, but the trade-offs between economic growth and energy security, and the consideration of energy security in a broader sense that includes environmental, social, international policy, and other considerations, are likely to figure more prominently in discourse over energy planning going forward.

David F. VON HIPPEL
Nautilus Institute for Security and Sustainability

James H. WILLIAMS
Monterey Institute of International Studies

Frederich KAHRL
Energy and Environmental Economics Inc.

Peter HAYES
Nautilus Institute at Global Studies, RMIT University

See also Association of Southeast Asian Nations (ASEAN); China; Energy Industries—Nuclear; Energy Industries—Renewables (China); Energy Industries—Renewables (India); Five-Year Plans; Green Collar Jobs; India; Japan; Korean Peninsula; Three Gorges Dam; Utilities Regulation and Efficiency; Water Security

FURTHER READING

Bloomberg News. (2011, November 22). Russia to lend Vietnam $9 billion for first nuclear plant. Retrieved January 13, 2012, from http://www.bloomberg.com/news/2011-11-22/russia-to-lend-vietnam-9-billion-for-first-nuclear-plant.html

British Petroleum Co. (BP). (2011, June). BP statistical review of world energy. Retrieved January 13, 2012, from http://www.bp.com/sectionbodycopy.do?categoryId=7500&contentId=7068481

Clawson, Patrick. (1997, November). *Energy security in a time of plenty* (Strategic Forum, No. 130). Washington, DC: National Defense University Institute for National Strategic Studies.

Community for Energy, Environment and Development (COMMEND). (2012). Homepage. Retrieved January 13, 2012, from http://www.energycommunity.org/

Harris, Jeffrey. (2008, April 3). Written testimony of Jeffrey Harris, Chief Economist, before the Committee on Energy and Natural Resources United States Senate. Retrieved January 13, 2012, from http://www.cftc.gov/ucm/groups/public/@newsroom/documents/speechandtestimony/opaharris040308.pdf

Hayes, Peter, & von Hippel, David. (2006). Energy security in northeast Asia. *Global Asia*, 1(1), 91–105. Retrieved January 13, 2012, from http://globalasia.org/pdf/issue1/Hayes,Hippel_GA11.pdf

International Atomic Energy Agency (IAEA). (2007, October 30). *Asia leads way in nuclear power development: Japan, South Korea, China and India driving present global nuclear power expansion* (staff report). Retrieved January 13, 2012, from http://www.iaea.org/NewsCenter/News/2007/asialeads.html.

Matthew, Richard. (1995). Environmental security: Demystifying the concept, clarifying the stakes. In P. J. Simmons (Ed.), *Environmental change and security project report* (pp. 14–23). Washington, DC: Woodrow Wilson Center for International Scholars.

Reuters. (2008a, July 9). FOREX-Dollar falls as oil prices rise on Iran news. Retrieved January 13, 2012, from http://www.reuters.com/article/usDollarRpt/idUSN0943813620080709

Reuters. (2008b, July 11). Oil hits record above $147. Retrieved January 13, 2012, from http://www.reuters.com/article/topNews/idUST14048520080711

Samuels, Richard J. (1997). Securing Asian energy investments. *The MIT Japan Program Science, Technology and Management Report*, 4(2).

Singleton, Kenneth J. (2011, July 22). *Investor flows and the 2008 boom/bust in oil prices*. Retrieved January 13, 2012, from http://www.stanford.edu/~kenneths/OilPub.pdf

Schneider, Mycle. (2011, September 9). Fukushima crisis: Can Japan be at the forefront of an authentic paradigm shift? *Bulletin of the Atomic Scientists*. Retrieved March 6, 2012, from http://www.thebulletin.org/web-edition/features/fukushima-crisis-can-japan-be-the-forefront-of-authentic-paradigm-shift

Suzuki, Tatsujiro; von Hippel, David; Wilkening, Ken; & Nickum, James. (1998, June). *A framework for energy security analysis and application to a case study of Japan* (Nautilus Institute report). Retrieved January 13, 2012, from http://oldsite.nautilus.org/archives/pares/PARES_Synthesis_Report.PDF

Swisher, Joel N.; Jannuzzi, Gilberto de Martino; & Redlinger, Robert Y. (1997, November). *Tools and methods for integrated resource planning*. United Nations Environment Programme. Retrieved January 13, 2012, from http://uneprisoe.org/IRPManual/IRPmanual.pdf

Takubo, Masa. (2011). Nuclear or not? The complex and uncertain politics of Japan's post-Fukushima energy policy. *Bulletin of the Atomic Scientists*, 67(5), 19–26.

United States Department of Energy, Energy Information Administration (USDOE EIA). (2011). NYMEX light sweet crude oil futures prices. Retrieved December 16, 2011, from http://www.eia.doe.gov/emeu/international/crude2.html

von Hippel, David F. (2004, December). Energy security analysis: A new framework. *reCOMMEND*, 2(1), 4–6. http://www.energy-community.org/reCOMMEND/reCOMMEND2.pdf

von Hippel, David F.; Savage, Timothy; & Hayes, Peter. (2011). Introduction to the Asian Energy Security project: Project organization and methodologies. *Energy Policy* (Asian Energy Security special section), 39(11), 6712–6718.

von Hippel, David F.; Suzuki, Tatsujiro; Williams, James H.; Savage, Timothy; & Hayes, Peter. (2011a). Energy security and sustainability in northeast Asia. *Energy Policy* (Asian Energy Security special section), 39(11), 6719–6730.

von Hippel, David F.; Suzuki, Tatsujiro; Williams, James H.; Savage, Timothy; & Hayes, Peter. (2011b). Evaluating the energy security impacts of energy policies. In Benjamin K. Sovacool (Ed.), *The Routledge handbook of energy security* (pp. 75–95). Oxon, UK: Routledge.

World Nuclear Association. (2010, February). Nuclear power in the United Arab Emirates. Retrieved January 13, 2012, from http://www.world-nuclear.org/info/UAE_nuclear_power_inf123.html

F

Fisheries (China)

China is the largest producer and consumer of fish in the world. As a result, Chinese fishing and marine environment policy is important not just nationally but also internationally. While the Chinese government seeks to implement a sustainable fisheries policy within China, it faces a number of challenges, including a lack of coordination between sister agencies, proliferation of enforcement actors, and inadequate deterrence.

Ocean fisheries are under extreme stress worldwide. In *The State of World Fisheries and Aquaculture 2010*, the Food and Agriculture Organization of the United Nations (FAO) observed that only 15 percent of the commercial stocks remain open to new fishing ventures, as more than half of the marine fishing stocks (53 percent) were fully exploited, 28 percent of the remaining stocks were overexploited, 3 percent were depleted, and a mere 1 percent were recovering from depletion. In the People's Republic of China (China), one scholar observed that "the development of our nation's fishing industry has reached an extremely important juncture. Most—if not all—of the fisheries have been fully exploited, and many are already exhausted" (Mu 2006, 292). China plays a key role in ensuring the sustainability of fisheries resources both globally and in the Asia Pacific region.

Chinese Fish Consumption and Production

China is the number-one consumer of fish internationally as measured by quantity of fish and seafood purchases (Pew Environment Group 2010). Between 1961 and 2007, Chinese consumption of fish products grew approximately 5.7 percent per year due largely to aquaculture (FAO 2010, 66). Of the 111 million tons of fish produced for the markets during 2007, China consumed 34.9 million tons or approximately 31 percent of the world's marketed fish (FAO 2010, 66).

China is also the number-one fishing nation for cumulative marine catches and aquaculture. In 2008, the country produced 47.5 million tons of fish, with the majority of that production (32.7 million tons) coming from cultivation (FAO 2010, 4). Aquaculture is currently responsible for 46 percent of the world's total fish supply (FAO 2010, 3), with China producing more than half of that (FAO 2010, 6). Just over 80 percent of the aquaculture products produced in China is consumed within China (FAO 2010, 18). Not all of these cultured fish are, however, destined for human plates; some cultured fish such as carp become feed fish for higher value aquaculture production (FAO 2010, 25). Many of the fish that are cultured in China are species that have been introduced from elsewhere, including North American largemouth black bass, North American channel catfish, North American bay scallops, South American pacu, Southeast Asian giant river prawns, and European eels (FAO 2010, 25–26).

Fishing in China accounts for almost 10 percent of the world's exports of fish in terms of quantity (FAO 2010, 49). China has the largest number of individuals in the world employed in the fishing industry (FAO 2010, 7), with marine capture and aquaculture directly employing 13.3 million people, 8.5 million of those jobs being full time (FAO 2010, 27). While the number of individuals employed in fishing in China is about 3 million more than the number of individuals employed in aquaculture, employment in the fishing industry is shrinking while employment in the aquaculture industry has been rapidly expanding (FAO 2010, 28).

Numerous other jobs are created indirectly by the fishing industry. The FAO estimates that each person employed in capture fisheries and aquaculture production generates three additional jobs in processing, equipment manufacturing, equipment maintenance, and other fishing-related work (FAO 2010, 29). While these jobs are not reported as fishing jobs, in the case of China they may generate around 40 million additional jobs, meaning that approximately 53 million individuals rely on fishing either directly or indirectly for income. In 2003, approximately 816.2 million Chinese citizens were employed (US CIA 2011), meaning that the fishing industry is responsible for nearly 6.5 percent of employment in China.

As the primary producer and consumer of fish in the world, China faces a number of sustainability challenges. For one, it continues like many other nations to have an overcapacity of fishing vessels, leading to a race by individual fishers to extract resources. China had 288,779 marine fishing vessels in 2007 and hoped to reduce the fleet to 192,390 vessels by 2010 (FAO 2010, 34).

Chinese fishermen focus most of their marine fishing efforts on the East China Sea, followed by the South China Sea, and finally the Yellow Sea (Goldstein 2009). In the East China Sea, however, fishermen have fished down the food chain so that annual catch levels have plummeted (Chen and Shen 1999). Likewise, in the South China Sea, dozens of species are disappearing; for example, a 2011 study showed that, of 109 shark species historically present in the South China Sea, only 18 have been recorded in recent surveys (Lam and Sadovy de Mitcheson 2011).

Government Responses

The Chinese government has responded to the threats to overfishing of marine fisheries by providing subsidies to assist marine fishermen in transitioning to other employment, supporting the development of the aquaculture sector, and designating marine reserves to help resources recover. Legal reforms since the 1990s have sought to reduce overfishing. Seasonal moratoria have been in place on the Yellow Sea, the East China Sea, and the Bohai Bay for over a decade (Xue 2005, 110–118). China has also attempted to rationalize fishing by vessels under its control by imposing conservation and management measures, including requiring fishing vessels to register with government authorities and to obtain fishing authorizations. Under the Fisheries Law of the People's Republic of China, China requires licensing of fishing vessels operating within areas under Chinese jurisdiction (People's Republic of China 2009a, Article 16). In order to address habitat degradation, the Chinese government has also responded to pollution threats to fisheries with its passage of the Marine Environment Protection Law of the People's Republic of China, which prohibits pollution activities that damage the marine environment.

China is an active participant in international fishery arrangements. It is a member of the United Nations Convention on the Law of the Sea as well as parallel regional fishery treaties involving primarily tuna. These treaties generally defer to the flag state for enforcement of conservation and management measures and rely on China to implement its international obligations through domestic measures. In addition to its participation in treaty regimes, China has participated actively in high seas enforcement exercises, including cooperating with the US Coast Guard to enforce a United Nations prohibition on drift net fishing (Xue 2005, 150).

In spite of the presence of both domestic and international legal regimes supported by political will at the highest levels of central lawmaking, there remain numerous challenges for China in the area of translating its written legal rules into actual local enforcement of fishery and pollution laws. The first challenge is a lack of necessary coordination between sister agencies. The primary institution responsible for fishery enforcement is the Fisheries Law Enforcement Command, which operates under the Ministry of Agriculture but lacks sufficient budget to be effective (Goldstein 2009). As a result of being unable to work effectively with its sister police agencies, the Fisheries Law Enforcement Command has generally underenforced national fishery laws (He et al. 2007). In some instances, agencies that derive their authority from different groups find themselves embroiled in a conflict of interest. The interests of provincial governments often clash with federal interests resulting in, for example, different interpretations of what is a sustainable yield for a given localized fishery.

The second challenge to achieving sustainability through the existing law is a tendency of certain environmental laws to encourage a proliferation of uncoordinated enforcement actors. For example, pollution enforcement under the national law relies on participation by numerous diverse agencies that may or may not be able to coordinate their efforts effectively to achieve overall pollution reduction. The Marine Environment Protection Law provides an example. Under the existing law, the State Council's Environmental Protection Department has ultimate administrative authority to protect the marine environment in China from pollution; the monitoring and enforcement work is undertaken by numerous other agencies. The State Administrative Department of Marine Affairs is responsible for providing oversight for offshore oil exploration and exploitation and for the dumping of wastes into the sea. The Harbor Superintendency Administration is responsible for preventing vessel pollution in nonfishing harbors. The State Fisheries Administration and Fishing Harbor

Superintendency are responsible for monitoring fishing vessels. The Environmental Protection Department of the Armed Forces oversees military vessels and naval ports. Finally, the environmental protection departments of the coastal provinces, autonomous regions, and municipalities under the central government are responsible for controlling pollution from coastal construction projects and land-sourced pollutants. In spite of this devolution of enforcement, it is unclear which of the groups are successfully fulfilling their mandate since large-scale pollution continues unabated. In a 2010 report from the State Oceanic Administration, administrators reported that 147,000 square kilometers (somewhat larger than the US state of New York) of China's coastal waters failed to meet standards for "clear water," an increase of 7.3 percent over 2008 (Xinhua News Agency 2010).

A third challenge for Chinese fisheries governance involves adequate deterrence. The existing laws provide the government with a great deal of flexibility in seeking liability from violators, ranging from issuing a warning to criminal prosecution. In spite of enforcement opportunities, the levels of environmental law enforcement may be quite low depending on institutional constraints (Wang 2007, 170). For example, in the case of the Department of Fishery Administration, the department has no independent authority to enforce its regulatory decisions and so has little motivation to make such decisions (McMullin 2009, 157).

A fourth challenge for China is to provide sufficient oversight of both its vessels and its people when they fish outside of Chinese-controlled waters. While China has a domestic, albeit uncoordinated, strategy to address the condition of the fisheries within its territorial waters and exclusive economic zone (waters internationally recognized as under the jurisdiction of the coastal state), other nations have growing global concerns that China is redeploying its excess fishing capacity into fishing activity in distant waters, which could impact the ecological sustainability of global fisheries. Chinese domestic law favors this approach with specific language in the 2009 Fisheries Law providing that the state will give preferential treatment in the form of funds, materials technology, and favorable taxation to offshore and deepwater fishing ventures (People's Republic of China 2009a, Article 15). As of 2006, China had approximately two thousand ships engaged in distant-water fishing (Xue 2006, 653) including numerous fishing vessels operating in and near African waters. In addition to these Chinese-flagged vessels, which are expected to comply with Chinese law, there is also a number of distant-water fishing vessels that are flagged under non-Chinese flags of convenience but are likely under Chinese operation and ownership, as well as Chinese-owned vessels operating under no flag. These ships are not adequately regulated under either China's fishing laws or the fishing law of the government that has permitted the vessel to be registered under its flag.

It is not surprising that China faces numerous institutional and enforcement challenges. As the biggest consumer and producer of fish, China is confronted with the daunting feat of controlling a complex, nontransparent, million-plus actor industry. Yet, the future of many commercial fisheries, and not just fisheries in China, depends on China having enforceable fishery and marine environmental policies.

Outlook

China has been proactive in trying to achieve sustainability, particularly in its domestic fisheries, by pursuing nationwide policies of minus-growth for marine capture and domestically pushing for investment in aquaculture. While these are positive developments from the perspective of sustainable fishery development, China has also contradicted the international goals of sustainable development by simultaneously extending the reach of its fishing fleets to distant waters where these fleets are impacting the sustainable development choices of other nations.

The future of global fisheries depends on the good faith effort of China to pursue a balance between conservation and use in both its domestic fisheries and its international fishing efforts. Fishery sustainability within China will certainly require greater collaboration among Chinese agencies. Also crucial is a commitment by the government to dedicate adequate enforcement resources to ensuring compliance with existing laws; toothless laws are easily discarded when parties have difficult resource choices to make. Outside of China, fishery sustainability requires a greater commitment by the Chinese government to investigating and prosecuting its nationals who fail to comply with international conservation and management agreements. In particular, China must be prepared to exercise its jurisdiction over its nationals who use either a flag of convenience or no flag as a shield against liability.

A proverb attributed to the Chinese neatly sums up the future of sustainable fisheries: "If we do not change our direction, we are likely to end up where we are headed." The Chinese recognize through their policies that the current trends of chronic species exploitation and habitat degradation need to be changed, but the question is whether China can effectively enforce these changes among its people without generating local backlash.

Anastasia TELESETSKY
University of Idaho College of Law

See also Association of Southeast Asian Nations (ASEAN); Biodiversity Conservation Legislation (China); China; Consumerism; Corporate Accountability (China); Education, Environmental (China); Five-Year Plans; Huang (Yellow) River; Mekong-Lancang River; National Pollution Survey (China); Rule of Law; Yangzi (Chang) River

FURTHER READING

Chen, Ya Qu, & Shen, Xin-Qiang. (1999). Changes in the biomass of the East China Sea ecosystem. In Kenneth Sherman & Qisheng Tang (Eds.), *Large marine ecosystems of the Pacific Rim: Assessment, sustainability, and management* (pp. 221–239). Malden, MA: Blackwell Science, Inc.

Food and Agriculture Organization (FAO) of the United Nations. (2010). *The state of world fisheries and aquaculture 2010.* Retrieved January 25, 2012, from http://www.fao.org/docrep/013/i1820e/i1820e.pdf

Goldstein, Lyle. (2009, August 7). China's fishing fleet sets challenge to US. *Asia Times.* Retrieved January 25, 2012, from http://www.atimes.com/atimes/China/KH07Ad01.html

He Zhonglong, Ren Xingping, Feng Shuili, Luo Xianfen & Liu Jinghong. (2007). *Research on the building of the Chinese Coast Guard.* Beijing: Ocean Press.

International Convention for the Conservation of Atlantic Tunas. (1966). Final act of the Conference of Plenipotentiaries on the conservation of Atlantic tunas. Retrieved February 9, 2012, from http://www.fao.org/Legal/treaties/014t-e.htm

Lam, Vivienne, & Sadovy de Mitcheson, Yvonne. (2011). The sharks of South East Asia: Unknown, unmonitored and unmanaged. *Fish and Fisheries, 12*(1), 51–74.

McMullin, Joseph. (2009). Do Chinese environmental laws work? A study of litigation as a response to the problem of fishery pollution in China. *UCLA Pacific Basin Law Journal, 26*(2), 142.

Mu Yongtong. (2006). *Fisheries management: Focusing on a rights-based regime.* Qingdao: Ocean University of China Press.

People's Republic of China. (2009a, June 23). Fisheries Law of the People's Republic of China. Retrieved January 25, 2012, from http://english.agri.gov.cn/ga/plar/200906/t20090623_1080.htm

People's Republic of China. (2009b, June 23). Marine Environment Protection Law of the People's Republic of China. Retrieved January 25, 2012, from http://english.agri.gov.cn/ga/plar/200906/t20090623_1114.htm

Pew Environment Group (2010, September 22). China tops world in catch and consumption of fish. *ScienceDaily.* Retrieved January 25, 2012, from http://www.sciencedaily.com/releases/2010/09/100922121947.htm

United Nations Convention on the Law of the Sea. (1982, December 10). Retrieved February 9, 2012, from http://www.un.org/depts/los/convention_agreements/convention_overview_convention.htm

United States Central Intelligence Agency (US CIA). (2011). The world factbook. East and Southeast Asia: China. Retrieved February 12, 2012 from https://www.cia.gov/library/publications/the-world-factbook/geos/ch.html

Wang, Canfa. (2007). Chinese environmental law enforcement: Current deficiencies and suggested reforms. *Vermont Law Journal, 8*(2), 159–190.

Western and Central Pacific Fisheries Commission. (2000, September 5). Convention on the Conservation and Management of Highly Migratory Fish Stocks in the Western and Central Pacific Ocean. Retrieved January 25, 2012 from http://www.wcpfc.int/doc/convention-conservation-and-management-highly-migratory-fish-stocks-western-and-central-pacific-

Xinhua News Agency. (2010, March 12). 147,000 sq km of China's sea below clean water standard. *China Daily.* Retrieved January 25, 2012, from http://www.chinadaily.com.cn/china/2010-03/12/content_9576742.htm

Xue Guifang. (2005). *China and international fisheries law and policy.* Leiden, The Netherlands: Martinus Nijhoff.

Xue Guifang. (2006). China's distant water fisheries and its response to flag state responsibilities. *Marine Policy, 30*(6), 651–658.

Berkshire's authors and editors welcome questions, comments, and corrections. Send your emails about the *Berkshire Encyclopedia of Sustainability* in general or this volume in particular to: sustainability.updates@berkshirepublishing.com

Five-Year Plans

Centralized and integrated national economic programs, called five-year plans, have played an important role in the economies of China and India since 1953 and 1951, respectively. Five-Year Plans since the 1980s have paid particular attention to sustainability and environmental measures. The Twelfth Five-Year Plans in India and China are the greenest yet, but local implementation in both countries does not always match ambition.

Five-Year Plans (FYPs) are centralized and integrated national economic programs. Joseph Stalin implemented the first FYP in the Soviet Union in the late 1920s. Most communist states and several capitalist countries subsequently have adopted them. China and India both continue to use FYPs, although China renamed its Eleventh FYP, from 2006 to 2010, a guideline (*guihua*), rather than a plan (*jihua*), to signify the central government's more hands-off approach to development. India launched its First FYP in 1951, and China began its plan in 1953. Both countries are now in their Twelfth FYP.

India and China initially adopted FYPs to emulate the Soviet Union's early rapid industrialization. In the Communist-ruled People's Republic of China an influx of Soviet technical advice and aid shaped the first plan. India introduced socialist planning for more pragmatic purposes, to take a "neutral" position between the ideologies of the postindependence nation's first leaders—the rural reconstructionism of Mohandas Gandhi and the industrial modernism of Jawaharlal Nehru. Both countries first introduced environmental topics in their FYPs in the 1970s and 1980s. Sustainability is now a significant component of central planning in both countries.

China

China launched its First FYP in 1953, four years after the founding of the People's Republic. The plan stressed rapid growth and increasing government control of heavy industry as well as agricultural collectivization. The State Planning Commission compiled the central plan. China's initial FYP introduced the first national census under its new government, revealing a larger than expected population of 583 million. This number was a cause for celebration at the time because Mao Zedong's government actively encouraged rapid population growth (Shapiro 2001, 33). China judged its First FYP to be mostly a success. Iron, steel, and cement production expanded significantly.

China's Second FYP, from 1958 to 1962, spanned the period of the Great Leap Forward, an era marked by the push for ever more ambitious production targets. An editorial in the official Communist Party newspaper *People's Daily* in 1956 suggested that China achieve the goals of the Second FYP ahead of schedule and above target (Shapiro 2001, 72). The reality of frenzied production initiatives did not match the slogan in that editorial: "Greater, Faster, Better, More Economical." Millions starved, partly as a result of catastrophic mismanagement and the diversion of agricultural labor into industrial production.

The period also saw the Maoist project Wipe Out the Four Pests, a synchronized mass campaign to eliminate the nation's rats, mosquitoes, flies, and sparrows, which were targeted because they ate grain seeds. This campaign was not only an apt symbol of the widespread ecological destruction under Mao—deforestation increased rapidly during the period, the agricultural sector widely misused pesticides, and poorly built irrigation projects led to disasters—but it also illustrates the unsustainable and counterproductive results of such campaigns: the birds, which were driven close to extinction, ate insects. Infestations of locusts and other insects spread after 1958, ruining a sizable proportion of the crop (Dikötter 2010, 188).

After the disaster of the Second FYP, China did not implement the next plan until 1966, at the start of the Cultural Revolution. That plan and the Fourth FYP, from 1971 to 1975, were the final plans of the Mao era. The Ten Year National Economic Development Plan Outline, from 1976 to 1985, set the stage for a new period of rapid economic growth, known as the period of Reform and Opening Up, under Deng Xiaoping's leadership (Hilton 2011, 5).The breakneck pace of development during this period came with such social and environmental costs that, for the first time, Five-Year Plans began to include measures to adjust economic growth targets downward, reduce energy and material consumption, slow population growth, and improve environmental protection. The Sixth FYP, from 1981 to 1985, included a national energy conservation program.

This trend toward a more sustainable model of development became clearer in the Eleventh FYP, from 2006 to 2010. This plan stressed a move away from the "getting rich first" model of rapid, often highly unequal development toward building the "harmonious socialist society" through support for more disadvantaged regions and sectors of society and for stronger environmental and energy-saving measures (Fan 2006, 708). China judged many of the programs under this FYP—measures to close small, inefficient plants; the Top 1,000 Enterprises Program for industrial energy efficiency, which fostered significant technological upgrades in large enterprises; and the Ten Key Energy Conservation Projects, which included green lighting projects and combined heat and power (cogeneration) programs—to be successful.

The most high-profile goal in that plan attracted more controversy: reduce the country's energy intensity (energy consumed per unit of gross domestic product) by 20 percent. This plan was the first quantitative and binding goal on energy efficiency in a Five-Year Plan, and one that translated into an estimated annual emissions reduction of over 1.5 billion tonnes of carbon dioxide. Against the background of the global economic crisis and the stimulus measures that ensued, however, local authorities struggled, some reportedly cutting power supplies to factories, traffic lights, and even hospitals in a late rush to meet the targets. This push to succeed also underscores the extent to which target-responsibility systems increasingly held local officials to account for their performance in meeting goals. The country ultimately achieved a 19.06 percent energy intensity reduction over the Eleventh FYP, less than a percentage point shy of the 20 percent goal.

The State Planning Commission became the National Development and Reform Commission (NDRC) in 1998. Once the NRDC sets the central macroeconomic and social policy, ministries and agencies, such as the Ministry of Environmental Protection, spend about a year producing their own documents interpreting the goals of the plan for implementation.

India

In the 1930s India was still a British colony, and as India's future leaders debated their vision of a modern, postindependence nation, they reached no clear consensus about policy making. The key ideological difference was between Mohandas Gandhi, who favored progress through rural reconstruction, and Jawaharlal Nehru, later the country's first prime minister, who wanted India to emulate the model of industrialized Western countries. India's socialist-influenced planning was a compromise between these two schools of thought. The government formed the National Planning Committee in 1937 as a "neutral" group that could find a way past the ideological conflict between the Gandhians and the Nehruvians (Chatterjee 2001, 273). After independence in 1947, this committee reemerged as a group of appointed experts from various fields, known as the Planning Commission, which set the FYPs.

India's First FYP ran from 1951 to 1955. It heavily emphasized agriculture, irrigation dam construction, and transportation and communication infrastructure development. The plan also stressed infant mortality reduction. Its underlying concern was to push up savings and capital formation within the country, the lack of which the planners saw as a major constraint on progress. The plan was a success from a growth perspective. India registered a 3.6 percent annual gross domestic product growth over the five years, exceeding its target of 2.1 percent.

The Second FYP, from 1956 to 1961, focused on heavy industry. The plan created a large number of public-sector companies producing steel, fertilizer, and coal. Railways expanded notably. The Third FYP, from 1962 to 1966, brought the focus back to agriculture. A period of crisis, marked by political instability and wars with China and Pakistan, followed that plan and lasted about fifteen years. The nationalization of the banks and the Green Revolution were notable achievements during that period. The general consensus, however, is that any plans during that period left the core issues affecting the broad mass of the population unattended. India often suspended its FYPs during the period and carried out annual plans instead.

International developments around the United Nations Conference on the Human Environment in Stockholm in 1972 were hugely instrumental to the environmental turn in policy making in India, even though sustainability was not included until the Sixth FYP, from 1980 to 1985. As a signatory of the Stockholm Declaration, the government established in 1972 the National Council for Environmental Policy and Planning, within the Department of Science and Technology, which evolved in 1985 into a full-fledged Ministry of Environment and Forests.

Although the government passed many laws that regulated natural resources prior to the 1972 Stockholm conference—the Indian Forest Act of 1927; the Mines Act of 1952; the Mines and Minerals (Development and Regulation) Act of 1957; the Petroleum, Oil, and Natural Gas Rules of 1959—the early plans primarily aimed such laws and regulations at the issues of licensing and the movement of goods rather than conservation of the environment.

The draft Fifth Plan, however, from 1974 to 1979, declared that the pursuit of developmental goals should not cause a quality-of-life reduction through deteriorating environmental conditions. India strove to maintain a balance between development and environmental management. The Sixth FYP, from 1980 to 1985, devoted an entire chapter to the environment. It noted, "The environment must not be considered as just another sector of national development. It should form a crucial guiding dimension for Plans and programs in each sector" (Government of India 1980). It was the first clear recognition of human-caused environmental problems.

The Fifth and Sixth FYPs adopted some important legal measures to achieve these objectives. The government amended the Water (Prevention and Control of Pollution) Act in 1974, set up the Central Pollution Control Board, introduced the Air (Prevention and Control of Pollution) Act in 1981, passed the Atomic Energy Act of 1982 to regulate handling of radioactive materials, and enacted the Forest (Conservation) Act of 1980 to protect natural resources. These measures reflected the broader policy guidelines that the plan documents framed.

Environmental concerns have become increasingly significant, as more recent FYPs in India have engaged the question of integrating growth with environmental issues. The Eleventh FYP, from 2007 to 2012, noted that one of the strategies for achieving faster growth with greater inclusiveness is protection of the environment. Per capita availability of scarce resources such as water and land are diminishing, it acknowledged, because of the irrational exploitation of the commons. It recognized that "[t]he pressing need to accelerate agriculture growth should not be at the cost of sustainability of our natural resource base, which is starkly limited" (Government of India 2008).

Development planning at all levels in India's Eleventh FYP gave environmental sustainability a very high priority. The state strengthened enforcement mechanisms for dealing with industrial and vehicular pollution on the principle that "the polluter pays." The plan focused attention on environmental management; for example, the plan integrated sewage treatment with water conservation. The FYP introduced the River Conservation Programme, particularly the Comprehensive Action Plan for Yamuna and other important rivers. The government added amendments to the existing Forest Conservation Act to involve communities in forest management. Finally, the plan chalked out a concrete plan for climate change action. This plan took a positive stance toward adaptation and also engaged constructively with the international community to reach a consensus on mitigation based on fair principles of burden sharing. The promotion and development of low-carbon and energy-efficient technologies with reasonable costs became priorities. It is also during this plan period that the National Action Plan on Climate Change took shape.

The Future of Sustainability

China's Twelfth FYP, from 2011 to 2015, focuses considerably on the environment. Of the plan's many targets, excluding population-related measures, the resource and environmental goals account for 33.3 percent of the total, up from 27.2 percent in the Eleventh FYP (Hu and Liang 2011, 20). These plans include binding targets on energy and resources and on environmental protection as well as the country's first target on carbon intensity (carbon dioxide emitted per unit of gross domestic product), a 17 percent reduction from 2011 to 2015. China's plan also includes a 16 percent reduction in energy intensity, an 8 percent reduction target for sulfur dioxide and chemical oxygen demand (which were also in the Eleventh FYP), and a 10 percent reduction target for ammonia nitrogen and nitrogen oxides (which were new targets). Water intensity (water consumed per unit of industrial added value) has a reduction target of 30 percent, and China aims to boost its forest cover to 21.66 percent and increase forest stock by 600 million cubic meters.

The environmental components of the plan focus not only on protecting China's natural resources and environment, but also on "moving up the value chain" (i.e., moving toward a higher-technology, more efficient, service-oriented, and ultimately postindustrial economy) and growing the country's role in clean-energy innovation. The plan expects investment in environmental protection and clean technology to surpass 3 trillion yuan (US$476 billion) over the five years, including wind, solar, and nuclear energy infrastructure and public transportation. The Chinese government will prioritize the development of seven Strategic Emerging Industries: biotechnology; new energy; high-end equipment manufacturing; energy conservation and environmental protection; clean energy vehicles; new materials; and next-generation information technologies. The plan also discusses at great length market mechanisms, including carbon-trading programs.

The environment is also at the center stage of India's Twelfth FYP, from 2012 to 2017. In the draft plan, entitled "Faster, Sustainable and Inclusive Growth," the tenth plan for the Ministry of Environment and Forestry aims for an increase of 57.86 percent in total outlay of funds. Some of the concrete plans stated aim to increase forest and tree cover by 5 percent, to attain World Health Organization standards of air quality in all major cities, to treat all urban wastewater, and to increase energy efficiency by 20 percent by 2016–2017.

In keeping with the dual aim of achieving inclusive growth and environmental sustainability, attention has come to rest on the natural resources of land and water. As foreign investment in industry puts demands on the governing of these natural resources, the plan has provided guidelines to deal with them. In the interests of food security, the draft places reasonable restrictions on foreign acquisition of multicrop irrigated land, without making government land acquisition impossible for roads and railways or for security purposes. Considering the sensitivity of implementing water pricing, the plan proposes differential water pricing to ensure efficient use of scarce resources. The plan recommends rational pricing and water rationing to reflect industrial, commercial, and agricultural uses. In short, the FYP rules out economic development at the expense of ecology through legal measures as well as incentive structures.

Outlook

In China, policy makers have debated the Twelfth FYP's target for carbon intensity and its regional distribution. Environmentalists pushed for an ambitious goal of a more than 18-percent reduction by 2015, which they argued would keep the pressure on local governments that might otherwise opt for high-carbon growth models (Yang, Hou, and Li 2011). Others argued that once the country shut down small power plants and inefficient steel plants that had been developed under the previous plan (so-called low-hanging fruit), it would be far more difficult to achieve energy savings. For the sake of development in poorer regions, these policy makers contended, the country should revise the target downward to around 16 percent on average and institute a trading program so provinces that could not meet the targets could buy credits from more energy-efficient provinces (Liu 2011). These factions, provincial governments, and powerful industry stakeholders (people who have a stake in an enterprise) compromised on a final target of 17 percent.

Many overseas environmentalists, including some in the United States, have expressed admiration for the environmental ambition in China's latest economic blueprint. The US environmentalist Jake Schmidt of the National Resources Defense Council wrote, "Policymakers in the United States are following China's movements very closely. So it is my hope that China's ambition is matched and exceeded by US resolve. A clean-energy race to the top is our best solution to climate change" (Ellis 2011, 42).

There is a difference, however, between the objectives of China's central planning and the deteriorating environmental situation on the ground. In early 2011, China's top environment minister Zhou Shengxian said in remarks on his ministry's website, "Natural resources are shrinking, degenerating and drying up. Ecological and environmental decay has become a bottleneck and a serious obstacle to our economic and social development. If our homeland is destroyed and we lose our health, then what good does development do?" (Hook 2011).

Many Chinese environmentalists believe reversing this trend will mean going beyond investment and top-down targets. China must redefine development to (1) take account of externalized costs, from natural resource depletion to pollution-related diseases, (2) overcome long-standing systemic obstacles to the local enforcement of central government regulations, and (3) help civil society, lawyers, and journalists to pressure local bodies that continue to prioritize economic growth over environmental protection.

Indian planning has focused on the search for pathways to inclusive growth. It has included environmental plans for this overarching concern. There is a tension between policy makers who aim for high growth rates (of 9–10 percent) and those who prefer implementing only modest measures on the environmental front. For many, what is missing is a focus on reducing inequality of access to the commons. This aspect of per capita availability of natural resources is absent in India's Twelfth FYP. Civil society groups are demanding more decentralized energy planning. Others have criticized the role of the central Planning Commission in a pluralist democracy (Bagchi 2007; Pellissery 2010). Expert plans often reach crisis at the initial stage of implementation because multiple aspirations that the experts have not considered cause friction among participants at the ground level. There are also strong aspirational differences between the national level and local-level political classes in understanding the plan's goals.

Sam GEALL
chinadialogue

Sony PELLISSERY
Institute of Rural Management, Anand

See also Activism, Judicial; China; Energy Security (East Asia); Gandhism; Great Green Wall (China); India; Microfinance; National Pollution Survey (China); One-Child Policy; Public-Private Partnerships; Reforestation and Afforestation (Southeast Asia); Rule of Law; Rural Development; Rural Livelihoods; South-North Water Diversion; Three Gorges Dam; White Revolution of India

FURTHER READING

Bagchi, Amaresh. (2007). Role of the planning and the planning commission in the new Indian economy. *Economic and Political Weekly*, 44(42), 92–100.

Chatterjee, Partha. (2001). Development planning and the Indian state. In Partha Chatterjee (Ed.), *State and politics in India* (pp. 271–297) New Delhi, India: Oxford University Press.

Dikötter, Frank. (2010) *Mao's great famine*. London: Bloomsbury.

Fan, C. Cindy. (2006). China's eleventh five-year plan (2006–2010): From "getting rich first" to "common prosperity." *Eurasian Geography and Economics*, 47(6), 708–723.

Ellis, Linden. (2011). Meanwhile in America. In Isabel Hilton (Ed.), *China's green revolution: Energy, environment and the 12th five year plan* (pp. 5–11). London: chinadialogue.

Government of India. (1980). Sixth Five Year Plan, 1980–1985. Retrieved April 2, 2012, from http://planningcommission.nic.in/plans/planrel/fiveyr/welcome.html

Government of India. (2008). Eleventh Five Year Plan, 2007–2012. Retrieved April 2, 2012, from http://planningcommission.nic.in/plans/planrel/fiveyr/welcome.html

Hilton, Isabel. (2011). Introduction: The evolving blueprint. In Isabel Hilton (Ed.), *China's green revolution: Energy, environment and the 12th five year plan* (pp. 5–11). London: chinadialogue.

Hook, Leslie (2011, February 28). China pollution "threat to growth." *Financial Times*. Retrieved April 2, 2012, from http://www.ft.com/cms/s/0/3671a476-4359-11e0-8f0d-00144feabdc0.html#axzz1qhNcU6Xg

Liu Jianqiang. (2011). Reining in China's energy targets. In Isabel Hilton (Ed.), China's green revolution: Energy, *environment and the 12th five year plan* (pp. 23–26). London: chinadialogue.

Mandal, Tirthankar. (2009, September). Five-year plans: Analysing environmental planning in India. *TerraGreen*, 2(6), 26–33.

Pellissery, Sony. (2010). Central agency in plural democracy. *The India Economy Review*, 7(3), 12–16.

Shapiro, Judith. (2001) *Mao's war against nature: Politics and the environment in revolutionary China*. Cambridge, UK: Cambridge University Press.

Yang Fuqiang; Hou, Yanli; & Li Jingjing. (2011). China needs higher targets. In Isabel Hilton (Ed.), *China's green revolution: Energy, environment and the 12th five year plan*. London: chinadialogue.

G

Gandhism

The philosophy of Mohandas Gandhi centers on a full realization of Truth, including the understanding that people are one with the world in which they live. The basic principles of nonviolence, selflessness, and economic freedom that are based on this understanding lead naturally to sustainable practices, and have influenced the development of many ecologically focused movements and philosophers.

Practices of sustainability, for Mahatma Mohandas Gandhi (1869–1948), follow naturally from an emphasis on nonviolence, selflessness, and economic freedom—concepts that are of primary importance in Gandhian philosophy. These principles are part of a fully encompassing and integrated philosophical system necessary for the realization of Truth (which Gandhi took to be humans' constant aim). For Gandhi, sustainability thus was as much a religious commitment as a civic virtue, in keeping with the lack of distinctions he drew between different spheres of life.

Philosophical Principles

Gandhian nonviolence involves extinguishing desires for that which is unnecessary. Once we have let go of cravings for more, people no longer will see the need for much of our violent behavior, since, for Gandhi, that which is truly necessary does not require the use of violence for its defense. Fully adopting Gandhian nonviolence means taking no more from nature than is truly necessary. This means that human practices will be sustainable, as the resources provided by the environment are sufficient for all people to obtain what they need.

When, for example, we desire warmth and convenience in travel to the extent that we endanger the world's oil supply, we accept violence as a legitimate means for preserving our lifestyle. On the contrary, when we can be content with just what we need to survive decently, we do not rely on violence to preserve our lifestyle. Our contentment is of infinitely greater value than, say, the latest model of an envy-provoking automobile.

To realize a world of genuine contentment and nonviolence (and thus sustainable practice), Gandhi held that humanity must first attain significant levels of selflessness. As he sought this end, he renounced self-centered practices. In keeping with his understanding of Hindu thought, he saw these renouncement practices as aiming for the eradication of the everyday, psychological (*jiva*) self that people commonly identify with. Attaining selflessness for Gandhi literally entailed minimizing to the furthest extent possible what one has taken to be himself. Perpetuating this self results from pursuing our desires, and while this self is being perpetuated, we are kept from realizing our True Self (*atman*). Realizing who one really is, for Gandhi, is the same as recognizing Truth, defined as the ultimate Reality that we are one with. Genuine selflessness thus rules out the self-indulgence that makes sustainability impossible.

Gandhi's ideas about economic freedom (*swaraj*) also relate to sustainability. Essential to this kind of economic freedom is local production of the basic goods a community consumes. Local control means that communities do not rely on far-removed, centralized systems for attaining basic necessities. An economic downturn in a distant country that is driven by unconstrained self-indulgence therefore would not affect a community's ability to provide for itself.

For Gandhi, a consequence of this kind of freedom is that it serves as a natural buffer against overproduction. Instead of constantly pursuing new markets and consumers as a means for economic survival, self-sufficient communities produce what they need for themselves in response to their own intimate knowledge of their particular situation and in a way that allows them to notice destructive practices and stop them. Resources are not excessively consumed in producing greater quantities of goods than could ever be considered reasonable. For Gandhi, sustainability naturally follows from this kind of genuine economic freedom.

Practical Movements

The influence of Gandhian philosophy on Western environmental movements is perhaps most evident in the example of the deep ecology movement. The Norwegian philosopher Arne Naess, founder of deep ecology, openly espoused Gandhian ideas about realizing one's true identity. In India, Gandhi's influence on environmental movements is evident in the Chipko ("to cling to") campaigns that began in the early 1970s. Members of this movement, based on principles of nonviolence, have been recognized as among those who have shaped present-day India. They have also inspired subsequent environmental movements throughout the world. In less obvious and profound ways, Gandhian ideas can be seen in present-day attempts to live simply and buy locally.

It is important to stress that for Gandhi, sustainable practices, like all activities, must be consciously based on the pursuit of Truth to be truly viable. Though such practices, like nonviolence itself, have great practical value, their acceptance should ultimately follow from deep metaphysical commitments. For Gandhi, it is only when such commitments are in place that one can truly maintain the right practices. Without this foundation, one's wishes and one's acts are liable to be in disharmony. This disharmony is ultimately counterproductive, since actual realization of Truth (our ultimate aim) requires affirmation of that Truth from within our deepest selves. For Gandhi, it is thus preferable to use more resources than absolutely necessary while acknowledging the need for progress than it is to have an ideal impact on the environment yet desire to live extravagantly.

Gandhian philosophy is inclusive. Gandhi himself did not think that the metaphysical commitments necessary for truly living in the right way had to be understood in the context of Hindu religious vocabulary. He famously declared that "Truth is God" and "God is the unbelief of the atheist." Such statements demonstrate the view that proper metaphysical understanding can be expressed in religiously neutral language, and that an emphasis on concepts like nonviolence, selflessness, and economic freedom are not the province of any one tradition. Indeed, for Gandhi, all great religious traditions emphasize such concepts at their core.

Sanjay LAL
Clayton State University

See also Activism, Judicial; Consumerism; Education, Environmental (India); Education, Female; India; Indigenous Peoples; Media Coverage of the Environment; Microfinance; Nongovernmental Organizations (NGOs); Outsourcing and Offshoring; Public Health; Religions; Rule of Law; Traditional Knowledge (India); White Revolution of India

FURTHER READING

Bose, Nirmal Kumar. (1940). *Studies in Gandhism*. Ahmedabad, India: Navajivan Publishing House.

Chatterjee, Margaret. (1985). *Gandhi's religious thought*. Basingstoke, UK: Palgrave Macmillan.

Gandhi, Mahatma. (n.d.). Hind swaraj and Indian home rule. Retrieved January 30, 2012, from http://www.mkgandhi.org/swarajya/coverpage.htm

Gandhi, Mahatma Mohandas. (2002). *The essential Gandhi: An anthology of his writings on his life, work, and ideas* (Louis Fischer, Ed., 2nd ed.). New York: Random House.

Gandhi, Mohandas Karamchand.(1971). *Gandhi: An autobiography. The story of my experiments with truth*. Boston: Beacon Press.

Grimes, William. (2009, January 5). Arne Naess, Norwegian philosopher dies at 96. *New York Times*. Retrieved February 18, 2012, from http://www.nytimes.com/2009/01/15/world/europe/15iht-15naess.19376594.html

Gruzalski, Bart K. (2002). Gandhi's contribution to environmental thought and action. *Environmental Ethics, 24*, 236.

Haynes, Jeffery. (2002). *Politics in the developing world: A concise introduction*. Hoboken, NJ: Wiley-Blackwell.

Jack, Homer A. (Ed.). (1956). *The Gandhi reader*. Bloomington: Indiana University Press.

Lal, Sanjay. (2006). *The tension and coherence of love, identification, and detachment in Gandhi's thought*. Knoxville: University of Tennessee.

Lal, Sanjay. (2008, July). Gandhi's universal ethic and feminism: Shared starting points but divergent ends. *Asian Philosophy, 18*(2), 185–195.

Lal, Sanjay. (2010). Globalization, Gandhism, and free trade. *Man in India, 90*(1–2), 3–10.

Naess, Arne. (1989). *Ecology, community, and lifestyle: Outline of an ecosophy*. Cambridge, UK: Cambridge University Press.

Verma, Surendra. (1970). *Metaphysical foundation of Mahatma Gandhi's thought*. New Delhi: Orient Longmans Press.

Ganges River

The Ganges, or Ganga, River begins in the western Himalaya along the Tibetan border in the Indian state of Uttarakhand and flows southeast across the Gangetic Plain of northern India into Bangladesh, where it empties into the Bay of Bengal. The Ganges basin is also drained by parts of Nepal and China. A sacred river for Hindus, the Ganges suffers from intensive pollution and other environmental threats.

The Ganges River originates 3,959 meters above sea level in the Himalaya Mountains of India, flowing from the Gangotri glacier, which bears ice that is four thousand years old. The Ganges flows through many important Indian cities, including Kanpur, Allahabad, Varanasi, Patna, and Kolkata (Calcutta), before it reaches the Bay of Bengal. About 40 percent of the Indian population lives in the Ganges watershed; as of 2011, about 400 million people live along the banks of the Ganges River (Najar 2011). At 2,525 kilometers, the Ganges ranks among the largest in the world in both drainage area and length. It brings sustenance to the alluvial Indo-Gangetic Plain, which is one of the world's most bountiful food-growing areas. Having a rich biodiversity (biological diversity as indicated by numbers of species of animals and plants), with fifteen species of mollusks, fifty-one species of insects, four species of freshwater prawns, eighty-three species of fish, twelve species of freshwater turtle, and three species of river dolphins, the river is a lifeline for many aquatic creatures (Rao, Sahu, and Pandit 1995). It has many tributaries, the largest of which is the Ghaghara River that meets the Ganges before Patna. Two major dams on the Ganges, one at Hardwar and the other at Farakka, have a crucial impact on the flow of the river. The Hardwar dam diverts much of the Himalayan snowmelt into the Upper Ganges Canal, built by the British in 1854 to irrigate the surrounding land.

Experts contend that this has caused severe deterioration to the flow in the river and is also a major cause for the decay of the Ganges as an inland waterway. The Tehri Dam on the Bhagirathi River, a tributary of the Ganges, has been controversial because the site is considered to be an earthquake-prone area (Brune 1993).

Although the Ganges is associated with myth, and its water is considered to be holy and to have healing properties, rampant pollution has marred its water quality. Among the most polluting industries on the Ganges are tanneries, especially near Kanpur, which empty toxic chrome into the river (Rao et al. 2009). The river basin also has sugar and paper mills; woolen, cotton, and rayon mills; battery industries; ordnance factories; thermal powerhouses; distilleries; and fertilizer corporations. Heavy metals such as cadmium, zinc, nickel, lead, chromium, and copper are concentrated in the river water and the sediments. In 1995, the Central Pollution Control Board (CPCB) listed 191 polluting industries in the state of Uttar Pradesh, 6 in the state of Bihar, and 67 in West Bengal (Alley 2002, 53). These industries were found to be discharging toxic substances into effluent flows with biological oxygen demand (BOD) concentrations of more than 100 milligrams per liter. Industry is not the only source of pollution, however. About 1 billion liters of untreated municipal waste also flow into the river daily. In addition, inadequate cremation procedures and surface runoff from farmlands where chemical fertilizers and pesticides are applied contribute to pollution of the Ganges. Organic waste decomposes faster in the Ganges than in other rivers, but the river cannot compensate for the high quantity of organic waste that is poured into its waters from the cities along its banks (Krishna Murti et al. 1996). In Varanasi, for example, fecal coliform levels have been recorded as high as 100,000 per 100 milliliters.

Another threat looming over the Ganges is silt that is deposited in its higher reaches in the Himalaya. Taking stock of the situation, the Uttar Pradesh Forest Department is planting trees in the catchment areas (areas where water gathers) to prevent soil erosion. At the current rate of 3,000 hectares of forest a year, however, it will take 150 years to arrest siltation fully. In response, the Chipko movement was launched in the Raghwal hills of Indian in the 1970s (Bandopadhyay and Shiva 1987). Chipko movement activists, who are mostly local villagers, are demanding a stop to tree felling in the Himalaya so that floods in the Ganges basin can be checked.

To combat pollution, the $270 million Ganges Action Plan (GAP) was started in 1986. GAP Phase I aimed at building waste-treatment facilities with Dutch and British support. Rakesh Jaiswal, executive secretary of the Kanpur-based nongovernmental organization EcoFriends, said that nearly $150 million pumped into Phase I was misspent mainly due to bureaucratic delays and indifference (personal communication with author, July 2002). In fact, sewage treatment plants under the plan have not been completed. Electric crematoria are standing like white elephants, entirely nonfunctional. The plan did not work satisfactorily largely because of the lack of participation by people along the river. The Indian activist and Supreme Court lawyer M. C. Mehta claimed that GAP has failed because politicians have sided with industrialists (personal communication with author, March 2002). The GAP was renamed as the National River Conservation Plan (NRCP), and GAP Phase I ended in 2000. GAP Phase II was approved by the Supreme Court in 1993. It was designed to clean the tributaries of the Ganges—the Yamuna River, which flows past New Delhi and the Taj Mahal, and the Gomti River, which flows through the historic city of Lucknow. The Mohananda River was also included in the plan in 2005–2006. The plan, however, has so far failed (Haberman 2006, 277). In 2007, the Ganges River was ranked among the top-five most polluted rivers in the world, dangerous for more than 140 fish species, 90 amphibian species, and the Ganges River dolphin (CNN-IBN 2007).

Tirtho BANERJEE
Journalist, Lucknow, India

See also Agriculture (South Asia); Delhi, India; Dhaka, Bangladesh; Education, Environmental (India); Gandhism; The Himalaya; Huang (Yellow) River; India; Mekong-Lancang River; Public Health; Religions; Tibetan Plateau; Traditional Knowledge (India); Transboundary Water Issues; Water Security; Water Use and Rights (India); Yangzi (Chang) River

FURTHER READING

Alley, Kelly D. (2002). *On the banks of the Gaṅgā: When wastewater meets a sacred river*. Michigan: University of Michigan Press.

Arnold, Guy. (2000). *World strategic highways*. London: Taylor & Francis.

Bandopadhyay, J., & Shiva, Vandana. (1987). The Chipko movement against limestone quarrying in Doon Valley. *Lokayan Bulletin, 5*(3), 19–25.

Brune, James N. (1993). The seismic hazard at Tehri dam. *Tectonophysics, 218*(1–3), 281–286.

D'Monte, Darryl. (1996). Filthy flows the Ganga. *People and the Planet, 5*(3), 20–22.

CNN-IBN. (2007, June 27). 30 Minutes: The Ganga is dying. Retrieved January 03, 2011, from http://ibnlive.in.com/news/30-minutes-the-ganga-is-dying/36796-3.html

Haberman, David L. (2006). *River of love in an age of pollution: The Yamuna River of northern India*. Berkeley: University of California Press.

Islam, M. Rafiqul. (1987). The Ganges water dispute: An appraisal of a third party settlement. *Asian Survey, 27*(8), 918–934.

Krishna Murti, C. R.; Das, T. M.; Bilgrami, K. S.; & Mathur, R. P. (Eds.). (1996). *The Ganga: A scientific study*. New Delhi: Northern Book Centre.

Najar, Nida. (2011, June 14). India aims $1 billion at sacred but filthy Ganges. Retrieved February 10, 2012, from http://www.nytimes.com/2011/06/15/world/asia/15ganges.html

Rao, R. T.; Sahu, S. K.; & Pandit, R. K. (1995). *Studies on biological restoration of Ganga in Uttar Pradesh: An indicator species approach* (Final technical report, 1995). Gwalior, India: School of Studies in Zoology, Jiwaji University.

Rao, D. P.; Saxena, Rajul; Saxena, Vishal; and Singh, Abha. (2009). Toxic load of tannery industries situated in Kanpur. *International Journal of Applied Environmental Sciences, 4*(3), 327–335.

Sampat, Payal. (1996, July–August). The river Ganges' long decline. *World Watch, 9*(4), 24–32.

Sharma, Ramesh C.; Bahuguna, Manju; and Chauhan, Punam. (2008). Periphytonic diversity in Bhagirathi: Preimpoundment study of Tehri dam reservoir. *Journal of Environmental Science and Engineering, 50*(4), 255–262.

Shukla, Ashok Chandra., & Vandana, Asthana. (1995). *Ganga: A water marvel*. New Delhi: APH Publishing Corporation.

Gender Equality

Women in China, India, and East and Southeast Asia have made strides toward gender equality—equal treatment and opportunities for men and women—but they have a long way to go. Women have not reached full economic and political participation, they do not have the same educational opportunities as men, and they are more vulnerable than men to natural disasters. Gender equality as an issue of sustainable development remains a challenge.

Gender equality and empowerment are two sides of the same coin. Although *gender* and *sex* are often used interchangeably, they are different concepts. *Sex* refers to an individual's biology. *Gender,* on the other hand, is socially constructed and comprises the roles, rights, and obligations attached to people on the basis of their sex. *Gender equality* refers to women's greater self-reliance and the participation of both women and men in productive and reproductive life. When both men and women realize their full potential, they achieve gender equality, a condition essential for the accomplishment of sustainable development. It is the women who are primarily affected by gender inequality. Women experience poverty differently from men as they are denied equal rights and opportunities. They lack access to resources and services and are excluded from important decisions. These inequalities between men and women adversely affect the lives of women and the quality of life for the society as a whole, hindering the process of sustainable development. A full understanding of the dimensions of gender equality is necessary if the rights and needs of women and men are to be met equally and sustainable development is to be attained (Irish Aid n.d.).

Dimensions

Researchers examine women's economic participation, educational attainment, political participation, health and survival as well as vulnerability to environmental degradation when they study gender equality in China, India, and East and Southeast Asia. Some Asian countries are closing the gender gap more successfully than others. (See table 1 on the next page.) The Philippines tops the list, closing 76 percent of its gender gap. China, Bangladesh, and India have reduced the gender gap by 68 percent, 67 percent, and 61 percent respectively. Although China has made remarkable progress in narrowing the gender gap, it comes in second to last on the health and survival subindex (133 out of 134), partly because its one-child policy—which restricts urban married couples to one child per family and has led to selective abortion and female infanticide—has resulted in a highly disproportionate sex ratio at birth.

Economic Participation

Gender inequity exists in the economic involvement of women. Women's employment status between South and East Asia shows a sharp contrast. About 67 percent of women work for pay in East Asian countries such as China, Cambodia, and Vietnam. Fewer than 36 percent of women do paid work in South Asian countries such as India and Pakistan (UNDP 2010).

Seventy-five percent of females are in paid work in China, compared to 85 percent of males. Women constitute 45.3 percent of the total labor force in the manufacturing sector (ILO 2010). Women's contribution in China runs parallel to the country's long-term growth

Table 1. Gender Gap Rankings in South, East, and Southeast Asia

Country	Economic Rank	Political Rank	Educational Rank	Health Rank	Overall Score*	Overall Rank
Philippines	13	17	1	1	0.7654	9
Sri Lanka	89	6	57	1	0.7458	16
Singapore	20	79	103	100	0.6914	56
Thailand	36	94	84	1	0.6910	57
China	46	56	88	133	0.6881	61
Vietnam	33	72	106	127	0.6776	72
Bangladesh	117	12	108	122	0.6702	82
Japan	1	101	82	1	0.6524	94
India	128	23	120	133	0.6155	112
Nepal	112	44	126	110	0.6084	115
Pakistan	133	52	122	127	0.5465	132

Source: Hausmann, Tyson, and Zahidi (2010).

*Scale of 0 to 1, where 0 = inequality and 1 = equality.

and industrialization (UNDP 2010). Women work predominantly in the service sector in East Asia, which accounts for 76 percent of all female employment. Most women in India (55 percent) work in agriculture (United Nations Statistics Division 2010); only 7 percent work in professional or technical occupations (Kishor and Gupta 2009). The majority of women workers in this region work in "vulnerable" employment, that is, low-paid work that is not secure, such as family work and own-account work. They are unlikely to have job security, adequate pay, or decent working conditions. They may serve as domestic workers away from home throughout the year.

Access to land and ownership anchors women's economic development to a large extent. Women in South Asia mostly have user rights and are less likely to own land. Custom and religious laws discriminate against women (Halim 2011, 11). Discrimination in land ownership in China and Vietnam is not as stark as in South Asia. Although China's 2003 agrarian reform allowed women to benefit from equal land distribution, in practice women do not own much land (Rao 2011; Costa 2010).

The wage gap remains wide in both South and East Asian countries. Women in China earn 70 percent of what men do for performing similar work (Hausmann, Tyson, and Zahidi 2010). An average Bangladeshi woman earns half of what a man makes, which is more than what women make in India, Pakistan, and Afghanistan, but less than they do in China, Sri Lanka, and Nepal (Islam and Dogra 2011, 8). South Korea has one of the largest wage gaps in the world; women's wages in the manufacturing sector average only 57 percent of those of men (United Nations Statistics Division 2010). For comparison to industrialized countries, the gender gap in the United States in 2009 was 80.2 percent (Rampell 2010) and in Germany in 2008 was 76.8 percent (Spiegel Online 2010).

Political Participation

Women in China participate politically at relatively low percentages at all levels of government. Most women who participate in government are at the lower levels. They occupy only 12 percent of ministerial positions and only 21.3 percent of all positions in China's parliament; their participation rate ranks fifty-first out of 187 countries (IPU 2011).

India, the world's largest democracy, ranks ninety-eighth. India lags behind many countries, including its neighbors Bangladesh, Pakistan, and Nepal, when it comes to women's participation in politics. Women make up only 10.8 percent of the members of its lower house, and 10.3 percent in its upper house (IPU 2011). Bangladesh has a relatively high representation of women in national politics compared to many other countries in the region. Women occupy 16 percent of ministerial positions in Bangladesh compared to 10 percent in India and 6 percent in Sri Lanka (Hausmann, Tyson, and Zahidi 2010).

Educational Attainment

Gender disparities at all levels of education have been effectively eliminated in China. By the end of 2009, the primary net school enrollment rate for boys and girls had reached 99.36 percent and 99.44 percent respectively. The number of female students attending college/university accounted for 50.48 percent of the total. The biggest challenge China is currently facing, however, in terms of gender equality in education is the eradication of illiteracy. Women account for 70 percent of illiterate adults in China (UN System in China 2010).

In India, as in other countries, the gender disparity in literacy is much greater in rural than in urban areas; even in urban areas, however, 25 percent of women and more than 10 percent of men are illiterate (Kishor and Gupta 2009). Male-female disparities exist at the tertiary level in India, comprising 15.25 percent of males and 11 percent of females (Thorat 2006). Bangladesh has already achieved gender parity in primary education enrollment. The share of female students at the secondary level has exceeded 50 percent (World Bank 2009). In terms of tertiary enrollments, however, Bangladesh is staying far from the target of gender parity—only 5 percent of females compared to 9 of males are enrolled at tertiary levels (Hausmann, Tyson and Zahidi 2010).

Health and Survival

Whereas average life expectancy at birth for females is higher in most Asian countries, the infant mortality rates in India and China are abnormally high for females. (See table 2 below). In India the child mortality rate for girls is 61 percent higher than for boys (Kishor and Gupta 2009).

Since the 1980s, China has seen a considerable decline in its infant mortality rate. The preference for sons differentially affects girls' survival by subjecting them to gender-based discrimination in terms of access to life-sustaining resources. The male infant mortality rate declined by a large margin while the female rate saw only a minor drop both in rural and urban areas. Not only has the infant mortality rate risen since the 1980s, but the sex ratio of males to females at birth has risen abnormally in both China and India. Sexual selection—the "before birth" solution and "after birth" solution—reflects sexual discrimination in childbirth and child survival. The high male-to-female birth ratio and the low ratio of males among infant deaths are two sides of the same coin (Li, Wei, and Jiang 2006). The naturally occurring birth sex ratio is 100 girls to 106 boys, but the national ratio of China in 1996 was 100 to 111, demonstrating a considerable weighting toward boys (Edwards 2000, 75). For the generation born between 2005 and 2010, 100 girls were born for every 120 boys. China's one-child policy and the patrilineal family system, coupled with the country's

TABLE 2. Life Expectancy, Infant Mortality Rates, and Sex Ratio at Birth in South and East Asian Countries

Country	Life Expectancy at Birth Male	Life Expectancy at Birth Female	Infant Mortality Rate by Sex (per 1,000 live births) Male	Infant Mortality Rate by Sex (per 1,000 live births) Female	Sex Ratio at Birth
China	71.1	74.5	15.61	16.57	120
India	62.8	65.7	46.18	49.14	108
Japan	79.3	86.1	2.98	2.58	106
Bangladesh	67.4	68.3	53.23	48.13	105
Nepal	66.7	68.0	44.54	44.55	105
Sri Lanka	71.2	77.4	10.68	8.6	104
Afghanistan	47.2	47.5	152.75	145.47	106
Pakistan	63.8	65.4	66.52	59.85	105
Thailand	70.2	71.1	17.38	15.35	106
South Korea	76.5	83.3	4.37	3.93	110
Vietnam	72.3	76.2	21.27	20.48	105

Sources: Compiled from UN DESA (2011a and 2011b); US CIA (2011).

traditional culture, are the root causes for son preference. Sustained low fertility, immature social security systems, and the lower status accorded to Chinese women condition families to prefer sons. Sex-selection services, although illegal, are still available and affordable (Shuzhuo 2007), which has made it easy to terminate pregnancies of female offspring.

The war against baby girls exists not only in China. India, South Korea, and Taiwan also have unusually high numbers of male births. In India, people have practiced female infanticide for thousands of years. The availability of modern sex-determination techniques such as amniocentesis and ultrasound has made sex-selective abortion common (Grewal and Kishore 2004). In 1990, there were 35 million more males than females in India. Estimates as of 2009 place the figure at 50 million (Al Jazeera 2009). Economic and social motives encourage this culturally accepted elimination of girls in India. The son provides income for the family and eventually marries a wife with a large dowry (Grewal and Kishore 2004).

Vulnerability to Environmental Degradation

Environmental degradation has gender-specific impacts. Women rely on natural resources for their livelihoods more than men because they do not have equitable access to alternatives such as wage labor and the accompanying security and benefits. Degraded environment implies that women have to walk further to collect water and fuel wood (Irish Aid n.d.). Women generally assume primary responsibility for collecting drinking water and fuel for cooking. When environmental degradation occurs, women suffer the most because of this discriminatory division of labor. Garwal women protested such suffering in India by organizing the Chipko movement to stop felling trees for commercial purposes (Halim 2007, 103). Women in many parts of South and East Asia lack access to clean-energy fuels and improved stoves. Evidence from Bangladesh, Cambodia, and Laos shows that women in more than 80 percent of households heavily rely on solid fuels for cooking, exposing themselves to respiratory problems and diseases (United Nations Statistics Division 2010).

Natural disasters kill more women than men. Many more women died in the 2004 tsunami, as figures from India, Indonesia, and Sri Lanka suggest; women are more often at home (or on shore or other physically vulnerable locations) and stay behind to look for children and relatives, and more men can swim and climb trees to safety (Oxfam 2005). Similarly, when Bangladesh was hit by a devastating cyclone and flood in 1991, the death rate among women aged 20–44 was 71 per 1,000, compared to 15 per 1,000 for men (Irish Aid n.d.). The socially constructed roles and existing inequalities make the women more vulnerable than men to the impacts of environmental and natural disasters such as drought, floods, and cyclones.

Implications and Challenges

Gender inequality persists in India, China, and their neighboring countries. If government and society do not address the sex ratio imbalances in India and China, between 2015 and 2030 there will be a 25 percent disparity between the numbers of men and women, leading to an obvious bride shortage (United Nations Children's Fund 2008). The discrimination and neglect of women are visible in education, political representation, employment, and access to productive resources. Widespread poverty and environmental degradation aggravate the discrimination. Gender equality depends on gender parity in education, pro-women's laws of inheritance, minimizing all forms of deprivation, and emphasizing health and survival. Women's power to control their lives within and outside the home will allow them freedom to make choices.

Political participation is a powerful instrument toward meaningful progress in all spheres. Sustainable development cannot be made unless men and women participate equally in the highest development policy-making positions. Women's involvement in such positions would counter the current attitudes and practices that obliterate women's potential as true development partners. Although women have emerged as the main actors in different types of development programs in recent years, they still lack access to resources and services mainly due to their exclusion from decision-making power structures. Therefore, the link between gender equality and sustainability must be established through the transformation of subordination inimical to women. Due emphasis should be given to the redistribution of power so that poor women can participate in controlling and influencing the directions in which the development occurs. The challenge is mostly political; it requires policies and programs both on national and international levels.

Sadeka HALIM
University of Dhaka

Muhammad Zakir HOSSIN
ASA University Bangladesh (ASAUB)

See also Activism, Judicial; Education, Female; Five-Year Plans; Gandhism; Labor; Microfinance; One-Child Policy; Public Health; Rural Livelihoods

FURTHER READING

Al Jazeera. (2009, August 27). Female infanticide. Retrieved October 19, 2011, from http://english.aljazeera.net/programmes/101east/2009/08/2009826121857421605.html

Costa, Beatrice. (2010, March). *Her mile: Women's rights and access to land; The last stretch of road to eradicate hunger*. Milan: ActionAid.

Edwards, Louise. (2000). Women in the People's Republic of China: New challenges to the grand gender narrative. In Louise Edwards & Mina Roces (Eds.), *Women in Asia: Tradition, modernity and globalization* (pp. 59–84). Sydney: Allen & Unwin.

Grewal, Indu, & Kishore, J. (2004, May 1). Female foeticide in India. *International Humanist News*. Retrieved October 19, 2011, from http://www.iheu.org/female-foeticide-in-india

Halim. Sadeka. (2007). South Asia. In Suad Joseph et al. (Eds.), *Encyclopedia of women and Islamic cultures: Volume 4. Economics, education, mobility and space* (pp. 102–104). Leiden, The Netherlands: Brill.

Halim, Sadeka. (2011). Women's ownership rights to land: Barriers & challenges in Bangladesh. In *Asian regional workshop on women & land rights: Workshop proceedings* (pp. 11–25). Quezon, Philippines: Asian NGO Coalition for Agrarian Reform & Rural Development & Association for Land Reform & Development.

Hausmann, Ricardo; Tyson, Laura; & Zahidi, Saadia. (2010, December 7). *The global gender gap report 2010*. Retrieved July 17, 2011, from http://www3.weforum.org/docs/WEF_GenderGap_Report_2010.pdf

International Labor Organization (ILO) Laborsta Internet. (2010). Statistics by topic: Employment. Employment for detailed occupational groups by sex. Retrieved December 26, 2011, from http://laborsta.ilo.org

Inter-Parliamentary Union (IPU) (2011). Women in national parliaments. Retrieved July 31, 2011, from http://www.ipu.org/wmn-e/classif.htm

Irish Aid. (n.d.). Environment and gender equality (Irish Aid key sheet, Department of Foreign Affairs). Retrieved January 12, 2012, from http://www.irishaid.gov.ie/Uploads/6_Environment_and_Gender_Equality.pdf

Islam, M. Shahidul, & Dogra, Suvi. (2011, January 6). Women empowerment in Bangladesh: The rise of the other half (ISAS Working Paper 119). Singapore: National University of Singapore.

Kishor, Sunita, & Gupta, Kamla. (2009, August). *Gender equality and women's empowerment in India* (National Family Health Survey [NFHS-3], India, 2005–06). Mumbai, India: International Institute for Population Sciences.

Li, Shuzhuo; Wei, Yan; & Jiang, Quanbao. (2006). Girl child survival in China: Past, present and prospects for the future. *Market and Demographic Analysis, 1*, 2–16.

Oxfam. (2005, March 26). The tsunami's impact on women. Retrieved October 19, 2011, from www.oxfam.org/en/policy/bn050326-tsunami-women

Rampell, Catherine. (2010, July 13). The gender pay gap, by state. *New York Times*. Retrieved December 31, 2011, from http://economix.blogs.nytimes.com/2010/07/13/the-gender-pay-gap-by-state/

Rao, Nitya. (2011, September 20–23). Women's access to land: An Asian perspective (paper, Expert Group Meeting on Enabling Rural Women's Economic Empowerment: Institutions, Opportunities and Participation). Accra, Ghana.

Shuzhuo, Li. (2007, October 29–31). *Sex ratio at birth and comprehensive intervention in imbalanced China*. Retrieved December 26, 2011, from www.unfpa.org/gender/docs/studies/china.pdf

Spiegel Online International. (2010). Gender inequality. Retrieved December 31, 2011, from http://www.spiegel.de/international/europe/0,1518,682026,00.html

Thorat, Sukhadeo. (2006, November 24). Higher education in India: Emerging issues related to access, inclusiveness and quality (Nehru Memorial Lecture). University of Mumbai, India.

United Nations Children Fund (UNICEF). (2008). The state of the world's children 2008: Child survival. Retrieved October 19, 2011, from http://www.unicef.org/sowc08/

United Nations Department of Economic and Social Affairs (UN DESA). (2011a). World population prospects: The 2010 revision. Table 2: Selected demographic indicators: Fertility, 2005–2010. Retrieved October 19, 2011, from http://esa.un.org/wpp/Sorting-Tables/tab-sorting_fertility.htm

United Nations Department of Economic and Social Affairs (UN DESA). (2011b). World population prospects: The 2010 revision. Table 3: Selected demographic indicators: Mortality, 2005–2010. Retrieved October 19, 2011, from http://esa.un.org/wpp/Sorting-Tables/tab-sorting_mortality.htm

United Nations Development Programme (UNDP). (2010). *Human development report 2010*. New York: United Nations.

United Nations Statistics Division. (2010). *The world's women 2010: Trends and statistics*. New York: United Nations.

United Nations System in China. (2010). China's progress towards the Millennium Development Goals 2010 report. Retrieved November 13, 2011, from http://www.un.org.cn/public/resource/China_MDG_Progress_report_2010_e.pdf

United States Central Intelligence Agency (US CIA). (2011). The world factbook: Country comparison; Infant mortality rate. Retrieved October 19, 2011, from https://www.cia.gov/library/publications/the-world-factbook/rankorder/2091rank.html

World Bank. (2009). *Education development index for Bangladesh: In quest of a mechanism for evidence based decision making in primary education*. Dhaka, Bangladesh: World Bank.

Genetic Resources

Genetic material from plants, animals, and microorganisms makes up genetic resources, which have many uses, including the manufacture of pharmaceuticals and the improvement of crops and livestock, among others. Seventeen countries, known as megadiversity countries, house 60-80 percent of the world's species. The Nagoya Protocol to the Convention on Biological Diversity focuses on access to genetic resources and benefit sharing.

Genetic resources originate from biological organisms—plants, animals, or micro-organisms—or viruses that are actually or potentially available for human exploitation. These resources include genetic material, genetic information, and traditional knowledge. Both traditional medicine and today's pharmaceutical industry use genetic resources to develop medicines. Species diversity forms a base for genetic resources. Genetic diversity in each species is also important in distinguishing different breeds or races. This diversity provides the basis for plant species that adapt well to local conditions and for developing improved strains of crops and livestock (TEEB 2010, 37). *Bioprospecting* involves collecting biological samples and searching for genetic resources. *Biopiracy* is the act of bioprospecting illegally or unethically, for example, infringing on the sovereign rights of nations or the intellectual property rights of indigenous people. For the sustainable use of genetic resources that derive from biological diversity, the Convention on Biological Diversity (CBD) designates the sovereignty of the country of origin over its own genetic resources. Much of the operational aspect, however, is left to each country's domestic law, including the evaluation of traditional knowledge about genetic resource utilization.

The Nagoya Protocol

The Nagoya Protocol on Access to Genetic Resources and the Fair and Equitable Sharing of Benefits Arising from Their Utilization to the Convention on Biological Diversity is an international agreement that aims to share the benefits arising from the utilization of genetic resources in a fair and equitable way. This is to be accomplished by appropriate access to these resources and by appropriate transfer of relevant technologies, taking into account all rights to those resources and technologies. It also addresses the issue of appropriate funding, thereby contributing to the conservation of biological diversity and the sustainable use of its components. The protocol was adopted by the Conference of the Parties to the CBD at its tenth meeting in October 2010 in Nagoya, Japan. The Nagoya Protocol was open for signature by Parties to the Convention from 2 February 2011 until 1 February 2012, and ninety-two countries signed to the protocol.

In the Nagoya Protocol, each party agreed to designate a national focal point on access and benefit sharing. The parties assign one or more checkpoints to monitor genetic resources and to enhance transparency in their use. Each will issue internationally recognized certificates of compliance (Secretariat of the CBD 2011). The domestic laws that correspond to the Nagoya Protocol differ (or are even under development) in each country.

Asian Megadiversity Countries

In Asia, the countries of China, India, Indonesia, Malaysia, and the Philippines are among the world's seventeen "megadiversity countries" (Mittermeier and Mittermeier 1997). These megadiversity countries house 60–80 percent of the world's species and a wealth of traditional knowledge. Most of these areas are in the tropics.

China is the third largest country on Earth and the largest of the megadiversity countries. More than 35,000 higher plant species have been recorded in China (Chinese Ministry of Environmental Protection 2008). Chinese medicine is an important genetic resource that has significant economic value. The Chinese government, in complying with the CDB, is greatly interested in protecting traditional knowledge, including that of traditional Chinese medicine. It takes integrated countermeasures for research, conservation, and quality improvement of seeds and genetic resources.

India houses 350 mammal species, ranking eighth on the world list; it also has 1,258 bird species (seventh in the world), 408 reptile species (sixth in diversity), and 206 amphibian species (ranking eighth). Fish diversity is also high with 2,546 species, which ranks in the top ten globally (Mittermeier and Mittermeier 1997). India passed the Biological Diversity Act (BDA) in 2002 to regulate access and benefit sharing by foreign individuals, organizations, and business enterprises. The government established the Biological Diversity Rules (BDR) in 2004 to enforce the BDA. The BDA and BDR also regulate intellectual property rights against biopiracy of endemic species such as turmeric, neem, and basmati rice.

Indonesia is one of the top two countries on Earth for biodiversity (along with Brazil) and the likely leader in marine biodiversity. Indonesia houses 17 percent of all biological species worldwide. It is second on the world mammal list with 515 species, fourth in reptile diversity with 511 species, fifth in bird diversity with 1,531 species, and sixth in amphibian diversity with 270 species. Indonesia is also in the top five in plant diversity with an estimated 38,000 higher plant species; it leads the world list in palm diversity with 477 species, and has over half of the 350 species of dipterocarp trees (an economically important group) found worldwide. Mittermeier and Mittermeier 1997). The Ministry of Environment is the national focal point for the CBD. The Ministry of Agriculture's programs focus on research and development of genetic resource potentials of critical and endangered domesticated animal and plant species. It endeavors to breed and to establish a gene bank for these species. It also aims to apply traditional knowledge in the use of biological resources, such as the harvest or the activity regulations called the *sasi* system in the eastern part of Indonesia (Indonesian National Development Planning Agency 2003).

Malaysia houses 10 percent of all living organisms worldwide with 15,500 species of higher plants, 300 species of mammals, 738 species of birds, 268 species of reptiles, and 189 species of amphibians. The Malayian Ministry of Science, Technology and Environment (MOSTE, which changed to the Ministry of Technology, Research and Innovation [MOSTI] in 2004) formulated the National Policy on Biological Diversity (NPBD) in 1998. To implement this policy, MOSTE created a federal-state consultative body, the National Biodiversity and Biotechnology Council (MOSTE 1998).

To provide a legal framework to the policy, the council set out three measures: the Biosafety Act (in place), the Access to Genetic Resources Act (in draft as of 2012), and the National Biodiversity Council Act (in draft) (Malaysian Ministry of Natural Resources and Environment 2009). The private company Nimura Genetic Solutions (NGS) opened in 2000; its head office is in Japan and its major research institute in Malaysia. Its objective is to explore tropical rain forests to find new bio-active compounds, in compliance with the CBD. The Malaysian government's national policy was one of the key motivations for NGS starting its activities there. The Forest Research Institute Malaysia (FRIM) and NGS entered into a research collaboration. In 2002, Malaysia's government, through FRIM, granted NGS research and development rights for the commercial use of Malaysia's bioresources in 2002. NGS established one of its research facilities inside the FRIM campus in Kuala Lumpur. The collaboration includes using microorganisms and plants as resources for finding bio-active substances with medical and/or environmental potentials.

In 2004, Sarawak Biodiversity Centre in the state of Sarawak in northern Borneo granted NGS the right to conduct similar activities. In 2005, through the collaboration between NGS and BioPERAK, a company partially owned by Perak State, the government granted NGS full access rights to all species inhabiting the Perak State primary forest near the northern Malaysia-Thailand border (UNU-IAS and JBA 2008).

The Philippines have at least 180 terrestrial- and 21 marine-mammal species, 556 species of birds, and 193 reptile species. Amphibians have comparatively low diversity with 63 species (Mittermeier and Mittermeier 1997). In the Philippines, the government has established three domestic laws referencing the CBD: National Integrated Protected Area System Law/Republic Act No. 7586; Executive Order No. 247 on Prospecting of Biological and Genetic Resources in the Country in May 1995; and the Indigenous Peoples Rights Act of 1997. Implementing Rules and Regulations on the Prospecting of Biological and Genetic Resources, Department Administrative Order No. 96–20, enforces Executive Order No. 247. It also includes requirements for prior informed consent of the concerned local communities, environmental impact assessment, and an arrangement about benefit sharing prior to bioprospecting. These requirements are too strict to fulfill for many foreign enterprises and have partly caused the delay of bioprospecting activities in the Philippines.

Outlook

The Nagoya Protocol grants a wide range of discretion to each country's domestic laws for the utilization of genetic resources, and it also includes a requirement that each party shall respect foreign systems. It is important internationally to deepen mutual understanding for effective internal measures that enable the sustainable use of genetic resources in the framework of access and benefit sharing.

TAKANO Takenaka Kohei
Research Institute for Humanity and Nature

See also Biodiversity Conservation Legislation (China); China; Endangered Species; India; Indigenous Peoples; Kuala Lumpur, Malaysia; Southeast Asia; Traditional Chinese Medicine (TCM)

FURTHER READING

Chinese Ministry of Environmental Protection. (2008). China's fourth national report on implementation of the convention on biological diversity. Retrieved April 2, 2012, from http://www.cbd.int/doc/world/cn/cn-nr-04-en.pdf

Convention on Biological Diversity (CBD). (n.d.). Country profiles. Retrieved December 26, 2011, from http://www.cbd.int/countries/

The Economics of Ecosystems and Biodiversity (TEEB). (2010). The Economics of Ecosystems and Biodiversity: Mainstreaming the economics of nature: A synthesis of the approach, conclusions and recommendations of TEEB. Retrieved January 31, 2012, from http://www.teebweb.org/TEEBSynthesisReport/tabid/29410/Default.aspx

Indonesian National Development Planning Agency. (2003). Indonesian biodiversity strategy and action plan. Retrieved April 2, 2012, from http://www.cbd.int/doc/world/id/id-nbsap-v2-p04-en.pdf

Japan Bioindustry Association. (n.d.). *Seibutsushigen e no akusesu to rieki haibun* [Access to bioresources and benefit sharing: Country information]. Retrieved December 26, 2011, from http://www.mabs.jp/countries/index.html

The Malaysian Ministry of Natural Resources and Environment. (2009). 4th national report to the Convention on Biological Diversity. Retrieved December 26, 2011, from http://www.cbd.int/doc/world/my/my-nr-04-en.pdf

The Malaysian Ministry of Science, Technology and Environment (MOSTE). (1998). Malaysia's national policy on biological diversity. Retrieved March 23, 2012, from http://www.arbec.com.my/NBP.pdf

Mittermeier, Russell A., & Mittermeier, Cristina Goettsch. (1997). *Megadiversity: Earth's biologically wealthiest nations*. Mexico City, Mexico: CEMEX/Agrupación Sierra Madre.

Secretariat of the Convention on Biological Diversity (CBD). (2011). Nagoya Protocol on Access to Genetic Resources and the Fair and Equitable Sharing of Benefits Arising from Their Utilization to the Convention on Biological Diversity. New York: United Nations. Retrieved March 2, 2012 from http://www.cbd.int/abs/doc/protocol/nagoya-protocol-en.pdf

United Nations University Institute of Advanced Studies (UNU-IAS & JBA). (2008). Collaborative work on ABS case studies. Retrieved December 26, 2011, from http://www.mabs.jp/archives/jba/pdf/IAS-JBAcaseStudies.pdf

Great Green Wall (China)

China's Great Green Wall is a government program to improve ecological conditions in the northern part of the country. The program promotes planting of trees where none had previously existed (a process known as afforestation) to combat desertification, protect farmland, and reduce soil erosion. Given limited funding and the difficulty of growing trees on dryland areas, the program has been at best a limited success.

China's Three-North Shelterbelt program, known as the Great Green Wall and instituted by the Chinese government in 1978, refers to the afforestation program to establish forests on land not previously forested to improve ecological conditions in the northern part of the country. The program planned to create 35.6 million hectares of protective forests in northeast, north, and northwest China (hence Three North), increasing forest cover from 5 percent to 15 percent (SFA 2008). Scheduled to last for seventy-three years (ending in 2050), the program aims to control land degradation and desertification. The program includes a swath 4,480 kilometers long and 560–1,460 kilometers wide, or 42.4 percent of China's land territory. The program affects a population of about 200 million. The Great Green Wall boasts the largest afforestation project in the world.

Much of the region covered by the Great Green Wall program in northern China is dry; it includes eight deserts, four sandy lands, and a large Gobi area. At the onset of the program in 1978, the erroneous land use policies of the Mao Zedong era had brought China to the brink of ecological collapse (Shapiro 2001). Northern China suffered from serious soil erosion and desertification.

The government designed the Great Green Wall program to build a lattice of forests to protect farmlands, reduce soil erosion, and control and reverse desertification. The State Forestry Administration (SFA) administers the Great Green Wall project and uses financial and administrative means to promote tree planting. The SFA has positioned staff at each level of the government. Local governments actively seek to engage in the Great Green Wall program because of funding opportunities. Central government funding comes with requirements for local matching in order to augment a total level of financial support for the program. The government also requires each laborer to perform mandatory work in planting trees.

The funding level, however, is rather limited. The total state investment in the Great Green Wall program during 1978–2007 totaled about 60 billion yuan (US$9.5 billion), of which state investment accounted for only 8.3 billion yuan (US$1.3 billion) (Sun 2009). This amount was clearly meager compared with the investment of US$40 billion for the Beijing Olympics. Matching funds from individuals (including labor cost) far surpassed state investment, making the program more of a local endeavor, albeit with a mandate from the central government.

Official reports from SFA have lauded the success of the Great Green Wall program, citing increases of tree cover and ecological improvements. By 2008, the SFA claimed to have established over 24 million hectares of forests, raising forest cover from 5.05 percent in 1978 to 10.51 percent in northern China (SFA 2008). The SFA also reported improvements in controlling sand, abating soil erosion, and increasing economic output in program areas. Calling the Great Green Wall a "great act of nature transformation," the state official rhetoric is filled with enthusiasm for both the program's achievements and its positive role in "building an ecological civilization" (SFA 2008).

Criticisms and Problems

Outside the Chinese official claims, however, ecologists have raised many concerns and criticisms for the Great Green Wall program. Critics say the program is an ecological mismatch. Much of northern China is on dryland with less than 380 millimeters of annual precipitation, which defines the lower boundary of precipitation necessary for rain-fed agriculture. Three-quarters of the program area has natural vegetation of grassland or desert, where trees do not grow naturally for lack of water. Tree planting on China's dryland has yielded a low survival rate of 15 percent (Cao 2008). Many of the trees that have survived have either lost their ability to protect the environment under harsh conditions or overdrawn the precious groundwater to exacerbate environmental decline (Ding, Xiao, and Jiang 2006). In Minqin county of Gansu Province, for example, where annual precipitation is 115 millimeters, workers planted 53,300 hectares of trees in the last few decades, but a quarter have died and the rest are dwarf trees. The groundwater level dropped 12–40 meters. Experts expect desert to swallow the area in the next decade (Bennett 2008). In Hunshandak Sandy Land of the Inner Mongolia Autonomous Region, despite numerous tree planting attempts, moving sand cover increased 50–70 percent in the twenty-first century from a mere 2 percent in the 1950s (Jiang 2006).

Single-species forestry is another problem with the Great Green Wall program. These forests help increase the government figures in trees, but they lack biodiversity and fail to improve the environment; they thus have been called "green deserts" (Jiang 2008a). In the Ningxia Hui Autonomous Region, for example, 70 percent of the trees planted are poplar and willow trees. In 2000, disease (*Anoplophora glabripennis*) destroyed a billion poplar trees and wiped out twenty years of planting effort (Yu, Li, and He 2008).

The Great Green Wall has produced limited local improvements. On the large scale, desertification in northern China remains one of the country's most challenging environmental problems (Chen and Tang 2005). Localized success stories in key project areas and experimental sites, which account for only about 10 percent of the area in northern China, justify the SFA's claim of success. Results can seem impressive in these select areas. China reports that the Ordos region of Inner Mongolia, a key project site, has increased vegetation cover from 30 percent to over 75 percent during 2000–2008 by planting trees and shrubs (Li et al. 2008). Geography of scale, local or regional, dictates different results; outcomes depend on the area examined.

Outlook

Scientists in China have long questioned the role of tree planting. In the 1980s, the geographer Huang Bingwei (1981) cautioned against the overestimation of forests' function to conserve water. Empirical studies in northern China since then have pointed to the problems of soil desiccation and groundwater depletion led by aggressive land improvement projects and tree planting (Chen, Wang, and Shao 2005). The Chinese ecologist Shixiong Cao and his colleagues pointed out that dryland precipitation cannot support trees on a large scale and that afforestation has exacerbated environmental degradation (Cao et al. 2010). Ecological problems elsewhere have long beset afforestation on areas not previously forested for generations (Farley, Jackson, and Jobbagy 2005). Stalin's shelterbelt program, part of his 1948 Great Plan for Transformation of Nature, is probably the most famous failure in dryland afforestation.

Scientist have studied alternative methods in dryland ecological recovery. They have found natural recovery and planting of local species much less costly and more effective (Jiang 2008b). China has yet to consider these methods as a replacement for the Great Green Wall program.

Hong JIANG
University of Hawaii at Manoa

See also Beijing, China; Biodiversity Conservation Legislation (China); China; Climate Change Mitigation Initiatives (China); Five-Year Plans; Genetic Resources; Huang (Yellow) River; Media Coverage of the Environment; Parks and Preserves; Reforestation and Afforestation (Southeast Asia); South-North Water Diversion; Transboundary Water Issues; Yangzi (Chang) River

FURTHER READING

Bennett, Karen. (2008). Swallowed by sand: China's billion-dollar battle against desertification. World Resources Institute. Retrieved March 1, 2012, from http://www.wri.org/stories/2008/08/swallowed-sand-chinas-billion-dollar-battle-against-desertification

Cao Shixiong. (2008). Why large-scale afforestation efforts in China have failed to solve the desertification problem. *Environmental Science & Technology, 42*, 1826–1831.

Cao Shixiong, et al. (2010). Damage caused to the environment by reforestation policies in arid and semi-arid areas of China. *AMBIO, 39*, 279–283.

Chen Hongsong; Wang Kelin; & Shao Ming'an. (2005). A review on the effect of vegetation rehabilitation on the deep soil layer on the Loess Plateau. *Scientia Silvae Sinicae, 41*(4), 155–161. [in Chinese]

Chen, Y., & Tang, H. (2005). Desertification in north China: Background, anthropogenic impacts and failures in combating it. *Land Degradation & Development, 16*, 367–376.

Ding Ming; Xiao Laisheng; & Jiang Xuecheng. (2006, October 8). Three north regrets: Dwarf trees for display. *Economics Reference News*, p. 4. [in Chinese]

Farley K. A.; Jackson, R. B.; & Jobbagy, E. G. (2005). Effects of afforestation on water yield: A global synthesis with implications for policy. *Global Change Biology, 11*(10), 1565–1576.

Huang Bingwei. (1981). Accurately assess the role of forest. *Geographical Knowledge, 1*(90), 1–3. [in Chinese]

Jiang Gaoming. (2006, March 30). Three mistakes in desertification control in China. *People's Daily*, p. 16. [in Chinese]

Jiang Gaoming. (2008a, January 10). China's "green deserts." Retrieved March 1, 2012, from http://www.sciencenet.cn/blog/user_content.aspx?id=14245 [in Chinese]

Jiang Gaoming. (2008b). Preface. In *Use nature's force to recover nature*. Beijing: Hydrological and Hydro-power Press. [in Chinese]

Li Bing; Pan Zhaodong; Hu Yihua; & Li Mingsheng. (2008). Model in realization of scientific development in western China–Analyzing the Ordos model. *Economy and Society, 9*, 24–26. [in Chinese]

State Forestry Administration (SFA). (2008). Review of thirty years of Three-North Shelterbelt program (1978–2008). *People's Net*. [in Chinese]

Shapiro, Judith. (2001). *Mao's war against nature: Politics and the environment in revolutionary China*. Cambridge, UK: Cambridge University Press.

Sun Chuihe. (2009). History and perspective of investment in Three North Shelterbelt Program. *Science & Technology of Protective Forestry* [*Fanghulin keji*], *91*(4), 59–61. [in Chinese]

Yu Lizhen; Li Wuzhong; & He Jingna. (2008). Problems and benefits of the Three-North Shelterbelt project in Ningxia Autonomous Region. *Journal of Northwest Forestry University, 23*(4), 228–232. [in Chinese]

Berkshire's authors and editors welcome questions, comments, and corrections. Send your emails about the *Berkshire Encyclopedia of Sustainability* in general or this volume in particular to: sustainability.updates@berkshirepublishing.com

Green Collar Jobs

Green collar jobs offer workers better wages and opportunities for career advancement while preserving or improving environmental quality. Globalization has shifted many green collar jobs to China and other countries in South and East Asia. Government support, worker training, and access of green industries to the grid are critical to the creation of green jobs.

Global concerns with climate change and slow economic growth have led to a growing interest in generating green collar jobs. Green collar jobs are assumed to improve environmental quality and offer more middle-class employment opportunities, providing solutions to both environmental and economic problems. These jobs often require additional training, but not necessarily a college education, and essentially entail manufacturing or contractor-type skill requirements.

Globalization and the Green Economy

The green economy has spread across the globe. The Asia Business Council (2011) created an index to measure the conditions for promoting green collar jobs in the region. The analysis suggests that China, Japan, and India have the most favorable conditions for creating green collar jobs, in part because of long-term, strong, and consistent government policies. As of 2011, China had six of the ten largest green companies in the world. Chinese companies account for more than half the world's green jobs, while Europe has about 28 percent, and the United States, approximately 17 percent (Siegel 2010). Chinese investments are expected to generate more than 30 million green jobs from 2005 to 2020 (Institute for Urban and Environmental Studies 2010).

Globalization of the green economy does not mean all countries follow the same path or focus on the same sectors of the industry. Each country must find its own niche in the green economy. Japan has effectively promoted biomass electricity generation, much of it from industrial (especially paper and livestock) and household waste. India is a regional leader in wind-power generation (Asia Business Council 2011) and is rapidly becoming a major global player in offshore wind deployment. The Philippines leads the region in the production of geothermal energy. Green companies in China and Korea have created export markets, particularly for wind, solar, and green materials, in the United States and Europe. Each country must take advantage of its own climate conditions, geographical factors, and industrial/human assets to identify a set of green industries that bring maximum benefits to its economy.

Cheap labor is one of the chief advantages China and other Asian countries have in the race to generate green collar jobs. Many green collar jobs, like other manufacturing jobs, have moved from the United States and Europe to low-cost areas. In a much-publicized case, Evergreen Solar, a solar panel manufacturer in Massachusetts, moved more than eight hundred jobs to China; General Electric has moved all its plants producing compact fluorescent lightbulbs to China.

In addition to providing cheap labor, Asian countries often offer firms substantial government subsidies. Japan and South Korea are probably the most proactive in government programs supporting green collar jobs. Japan has offered zero-interest loans for green companies, and South Korea has provided incentives to promote the use of renewable energy. India is actively restructuring its transportation system by assisting cities and states to develop green transportation options. The World Trade Organization (WTO) has recently challenged China's subsidies to wind turbine manufacturers, however, and as a result the Chinese are expected to drop these subsidies soon.

The international transfer of green technologies also has been crucial to the generation of green collar jobs (OECD 2011). Japan, the United States, and the European Union are home to the largest innovation centers, which include universities, corporate research and development, government-funded incubators, technology parks, and the like. Developing countries, especially China, receive the largest green technology transfers (Percival and Schreurs 2010). International green technology research cooperation between Asia and the rest of the world has also grown substantially in recent years. This cooperation greatly facilitates the growth of the green economy in Asia.

Industrial Sectors and Green Collar Jobs

Green collar jobs are located in four key sectors: renewable energy, energy efficiency, transportation, and prevention or mitigation of pollution. Although data sources are fairly weak, recent estimates suggest there are more than 2 million jobs worldwide in the renewable energy sector (World Watch Institute 2008).

China is the clear global leader in solar energy. The energy efficiency sector offers the most jobs globally. In India, biomass cooking techniques will replace traditional cook stoves, and their manufacture should provide more than 150,000 jobs. Transportation accounts for almost one-third of energy use, and most jobs in India are related to improving fuel efficiency and public transportation. China, India, and Pakistan have made huge investments in compressed natural gas vehicles in recent years, creating thousands of jobs. Recycling is probably the largest source of jobs in the pollution mitigation sector. China creates the most waste and probably has as many as 4 million jobs in this sector, although many of the jobs are informal and pay poorly.

While many industries create new green collar jobs, existing jobs in other industries are greened. Jobs in the renewable energy sector are mostly new because the industry is relatively nascent. Green jobs in transportation and the energy efficiency sectors, however, are rarely new. Both creating new jobs and changing the skills required for existing jobs are effective ways to promote green collar jobs.

Government Policy

Governments in Japan, South Korea, and China have been the most proactive in promoting green collar jobs in Asia. Japan has approximately 1.4 million workers employed in green industries and expects to create an additional 2.2 million green collar jobs in the next decade (Asia Business Council 2011). South Korea recently invested $30 billion in green industries with the hope of creating about a million jobs. In 2010, China led all countries in the world in investment in renewable energy. Over $40 billion of this investment was in wind energy production. India's investment during the same year grew 25 percent to about $4 billion.

One of the most effective policies for creating green collar jobs is the feed-in-tariff (FIT), a government policy that encourages renewable energy production. The FITs guarantee grid access, offer long-term contracts, and base prices on the cost of production. Guaranteed purchase prices based on cost of production are particularly important because they encourage a wide diversity of renewable energy producers. FITs were initiated in Europe but have spread to other countries (a total of sixty-three now) including China, India, Pakistan, and South Korea. In China, the Renewable Energy Act of 2005 provides FITs for wind and solar energy. Most analysts believe this act has contributed to the rapid rise in wind-energy production in China, which now accounts for one-half of the world's wind-energy market.

Policy makers in the region prioritize training for green collar jobs, especially those that target youth (OECD 2011). Although access to training programs is very limited for Asian workers and job seekers, several international nongovernmental organizations are working with employers and communities to make training available to them.

Government policies promoting the green economy are inadequate without the support of private-sector entrepreneurs and business leaders. The private sector increasingly recognizes the value of greening businesses, but successful green collar jobs initiatives are limited in scale. Although Asian governments have created policy environments conducive to the generation of green jobs, obstacles remain. Government agencies need to better coordinate with each other in the transition to the green economy before they can meaningfully engage business leaders. The challenge is to communicate to politicians and businesses that "green" is not a cost or job killer, but a transformational value creating opportunity for traditional industries.

Challenges

Efforts to generate green collar jobs face numerous challenges. The shift to a green economy will inevitably create winners and losers. Many regions and industries will suffer through the conversion process. For example, the greening of China's electricity industry has led to the unemployment of half a million workers (Ministry of Human Resources and Social Security 2010). These workers need help, especially job training and social services, as they retool for the low-carbon economy.

Most green collar jobs will not require major investments in job training, but instead will build on existing programs. Green collar jobs in the energy efficiency sector, for example, may simply require training workers with new material or products.

Green skill development continues to lag behind demand in many countries. Skill shortages pose a major barrier to the growth of green industries. A small number of training programs partner with companies in the green industries in designing the curriculum in China. In most cases, there is no systematic method for identifying green skill needs. A more comprehensive approach would ensure that the labor supply meets the demand.

Green job programs in Asia focus almost entirely on the number of jobs created and much less on the quality of jobs. Wind energy jobs in China pay better and have better working conditions and higher job satisfaction than traditional energy jobs (Ministry of Human Resources and Social Security 2010), but it is uncertain whether the remaining green jobs meet these criteria (World Watch Institute 2008). For the most part, the promise that green jobs would provide middle-class occupations remains unfulfilled in Asia. To date, most green jobs remain poorly paid manufacturing or contracting jobs.

One of the obstacles in creating green collar jobs in the renewable energy sector is the poor state of the grid for transporting energy. Regions with solar and wind energy potential need an adequate grid to realize that potential.

Many countries have adopted FITs as a policy tool to promote green jobs. FITs may raise energy costs to consumers in the short run, but the impact depends on the relative cost of fossil fuel as the alternative. An FIT is not a sustainable driver for the green economy as a whole. The creation of green jobs has been largely a top-down process that depends on government support. The market is expected to respond favorably in the near future as green industries mature. The labor market will also better adapt to the green economy as more training programs develop.

The lack of reliable data on green jobs restricts the policy-making capacity. There are far more estimates of potential numbers of green jobs in the future than counts of green jobs that are currently available.

Lack of consensus over the definition can also limit the creation of green collar jobs. In China, for example, green collar jobs are associated more with environmentally oriented worldviews and lifestyles than they are with the actual occupations and work conditions (Kong 2008). Most of the self-claimed green collar workers in China do not work in the green sector, as defined by policy makers. In light of this, countries need not only green skills training programs but also public education about what makes green jobs green.

Outlook

Across the globe the rapid increase in green investments has resulted in growth in green collar jobs. Government incentives and subsidies have driven part of the growth; lower production costs have led companies to move to Asia, especially to China. Will these trends continue? For East and South Asia, it is uncertain how green collar jobs can be a sustainable economic driver in the long run. In addition, the same factors that have led to the migration of many green collar jobs to China may ultimately lead to capital mobility to even lower-cost areas within the region or elsewhere. The challenge, then, is to overcome the forces that push wages and benefits down in the green economy.

Gary P. GREEN and Yifei LI
University of Wisconsin, Madison

See also Energy Industries—Nuclear; Energy Industries—Renewables (China); Energy Industries—Renewables (India); Energy Security (East Asia); Gender Equality; Information and Communication Technologies (ICT); Labor; Microfinance; Outsourcing and Offshoring; Utilities Regulation and Energy Efficiency

FURTHER READING

Asia Business Council. (2011). Research: Green jobs (PDF): Addressing Asia's new green jobs challenge. Retrieved June 27, 2011, from http://www.asiabusinesscouncil.org/ResearchGrnJ09.html

China Academy of Labour and Social Security, Ministry of Human Resources and Social Security, China. (2010). *Skills for green jobs in China: Unedited background country study*. International Labour Organization (ILO). Retrieved July 7, 2011, from http://www.ilo.org/wcmsp5/groups/public/@ed_emp/@ifp_skills/documents/publication/wcms_142486.pdf

Institute for Urban and Environmental Studies (IUE), Chinese Academy of Social Sciences (CASS). (2010). *Study on low carbon development and green employment in China*. International Labour Organization (ILO). Retrieved July 5, 2011, from http://www.ilo.org/beijing/whatwedo/publications/lang--en/docName--WCMS_155390/index.htm

Kong, Xiaowei. (2008). Analyzing "green collar." *Anhui Literature, 3*, 291. [in Chinese]

Lee, Soo Young; Jin, Mi Sug; & Song, Chang Yong. (2010). *Skills for green jobs in the Republic of Korea: Background country study*. International Labour Organization (ILO). Retrieved July 7, 2011, from http://www.ilo.org/wcmsp5/groups/public/@ed_emp/@ifp_skills/documents/publication/wcms_142476.pdf

Ministry of Human Resources and Social Security. (2010). Study on green employment in China. International Labour Organization (ILO). Retrieved July 4, 2011, from: http://www.ilo.org/beijing/areasofwork/lang--zh/facet--LOC.ASIA-_-ASIA.GRE-_-TYP-_-Publication-_-4070/WCMS_DOC_BJS_ARE_GRE_ZH/index.htm [in Chinese]

Organization for Economic Co-operation and Development (OECD). (2011). *Job-rich growth in Asia: Strategies for local employment, skills development and social protection*. Paris: OECD.

Percival, Robert V., & Schreurs, Miranda A. (2010). *Intellectual property rights and green technology transfer: German and U.S. perspectives*. Retrieved February 21, 2012, from http://www.aicgs.org/site/wp-content/uploads/2011/10/polrep45.pdf

Pernick, Ron, & Wilder, Clint. (2011). Clean energy trends 2011. Clean Edge, Inc. Retrieved July 7, 2011, from http://www.cleanedge.com/reports/pdf/Trends2011.pdf

Pew Charitable Trusts. (2011). *Who's winning the clean energy race? 2010 edition*. Retrieved June 29, 2011, from http://www.pewenvironment.org/uploadedFiles/PEG/Publications/Report/G-20Report-LOWRes-FINAL.pdf

Siegel, R. P. (2010, October 20). Green jobs are plentiful right now . . . in China. Retrieved June 28, 2011, from http://www.triplepundit.com/2010/10/green-jobs-plentiful-nowin-china/

Strietska-Ilina, Olga; Hofmann, Christine; Durán Haro, Mercedes; & Jeon, Shinyoung. (2011). *Skills for green jobs: A global view; Synthesis report based on 21 country studies*. International Labour Organization (ILO). Retrieved July 7, 2011, from http://www.ilo.org/wcmsp5/groups/public/@ed_emp/@ifp_skills/documents/publication/wcms_156220.pdf

World Watch Institute. (2008). Green jobs: Towards decent work in a sustainable, low-carbon world. Retrieved February 21, 2012, from http://www.unep.org/labour_environment/PDFs/Greenjobs/UNEP-Green-Jobs-Report.pdf

Guangzhou, China

8 million est. pop. 2010; part of "mega-region" est. pop. 120 million

The spectacular growth of Guangzhou's economy—a part of southern China's Pearl River Delta, known as the world's largest "mega-region"—has come at the expense of the environment, which experienced serious degradation during the city's prolonged development. Pollution statistics for the city have been alarming and have triggered the municipal government's determination to green its development strategy for the new millennium and to actively pursue urban sustainability.

Guangzhou (known historically in the West as Canton), the capital city of Guangdong Province, is the largest city and a major commercial center in the southern part of China, with an area of 7,434.6 square kilometers and a population of over 8 million in 2010 (Guangzhou Yearbook Editorial Committee 2011, 4–5). Guangzhou is a part of the urban "mega-region" of the Pearl River Delta, which encompasses Hong Kong-Shenzhen-Dongguan-Guangzhou. According to the 2010–2011 UN-Habitat biannual report *State of World Cities*, this is the world's largest mega-region, with an estimated total of 120 million residents in 2011 (UN-Habitat 2011). Among major Chinese cities, Guangzhou has been a forerunner in sustainable development and some consider it to be ahead of Beijing and Shanghai in the pursuit of urban sustainability.

At the turn of the millennium, after decades of single-mindedly focusing on achieving rapid economic growth, even when it was at the expense of the environment, the Guangzhou municipal government finally realized the need to green its development strategy and redirected the city's long-term development plans toward ecological harmony (Lo and Chung 2004). To this end, it reshaped the city's economic structure using a green format and tightened the regulatory control of polluting industries. In addition, the city invested in the education of its populace, making it more environmentally aware so as to build institutional strength and realize a green vision of urban development (Lo and Leung 2000; Lo, Fryxell, and van Rooij 2009).

Politics of a Green Vision

Guangzhou's commitment to sustainable development can be traced back to 1996, when the municipal government first decided to align itself with the national strategy by setting up the Guangzhou Agenda 21 Steering Group and Office. Later, in 1998, it released its local Agenda 21 (Lo and Chung 2004). Since then, senior municipal leaders have increasingly incorporated environmental protection as a major component of the city's development strategy, strongly desiring to give the city a green image. The city's underlying policy ideology has been one that coordinated development of the economy, society, and the environment, an ideology that acknowledges that "economic growth cannot directly solve all the problems related to sustainable development" (Guangzhou Agenda 21 Steering Group 1998). This paradigm shift has gradually tempered the pro-growth obsession of the municipal leadership, and increasingly recognized environmental well-being as a prerequisite for the city's sustainable development, as it moves steadily toward becoming an affluent society in the first decade of the twenty-first century.

In 2004, Guangzhou successfully bid to host the 2010 Asia Games (a multisport event that takes place every four years in Asia and includes the participation of athletes from all over the continent). And in 2006, with the support of a high-level group led by the mayor and deputy mayors, Guangzhou finally passed a comprehensive environmental assessment performed by the National Environmental Protection Administration to achieve national green city status. This achievement came after an eight-year period of hard work on citywide pollution cleanup and ecological restoration (*Pearl Environmental News* 2006). The presence of a determined provincial and municipal leadership that was committed to a green-city vision enabled the Guangzhou Environmental Protection Bureau (EPB) to strictly implement a six-year plan to reduce industrial pollution and improve air and water quality in order to deliver on the promise of organizing the Asian Games in an environmentally friendly fashion (Guangzhou EPB 2011a).

The political commitment of Guangzhou's municipal government to urban sustainability was further manifested in its 2009 Action Directive on Building Guangzhou into a Garden-Like City (2009–2015). According to this dictate, in order to transform into a national environmental model city, Guangzhou was to avail itself of opportunities arising from the fact that, in 2010, it was to host the Asian Games. Per the directive, Guangzhou was to "be built into a harmonious and beautiful Green Asian Games City" by 2010 and, by 2015, its "overall ecosystem environment [was] to reach first-class in the nation, the first step to a garden-like city" (Guangzhou Municipal Government 2009). There is no sign that the municipal government will step back from its green path toward urban development now that it has already hosted the Asian Games. In fact, in order to establish the city as a "garden city" by 2015, the municipal government has commissioned the Guangzhou Academy of Social Sciences to compile a set of metropolitan indicators to assess the city's urban sustainable development.

Economic Sustainability

Guangzhou has one of the fastest developing local economies in China, with a highly organized enterprise sector. In 2010, the city's gross domestic product (GDP) ranked third in China just behind Shanghai's and Beijing's, and amounted to over 1,074 billion yuan (Guangzhou Yearbook Editorial Committee 2011, 44). Because this economic status was cultivated under the model of "pollution first, remedy second," and because of the recognition that this pollution-dominated approach is not sustainable, the Guangzhou municipal government decided to base further economic development on technological innovation, with the intention of transforming the city's development trajectory from being quantity- to quality-oriented. Since taking this decision, the industrial restructuring has been guided by environmentally friendly concepts of cleaner production, restorative economy, and energy-saving emissions reduction. This, in turn, has resulted in the phasing out of polluting industries, the introduction of high-tech production, the technological upgrading of heavy industries, and the rapid expansion of the tertiary sector (the segment of the economy that is concerned with providing services, such as transportation and distribution centers, to other businesses, and with providing such services as utilities and food to both businesses and final consumers). This repositioning strategy has proved to be the correct move and has enabled Guangzhou to sustain a rapid economic growth while improving the quality of its environment.

With economic sustainability as the strategic focus, the long-term competitive advantage of the municipal economy was built around seven major industries, namely, automobiles, electronic information, pharmaceuticals, iron and steel, petrochemicals, fine chemicals, and textiles (*Nanfang Daily* 2004). At the same time, the tertiary sector's proportion of local GDP has steadily increased under the government's preferential investment policy from 49.82 percent, in 2000, to 61 percent in 2010. The growing predominance of a tertiary industry indicates that Guangzhou, while increasing its competitiveness, has already been transformed from an industrial to a commercial economy. It is a major center for such wholesale trade as shoes, garments, small electronic goods, and plastic products. In 2010 Forbes named it "the best commercial city in China" (Guangzhou Yearbook Editorial Committee 2011, 44). While reducing the ecological footprint of economic growth and directly addressing the issue of climate change on the national agenda, the municipal government responded positively to this changing national development strategy by setting a "low-carbon economy" as the chief development concept for Guangzhou's economic sustainability in the next five years (Guangzhou Urban Development Concept 2011).

Environmental Sustainability

Guangzhou has recently managed to reverse the downward trend of a prolonged period of environmental degradation and to steadily lift environmental quality during the first decade of the new millennium. The quality of the atmospheric environment has markedly improved as the amount of all major air pollutants and the frequency of acid rain have consistently decreased throughout the 2000s. (See table 1 on the next page.) The water quality has also improved, with the percentage of drinking water that meets the water quality standard rising from 67.86 percent in 2006 to 100 percent in 2010, and the sewage treatment rate surging from 26.28 percent in 2000 to over 85 percent in 2010.

In order to bring the city on board for the journey to environmental sustainability, in 1995 the Guangzhou municipal government upgraded the status of the municipal environmental agency from that of an office to that of a bureau, a move that automatically increased its budget and gave it additional manpower to strengthen its organizational capacity in combating pollution. When it resolved to transform Guangzhou into a green city and to host a green Asian Games, it tightened the enforcement of pollution control even further (Lo and Leung 2000; Lo, Fryxell, and van Rooij 2009). It also tried to systematically green local public transportation by phasing in liquid petroleum gas (LPG) on a large scale for use in buses and coaches, and constructed a comprehensive mass transit railway network. Lastly, it allocated more financial resources to supporting environmental protection; the amount of government spending on the environment increased from 13.67 billion yuan in 2000, to 24.33 billion yuan in 2010.

The period between 2000 and 2006 in Guangzhou was the turning point for the city's environmental sustainability, as there was a measure of urgency about prioritizing regulatory enforcement when the municipal government fully embraced the designation of "green model city." This led to the establishment of the Achieving Model City Target Responsibility System at all levels of the municipal government, with the purpose of rallying bureaucratic support for the municipal EPB in enforcing stringent environmental measures. At the same time, enforcement officials were told to become stricter with polluting enterprises regardless of their "connections". Evidence of improved enforcement effectiveness included the closure or relocation of 140 large polluting factories and the criminal prosecution of 2 firms. As a result, the number of administrative enforcement cases grew from 256 in 1998 to 1,547 in 2006, while the average fines rose from 5,207 yuan in 1998 to 45,639 yuan in 2006 (Guangzhou EPB 2011a). Perhaps the most eye-catching achievement of stringent regulatory control in this period, however, was the resumption, in 2006, of the Cross-Pearl River Swim in the Guangzhou segment, after the event had been put on hold for more than three decades because of heavy water pollution. From that time, the overall trend of environmental regulation has been to be tougher on pollution regulation violations and to give greater attention to the legal approach to regulatory enforcement (*Pearl Environmental News* 2006).

Social Sustainability

Socially, the citizens of Guangzhou, now in the fast lane toward economic affluence, have become more critical and less tolerant of industrial pollution than in the past; they constitute an altogether more environmentally aware society. The municipal government's effort in environmental education and socialization effected an environmental awakening among local people in the early

TABLE 1. Environmental Standards and Quality in Guangzhou Municipality, 2000, 2006–2010

	Item	Unit	Mandatory Standard	2000	2006	2007	2008	2009	2010
Atmospheric Environment	Respirable suspended particulates (RSPs)	mg/m^3 (annual concentration)	0.10[#]	n/a	0.076	0.077	0.071	0.07	0.069
	Sulphur dioxide	mg/m^3 (daily average value in urban area)	0.15[#]	0.045	0.054	0.051	0.046	0.039	0.033
	Nitrogen dioxide	mg/m^3 (daily average value in urban area)	0.12[#]	0.061	0.067	0.065	0.056	0.056	0.053
	Acid rain	Frequency	n/a	62.30%	75.40%	82.60%	77.80%	60.5%	50.7%
Water Environment	Industrial waste water discharged	Total volume discharged (up-to-standards discharge) (million tonnes)		241.23 (217.32)	204.45 (196.29)	211.03 (201.02)	344.75 (330.45)	260.23 (251.16)	236.04 (228.28)
		Up-to-standards discharge percentage		90.09%	96.01%	95.25%	95.85%	96.51%	96.71%
	Residential waste water discharged	million tonnes		713.11	1078.58	903.88	916.81	932.94	1020.6
	Sources of drinking water	Percentage of drinking water meeting the water quality standard		98.30%	67.86%*	75.99%*	80.96%*	82.23%	100%
	Sewage management	Sewage treatment rate		26.28%	71.64%	74.14%	n/a	81.06%	85.65%
Acoustic Environment	Traffic noise (main roads)	leq dB (A)	70 (day-time), 55 (night-time)	69.10	69.40	69.20	69.10	69.20	69.10
	Regional environmental noise	leq dB (A)	55 (day-time), 45 (night-time)	54.2	55.2	55	n/a	55.0	55.1
Total investment in environmental protection/ percentage of GDP		billion yuan	–	13.67	22.25	21.17	19.57	n/a	24.33
		%	–	5.75%	3.67%	2.96%	2.36%	n/a	2.48%

Notes: leq dB (A) is a measure of relative noise levels; 70 leq dB (A) is equivalent to passing vehicles at normal speed.

Sources: Guangzhou EPB (2011b and 2011c); Guangzhou Municipal Statistics Bureau and Guangzhou Survey Office of National Bureau of Statistics (2001, 2008, and 2010); Guangzhou Yearbook Editorial Committee (2011).

[#]indicates Grade II Standard, which is applied in urban residential and commercial areas.

*The dramatic reduction in the percentage of the drinking water that satisfies the water quality standards is partly due to the measurement change in the new policy announced in China's Eleventh National Five-Year Plan (2006–2010).

1990s, as shown by a 1996 survey in which local citizens showed their awareness of pollution problems, asked for greater government effort to protect the environment, and manifested their inclination toward the idea of a balanced nature. This level of environmental awareness has been promoted through the publication of the *Pearl Environmental News*, environmental publicity activities organized by the Guangzhou EPB in cooperation with other social organizations, and most importantly, through the public release of an annual report on changing environmental quality in Guangzhou (Lo and Chung 2004; Lo and Leung 2000). Today, the municipal environmental protection administration has become more transparent, and most environmental information and pollution statistics are available on the Guangzhou EPB's webpage (Guangzhou EPB 2011a).

Accompanying the steady improvement of living standards has been the ever-growing popular demand for reducing pollution. Since the late 1990s, local people can communicate their environmental grievances to the city's mayor through a dedicated hotline, or they can lodge their complaints with the petition unit of the Guangzhou EPB. The number of complaints about pollution soared from 5,300 in 1999 to a record high of 20,192 in 2006, and maintained a high figure of 17,182 in 2010 (Guangzhou Yearbook Editorial Committee 2011, 326). Since 2006, more and more people have used the media and the Internet as channels for voicing complaints on specific pollution cases and expressing their discontent over the slow progress in environmental improvement. On the whole, these changes indicate increasing environmental concern and a more favorable social attitude for the city in its pursuit of sustainable development.

Since the reform era was inaugurated in 1979, there is solid empirical evidence to show that Guangzhou has, in fact, undergone a true green transformation. After years of green capacity building in political, economic, environmental, and social aspects, the Guangzhou municipal government has already institutionalized the momentum in the city's quest for long-term urban sustainability. The prospects for this green revolution are quite promising as revealed by a recent strategic review in which the Guangdong Provincial Government fully aspired to greening its development model.

Carlos Wing-Hung LO and Pansy Hon-ying LI
The Hong Kong Polytechnic University

See also Beijing, China; China; Cities—Overview; Education, Environmental (China); Green Collar Jobs; Pearl River Delta; Public Transportation; Shanghai, China

Further Reading

Baeumler, Axel; Ijjasz-Vasquez, Ede; & Mehndiratta, Shomik. (2012). *Sustainable low-carbon city development in China*. Washington, DC: World Bank.

Chung, Shan Shan, & Lo, Carlos Wing-Hung. (2006). Sustainable development in urban cities in the Pearl River Delta region: Comparing Guangzhou and Hong Kong. In Anthony Gar-on Yeh, Victor Fung-shuen Sit, Gunaghan Chen & Yunyuan Zhou (Eds.), *Developing a competitive Pearl River Delta in South China under one country–two systems* (pp. 271–308). Hong Kong: Hong Kong University Press.

Guangzhou Agenda 21 Steering Group. (1998). Guangzhou Agenda 21. Guangzhou, China: Guangzhou Science Press. [in Chinese]

Guangzhou Environmental Protection Bureau (EPB). (2011a). *Collection of material on the work of environmental enforcement in Guangzhou (2004–2010)*. Guangzhou, China: Guangzhou EPB. Retrieved April 2, 2012, from http://www.gzepb.gov.cn/ [in Chinese]

Guangzhou Environmental Protection Bureau (EPB). (2011b). Ambient air quality standard. Retrieved April 4, 2012, from http://www.gzepb.gov.cn/zwgk/fgybz/dqhjzlbz/200311/t20031126_40979.htm [in Chinese]

Guangzhou Environmental Protection Bureau (EPB). (2011c). Standard of environmental noise of urban area. Retrieved April 4, 2012, from http://www.gzepb.gov.cn/zwgk/fgybz/zsbz/200311/t20031126_40902.htm [in Chinese]

Guangzhou Municipal Government. (2009). *Guān yú yìn fā: Guǎngzhōu shì jiàn shè huā yuán chéng shì xíng dòng gāng yào* [The action program of constructing Guangzhou into a Garden City (2009–2015)]. Retrieved March 22, 2012, from http://fgj.getdd.gov.cn/detail.asp?id=4393&FirstClassid=3&secondclassid=25

Guangzhou Municipal Statistics Bureau, & Guangzhou Survey Office of National Bureau of Statistics. (2001). Guangzhou statistical yearbook 2001. Beijing: China Statistics Press. [in Chinese]

Guangzhou Municipal Statistics Bureau, & Guangzhou Survey Office of National Bureau of Statistics. (2008). Guangzhou statistical yearbook 2008. Beijing: China Statistics Press. [in Chinese]

Guangzhou Municipal Statistics Bureau, & Guangzhou Survey Office of National Bureau of Statistics. (2010). Guangzhou statistical yearbook 2010. Beijing: China Statistics Press. [in Chinese]

Guangzhou Urban Development Concept: A low carbon economy, a smart city, a happy life. (2011). Retrieved March 22, 2012, from http://news.dayoo.com/guangzhou/201112/25/73437_21168024.htm [in Chinese]

Guangzhou Yearbook Editorial Committee. (2011). *Guangzhou yearbook 2011*. Guangzhou, China: Guangzhou Yearbook Press. [in Chinese]

Ikels, Charlotte. (1996). *The return of the god of wealth: The transition to a market economy in urban China*. Palo Alto, CA: Stanford University Press.

Kuhn, Robert Lawrence. (2009). *How China's leaders think*. Singapore: John Wiley & Sons.

Lo, Carlos Wing-Hung, & Cheung, K. C. (1998). Sustainable development in the Pearl River Delta region: The case of Guangzhou. In Joseph Y. S. Cheng (Ed.), *The Guangdong development model and its challenge* (pp. 379–404). Hong Kong: City University Press.

Lo, Carlos Wing-Hung, & Chung, Shan Shan. (2004). The responses and prospects of sustainable development for Guangzhou and Hong Kong. *The International Journal of Sustainable Development and World Ecology*, 11(2), 151–167.

Lo, Carlos Wing-Hung, & Fryxell, Gerald E. (2005). Governmental and societal support for environmental enforcement in China: An empirical study in Guangzhou. *The Journal of Development Studies*, 41(4), 558–589.

Lo, Carlos Wing-Hung; Fryxell, Gerald E.; & van Rooij, Benjamin. (2009). Changes in enforcement styles among environment officials in China. *Environment and Planning A, 41*(11), 2706–2723.

Lo, Carlos Wing-Hung, & Leung, Sai Wing. (2000). Environmental agency and public opinion in Guangzhou: The limits of a popular approach to environmental governance. *The China Quarterly, 163*, 677–704.

Nanfang Daily. (2004, July 6). Guangzhou to promote industrial competitiveness and in the future emphasize the development of the seven major industries. Retrieved March 22, 2012, from http://58.63.114.194:86/ssds/html/2004/12/200412131611481092.htm [in Chinese]

Pearl Environmental News. (2006). Constructing harmony, pursuing excellence: The first special issue on the original record of the Guangzhou classic on achieving a model city. Guangzhou, China: Guangzhou Environmental Education and Publicity Centre. [in Chinese]

Seabrooke, William; Yeung, Stanley C. W.; Ma, Florence M. F.; & Li, Yong. (2004). Implementing sustainable development at the operation level (with special reference to Hong Kong and Guangzhou). *Habitat International, 28*(3), 442–466.

United Nations Human Settlement Programme (UN-Habitat). (2011). *State of the world's cities 2010/2011: Bridging the urban divide.* London: Earthscan. Retrieved April 10, 2012, from http://www.unhabitat.org/pmss/listItemDetails.aspx?publicationID=2917

Wong, Siu Wai, & Tang, Bo-sin. (2005). Challenges to the sustainability of "development zones:" A case study of Guangzhou Development District, China. *Cities, 22*(4), 303–316.

Wong, Siu-Wai, & Tang, Bo-sin. (2006). Strategic urban management in China: A case study of Guangzhou Development District. *Habitat International, 30*(3), 645–667.

Xu, Jiang, & Yeh, Anthony G. O. (2003). Guangzhou. *Cities, 20*(5), 361–375.

Berkshire's authors and editors welcome questions, comments, and corrections. Send your emails about the *Berkshire Encyclopedia of Sustainability* in general or this volume in particular to: sustainability.updates@berkshirepublishing.com

H

The Himalaya

The Himalaya, an Asian mountain range that separates the Indian subcontinent from the Tibetan Plateau, is the world's youngest mountain range as well as its highest. The Himalaya faces sustainability challenges that include glacier retreat, biodiversity loss, urbanization and its accompanying pollution, and deforestation and soil erosion, among others. Many of these challenges are tied to local and international demand for the region's rich resources.

The Himalaya, an Asian mountain range whose name means "abode of the snows" in Sanskrit, divides the Tibetan Plateau of China from the Indian subcontinent to the south. It is an area of extreme biological, ecological, cultural, and linguistic diversity, which makes sustainability issues both urgent and challenging. The Himalayan mountain range covers an area of roughly 600,000 square kilometers, extending 2,500 to 3,000 kilometers in a roughly east–west arc. With its subranges and extensions, including the Karakoram, the Hindu Kush, and the Pamir, the Himalaya encompasses parts of Afghanistan, Pakistan, India, Burma, and China, as well as all of Bhutan and Nepal. Because of the difficulty in strictly defining this rugged transboundary region, as well as challenges in accurately counting the millions of farmers, herders, and traders dispersed through remote mountain settlements, human population estimates for the region range from 47 million people (Zurick et al. 2006) to 70 to 90 million (Ives 2004) to 210 million (ICIMOD 2011).

Verticality is the most significant feature of this region. Elevations in the Himalaya range from several dozen meters above sea level to 8,850 meters on top of Mount Everest (known as Sagarmatha in Nepali and as Chomolungma in Tibetan), the highest point in the world. The Himalaya is the world's youngest mountain range. The Indo-Australian tectonic plate collided with the Eurasian plate 40 to 50 million years ago to create the Himalaya. Neither plate gave way; the pressure of the collision moved the rock upward, eventually into the form of the jagged Himalayan peaks, which are still increasing in height. This dynamism is evident today. Frequent earthquakes, landslides, and avalanches, together with extreme topography, make agriculture, travel, transportation, and infrastructure development challenging. Steep mountainsides and rushing rivers separate valleys into isolated enclaves, where disparate languages, cultures, and organisms have developed over thousands of years. Rich in cultural diversity, the Himalayan region is also a vulnerable landscape, subject to sustainability challenges in the form of climate change, biodiversity loss, deforestation and soil erosion, and urbanization and pollution.

Climate Change and Water Supply

Climate change is the most significant sustainability issue for the Himalaya, "the water towers of the world." The glaciers capture and store winter snows, releasing meltwater slowly throughout the year. This glacial and snow melt is an essential source of consistent water for farming, energy, and ecological stability. The fast-running rivers of the Himalaya feed hydropower plants that produce clean energy. The Himalaya supplies water to rivers across Asia, including the Amu Darya, Indus, Ganges, Brahmaputra (Yarlungtsanpo), Irrawaddy, Salween (Nu), Mekong-Lancang, Yangzi (Chang), Huang (Yellow), and Tarim (Dayan), on which 1.3 billion people, or one-fifth of the world's population, depend.

Temperatures in the Himalaya are increasing faster than the global average. Climate change has affected the timing of the Asian monsoon that brings summer rains to the Himalaya. Increased temperatures lead to glacial melting, an unstable water supply, and erratic weather conditions, as well as challenges to human livelihoods. If current rates of glacier retreat continue, small glaciers below 5,000 meters of elevation are likely to disappear by the end of the century, while higher and larger glaciers will shrink (ICIMOD 2010). Glacial decline can lead to sudden surges in water—as in glacial lake outburst floods, when the moraine dams trapping meltwater suddenly release, inundating downstream valleys—followed by reduction in water supplies, as rivers and lakes dwindle. Glacial retreat threatens even India's sacred Ganges River. The glacier at Gaumukh-Gangotri, which supplies about 70 percent of the river's water, is shrinking by about 37 meters per year (Wax 2007). Without reliable water sources, mountain communities, as well as the hundreds of millions of downstream users who depend on river water, face an uncertain future.

Biodiversity Loss

Ecologists believe that the Earth is undergoing a mass extinction event, in which a large number of species are lost in a short amount of geologic time (Barnosky et al. 2011; Pereira et al. 2010). They observe this massive decline most sharply in areas like the Himalaya that have high biological diversity and a high degree of endemism, that is, a large number of species found only in a particular area. Located at the interface between the temperate Palearctic realm of Eurasia and the tropical Indo-Malayan realm of the Indian subcontinent, the Himalayan region hosts remarkable diversity. Nepal is home to sixty-one globally threatened species and subspecies, including the Bengal tiger (*Panthera tigris tigris*), greater one-horned rhinoceros (*Rhinoceros unicornis*), and musk deer (*Moschus chrysogaster*). The rare and beautiful snow leopard (*Uncia uncia*, or *Panthera uncia*), believed to have a population of only several thousand individuals left in the wild, ranges throughout the high Himalaya, from Pakistan and Ladakh, India, in the west, through Nepal, Bhutan, China, and northern India in the east. Their beautiful pelts make snow leopards a target for poachers, while climate change and human encroachment destroy their high elevation habitat and lead to more frequent human-wildlife conflicts when snow leopards prey on livestock.

Healthy ecosystems provide habitat for vulnerable species and resources for rural livelihoods. They also provide a wide variety of essential ecosystem services—waste decomposition, nutrient cycling, flood prevention, water purification—that support life far beyond their boundaries. The Himalaya supports a tremendous diversity of medicinal plants, many of which are still used by rural people. Less than 25 percent of the original vegetation of the Himalayan landscape, however, remains in pristine ecological condition (Conservation International 2007). Erosion, deforestation, and conversion of lands to agricultural use have reduced the forests of the eastern Himalaya by about two-thirds. For these reasons, the global environmental organization Conservation International identifies the Himalaya as one of twenty-five global biodiversity hotspots. It has based this designation on the area's exceptionally rich plant endemism—nearly one-third (3,160) of the estimated 10,000 species of plants found in the Himalaya are endemic—and increasing human demands for natural resources. Immigration, population growth, connections with global markets, poaching, extraction, grazing, agriculture, urbanization, pollution, and war threaten this biological diversity.

Bhutan has taken strong measures to counter the deforestation and biodiversity loss. Recognizing the opportunity to maintain its reservoir of biodiversity, the National Assembly mandated in 1974 that Bhutan's forest cover must never drop below 60 percent. The constitution adopted in 2008 requires that 60 percent of the country remain under forest cover in perpetuity. Thirty-six percent of the country was under direct conservation protection through parks and protected areas in 2008. Nearly two-thirds (64 percent) of Bhutan was under forest cover in 2009. When the total includes the biological corridors (another 9.5 percent of Bhutan's land area) running between the protected areas, Bhutan has almost half of its land area under protected area status, among the highest proportion of any nation.

Large tracts of uninterrupted, high-quality habitat are necessary for the survival of many wildlife species. Often, appropriate habitat spans international boundaries, making transboundary cooperation essential for biodiversity conservation. The governments of Bhutan and India have discussed creating a biodiversity protection area known as Greater Manas, which would span the existing Bhutanese Royal Manas National Park and adjoining Manas National Park and Tiger Reserve in Assam, India. Together, these two parks comprise an area of more than 1,500 square kilometers that encompasses one of the largest tiger populations in South Asia. Transboundary cooperation has been important in monitoring the rare black-necked crane (*Grus nigricollis*) which breeds on the Qinghai–Tibetan Plateau in China, and in Ladakh, India, and then migrates south to winter in Bhutan, Arunachal Pradesh, India, and the low elevation areas of the Qinghai-Tibetan and Yunnan-Guizhou plateaus in China. Since 2003, many of the major wintering areas have been protected as national parks and reserves. Another ambitious plan involves creating a tri-national peace park around Mount Kanchenjunga, which would encompass the Kanchenjunga Conservation Area of Nepal, a community-based biodiversity conservation project; the Kanchendzoga National Park of Sikkim, India; and an extension of the Quomolungma Nature Reserve in the Tibet Autonomous Region of China.

Deforestation and Soil Erosion

Deforestation for commercial exploitation, expansion of agricultural land and human settlements, and military security have changed the face of the Himalaya. Mismanagement of forests and land tenure policies, corruption, smuggling, and livestock grazing in forests have decreased the quality of remaining forest cover as well. The dynamics of deforestation and erosion vary greatly throughout the range; the western reaches are much drier and less forested than the moist, monsoon-fed eastern Himalaya. England exploited Indian forests for commercial purposes starting in the early 1800s. Indian teak supplied the lumber for the shipbuilding needs of deforested England during the Napoleonic wars and subsequent maritime expansion. The English later built plantations for the export of tea to world markets, replacing forests in some parts of the Indian foothills. During the period of the British Raj, the British decimated forests, particularly in Garwhal and Kumaon, to build the railroad, and began exploiting the sal (*Shorea robusta*) and deodar (*Cedrus deodara*) forests of the Himalaya for commercial use in the 1850s and 1860s. The Indian government established the Imperial Forest Department in the 1860s to oversee sustained yield from these forests, but some never recovered.

The forces leading to overexploitation of Nepal's forests were different. Under the Shah monarchy, government tax policies before 1950 gave rural peasants strong incentives to clear forests and convert lands to agriculture. In the 1970s, as foreign experts observed the erosive force of monsoonal rains that sent soil into churning rivers, they assumed that the clearing of hillside forests for farming had led to excessive erosion. The theory of Himalayan environmental degradation purported that downstream flooding and siltation in the plains of Bangladesh and India resulted from deforestation and poor farming practices that caused erosion in the Himalaya (Blaikie 1985; Ives and Messerli 1989). According to this theory, modernization of the farming practices could slow erosion and bring greater stability to the region. The theory ignored the Himalayan farmers' long-term experience with the steep hillsides and the traditional knowledge, such as terrace building, they had developed for effective farming. The theory also neglected the role of government policies and incentives in creating a climate that misused natural resources. Recent empirical work suggests that the theory of Himalayan environmental degradation was based on unreflective paradigms and convenient explanations (Ives 2004; Hofer and Messerli 2006). Ecologists in the 1990s and early-twenty-first century saw firewood harvesting as a significant threat to the forests of Nepal and India.

Local resource mismanagement is not the sole cause of deforestation and soil erosion in developing countries, however. State structures and activities, economic factors, and the uneven generation and deployment of knowledge add to the problems. Deforestation is a serious concern in southwestern China (an area that encompasses the southeastern Tibet Autonomous Region, western Sichuan, northern Yunnan, southwest Gansu, and southeast Qinghai provinces), where estimates suggest that 50 percent or more of forest cover in some areas has been destroyed (Cui and Graf 2009; Karan 2009). In the 1950s, the Chinese government designated the forests of this area as China's "second timber production base" and instituted large-scale timber extraction to support China's growing economy and rapid infrastructure development (Studley 1999). Reforestation has not kept pace with timber extraction, and the resulting deforestation contributes to soil erosion and river siltation. Expansion of the road network allows timber to be extracted from remote areas, while agricultural development, fuelwood needs, and urbanization also contribute to loss of forest cover. Degradation is thus linked to problems of structural social inequality, suggesting that governments need to effect fundamental social change to manage environmental dilemmas.

Urbanization and Pollution

Historically, the narrow valleys of the Himalaya limited the development of urban areas to a few broad valleys, such as Kathmandu, Nepal, and Srinagar, in northwestern India. Although much of the region's populace lives in dispersed villages and towns, with many rural villagers still engaged in subsistence agriculture and pastoralism, the Himalaya is not exempt from the global trends of urban expansion that have resulted in more than half the world's human population living in cities. Both "pull" factors, such as better employment opportunities, access to education and health care, and improved roads and infrastructure, and "push" factors, such rural poverty, discrimination, wildlife conflict, and environmental degradation, draw migrants to urban areas. Simultaneously, urban areas expand their footprints into the surrounding rural areas to accommodate their growing populations. The capital of Bhutan, Thimphu, became one of the fastest growing cities in Asia in the early years of the twenty-first century, growing at a rate of 7–10 percent annually (RGOB 2006). Similarly, the Leh District of Ladakh, in the western Indian Himalaya, experienced an annual population growth rate of 5.92 percent in the urban areas in the years 1981–2001, well above the average urban population growth rate of 2.95 percent for India as a whole (Goodall 2004). At these rapid growth rates, it is difficult for municipal and national governments to keep pace with the ever-expanding need for urban services, such as sanitation, hygiene, garbage collection, pollution control, and land-use planning. In Gilgit-Baltistan, Pakistan, wood burning for winter heating causes a pall of smoke to hang over urban areas (Mir 2011). Rapidly growing cities tend to expand their geographical footprints in an uncontrolled manner. For example, with a population of 1.4 million, Srinagar, the capital of Kashmir, has encroached on surrounding agricultural land and wetlands, degrading water quality, and threatening the area's famous lakes (Fazal and Amin 2011).

The sustainability challenges of rapid urbanization and pollution can be seen in the case of the Kathmandu Valley of Nepal, which was for centuries a trading crossroads between India and Tibet. This example suggests some of the challenges that rapidly growing towns of the Himalaya may have ahead of them.

Economic expansion in the 1980s brought a significant increase in the material living standards in Kathmandu. Drawn by hopes of better health care and education, migrants flooded into the city, quadrupling the population to 414,000 between 1951 and 1991 (Liechty 2003, 53). Along with material exuberance, however, came uncontrolled pollution of air, urban waterways, and public spaces. During the Nepal Civil War, which lasted from 1996 to 2006, when Maoist rebels faced off against government forces, villagers streamed into Kathmandu to avoid being conscripted to fight for the warring parties. By 2001, the population of an overcrowded and chaotic Kathmandu had more than doubled again, reaching 1.1 million, according to the United Nations Environment Programme.

This rapid growth overtaxed solid waste and wastewater management systems. Households, factories, and slaughterhouses left solid waste to decay on the streets or indiscriminately dumped it in waterways. Wastewater and industrial effluent often ran directly into the Bagmati and Bishnumati rivers that thread through the valley. The historically pristine views of the Himalaya's snow-covered peaks disappeared into a haze of exhaust fumes that represented some of the worst urban air quality in Asia and took a toll on human health. Most people lacked safe drinking water or even adequate water for washing and hygiene. Waterborne diseases, such as diarrhea, dysentery, giardiasis, and cholera, were widespread. As residents and tourists complained about the abysmal conditions, government agencies and international aid organizations began studying the challenges rapid urbanization brought. Lack of urban environmental management policies, of consistent implementation strategies, and of a stable government hampered the ability to make major inroads on Kathmandu's urban problems.

The Future

As these examples show, the Himalayan region faces complex and interconnected sustainability challenges closely tied to the unique social and physical geography of the region. These "wicked problems" have no single correct answer and no defined conclusion. These challenges are tied to social conditions: poverty; war and unrest; population growth, both regionally and globally; and the status of women. Improvements in these social indicators, together with well-planned and implemented national and international environmental policies, may slow the environmental degradation of the Himalaya. Governments have made efforts to improve the lives of rural residents through, for example, the promotion of the community forestry concept that builds on traditional communal land management practices. Governments have developed compensation programs that reimburse farmers who lose livestock to wildlife predation. The development of satellite cities or regional towns takes pressure off the major urban areas and slows rural-urban migration by providing the health care, education, communication, government, and cultural services that people seek in moving to urban areas. Some ecotourism projects bring much needed cash income to rural areas. As governments acknowledge the sustainable practices and traditional ecological knowledge that long-term residents of the region have developed, they may discover ingenious indigenous strategies for increasing sustainability.

Elizabeth ALLISON
California Institute of Integral Studies

See also Biodiversity Conservation Legislation (China); China; Ganges River; Genetic Resources; Huang (Yellow) River; India; Indigenous Peoples; Mekong-Lancang River; Parks and Preserves; Public Health; Reforestation and Afforestation (Southeast Asia); Rural Development; Rural Livelihoods; Tibetan Plateau; Traditional Chinese Medicine (TCM); Transboundary Water Issues; Water Security; Yangzi (Chang) River

FURTHER READING

Barnosky, Anthony D., et al. (2011). Has the Earth's sixth mass extinction already arrived? *Nature, 471*(7336), 51–57.

Blaikie, Piers M. (1985). *The political economy of soil erosion in developing countries*. London: Longman.

Conservation International. (2007). Biodiversity hotspots: Himalaya. Retrieved October 5, 2011, from http://www.biodiversityhotspots.org/xp/hotspots/himalaya/Pages/default.aspx

Cui, Xuefeng, & Graf, Hans F. (2009). Recent land cover changes on the Tibetan Plateau: A review. *Journal of Climatic Change, 94*(1–2), 47–61.

Fazal, Shahab, & Amin, Arshad. (2011). Impact of urban land transformation on water bodies in Srinagar City, India. *Journal of Environmental Protection, 2*(2), 142–153.

Gadgil, Madhav, & Guha, Ramachandra. (1992). *This fissured land: An ecological history of India.* Delhi: Oxford University Press.

Goodall, Sarah. (2004). Rural-to-urban migration and urbanization in Leh, Ladakh. *Mountain Research and Development, 24*(3), 220–227.

Guha, Ramachandra. (1983). Forestry in British and post-British India: A historical analysis. *Economic and Political Weekly, 18*(44), 1882–1896.

Guha, Ramachandra. (2000). *The unquiet woods: Ecological change and peasant resistance in the Himalaya.* Berkeley: University of California Press.

Hofer, Thomas, & Messerli, Bruno. (2006). *Floods in Bangladesh: History, dynamics and rethinking the role of the Himalayas.* Tokyo: United Nations UniversityPress.

International Centre for Integrated Mountain Development (ICIMOD). (2010). Melting Himalayas: ICIMOD's comments on a turbulent debate. Retrieved February 28, 2010, from http://www.icimod.org/?page=737

International Centre for Integrated Mountain Development (ICIMOD). (2011). Hindu Kush-Himalayan region. Retrieved October 3, 2011, from http://www.icimod.org/?q=1137

Ives, Jack D. (2004). *Himalayan perceptions: Environmental change and the well-being of mountain peoples.* New York: Routledge.

Ives, Jack D., & Messerli, Bruno. (1989). *The Himalayan dilemma: Reconciling development and conservation.* New York: Routledge.

Karan, Pradyumna P. (2009). The new Tibet. *FOCUS on Geography, 52*(2), 7–13.

Liechty, Mark. (2003). *Suitably modern: Making middle-class culture in a new consumer society.* Princeton, NJ: Princeton University Press.

Mir, Shabbir. (2011). Environmental problems: Bad air causing eye infections in Gilgit. *Express Tribune.* Retrieved January 19, 2012, from http://tribune.com.pk/story/99785/environmental-problems-bad-air-causing-eye-infections-in-gilgit/

Metz, John J. (1991). A reassessment of the causes and severity of Nepal's environmental crisis. *World Development, 19*(7), 805–820.

Pereira, Henrique M., et al. (2010). Scenarios for global biodiversity in the 21st century. *Science, 330*(6010), 1496–1501.

Rangan, Haripriya. (2000). *Of myths and movements: Rewriting Chipko into Himalayan history.* London: Verso.

Royal Government of Bhutan (RGOB), Office of Census Commissioner. (2006). *Population and housing census of Bhutan 2005.* Thimphu, Bhutan: RGOB.

Studley, John. (1999). Forests and environmental degradation in SW China. *International Forestry Review, 1*(4), 260–265.

Thompson, Michael; Warburton, Michael; & Hatley, Tom. (1986). *Uncertainty on a Himalayan scale: An institutional theory of environmental perception and a strategic framework for the sustainable development of the Himalaya.* London: Milton Ash Editions/Ethnographica.

Tucker, Richard P. (1987). Dimensions of deforestation in the Himalaya: The historical setting. *Mountain Research and Development, 7*(3), 328–331.

Wax, Emily. (2007, June 17). A sacred river endangered by global qarming: Glacial source of the Ganges is receding. *Washington Post.* Retrieved December 4, 2011, from http://www.washingtonpost.com/wp-dyn/content/article/2007/06/16/AR2007061600461.html

Zurick, David; Pacheco, Julsun; Shrestha, Basanta Raj; & Bajracharya, Birendra. (2006). *Illustrated atlas of the Himalaya.* Lexington: University Press of Kentucky.

Huang (Yellow) River

Since ancient times, the Huang (Yellow) River has driven trade and defined political power in China. Prone to flooding, silting, and changing course, this unreliable river is nonetheless relied upon by the nation to support population and economic growth. But environmental degradation is impairing the river's ability to do this, forcing the nation to find sustainable solutions for both national and ecosystem survival.

The Huang (Yellow) River, at 5,400 kilometers in length, is China's second-longest river. It originates in Qinghai Province and flows northeast and then east across the top of its great bend. At Hekouzhen in Inner Mongolia, the river turns south for 800 kilometers before again turning northeast to cross the North China Plain and reach the sea at its delta at the Bohai Gulf. The river's drainage area of 745,000 square kilometers ranks it twenty-ninth among the world's rivers, but its discharge of 1,365 cubic meters per second is far less than that of many rivers of comparable drainage area. The Mekong River, for example, has a similar drainage area but more than ten times the flow of the Huang River.

In spite of its small flow, the Huang River has been infamously difficult to control, repeatedly flooding and changing course throughout history. Two main factors contribute to the river's tendency to flood. The first is a seasonal rainfall pattern that causes extreme and often sudden variations in water levels, particularly in summer and fall. The second factor is the river's massive silt burden. As the river travels south between Shanxi and Shaanxi provinces, it crosses a highly eroded loess plateau. Loess is a fine-grain, nutrient-rich but easily eroded soil that gives the river its characteristic yellow color. In the rainy season, sudden downpours in the barren erosion gullies of the loess plateau send streams of mud cascading into the river. This results in a silt content that has been measured as high as 37 kilograms of silt per cubic meter of water. When the river leaves the mountains and turns east to cross the relatively flat North China Plain, perhaps one-third of this silt settles out, causing the river channel to fill and rise. Eventually the river breaks out of its elevated bed and finds a new, lower course to the sea.

All of China's early dynasties emerged on or near the Huang River, and river control played an important part in imperial politics from earliest times. Emperor Yu, the legendary founder of China's first dynasty, the Xià (2100–1766), supposedly established his right to the throne by subduing the Huang River. The Yuán dynasty (1279–1368) marked the beginning of a more active approach to controlling the river. The Yuán constructed the Grand Canal to allow the shipment of grain from the Yangzi (Chang) River valley to the capital at Beijing. Because the canal incorporated part of the Huang River, controlling the river became a central concern of the imperial state. The Ming (1368–1644) and Qīng (1644–1911/12) dynasties created an extensive system of dikes, locks, spillways, and revetments (embankment facings) to keep the river in its bed and the grain flowing north. By the middle of the nineteenth century, the Huang River control system was one of the largest and most expensive projects of imperial administration, but devastating floods continued to be a problem.

A series of floods in the 1840s and 1850s, combined with the disruption of the grain tribute caused by the Taiping Rebellion in south China, finally led the imperial state to abandon its efforts to control the lower reaches of the Huang River. The river was allowed to remain in a new, northerly course that emptied into the Bohai Gulf. Along much of the new course, river control efforts were turned over to local officials and communities. The result was repeated flooding and severe economic and social dislocation for many parts of the North China Plain. In the Republican era (1911/12–1949), massive floods continued to cause widespread devastation.

Beginning in the 1950s, the People's Republic of China attempted to use both reforestation of the loess plateau and construction of dams to reduce silting and regulate the flow of the Huang River. Initial efforts at reforestation failed, and silting behind Huang River dams has severely limited or eliminated their hydroelectric potential. Since the early 1990s, soil conservation efforts in the loess plateau have reduced the silt burden carried by the river, but extensive agricultural use of water in the upper reaches so reduced flow that the downstream bed went dry for extended periods.

Stepped-up conservation efforts in the 1990s improved the river's condition, but numerous challenges remain. Many of the dams built to reduce flooding in the upper reaches of the river are decayed and some in danger of collapse. China's rapid industrialization has resulted in widespread air and water pollution along the Huang River valley, so that the river's water is unsafe for drinking or swimming along much of its course. Chemical discharges and oil spills have damaged the ecosystem. It is estimated that one-third of the fish species once native to the river have disappeared from its waters.

At the same time that global warming is shrinking the glaciers that feed the river and reducing flow, the Huang River is being called upon to help ease the Beijing region's growing demand for water. Just as in ancient times the government's ability to control the Huang River symbolized the strength or weakness of the state, so today the government's ability to preempt the collapse of the Huang River ecosystem may be a harbinger of China's ability to survive the environmental consequences of its rapid industrialization.

Randall DODGEN
Sonoma State University

See also Agriculture (China and Southeast Asia); Beijing, China; Education, Environmental (China); Fisheries; Ganges River; Mekong-Lancang River; National Pollution Survey (China); South–North Water Diversion; Three Gorges Dam; Transboundary Water Issues; Water Security; Yangzi (Chang) River

FURTHER READING

Dodgen, Randall. (2001). *Controlling the dragon: Confucian engineers and the Yellow River in late imperial China*. Honolulu: University of Hawaii Press.

Economy, Elizabeth. (2004). *The river runs black: The environmental challenge to China's future*. Ithaca, NY: Cornell University Press.

Greer, Charles. (1979). *Water management in the Yellow River basin of China*. Austin: University of Texas Press.

Leonard, Jane Kate. (1996). *Controlling from afar: The Daoguang emperor's management of the Grand Canal crisis, 1824–1826*. Ann Arbor: University of Michigan Press.

Needham, Joseph; Ling, Wang; & Gwei-djen, Lu. (Eds.). (1971). *Science and civilisation in China: Vol. 4(3). Civil engineering and nautics* (pp. 211–378). Cambridge, UK: Cambridge University Press.

Pomerantz, Kenneth. (1993). *The making of a hinterland: State, society and economy in inland North China, 1853–1937*. Berkeley: University of California Press.

---

chat

Berkshire's authors and editors welcome questions, comments, and corrections. Send your emails about the *Berkshire Encyclopedia of Sustainability* in general or this volume in particular to: sustainability.updates@berkshirepublishing.com

I

India

1.2 billion est. pop. 2010

India is the seventh-largest (by geographical area) and the second-most populous country in the world. With Pakistan to its west, China, Nepal, and Bhutan to the northeast, and Myanmar (Burma) and Bangladesh to the east, India is surrounded by the Indian Ocean on the south, the Arabian Sea on the southwest, and the Bay of Bengal on the southeast. This home of many ancient civilizations is one of the fastest growing economies today. Although India is the world's largest democracy, its people are divided by deep disparities of income, economic opportunity, and privilege.

India is a country whose environment is a study in contrasts. Environmental issues, especially those of forest access, air quality, and water use, are keenly contested in a deeply unequal society with a vibrant democracy. Questions of livelihood loom large, because more than 37 percent of India's 1.2 billion people are poor (Nanda 2010), 74 percent of adults are literate (Census of India 2011), and 47 percent of the children are malnourished (Gragnolati et al. 2005). Urban middle-class groups similar to those in developed countries at times sharply differ with the livelihood-based agendas of the poor. The latter include 6 million coastal fishers, 80 million Scheduled Tribals (indigenous groups who are eligible for positive discrimination under India's constitution), and others who rely on forest resources. Displacement by development projects is a major public issue.

The legacies of British colonial rule until 1947 and the subsequent model of development are central forces in reshaping the environment. The voter turnout in state and federal elections averages more than 60 percent; more than 3 million representatives hold offices at local, state, and federal levels. But India's people are divided by deep disparities of income, economic opportunity, and privilege. Livelihood in rural settlements, which account for 73 percent of the population, is still heavily reliant on the use of land, water, and biomass (the amount of living matter). Conversely, India has been a nuclear-capable country since 1974 and has the third-largest pool of scientific and technical labor power in the world. By 2009, the Indian life span had risen to sixty-four years (from twenty-seven in 1951) (World Bank 2011), but issues of quality of life and sustainability are more contentious than ever.

Climate and Geography

India has four times the population of the United States on one-third the land area. One-half the land of India is arable (suitable for irrigation). Major regions include the Indo-Gangetic Plain, the Himalaya Mountains, the peninsula, and the Northeast, which borders on Myanmar (Burma). The floodplains of the Indus, Ganges, and Brahmaputra rivers make up one of Asia's largest expanses of lowland river plains. To the north, the geologically young Himalaya stretch from west to east. They moderate the cold winds from the Tibetan Plateau, and they block the clouds brought in by the southwest monsoon from the Bay of Bengal in the east. The subcontinent is drier to the west, but the pattern does not always hold true. The Western Ghat Mountains, which run parallel to the western coast, form a barrier to the monsoon clouds coming in from the Arabian Sea.

There are significant contrasts between the north and the south. All regions have a well-defined rainy season, the monsoon (from the Arabic *mausam*, meaning "season"). Northern rivers are perennial, fed by the snows of the Himalaya ("the abode of snow"; *him = snow, alaya = home*). Southern rivers, including the Kaveri, Tambrapani, Mahanadi, Godavari, and Krishna, are seasonal, not perennial. The plains and river valleys in the south and peninsula are also less extensive, with no vast expanse that can compare to the Indo-Gangetic Plain. The peninsula, lying south of the Vindhya hills, is marked by undulating ground. There are several smaller ranges of mountains and hills—the Ashambu, the Cardamoms, and the Eastern Ghats; much of the peninsula, especially the Deccan Plateau, is composed of older basalt and granite outcrops.

The Thar Desert lies at the end of the range of the monsoon winds in the northwest. The Ladahk desert in the Ladakh Plateau has subzero temperatures. Nearly 40 percent of India is semiarid, with fluctuations in rainfall historically being a major factor in determining crop output. By contrast, in the Northeast the hill ranges receive heavy rains, with Cherrapunji recording more than 1,000 centimeters a year.

Ecological Diversity

The diversity of terrain and habitats explains why a country of 1 billion people is also one of the world's twelve mega biodiversity regions (the World Conservation Union designates biological diversity by the numbers of species of animals and plants). India is that rare country where the three great zoogeographic (relating to the geographic distribution of animals) regions—the Ethiopian, the Oriental, and the Alpine—overlap (Rangarajan 2001). The Ethiopian is represented by lions in the Gir Forest (their only surviving habitat in Asia) and by gazelle, antelope, and acacia trees. The Oriental is represented by tigers, sloths, and a variety of deer species. The Alpine, or Himalaya, is represented by fauna and flora often more typical of Europe: brown bears, a subspecies of the red deer, mountain sheep and goats, pines, oaks, and rhododendrons. There are more than forty thousand species of plants and twelve hundred bird species, many of them native, especially in the Western Ghats.

Demographic Expansion and Economic Growth

The increase in the human population and its economy reshaped India's landscape, especially in the twentieth century. According to the 2011 census of India, India's population density of 382 people per square kilometer masks great variations between regions. The Hindi-speaking states of the north, which cover most of the Ganges River basin or are adjacent to it, make up 45 percent of the population. In the east, Arunachal Pradesh State records densities as low as 17 people per square kilometer.

Much of the population growth is relatively recent. Estimates place India's population in 1596 at 114 million. Even in 1900, India had only 240 million people. The rate of population growth exceeded 0.5 percent a year only after 1921. In 1951, there were 360 million people, and the population growth rate was more than 2 percent a year until 1981 (Sinha and Zacharia 1986, 291). It has slowed since then, mainly due to better health care facilities, expansion of women's literacy, better social services, and government-sponsored family planning. India's population is now growing at 1.4 percent a year (World Bank 2011).

The transformation of the landscape owes much to major socioeconomic changes. The advance and retreat of forests due to ax and plow are not new, with the Indus River basin experiencing a first wave of urbanization around 3000 BCE with the Harappan culture (Mughal 2011). A second wave of urban settlement in the Ganges River valley occurred around 600 BCE. Even during the Mughal Empire (1526–1857), Asian elephants were captured in parts of central India where they are now extinct; the greater one-horned rhinoceros was hunted in the Indus River basin (Habib 1982). By the late eighteenth century, there were already significant and irreversible changes in certain regions. Economic and cultural changes under British rule unleashed new forces of change.

Precolonial Legacies

The advent of British colonialism in the eighteenth and nineteenth centuries marked a major watershed for India. Historians are divided on what colonialism meant and why, and the division arises partly from radically varying views of precolonial society in India. The institution of caste—which entails a division of labor in a sharply unequal system, with closed marriage circles—is central to one view of India's ecological history (Gadgil and Guha 1992, 91–111). Different castes had differential access to resources at the village level, and there was less intervention by the state in local affairs until the coming of colonial rule. Colonialism displaced marginal social groups who relied on fodder, game, wood, and other land- and water-based resources. Caste- and kin-based systems underpinned a more ecologically prudent social order.

A contrasting view of India's ecological history shows much more fluidity before the colonial era (Arnold and Guha 1995). Ethnic groups were not fixed in particular sites, and the level of mobility was high because there was more land per laborer. Forests, far from being cut off from wider society, were resources in times of scarcity and a political base for rival claimants for political power.

Archival and archaeological evidence does not support the notion of a long period of stability, as groups often combined activities, such as hunting, herding, and slash-and-burn cultivation, with settled agriculture. The late nineteenth century was indeed a break, but in this view, mainly because the British drew a *cordon sanitaire* (a protective barrier) around forests and hills, securing them for timber and for strategic reasons.

Imperial Impact: The Debate

The colonial era marked a break because of the new intensity of resource use and regulation (Grove 1995). Although the British first took control of Bengal Province in 1757 and expanded their power steadily, the impact unfolded only over time. Unlike previous Indian regimes, the British had a deep distrust of mobile herders and traders and a strong preference for those who had a fixed home. The British also had a deep prejudice that mobility signified lack of thrift and could damage forests and the land itself.

In one interpretation, strategic and commercial interests shaped British policy. Securing timber for the navy led to forest reservation—the annexation of forest land by the government—for teak in Malabar in 1807. Expanding the rail network led to a timber shortage and creation of the Forest Department in 1864. By 1900, one-fifth of British India was administered by foresters who imposed new regulations on customary uses. Commercial interests led to tensions between the British administrators and indigenous peoples who had had access to the forests. The expansion of canal networks proceeded on a parallel course. Although irrigation increased crop yields and expanded plowed acreage, salinity, waterlogging, and the spread of malaria caused new problems. The building of water-control systems on an unprecedented scale often caused unintended damage in the deltas of peninsular rivers such as the Mahanadi.

Another interpretation emphasizes the ideological and scientific currents among British decision makers, rather than British imperial political economy. Colonial regulations aimed to halt the negative impact of clearing vegetation on water supplies and agricultural prosperity. The East India Company, which governed India until 1858, had a small but influential cadre of botanists and other scientists who anticipated many twenty-first-century concerns about species extinction, climate change, and the links between vegetation and water runoff. Policy initiatives were often driven by such concerns. The Indian princes, who ruled over one-third of the land as junior partners of the British, also supported zoology and forestry, often creating the nuclei of modern scientific investigation.

The British had to try to devise methods of irrigation and forestry and game control strategies that suited South Asia's specific ecological and social conditions. But the outcomes and responses were often radically different from what they expected (Whitcombe 1995). The canal networks in colonial India were among the world's largest, but often they led to increased waterlogging and salinity and contributed to the spread of malaria. In the Himalaya, hill peasants protested levies of forced labor. They also resisted when foresters replaced mixed oak forests with pine monocultures. In central India, there were even sharper tensions. A tribal uprising in Bastar, for example, was sparked in part by curbs on shifting cultivation. In central and eastern India, denial of access to the forest for wood, hunting, fodder, and cultivation was at issue. In the foothills of the Himalaya, shepherds bore the brunt of exclusion.

Independence and Development

After independence in 1947, India drew much from the philosophy of nonviolent resistance developed by the nationalist Mohandas Gandhi (1869–1948). India drew less from his critique of development and the ecological insights that led to alternative development paths. India followed the model of a mixed economy with an emphasis on capital-intensive technology in a quest for economic self-reliance. Many middle-class Indians hoped to modernize faster than their former imperial masters had let them.

Environmental concerns took a generation to emerge fully, although they had older historical roots. Initially dissent was muted, but since about 1970 the environment as an issue has become central to public debate. Not surprisingly, Gandhi's ideas have often been drawn upon by critics of the dominant model of development. The courts, the media, citizens associations, political parties, and scientists have been prominent in a variety of debates, resulting in a series of reports on the environment by citizen groups.

Environmental Movements

The fate of the forests has been an issue marked by deep divisions. Two attempts to enact legislation on forests, in 1982 and 1994, failed due to protests by tribal and other forest-reliant peoples. Many of the protesters were marginal agriculturalists for whom forests were a critical supplementary resource. Underprivileged groups blame industry and urban demand and the commercial orientation of the Forest Department for the loss of forest cover. Gender concerns about access and equity have also come into sharp focus. Women have been active in voicing demands for more access to forests and fisheries for sustaining livelihoods (Shiva 1988). The expansion of cultivation and the growth of human and livestock populations are singled out by those who favor stringent measures to protect remaining forest cover, now less than 11 percent of the landscape. Since 1990, many states, especially West Bengal, have attempted more participatory arrangements, with resource sharing with villages. These plans appear to work best in regions with less-polarized land ownership. Known as joint forest management, these plans will either evolve into an alternative or merely complement the dominant model of forestry.

About 5 percent of the Indian landmass is set aside in protected areas, often with intact assemblages of flora and fauna. Many areas are former forest or hunting reserves of the British or of the Indian princes. India, despite its population, has more tigers and Asian elephants than any other Asian country (Seidensticker, Christie, and Jackson 1999). Here, too, legacies of exclusion clash with the call for more participation by local people. An estimated 3 million people rely on parks and sanctuaries for their livelihood. It is still unclear how increased resource sharing is to be accomplished while retaining biodiversity. Alternatives range from microreserves run by communities to resource sharing on the periphery of large parks. Who is to enforce what control regime and how remain contentious issues.

Dams also have been a major issue. After independence, they were seen as critical to achieving self-sufficiency in producing food and generating power for industry. The ecological and social costs were widely questioned (Singh 1997). In 1980, concern about the loss of rain forest stalled construction of a dam in Silent Valley, Kerala. More recently, controversy has centered on the displacement of more than 100,000 people by large dams on the Narmada River in central India (Dreze, Sampson, and Singh 1997). Most controversial of these is the Sardar Sarovar dam. Whether and under what conditions displacement was justified raise significant issues. Most of the displaced are from Madhya Pradesh State, whereas the benefits of irrigation will primarily flow to the richer state of Gujarat. Many of the displaced are tribal peoples whose social and political rights are prominent in Indian politics. Although the controversial Sardar Sarovar dam is proceeding after a favorable judicial verdict, the wider debate continues. In some parts of India, the tribal people are also in conflict with the government in order to assert their right to forest access (Aufschnaiter 2009).

The Challenge

The central challenge is simple but daunting: to achieve a better standard of living for 1 billion people and to do so in a sustainable manner via a democratic polity. A growing media and a range of citizens groups are often in conflict with each other in courts and in public spaces. The century ahead will be one of crises but also one of new opportunities.

Mahesh RANGARAJAN
University of Delhi

See also Activism, Judicial; Agriculture (South and East Asia); Chennai, India; Delhi, India; Education, Environmental (India); Five-Year Plans; Gandhism; Ganges River; The Himalaya; Indigenous Peoples; Mumbai, India; Parks and Preserves; Reforestation and Afforestation (Southeast Asia); Religions; Traditional Knowledge (India); Water Use and Rights (India); White Revolution of India

This article was adapted by the editors from Mahesh Rangarajan's article "India" in Shepard Krech III, J. R. McNeill, and Carolyn Merchant (Eds.), *Encyclopedia of World Environmental History*, pp. 668–672. Great Barrington, MA: Berkshire Publishing (2003).

FURTHER READING

Agarwal, Anil; Chopra, Ravi; & Sharma, Kalpana. (Eds.). (1982). *The first citizen's report on the environment in India*. New Delhi: Centre for Science and Environment.

Agarwal, Anil; Narain, Sunita; & Sen, Srabani. (Eds.). (1999). *The citizen's fifth report on the environment in India*. New Delhi: Centre for Science and Environment.

Agrawal, Arun, & Sivaramakrishnan, K. (Eds.). (2000). *Agrarian environments: Resources, representations, and rule in India*. Durham, NC: Duke University Press.

Arnold, David, & Guha, Richard. (1995). *Nature, culture, imperialism: Essays on the environmental history of south Asia*. New Delhi: Oxford University Press.

Aufschnaiter, Claudia. (2009). *Adivasi land rights struggles in south India: Indigenous resistance strategies and the (inter)national law context*. Saarbrücken, Germany: VDM Publishing House.

Bayly, Christopher. Alan. (1988). *The new Cambridge history of India: Indian society and the making of the British Empire, 1780–1870* (Vol. 2.1). Cambridge, UK: Cambridge University Press.

Census of India. (2011). Literates and literacy rates by sex: 2011 (Office of the Registrar General and Census Commissioner, India, Ministry of Home Affairs, Government of India). Retrieved January 5, 2012, from http://www.censusindia.gov.in/2011-prov-results/data_files/india/Table-2(3)_literacy.pdf

D'Monte, Darryl. (1985). *Temples or tombs? Industry versus environment: Three controversies*. New Delhi: Centre for Science and Environment.

Dreze, Jean; Sampson, Meera; & Singh, Satyajit. (1997). *Dam and the nation: Displacement and resettlement in the Narmada Valley*. New York: Oxford University Press.

D'Souza, Rohan. (2002). Colonialism, capitalism and nature: Debating the origins of the Mahanadi Delta's hydraulic crisis. *Economic and Political Weekly, 37*(3), 1261–1272.

Gadgil, Madhav, & Guha, Richard. (1992). *This fissured land: An ecological history of India*. New Delhi: Oxford University Press.

Gadgil, Madhav, & Guha, Richard. (1995). *Ecology and equity: The use and abuse of nature in contemporary India*. London: Routledge.

Gilmartin, David. (1996). Scientific empire and imperial science: Colonialism and irrigation technology in the Indus basin. *Journal of Asian Studies, 53*(4), 1127–1154.

Gragnolati, Michele; Shekar, Meera; Das Gupta, Monica; Bredenkamp, Caryn; & Lee, Yi-Kyoung. (2005). *India's undernourished children: A call for reform and action* (HNP Discussion Paper). Washington, DC: The World Bank.

Grove, Richard H. (1995). *Green imperialism, colonial expansion, tropical island Edens and the origins of environmentalism, 1660–1860*. New Delhi: Oxford University Press.

Grove, Richard H.; Damodaran, Vinita; & Sangwan, Satpal. (1998). *Nature and the Orient: Essays on the environmental history of South and Southeast Asia*. New Delhi: Oxford University Press.

Guha, Ramachandra. (1989). *The unquiet woods: Ecological change and peasant resistance in the western Himalaya*. Berkeley: University of California Press.

Guha, Sumit. (1999). *Environment and ethnicity in India, 1200–1991*. Cambridge, UK: Cambridge University Press.

Guha, Sumit. (2001). *Health and population in south Asia from earliest times to the present*. London: Hurst.

Habib, Irfan. (1982). *An atlas of the Mughal Empire*. Cambridge, UK: Cambridge University Press.

Hazarika, Sanjoy. (1999). *Bhopal: The lessons of a tragedy*. Delhi: Penguin.

Jeffery, Roger, & Sundar, Nandini. (1999). *A new moral economy for India's forests? Discourses of community and participation*. Thousand Oaks, CA: Sage.

Kothari, Ashish; Anuradha, R. V.; Pathak, Neema; & Taneja, Bansuri. (Eds.). (1998). *Communities and conservation in South and Central Asia*. New Delhi: Sage.

Mughal, Muhammad Aurang Zeb. (2011). Mohenjo-daro's sewers. In Alfred J. Andrea (Ed.), *World History Encyclopedia* (Vol. 3, pp. 121–122). Santa Barbara: ABC-CLIO.

Nanda, Rupashree. (2010). It's official: 37 pc live below poverty line. IBN Live India. Retrieved January 5, 2010, from http://ibnlive.in.com/news/its-official-37-live-below-poverty-line/113522-3.html

Rangarajan, Mahesh. (1996). *Fencing the forest, conservation and ecological change in India's central provinces, 1860–1914*. Oxford, UK: Oxford University Press.

Rangarajan, Mahesh. (2001). *India's wildlife history: An introduction*. New Delhi: Permanent Black.

Rangarajan, Mahesh. (2002). Polity, ecology and landscape: New writing on south Asia's past. *Studies in History, 18*(1), 135–147.

Saberwal, Vasant. (1998). *Pastoral politics, shepherds, bureaucrats and conservation in the western Himalaya*. New Delhi: Oxford University Press.

Saberwal, Vasant, & Rangarajan, Mahesh. (Eds.). (2003). *Battles over nature: Science and the politics of conservation*. New Delhi: Permanent Black.

Seidensticker, John; Christie, Sarah; & Jackson, Peter. (Eds.). (1999). *Riding the tiger: Tiger conservation in human-dominated landscapes*. Cambridge, UK: Cambridge University Press.

Shiva, Vandana. (1988). *Staying alive: Women, ecology and survival in India*. New Delhi: Zed Press.

Sinha, V. C., & Zacharia, E. (1986). *Elements of demography*. New Delhi: Allied Publishers Private Limited.

Singh, Satyajit. (1997). *Taming the waters: The political economy of large dams in India*. New Delhi: Oxford University Press.

Sivaramakrishnan, K. (1999). *Modern forests, state making and environmental change in colonial eastern India*. Palo Alto, CA: Stanford University Press.

Sundar, Nandini. (1997). *Subalterns and sovereigns: An anthropological history of Bastar, 1854–1996*. Oxford, UK: Oxford University Press.

Sundar, Nandini; Jeffery, Roger; & Thin, Neil. (2001). *Branching out: Joint forest management in India*. Oxford, UK: Oxford University Press.

Whitcombe, Elizabeth. (1995). The environmental costs of irrigation in British India. In David Arnold & Ramachandra Guha (Eds.), *Nature, culture, imperialism: Essays on the environmental history of south Asia* (pp. 237–259). New Delhi: Oxford University Press.

World Bank. (2011). India at a glance. Retrieved January 5, 2011, from http://devdata.worldbank.org/AAG/ind_aag.pdf

Indigenous Peoples

Due to their dependence on natural resources anchored to development activities, indigenous peoples are forced to adopt environmental practices currently considered unsustainable. Their struggles in India, China, and Southeast Asia epitomize the intricate nexus of sustainability, development practices, and indigenous resource management. Indigenous peoples are rendered resilient, however, by their knowledge systems and rights-based aspirations, both key to sustainability. Consequently, they can be powerful partners for institutions and governments facing sustainability challenges.

The term *indigenous peoples* is popularly used to refer to traditional peoples worldwide (though not all traditional peoples are classified as indigenous). While there is no universally accepted definition of indigenous peoples, they are referred to by various names such as "ethnic minorities," "tribal groups," "cultural minorities," and "scheduled tribes" among others. Part of the terminological quandary results from the fact that definitions can be, and have been, used as political tools in pursuing social and economic agendas (Bowen 2000; Sanders 1999). Indigenous peoples have always been victimized by misleading definitions or by the outright absence of legal, and therefore binding, definitions. For example, in drafting its numerous development policies, the World Bank has not attempted to articulate a definition of its own for indigenous peoples because of the varied and changing contexts in which they live, and because there is no universally accepted definition. In its Operational Directive 4.10, the World Bank opted to refer to indigenous peoples as "indigenous ethnic minorities," "aboriginals," "hill tribes," "minority nationalities," "scheduled tribes," or "tribal groups," depending on the countries within the confines of which they were located. The same holds true for the United Nations (UN), which to date has not chosen to adopt any specific definition and instead has developed broad category-based criteria for identifying indigenous peoples, which include one or more of the following conditions: self-identification at the individual level and acceptance by the community as members; historical continuity with precolonial or presettler societies; a strong link to territories and surrounding natural resources; a distinct economic or political system; a distinct language, culture, and beliefs; nondominance within the societies they live in; and a resolve to remain as distinctive peoples and communities and maintain and reproduce ancestral environments and systems (ADB 1998; UN 1986).

This question of identity, whether characterized by the absence or presence of specific or broad definitions, has impacted the indigenous peoples' opportunities to improve their lives and chances of survival. Speaking at the Fifty-Third session of the United Nations Commission on Human Rights, Long Xuequn, adviser of the Chinese delegation, warned that the justification and scope of application for the Declaration on the Rights of Indigenous Peoples would be subject to much criticism in the absence of a definition that truly applies to genuine indigenous peoples (Chinese Embassy 1997).

Relationship to the Natural Environment

Generally speaking, the lifestyles of traditional peoples reflect the dynamics of sustainability. Indigenous peoples "traditionally have a harmonious and symbiotic relationship with the natural environment" (ACPP 2009, 1), although there are some traditional peoples who are not good environmental managers and are not managing sustainably. All indigenous communities depend on the natural resources available in their habitats and territories.

Ironically, this dependence is the very factor that has induced them to develop what may be described today as unsustainable environmental practices. The reasons for this are twofold and mutually reinforcing: indigenous peoples suffer from encroachment on, and dispossession of their territories by settlers, companies, and state agencies. Consequently, their right to self-govern is compromised, and their sources of livelihood are threatened (see Johnson 1992; Erasga 2008; ADB 1998). This, in turn, renders them vulnerable to development processes and practices, which has led them to devise resource-extractive means of survival (Charters and Stavenhagen 2009; de Varennes 1996; Indigenous Peoples Plan 2002).

Sustainability Predicaments

The twin issues of vulnerability and poverty have always been at the root of the hesitation, on the part of states and governments, to define their own responsibilities toward indigenous peoples or their rights-based agenda. A corpus of research-based statistics has documented the plight of indigenous peoples around the world (Howitt, Connell, and Hirsch 1996). Given their socioeconomic, political, and linguistic uniqueness in relation to the general population to whom they have been compared, they have often experienced the burdens of being "second class citizens" and of being treated as such even in their own countries (Erasga 2008; Errico 2007; Tennant 1994). The forces of globalization have been responsible for this phenomenon. All over the world indigenous cultures are threatened by the persistent spread of Western culture with its emphasis on individualism, competitiveness, consumerism, and technological advancement (ADB 1998; Perera 2009). So-called progress has been synonymous with the forced assimilation of indigenous people so that they might have a chance of survival. A consequence of this forced assimilation is the massive loss of indigenous traditions, bringing about the endangerment of human cultures and, especially, the endangerment of traditional resource management practices (Howitt, Connell, and Hirsch 1996; IFAD 2003; IUCN 1997; Witzig and Ascencios 1999).

India, China, and Southeast Asia

The plight of indigenous peoples in India, China, and Southeast Asia typify the problems faced worldwide vis-à-vis the forces of globalization. In India, the forest has become an icon of their struggles; in China, sustainable water management has brought to the forefront the human-induced environmental problem of drought; and in Southeast Asia, the oil palm industry expansion has jeopardized customary environmental management practices through land expropriation by private and government entities.

India

India's ethnic groups are politically known as the Scheduled Tribes. They are traditionally referred to as Adivasis, which literally means "indigenous peoples" (Bijoy and Raman 2003). There are approximately 622 Scheduled Tribes with an "estimated population of 84.3 million comprising 8.2% of the total population.... The largest populations of IPs are concentrated in the so-called central tribal belt stretching from Rajasthan to West Bengal in the seven states of northeast India" (Karlsson 2008, 24). There are still as many as 635 ethnic groups that qualify for Scheduled Tribes status but are not officially recognized (Mathur 2009).

India has a long history of indigenous peoples' movements aimed at asserting their rights and fighting the violations thereof (Karlsson 2008; Wessendorf 2011). The country has existing laws and legal provisions, such as the Fifth Schedule for mainland India and the Sixth Schedule for certain areas of northeast India, which recognize indigenous peoples' rights to land and self-governance and are aimed at protecting them. The legal measures, however, have numerous loopholes, and their implementation is far from satisfactory (Barsh 1989; Reisman 1995; Singh 1986). Consequently, despite these laws, the Adivasis continue to face civil and political rights violations, land alienation, displacement, and false prosecution for accessing minor forest produce (Rath 2006). With a booming economy, India requires an ever-growing number of resources, and the indigenous peoples' land and resources are being grabbed from them (Mathur 2009). The result is a strong sense of alienation among the indigenous peoples and an exacerbation of conflicts, exemplified by the 2003 "Muthanga incident," in which a major land-occupation movement was conducted by members of the Kadar tribe, which resulted in a confrontation with authorities and fatalities on both sides of the conflict (Bijoy and Raman 2003; Roy 2009; Wessendorf 2011).

China

With an immensely diverse terrain and climate, China also boasts a great diversity of people. The 2000 census reported 105,226,114 people belonging to ethnic minority groups comprising 8.47 percent of the total population of China. The largest ethnic minority group consists of the Han Chinese, numbering 900 million and residing in every region of the country. The smallest group consists of the Hezhen, living in the far northeast, with fewer than 2,000 people (Wessendorf 2011, 244). The Chinese government has not officially recognized the existence of "indigenous peoples" in China. Instead, it refers to its ethnic minorities as "minority groups." Although in principle it is open to recognizing any of these minority groups as its very own indigenous peoples, the present government has not established any clear mechanisms and procedures that may clearly identify which among these ethnic minority groups qualify as indigenous peoples (Chia 2010; Hannum 2011; Sanders 1999). Geographically, these ethnic minorities can be found in the southwest of the country, in the north (a few groups), in the east, and on Hainan Island, where most are subsistence farmers with illiteracy rates of over 50 percent (Wessendorf 2011).

The devastating drought that hit China's southwest provinces starting in the autumn months of 2009 and continuing through the spring of 2010 can be considered a turning point in exploring the issue of Chinese ethnic minorities and the politics of environmental challenges. In its attempts to assess the cause and effects of the disaster, the Chinese government recognized that the drought had undermined the water conservation and irrigation infrastructure of the southwest provinces. The government's proposed solution was to enhance the hydrological facilities in the region, and implement additional engineering projects in order to strengthen the ability to combat future droughts. What the government failed to realize is that the environmental devastation of the southwest provinces—areas inhabited by ethnic minority peoples—was in fact the direct result of the economic development process and of overexploitation of the land (Wessendorf 2011). The encroachment of the lands that have traditionally and historically been occupied by ethnic minorities, on the part of government agencies operating "in the name of development," further exacerbates the environmental impacts of natural disasters.

Southeast Asia

An estimated two-thirds of the total 300 million population of indigenous peoples worldwide live in Asia. The forested regions of Southeast Asia are home to a large number of indigenous peoples. As in China, few states in Southeast Asia recognize their indigenous peoples, and even if they do, they do not take into account their identity during preparations of national censuses. It is therefore very difficult to give accurate or even approximate figures for the populations of indigenous peoples in the Southeast Asia region (AIPP, IWGIA, and FORUM-ASIA, 2010).

There are many issues confronting the ethnic minorities of the Southeast Asian region vis-à-vis their natural resources and global trades. Of note is the expansion of the oil palm industries in the countries of Indonesia, Philippines, Malaysia, Vietnam, Cambodia, and Thailand. The Forest Peoples Programme, *Sawit Watch* (an Indonesian organization that is against oil palm plantations), and other partners have documented and published the implications of these expansions in several installments. According to the sixth volume of the regional study, the oil palm industry expansion has wrought unexpected consequences that transformed "land tenure systems and foster[ed] insecurities of subsistence livelihoods, conflicts and resentments, landlessness and evictions, re-arrangements of ownership, management, occupation, exploitation and utilization of land, forest, water and other natural resources" (Colchester and Chao 2011, iii).

The general principles uncovered by the regional study suggest that land allocations and land use planning carried out by government agencies in areas inhabited by indigenous peoples have inevitably transformed the latter's resource management practices (e.g., slash-and-burn agriculture, which involves cutting and burning forested areas to create fields) into destructive forest activities. Legal discourse has it that fallows (fields that are left unused during a growing season) are simply "unused lands," and are therefore suitable for reforestation. If fallow areas are planted with trees, indigenous peoples have "no choice when the time comes to re-use the land other than to clear another area for their crops or to cut down the planted trees" (Lang 2002, as cited in Colchester and Chao 2011, iii).

Aspirations and Sustainability

Indigenous peoples' aspirations are critical starting points toward a sustainable course of action that can be undertaken not only *by* international institutions and states on their own, but *in unison with* the ethnic minorities themselves. It was along this line of thought that the

International Fund for Agricultural Development (IFAD) was established in 1976 with the mandate "to combat hunger and rural poverty in developing countries, especially low-income, food-deficit countries, and to improve the livelihoods of rural poor people on a sustainable basis" (IFAD 2003, ii). The IFAD mandate defines hunger "not just as a food production and supply issue, but also as a livelihood issue" (IFAD 2003, ii). IFAD also recognizes that, among the poor, the indigenous peoples continue to be the poorest and most affected by hunger and hence need the most attention. In its discussion paper on the nexus of indigenous peoples and sustainable development, IFAD lists four key principles defining the rights-based aspirations of indigenous peoples: recognition and respect of indigenous peoples' rights; respect of indigenous peoples culture and knowledge system; right to meaningful participation; and autonomy of action (IFAD 2003, 16–17).

Interestingly, these rights-based aspirations are both sustainable and environmental in orientation. Governments, institutions, and indigenous people can find common grounds for collaboration. IFAD has already identified three areas that can serve as a valuable starting point: strengthening or recovering peoples' rights to their ancestral lands and related resources; supporting the preparation and implementation of land management plans incorporating indigenous knowledge systems; and working out innovative mechanisms for compensating indigenous peoples for the environmental services they provide to the global economy (IFAD 2003, 14–15). The benefits of these collaborative efforts would likely be valuable on national, regional, and global levels.

Dennis S. ERASGA
De La Salle University–Manila

See also China; Ecotourism; Education, Female; India; Microfinance; Nongovernmental Organizations (NGOs); Property Rights (China); Public Health; Religions; Rural Development; Rural Livelihoods; Southeast Asia; Three Gorges Dam; Traditional Chinese Medicine (TCM); Traditional Knowledge (China); Traditional Knowledge (India)

FURTHER READING

Asia Indigenous Peoples' Pact (AIPP), the International Work Group for Indigenous Affairs (IWGIA) & Asian Forum for Human Rights and Development (FORUM-ASIA). (2010). ASEAN's indigenous peoples. Chiang Mai, Thailand: AIPP/IWGIA/FORUM-ASIA.

Asian Center for the Progress of People (ACPP). (2009). Backgrounder on situation of Adivasis in south India. Retrieved March 14, 2012, from http://www.acpp.org/uappeals/bground/Adivasis%20in%20SIndia.htm

Asian Development Bank (ADB). (1998). The bank's policy on indigenous peoples. Mandaluyong City, Philippines: ADB.

Asian Indigenous and Tribal Peoples Network (AITPN). (2009). The state of India's indigenous and tribal peoples. Retrieved Sept 12, 2011, from http://www.aitpn.org/Reports/Tribal_Peoples_2009.pdf

Barsh, Russel Lawrence. (1989). United Nations seminar on indigenous peoples and states. *The American Journal of International Law, 83*(3), 599–604.

Bijoy, C. R., & Raman, K. Ravi. (2003). Muthanga: The real story; Adivasi movement to recover land. *Economic and Political Weekly, 38*(20), 1975–1977, 1979–1982.

Bowen, John R. (2000). Should we have a universal concept of "indigenous peoples" rights? Ethnicity and essentialism in the twenty-first century. *Anthropology Today, 16*(4), 12–16.

Burman, J. J. Roy. (2009, July 25). Adivasi: A contentious term to denote tribes as indigenous peoples of India. *Mainstream, 47*(32). Retrieved August 20, 2011, from http://www.mainstreamweekly.net/article1537.html

Charters, Claire, & Stavenhagen, Rodolfo. (Eds.). (2009). *Making the declaration work: The United Nations Declaration on the Rights of Indigenous Peoples.* Copenhagen, Denmark: IWGIA.

Chia, Tek khiam. (2010). Taiwan: No indigenous people claimed China. Retrieved August 20, 2011, from http://www.indigenousportal.com/heritage/taiwan-no-indigenous-people-claimed-china.html

Chinese Embassy. (1997, April 1). China concerned with protection of indigenous peoples' rights. Retrieved August 12, 2011, from http://www.china-embassy.ch/eng/ztnr/rqwt/t138829.htm

Colchester, Marcus, & Chao, Sophie. (Eds.). (2011). Oil palm expansion in South East Asia: Trends and implications for local communities and indigenous peoples. Forest Peoples Programme. Retrieved March 5, 2012, from http://www.forestpeoples.org/sites/fpp/files/publication/2011/11/oil-palm-expansion-south-east-asia-final.pdf

Davis, Sheldon. (1988). *Indigenous peoples, environmental protection and sustainable development.* Gland, Switzerland: IUCN.

de Varennes, Fernand. (1996). *Internationale Zeitschrift für Erziehungswissenschaft: Revue Internationale de l'Education* [Minority aspirations and the revival of indigenous peoples: International review of education]. *The Education of Minorities, 42*(4), 309–325.

Downing, Theodore; Moles, Jerry; McIntosh, Ian; & Garcia-Downing, Carmen. (2002). Indigenous peoples and mining encounters: Strategies and tactics (MMSD Working Paper No. 57). International Institute for Environment and Development (IIED). Retrieved August 28, 2011, from http://pubs.iied.org/pdfs/G00548.pdf

Erasga, Dennis. (2008). Ancestral domain claim: The case of the indigenous people in Muslim Mindanao (ARMM). *Asia-Pacific Social Science Review, 8*(1), 33–44.

Errico, Stefania. (2007). The draft UN Declaration on the rights of indigenous peoples: An overview. *Human Rights Law Review, 7*(4), 741–755.

Hannum, Emily. (2011). Ethnic disparities in China: Geography, rurality, and socioeconomic welfare. (Indigenous Peoples, China Country Brief No 3). Washington, DC: World Bank.

Herz, Richard. (1993). Legal protection for indigenous cultures: Sacred sites and communal rights. *Virginia Law Review, 79*(3), 691–716.

Howitt, Richard; Connell, John; & Hirsh, Philip. (Eds.). (1996). Resources, nations and indigenous peoples: Case studies from Australasia, Melanesia and Southeast Asia. Melbourne, Australia: Oxford University Press.

Indigenous Peoples' Plan of Implementation on Sustainable Development. (2002). Retrieved September 10, 2011, from http://www.dialoguebetweennations.com/ir/english/kariocakimberley/IndigenousPeoplesPlan.htm

International Fund for Agricultural Development (IFAD). (2003). Indigenous peoples and sustainable development. Roundtable discussion paper for the twenty-fifth anniversary session of IFAD's governing council. Retrieved September 23, 2011, from http://www.ifad.org/gbdocs/gc/26/e/ip.pdf

International Labour Organization (ILO). (1989). Convention (NO.169) concerning indigenous and tribal peoples in independent countries. *International Labour Office, Official Bulletin, 72*, series A, number 2.

International Union for the Conservation of Nature (IUCN) Inter-Commission Task Force on Indigenous Peoples. (1997). *Indigenous peoples and sustainability: Cases and actions*. Utrecht, The Netherlands: International Books.

Johnson, Martha. (Ed.). (1992). *Lore: Capturing traditional environmental knowledge*. Ottawa, Canada: IDRC.

Karlsson, Bengt. (2008). Asian indigenousness: The case of India. *Indigenous Affairs*, 3–4. Copenhagen, Denmark: IWGIA.

Lang, Chris. (2002). *The pulp invasion: The international pulp and paper industry in the Mekong Region (Thailand, Laos, Vietnam, Cambodia)*. Montevideo, Uruguay: World Rainforest Movement.

Mathur, Hari Mohan. (2009). Tribal land issues in India: Communal management, rights, and displacement. In Jayantha Perera (Ed.), *Land and cultural survival: The communal land rights of indigenous peoples in Asia* (pp. 163–192). Mandaluyong City, Philippines: Asian Development Bank.

Mitra, Kinsuk, & Gupta, Radhika. (2009). Indigenous peoples' forest tenure in India. In Jayantha Perera (Ed.), *Land and cultural survival: The communal land rights of indigenous peoples in Asia* (pp. 193–211). Mandaluyong City, Philippines: ADB.

Perera, Jayantha. (2009). Scheduled tribes and other traditional forest dwellers (Recognition of Forest Rights) Act 2006: A charter of forest dwellers' rights? In Jayantha Perera (Ed.), *Land and cultural survival: The communal land rights of indigenous peoples in Asia* (pp. 213–223). Mandaluyong City, Philippines: ADB.

Rath, Govinda C. (2006). *Tribal development in India: The contemporary debate*. Delhi: Sage Publications.

Reisman, Michael. (1995). Protecting indigenous rights in international adjudication. *The American Journal of International Law, 89*(2), 350–362.

Roy, Chandra. (2009). Indigenous peoples in Asia: Rights and development challenges. In Claire Charters & Rodolfo Stavenhagen (Eds.), *Making the declaration work: The United Nations Declaration on the Rights of Indigenous Peoples* (pp. 216–231). Copenhagen, Denmark: IWGIA.

Sanders, Douglas. (1999). Indigenous peoples: Issues of definition. *International Journal of Cultural Property, 8*, 4–13.

Shelton, Dinah. (1991). Human rights, environmental rights, and the right to environment. *Stanford Journal of International Law, 28*, 103–138.

Singh, Chhatrapati. (1986). *Common property, common poverty: India's forests, forest dwellers and the law*. Oxford, UK: OUP.

Stevens, Stan. (Ed.). (1997). *Conservation through cultural survival: Indigenous peoples and protected areas*. Washington, DC: Island Press.

Tennant, Chris. (1994). Indigenous peoples, international institutions, and the international legal literature from 1945–1993. *Human Rights Quarterly, 16* (1), 1–57.

UN Framework Convention on Climate Change (UNFCCC) Intersessional Meeting. (2009). Indigenous peoples and climate change (briefing paper). Retrieved March 29, 2012, from http://www.iwgia.org/iwgia_files_publications_files/0515_Briefing_paper_IPsCC_final.pdf

Wessendorf, Kathrin. (2011). *The indigenous world*. Copenhagen, Denmark: IWGIA.

Witzig, Richard, & Ascencios, Massiel. (1999). The road to indigenous extinction: Case study of resource exportation, disease importation, and human rights violations against the Urarina in the Peruvian Amazon. *Health and Human Rights, 4*(1), 60–81.

World Bank. (2011). Indigenous peoples: Still among the poorest of the poor. Retrieved Oct 7, 2011, from http://siteresources.worldbank.org/EXTINDPEOPLE/Resources/407801-1271860301656/HDNEN_indigenous_clean_0421.pdf

Share the *Encyclopedia of Sustainability*: Teachers are welcome to make up to ten (10) copies of no more than two (2) articles for distribution in a single course or program. For further permissions, please visit www.copyright.com or contact: info@berkshirepublishing.com

Information and Communication Technologies (ICT)

Information and communication technologies (ICT) play a prominent role worldwide, especially in South and East Asia. India and China, the two largest countries in the region and world, have used ICT to promote economic growth and transform their standards of living. Mobile phones and the Internet impact myriad life-changing sectors, such as education and health, to build and sustain the overall growth of these nations. The downside, however, is the e-waste generated, the consequences of which remain a challenge.

Late in the twentieth century, information and communication technologies (ICT) emerged as a major force in the world, changing the way people live, work, communicate, entertain, and govern. South and East Asia were not left untouched, and the region has adopted ICT to drive rapid economic growth and societal changes, leaving behind the legacy of centuries of colonialism. India and China in particular have effectively used ICT as an instrument to propel their economy. Internet and communication technologies have had an impact on livelihood, education, health, financial access, and production and distribution in their rural and remote areas. And yet there is a downside: ICT have started to generate a huge amount of e-waste, and attempts to deal with it have just begun. Nevertheless, most researchers in the field believe in the potential of ICT to further transform these Asian nations in the years to come.

Emergence of ICT

In the 1970s three major technological breakthroughs brought ICT center stage. The first was digitization of signals and systems. The early electrical signals we encountered, such as voice, pictures, and video, were all analog electrical signals. Analog signals are continuous in time (implying that they need to be defined for all time instants) and continuous in amplitude (they can take any amplitude value). The Swedish American engineer Harry Nyquist discovered a sampling theorem (Marks 1991) several decades before the 1970s to enable analog signals to be sampled or discretized in time (Haugen 2005) without any loss of signal. An analog signal could thus be quantized (Rabaey 2003) or discretized in amplitude domain, and the resulting digital signal could now be represented by a string of numbers (for example, 10110010110, if coded using a binary number system). Furthermore, these digitized voice/video signals could be stored digitally and, more importantly, processed digitally. Systems themselves became digital, whether they were communication systems like telephones or entertainment systems like television.

A breakthrough came with the advent of the integrated circuit (IC) technologies (Luo, Hong, and Rashid 2005). Circuits could now be manufactured as ICs, using a process similar to printing. Most of the costs for ICs were in the design and the development of masks (i.e., IC layouts) used for production; production of ICs involved little additional cost. Also, the IC-making process could be improved year after year to reduce cost, size, and power consumption. The well-known concept of "Moore's law" captures this phenomenon in which the "size, cost and power-consumption of digital ICs halve every eighteen months" (Marks and Gray 1954). This exponential phenomenon implies that a digital IC would cost one thousand times less in fifteen years when produced in large numbers and a million times less in thirty years. So far, at least into the second decade of the twenty-first century, Moore's law has held, and the prices of electronic goods have fallen year after year. Furthermore, ICs make electronic systems highly reliable, enabling them to be operated twenty-four hours a day and seven days a week without being switched off.

Another breakthrough was the design of a processor IC, where the software drives the kind of processing that will be carried out (Anderson 2005). So instead of building different circuits to carry out different types of processing, a system could be designed using a microprocessor or digital signal processor (DSP), and relevant software could be used to drive the processor to carry out the required processing at different times (Porat 1996). This had several implications. First, hardware design became simpler; instead of designing different circuits for different kinds of processing, a single processor would suffice. Second, the system design would now primarily involve the design of software to carry out the various required processing. The latter had profound impact especially on India, as the country used its software skills to become a forerunner in ICT system design.

These three sets of innovation came together, allowing ICT to prevail. Things that could barely be imagined earlier could now be built, and these things could be mass-produced with a high degree of reliability. More importantly, their cost and power consumption would continuously decrease, thereby becoming highly affordable.

Telephony, Television, Computers, and Internet

Among the large number of tools and appliances provided by information and communications technologies, telephony, television, computers, and Internet have perhaps made the largest impact. Emerging nations of South and East Asia had very few telephones for their large population until around 1990, as the investment required for each line was quite high. The digitalization of telephony started in the late 1970s with long-distance lines adopting digital communications, initially on copper wires (Manning 1999). Soon microwave communication links (IEEE 2008) and fiber optic communication links (Graham-Smith 2000) were adopted for interexchange and long-distance trunks. This made the intercity calls reliable and inexpensive. As telephone exchanges got digitized using digital switching and computers for controls (Harte 2003), costs decreased drastically. But the local loop, the buried copper line between an exchange and the subscriber's home/office, remained expensive and difficult to install (Jhunjhunwala, Jalihal, and Giridhar 2000). Mobile telephony made this local loop wireless and also enabled subscribers to communicate even on the move (Klingenbrunn and Mogensen 1998). Complete digitalization of telephone networks (true to plan according to Moore's law) took a few more years to bring down the cost, thereby making telephony highly affordable. As of 2011 China had 916.53 million and India had 892.55 million mobiles and telephones empowering them not only to communicate, but also to carry out their business more efficiently (Reuters 2011; TRAI n.d.). (See figure 1.) Most of these are mobile phones, however, and

Figure 1. Number of Telephones in India and China (in Millions)

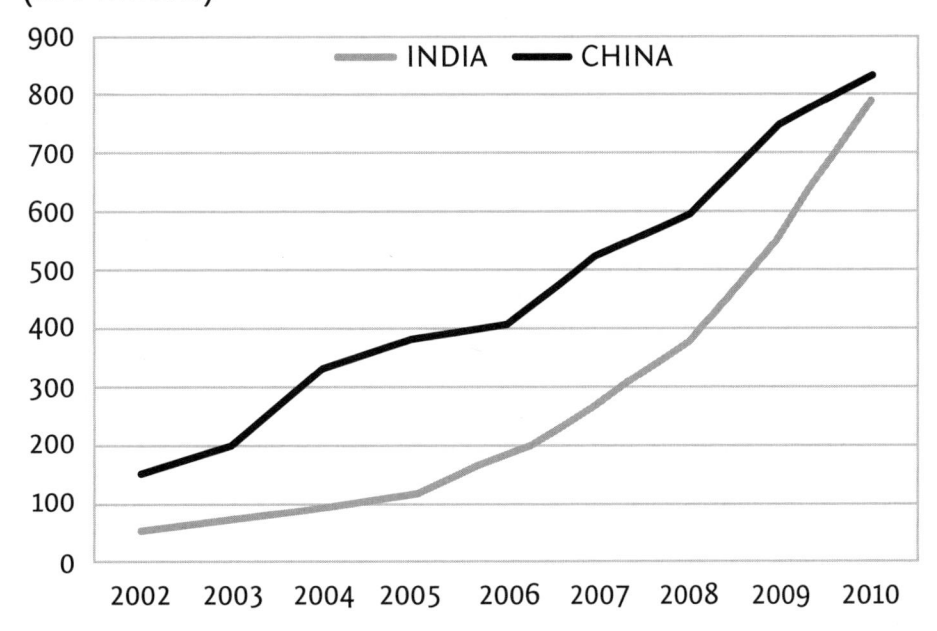

Source: (India) TRAI (n.d); (China) National Bureau of Statistics of China (2011).

Millions and millions of mobile phones empower people in India and China not only to communicate, but also to better conduct their business.

the number of landlines in these countries is small. The implication is that, unlike the West, even for Internet, both countries have to depend on wireless communications.

Television has also grown in India and China. For example, India had barely 10 million television sets in early 1990s, while the number of televisions owned in 2011 was nearly 116.5 million (Government of India 2011b). The use of ICs lowered the costs of television sets enabling many Indian homes to acquire them. These TVs were initially cable TVs, where a large satellite dish in the neighborhood received analog TV signals from the satellite and distributed it to nearby homes (Goodman 1996; US Congressional Record 2000). Digitization of video signals, however, enabled direct-to-home (DTH) TV, where a much smaller dish could receive the digitized TV signals directly from satellite, increasing the quality and reach (Bhasi 2003).

Indian academia had adopted computers even in the 1960s, and a good number of students were trained to program and use them. The advent of computerization of businesses and offices in the West created a huge demand for trained personnel proficient in handling computers, and some computer-literate youth from India migrated to the United States and Europe to take up these positions. But late in the 1970s, as the prices of the computers fell and some communication links from the West to India became available, Indian entrepreneurs found an opportunity to get computer work outsourced from the West to India. Leveraging India's computer skills and its English-language fluency, this information technology (IT) outsourcing industry continued to grow and has become one of the largest employers in India. In 2010, IT outsourcing revenue was 23.4 billion USD and it contributed to 7 percent of India's GDP (Maps of India 2011). China has also seen a great potential in the IT services industry, but could not build it significantly due to its weaker computer and language skills. China has a massive program to overcome these weaknesses and expand its IT services industry (Schwarz 2006).

As microprocessors transformed computers for personal use their prices (helped by Moore's law) continued to decline, and they became affordable to people from upper- and middle-class backgrounds in India and China. Business and offices were the first to take advantage, resulting in a huge gain in productivity. Home computers were still limited, however, until the Internet became available. The Internet, to which computers connect by servers, presented users with the opportunity to access data, whether through servers located at an office, school, or other public institution. The Internet was no longer merely a data source (Deitel, Deitel, and Goldberg 2003); the World Wide Web further enhanced the types of data that users could access and enabled access to all kinds of information and services. The Web gradually became a platform for entertainment, education, and conducting business. Voice and video on the Internet further enriched it (DeSantis 2006).

Internet services and applications, however, require a reasonably high bit-rate Internet link in the twenty-first century. Low bit-rate data communication on telephones and 2G mobiles, used widely in Asia, were not adequate for this purpose (Selian n.d.; Stoefga and Llamas 2009). The nations needed to extend broadband data communication to the homes and offices of their citizens. China did just that, enabling 420 million broadband connections for its citizens (Internet World Statistics 2010) using a mixture of 3G mobile and wired broadband to get there (Trillium Digital Systems 2000). (See figure 2). India has lagged, having just about 12.32 million broadband connections in 2011 and only 100 million of its 1.2 billion people connected to the Internet (MediaNama 2011). The 3G and 4G mobiles are just being introduced with a hope of accelerating this pace.

China is a large country with a huge population speaking many dialects and languages. In order to surmount the language barrier, the country made efforts to indigenize its computers and Internet with characters in Mandarin (the country's "common tongue" taught in schools and understood by most Chinese throughout the world) (Su 2012). A vast amount of content, combined with a plethora of services, became available in Mandarin. China had an estimated 240 million Internet users in 2010, representing roughly 23 percent of the world's Internet users (Internet World Stats 2011). People in India speak as many as twenty major languages but the country does not have a common script or language (Maps of India 2001). English, therefore, has become the common language, even though only about 10.4 percent of its population can read and write it (*Times of India* 2010; Graddol 2010). Many Indians from the lower middle class and poorer sections of the society are not comfortable using the Internet because it lacks Indian-language content.

Leveraging ICT

South and East Asia, particularly China and India, have leveraged ICT to enhance their respective economic development. In the 1980s China became the outsourcing destination for manufacturing. Companies in the West shifted their manufacturing facilities to China, primarily because of its abundant supply of disciplined low-cost labor. As a consequence, the use of ICT for managing the supply chain and manufacturing began.

Electronics assembling and manufacturing, including integrated circuit (IC) manufacturing, was one major industry that expanded through outsourcing. By the 1990s, China had acquired significant skills in this area. The Chinese government, seeing an opportunity, encouraged the local electronics industry by providing tax

Figure 2. Number of Internet Users in India and China (in Millions)

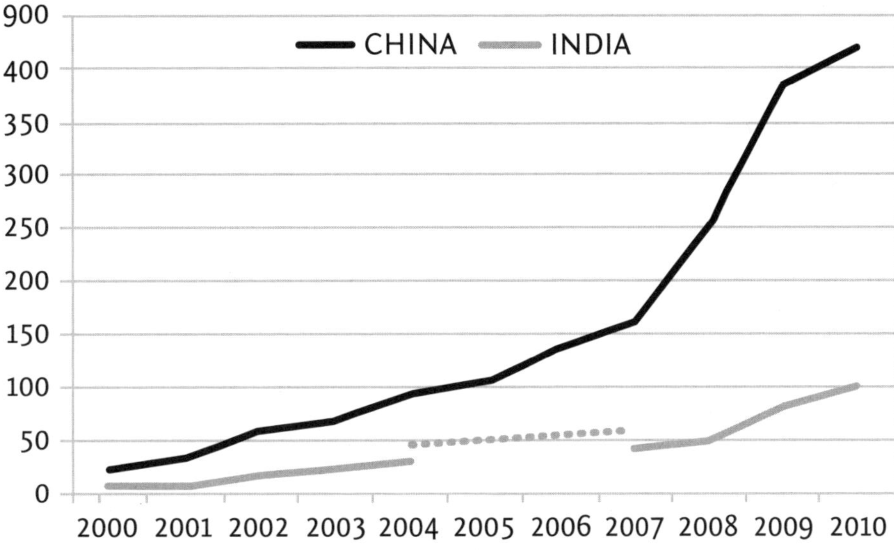

Source: (India) TRAI (n.d); (China) National Bureau of Statistics of China (2011).

Broadband penetration in both the countries over the years (the dotted line indicates that data for India from 2004 to 2007 is unverifiable).

incentives, market protection, infrastructure creation, and investments. By the year 2000, electronics hardware manufacturing became China's strength. With huge investments from the industry and the government in research and development (R&D), China soon became the center of hardware design and manufacturing. Subsequently the major industry of Chinese products emerged, and Chinese companies such as Huawei and ZTE are amongst the leading telecom product companies in the world (Australian Business Forum 2011; Lynch 2012). Companies such as Foxconn, SMIC, and Hynix STM are the leading IC foundries (Chai 2011). At the same time, a major chunk of electronics manufacturing (of mobile phones, televisions, set-top converter boxes, computers, and so forth) is done in China. In 2007, the manufacturing industry contributed to almost 50 percent of China's GDP (Cho 2009).

While China built its ICT hardware industry, India focused on its software industry. In the 1980s India had set up numerous software outsourcing companies, which carried out software development and maintenance for companies around the world (Overby 2010). Leveraging its skilled manpower and using simple computers and communication links, work for Western companies was carried out in India. It started with low-end software and data-entry work, but in a decade and a half it graduated to complex software and designs. By the turn of the century, India had become the software outsourcing capital of the world. In 2010, the industry employed 2.3 million people and contributed to 6.4 percent of India's GDP (CII 2011).

At the same time, both countries extended ICT-based telephone and Internet services to their citizens. But these countries went far beyond providing mere telecom and Internet services in the first decade of the twenty-first century. Banking has been transformed in both the countries using core banking; anywhere, anytime, electronic banking is now available with major banks. Vigorous efforts are being made to provide banking services on mobile phones. In India, local language voice banking is being introduced to cater to its semiliterate and illiterate population, where a customer just talks to the bank's computer using a phone to carry out banking transactions (Jhunjhunwala and Rangarajan 2011). ATMs are proliferating in cities, and India is now installing solar-powered rural ATMs in its villages (Vortex 2011). At the same time, India has converted some of its retail shops to provide banking services (including deposits and withdrawals) using Banking Correspondents (RBI 2006). Tax payment and filing are now available on the Internet, and registered companies can carry out their accounts filing electronically. Most companies, large- as well as medium-sized, have started using ICT internally to enhance efficiency. Accounts procurement, human resources services, production management, supply-chain management, and delivery are being increasingly computerized. A few companies have also been using ICT to enhance their market reach, though such applications have a long way to go. Small companies, however, have yet to leverage ICT. China has a very mature e-market (China Internet Watch 2011), whereas India (though lagging) had around 50–80 million online customers in 2010 (Online Trends 2010). Digital advertising is therefore making its mark. Travel tickets and hotel booking are all being done online. Takeoff of e-governance services, however, has been slow even though there are strong government programs supporting it (Jhunjhunwala 2011b).

On the whole, South and East Asia have leveraged ICT services well, both for leapfrogging their economy, as well as for enhancing efficiency in manufacturing and service delivery.

Empowering Rural Areas Through ICT

Though there has been significant rural-to-urban migration, a large percentage of the population in India and China (68 percent in India [Government of India 2011a] and 50 percent in China [National Bureau of Statistics of China 2011]) continue to live in rural areas. The overall economy of these nations has been growing rapidly, but their rural economies continue to trail their urban counterparts (*Financial Express* 2011; *Economic Times* 2011; *China Daily* 2010). This is a major problem and a source of considerable tension. The first benefit of ICT that rural India and China have received is in the form of mobile phones and television (some DTH and some cable TV). As a result, they are better connected to the world, and mobile phones have enabled them to access market prices for their agricultural produce as well as for inputs. In China, rural people have started getting broadband on mobiles, enabling them to access many new services; rural India has yet to experience such benefits.

ICT has an as yet unrealized potential to bridge this urban–rural gap and empower rural people. Many interesting experiments are being conducted toward using ICT as a tool for overcoming the urban–rural divide. Over the last decade there has been a large focus on setting up telecenters in villages both in India and China (IL&FS 2006; Soriano 2007). They have failed, however, to make any remarkable impact so far (Jhunjhunwala and Ramachandran 2004). Other kinds of ICT initiatives, some of which are described in the following section, appear to have greater potential.

ICT-Based Outsourcing of Manufacturing and Services

In the twentieth century rapid developments took place first in East Asia, when manufacturing was outsourced from the West to this region to take advantage of lower labor costs. China significantly benefited from this outsourcing. Later in the century a flurry of outsourcing of IT-based services occurred from the West to East Asia, particularly India, driven mainly by the availability of an abundance of trained personnel who could be hired for low wages. Asian nations used this huge available human resource to bring in manufacturing and services to their countries, consequently developing their regions.

In the early twenty-first century, similar large differences exist between the urban and rural parts of these nations. Labor is inexpensive and abundant in rural India and China as compared to their urban areas. Is it possible to outsource IT-based services and manufacturing from urban areas to rural areas?

In India several IT-enabled service companies like DesiCrew (2009) and Rural Shores (n.d.) have emerged, which are setting up their service centers in villages. They obtain the work from urban areas and transfer it to these rural centers for execution. Training, delivery management, and quality management are all done remotely from their urban centers. On one hand, the companies are leveraging the low-cost resources in villages. On the other hand, such initiatives encourage the educated younger generation to stay in villages instead of migrating to urbanized cities. For the village this generates some wealth and also instills confidence in the rural youth that deliver quality services to urban India. Still in its nascent stage, this rural business process outsourcing (BPO) is likely to create massive employment in the future, as larger IT companies see it as a means to enhance their cost efficiency.

While the rural BPO employs educated youth in villages, another kind of distributed IT-enabled enterprise, which outsources manufacturing to rural India, is emerging. Once again orders are obtained in urban India and manufacturing is carried out in rural India. The initial focus is on products that do not require heavy machinery or large amounts of electric power. Furthermore, some of the raw materials for these products are obtained from rural areas. ROPE (2011), a startup of the Rural Technology and Business Incubator (RTBI 2010) of IIT Madras, has set up manufacturing outfits in several villages and uses natural fiber made out of bamboo as a raw material. By obviating the need to travel to find work, and by providing a safe workplace, women employees especially value ROPE-sponsored programs. ROPE uses ICT for training, process control, and quality control and is setting up remote video facilities in some of their centers.

The Chinese government has also been focused on moving manufacturing from coastal areas by encouraging enterprises to set up production in inland and minority-dominated areas and by using ICT to manage production. This has been coupled with offers of tax deductions and exemptions for such enterprises. Also the Chinese *hukou* (household registration) system (Congressional Executive Commission of China 2006; Chan and Zhang 1998), which enables residents to access healthcare and education only in their hometowns, provides an added incentive for migrants to return inland, reducing labor costs there (*Economist* 2012).

Outsourcing of manufacturing and IT-enabled services may be an important source of livelihood in the years to come for rural areas, therefore slowing down the rural-to-urban migration. The youth who thereby decide to remain in their Asian villages may prove to be instrumental in refurbishing them.

Rural ICT-Based Education and Health Care

Rural areas in India and China lack quality education and health care facilities. Even where health centers and hospitals exist, there is a dearth of efficient doctors. Many Indian rural teachers lack the ability to impart quality education. It is here that ICT-based education and health care promise to be magic tools. Since the year 2000, a number of experiments in these sectors have been conducted. Unfortunately most have not been able to become financially self-sustainable and scalable, and most have failed. Despite these failures, there are glimpses of solutions emerging, bringing some new hope. This section briefly touches upon a few of these experiments in India.

Around the year 2000, several village Internet centers in the southern part of India started taking photographs of the eyes of patients and sending them to doctors in urban hospitals to obtain diagnoses and opinions on treatment (Jhunjhunwala, Ramachandran, and Bandyopadhyay 2004). Doctors diagnosed some patients suffering from acute cataracts, a condition requiring immediate surgery. Email and photographs were soon replaced by low-resolution video-conferencing between rural patients and urban doctors, which proved to be fairly successful for eye care, skin care, and sometimes even psychiatric care. The tool was also used for getting urban veterinarians to treat animals. As doctors expressed the need to examine patients beyond what video conferencing made possible, a startup company, Neurosynaptic (2010), took the initiative of designing and commercializing an Internet-based, low-cost, remote telemedicine kit. This enabled doctors to measure the temperature, blood pressure, pulse count, heartbeat, and ECG of the patients remotely. As several centers started using the kit, many reached the consensus that there was a need to distribute medicines in villages. Despite making headway, this service could not be made financially sustainable.

Another experiment (First Care 2010) involved village health practitioners (VHPs) who do not have the requisite qualification to practice as a doctor. But in absence of qualified doctors, VHPs end up providing the medical services in the village. The efforts of First Care involved the use of ICT to train these VHPs to address some simple ailments but to refer patients to town doctors in case of serious illness. Mobile phones were used to get the VHPs to consult doctors for the treatment and suggest test labs if appropriate. Phones also provided a basic patient health record on the Internet cloud, which could be maintained and referred to by VHPs. The experiment did yield positive results, but the Medical Council of India (MCI) objected to the use of VHPs to provide even basic care. Many feel, however, that combining the remote tele-diagnostic methods with the use of trained VHPs could possibly provide sustainable health care in villages.

There have been a number of attempts to strengthen education in rural India using computers and communications. The Azim Premji Foundation (2012) has prepared a large amount of material to make learning more interesting and conceptual. Similarly, IL&FS took an initiative (K-yan n.d.) to prepare computer-based educational materials from kindergarten to the twelfth grade. IIT Madras came up with material to provide better coaching to those rural students who were going to take school-leaving (i.e., graduate certification) board exams (RTBI 2009). InOpen, a company incubated by IIT Bombay, has come up with computer-based learning materials called Computer Masti (2012), which are to be offered to schools. A number of states have taken the initiative to install computers and provide connectivity in some rural schools. All these initiatives have so far failed to come up with a delivery model that works in villages, however, where the electric-grid supply is unreliable (power failure could be as high as twenty hours a day) and school buildings are often in shambles. Private initiatives to set up computer-based learning centers have sometimes worked in towns, but rarely in small villages.

Even among these failures, there have been some isolated successes. In the absence of better alternatives, experiments on ICT-based health care and education delivery may have to be continued to come up with answers.

The Downside of ICT Expansion

Even though ICT has indeed empowered East Asia, the downside of the technologies, which include the increased use of energy, increased radiofrequency (RF) radiation, and the generation of e-waste, requires monitoring.

ICT significantly increases the use of electrical power. India and China depend primarily on coal to generate their electrical power, and thus this increased use of electricity impacts the environment adversely.

Figure 3a. India's Fuel Generation Capacity (in megawatts)

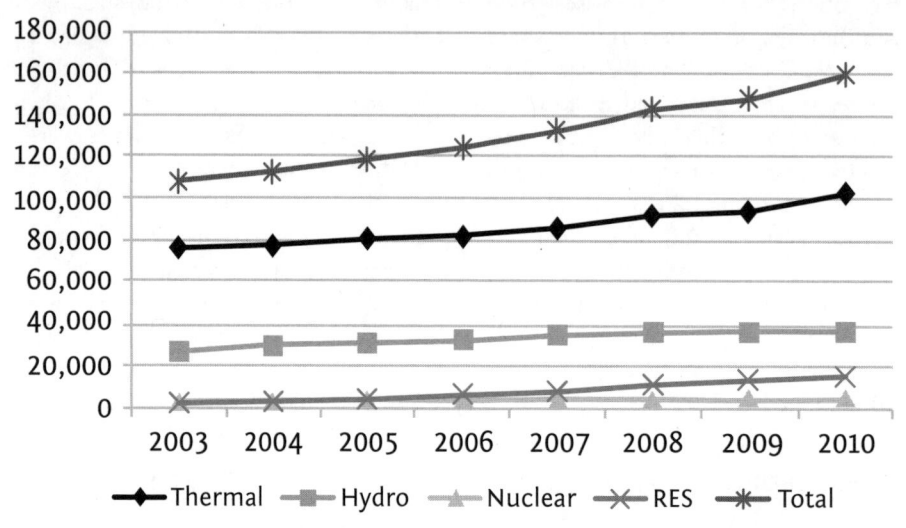

Source: Jhunjhunwala (2011).

Figure 3b. China's Fuel Generation Capacity (millions of tonnes of oil equivalent)

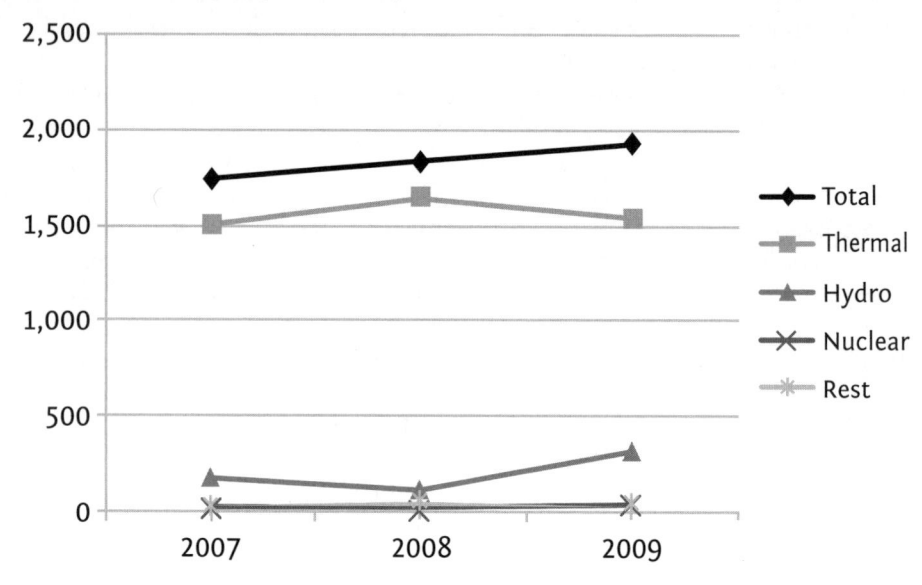

Source: EIA (2012).

Figures 3a (for India from 2003 to 2010) and 3b (for China from 2007 to 2009) track the countries' total capacity for generating fuel capacity based on using several types of power.

(See figures 3a and 3b.) The problem is exacerbated because these nations face huge power shortages, especially in their hinterlands, and they have started using inefficient diesel-power generation and battery backups. Fortunately, Moore's law is helping reduce the power consumption of all electronic items every year, thereby partially alleviating the problem. As of 2011, India and China have also started using decentralized solar-power generation, which is far more environmentally friendly.

The increased use of wireless communication between people and things also results in the proliferation of RF radiation from a large number of wireless devices. Even though the radiation level emanating from most devices is very low, the long-term impact of such continuous radiation on any form of life is not yet known. The larger culprit may be the cellular base stations on towers. As more and more spectrum is used for broadband communication, the power transmitted by these base stations is likely to increase significantly. Even though the total radiation is below the internationally accepted norm, it is imperative that R&D teams come up with architectures to reduce the power transmitted per bit by a factor of ten or even one hundred, to alleviate any long-term consequences.

"E-waste is the third direct impact of increasing use of ICT. It refers to any electrical appliance which is old, obsolete, having reached the end of its life and which has been discarded by its owners" (MAIT, GTZ, and IMRB 2007). Obsolete computers, mobile phones, radios, TV sets, and so forth are all examples of e-waste. All the e-wastes generated from electronic devices contain precious metals such as gold, palladium, and silver as well as poisonous substances like lead, mercury, and cadmium. Recycling of e-wastes is not environment friendly because of the emission of toxins that are hazardous to not just humans but also to flora and fauna.

With the rapid strides that India and China have taken in the ICT sector, they have also become the dumping yard for the e-wastes generated from all over the world. Several prevalent e-waste disposal methods exist in both countries, and their governments have instituted and adopted policies in recent times to tackle the environmental issues posed by e-waste.

"According to a survey by IRG [International Resource Group] systems South Asia, a subsidiary of the IRG, Washington DC, USA, the total waste from electronic and electrical equipment in India has been estimated to be 146,180 tonnes per year" (Waste2resource 2009). According to a MAIT-GTZ report, India had generated 332,979 tonnes of e-waste in 2007 (MAIT, GTZ, and IMRB 2007). (See table 1.) Furthermore, 50,000 tonnes were illegally imported. The e-wastes processed were just 19,000 tonnes, or merely 5 percent of the total quantity generated. The remaining e-waste either proliferated into the recycling sector, mainly in the form of TVs and mobile phones, or remained in the company warehouses. The report has also pointed out that about 94 percent of the organizations that were a part of the survey conducted did not have any e-waste disposal policy.

Until 2011, India did not have any effective e-waste management policy in place. In 2011, the Department of Information Technology (government of India) instituted the National Electronics Policy 2011 (NEP 2011) to facilitate, in part, best practices of e-waste handling. The policy includes: (a) creating a system in tandem with industry to streamline the implementation of e-waste Management and Handling Rules 2011; (b) streamlining procedures to prevent e-waste dumping in India; (c) facilitating the implementation of the Extended Producers Responsibility clause under the e-waste Management and Handling Rules 2011; (d) promoting development of the e-waste recycling industry for e-waste produced in the country; and (d) creating a specific motivation within the Electronic Development Fund for the development of IPR and electronics products in green technologies (NEP 2011). The impact of this policy in improving the e-waste recycling scenario can be known only in the future.

In 2007, more than 70 percent of the e-wastes generated in the United States were exported to China. More than 80 percent of people in the Guiyu district have been involved in the unregulated, non-ecofriendly e-waste recycling industry, which results in uncontrolled emissions of toxic substances in the environment. The e-waste statistics for China for 2007 are split as follows: 500,000 tonnes from refrigerators, 1.3 million tonnes from TVs, 300,000 tonnes from personal computers (Johnson 2006; *Science Daily* 2010). The

TABLE 1. E-Waste Data for India, 2007 (in tonnes)

	Components	Generated	Available for Recycling	Processed
Annual e-waste generated: 332,979 tonnes	Computer	56,324	24,000	12,000
E-waste available for recycling: 144,143 tonnes	Mobile phones	1,655	143	7,000
	TVs	275,000	70,000	
E-waste processed 19,000 tonnes	Imports		50,000	
	Total	332,979	144,143	19,000

Source: MAIT, GTZ, and IMRB (2007).

Problems associated with e-waste, present in India as indicated by the figures in this table, contributed to policies instituted by the government in 2011 that aimed to implement best practices in e-waste handling and management.

Chinese government has identified the dangers involved in e-waste recycling in China, and in a bid to ensure environmentally friendly recycling of e-wastes it has come up with a series of regulations. China has used an accommodation policy to regulate e-waste. The Chinese government has set up industrial parks in places like Tianjin, Ningbo, and Zhangzhou for the recycling of e-wastes. These industrial parks are equipped with efficient treatment facilities and are aimed at integrating all the individual efforts through a centralized management of the recycling activities. Most of the recycling activities in these parks are done manually, thereby providing more job opportunities to its populated labor resources. In January 2011, China formulated a new regulation called Regulation on the Administration of the Recovery and Disposal of WEEE [waste electrical and electronic equipment], where the manufacturers and producers are held responsible for the products that they manufacture. In order to help the producers adhere to the new regulation, the government has started a fund to provide subsidies for formal collection and recycling of e-waste. The efficacy of the regulation will be known only after some time has elapsed (Streicher-Porte et al. 2010).

Harnessing the Promises of ICT

ICT, however, promises to make a positive impact in several ways in different parts of the world, and some of these are also in the early stages of implementation in South and East Asia.

Communication technologies promised a reduction in travel, at least work-related travel, as voice and video conferencing became increasingly accessible. As communications emerged, however, the world became more integrated and modes of transportation became more efficient and affordable; thus travel related to work increased as well. Nevertheless, a significant amount of coordination work gets done using voice teleconferencing, and in 2012 technologies continue to improve. Teams distributed in different parts of a country, and even those distributed across the world, work together with regularly scheduled multiparty voice conferencing. Solutions like Skype are being used as a platform for working and for the sharing of ideas by several institutions, both public and private. High-quality video conferencing has also emerged since about 2010, and for the first time it seems that some work-related travel will become unnecessary. This trend can only increase in times to come.

In a similar manner China, and to a lesser extent India, has taken up online consumerism. More and more urban people have access to the Internet and are making purchases online. While buying online does reduce some local travel, it does increase the transport of goods with individualized delivery, and whether online shopping saves energy or not remains to be seen.

In the same fashion, work from home (telecommuting), at least in certain sectors, is on the rise. This may reduce some need for work-related travel, but it increases the risk of blurring work–leisure boundaries. Oftentimes colleagues, business partners, and customers demand instantaneous response from telecommuters; ICT has made this possible.

ICT had already brought increased efficiency to the organization of manufacturing and production. Material handling and logistics, as well as the transport industry, have been transformed. Now decentralized manufacturing is also becoming a reality. Manufacturing trends across the world are coming full circle; the Industrial Revolution centralized manufacturing and now ICT is bringing manufacturing back to local communities. Similarly, the Industrial Revolution moved production from the East to the West; ICT is bringing the manufacturing and services sectors back to the East. Wealth drained from East is now flowing back. This trend promises to continue in the years to come.

Likewise, power generation and distribution were also centralized. The world moved away from using distributed and renewable resources like sun, wind, and small river streams to using fossil fuels like oil and coal. The threat of global warming, the need for rural communities to stand up to the nonrenewable energy sector, and the proliferation of ICT technologies like smart grids are bringing back the use of renewable energy resources.

In other words, ICT give sustainability a lever. The potential, however, needs to be harnessed by the human mind, will, and effort. Information and communication technologies are merely a tool that, alone, would not drive the world in a different direction. But India and China have a great opportunity to harness the potential of ICT to change the world. Their own compulsions may push them a bit in that direction. How far they succeed will become apparent in coming decades.

Ashok JHUNJHUNWALA
Indian Institute of Technology (IIT) Madras

Janani RANGARAJAN
IIT Madras's Rural Technology and Business Incubator (RTBI)

See also Consumerism; Corporate Accountability (China); E-Waste; Green Collar Jobs; Labor; Media Coverage of the Environment; Microfinance; Nanotechnology; Outsourcing and Offshoring; Public Health; Public-Private Partnerships; Rural Development; Rural Livelihoods; Utilities Regulation and Energy Efficiency

Further Reading

Anderson, John B. (2005). Digital transmission engineering: Volume 12 of IEEE series on digital & mobile communication (2nd ed.). Hoboken, NJ: John Wiley & Sons.

Australian Business Forum. (2011, May 4). Huawei becomes world's number two telecom company by revenue. Retrieved April 11, 2012, from http://www.australianbusinessforum.com.au/_blog/ITmatters_Articles/post/Huawei_becomes_world's_number_two_telecom_company_by_revenue/

Azim Premji Foundation. (2012). Homepage. Retrieved April 9, 2012, from http://www.azimpremjifoundation.org/home.html

Bhasi, K. C. (2003, August). Direct-to-home TV: Transmission and reception. Retrieved April 9, 2012, from http://www.electronicsforu.com/EFYLinux/efyhome/cover/aug2003/DTH-TV.pdf

Chai, Nobunaga. (2011, January 24). Greater China IC foundry overview. Retrieved April 5, 2012, from http://www.digitimes.com/Reports/Report.asp?datepublish=2011/1/24&pages=RS&seq=400&read=toc

China Daily. (2010, January 22). China's urban rural income gap widens. Retrieved April 9, 2012, from http://www.chinadaily.com.cn/bizchina/2010-01/22/content_9361049.htm

China Internet Watch. (2011, July 26). China online shopping market reached 179.2 billion yuan in Q2. Retrieved April 9, 2012, from http://www.chinainternetwatch.com/1202/china-online-shopping-q2/

Chan, Kam Wing, & Zhang, Li. (1998). The hukou system and rural-urban migration in China: Processes and changes. Retrieved April 5, 2012, from http://csde.washington.edu/downloads/98-13.pdf

Cho, John H. (2009). Transforming China's electronics industry: A roadmap for increasing business value through collaboration and ICT integration. Retrieved April 5, 2012, from http://www.cisco.com/web/about/ac79/docs/pov/China_Electronics_VC_Collab_WP_121109.pdf

Computer Masti. (2012). Homepage. Retrieved April 9, 2012, from http://computermasti.com/

Confederation of Indian Industry (CII). (2011). Changing landscape and emerging trends: Indian IT/ITeS industry. Retrieved April 5, 2012, from http://www.pwc.com/en_IN/in/assets/pdfs/publications-2011/Indian_IT-ITeS_Industry_-_Changing_Landscape_and_emerging_trends.pdf. [Report]

Congressional-Executive Commission on China. (2006). China household registration system: Sustained reform needed to protect China's rural migrants. Retrieved April 4, 2012, from http://www.cecc.gov/pages/news/hukou.php

Deitel, Harvey M.; Deitel, Paul J.; & Goldberg, Andrew B. (2003). *Internet and World Wide Web: How to program* (3rd ed.). Upper Saddle River, NJ: Prentice-Hall.

DeSantis, Matthew. (2006). Understanding voice over Internet protocol (VoIP). Retrieved on April 4, 2012, from http://www.us-cert.gov/reading_room/understanding_voip.pdf

DesiCrew. (2009). Homepage. Retrieved April 9, 2012, from http://desicrew.in/

Economic Times. (2011, May 31). Per capita income in 2010–11 at Rs.54,835. Retrieved April 5, 2012, from http://articles.economictimes.indiatimes.com/2011-05-31/news/29604458_1_capita-income-national-income-economy-at-current-prices

Economist. (2012, February 25). Changing migration patterns: Welcome home. Retrieved April 9, 2012, from http://www.economist.com/node/21548273

Financial Express. (2011, March 8). India's per capita income jumped 14.5%. Retrieved April 5, 2012, from http://www.financialexpress.com/news/india%5Cs-per-capita-income-jumped-14.5/759519/

First Care. (2010). Homepage. Retrieved April 9, 2012, from http://firstcarehealth.in/aboutus.asp

Goodman, Robert L. (1996). *Digital satellite services: Installation and maintenance* (1st ed.). New York: McGraw-Hill and Tab Electronics.

Goodwin, Graham C. (2007). *Sampling of signals*. Newcastle, Australia: University of Newscastle.

Government of India. Ministry of Home Affairs. (2011a). Census of India. Retrieved on April 5, 2012, from http://censusindia.gov.in/

Government of India. Ministry of Home Affairs. (2011b). Census of India: Houselisting and housing census highlights 2011. Retrieved April 12, 2011, from http://www.censusindia.gov.in/2011census/hlo/hlo_highlights.html

Graddol, David. (2010). English next India: The future of English in India. Retrieved April 11, 2012, from http://www.britishcouncil.org/learning-english-next-india-2010-book.pdf

Graham-Smith, Sir Francis. (2000). *Optics and photonics: An introduction* (1st ed.). Hoboken, NJ: John Wiley and Sons.

Harte, Lawrence. (2003). Introduction to telecom switching: Circuit switching, packet switching, optical switching, crossbar, TSI, data routing, and virtual circuits. Fuquay Varina, NC: Althos Publishing.

Haugen, Finn. (2005). Discrete-time signals and systems. Retrieved April 9, 2012, from http://techteach.no/publications/discretetime_signals_systems/discrete.pdf

Infrastructure Leasing & Financial Services Limited (IL&FS). (2006). The common services centre scheme. Retrieved April 5, 2012, from http://www.ilfsindia.com/downloads/bus_concept/CSC_ILFS_website.pdf

Institute of Electrical and Electronics Engineers (IEEE) Global History Network. (2008). Microwave link networks. Retrieved April 5, 2012, from http://www.ieeeghn.org/wiki/index.php/Microwave_Link_Networks

Internet World Stats. (2010). China: Internet usage stats and population report. Retrieved April 5, 2012, from http://www.internetworldstats.com/asia/cn.htm

Internet World Stats. (2011). Top 20 countries with the highest number of Internet users. Retrieved April 18, 2012, from http://www.internetworldstats.com/top20.htm

Jhunjhunwala, Ashok. (2011a). Back-to back: End basics. Retrieved April 9, 2012, from http://egov.eletsonline.com/2011/01/back-to-back-end-basics/

Jhunjhunwala, Ashok. (2011b). Technologies enabling collaborations in Indian context. Retrieved April 9, 2012, from http://www.tenet.res.in/Publications/Presentations/pdfs/Technologies_Enabling_Collaborations_-_F.pdf

Jhunjhunwala, Ashok; Jalihal, Devendra; & Giridhar, Jalihal K. (2000). Wireless in local loop: Some fundamentals. *Journal of IETE, 46*(6).

Jhunjhunwala, Ashok, & Ramachandran, Anuradha. (2004). N-Logue: Building a sustainable rural services organization (Case study: Communication for rural and remote areas.) Retrieved April 9, 2012, from http://www.itu.int/ITU-D/fg7/case_library/case_study_2/Asia/India2.pdf

Jhunjhunwala, Ashok; Ramachandran, Anuradha; & Bandyopadhyay, Alankar. (2004). N-Logue: The story of a rural service provider in India. *Journal of Community Informatics, 1*(1), 30–38.

Jhunjhunwala, Ashok, & Rangarajan, Janani. (2011). Connecting the next billion: Empowering rural India. *IT Professional, 13*(4), 53–55.

Johnson, Tim. (2006, April 9). E-waste dump of the world. Retrieved April 5, 2012, from http://seattletimes.nwsource.com/html/nationworld/2002920133_ewaste09.html

K-Yan. (n.d.). Homepage. Retrieved April 9, 2012, from http://www.k-yan.com/

Klingenbrunn, Thomas, & Mogensen, Preben. (1998). *Capacity of a wireless local loop network based on GSM*. Aalborg, Denmark: Centre for Person Kommunikation, Aalborg University.

Luo, Fanglin; Ye, Hong; & Rashid, Muhammad H. (2005). *Digital power electronics and applications*. San Diego, CA: Academic Press.

Lynch, Grahame. (2012, March 4). Analysis: Global telecommunications with Chinese characteristics. Retrieved April 11, 2012, from http://www.commsday.com/commsday/2012/analysis-global-telecommunications-chinese-characteristics/

Manufacturer's Association for Information Technology (MAIT); The Deutsche Gesellschaft für Technische Zusammenarbeit (German Society for Technical Cooperation) (GTZ); & Indian Market Research Bureau (IMRB). (2007). E-waste Inventorisation in India: MAIT-GTZ study, 2007. New Delhi: IMRB Publications.

Manning, Trevor. (1999). *Microwave radio transmission design guide* (Artech House microwave library). Boston: Artech House Publishers.

Maps of India. (2001). Indian language map. Retrieved April 5, 2012, from http://www.mapsofindia.com/culture/indian-languages.html

Maps of India. (2011). India GDP. Retrieved April 5, 2012, from http://business.mapsofindia.com/india-gdp/

Marks, Robert J. (1991). *Introduction to Shannon sampling theory*. New York: Springer Publications.

Marks, Robert J., & Gray, Truman S. (1954). Applied electronics: A first course in electronics, electron tubes, and associated circuits. Cambridge, MA: The MIT Press.

MediaNama. (2011). June 2011: India has 12.32M broadband connections; 594.73M active mobile. Retrieved April 5, 2012, from http://www.medianama.com/2011/08/223-june-2011-india-has-12-32m-broadband-connections-69-83-of-851-70m-mobile-are-active/

National Bureau of Statistics of China, Government of China. (2011). Communiqué of the National Bureau of Statistics of People's Republic of China on major figures of the 2010 population census (No. 1). Retrieved April 5, 2012, from http://www.stats.gov.cn/english/newsandcomingevents/t20110428_402722244.htm

National Electronics Policy (NEP). (2011). Report of Department of Information Technology, Ministry of Communications and Information Technology, Government of India. Retrieved April 10, 2012, from http://mit.gov.in/sites/upload_files/dit/files/Draft-NationalPolicyonElectronics2011_3102011.pdf

Neurosynaptic. (2010). Homepage. Retrieved April 9, 2012, from http://www.neurosynaptic.com/

Online Marketing Trends. (2010, January 26). India to have 3rd largest online users by 2013. Retrieved April 9, 2012, from http://www.onlinemarketing-trends.com/2010/01/indian-to-have-3rd-largers-online-users.html

Overby, Stephanie. (n.d.). Outsourcing definition and solutions. Retrieved April 5, 2012, from http://www.cio.com/article/40380/Outsourcing_Definition_and_Solutions#disqus_thread

Porat, Boaz. (1996). *A course in digital signal processing*. Hoboken, NJ: John Wiley and Sons Inc.

Qiang, Christine Zhen-Wei; Bhavnani, Asheeta; Hanna, Nagy K.; Kimura, Kaoru; & Suda, Randeep. (2009). *Rural informatization in China* (World Bank working paper #172). Washington, DC: World Bank.

Rabaey, Jan M. (2003). *Digital integrated circuits* (2nd ed.). Upper Saddle River, NJ: Prentice Hall Publications.

Reserve Bank of India (RBI). (2006). Financial inclusion by extension of banking services: Use of business facilitators and correspondents. Retrieved April 5, 2012, from http://rbi.org.in/scripts/BS_CircularIndexDisplay.aspx?Id=2718

Reuters. (2011, August 23). *China's mobile subscribers rise by 1.1 pct to 916.53 mln*. Retrieved April 5, 2012, from http://www.reuters.com/article/2011/08/23/china-mobile-idUSL4E7JM16420110823

Rocchesso, Davide. (2003). *Introduction to sound processing*. Retrieved April 5, 2012, from http://www.e-booksdirectory.com/details.php?ebook=29

ROPE. (2011). Homepage. Retrieved April 9, 2012, from http://ropeinternational.com/

Rural Technology & Business Incubator (RTBI). (2009). IITM's Rural Technology and Business Incubator: Annual report. Retrieved April 5, 2012, from http://www.rtbi.in/AnnualReport_2009.pdf

Rural Technology & Business Incubator (RTBI). (2010). Homepage. Retrieved April 9, 2012, from http://www.rtbi.in/

Rural Shores. (n.d.). Homepage. Retrieved April 9, 2012, from http://ruralshores.com/

Schwarz, Brian. (2006, September 7). China's push to outsourcing. Retrieved April 5, 2012, from http://www.atimes.com/atimes/China_Business/HI07Cb01.html

Science Daily. (2010, February 22). *Hazardous e-wastes surging in developing countries*. Retrieved April 5, 2012, from http://www.sciencedaily.com/releases/2010/02/100222081911.htm

Selian, Audrey. (n.d.). *3G mobile licensing policy: From GSM to IMT-2000; A comparative analysis* (International Telecommunication Union [ITU] Series). Geneva: ITU.

Soriano, Cheryll Ruth R. (2007). Exploring the ICT and rural poverty reduction link: Community telecenters and rural livelihoods in Wu'an, China. *Electronic Journal on Information Systems in Developing Countries, 32*(1), 1–15.

Stofega, William, & Llamas, Ramon T. (2009). *The OMH initiative: Enhancing CDMA device availability*. Costa Mesa, CA: CDMA Development Group (CDG).

Streicher-Porte, Martin; Chi, Xinwen; Wang, Mark Y. L.; & Reuter, Markus A. (2010). Informal electronic waste recycling: A sector review with special focus on China. *Waste Management, 31*(4), 731–742.

Su, Qui Gui. (2012). *Introduction to Mandarin Chinese*. Retrieved April 5, 2012, from http://mandarin.about.com/od/chineseculture/a/intro_mandarin.htm

Telecom Regulatory Authority of India (TRAI). (n.d.). Annual reports. New Delhi: TRAI. Retrieved April 9, 2012, from http://www.trai.gov.in/Content/Annual_Reports.aspx

Times of India. (2010, March 14). Indiaspeak: English is our 2nd language. Retrieved April 5, 2012, from http://articles.timesofindia.indiatimes.com/2010-03-14/india/28117934_1_second-language-speakers-urdu

Trillium Digital Systems, Inc. (2000). Third generation (3G) wireless. Retrieved April 9, 2012, from http://srohit.tripod.com/wp_3g.pdf

United States (US) Congress. (2000). US congressional record. Washington, DC: Government Printing Office.

United States Energy Information Administration (EIA). (2012). AEO2012 early release overview. Retrieved April 9, 2012, from http://www.eia.gov/forecasts/aeo/er/

Vastra. (n.d.). Homepage. Retrieved April 9, 2012, from http://www.indiamart.com/vastragarments/

Vortex. (2011). Homepage. Retrieved April 9, 2012, from http://vortexindia.co.in/

Waste2resource.com. (2009, July 21). Waste piling up in India. Retrieved April 5, 2012, from http://www.waste2resource.com/2009/07/statistics-waste-piling-up-india/

Xinmin, Gao. (2009). *IPTV based rural information service in Ningxia: A successful case*. Retrieved April 5, 2012, from http://www.unescap.org/idd/events/2009_RW-AP%20Knowledge-hubs/Presentation%20in%20PDF/China-Ningxia-Paper.pdf

J

Jakarta, Indonesia

9.6 million est. pop. 2010

The city of Jakarta is plagued with polluted waterways, poor air quality, continuous traffic jams, and a host of other problems that make the city environmentally unsustainable. Steps have been taken to improve the infrastructure, reduce air pollution, raise environmental awareness, and provide more services to Jakarta's residents; however, the increasing population and lack of environmental education marginalize these steps and are barriers to sustainability in the area.

The bustling city of Jakarta is the capital of the Republic of Indonesia, a sixteen-thousand-plus island archipelago in Southeast Asia. The city, also officially a province, is located on the northwestern coast of Java at the mouth of the Ciliwung River. Jakarta spreads out from the coast along a flat alluvial plain encompassing 662 square kilometers of terrain. Approximately 60 percent of the city is 7 meters above sea level, while the other 40 percent is just below sea level. On average Jakarta receives 1,760 millimeters of rain annually, with January and February being the wettest months.

According to the Central Bureau of Statistics, Jakarta's population equaled 9,607,787 in 2010, making it the tenth-most-populated city in the world. The city grew at an annual rate of 1.4 percent from 2000 to 2010, a fairly large increase compared to the annual growth rate of 0.17 percent between 1990 and 2000, but rather low compared to the growth rate of Jakarta's outlying region, known as Bodetabek, which grew at an annual rate between 2.39 and 4.74 percent from 2000 to 2010 and is home to 18.3 million people. The population growth in these outlying areas creates roadblocks to sustainability in Jakarta because many residents commute to the already overcrowded metropolis. Jakarta has a population density ranging from ten- to twenty-thousand people per square kilometer, with 60 percent living in underdeveloped residential areas known as *kampungs* (Steinberg 2007, 356). In some areas, affluent neighborhoods border the *kampungs*, separated by high walls lined with barbed wire and glass shards. The economic disparity, high population density, geographic location, and the lack of sound urban planning have created environmental headaches and obstacles to sustainability for the millions of residents living in Jakarta; some efforts are being made, however, to reduce these roadblocks and make Jakarta a more environmentally friendly place to live.

Early Environmental and Health Concerns

Dutch colonization of Indonesia from the early 1600s until the beginning of World War II influenced how planners designed and structured Jakarta's network of streets, alleys, railroads, and canals. The Dutch-built irrigation canals were ineffective in dealing with the heavy monsoons and flooding common in Jakarta and were filled with waste and debris, creating a stench unbearable in the city's sweltering heat. In the early to mid-eighteenth century, Dutch colonists living in Jakarta, then called Batavia, began moving outside the city walls to get away from the stench in the urban center. The filth from the canals and the stagnant water on the ground also led to malaria, typhoid, and dysentery outbreaks, providing even more reason for colonists to spread outward from the city center. It was not until 1918 that the Dutch engineer Herman van Breen proposed construction of the East and West Flood canals to alleviate some of the problems earlier colonists had complained of.

Sewage, Waste Removal, and Flood Control

Some of the Dutch-built canals that stretched through Jakarta in the eighteenth century still exist, causing some of the same problems they did when they were first built. In many areas of the city, water from canals is used for washing, cleaning, and fishing, while upstream the same water is used to flush out waste and sewage. Approximately 1.2 billion liters of sewage are created every day in Jakarta, but only 600,000 liters can be treated by the sewage plants throughout the city, with much of the waste winding up in the city's canals and rivers (Steinberg 2007, 359). Industrial waste, refuse, and untreated sewage have been blamed for the thousands of dead fish that washed ashore in Jakarta Bay in 2004. Of the 23,400 cubic meters of garbage created every day in Jakarta, only 14,700 cubic meters is disposed of by the City Sanitation Office, with much of the remaining waste finding its way into the canals and rivers. The Jakarta Environmental Management Agency has found *E. coli* bacteria in all of Jakarta's thirteen rivers, and illegal dumping in Jakarta's waterways has caused rivers like the Angke to shrink by 5 to 10 meters, resulting in flood control problems and unsanitary living conditions.

Construction began on a twenty-four-kilometer section of the East Flood Canal in 2003, costing $210 million, but the project was not completed in time to prevent massive floods in 2007. Shrinking rivers and waste-filled canals were blamed for many of the problems associated with the 2007 floods, which inundated 70 percent of the city and displaced 450,000 people. The stagnant water left behind from the floods led to an increase in waterborne diseases, diarrhea, acute respiratory infections, dengue fever, and other health issues. The National Development Planning Agency estimated the economic costs of the floods to be $453 million, with even more unaccounted losses in private property and destroyed crops that grew along the riverbanks and in other areas of the city. In response to the floods, the government announced it would spend $300 million to complete the East and West Flood canals; by late April 2011, another $40.6 million was needed to finish the East Flood Canal, with only 67 percent of the project complete (Arditya 2011).

Besides causing major health problems and destroying private property and crops, heavy rains and flooding damage roadways and add more problems to the already heavily congested streets. Since 2007 the city has dredged canals and rivers and placed water pumps along major roadways to prevent flooding problems. These measures were seen as a success by the government when 2009 precipitation levels were around the same as those in 2007, yet no major flooding occurred. In 2008 the World Bank granted a $150 million loan to the city and central government to revitalize the Ciliwung River and improve waterways; there is some controversy over the project because thousands of Jakartans living in project areas are expected to be relocated while work is underway.

Air Quality and Traffic Congestion

It was estimated that Jakarta would have approximately 12 million vehicles operating in the city by the end of 2011, with the majority of these being motorcycles and mopeds, and only 2 percent of all vehicles being used for public transportation (Fasila 2011). These vehicles account for about 70 percent of the air pollution in Jakarta, with the other 30 percent coming from industry. Although the Jakarta Environmental Management Agency proposed a law requiring motor vehicles to pass an emissions test before drivers are given their vehicle licenses, it is unlikely that this will have much of an impact on air quality, since only 85 percent of drivers extend their licenses and many more vehicles remain unregistered (*Jakarta Post* 2011). Pollution from motorized vehicles comprises 68.8 percent of the nitrogen oxide (NO_X) and 14.6 percent of the sulfur dioxide (SO_2) found in the city's air, with buses and trucks being the biggest emitters of particulate matter. Compared to other Southeast Asian cities, Jakarta falls somewhere in the middle in terms of the amount of SO_2 and NO_X each person emits annually. In 2000 Jakarta residents emitted 0.89 kilograms of SO_2 and 10.78 kilograms of NO_X per person. By comparison, residents of Bangkok, Thailand, emitted 3.29 kilograms of SO_2 and 21.09 kilograms of NO_X per person, while in Manila, Philippines, inhabitants emitted 1.3 kilograms of SO_2 and 8.33 kilograms of NO_X per person. Residents in both Ho Chi Minh City, Vietnam, and Kuala Lumpur, Malaysia, emitted less SO_2 and NO_X per person than Jakartans, while Singapore emitted more for the same year (Ooi 2008, 200).

The economic losses to traffic congestion are estimated to be around $1 billion per year, and with the rate of vehicle ownership going up by 9 percent annually it is predicted the city will be in total gridlock by 2014 if nothing is done to mitigate the problem (*Economist* 2010). To help lower these costs, reduce air pollution, and manage traffic congestion, a bus rapid transit (BRT) system began operating in January 2004. The BRT provides designated lanes for buses, and as of March 2011 there were ten such lanes in operation and another five planned or under construction. These lanes, or busways, help to reduce emissions and travel times, but air quality continues to be a problem, and Jakarta's *macet*, or traffic jams, are still some of the worst in the world.

Construction began on a privately funded monorail project in 2004 to manage the traffic problems and reduce air pollution further, but the project was halted in 2008 due to legal and financial problems; as of early 2011 it remained unfinished. Also in the works is a publicly funded rail project called Mass Rapid Transit (MRT) Jakarta. The Japan International Cooperation Agency is providing the loans for the project, with funding made available by DKI Jakarta provincial government and the Indonesian central government. The basic engineering design for phase one of the North–South line was completed in January 2011, with expectations for the line to be operational by 2016. It is estimated the MRT will reduce up to 0.7 percent of the total carbon dioxide (CO_2) emissions per year while increasing public transportation capacity and significantly improving travel times (MRT Jakarta n.d.).

To reduce air pollution and prevent total gridlock by 2014, the local government is working to implement an electronic road pricing system, which will require drivers of privately owned vehicles to pay a fee when entering major thoroughfares (Arditya 2011). The local government also hopes to improve pedestrian and bicycle pathways, increase the number of parking spaces throughout the city, encourage drivers to use park-and-ride systems, and ban vehicles all together along Sudirman and M. H. Thamrin roads during car-free days, which take place twice a month.

Raising Environmental Awareness

To help raise awareness and educate the public about environmental issues, the Jakarta Environmental Management Agency launched a river cleanup competition in June 2011 and handed out awards to groups and individuals who helped develop water catchment systems, for using environmentally friendly plastic bags, and meeting other environmental management criteria.

Privately run businesses, nongovernmental organizations, and committed individuals are also doing their part to increase environmental awareness in Jakarta. In 2008 Jakarta's first environmentally friendly radio station, Green Radio 89.2 FM, was launched by radio broadcaster and journalist Tosca Santoso. The station, running on solar power, broadcasts out of East Jakarta for nineteen hours a day, with ten of those hours dedicated to discussion of environmental issues. The station is involved in environmental activities, including a reforestation program in the Gunung Gede Pangrango National Park, a primary water source for Jakartans.

In addition to the radio, print and online media also educate Jakartans about ongoing environmental issues in the city. To promote energy efficiency, improved infrastructure, and environmentally friendly development throughout Jakarta, a website titled the Sustainable Jakarta Convention (http://www.sjconvention.com) offers news and information on sustainability issues in Jakarta and lists workshops and events related to environmentally friendly development and construction in the city.

Also raising environmental awareness among Jakartans and the global community is Julia Genatossio, founder of Monsoon Vermont, a company that makes consumer products from trash found around Jakarta's streets, landfills, and waterways. The company was established in 2005 and sells items like backpacks, umbrellas, and wallets that are made entirely of recycled Jakartan trash. Monsoon Vermont has also teamed up with WatSan Action to develop "awareness of practical means of improving water, sanitation, and waste conditions," while also working to provide access to clean drinking water, provide solid-waste management practices, and improve latrines, drainage, and infiltration methods (Monsoon Vermont 2009).

Outlook

By improving the city's infrastructure and increasing environmental awareness, Jakarta's planners are taking steps needed to provide a more sustainable living environment throughout the city. The continually growing population poses serious challenges for city officials, however, and until a clear set of long-term environmental policies and goals are in place, officials will continue to react to issues of sustainability rather than addressing them before they come to a head. Corruption, interagency divisions, and poor planning and coordination among government officials will also continue to create barriers to sustainability, and until these problems are addressed, they will cause delays in infrastructure upgrades and better environmental policy implementation and enforcement. As environmental awareness and education increase, some of these roadblocks will be removed, but it will take the efforts of the average Jakartan, the city and national governments, and the international community to make Jakarta a greener, cleaner, and healthier city to live in.

Scott M. ALBRIGHT
University of Hawaii at Hilo

See also Automobiles and Personal Vehicles; Cities—Overview; Consumerism; Education, Environmental (*several articles*); Guangzhou, China; Kuala Lumpur, Malaysia; Media Coverage of the Environment;

Nongovernmental Organizations (NGOs); Public Health; Public Transportation; Reforestation and Afforestation (Southeast Asia); Singapore; Southeast Asia; Transboundary Water Issues; Water Security

FURTHER READING

Arditya, Andreas D. (2011, March 3). Jakarta govt gives up on monorail project. *The Jakarta Post*. Retrieved February 11, 2012, from http://www.thejakartapost.com/news/2011/03/10/jakarta-govt-gives-monorail-project.html

Arditya, Andreas D. (2011, April 21). Extra $41m needed for East Canal. *The Jakarta Post*. Retrieved February 11, 2012, from http://www.thejakartapost.com/news/2011/04/21/extra-41m-needed-east-canal.html

Arditya, Andreas D. (2011, June 25). One legal boundary to go for Jakarta ERP. *The Jakarta Post*. Retrieved June 29, 2011, from http://www.thejakartapost.com/news/2011/06/25/one-legal-boundary-go-jakarta-erp.html

Asri, Dail Umamil, & Hidayat, Budi. (2005). Current transportation issues in Jakarta and its impacts on environment. *Proceedings of the Eastern Asia Society for Transportation Studies*, 5, 1792–1798. Retrieved February 11, 2012, from http://www.easts.info/on-line/proceedings_05/1792.pdf

Badan Pusat Statistik [Central Bureau of Statistics]. (2010). Indonesian population by province, 1971, 1980, 1990, 1995, 2000 and 2010. Retrieved February 11, 2012, from http://www.bps.go.id/eng/tab_sub/view.php?tabel=1&daftar=1&id_subyek=12&notab=1

Cybriwsky, Roman, & Ford, Larry R. (2001). City profile Jakarta. *Cities*, 18(3), 199–210.

Dick, Howard; Houben, Vincent J. H.; Lindblad, J. Thomas; & Wie, Thee Kian. (2002). *The emergence of a national economy: An economic history of Indonesia, 1800–2000*. Honolulu: University of Hawaii Press.

The Economist. (2010, February 4). Traffic in Indonesia's capital, Jam Jakarta: The race to beat total gridlock. Retrieved June 29, 2011, from http://www.economist.com/node/15473915

Fadillah, Rangga D. (2011, June 7). People more concerned about pollution than renewable energy. *The Jakarta Post*. Retrieved February 11, 2012, from http://www.thejakartapost.com/news/2011/06/06/people-more-concerned-about-pollution-renewable-energy.html

Fasila, Dofa. (2011, June 21). Congested Jakarta must embrace public transportation: Fauzi. *Jakarta Globe*. Retrieved June 29, 2011, from http://www.thejakartaglobe.com/indonesia/congested-jakarta-must-embrace-public-transportation-fauzi/448307

The Jakarta Post. (2011, April 2). Govt proposes emission test for STNK. Retrieved June 29, 2011, from http://www.thejakartapost.com/news/2011/04/24/govt-proposes-emission-test-stnk.html

Lamoureux, Florence. (2003). *Indonesia: A global studies handbook*. Santa Barbara, California: ABC-CLIO.

Monsoon Vermont. (2009). Why water? Retrieved June 29, 2011, from http://monsoonvt.com/waste_couture.cfm.

Mass Rapid Transit (MRT) Jakarta. (n.d.). What benefits MRT Jakarta would bring? Retrieved June 29, 2011, from http://www.jakartamrt.com/index.php?option=com_content&view=article&id=64&Itemid=103&lang=en

Ooi, Giok-Ling. (2008). Cities and sustainability: Southeast Asian and European perspectives. *Asia Europe Journal*, 6(2), 193–204. doi:10.1007/s10308-008-0176-0

Steinberg, Florian. (2007). Jakarta: Environmental problems and sustainability. *Habitat International*, 31, 354–365.

United Nations, Executive Board of the United Nations Development Programme and of the United Nations Population Fund. (2010). Draft country programme document for Indonesia (DP/FPA/DCP/IDN/8). Retrieved February 11, 2012, from http://www.unfpa.org/exbrd/2010/second_session/dpfpa_dcp_idn8_en.pdf

World Bank. (2010, May 27). Grant agreement/letter to the Wildlife Conservation Society Global Conservation explaining the terms of the World Bank grant [TF096887] in support of Indonesia's Green PNPM. Retrieved February 11, 2012, from http:go.worldbank.org/EVRQDCU0P0

World Bank. (2011). Energy & mining in East Asia and Pacific: Indonesia and energy. Retrieved June 13, 2011, from http://go.worldbank.org/G86L8GYVC0

Share the *Encyclopedia of Sustainability*: Teachers are welcome to make up to ten (10) copies of no more than two (2) articles for distribution in a single course or program. For further permissions, please visit www.copyright.com or contact: info@berkshirepublishing.com

Japan

125 million est. pop. 2011

Japan has a varied and extensive history of environmental problems. Its early people employed farming techniques that caused population growth, leading to environmental stress, which increased exponentially when the country began industrializing in the late nineteenth century. Today, most of Japan's 125-plus million people live in cities. Much of the northeastern coast was devastated in 2011 by a tsunami that heavily damaged the nuclear reactor at the Fukushima Daiichi Nuclear Power Plant.

An industrialized nation of more than 125 million people, Japan is composed of four large islands and thousands of smaller islands in a chain between the Sea of Japan and the Pacific Ocean. In area, the country is slightly smaller than the US state of California, and it has nearly 30,000 kilometers of coastline. The geography is generally rugged and mountainous, making it unfavorable to large-scale agriculture, and it is relatively poor in natural resources. These qualities have significantly influenced the country's development to the point where Japan has become the world's largest importer of coal and liquefied natural gas—since it has virtually no fossil fuel reserves—and it is the world's second-largest importer of oil (US CIA 2011).

Ancient History

Around 400 BCE, people in Japan moved away from foraging techniques and began employing horticultural practices. As these expanded over centuries, the population grew from a few hundred thousand to some 7 million by 1200 CE. Then an array of social and agronomic changes began displacing the agricultural system with a much more intensive one, leading to further population growth—30 million by 1700. At that time the pulse of rapid growth faded, ushering in a time of demographic stasis and unprecedented environmental stress. From 1880 onward, industrial techniques based on fossil fuel use were adopted, triggering a new pulse of rapid growth that raised the population to over 125 million by 2000. Japanese industrialization created the full range of environmental issues that marks industrial society everywhere: pollution, resource depletion, and loss of biodiversity and natural habitat.

Intensive Agriculture (1200–1880)

Around 1200, elements of intensified agriculture began falling into place; fallowing gave way to fertilizing with ashes, mulch, and manure. Also, regularly irrigated wet rice, which can give much higher yields per hectare than dry grains, came to be planted more widely, with nurturing techniques much improved. These changes required more intensive labor and more communal cooperation in the use of land, labor, and water supplies, spurring the growth of larger, better-organized villages.

These trends were facilitated by the evolution of smallpox and measles from exogenous, highly fatal, epidemic diseases of adulthood to endemic illnesses of childhood. That helped stabilize local populations, enabling intensive tillage techniques to become ever more widely practiced despite centuries of violent political turmoil. Towns and trade grew, fostering crop specialization and market gardening. In consequence, the population kept growing, reaching 15 million by 1600.

By then, the broader environmental ramifications of growth and turmoil had become apparent. In particular, the expanding village demand for fertilizer, fuel, and fodder was met by more intensive cutting, raking, and gathering of wood, grass, and leaves from woodland and waste areas, which produced more eroded hillsides. Consequently, whereas there earlier had been only desultory government efforts (and those only in the vicinity of Kyoto and Nara) to protect woodlands by closing forests and issuing decrees to regulate land use, during the 1500s measures to regulate the exploitation of natural resources (woodland and water supplies in particular) became widespread, pursued most vigorously by villagers and regional barons.

Changes Around 1600

Centuries of recurrent warfare ended around 1600, when a strong dictatorship came to power. The synergies associated with this pacification produced a sharp, short-term acceleration in several trends, notably, increases in paddy-field acreage, construction activity, urbanization, mining, and deforestation. The expansion of paddy-field acreage shifted many dry-crop fields into wet-rice production, opened new areas of lowland near major rivers to tillage, gave Japan many new and elaborate irrigation systems, and enabled society to grow rapidly for a few decades.

Urban construction work of the late 1500s and early 1600s dotted the realm with an array of grand wooden monuments—palaces, castles, mansions, temples, and shrines—as well as large cities, lesser towns, and highway stations. This activity was abetted by a boom in mining that briefly made Japan the world's greatest producer of bullion. By 1630, however, bullion mining had gone into steep decline as deposits were consumed. By then, too, the construction boom was petering out, partly because much demand had been sated, and partly because most of the reasonably accessible high forest from Kyushu (the southernmost of Japan's four main islands) to the northern tip of Honshu (Japan's central island) had been consumed, and the cost of timber provisioning was becoming prohibitive.

The Eighteenth Century: Environmental Stress

By 1660, the age of land clearance and water-works expansion was also passing. As decades advanced, the consequences of excessive deforestation and land clearance became more and more evident: soil erosion, bald mountains, flooding, irregular stream flow, and harvest shortfalls. By 1700 the resulting stresses were starting to work their way through society. Deforestation caused more elaborate and tightly enforced woodland regulations, the beginnings of plantation forestry, and the emergence of the use of coal. Foreign trade was cut, and diverse forms of substitution and rationing were developed in order to cope with scarcities. To protect its irrigation systems, Japanese society committed itself to the long-term task of continual riparian maintenance: river dredging and dike, dam, and diversion-ditch construction and repair. To sustain soil fertility, farmers utilized increasing amounts of "night soil" (human waste), industrial waste, and fish meal, which spurred the expansion of coastal fisheries.

The challenge of surviving in a stressed ecosystem also transformed Japan's demographics. Roughly 75 percent of the archipelago's people maneuvered to limit family size as a way of sustaining their household well-being, the cumulative effect of which replaced population growth with stasis. The maneuvers included delayed and less fecund marriages, outplacement of surplus children, and abortion and infanticide despite official denunciation. The efforts to contain population growth were aided by a heightened frequency of famines and epidemics, which decimated the weak.

Villagers acted as they did because their choices were harsh. This is evidenced in many ways, such as increased tenancy and landlessness, as well as greater geographical mobility as more and more people pursued work away from home. There were more frequent peasant rebellions, more forceful armed suppressions, increased numbers of urban poor, and larger violent urban outbursts.

The Late Nineteenth Century

The ruling elite managed to stay in power until the 1860s. But then unprecedented demands from a new quarter—expansionist, early-industrial Europe (and its North American outpost)—presented problems that the elite class was unable to handle. During that decade, Japan slipped into political turmoil, and the old elite destroyed the existing polity, replacing it during the 1870s with a more centralized and powerful regime that started propelling Japan beyond its agricultural order into the age of industrialism, with all the associated social, cultural, and environmental change.

By the 1880s, the lowlands and valley floors of a once thoroughly forested realm had been opened to tillage, and nearby hillsides were barren or covered with scrub growth. The deeper mountains surrendered much of their old-growth timber, but most were still verdant, and significant tracts of inaccessible forest—not to mention nearly all of Hokkaido (the northernmost of Japan's four main islands)—remained untouched. Humans and their collaborating species and parasites had displaced earlier occupants from an appreciable part of the realm, mostly lowlands, and placed some creatures, such as the black bear and the wolf, at risk of or near extinction.

Having maximized paddy tillage by opening floodplains to cultivation, the populace found itself locked in a perpetual struggle to control river flow. Coastal fisheries were worked intensively, and the malign effects of mining, notably air and water pollution, were becoming evident from the late eighteenth century onward, as coal and metal mining began to expand.

Industrialism: 1880 to the Present

Industrial society is as different from agricultural society as the latter is from forager society, being distinguished by two basic environmental changes. One change is a shift from material dependence on the society's own terrain to dependence on a global resource base made accessible by some mix of politico-military and entrepreneurial means. The other change is a radical acceleration in the rate of human-controlled energy cycling, made possible by supplementing energy obtained from the living biome (food, fuel wood, and animal power) with energy obtained from past biomes (fossil fuel) and other sources (hydroelectric and nuclear).

Japan began the shift to industrialism around 1880 and became an industrial society after 1960. In the country's shift to global resources, before 1945 its leaders relied heavily on politico-military means (i.e., empire building) to expand their resource base. But after 1950 they favored an entrepreneurial strategy that exchanged finished goods and diverse services for imported raw materials, notably fossil fuel, metals, timber, and foodstuffs. The acceleration in energy cycling was achieved by heavy use of domestic coal, supplemented from the 1910s to the 1930s by development of hydropower; after 1960 by a shift to imported fuel oil and coal; and from the 1970s onward by the addition of nuclear power.

The shift to new energy sources had a broad range of environmental ramifications. But these problems associated with urbanization, agricultural practice, mining, fisheries, industrial chemistry, and forest use are of a sort familiar to all industrial societies and can be noted succinctly.

The explosive growth in Japan's population, roughly a tripling during the 1900s, was surpassed by the rate of urbanization, so that most Japanese have become urban dwellers. From the 1880s to 1950, cities were breeding grounds for one of the world's worst pandemics of tuberculosis, but with the development of antibiotics that problem was overcome. Today, Japan's cities and towns are some of the safest and healthiest places a human can live, and their residents enjoy, on average, the world's longest lifespans. Because this population's rate of material consumption is vastly higher than that of its ancestors, however, the urban sites produce immense quantities of effluent and trash that pollute widely and create chronic problems of waste disposal.

Consequences of Feeding a Dense Population

To feed this burgeoning population, Japanese agricultural leaders spurred domestic food production and achieved major increases in annual output. Since the 1950s, however, the effort has relied on chemical fertilizers and biocides, which have had the usual effect of polluting water and soil, with toxic effluents draining into lakes and coastal waters, in the process injuring diverse organisms. Whereas the people of pre-1860 Japan obtained all their caloric intake from domestic and near-shore production, by the 1990s over half of it came from abroad.

Part of the imported food has been of marine provenance. With motorized vessels, huge nets, and, by 1930, cannery ships and catcher boats, Japanese fishermen moved beyond coastal operations into pelagic (open sea) fisheries, in the process making Japan a significant participant in the global marine harvest. Meanwhile, as the twentieth century ended, overfishing and pollution ravaged Japan's coastal and inland fisheries. From the 1980s onward, moreover, the lower-wage pelagic fishing fleets of other countries became able to undersell Japan's own fishermen. These trends led to a gradual decline in the indigenous fishing industry, a decline that continues in the twenty-first century. During the 1990s, the level of seafood consumption also began dropping, as global overfishing and marine pollution decimated world supplies and prices increased.

Industrial Pollution

Much as industrial technology transformed farm and fishery operations, so it changed the mining industry. Metal and coal mining created downstream pollution problems by the early 1800s, and the rapid expansion of mechanized mining after 1880 led to a countrywide surge in mine output and environmental injury. The most notorious instance involved the Ashio copper mine north of Tokyo during the 1890s, during which mine tailings from the extremely productive mine were heaped on the banks of the Watarase River, to be dynamited and shoveled into the river by workers periodically when heavy rains arrived; this practice led to extensive flooding and pollution in downstream communities (Wilkening 2004, 64–65). Local, less visible cases of toxic effluent became widespread despite modest legislative attempts to contain pollutants and improve mine safety. By the 1960s, however, with many mines petering out, the government was promoting metal and coal imports. Thereafter, the domestic mining industry withered, and its environmental impact diminished.

Even as reliance on imports was shifting some of the environmental effects of industrial-age agriculture, fisheries, and mining offshore, the malign impact of other industries continued to grow within Japan. From the early 1900s onward, new types and uses of chemicals produced more pollutants that poisoned air, water, and soil, mainly downstream and downwind from factories and smokestacks. During the 1960s, a cluster of severe poisoning incidents involving mercury, cadmium, polychlorinated biphenyls (PCBs), petrochemicals, and other industrial products provoked public protests forceful enough to overwhelm industrial and government resistance and win modest remediation and the creation of an environmental regulatory system designed to minimize future problems. The proliferation of motor vehicles since the 1950s and the use of more and newer chemicals and pharmaceuticals perpetuated the production of pollutants, many of them unregulated and unmeasured, and their impacts on the biosystem are slowly becoming apparent.

Japan's Forests in the Industrial Age

Perhaps the most interesting environmental story of industrial-age Japan (interesting because it is abnormal) is that of its forests. The modest gains in woodland management and reforestation of the eighteenth and nineteenth centuries were largely undone by the political turmoil of the 1860s and 1870s. Starting about 1875, an explosion in demand for timber to build cities, factories, railroads, and so forth combined with access to new logging technology to produce a surge in timber harvesting that denuded more mountainsides. Together with expanded consumption of mulch and fodder materials, this surge led to escalating erosion, flooding, and downstream devastation. During the early twentieth century, remedial measures slowly brought the situation under control as the government employed its powers of regulation, the technology of concrete construction, and a somewhat improved silviculture to manage woodland use, promote reforestation, and control erosion and water flow.

By the late 1930s, many areas had been reforested and many waterways effectively controlled. The warfare and urban reconstruction of 1937–1950, however, consumed most of Japan's timber and led during the 1950s and 1960s to a massive nationwide program of reforestation that by 1990 had transformed about 40 percent of the country's woodland into even-aged monoculture conifer stands. But trends in international trade have made timber imports cheaper, leaving Japan with vast acreages of hand-planted conifer stands that are aging poorly, with overcrowded trees growing spindly and becoming subject to windthrow (uprooting and overturning by wind) and snow breakage. In a happy trade-off, however, as the stands disintegrate, the forest floor is exposed to sunlight, varied new growth starts, and a habitat more favorable to birds and other creatures reestablishes itself.

The gradual disintegration of hand-planted conifer stands, a trend lamented by professional foresters, constitutes a bright spot—perhaps the only bright spot—in the broader story of biodiversity in industrial Japan. Otherwise the story is the poorly documented one found everywhere of vulnerable species being crippled and consumed by environmental pollution, losing habitat, and being pushed out by exotic competitors. Agricultural and industrial contaminants achieve the first result; diverse forms of urban sprawl accomplish the second; and imports, mainly accidental, introduce the third. There seems to be, in Japan as elsewhere, only minimal countermovement to these trends despite the presence of a small but dedicated and sometimes vocal environmentalist movement.

Modern Day Issues: The Triple Disaster of 2011

In March 2011, an earthquake off Japan's northeast coast triggered a tsunami that caused widespread damage to the country. Thousands are missing, injured, or dead, and the nuclear reactor at the Fukushima Daiichi Nuclear Power Plant was heavily damaged. Water entered the complex and caused some generators to stop working, while the earthquake had split some reactors and caused radiation leakage. The plant's cooling system also failed. A 20-kilometer evacuation zone was set up. As yet, there have been no reported deaths as a result of the radiation (BBC 2011) but it may be too soon to tell. The future of the nuclear power industry in Japan is difficult to foresee as a result. Analysts and energy officials continue to describe nuclear energy as Japan's best energy option, but the country's citizens have turned against nuclear energy to such an extent that many of Japan's fifty-four undamaged nuclear power plants have been idled in the months since the tsunami, causing an energy crisis (Fackler 2012). The crisis contributed to the end of Naoto Kan's administration as prime minister in August of 2011; this was but one of many signs that the Japanese people's faith and trust in the government was sorely tested by the triple disaster of earthquake, tsunami, and subsequent nuclear meltdown (*The Economist* 2012). Future chapters of the story surely will be instructive.

Conrad TOTMAN
Yale University, Emeritus

See also Agriculture (China and Southeast Asia); Agriculture (South and East Asia); Consumerism; E-Waste; Education, Environmental (Japan); Energy Industries—Nuclear; Energy Security (East Asia); Public Health; Public Transportation; Reforestation and Afforestation (Southeast Asia); Tokyo, Japan; Utilities Regulations and Efficiency

This article was adapted by the editors from Conrad Totman's article "Japan" in Shepard Krech III, J. R. McNeill, and Carolyn Merchant (Eds.), the *Encyclopedia of World Environmental History*, pp. 724–728. Great Barrington, MA: Berkshire Publishing (2003).

FURTHER READING

BBC. (2011). *How does Fukushima differ from Chernobyl?* Retrieved November 3, 2011, from http://www.bbc.co.uk/news/world-asia-pacific-13050228

The Economist. (2012, March 10). Japan after the 3/11 disaster: The death of trust. Retrieved March 26, 2012, from http://www.economist.com/node/21549917

Fackler, Martin. (2012, March 8). Japan's nuclear energy industry nears shutdown, at least for now. *New York Times.* Retrieved March 26, 2012, from http://www.nytimes.com/2012/03/09/world/asia/japan-shutting-down-its-nuclear-power-industry.html?_r=1

George, Timothy S. (2001). *Minamata: Pollution and the struggle for democracy in postwar Japan.* Cambridge, MA: Harvard University Asian Center.

Huddle, Norie, & Reich, Michael. (1975). *Island of dreams: Environmental crisis in Japan.* Tokyo: Autumn Press.

Jannetta, Ann Bowman (1987). *Epidemics and mortality in early modern Japan.* Princeton, NJ: Princeton University Press.

Johnston, William. (1995). *The modern epidemic: A history of tuberculosis in Japan.* Cambridge, MA: Harvard University Press.

Kiple, Kenneth F. (Ed.). (1993). *The Cambridge world history of human disease.* Cambridge, UK: Cambridge University Press.

Kurosu, Satomi. (2002). Studies on historical demography and family in early modern Japan. *Early Modern Japan, 10*(1), 3–21, 66–71.

Morris-Suzuki, Tessa. (1998). Environmental problems and perceptions in early industrial Japan. In Mark Elvin & Ts'ui-jung (Eds.), *Sediments of time: Environment and society in Chinese history* (pp. 756–780). Cambridge, UK: Cambridge University Press.

Souyri, Pierre Francois. (2001). *The world turned upside down: Medieval Japanese society.* New York: Cambridge University Press.

Taueber, Irene. (1958). *The population of Japan.* Princeton, NJ: Princeton University Press.

Totman, Conrad. (1993). *Early modern Japan.* Berkeley: University of California Press.

Totman, Conrad. (2000). *A history of Japan.* Oxford, UK: Blackwell Publishers.

Tsurumi, E. Patricia. (1990). *Factory girls: Women in the thread mills of Meiji Japan.* Princeton, NJ: Princeton University Press.

United States Central Intelligence Agency (US CIA). (2011). World factbook: Japan. Retrieved November 3, 2011, from https://www.cia.gov/library/publications/the-world-factbook/geos/ja.html

Walker, Brett L. (2001). Commercial growth and environmental change in early modern Japan: Hachinohe's wild boar famine of 1749. *Journal of Asian Studies, 60*(2), 329–351.

Walker, Bybrett L. (2001). *The conquest of Ainu lands: Ecology and culture in Japanese expansion, 1590–1800.* Berkeley: University of California Press.

Wilkening, Kenneth E. (2004). *Acid rain science and politics in Japan: A history of knowledge and action toward sustainability.* Cambridge: Massachusetts Institute of Technology Press.

Berkshire's authors and editors welcome questions, comments, and corrections. Send your emails about the *Berkshire Encyclopedia of Sustainability* in general or this volume in particular to: sustainability.updates@berkshirepublishing.com

K

Korean Peninsula

South Korea: 48.8 million est. pop. 2012
North Korea: 24.5 million est. pop. 2012

South and North Korea are located on a mountainous peninsula in northeast Asia that is home to around 73 million people. The two countries are ethnically similar but radically different in political economies. Both South Korea and North Korea ranked low on the 2005 Environmental Sustainability Index (122nd and 146th—last—respectively). South Korea recently funded major sustainability initiatives, as it imports 97 percent of its fuel. The demilitarized zone (DMZ) between the two Koreas is the most heavily fortified border in the world and, given its lack of development, acts as a de facto nature reserve.

The Korean peninsula was home to one nation from the late 600s to the mid-1900s. The name *Korea* is derived from *Koryo*, a tenth- to fourteenth-century dynasty. Korea is remarkably uniform in ethnicity, even after splitting into two countries in 1948. Daehan Minguk is the term Koreans use for the Republic of Korea (South Korea), which has a population of nearly 49 million people (ranked twenty-fifth globally). The Democratic People's Republic of Korea (North Korea), called Chosun Minchu-chui Inmin Konghwa-guk, has a population of approximately 24.5 million people (ranked forty-ninth globally) (US CIA 2012).

The two Koreas are situated on a mountainous, peninsular region of 222,073 square kilometers—roughly the size of Great Britain. The Amnok and Tuman rivers form its northern border with the Chinese region of Manchuria and with 20 kilometers of eastern Russia. The Sea of Japan separates Korea from the main Japanese island of Honshu by approximately 200 kilometers, while the East China and Yellow seas form the south and west boundaries, respectively.

South Korea has a capitalist economy so successful that it was labeled as one of the four "Asian Tigers" of the global economy in the 1980s and 1990s (along with Hong Kong, Singapore, and Taiwan). Much of its early rise after the Korean War (1950–1953) was through state-sponsored capitalism of family-owned industrial conglomerates, known as *chaebol*. Today Korean firms such as Hyundai and Samsung are known around the world. South Korea has the third largest economy in East Asia and the thirteenth largest globally (Watts 2009). Initially North Korean industry also grew rapidly, building on a base of preexisting Japanese infrastructure, but it has stagnated under current isolationist, Marxist policy.

While South Koreans' average living standards are now far above that of the North Koreans, as in many nations critiques still exist there about the capitalist effects on cultural traditions and quality of life across social classes. Major religions in South Korea are Buddhism and Christianity, each followed by approximately 25 percent of the population, with the other half proclaiming no religion (US CIA 2012). Christianity became popular through public resistance to the 1910–1945 Japanese occupation by missionaries. Religion is supposedly practiced in North Korea but in effect is repressed.

The legacy of Confucianism, introduced in the early 1400s, influences Korean cultural practices through an emphasis on paternalistic hierarchy. South Korea ranked 115th out of 134 countries in the World Economic Forum's 2009 index of gender equality. But approximately 60 percent of South Korean women now enter college; fewer than 10 percent did so in 1981 (Sang-Hun 2010). Many women now work in the less-discriminatory public sector and marry in their late twenties and early thirties. Intermarriage with other nationalities is also beginning to break down the unusually homogenous ethnicity of South Korea.

Personal relationships, operating on the concept of maintaining harmony, are highly valued in business. New sustainability practices thus may need to be introduced through third-party introductions. *Kibun* is the concept of face, feelings, or pride, constantly monitored through body language and speech, which must not be damaged in relationships. Intrafamily relationships are also highly valued in Korea.

Relations between North and South Korea are tense. The demilitarized zone (DMZ) between North and South Korea is the most heavily fortified border in the world and, given its lack of development, acts as a de facto nature reserve. In 1997, Kim Dae Jung became the first South Korean opposition leader elected to the presidency. He won the 2000 Nobel Peace Prize for his efforts to repair relations with North Korea.

Natural Resources

Approximately three-fourths of the Korean peninsula is uninhabitable due to steep topography. The peninsula tilts down from east to west, through a process that began approximately 100 million years ago in the late Mesozoic era. Most of the peninsula has a granite basement overlain with mountains of sandstone and marble. The rugged T'aebaek Sanmaek Mountains, home of the 2018 Winter Olympics, drop swiftly to the unbroken shoreline of the east coast, while the west coast is more rolling, with a highly indented shoreline and strong tidal influence. Volcanic mountains include the highest peaks at the northern and southern ends of the peninsula.

The climate is dominated by late summer monsoons, when half the annual 1,000 millimeters of rain falls, and by a dry season from October through March. Precipitation is approximately twice mainland China's and half of Japan's. The Hangang River (514 kilometers long, flowing through Seoul) is the largest river in water volume within the Korean peninsula.

Vegetation reflects the varied climate, with subtropical vegetation at the southern tip and islands, temperate deciduous forest at low and middle elevations, and coniferous forests at northern latitudes and higher elevations. Forested land accounts for 65 percent of the landscape, with almost half of that consisting of coniferous forests. Major tree species include red pine, Korean white pine, larch, and oak.

Common fauna include river deer, fox, and ring-necked pheasant, while black bear, lynx, squirrel, tiger, and weasel are less common. Endangered species include the white-bellied black woodpecker, Japanese crested ibis, white stork, black stork, whooper swan, Manchurian crane, musk deer, and golden eagle. Any remaining tigers are thought to live near Korea's highest elevation of Mount Paekdusan, 2,744 meters above sea level, on the Chinese border.

Historical Environmental Issues

The Three Kingdoms Period, prior to early Korean unification, saw mass-produced agricultural implements, new road construction, and plowing of fields. From being communally owned, land became the property of the monarchy, aristocracy, and Buddhist temples. The Unified Shilla kingdom (668–935 CE) unified Korea for the first time in the late seventh century, creating a major capital in Gyeongju and expanding foreign trade from raw materials to manufactured goods.

The subsequent Koryo dynasty (918–1392), contemporary with Mongol dominance in China, called its capital of 500,000 people Song-ak (present-day Gaesong, North Korea)—the "pine tree" capital. Pines, with their four points of beauty (color, form, perfume, and resistance to lightning), feature regularly in Korean art, which also commonly depicts cranes, tigers, and other wildlife.

The Choson (Yi) dynasty assumed power in 1392, holding it until 1910. In this period land ownership largely shifted from the monarchy to private ownership by upper-class government officials. Conversion of land to agricultural use increased cropland to three times its Koryo period extent. Despite historically large populations, as in many East Asian nations, most environmental change occurred with twentieth-century technology.

Japan became the first industrialized Asian nation, gaining power and annexing Korea in 1910. During this period modern technology began severely damaging the environment: road and rail networks were extended in the 1920s, and logging came to affect 72 percent of the forest landscape. Korea's population grew from over 13 million in 1910 to almost 26 million in 1944. Some flora and larger fauna species disappeared, while populations of others declined. Industrialization and associated pollution was, however, still relatively dispersed and moderate.

The more rural, less wealthy North had long been resentful of the South, but external Cold War factors mostly led to a Russian-supplied invasion in June 1950. In the subsequent Korean War, much urban and rural landscape was ruined, 2 million people died, bombing damaged the forest cover, and the partitioning of Korea became permanent. Postwar poverty, exacerbated by an influx of 4.8 million North Korean refugees to South Korea, led to increased logging to obtain inexpensive fuel. Contemporary photographs reveal denuded hillsides, which frequently suffered erosion and landslides in monsoon rains.

Over 80 percent of South Korea's forests had been damaged by the end of the Korean War. In 1961 the

Forest Law was enacted, and in 1973 the Forestry Administration embarked on a ten-year National Forest Basic Plan. Since 80 percent of South Korea's forests are under forty years old and are not yet fully productive, Korea produces less than 5 percent of its own timber (Edmunds and Wollenberg 2001). South Korea imports forest products from over twenty countries, including Malaysia, Papua New Guinea, the United States, Chile, and New Zealand.

South Korea's labor-intensive postwar industrialization brought rapid urbanization with associated housing and infrastructure problems. The use of industrial coal caused carbon monoxide and sulfur dioxide pollution, the effects of which were compounded by poor working conditions and the close proximity of industrial and residential areas.

An industrial decentralization policy simply relocated pollution, causing problems such as coastal water pollution and acid rain. Farmers increased yields through the Green Revolution yet suffered from high chemical costs. The environment had become a controversial topic by the late 1970s, but media was controlled and general student protests were violently repressed. Public pressure eventually led to most environmental reforms.

The late 1980s and 1990s saw continued industrial and economic growth, and sulfur dioxide levels in Seoul, Incheon, and Pusan reached six times permitted levels (0.05 parts per million) by 1990. Urban growth in the Seoul region reduced open space and habitats, and construction of deepwater ports reduced the extent of coastal wetlands. Though South Korea is now following the West in building its service sector—which is less polluting—environmental problems persist. Major environmental laws of 1977 were overhauled in the early 1990s to improve pollution control and introduce aggressive recycling incentives.

North Korean industrial pollution, some related to mineral exploitation, has been less severe than in the South. It has far fewer cars and associated emissions. North Korea, however, has done less reforesting in the postwar period. Recent natural disasters, such as floods, combined with deforestation, erosion, and economic collapse, led to large-scale famine beginning in the 1990s.

Current Environmental Issues

Air and water pollution are major domestic environmental issues today in both Koreas. North Korea is especially concerned with inadequate supplies of potable water, waterborne disease, deforestation, and soil erosion. Less modernization in the North means that many important natural sites, including Mount Paekdusan and the Tuman River wetlands, remain relatively unspoiled.

In South Korea, environmental organizations address a full range of issues, including biotechnology, environmental economics, environmental law, genetically modified organisms, industrial ecology, religious (Buddhist and Christian) ecology, sustainable development, urban issues, water, and wetlands. The 40,000-hectare Saemangum wetland reclamation project on the west coast of South Korea is particularly controversial. Green Korea United is a major nongovernmental organization with ten chapters and fifteen thousand members. An issue common to both North and South Korea is a proposal, backed by world-renowned biologists, to make the DMZ into a formal nature reserve.

South Korea is party to many international treaties addressing Antarctica, biodiversity, climate change, desertification, endangered species, hazardous wastes, marine dumping, nuclear testing, ozone layer protection, ship pollution, tropical timber, wetlands, and whaling. It has signed but not ratified the Kyoto Protocol regarding climate change. North Korea is party to international treaties addressing Antarctica, biodiversity, climate change, environmental modification, ozone layer protection, and ship pollution. It has signed but not ratified the Protocol on Environmental Protection to the Antarctic Treaty (Antarctic-Environmental Protocol) and the United Nations Convention on the Law of the Sea.

Unique international environmental issues that draw attention to Korea include drift-net fishing (South Korea) and nuclear energy and arms (North Korea). Green trade is of particular concern, in view of South Korea's increased ability to import products. Committee discussions within the World Trade Organization and the Association of Southeast Asian Nations (ASEAN) are attempting to curb the detrimental effects of free trade, including the decline of global fisheries and tropical deforestation with its associated loss of biodiversity.

Outlook for Sustainability

South Korea was ranked low (score 43.0, 122nd out of 146 countries) on the 2005 Environmental Sustainability Index (ESI), which measure countries' relative abilities to maintain environmental sustainability relating to twenty-one key sustainability indicators (Esty et al. 2005). (A high ESI score indicates that a country is in a good position to maintain favorable environmental conditions into the future.) Lower scoring categories were in reducing air pollution (lowest), reducing environmental stress, natural resource management, reducing water stress, biodiversity, reducing natural disaster vulnerability, and water quantity. The highest scoring categories were in science and technology (highest), reducing population stress, and water quality. Its scores were moderately positive in environmental governance and private sector responsiveness.

North Korea ranked the lowest of any nation on Earth (29.2, 146th out of 146) on the ESI. Its lower categories were in reducing natural disaster vulnerability (lowest), greenhouse gas emissions, international collaborative efforts, environmental governance, and reducing air pollution. The country's only moderately positive category was in reducing population stress. The highest ranking nation was Finland (score 75.1). The highest ranking Asian nation was Japan (score 57.3, 30th), followed by the less developed South and Southeast Asian nations of Bhutan (43rd), Myanmar (46th), Laos (52nd), and Cambodia (68th) (Esty et al. 2005).

North Korea's lack of development offers positives in reducing population pressure and protection of remote habitats. Low negative scores, however, in greenhouse gas emissions, lack of collaboration, environmental governance, and other areas will likely continue to outweigh the positives.

South Korea has numerous sustainable development policy initiatives, including a National Action Plan for Agenda 21, an Environmental Vision for the New Millennium, an Act to Promote Shifting to an Environmentally Friendly Industrial Structure, and a Presidential Commission on Sustainable Development.

Responsiveness in the private sector is another positive, including energy-saving initiatives by major firms. A recent corporate responsibility study of South Korean firms, however, found few reporting and, of those participating, strong reporting on environmental issues but poor reporting on social issues, including human rights. A traditional culture of limited corporate transparency thus may limit "win-win" improvements such as building sustainability into the core business model and life cycle of products (Boston Common Asset Management 2010; Perks 2012).

Hope may lie in accentuating positive trends in science and technology and environmental governance. The nation is 97 percent dependent on expensive imported fuel. A recent financial stimulus package included 81 percent (approximately $37 billion) for green initiatives such as bike trails, mass transit, and energy-saving technologies. Activists are skeptical, given calls for increased nuclear energy and river restoration projects that pave streams. Offshore wind energy may attract $9 billion in investment, while wave and tidal power may offer added power (Watts 2009). South Korea is also looking at tapping geothermal energy potential in the Philippines. International collaboration, currently with a low positive score, may be where increased efforts by South Korea have the widest-ranging impact, addressing effects of consumption on global resources.

William FORBES
Stephen F. Austin State University

See also China; Energy Industries—Nuclear; Energy Security (East Asia); India; Japan; Nongovernmental Organizations (NGOs); Public Transportation; Public-Private Partnerships; Southeast Asia

FURTHER READING

Boston Common Asset Management. (2010, April 21). South Korean companies embrace environmental sustainability, but human rights and board independence remain key challenges. Retrieved April 9, 2012, from http://www.csrwire.com/press_releases/29426-South-Korean-companies-embrace-environmental-sustainability-but-human-rights-and-board-independence-remain-key-challenges

Chung, Jae-Yong, & Kirkby, Richard J. (2002). *The political economy of development and environment in Korea*. London: Routledge Press.

Edmunds, David, & Wollenberg, Eva. (2001). Historical perspectives on forest policy change in Asia: An introduction. *Environmental History*, 6(2), 190–212.

Esty, Daniel C.; Levy, Marc; Srebotnjak, Tanja; & de Sherbinin, Alexander. (2005). *2005 Environmental Sustainability Index: Benchmarking national environmental stewardship*. New Haven: Yale Center for Environmental Law & Policy. Retrieved April 7, 2012, from http://sedac.ciesin.columbia.edu/es/esi/index.html

International Institute for Sustainable Development. (2004). Republic of Korea case study (Unedited working paper). Retrieved April 7, 2012, from http://www.iisd.org/pdf/2004/measure_sdsip_korea.pdf

Joe, Wanne J., & Choe, Hongkyu A. (1982). *Traditional Korea: A cultural history*. Seoul: Chung'ang University Press.

Korea.net. (2012). Homepage. Retrieved April 7, 2012, from http://www.korea.net/main

Ministry of the Environment, Republic of Korea. (n.d.). Presidential commission on sustainable development. Retrieved April 7, 2012, from http://eng.me.go.kr/content.do?method=moveContent&menuCode=pol_pol_edu_gov_presidential

Perks, Jason. (2012, March 27). Sustainability: Why South Korea's industrial firms need to do more. *The Guardian*. Retrieved April 7, 2012, from http://www.guardian.co.uk/sustainable-business/south-korea-industry-sustainability-strategy

Sang-Hun, Choe. (2010, March 1). Korean women flock to government. Retrieved April 10, 2012, from http://www.nytimes.com/2010/03/02/world/asia/02iht-women.html

Suh, Moon-Gi. (1998). *Developmental transformation in South Korea: From state-sponsored growth to the quest for quality of life*. Santa Barbara, CA: Greenwood Publishing Group.

Tay, Simon S. C., & Esty, Daniel C. (Eds.). (1996). *Asian dragons and green trade: Environment, economics, and international law*. Singapore: Times Academic Press.

United States Central Intelligence Agency (US CIA). (2012). The world factbook: Korea, South, and Korea, North. Retrieved April 9, 2012, from https://www.cia.gov/library/publications/the-world-factbook/geos/ks.html and https://www.cia.gov/library/publications/the-world-factbook/geos/kn.html

Watts, Jonathan. (2009, April 20). South Korea lights the way on carbon emissions with its £23bn green deal. Retrieved April 9, 2012, from http://www.guardian.co.uk/environment/2009/apr/21/south-korea-enviroment-carbon-emissions

Kuala Lumpur, Malaysia

1.6 million est. pop. 2006 (includes Federal Territory only)

The city of Kuala Lumpur industrialized rapidly following its independence from Britain in 1957. With the formation of the nation of Malaysia in 1963, the city took center stage in national development and, since the 1980s, has seen extensive building projects and technology networks. The material and symbolic transformations of Kuala Lumpur is both a vibrant expression of postcolonial nation building and global political Malay identifications.

The Federal Territory of Kuala Lumpur, formed in the 1850s at the confluence of the Klang and Gombak rivers (in Malay, *kuala* means "muddy confluence"), is the national capital of Malaysia, although administrative functions are located at Putrajaya, a purpose-built government city located 25 kilometers south of Kuala Lumpur. In this overview, Kuala Lumpur is defined to include primarily the Federal Territory of Kuala Lumpur, which has its own city council (Dewan Bandaraya Kuala Lumpur, or DBKL). Its suburbs, including principally Petaling Jaya, while regarded as part of the Kuala Lumpur conurbation, are technically within the state jurisdiction of Selangor.

History and Development

In 1857 a group of Chinese miners began mining tin in the area where the Klang and Gombak rivers come together, and a member of the Selangor royal family, Raja Abdullah, opened up the Klang Valley for additional tin prospecting. As miners came to the area, a new settlement began grow. Prosperity drew a large population, making Kuala Lumpur an overcrowded and unhealthy place, often damaged by floods or fire. Much of the early trading-post town was destroyed in the fire and subsequent floods of 1881 because of the ephemeral quality of the building materials, which were wood and *atap* (thatch roof) (Sulaiman and Zubir 2004). From 1884 to 1890, the population grew from 4,500 to 20,000. The rapid expansion, particularly with the construction of a railway line between the harbor town of Klang and Kuala Lumpur (completed in 1886) also led to widespread development of rubber estates around Kuala Lumpur. Piped water in the late 1890s and then a town electricity supply a few years later served a growing population. By 1920 the population of Kuala Lumpur had grown to 80,000 (Gullick 2000).

In 1972 Kuala Lumpur was given city status, and in 1974 it became a separate Federal Territory. The handing over of 243 square kilometers of land to the federal government on 1 February 1974 marked a new beginning for Kuala Lumpur and heralded a progressive enlargement of its territorial boundaries. The city continued to grow despite the two World Wars, and following independence from British rule in 1957 and the formation of Malaysia in 1963, it became the administrative center and took center stage in national development. By the 1970s the demarcated area of the city held a population of about 450,000 and grew steadily due to a combination of industrialization as well as a concentration of federal and state government employees. This city is now known more formally as Wilayah Persekutuan (Federal Territory) Kuala Lumpur and has an estimated population of 1.6 million (according to a 2006 census).

Beginning in the mid-1980s, Kuala Lumpur underwent policy shifts, notably privatization and economic liberalization, and has become the locus of spectacular megaprojects such as the Menara Maybank, the Kuala Lumpur City Centre (KLCC) project, the PETRONAS Twin Towers, the Hiijas Kasturi (LUTH) tower, and the more recent Telecoms Tower (2002). While the constitutional division of state and federal powers over green practices for sustainable development is complex and frequently difficult to ascertain, reports such as that of EarthCheck (n.d.), a global sustainable travel and tourism certification organization, reveal that there is a concerted effort to improve and sustain green practices in development. The EarthCheck report indicates that KLCC became the first convention center in Asia to achieve EarthCheck Benchmarked status, which means it has developed a sustainability policy and measured its performance indicators above a baseline level (the audit covered the period 2005–2010).

Infrastructure development was a major priority in the 1984 Kuala Lumpur Structure Plan. Modern telecommunications and transport infrastructures were emphasized to ensure that Kuala Lumpur was building for a global network. The National Information Technology Agenda (NITA) was formulated in 1996 and provided the framework for the development of an extensive infrastructure to support an information and communication technologies (ICT) network that would encompass Kuala Lumpur and the wider Klang Valley region. This multimedia super corridor embedded through the center of Kuala Lumpur city—designated a world test site for ICT developments and supported by a set of world-leading cyberlaws—became the centerpiece for a city and a state that was simultaneously modern and Muslim (a majority of the national population are Malay Muslims).

Construction of a new light rapid transit system, a commuter train network, and the people-mover rapid transit tract in the commercial core of Kuala Lumpur began in 2005. Phased to be completed in 2015, this network, also known as the Kuala Lumpur Sentral, comprises the central station, corporate office towers and business suites, five-star international hotels, luxury condominiums, and a shopping mall. The globalization of greater Kuala Lumpur in the first decades of the twenty-first century has been manifested in its extensive landscape transformation and is the clearest sign of the city's increased role in global financial networks. These strategies through which the Malaysian state has sought to position itself in these transnational, networked times has also raised questions of what effect private-sector-driven development of wired urban living and working spaces and their world-class exclusivity (Bunnell and Nah 2004) has on new possibilities of social and spatial fragmentation and decay.

Human and Physical Geography

When the multimedia super corridor became a reality, architectural icons such as the KLCC project were the first to incorporate the idea of a city within a city, connecting the Golden Triangle (Kuala Lumpur's business hub) and making the area more accessible through a maze of covered verandaways of building or tree pathways, accessible only on foot (Sulaiman and Zubir 2004). The KLCC project development encompassed a freehold prime property of nearly 40.5 hectares, enclosing the PETRONAS Twin Towers and divided into sections of office buildings, hotels, retail stores, a convention center, and residential and recreational facilities. Incorporation of the pathways was meant to contribute to sustainable practices such as reduced fuel use and air pollution, as well as promote recreation and wellness activities such as walking for the urban population.

The announcement of the plans to build a new multimedia super corridor in 1996 put in place a vast but interconnected urban region, now known as the Kuala Lumpur Metropolitan Area. A series of new transport projects would now integrate Kuala Lumpur with Kuala Lumpur International Airport (KLIA) and Putrajaya and include the new "intelligent" city, Cyber Jaya, with the broader Klang Valley region. The whole corridor extending from KLCC in Kuala Lumpur to KLIA has been built on a fiber optic backbone, both to attract world-class information technology companies and to connect the greater metropolitan area into an emerging global information economy and society. Despite regional redistribution goals, particularly following the New Economic Policy from the early 1970s (Bunnell, Barter, and Morshidi 2002), urban development has been undertaken at a rate that has made the express policy of sustainable development itself difficult to sustain. Similar indications have been made by the Canadian researcher Andrew Harding and the Malay researcher Azmi Sharom:

> What is clear from the legislation, apart from certain sections of the TCPA [the Town and Country Planning Act 1976] and the EIA [Environment Impact Assessment] requirements of the EQA [the Environmental Quality Act, passed in 1974, established the Department of Environment within the Ministry of Science, Technology and Environment] is that there is precious little room for the public to take part in any decision-making. (Harding and Sharom 2007, 152)

The public is therefore left with post-decision-making decisions, which can take two forms: to litigate or to object (Harding and Sharom 2007, 152).

The center of Kuala Lumpur still retains some of his historical character, especially around sites such as Chinatown and the Merdeka (Independence) Square and some of its surrounding public buildings. Most of these buildings now are adapted to others uses, such as the National Museum, but are also connected to the modern architecture through the rapid transport system.

Major urban landscape change in the 1990s also gave rise to a new southern corridor, namely the extended Kuala Lumpur Metropolitan Area, which, with increased demands for urban space, was contested vigorously within new and evolving systems of evaluation about land use.

An amended Land Acquisitions Act of 1991 now enables the state authority, without provision for judicial review, to alter or invalidate any previously disposed land in the name of "general public good," specifically, to acquire land that is "needed by any person or corporation for any purpose which in the opinion of the State Authority is beneficial to the economic development of Malaysia or any part thereof or to the public generally or any class of the public" (Land Acquisition [Amended] Act 1991, s.3(b)). Whether this will contribute to sustainable development is difficult to ascertain, particularly as the demand for space and land has intensified—and various levels of contestations exist at local municipality, state, and federal aspirations and ambitions.

Environment and Housing

The Environmental Quality Act 1974 (EQA) is administered through the federal Ministry of Science, Technology and Environment. With the abolition of local government elections (Federal Capital Act 1960, rev. 1970, Act 190), the appointment of the mayor and councilors is relegated to state authorities (since 1965), and with DBKL placed under the prime minister's department, the constitutional division of state and federal powers over environmental matters is complex. The absence of local electoral accountabilities and of autonomous authority for local authorities also makes it extremely difficult for the public to determine unaccountability and threats to the local environment. Avenues for citizens of the city to determine measures to protect the environment can also be limited and complicated. A review of local newspapers during four weeks in June–July 1995 revealed "an extraordinary array of environmental problems in KL, but also a corresponding awareness and concern" (Harding and Sharom 2007, 127). The main concerns raised were inadequate housing, lack of "green lungs" areas, air pollution, haze from forest fires nearby (inclusive of Indonesia), and water pollution. The provision of housing for low-income groups remains perhaps the single most significant problem facing planners in Kuala Lumpur (Bunnell, Barter, and Morshidi 2002).

The 2006 census shows that Kuala Lumpur is now home to 1.6 million people, with an estimated growth to 2.2 million expected by the year 2020. (The population is estimated to be around 5.9 million if the surrounding urban areas are taken into consideration [Demographia 2011 4, 15].) As a socially and economically dynamic city in which the definition of poverty is changing rapidly (Harding and Sharom 2007), the city provides insight into what is an increasingly complex and interwoven confluence of people, settlements, and development agendas. The Kuala Lumpur Plan 2020 stipulates that Kuala Lumpur is set to become a world-class city by 2020 in the areas of living environment, working environment, business environment, and city governance. It is emblematic of a pattern across former colonies to replace a former colonial city with one that symbolizes the state's national ideology and aspirations. As such, the evolving city of Kuala Lumpur is both a vibrant expression of postcolonial nation building and a site of continuing debate over what is national, what is global, and what inevitably is rooted in local sensibilities.

Yaso NADARAJAH
Royal Melbourne Institute of Technology (RMIT)

See also Activism, Judicial; Cities—Overview; Education, Environmental (*several articles*); Genetic Resources; Information and Communication Technologies (ICT); Media Coverage of the Environment; Nongovernmental Organizations (NGOs); Public Transportation; Rule of Law; Southeast Asia

FURTHER READING

Azizah, Kassim. (1983). The genesis of squatting in west Malaysia with special reference to the Malays in the Federal Territory. *Malaysia in History, 26*, 60–83.

Bunnell, Tim; Barter, Paul A.; & Morshidi, Sirat. (2002). Kuala Lumpur metropolitan area: A globalizing city-region. *Cities, 19*(5), 357–370.

Bunnell, Tim, & Nah, Alice M. (2004). Counter-global cases for place: Contesting displacement in globalising Kuala Lumpur metropolitan area. *Urban Studies, 41*(12), 2447–2467.

Demographia. (2011). Demographia world urban areas (world agglomerations). 7th Annual Edition. Retrieved March 30, 2012, from http://www.demographia.com/db-worldua.pdf

EarthCheck. (n.d.). Kuala Lumpur Convention Center. Retrieved January 12, 2012, from http://www.earthcheck.org/media/2563/cs22_kuala_lumpur_convention_centre_case_study.pdf

Gullick, John. (2000). *Kuala Lumpur 1857–1939* (MBRA Monograph no.29). Kuala Lumpur: Kuala Lumpur Malaysia Branch of the Royal Asiatic Society.

Harding, Andrew, & Sharom, Azmi. (2007). Access to environmental justice in Malaysia. In Andrew Harding (Ed.), *Access to environmental justice: A comparative study* (pp. 125–156). Leiden, The Netherlands: Koninklijke Brill Nv.

Morshidi, Sirat, & Suriati, Ghazali. (1999). *Globalisation of economic activity and third world cities: A case study of Kuala Lumpur.* Kuala Lumpur: Utusan.

Nadarajah, Yaso. (2010). Kuala Lumpur, Malaysia. In *Annual Review 2010, Global Cities* (pp. 88–97). Melbourne, Australia: Global Cities Research Institute, RMIT University.

Phang, Siew N.; Kuppusamy, Singaravelloo; & Norris, Malcolm W. (1996). Metropolitan management of Kuala Lumpur. In Jurgen Ruland (Ed.), *The dynamics of metropolitan management in Southeast Asia* (pp. 133–167). Singapore: Institute of Southeast Asian Studies.

Ong, Aihwa. (1999). *Flexible citizenship: The cultural logics of transnationality.* London: Duke University Press.

Sardar, Ziauddin. (2000). *The consumption of Kuala Lumpur.* London: Reaktion Books.

Sulaiman, Wan Azhar, & Zubir, Syed Sobri. (2004, June 9–11). Verandahways as catalysts for walking in a tropical city (paper, Fifth International Conference on Walking in the 21st Century, "Walk21-V Cities for People"). Copenhagen, Denmark.

Tay, Lillian, & Ngiom Lim Teng. (Eds.). (2000). *80 years of architecture in Malaysia.* Kuala Lumpur: Pertubuhan Akitek Malaysia.

L

Labor

In many countries economic growth has increasingly become capital and skill intensive, depriving a vast section of the unskilled and semiskilled workers from accessing productive jobs. In the broad context of globalization, the need for competitiveness has forced many countries to pursue strategies that deny labor its due share. Interventions in various forms are essential for a just society and for development to be sustainable.

Both China and India are witnessing rapid economic growth; labor intensive Chinese consumer goods have flooded the international market. Both countries hold a great potential to emerge as the major markets in the world economy because the vast middle income group is expected to generate enormous demand. In addition, the cost advantages in both the countries are likely to attract producers worldwide, which in turn may contribute to future economic growth in these countries and benefit others as well. Growth has been impressive in some of the other Asian countries also, although it has been sluggish; persistent poverty remains in certain other parts of the continent. The question is whether countries with faster growth have experienced rapid employment growth. Roughly 40 percent of the world's poor live in South Asia. Poverty reduction strategies need to generate productive employment in the process of growth.

The relationship between economic growth and poverty is complex. It has long been recognized that growth alone cannot reduce poverty, though it may be a necessary condition for poverty reduction. Further, globalization forced many countries to pursue a growth-oriented approach, which did not necessarily lead to significant reductions in poverty. The structural elements at the country level therefore need to be modified to derive greater benefits from growth, particularly keeping in view the long-standing goals of poverty reduction in these countries. A number of countries have not experienced the standard *poverty-growth elasticity* (i.e., proportionate fall in the poverty due to proportionate rise in economic growth) of –2, which means that a 1 percent increase in growth reduces poverty by 2 percent. Poverty rates in some middle-income countries are far higher than predicted, possibly indicating that the changes in income distribution are weakening the expected impact of growth, and/or the income distribution around the poverty line might be changing with an increased differentiation (i.e., rising inequality) among the poor (Weiss and Khan 2006).

Market Indicators

Labor market analysis can be pursued at the aggregate level by examining the labor force participation rate (LFPR), which is the proportion of labor force—the workforce plus the unemployed—to the total population. The work participation rate is the proportion of working persons to the total population. Both these ratios are a function of a large number of variables falling into the domain of social, cultural, demographic, and economic aspects of life. Some supply-side variables like fast natural population and immigration growth raise the supplies of labor. Others, like a rise in school enrollment and human capital formation, reduce labor-force participation in the short run. On the other hand, demand-side factors like rapid urbanization, industrialization, and commercialization provide an impetus to work participation. Work participation rates in general and for women are at times largely an outcome of supply-side variables. Poor households cannot afford to remain unemployed for long and join the entry-free low-productivity informal sector in the absence of any alternative. A high work participation rate and poverty can coexist. Women are often burdened by household responsibilities, which reduce their participation in the labor market. Their low work participation rate thus does not necessarily translate into a low demand for women's labor.

The Key Indicators of Labour Market (KILM), Sixth Edition dataset of the International Labour Organization (ILO) shows that the female labor participation varies considerably across countries. At two time points (1980 and 2006), India, Pakistan, and Sri Lanka show a participation rate of less than 35 percent. Cambodia, China, Papua New Guinea, Thailand, and Vietnam, on the other hand, show a rate of nearly 70 percent or more (ILO 2010). Factors like education, cultural attitudes toward female work, and other socioeconomic conditions that influence the female work participation rate cannot be ruled out in these cross-country variations. Over time these variations are declining, possibly indicating that some of the countries with low female labor participation rates are catching up.

In contrast to female labor-force participation rate, the male LFPR shows fewer variations across countries. The ratio of female-to-male participation rate, however, shows wide variations—from 0.45 to 0.92—implying that in some of the countries women's labor participation rate is less than half of its male counterpart, whereas in others it is as high as that of the males (ILO 2010). The female-male differences are extremely high in India, Pakistan, and Sri Lanka, whereas Vietnam; Vanuatu; Papua New Guinea; Macao, China; and Thailand show minimal differences between the sexes. The correlation coefficient reflecting on the degree of association between the female and male labor force participation is very low (0.18 for 2005), as seen from ILO dataset (ILO 2010). The positive correlation, however, possibly indicates that as economic activities expand, opportunities for both male and female labor increase, to which the supplies respond positively. In other words, the hypothesis of male labor being substituted by female labor because of wage differences does not seem to always be valid. But given the fact that the complementary relation is not too strong, countries must not leave low women's participation to the market forces and wait for demand to grow and bridge the gender gap. Their policies need to address this problem so that women's participation in the labor market increases rapidly.

Growth and Technology

Globalization has detrimentally affected employment in many countries. The growth process and technological progress seem to have become increasingly more capital and skill intensive; opportunities for unskilled and semi-skilled workers are meager. The relatively low skill base of a large number of workers deprives them of upward mobility.

The diffusion of primary education in East Asia has been possibly the single most important factor reducing poverty and income inequality. These countries generally allocated a much larger proportion of their public investment for agriculture and rural development than most other developing countries at comparable stages of their development. Growth became broad based and labor intensive with improved income distribution (Hashim 1998). Investment in physical and human capital with special emphasis on developing human resources and effective participation in international markets, leading to expanding employment at higher productivity, contributed to both reduction in poverty and enhancement of growth.

Women's employment share in agriculture is high in countries with low per capita income (ILO 2000). The percentage of the female workforce engaged in agriculture has been larger than its male counterpart in Bangladesh, Cambodia, Korea, Malaysia, Pakistan, Sri Lanka, and for some of the years in Thailand. As men look for better employment opportunities outside agriculture, women pursue work on family farms. Rapid industrialization has led to a larger percentage of workers in manufacturing in some countries. In other countries, however, the services sector grew before the manufacturing sector could absorb a sizable chunk of the work force. In the case of female workers this can be partly rationalized in terms of their strong preference to work in the services sector (Mitra 2010). Because of low human capital endowment, workers can afford to enter the services sector relatively more easily compared to manufacturing.

Yet we also need to recognize the fact that several countries are experiencing rapid tertiarization—that is, the services sector has become the largest segment of the economy—in response to demand for new services, introduction of information technology (IT) and IT-related services, outsourcing of business services by the developed countries to the developing countries, and so on. These factors have led to increased labor absorption in the services sector. Most of the advantages, however, have reached only those who have higher levels of human capital endowments because many services such as accounting and medical services need skilled workers. On the other hand, within the vast spectrum of the services sector, there are many pockets that do not require skill, for example personal services and retail trade, and are grossly characterized by low productivity.

Manufacturing is both capital and skill intensive. Poor resource endowment and limited human capital formation mean that fewer people are employable in the high productivity manufacturing sector. Further, the limited spread of the high productivity manufacturing sector in many countries and/or the import of capital-intensive technology from the Western world have restricted workers' entry into the high-productivity industrial sector (Mitra 2009). Domestic innovation measured in terms of research and development expenditure as a percentage of total sales or profits is incredibly low in many sectors, implying inadequate efforts made by the domestic firms to innovate technology that suits the domestic labor market. On the other hand, reduction in import tariffs and other trade reforms have facilitated the free flow of technology across borders, which is highly capital intensive in nature. Although this process is favorable to total factor productivity growth, employment growth in the manufacturing sector has remained sluggish. In fact, in Bangladesh, Indonesia, Laos, Mongolia, Pakistan, and the Philippines, the pace of workers entering the industrialization sector has been quite slow. For India there is a sizable discrepancy between the changes that are occurring in the composition of value added and those in the occupational structure (Mitra 2008). And this is usually explained, as mentioned above, in terms of the nature of technology, factor price distortions (the relative price of capital being kept at a low), and sluggish or no growth in the production of labor-intensive manufacturing goods, leading to a slow demand for labor. Competitiveness has forced many countries to reduce the share of labor in value added, that is, the proportion of wage income to value added. Though this process helps capture the external (foreign) market, issues relating to inequality and poverty are unlikely to get settled.

Informal Sector

The relative size of the informal sector is dominant both in the rural and the urban areas, particularly in South Asia. While most of the rural workers would fall within the domain of the informal sector, in the urban areas the share of the informal sector is at least 50 percent (Mitra 2001). The composition of rural informal or unorganized sector employment shows that a large majority is located in the agricultural activities. In some of the regions the rural nonfarm sector has witnessed the growth of the demand-induced component whereas in several others the informal sector is a manifestation of supply-push phenomenon (i.e., large supplies of labor relative to demand forcing many to pick up residual or marginal activities). East Asia is the role model for the demand-induced growth of the rural nonfarm sector. Agricultural and urban-based activities complement each other, thus contributing substantially to growth in employment opportunity for the rural population.

The urban informal sector comprises both manufacturing and tertiary activities. In many countries, informal sector workers earn low wages because supplies of labor exceed demand and because products manufactured in the informal sector are of poor quality and have a limited market (Mitra 2001). Most of the informal sector workers are outside the purview of any labor market protection (Mitra 1994). Intense informalization is accompanied by high levels of morbidity, a large reserve labor supply, and low job security (Salway, Rahman, and Jesmin 2003). Capital-intensive forms of production meet the growing demand of the middle class for higher-quality standardized products, thus excluding low-skilled poor workers (Wood and Salway 2000). China may be an exception in this respect as the products of small manufacturing enterprises have captured the world market. Similarly some of the East Asian economies have many success stories. The episodes of vulnerability, however, are enormous in many other parts. Other than the informal sector employment, what has become increasingly evident is informal employment, which includes casual and contractual employment, in the formal sector. In the era of globalization, several countries have introduced labor market reforms directly or indirectly that have substantially raised the incidence of informal employment in the formal sector (Mitra 2008).

Networks

The concept of "social capital" provides a substantive basis to the understanding of how labor markets in developing countries function and how individuals, particularly those with low incomes, access jobs. Job seekers use caste/kinship bonds and contacts through co-villagers and co-residents of the cluster in which they live to pursue a rural-based search for urban jobs and to migrate to urban areas for employment (Mitra 2010). Most networks are informal. Private contractors have taken a role in rural-to-rural and rural-to-urban migration.

There is no strong evidence to confirm that workers can improve their earnings through networks. On the contrary, traditional networks reduce the possibility of upward mobility by creating information asymmetry and excess supplies of labor in certain pockets and activities. On the other hand, labor intermediaries, who have grown sizably, particularly in the post-globalization period, squeeze a substantial part of the remuneration that the workers receive.

The Future

Areas in which social capital plays a dominant role need to be identified. Government initiatives must complement individual efforts so that the measures remain cost efficient, creating possibilities of public-private partnership development. State interventions and the role of civil society are essential to remove information asymmetry and gross inequalities leading to social and economic deprivation of certain sections of the population, and to create economic opportunities for all in the process of growth. Investment in physical infrastructure and basic amenities for the poor is necessary. Issues relating to livelihood, microcredit, job training and skills upgrading, institutional support, and health benefits to low-income workers need immediate attention.

Arup MITRA
Institute of Economic Growth, Delhi

See also Consumerism; Education, Female; Gender Equality; Green Collar Jobs; Information and Communication Technologies (ICT); Microfinance; Outsourcing and Offshoring; Rural Development; Rural Livelihoods; Steel Industry

FURTHER READING

Hashim, S. R. (1998). Foreword. In Ashoka Chandra, Horst Mund, Tripurari Sharan & C. P. Thakur (Eds.), *Labour, employment and human development in South Asia*. Delhi: B. R. Publishing Corporation.

International Labour Organization (ILO). (2010). *Key indicators of the labour market* (6th ed.). Geneva: ILO.

International Labour Organization (ILO). (2000). Towards full employment: 2.4 Gender inequalities. ILO, Regional Office for the Asia and the Pacific, Bangkok. Retrieved October 6, 2011, from http://www.ilo.org/public/english/region/asro/bangkok/feature/f-emp24.htm

Mitra, Arup. (1994). *Urbanisation, slums, informal sector employment and poverty: An exploratory study*. Delhi: B. R. Publishing Corporation.

Mitra, Arup. (2001). Employment in the informal sector. In Amitabh Kundu & Alakh N. Sharma (Eds.), *Informal sector in India: Perspectives and policies* (pp. 85–92). Delhi: Institute for Human Development and Institute of Applied Manpower Research.

Mitra, Arup. (2008). The Indian labour market: An overview (ILO-Asia Pacific Working Paper Series). New Delhi: International Labour Organization.

Mitra, Arup. (2009). Technology import and industrial employment: Evidence from developing countries. *LABOUR, 23*(4), 697–718.

Mitra, Arup. (2010). Migration, livelihood and well-being: Evidence from Indian city-slums. *Urban Studies, 47*(7), 1371–1390.

Mitra, Arup. (2011). Trade in services: Impact on employment in India. *Social Science Journal, 48*(1), 72–93.

Salway, Sarah; Rahman, Shahana; & Jesmin, Sonia. (2003). A profile of women's work participation among the urban poor of Dhaka. *World Development, 31*(5), 881–901.

Weiss, John, & Khan, Haider A. (2006). *Poverty strategies in Asia: A growth plus approach*. Cheltenham, UK: Asian Development Bank Institute & Edward Elgar.

Wood, Geof, & Salway, Sarah. (2000). Introduction: Securing livelihoods in Dhaka slums. *Journal of International Development, 12*(5), 669–688.

M

Media Coverage of the Environment

As environmental problems have become more visible, media coverage about sustainability issues has grown across Asia. In both India and China, environmental journalists have found an increasingly important social role as watchdogs in fast-growing economies where environmental concerns can sometimes be sacrificed for the sake of rapid development. In China, environmental reporting has played an important role in a nascent civil society.

Media coverage of sustainability topics has increased in Asia as public concern has grown regarding many environmental issues, from water scarcity to food safety, from the impacts of large infrastructure projects to climate change. Journalism has both reflected and influenced public opinion on these issues across Asia, and there have been a number of notable policy reversals and changes across the region as a result of media pressure. This article focuses on the two largest players in Asia (India and the People's Republic of China) and on their notably contrasting approaches to journalism about the environment.

In China, government efforts to limit the scope and effectiveness of journalism are common. Online opinion and reporting are subject to wide-ranging and sophisticated censorship. Information about environmental incidents and protests is sometimes tightly controlled. For nine days in July 2010, for example, the Zijin Mining Company managed to avert media reports about a massive leak from one of its copper mines into the Ting River in Fujian Province. The leak caused the death of more than 1,500 tonnes of fish. The jailing and harassment of reporters that cover sensitive topics, including environmental investigations, continues. The Press Freedom Index 2011–2012—an annual report of the measured degree of freedom enjoyed by journalists and media in over 170 countries—published by Reporters Without Borders, ranked China fifth from the bottom in its ranking of 178 nations. Nevertheless, environmental reporting in China has grown to become an important and dynamic part of the media landscape.

Media sources have multiplied rapidly and partially liberalized in China, particularly since the early 1990s. Over two thousand newspapers and about ten thousand periodicals and magazines are published. By 2008 China was home to the largest number of Internet users in the world. Private and local government–owned newspapers and magazines increasingly compete for readers, leading to a declining audience for central government–controlled media. Many of these more independent publications—including *Caijing*, *New Century Weekly*, *Economic Observer*, and *Southern Weekend*—are known for their hard-hitting investigative reports, particularly where environmental topics are concerned.

China's oldest and largest environmental nongovernmental organization (NGO), Friends of Nature, has conducted studies that show an increasing frequency of environmental terms in Chinese newspapers since the mid-1990s. This trend intensified during the following decade, notably around 2007, when Chinese television and newspaper coverage of climate change increased significantly after the publication of the Fourth Assessment Report by the Intergovernmental Panel on Climate Change. This report addressed scientific, technical, and socioeconomic aspects of global warming. In 2010 a number of Chinese newspapers (*Southern Weekend* and *21st Century Business Herald*, for example) launched environmental sections, and popular websites, portals, and online messaging services (such as Tencent QQ, a free online messaging service), set up environment channels. Specialized environmental publications (such as the daily *China Environment News*) also exist in China.

Since environmental reports are seen as less sensitive than political or human-rights stories in China, articles about sustainability-related topics are often used as vehicles for addressing social issues, from institutional corruption to the lack of transparency or public participation in policy making. One of China's best-known environmental journalists, Liu Jianqiang, summed up this phenomenon in a 2010 interview: "The environment in China is not politics; politics is very sensitive. Journalists do find it easier to report about the environment. But my question has always been who is really harming China's environment? It's not you, me or the common people. It's the huge interest groups out there. From local governments to companies and corporations, there are huge stakes in maximizing profit" (Liu 2010, 1).

The media landscape in India is older, more diverse, better established, and more vocal than it is in China. Like China, India is also a fast-growing market, with a rapidly growing online population. Sustainability-focused publications, such as the biweekly magazine *Down to Earth*, do exist in India. But because other forms of investigative journalism are also permitted there—and sustainability-focused reporters compete with more sensational genres—environmental journalism occupies a less prominent public role in India than it does in China.

Nevertheless, many environmental stories have emerged in India and have captured the imagination of the public both at home and beyond. The first such one arose in the mid-1970s, when the women of the so-called Chipko movement hugged trees in an act of Gandhian, nonviolent protest, to prevent them from being felled. As in other parts of Asia (notably Indonesia), deforestation has been a contentious issue for decades in India and has been covered frequently by the Indian media. Since the government has tended to blame the slash-and-burn agricultural techniques of tribal peoples—whereby sections of forests are burned to create open fields—for the problem of deforestation, environmental reporters have played a central role in exposing the role of industry and the timber lobby in deforestation and defending the traditional livelihoods of indigenous peoples.

It was the Bhopal tragedy of 1984, however, that is cited by many environmental reporters as their introduction to the field of environmental reporting. During this incident, methyl isocyanate gas (a highly toxic substance) and other chemicals leaked from a pesticide plant owned by Union Carbide, resulting in the exposure of hundreds of thousands of people to the harmful substances. The death toll released by the state government of Madhya Pradesh, in central India, was 3,787; around 40,000 people were left disabled or suffering from serious illnesses. Other sources report as many as 8,000 deaths, initially, with 20,000 to 30,000 subsequent deaths. The Mumbai-based journalist Kalpana Sharma explained that

> [the Bhopal disaster] revealed the indifference of policy makers to the interests of poor people who were allowed to live in the vicinity of such a hazardous industry without knowledge of what to do in an emergency.... Bhopal is an environmental story but also a political one. It has already illustrated the power of big industry over government. It has shown how difficult it is for victims who are also poor to get their voices heard." (Sharma 2012)

In 2009, protests against the mining operations of the UK-headquartered company Vedanta Resources became a major focus of media coverage when critics said that a proposed bauxite mine in Orissa (in eastern India) would threaten indigenous livelihoods and an important wildlife habitat.

Much as in China, reports about climate change have been on the rise in India since 2007. The tone of the coverage in India, however, has often been anticolonial or nationalistic—its main emphasis being the risks borne by India and the responsibilities of developed countries to act—a perspective honed during the 1990s by writers and campaigners (such as Anil Agarwal and Sunita Narain) from India's environmental movement. By contrast, Chinese-language coverage of the topic increasingly tends to emphasize the economic benefits of the low-carbon economy for China. In 2010, Zou Xi, a journalist for the *Beijing Science & Technology Report,* explained this phenomenon this way: "This is not a right-or-wrong issue. It's only about negotiation. Everyone is trying to grasp opportunities in this green wave and make a compromise at the same time" (Liu 2009, 1).

Key Campaigns and Controversies

In 2004 the Chinese environmental movement had its first major success, when a proposed cascade of dams on Asia's longest undammed river, southwest China's Nu River—known as the Salween when it flows into Thailand and Myanmar (Burma)—was shelved after Premier Wen Jiabao personally intervened. The campaign started with an investigation by journalists, photographers, and scholars from Beijing, who applied pressure in the media after joining with local grassroots activists and campaigners from downstream countries. The following year, a media outcry also helped to spark China's first state-level public environmental hearing—overseen by the then outspoken and media-friendly environmental official Pan Yue—investigating the lack of an environmental impact assessment for the laying of an impermeable plastic lining on a lake-bed at the Old Summer Palace (an important historical site in Beijing). The academic Zhang Zhengchun initially published an article about the project on the website of the *People's Daily* newspaper, but not long after the story was featured across a number of outlets including *Southern Weekend*. Partly based on an analysis of the Nu River campaign, the sociologists Guobin Yang and Craig Calhoun wrote that China has seen the emergence of a "green public sphere," with mass media, the Internet, and unofficial green publications as its main channels of communication (Yang and Calhoun 2007, 211).

In India the ongoing struggle over the Sardar Sarovar Project, one of a number of large dams planned on the Narmada River in the western state of Gujarat, has been a contentious issue and a major story for many environmental reporters. The prominent documentary filmmaker Anand Patwardhan weighed in on this debate with his 1995 film *A Narmada Diary*, coproduced and codirected with the activist Simantini Dhuru. Kalpana Sharma wrote of the campaign: "The resistance to the construction of the dam by the [Save Narmada Movement] brought into the public arena the concept of 'destructive development.' Till then all development was considered good. Dams were the temples of modern India, people were told" (Sharma 2012, 1).

Another controversial environmental debate that questioned concepts of development and was played out in the Indian media was the public uproar over biotechnology that led to a moratorium in 2010 on Bt brinjal, a type of genetically modified (GM) eggplant developed by India's Maharashtra Hybrid Seeds Company (Mahyco) in partnership with the US-based multinational Monsanto. Some news reports claimed that eating the vegetable "can make you sick" (Sharma 2011, 1); others said its development may have "violated a law" (*The Telegraph* 2010, 1) protecting the country's genetic resources. Contrary reports in the Indian media, however, argued that farmers would bear the costs of such a ban, that India had missed a "window of opportunity to leap forward" (Padmanaban 2011, 157), and that green NGOs had used "falsehoods, scare stories and pseudo-science to pressure governments to block proven agricultural technology" (Wager 2011, 1). In the middle-ground were analyses found in publications like *Economic and Political Weekly*, which claimed the key issue was not the ecological or health risks of GM but, rather, "who controls Indian agriculture and therefore who controls food security in India" (Purkayastha and Rath 2010, 42). This question, they argued, should be at the center of a less emotional debate.

This episode can be compared to the debate around transgenic rice in China. A number of GM crops are already grown in China, which has also authorized the importation of GM soya and corn. Two strains of GM rice were approved for testing in China in 2009, but none was approved for commercial sale. In April 2011, however, *Southern Weekend* reported that government officials had admitted that "illegal GM [rice] seeds are present in several provinces because of weak management" (Cambreleng 2011, 1).

Since rice is a staple food strongly associated with traditional Chinese culture, this news fed into fierce discussions, with one respected agronomist, Tong Pingya, accusing

Chinese scientists of "treating the people like guinea pigs" and many signing online petitions and expressing their upset in the media (Cambreleng 2011, 1). But a number of science and environment commentators—such as Li Hujun, a well-known journalist for *New Century Weekly*—have argued that while such episodes show the need for improvements in government transparency, environmental and health concerns around GM rice had been exaggerated.

Key Figures

The rise of environmental reporting in China mirrors the growth of Chinese civil-society groups focused on sustainability issues. Environmental NGOs have traditionally helped to make up for the lack of central state capacity in China. Regulations drawn up in Beijing are often not implemented at the local level, and the Ministry of Environmental Protection (formerly the State Environmental Protection Agency, a subministerial agency) has often encouraged and relied on grassroots groups to oversee the work of local-level officials, whose focus on economic growth often conflicts with environmental directives. In a similar fashion, journalists have often been known to bring attention to lax enforcement by local levels of government with the tacit support of the central government.

It is not surprising, therefore, to find that many prominent Chinese environmental activists started out as journalists. One of the most famous and controversial is Dai Qing, an activist and reporter for the national newspaper *Guangming Daily*, who became known in the 1980s for her outspoken opposition to the Three Gorges Dam project—a huge hydroelectric project that was completed in 2008 in Hubei Province. Dai's book opposing the dam, *Yangtze! Yangtze!*, was banned, and she was later imprisoned for her involvement in the 1989 student protests in Tiananmen Square in Beijing. She remains an activist campaigning on the environment and other issues. A less confrontational figure is Ma Jun, a former journalist at the *South China Morning Post*, whose 1999 book *China's Water Crisis* has often been described as a call-to-arms for Chinese environmentalists. Ma later founded the Institute for Public and Environmental Affairs, which uses open government information to campaign against water and air pollution.

In India some of the country's best-known environmental journalists have also founded NGOs. Anil Agarwal, who started as a reporter at the Delhi-based *Hindustan Times* in 1973 and reported on the Chipko movement, founded the Centre for Science and Environment in 1980, which pioneered the study of sustainability in the Indian context. Agarwal continued to write on environmental topics until his death in 2002. Darryl D'Monte was an editor at the *Times of India* and the *Indian Express* before he became the chairperson of the Forum of Environmental Journalists of India (FEJI) and the founder-president of the International Federation of Environmental Journalists (IFEJ). In south Asia, however, environmental journalism, as a "category" of journalism, has been the subject of more criticism than is often seen in the Chinese context. Kunda Dixit, a prominent Nepali journalist and editor, has written, "One of the greatest disservices we have done to the cause of environmental protection is to invent a separate category of reporting called 'environmental journalism.' . . . These issues are important in their own right, not because some donor finds them important and is willing to cough up money to get them covered. There has to be a distance between the NGO and media worlds, getting too close hurts the credibility of both" (Dixit 2010, 16).

Sam GEALL
chinadialogue

See also Activism, Judicial; Agriculture (China and Southeast Asia); China; Consumerism; Education, Environmental (*several articles*); Gandhism; India; Information and Communication Technologies (ICT); National Pollution Survey (China); Nongovernmental Organizations (NGOs); Public Health; Rule of Law; Three Gorges Dam

FURTHER READING

Acharya, Keya, & Noronha, Frederick. (2010). *The green pen: Essays on environmental journalism from India and South Asia*. New Delhi: Sage Publications.

Calhoun, Craig, & Yang, Guobin. (2007). Media, civil society, and the rise of a green public sphere in China. *China Information, 21*, 211–236.

Cambreleng, Boris. (2011, June 22). GM rice seeds spread illegally, prompt heated debate in China. *Manila Bulletin Publishing Corporation*. Retrieved March 20, 2012, from http://mb.com.ph/node/323710/gm-rice-

Dixit, Kunda. (2010). This separate category. In Keya Acharya & Frederick Noronha (Eds.), *The green pen: Essays on environmental journalism from India and South Asia* (pp. 16–22). New Delhi: Sage Publications.

Geall, Sam. (2011). *Climate-change journalism in China: Opportunities for international cooperation*. Retrieved August 23, 2011, from http://www.chinadialogue.net/content/file_en/4289/climatejournalism.pdf

Litzinger, Ralph. (2007). In search of the grassroots: Hydroelectric politics in northwest Yunnan. In Elizabeth J. Perry & Merle Goldman (Eds.), *Grassroots political reform in contemporary China* (pp. 282–300). Cambridge, MA: Harvard University Press.

Liu, Alice Xin. (2009, October 2). China is taking the climate change issue seriously and cautiously. Retrieved March 20, 2012, from http://www.danwei.org/media/zou_xi_from_beijing_science_te_1.php

Liu Jianqiang. (2010). China's environmental movement; A journalist's perspective. Retrieved March 20, 2012, from http://asiasociety.org/policy/environment/climate-change-and-energy/china's-environmental-movement-journalist's-perspective

Padmanaban, G. (2011, January 25). GM technology in India: is it a quiet burial? *Current Science, 100*(2) 157.

Purkayastha, Prabir, & Rath, Satyajit. (2010). Bt brinjal: Need to refocus the debate. *Economic & Political Weekly, 45*(20), 42–48.

Shanahan, Michael. (2009). Time to adapt: Media coverage of climate change in nonindustrialised countries. In Tammy Boyce & Justin Lewis (Eds.), *Climate change and the media* (pp. 146–157). Retrieved August 23, 2011, from http://pubs.iied.org/pdfs/G02512.pdf

Sharma, Dinesh. (2011, January 17). Bt brinjal can damage liver, hit immunity: Study. *India Today*. Retrieved March 20, 2012, from http://indiatoday.intoday.in/story/bt-brinjal-can-damage-liver-&-hit-immunity-of-a-human-being./1/126821.html

Sharma, Kalpana. (2012). Trailing ignorance. Retrieved March 20, 2012, from http://www.briangwilliams.com/environmental-journalism/trailing-ignorance.html

The Telegraph. (2010, March 2). Glare on brinjal genetic study. Retrieved March 20, 2012, from http://www.telegraphindia.com/1100302/jsp/nation/story_12165512.jsp

Tolan, Sandy. (2007). Coverage of climate change in Chinese media: Human Development Report 2007 Occasional Paper. Retrieved August 23, 2011, from http://hdr.undp.org/en/reports/global/hdr2007-2008/papers/tolan_sandy.pdf

Wager, Robert. (2011, July 13). Future of Bt brinjal. *The Financial Express*. Retrieved March 20, 2012, from http://www.financialexpress.com/news/Column--Future-of-Bt-brinjal/817290/

Yang, Guobin. (2010). Brokering environment and health in China: Issue entrepreneurs of the public sphere. *Journal of Contemporary China, 19*(63), 101–119.

Yang, Guobin & Calhoun, Craig. (2007). Media, civil society, and the rise of a green public sphere in China. *China Information, 21*(2), 211–236.

Share the *Encyclopedia of Sustainability*: Teachers are welcome to make up to ten (10) copies of no more than two (2) articles for distribution in a single course or program. For further permissions, please visit www.copyright.com or contact: info@berkshirepublishing.com

Mekong-Lancang River

The Mekong-Lancang River is the source of life and livelihoods binding the histories, economies, and environments of China, Myanmar (Burma), Laos, Cambodia, Thailand, and Vietnam. Just as the river's flow is rapid in its upper reaches and relatively slow in the downstream countries, the characteristics of the socioeconomic context change along the river's course. Cooperation among the riparian countries is still in the early stages.

The Mekong-Lancang River is the tenth longest river in the world at a total length of 4,909 kilometers (Mekong River Commission [MRC] 2010). (Documented length varies somewhat depending on the source.) The river emerges in the Qinghai-Tibetan Plateau and flows south-southeastward through Tibet (Xizang) Autonomous Region (TAR) in China, the western Chinese province of Qinghai, and the southern Chinese province of Yunnan. From there, the river flows briefly toward the southwest, defining the border between Laos (to the east) and Myanmar (Burma), to the west, then eastward and southward through Laos and Thailand (defining a portion of the border between them), and finally southward through Cambodia and Vietnam where it empties into the South China Sea. In its upper reaches (extending from the Qinghai-Tibetan Plateau in the north and southward through the regions known as the Three Rivers Areas and the Lancang Basin), the river is known as the Lancang. In its southern reaches (starting in Myanmar and Laos and ending at the South China Sea) the river is called the Mekong. The two sections of river are not quite equal in length; the Lancang portion is about 500 kilometers shorter.

The history of the Mekong-Lancang River has long been tied to geopolitical movements between the countries through which it flows. Rapid economic growth in the region, together with the potential impacts of climate change, poses new risks to the Mekong-Lancang River basin and its residents. While these risks will exacerbate existing challenges, the potential for sustainable development is considerable.

Description

The headwaters of the Mekong-Lancang River are fed by the meltwaters of one of the most densely glaciated regions of the world. As it flows southward through the Three Rivers Area (the Salween River and the Yangzi [Chang] River flow alongside the Lancang in this area) the river flows rapidly through the steep mountainous region, dropping by as much as 2,500 meters in elevation in some places. Further south, the river passes through the Lancang Basin, which consists of highlands and plateaus in its northernmost portions (and is between 2,000 and 3,000 m above sea level despite being part of a basin), and then enters the Pu'er and Xishuangbanna prefectures where its floodplains widen and its flow slows. The river's mineral-rich sediments, together with its water, render the land along its course so rich in natural resources and biota that the region is referred to as "the kingdom of plants and animals" and "the kingdom of nonferrous metal" (WWF n.d.).

The downstream half of the river, the Mekong, flows through the Northern Highlands region of northeastern Myanmar and northern Thailand and Laos, then southeastward through the Khorat Plateau of northeastern Thailand and of Laos. Unlike stretches further upstream, the Northern Highlands stretch of the river receives water (and sediment) from large tributaries originating in the upland regions of Myanmar, the high rainfall areas of northern Laos, and the low rainfall areas of northern Thailand (MRC 2009). From here on, the river meanders relatively gently through the downstream countries.

When the river enters the Tonle Sap Basin, just north of Pakxe, Laos, it plunges suddenly in Cambodia at

Khone Falls. From there rapids interspersed with alluvial plains characterize the Mekong until it reaches Kratie (Cambodia). In Cambodia, the Mekong is connected to the Tonle Sap Great Lake system (the largest freshwater lake in South East Asia and an ecological hot spot) by the Sap River. South of Kompong Cham the river's gradient becomes gentle. When it enters the Mekong Delta in Vietnam, the river opens up into a wide system of distributaries and drains into the South China Sea.

Social Context

Because the upper Lancang region is mountainous, cold, and remote, and because the river flows through it at high speeds, the region is sparsely populated and has limited transportation and infrastructural facilities. Environmental damage (such as deforestation) in this area is subject to long recovery periods due to the high elevation and steep slope, which results in greater erosion.

Further downstream, an expanding transportation network bolsters the economy of the local people. In Lincang, Pu'er, and Xishuangbanna prefectures it provides a market for cash crops (readily salable crops) of tea, coffee, and sugar. Even so, the region is still poorer than other parts of China, and urban and rural poverty persist alongside the plantations. In Yunnan Province, 5.55 million people lived below the national poverty line as of 2008 ($176 per capita) (Li, 2010). These people account for 13.8 percent of the nation's poor (Zhang, 2011). Yunnan also has the second highest number (25) of ethnic groups among the provinces in China, with 38 percent from minority communities.

South of Yunnan, the meandering river provides ample opportunities for economic growth, a habitat for humans and animals alike, and the river and its banks are bustling with activity and life. The people in the riparian zone depend on the river for their livelihood—farming and fishing. Most of these activities, however, are small-scale in nature. Poverty and cross-border migration are critical issues here. Human trafficking for unskilled labor and the sex industry are major social problems. Other social problems include money laundering, insurgency, and border disputes created by local conflicts of interest. In addition, economic disparities and benefits abound from activities such as the development of infrastructure and economic corridors, construction of dams, and unevenly distributed fisheries.

Sustainability Challenges

The wild and turbulent Lancang is being tamed to meet human needs. Hydropower development (primarily in the form of the construction and operation of dams along the river's course) provides electricity and makes possible the control of water flow, but it will likely also impact the river's health (Molle et al. 2009). While the river supports a range of economic activities (fishing, agriculture, and transportation, for example), it also suffers from rapid land-use changes, unsustainable land-use practices, and increasing tourism. Even though the river is relatively unpolluted, riverside industrialization and urbanization, soil erosion, landslides, and increased sediment loads, will affect fisheries, the quality of drinking water, and irrigation. They will bring about habitat fragmentation and species loss, and these, in turn, will affect those dependent on the river for their livelihoods. The key question for local governments is how to sustainably develop the region and raise the income of those whose livelihoods are tied to the river while preserving valuable riparian environmental functions.

One crucial issue in the lower Mekong Basin is the negative impact of dams on the productivity of fisheries in Tonle Sap Lake in northwestern Cambodia, connected to the Mekong via the Tonle Sap River. During the wet season, the lake absorbs floodwater from the Mekong River and expands by about six times its dry season size. This helps protect the downstream locations from flooding. During the dry season, the flow of the stream between the Tonle Sap Lake and the Mekong River reverses, and the lake empties into the Mekong, thereby bringing much-needed water to the otherwise dry downstream locations and preventing saltwater intrusion from the Mekong Delta (saltwater intrusion threatens Vietnamese crops, especially rice crops). About a quarter of the population living beside the lake depends on the lake's fisheries for its livelihood (Middleton 2007). The presence of the dams has altered the flow of water and sediment transport in the river, which in turn has altered the flood pulse system between the lake and the river and therefore threatens the fisheries (Kummu and Sarkkula, 2008).

The lower Mekong Basin also suffers from recent land use changes. Large areas in different parts of Thailand have been converted from lowland forests to rubber and palm oil plantations, and rubber plantations are on the rise in Laos. Such changes in land use patterns alter the demand for water. Further, interstate conflicts such as the Thailand–Cambodia border tension, the complex Cambodia–Vietnam relationship, and the increasing role of China and Vietnam in Laos are challenges that could affect cooperative relations in the lower Mekong region.

In addition, climate change may lead to a number of problems, including rising temperatures; an increase in the number of forest fires during the summer months; hurricanes; cooling in the winter; an increase in the number of mudslides, landslides, and floods from heavy rainfall; droughts in the Lancang; and flooding, droughts and sea level rise (and resulting salt water intrusions) in the lower Mekong Basin (Eastham et al. 2008; MRC 2009; TKK & SEA START RC 2009). These problems, along with the karst topography (which does not retain water) in the Lancang Basin, and the undeveloped economy along most of the Mekong's course, render rural households ever more vulnerable.

Governance

Historically, the split name of the river has reflected the divided nature of governance in this region. The Changjiang Water Resources Commission (CWRC) of the Ministry of Water Resources (MWR) of China, has administrative and legal control over the Lancang portion of the river. The CWRC aims for integrated water resources management for the basin and stewardship of local government-owned assets. Autonomous villages, held together by informal ties such as race and lineage, hold farmland rights and decide on water use rights. The county steers regional development through resource allocation, land rights, and spatial planning. The provincial government is responsible for regional water utilization and economic development.

Each of the downstream countries has its own system of managing the river and its resources. A common approach adopted by them, however, is the management of water resources through the formation of river basin organizations (RBOs) with participation from stakeholders at different administrative levels. The RBOs consist of a multitude of actors, from national governments, to private investors, to local and international campaigners. Each of these players brings its own set of interests to the management process. Water resource governance and planning are mainly expert-driven with significant focus on procedures and targets. Laws and policies exist at the national level, formulated mainly by top-level officials with expert involvement but less input from stakeholders (i.e., those people who have a stake in an enterprise). Many of these policies are also not implemented at the local level. For example, the Law on Water Resources Management of the Kingdom of Cambodia of 2007 emphasized stakeholder participation in water management. This led to many smaller irrigation systems being handed over to farmer water user committees (FWUCs). But government experts mostly dominated the process marginalizing the FWUCs. Such dominance discourages the effective involvement of FWUCs and other involved NGOs. The region has thus been unable to make the shift to a more participatory process of decision making to involve users, actors, and government agencies (IWMI 2006).

International Level

In 1995, four downstream countries (Cambodia, Laos, Thailand, and Vietnam) coordinated their Mekong River governance through the Mekong Agreement. Following this, they established the Mekong River Commission (MRC) as an intergovernmental agency in the Lower Mekong Basin. The MRC is the main entity responsible for planning and development of the river (Dore and Lazarus, 2009, Sneddon and Fox 2007). Although not members, Myanmar and China are dialogue partners as of 1996.

Historically, the management of the river as a whole has been a source of tension between China and countries along the lower section. China's ability to undermine downstream cooperation is enhanced by its more powerful economic stature in the world, and by the fact that it controls the upstream reaches of the river. Its incentive to cooperate with downstream regimes is thus reduced. The role of China as a dialogue partner is a first step toward more comprehensive cooperative management of the river. China engages in bilateral and multilateral discussions with the Mekong countries but does not participate in the Mekong River Summit.

Many international organizations and aid agencies are active in this region. For example, the United Nations Development Programme (UNDP) supports regional cooperation projects, including the Greater Tumen Initiative (an intergovernmental platform for economic development within Northeast Asia) and the Cross-border Economic Cooperation Development program (which promotes business across the China-Vietnam border). Similarly, a Core Agricultural Support Program for the Greater Mekong Subregion (part of the Asian Development Bank) is an important initiative that contributes to economic growth along the Lancang-Mekong's course in China, Myanmar, Thailand, Laos, Cambodia, and Vietnam.

Future Challenges

In the second decade of the twenty-first century, China is emerging as a major global, political, and economic power with high demands for resources and energy. Southeast Asia is also developing rapidly. The relative lack of development along the Lancang River may attract investors to this resource-rich region, which will generate new economic challenges.

The existing and potential hydropower development projects involving a cascade of dams along the mainstream river flowing through China and Laos, and along the downstream tributaries, may further affect the region and its interstate relationships. The potential expansion of irrigation facilities in northeastern Thailand, in Laos, and in Cambodia (IWMI 2006; Molle et al. 2009) could result in additional water extraction from the river and in increased pollution of the river. Climate change could further exacerbate the hydrological circumstances and expose the population to increased floods, droughts, and saltwater intrusion.

The density of the population, the rate of economic growth, and the wealth of resources of the region, however, could collectively contribute to the well-being of its people. In order for this to happen, the existing and potential tensions that are present on all levels, from local to regional, must be well managed. Otherwise, these collective assets could become a source of continuous stress.

Joyeeta GUPTA
*UNESCO-IHE Institute for Water Education,
Delft, The Netherlands*

Hao LI
*Chanjiang River Scientific Research Institute,
Wuhan, China*

Ram Chandra BASTAKOTI
*Asian Institute of Technology, Klong Luang,
Pathumthani, Thailand*

See also China; Fisheries (China); Ganges River; The Himalaya; Huang (Yellow) River; Indigenous Peoples; Pearl River Delta; Reforestation and Afforestation (Southeast Asia); Rural Development; Rural Livelihoods; Southeast Asia; South-North Water Diversion; Three Gorges Dam; Tibetan Plateau; Transboundary Water Issues; Water Security; Yangzi (Chang) River

FURTHER READING

Dore, John, & Lazarus, Kate. (2009). Demarginalizing the Mekong River Commission. In François Molle, Tira Foran & Mira Käkönen (Eds.). *Contested waterscapes in the Mekong Region: Hydropower, livelihoods and governance* (pp. 357–382). Oxford, UK: Earthscan.

Eastham, Judy, et al. (2008). *Mekong River Basin water resources assessment: Impacts of climate change.* (Water for a Healthy Country National Research Flagship Report). Canberra, Australia: CSIRO.

He Da-ming; Feng Yan; & Hu Jin-ming. (2007). *Utilization of water resources and environmental conservation in the international rivers, southwest China* (in Chinese). Beijing: Science Publisher.

Helsinki University of Technology (TKK), & Southeast Asia START Regional Center (SEA START RC). (2009). *Water and climate change in the Lower Mekong Basin: Diagnosis & recommendations for adaptation.* Espoo, Finland & Bangkok, Thailand: Water and Development Research Group, TKK, SEA START RC, Chulalongkorn University.

International Water Management Institute (IWMI). (2006). *Water governance in the Mekong region: The need for more informed policymaking.* Water Policy Briefing, Issue 22. Battaramulla, Sri Lanka: IWMI.

Kummu, Matti, & Sarkkula, Juha. (2008). Impact of the Mekong River flow alteration on the Tonle Sap flood pulse. *Ambio, 37*(3), 185–192.

Li Guo-qiong. (2010). The thinking of Constructing Yunnan Rural Social Security System. *Journal of Yunan Agricultural University, 4*(3), 10–14.

Mekong Committee Secretary. (1993). *Annual report of Mekong Committee Secretary.* Bangkok, Thailand: Mekong Committee Secretary.

Mekong River Commission (MRC). (2009). *Adaptation to climate change in the countries of the Lower Mekong Basin: Regional synthesis report.* MRC Technical Paper No. 24. Vientiane, Laos: MRC.

Mekong River Commission (MRC). (2010). *State of the Basin report 2010.* Vientiane, Laos: MRC.

Middleton, Carl. (2007). Protecting the Fisheries of Tonle Sap Lake. Retrieved March 18, 2012, from http://www.internationalrivers.org/southeast-asia/mekong-mainstream-dams/protecting-fisheries-tonle-sap-lake-0

Molle, François; Foran, Tira; & Käkönen, Mira. (Eds.). (2009). *Contested waterscapes in the Mekong Region: hydropower, livelihoods and governance.* Oxford, UK: Earthscan.

Sneddon, Chris, & Fox, Coleen. (2007). Power, development, and institutional change: Participatory governance in the Lower Mekong Basin. *World Development, 35*(12), 2161–2181.

World Wide Fund for Nature (WWF). (n.d.). Upper Mekong Basin Project. Retrieved March 17, 2012, from http://www.wwfchina.org/english/downloads/Kunming/Upper%20Mekong%20Basin%20Project.pdf

Zhang You-fu. (2011). Research on new countryside construction planning in minority areas. *Journal of Yunnan Administration College, 1,* 2011, 158–161.

Microfinance

Microfinance has evolved beyond simple microloans to include the provision of various small-scale financial services. While many of Asia's poor remain without access to any formal financial services, Asia is also home to some of the largest, most innovative microfinance markets in the world. These innovations include advances toward meeting a triple bottom line of "profits, people, and planet" that explicitly includes environmental sustainability as a core commitment.

Microfinance, defined as the provision of small-scale financial services to the world's poor, originated in Asia. Many of the best microfinance institutions by any measure of performance are still located there today. Pioneers of the movement, the most well known being the joint recipients of the 2006 Nobel Peace Prize, Muhammad Yunus and the Grameen Bank in Bangladesh, inspired a movement that has spread around the world.

In 1976, Yunus, then a professor of economics at Chittagong University, made one of the first-ever microloans: $27 from his own pocket to a group of poor women in the village of Jobra, near his university. This experiment prompted Yunus to volunteer to serve as the guarantor of a larger loan made to the poor by a traditional bank. The repayment rates were high, higher than at any of the other traditional commercial banks in Bangladesh, which violated the accepted economic theory of the time, that the poor were not reliable borrowers. What became known as the Grameen Project eventually launched a revolution in the way financial services are administered to the poor.

As of 2012, microfinance institutions serve an estimated 175 million people around the globe (Maes and Reed 2012). At the same time, an estimated 2.7 billion people remain without access to formal financial services (CGAP and World Bank 2010). China and India, the two most populous countries in the world and home to most of the world's poor, illustrate this dichotomy. India is one of the largest and most innovative microfinance markets in the world. In China, microfinance is still a nascent industry, with services mostly limited to traditional microcredit.

When most people think of microfinance, the image that comes to mind is usually something similar to the original Grameen Bank model: small loans to groups of female microentrepreneurs who take loans individually but agree to share joint liability for each member's repayment. But since the launching of the microfinance revolution, the microfinance industry has continued to innovate. Microfinance increasingly serves men as well as women, and microfinance institutions increasingly offer clients the option of individual loan contracts—not necessarily just for business investments—with flexible repayment plans rather than only group lending programs with rigid repayment schedules.

And microfinance is no longer just about loans. One of the most significant innovations has been the acknowledgement that the poor need more than just credit. The poor face not just low income, but highly variable income. In that regard they have even more need than the rich for financial services that go beyond microcredit and include services, such as savings, which will allow them to manage their limited cash flow and to become a little less vulnerable to unexpected shocks like illness and natural disasters. Recognition of this need has inspired many microfinance institutions to move beyond the traditional provision of microcredit to include microsavings and even more sophisticated financial services, such as insurance and pensions.

Information technology is also transforming microfinance. The success of Kenya's mobile phone–based money transfer service, M-PESA, has raised hopes that mobile banking may be a low-cost way to reach the majority of those who today remain without access to financial services. In Asia, mobile-banking initiatives such as FINO (Financial Information Network & Operations Ltd.) in India and Smart Money in the Philippines now have more active clients than the largest "brick and mortar" microfinance institution in those countries (CGAP 2010).

Double Bottom Line

Part of the attraction of microfinance is the promise of "doing well by doing good," that is to say, the notion that microfinance can be profitable. In some cases, the profits in the industry have attracted private sector commercial banks like Indonesia's Bank Tabungan Pensiunan Nasional (BTPN), which reported a 14 percent net interest rate margin on its microloans in 2011. Another Indonesian example, the famous Bank Rakyat Indonesia (BRI), today one of the world's largest and most profitable microfinance institutions, started out as a government bank. In other cases, microfinance institutions that started out as small nonprofit organizations "commercialize" and become for-profit institutions pursuing the double bottom line of social objectives and financial sustainability simultaneously. In 2010 India's largest microlender, SKS, which had started out as an nongovernmental organization (NGO) twelve years earlier, raised $350 million by selling a 21.6 percent stake in an initial public offering (IPO) that was thirteen times oversubscribed. Other microfinance institutions, like the Khushhali Bank in Pakistan, now skip the initial NGO phase and start out with a clear vision as a commercial bank.

This trend toward profitability has brought on a heated debate about the pros and cons of commercialization in microfinance. This debate has raged since the 1990s. But in the early 2000s the governments of Bangladesh and India, the largest microfinance markets in the world, seem to be siding with those who believe that the cons of commercialization (the danger that a focus on profits will lead microfinance institutions down the path of "mission drift," from which they forget their original social mission), outweigh the pros of commercialization (faster growth and outreach to more clients).

Bangladesh has capped the interest rates that microfinance institutions can charge, and officials in the natural-disaster-prone Indian state of Andhra Pradesh have passed a series of new regulations on microfinance institutions after an alarming spate of suicides by over-indebted poor, some of them clients of microfinance institutions.

Triple Bottom Line

Even as the debate of financial sustainability continues to rage, the microfinance industry focuses increasing attention to environmental sustainability as well. For some microfinance institutions like ACLEDA in Cambodia, which reports on environmental performance in addition to social and economic performance, the triple bottom line of "profits, people, and planet"—maintaining financial sustainability while advancing the original social mission of microfinance *and* protecting the environment—has become an institutional commitment.

Why? Even though the scale of the microenterprises targeted by microfinance are small, meaning that individually they have little impact on the environment, collectively they contribute to environmental damage, at a minimum through pollution and unsustainable use of natural resources.

For some microfinance institutions, policies to mitigate this damage may be consistent with their core mission and seem simply the right thing to do. Others may join the movement for image or branding incentives, or because institutions that finance microfinance, including private institutions such as the Calvert Foundation, Triodos, and the Bill and Melinda Gates Foundation, increasingly value environmental sustainability and include environmental criteria in their funding decisions. Responding to this trend, microfinance-rating agencies such as M-Cril, MicroFinanza, and Planet Rating have all defined some environmental indicators to include in their assessments.

Other immediate reasons exist for microfinance institutions to get involved in protecting the environment. Microenterprises are not only agents of environmental damage; they are victims of it. As policy makers from poor countries often point out, poor countries have the right to develop, and that requires energy. But the poor cannot simply dismiss the negative effects of environmental degradation as a problem of the rich world. The impact of climate change is predicted to fall disproportionately in tropical regions—home to many of the world's poor countries. Within those countries, the costs of environmental degradation will fall disproportionately on the poor. The poor are often more dependent on natural resources for their livelihoods. They are more likely to succumb to illness or reduced productivity due to pollution or inadequate waste disposal. The extreme weather conditions resulting from climate change tend to hurt the poor more—for example by destroying their homes and livelihoods—and the poor have fewer options to financially cushion themselves from these events. Because the costs of environmental degradation will disproportionately affect their clients, even microfinance institutions that place human security squarely above environmental concerns cannot ignore completely the question of environmental sustainability.

Environmentally Sustainable Microfinance

Microfinance institutions are responding to this environmental sustainability challenge in a variety of innovative ways. Many microfinance institutions, like XacBank in Mongolia, may start by including the environment in their mission statement and working to reduce their own ecological footprint. Often, this environmentally oriented mission influences the activities they choose to support. Some microfinance institutions, like ACLEDA in Cambodia or KASHF in Pakistan, have created an exclusion list of microentrepreneurial activities that are not environmentally sustainable, which they will not finance. Other microfinance institutions may not go so far, but at least limit the percentage of their portfolio allocated to "A list" industries that are particularly damaging to the environment.

Other microfinance institutions provide "green microcredit" to promote environmentally friendly activities or green technologies. For example, Ningxia CEPA in China and BASIX in India provide green microcredit to renewable energy solutions. In India, the Self-Employed Women's Association (SEWA) has partnered with SELCO, a supplier of solar panels, to bring solar energy systems into the homes of the poor and set up training programs for smokeless home stoves. Also in India, Wesco Credit has partnered with Green Microfinance to provide a solution to waste management and disease control with biogas plants that use biodegradable waste to provide renewable energy (and, as a side product, organic fertilizer) for home stoves. In Bangladesh, a developmental organization called BRAC (affiliated with BRAC University), and Grameen Shakti (part of the Grameen family) are involved in similar green microfinance, extending loans to households for the purchase of home solar energy systems, biogas plants, and improved cook stoves, while the NGO Proshika has had a successful experiment using microfinance to motivate poor households to participate in reforestation.

Outlook

Looking forward, these kinds of environmentally sustainable innovations in the field of microfinance will continue to expand. In the past thirty years microfinance has evolved to a scale and level of sophistication that few would have imagined when Muhammad Yunus made his first microloan to a poor woman in Bangladesh. Although many of world's poor remain without access to any formal financial services, the field of microfinance now serves an estimated 175 million people and includes a wide variety of financial instruments such as savings and even pensions and insurance.

The success of some microfinance institutions in meeting the so-called double bottom line of profitability and social objectives has contributed to a trend of commercialization in the industry. This shift includes large commercial banks downscaling to include microfinance in their portfolio of services, and small, nonprofit organizations transforming into licensed, regulated, financial institutions. This trend and recent tragic events in the Indian state of Andhra Pradesh have renewed a heated debate about the pros and cons of commercialization in microfinance.

Even if responses to the events in Andhra Pradesh mean that growth in the microfinance industry plateaus or even reverses in the next few years, it is likely that innovations in green microfinance will continue. Microfinance institutions must increasingly embrace a triple bottom line of "profits, people, and planet" that includes environmental sustainability. Assessment and access to financing for microfinance institutions is increasingly dependent upon environmental criteria in addition to social objectives and financial performance. The main clients of microfinance institutions, the poor, are also the main victims of environmental degradation. The poor rely more upon natural resources for their livelihoods. They are more vulnerable to illnesses and lowered productivity as a result of environmental damage. They tend to live in areas that are more susceptible to extreme weather conditions and they are less able to cushion themselves financially from the damage of natural disasters. For all these reasons, in the coming years microfinance will be one of the industries at the forefront of environmental sustainability.

Heather A. MONTGOMERY
International Christian University

See also Climate Change Migration (India); Corporate Accountability (China); Education, Female; Five-Year Plans; Gender Equality; Green Collar Jobs; Information and Communication Technologies (ICT); Labor; Nongovernmental Organizations (NGOs); Outsourcing and Offshoring; Public Health; Public Transportation; Public-Private Partnerships; Rural Development; Rural Livelihoods; White Revolution of India

FURTHER READING

Consultative Group to Assist the Poorest (CGAP). (2010). *Scenarios for branchless banking in 2020* (CGAP focus note no. 57). Washington, DC: CGAP.

Consultative Group to Assist the Poorest (CGAP). (2010). *Andhra Pradesh 2010: Global implications of the crisis in Indian microfinance* (CGAP focus note no. 67). Washington, DC: CGAP.

Consultative Group to Assist the Poorest (CGAP) and World Bank. (2010). *Financial access 2010*. Washington, DC: CGAP and the World Bank.

Chen, Greg; Rasmussen, Stephen; Reille, Xavier; & Rozas, Daniel. (2010). *Indian microfinance goes public: The SKS Initial Public Offering* (CGAP focus note no. 65). Washington, DC: CGAP.

Hall, Joan; Collins, Liam; Israel, Elizabeth; & Wenner, Marc. (2008). *The missing bottom line: Microfinance and the environment.* Washington, DC: GreenMicrofinance Center.

Maes, Jan, & Reed, Larry. (2012). *State of the Microcredit Summit Campaign Report 2012*. Washington, DC: The Microcredit Summit Campaign.

Microfinance Information eXchange (MIX). (2010.) *2009 MIX Global 100: Ranking of microfinance institutions.* Washington, DC: MIX.

Montgomery, Heather. (2005, November). *Meeting the double bottom line: The impact of Khushhali Bank's microfinance program in Pakistan* (Asian Development Bank Institute policy paper no. 8). Tokyo: Asian Development Bank.

Rippey, Paul. (2009). *Microfinance and climate change: Threats and opportunities.* (CGAP focus note no. 53). Washington, DC: CGAP.

Berkshire's authors and editors welcome questions, comments, and corrections. Send your emails about the *Berkshire Encyclopedia of Sustainability* in general or this volume in particular to: sustainability.updates@berkshirepublishing.com

Mumbai, India

22 million est. pop. 2012

Mumbai is India's biggest city and leading business center; it is the home of Bollywood, India's leading film industry community. The wealthiest city in one of India's richest states (Maharasthra), it also harbors abject urban poverty; about half of the population lives in slums. It is situated on a low-lying, monsoon-affected peninsula with high population densities. Among the main environmental problems are flooding and poor drainage, water pollution, clean water provision, and sewage and garbage disposal.

By a wide range of measures, Mumbai (formerly called Bombay in English) is the leading city in India. It is India's largest city, with nearly 22 million people in the urban region; it boasts the largest airport; it houses the biggest stock exchange; it is home to the headquarters of the Reserve Bank of India, the State Bank of India, and the Western and Central Railway Zones; it has the largest share of bank credits of any city in India as well as the largest share of bank deposits and income tax revenues; and Mumbai has the largest share of telephones. Mumbai is also the country's main juncture with the global economy and the most globally connected city in India. For example, its airport services more international passengers than any other in India; the seaport registers more international cargo than any other in the nation; Mumbai houses more transnational companies than any other city; it has the largest share of foreign collaborations; it has the largest share of foreign direct investment as well as the largest share of international trade and customs duties; it is the home of India's major film industry, Bollywood (see sidebar on page 257); and it has more Internet connections than any other city in India. As this vital urban center continues to grow, providing adequate resources for a sustainable, healthy environment will require significant development of infrastructure, especially water, sewage, and garbage disposal systems, as well as attention to transportation, housing, and slum redevelopment.

Geography

Greater Mumbai comprises the peninsula bound by the Arabian Sea to the west, Thane Creek to the east, and Vasai Creek and the Ulhas River to the north. It is connected to the mainland in the north and northwest. The area's dimensions are about 50 kilometers from north to south and an average of 10 kilometers from west to east. On the peninsula, the current population is around 12 million people, and the average population density is twenty-four thousand people per square kilometer. The city grew spectacularly in the decades following independence from British rule in 1947, and its geography became increasingly dense. Recent decades witnessed a shift of population from the south to the northern suburbs.

The geographical constraints of the Island City (a common reference to the peninsula) put a premium on space and have historically influenced land values and land use in the city. There has been a steep gradient in land values from the south to the north. In the mid-1990s, an unprecedented influx of foreign corporations contributed to an extreme escalation of land values, making Mumbai for some time the most expensive city in the world.

In the southwestern part of the city, land reclamations in the 1960s added a valuable sliver of real estate along the Arabian Sea. It was there, in the business district of Nariman Point, that land values reached enormous heights, and it is still one of the most prized areas in the city for office space, especially for international businesses.

In subsequent years, expansion followed in the northeast and on the mainland in what is known as Navi Mumbai (New Mumbai), and this area too has developed very rapidly. Together, greater Mumbai and Navi Mumbai constitute Mumbai District, which has a population of about 22 million people.

Historical Background

From a historical perspective, global connections are far from new to this city. Known to the British as Bombay, it emerged as a major city in the second half of the nineteenth century. This was the era of industrial development, textile mills, railroads, and steamships. From Mumbai, British industrial interests in South Asia were coordinated, and the city functioned as a major link in the colonial commodity chain. The industrial revolution was a widespread phenomenon, but the ways in which the textile mills, railroads, and steamships shaped Mumbai must be understood in the context of the city's contemporary global linkages: Mumbai, as a place, was in essence the product of colonialism.

The spatial layout of the city was organized around the port. The city functioned as a central node in the trade network between its hinterland and England. As such, it was strategically located to link rail lines and shipping routes. The docks, warehouses, and railroad terminals highlight these functions of trade, storage, and distribution. Adjacent to the port area was a well-defined European business district that functioned as the designated location for foreign companies. Most economic activities in the European commercial area involved trade, distribution, transport, banking, and insurance. Zoning and building codes were strictly enforced to maintain an orderly European character and atmosphere in the district. Traditional markets or bazaars, however, were located in a business district in the "Native Town," which comprised a mix of commercial and residential land uses. Much commercial activity there involved trade of agricultural produce and crafts, small-scale industry, and retailing. The European Town and the Native Town were physically separated by the Esplanade, a green area that served recreational purposes and that was already laid out by the Portuguese in the sixteenth century.

The city underwent some important transformations in the wake of independence. Rapid overall population growth resulted in significant northward expansion on the peninsula, mainly along the railroad tracks and main highways. The former European Town in the south was quickly de-Europeanized and "nationalized," politically and economically. Administrative and military functions in the area were taken over by the Indian government. New large domestic companies favored a location in this area, which led to a steadily growing corporate density and a large majority of domestically controlled companies. The area was nationalized in a symbolic sense with the locating there of the newly established Central Bank, the stock exchange, and state-controlled companies.

With the beginning of liberalization and deregulation across India in the early 1990s, Mumbai's economic geography again underwent substantial changes. Foreign investment increased, land values increased, and deindustrialization in certain sectors (especially textile mills) accelerated, while producer services, finance, and the information technology sector expanded. Although the new middle class and its purchasing power increased conspicuously, so did the gap between rich and poor. Overall population growth from 2001 to 2011 was about 12 percent, and the share of the slum population remained at about 52 percent.

Sustainable Development Challenges

Obstacles to Mumbai's sustainable development and a healthy environment seem almost insurmountable, with enormous population densities, extreme poverty, ferocious monsoon downpours, and the geographical constraints of a peninsula with large swaths of land below sea level. The environmental conditions of many slums are appalling as they often lack proper sanitation, and sewage and garbage disposal. In all, however, and given the scale of the obstacles, the accomplishments of government should not be downplayed—there is an elaborate system of garbage collection, public transportation, and water provision, along with a range of efforts to control pollution, such as the prohibition of thin plastic bags (often used in shops) that are known to clog drainage systems throughout the city. Many problems remain, however, with housing among the most acute.

The city's housing problems have been on record for over 150 years, ever since it became an urban center of significance. At the middle of the nineteenth century, after a couple of decades of rapid growth, the city's population reached half a million. The urban area then was, of course, much smaller than it is now and covered only the southern extension of the peninsula. Most parts of Mumbai had a population density thirteen times higher than London at the time. The city's growth in population led to an acute shortage of housing and serious problems with the provision of water, sanitation, and drainage. There was a big difference between European and native residential quarters, with the slums heavily concentrated in the latter. The Native Town grew virtually unplanned and without any consideration of the quality of life of its inhabitants. Despite the fact that the housing problems in the Indian quarter were common

BOLLYWOOD AND SUSTAINABILITY

Some industries in Mumbai show signs of breaking away from the pattern of environmental degradation that is all too common in the city. One of them is the film industry. Mumbai is home to India's largest film producing community, well known throughout the world as Bollywood (a portmanteau word combining "Hollywood" with Mumbai's former name, Bombay). With an eye on environmental sustainability and minimizing the industry's impact on the city's environment, Bollywood is building Parinee I, an innovative and ecofriendly structure, for its new offices. Building materials are composed of low-volatility organic compounds; the structure utilizes a rainwater harvesting and treatment system to provide water for washrooms, and includes a sewage reclamation plant. The futuristic-looking building features oddly angled sides that help regulate temperature in Mumbai's hot, often wet, climate, and keep energy efficiency high (Sajnani 2011). With Bollywood as a leading example, state-of-the-art buildings like Parinee I may increase in number, aiding in the effort to mitigate environmental concerns like clean water, energy efficiency, and sewage systems.

The Editors

---

knowledge, no substantial measures were taken by colonial governments.

Since independence, despite a range of successive policies to reduce the slums, those areas have steadily grown and now house at least half of the total population of greater Mumbai. Slums are scattered across the city and have very high densities, though they occupy only about 12 percent of the land. The most recent slum redevelopment scheme dates from 1995 and is closely related to the liberalization of the urban land market and rapidly increasing real estate values. While private developers have brought large numbers of new expensive homes on the market that are out of reach of most Mumbaikars, slum redevelopment has stalled.

More generally, Mumbai is facing at least four interrelated environmental challenges. First, there is widespread lack of access to clean drinking water resulting from inadequate infrastructure combined with excessive population densities and extreme poverty. This, in turn, causes major health problems with high incidence of cholera, intestinal diseases, infectious diseases, and infant mortality. Only about 70 percent of Mumbai's population has access to piped drinking water, the remainder being dependent on provision by water trucks or pumps. Water contamination, even occasionally of piped water, is not uncommon.

Second, drainage and sewage problems also stem from the lack of adequate infrastructure. This is especially evident during the monsoon. Across the city, flooding is common during the heavy rains, leading to traffic jams, electricity outages, and a range of safety hazards. Mumbai has separate sewage and storm-water systems, but they are connected and overflow routinely, especially during floods. This mixing of sewage and storm water is especially evident in slum areas where there is a dire lack of proper sanitation. Across Mumbai's slums, it is estimated that there is one toilet for every 200–800 residents, with the majority of people not using a closed sewage system. This causes widespread health problems, especially among women (for whom access to toilets is especially difficult), and it also compounds pollution of water and soil. Since most of the slums are built on less desirable low ground, this is where health problems from poor drainage and sewer systems are greatest and at the same time is where access to health care is the most limited.

Third, traffic congestion has escalated since liberalization in the early 1990s. The number of cars on Mumbai's already strained road network is enormous, and public transportation seemed to have reached its limits already long ago. Today, it is estimated that around 7 million people use the urban railway system every day, and commutes are getting longer all the time. For many years there has been talk about plans to connect south Mumbai to the mainland in order to relieve pressure on the peninsula, but nothing has materialized. The average one-way commute for Mumbai workers is about forty-five minutes, and for the great majority this involves public transportation. Automobile ownership has increased rapidly, at about 5 percent annually in recent years, and traffic congestion has worsened.

Fourth, Mumbai faces substantial difficulties in managing garbage disposal. The city generates over 7,000 tons of garbage daily with only three active dumping grounds (in the Borivali, Mulund, and Deonar dumping grounds), all far from the central city in the south. Garbage collection requires a herculean effort: it involves some 3,800 personnel and 800 vehicles, and about 2,000 truck dumpings per twenty-four-hour period. It is estimated that about 95 percent of all generated waste is actually collected—but that leaves at least around 300–400 tons of uncollected garbage every day. Much of that is burned locally or deposited illegally in the city's creeks and elsewhere, causing a range of pollution problems. At the official dumping grounds, the encroachment of slums has been an issue of concern.

Mumbai has always had active citizen groups and more recently nongovernmental organizations (NGOs) that seek to bring improvements, hold local government accountable, and support private initiatives to "clean up" Mumbai. This has had some positive effects in particular localities, such as in the more affluent communities along the western coast. Overall, however, environmental improvements in Mumbai have seen little progress. With the population expected to increase further (even if at a lower rate), with consumption estimated to go up, without large-scale capital investment in infrastructure, and without apparent solutions to the conditions in the slums, Mumbai's environmental problems are likely to get worse in the coming years.

Jan NIJMAN
University of Amsterdam

See also Chennai, India; Cities—Overview; Climate Change Migration (India); Delhi, India; Dhaka, Bangladesh; Five-Year Plans; Gender Equality; Labor; Microfinance; Public Health; Public Transportation; Rule of Law; Water Security; Water Use and Rights (India)

FURTHER READING

Dossal, Mariam. (1991). *Imperial designs and Indian realities: The planning of Bombay City 1845–1875*. Delhi: Oxford University Press.

McKenzie, David, & Ray, Isha. (2009). Urban water supply in India: Status, reform options and possible lessons. *Water Policy, 11*(4), 442–460.

Nijman, Jan. (2012). India's urban challenge. *Eurasian Geography and Economics, 53*(1), 7–20.

Nijman, Jan. (2010). A study of space in Mumbai's slums. *Tijdschrift voor Economische en Sociale Geografie* [Journal of Economic and Social Geography], *101*(1), 4–17.

Sajnani, Babita. (2011, July 25). Parinee I: Sustainable "Bollywood" offices project designed by James Law Cybertecture. Retrieved April 6, 2012, from http://www.ecofriend.com/entry/parinee-sustainable-bollywood-offices-project-designed-james-law-cybertecture/

Yedla, Sudhakar. (2006). Dynamics of environmental problems in Mumbai. *Clean Technologies and Environmental Policy, 8*(3), 182–187.

N

Nanotechnology

Nanotechnology has rapidly emerged as one of the most commercially promising sciences. China, Taiwan, and India, in their aim to shift from manufacturing to knowledge-based economies, are trying to position themselves as global leaders in nanotech research and development. Their success will depend on critical factors such as the design of regulatory frameworks and the promotion of research and development, both of which they approach very differently.

Nanotechnology is the science of manipulating matter at the atomic and molecular scale. The dimensions refer to structures of 1–100 nanometers—1 nanometer is one-billionth of a meter. Nanotechnology covers a broad range of (potential) applications in fields such as medicine, electronics, physics of molecular-level semiconductors, materials, polymers, and composites. It has already become a part of our daily life, in the form of scratch-resistant sunglasses, drag-reducing aircraft shells, wrinkle-free shirts, wound dressings, and many other products. Viewed in the context of the manifold potential opportunities for utilization, however, nanotechnology is still in its infancy and will be one of the strongest growth industries in the near future.

Historical Development of Nanotechnology

While the first theoretical introduction of the manipulation of materials on the nanoscale was presented in 1959 by the US scientist (and later Nobel laureate) Richard P. Feynman, the term *nanotechnology* was not coined until 1974 by Norio Taniguchi of Tokyo Science University (Palmberg, Dernis, and Miguet 2009, 16). In 1981, the US engineer K. Eric Drexler began to publish works about the use of molecular machine systems for construction involving atomic precision. With these publications, he achieved an essential change in the view of physics, which, from that point forward, would no longer be seen as a science in which matter can only be manipulated downward, but as one that allows for "bottom-up" construction from the nanoscale (Peterson 2004). As is often the case with new forms of technology, once research into its possible applications gained momentum in the late 1980s, potential negative aspects, such as harmful impacts on the environment and on health, and problematic applications, such as nanotechnology-based warfare, also began to surface.

Today, there is still no unified definition of nanotechnology. Organizations and programs such as the US National Nanotechnology Initiative, the EU's seventh Framework Programme (2007–2013), the Second Japanese Science and Technology Basic Plan, the International Organization for Standardization (ISO), and the European Patent Office are each operating according to their own working definitions. All these definitions, however, include three common attributes of nanotechnology: it involves the intentional manipulation of matter at a very small scale; it refers to quantities where the rules of physics allow for quantum mechanical effects (<100 nanometer); and it makes possible innovative products and industrial procedures (Palmberg, Dernis, and Miguet 2009).

Impact on Sustainability in Asia

Risk assessment and management are crucial elements of the sustainability of nanotechnology development around the world. One reason for this is that, despite the apparent commercial benefits associated with nanotechnology development, the application of nanotechnology, (e.g. in carbon nanotubes), bears potential health threats that could be as harmful as those associated with asbestos fibers (Greenemeier 2008). Other potential threats to social and environmental security result from the assumed inverse relationship between nanotoxicity and particulate size, meaning that the smaller the nanomatter, the more toxic such particulates can be (Maynard 2006). The approaches of China and India to nanotechnology development, however, show that the primary focus is currently on the marketization and commercialization of nanotechnology products, while assessment and management of potential risks are of secondary importance. The Taiwanese government, by contrast, has recognized the need to consider environmental issues related to nanotechnology and the need to design laws, regulations, and standards, accordingly, to meet risk challenges.

India

In India, risk assessment related to nanotechnology is limited to a few individual toxicity projects, while studies and overall spending on toxicology research are marginal. Although the legislative community has started to pay more attention to the topic, there are currently no laws or regulations in India that deal specifically with nanotechnology. Most products—for example, nanotechnology-based pharmaceuticals or pesticides—are subject to corresponding medical or chemical regulation, but are not subject to any regulation that specifically addresses their status as products of nanotechnology (Jaspers 2010).

China

China has established an advanced and sophisticated regulatory framework, with the National Nanotechnology Standardization Committee (NSTC) in charge of reviewing standards and the Technical Committee 279 (a specialized subcommittee under the Standardization Administration of China) responsible for drafting essential nanotechnology standards as well as test protocols (Jarvis and Richmond 2011). In 2010, China also decided to adopt China REACH, a concept comparable to the EU REACH (Registration, Evaluation, Authorisation and Restriction of Chemical Substances) regulation framework, which dictates that all domestically produced or imported chemicals are subject to the regulatory oversight of a single authority.

Taiwan

In Taiwan, the National Science and Technology Committee (NSTC) and the National Science Council (NSC) are in charge of national science and technology policy, while the Industrial Technology Research Institute (ITRI) is the central organization for nanotechnology research. Technical standards for nanotechnology are set by the Bureau of Standards, Measurement, and Inspection (BSMI), through its oversight of the Taiwan Nanotechnology Standards Council (TNSC), which is also representing Taiwan at the International Organization for Standardization (ISO). Joint efforts with the Environmental Protection Agency (EPA) led to the development of Taiwan's Strategic Plan for Responsible Nanotechnology. Taiwan has not only integrated social and environmental sustainability concerns into its policies concerning nanotechnology, but has also dedicated significant parts of its research to environmentally friendly nanotech products (Purra and Richmond 2010).

Dynamics Between China, Taiwan, and India

The economic impact of nanotechnology on a country's overall economy varies extensively among Asian countries. Benchmarked against a value of 100 (set for the United States, the global leader), the economic impact of nanotechnology in China is 89, in India is 5, in Japan is 29, in South Korea is 25, and in Taiwan is 9 (Cientifica 2011).

The support of research and development in nanotechnology has become a relevant tool for establishing growth-oriented policy in China, which aims to graduate from an economy mainly based on manufacturing to one based on knowledge and service. It was not until the middle of the first decade of the twenty-first century, however, that the Chinese government began to consider nanotechnology a key part of China's strategic national science development plan.

India started investing in nanotechnology research and development in 1997. During the five-year period between 2002 and 2007, India invested $22.8 million in nanotechnology research, compared to the $230 million invested by China for the four-year period from 2000 to 2004 (Meridian Institute 2007). Ten years later, the Nano Mission was established under India's Department for Science and Technology, at which point significant financial resources began to be allocated to nanotechnology research and development.

When the government of Taiwan launched its National Nanotechnology Program (NNP) in 2002, it was endowed with $559 million for six years. Major shares went into ITRI's Industrialization Program, which allocated 20 percent of the funds for short-term projects, 60 percent for medium-term projects, and another 20 percent for long-term projects (Purra and Richmond 2010).

In terms of innovation in nanotechnology, China is far ahead of Taiwan and India. While India filed 167 patents between 1990 and 2007 (Gupta 2009a), and Taiwan had filed 300 by 2005 (Kanama 2006), Chinese authorities received more than 4,500 patent applications in 2005 alone (Liu 2008). In 2005, Chinese scholars published about 9,000 articles on nanotechnology (Appelbaum and Parker 2008), whereas Taiwanese and Indian researchers published around 8,000 (Youtie, Shapira, and Porter 2008) and 1,300 publications (Gupta 2009b), respectively, in the same year.

Different Approaches

China's approach to nanotechnology and its regulation is closely linked to the national political agenda. As one of China's four science-based megaprojects (a large-scale project involving substantial investment), nanotechnology is subject to centralized economic-planning processes and therefore bears the burden of contributing to China's economic growth through substantial, commercially viable outcomes. As a result, there is limited room for political disagreement or interference on the part of the public, as this would be perceived as a potential threat to the country's growth aspirations.

While the promotion of nanotechnology in China is driven by the national government, in India it is the private sector that has taken the lead in investing in research and development. The private sector is dominated by a few major companies, including Reliance (energy and materials), Birla (metals, cement, textiles, and communications, among others), and Tata (communications, energy, textiles, engineering, and chemicals, among others). Leading patent holders are Ranbaxy Laboratories and Stempeutics (Jaspers 2010), both involved in the business of pharmaceuticals. In India, the political system allows for more public participation, which is why civil society organizations like The Energy and Resource Institute (TERI) have started to energetically contribute to the public discourse (e.g., through calls for changes of legislation or for better monitoring of the regulatory framework) (Observatory Nano 2010).

In Taiwan, the government has been a dynamic actor in the promotion of nanotechnology development, aiming at the creation of a globally competitive scientific and industrial cluster. The Taiwanese investment structure is thereby replicating the National Nanotechnology Initiative of the United States (Purra and Richmond 2010). While the market in India is dominated by large firms, the Taiwanese industry structure is characterized by small and medium-size companies with a paid-in capital of less than $3 million (Su et al. 2007).

Perspectives in Asia

The critical factors for sustainability in India in the short run will be the development of an effective regulatory framework. Since the institutional responsibility for nanotech policy lies with the Ministry of Science and Technology, it is expected to take the lead on this matter. While India's work on nanotechnology has heretofore been a rather domestic affair, in the near future it will look increasingly to international cooperation for both research and regulatory mechanisms.

With the exception of China and Taiwan, most South, East and Southeast Asian countries are lagging behind the leading Western countries in terms of the volume of their nanotechnology industries, their spending on research and development, and the number of patents they file. China and Taiwan also have an advanced regulatory framework for managing risks associated with nanotechnology. It is too early to conclude, however, whether nanotechnology will be able to accelerate the progress from industry- to knowledge-based economies in these countries.

Tim HILGER and Darryl S. L. JARVIS
National University of Singapore

See also Biosafety Legislation (China); Consumerism; E-Waste; Five-Year Plans; Genetic Resources; Green Collar Jobs; Information and Communication Technologies (ICT); Public Health; Steel Industry

FURTHER READINGS

Appelbaum, Richard P., & Parker, Rachel. (2008). China's bid to become a global nanotech leader: Advancing nanotechnology through state-led programs and international collaborations. *Science and Public Policy, 35*(5), 319–334.

Cientifica. (2011). Global funding of nanotechnologies. Retrieved November 25, 2011, from http://www.cientifica.com/research/market-reports/nanotech-funding-2011/

Greenemeier, Larry. (2008, May 20). Study says carbon nanotubes as dangerous as asbestos. Retrieved November 25, 2011, http://www.scientificamerican.com/article.cfm?id=carbon-nanotube-danger

Gupta, Vinod K. (2009a). Indian patents output in nanotechnology. *Journal of Intellectual Property Rights, 14*, 164–165.

Gupta, Vinod K. (2009b). Indian publications output in nanotechnology during 1990–2008. *Advanced Science Letters, 2*, 402–404.

International Risk Governance Council. (2007). Nanotechnology risk governance: Recommendations for a global, coordinated approach to the governance of potential risks. Retrieved November 24, 2011, from http://www.irgc.org/IMG/pdf/PB_nanoFINAL2_2_.pdf

Jarvis, Darryl S. L., & Richmond, Noah. (2011). Regulation and governance of nanotechnology in China: Regulatory challenges and effectiveness. *European Journal of Law and Technology, 2*(3), 1–11.

Jaspers, Nico. (2010). International nanotechnology policy and regulation: Case study: India. Retrieved November 30, 2011, from http://www2.lse.ac.uk/internationalRelations/centresandunits/regulatingnanotechnologies/nanopdfs/India2010.pdf

Kanama, Daisuke. (2006). Patent application trends in the field of nanotechnology. Retrieved November 29, 2011, from http://www.nistep.go.jp/achiev/ftx/eng/stfc/stt021e/qr21pdf/STTqr2105.pdf

Liu, Deming. (2008). Nanotechnology in China: Regulations and patents. *Nanotechnology Law & Business, 5*(4), 465–491.

Maynard, Andrew D. (2006). Nanotechnology: A research strategy for addressing risk. Retrieved November 25, 2011, from http://www.nanotechproject.org/file_download/files/PEN3_Risk.pdf

Meridian Institute. (2007). Nanotechnology, commodities & development: Background paper for the International Workshop on Nanotechnology, Commodities, and Development. Retrieved November 25, 2011, from http://sites.merid.org/nano/commoditiesworkshop/files/Comm_Dev_and_Nano_FINAL.pdf

Observatory Nano. (2010). Developments in nanotechnologies: Regulation and standards 2010. Retrieved November 25, 2011, from http://www.observatorynano.eu/project/filesystem/files/ObservatoryNano_Nanotechnologies_RegulationAndStandards_2010.pdf

Palmberg, Christopher; Dernis, Hélèn; & Miguet, Claire. (2009, June 25). Nanotechnology: An overview based on indicators and statistics. Retrieved March 23, 2012, from http://www.oecd.org/dataoecd/59/9/43179651.pdf

Peterson, Christine L. (2004). Nanotechnology: From Feynman to the grand challenge of molecular manufacturing. *Technology and Society Magazine, 23*(4), 9–15.

Purra, Mika, & Richmond, Noah. (2010). Mapping emerging nanotechnology policies and regulations: The case of Taiwan. Retrieved November 25, 2011, from http://www.risk-and-regulation.com/wp-content/uploads/2010/07/Case-study-of-Taiwan.pdf

Su, Hsin-Ning; Lee, Pei-Chun; Tsai, Min-Hua; & Chien, Kuo-Ming. (2007). Current situation and industrialization of Taiwan. *Journal of Nanoparticle Research, 9*(6), 965–975.

Youtie, Jan; Shapira, Philip; & Porter, Alan L. (2008). Nanotechnology publications and citations by leading countries and blocs. *Journal of Nanoparticle Research, 10*(6), 981–986.

Share the *Encyclopedia of Sustainability*: Teachers are welcome to make up to ten (10) copies of no more than two (2) articles for distribution in a single course or program. For further permissions, please visit www.copyright.com or contact: info@berkshirepublishing.com

National Pollution Survey (China)

Rapid industrialization, high population growth, and increasing imports of the world's garbage are putting pressure on China's ecosystem sustainability and social fabric. As these pressures increase, China will have to develop its own country-specific plans and policies to avoid further environmental degradation.

At the turn of the twenty-first century, news stories such as those of cancer villages—clusters of cancers occurring near industrial sites—have become much more common in China as breakneck economic growth increasingly takes its toll on the nation's health environment (Watts 2010b). Nationwide, cancer rates have surged since the 1990s to become the nation's biggest killer. In 2007, the disease was responsible for one in five deaths, up 80 percent since the start of economic reforms thirty years earlier (Watts 2010a). Elsewhere, citizens have protested against chemical factories that are blamed for carcinogens that enter water supplies and the food chain.

The conflict between China's natural environment and its economic development is extremely serious. If China wants to quadruple its economic output before 2030 with no more serious damage to the environment, the country will have to use resources more efficiently and implement environmental laws more strictly; otherwise, the country will have to pay a high price in the future. The first national pollution sources census of China, carried out from 2008 to 2010, represented a small step forward for China in terms of transparency. It raised serious questions about the shortcomings of China's previous pollution data and suggested that in spite of limited progress in some areas, the country still had a long way to go to clean its waterways, air, and soil (National Bureau of Statistics 2010).

Water Contamination

In the early 1980s, water pollution of major lakes and rivers became one of China's most pressing national environmental concerns. At the same time, water pollution control significantly reduced the discharge of industrial effluents on a per yuan output basis. Despite this progress, water pollution in China still caused a direct economic loss of about 147 billion yuan (about $23 billion) a year.

Industrial Pollution

The national pollution survey targeted nearly 6 million industrial sources, with data showing about 209 billion tonnes of wastewater; 30 million tonnes of chemical oxygen demand (organic pollutants); 1,730,000 tonnes of ammonia; 5 million tonnes of total nitrogen; 423,000 tonnes of total phosphorus; 782,000 tonnes of petroleum; and 900 tonnes of heavy metals (cadmium, chromium, arsenic, mercury, lead) in 2007 (National Bureau of Statistics 2010). These data clearly demonstrate serious structural pollution problems.

Pollutants are mainly concentrated in several chemical industries. Chemical oxygen demand and ammonia-nitrogen emissions in papermaking, chemicals, textiles, and a few other industries make up a large proportion of all industrial emissions (Dong 2011). According to the 2006–2010 pollution prevention program of the upper-middle Huang (Yellow) River, in the Huang River basin, for example, a well-developed chemical industry on its upper-middle reaches and the presence of coal and oil industries with low energy efficiency are producing high emissions intensity. In addition, few financial resources go into pollution treatment and most of the basin's enterprises continue to use outdated manufacturing techniques with a very low utilization ratio of energy, raw materials, and water to output. Some factories even illegally exhaust mercury, cadmium, lead, arsenic, hexavalent chromium, volatile phenol, cyanide, and other toxic substances (Dong 2011). Consequently, pollution in the Yellow River basin is worsening and is beyond the load capacity of the river's water.

Agricultural Pollution

Agricultural pollution, consisting of wastes, emissions, and discharges arising from farming activities, made an even greater contribution to China's water deterioration than did industry. Chemical oxygen demand accounted for about 13,240,000 tonnes of emissions; nitrogen, 2,704,000 tonnes; and phosphorus, 285,000 tonnes; respectively occupying 43.7 percent, 57.2 percent and 67.4 percent of the national total (National Bureau of Statistics 2010). Total nitrogen and phosphorus emissions of livestock and poultry accounted for 94 percent of China's agricultural pollution.

China used nearly a third of the world's total of nitrogen fertilizer in 2011, and its utilization ratio (the amount that is actually taken up by growing plants) is only 30 percent, far below the world average level (compared with the United States at 52 percent and Europe at 68 percent) (Jiang 2011). The low utilization ratio of fertilizer during the growing season has many environmental implications, the most significant being that a large amount of nitrogen, phosphorus, and potassium is released into the air or left in the soil, and it eventually contaminates groundwater or surface water: soil structure deteriorates, eutrophication (a buildup of dissolved nutrients) occurs in surface water, high levels of nitrates appear in vegetables and groundwater, nitrous oxide emissions increase, and the overall environmental bearing capacity deteriorates.

The Ministry of Environmental Protection studied the basic environmental condition of drinking water from 2007 to 2010. Its survey showed that about one-fifth of the land from which drinking water is drawn is also subject to the discharge of excessive pollutants that exceed legal standards (Tang 2010). The causes of contamination vary. For example, excessive pollutants in rivers mainly stem from ammonia, total nitrogen, total phosphorus, fecal coliform bacteria, organic compounds, volatile phenol, and oil. In lakes, pollution mainly comes from nitrogen, phosphorus, and algae. Toxic organic pollutants have not been monitored or regulated in many places, however, although they are undoubtedly a contributor. The environmental management of drinking water sources is limited to the major pollutants.

Air Pollution

Technology improvements that occurred alongside economic growth have resulted in much-improved resource utilization: ambient concentrations of particulate matter and sulfur dioxide in cities have gradually decreased since 1985. At the same time, all sorts of old and new air pollution challenges have been created, which explains why the air pollution index still remains high. Air quality in several cities with a population of more than 1 million regularly exceed the government's standard, owing much to the high air pollution index, especially the sulfur dioxide and particulate matter. As the national pollution survey shows, in 2007, the whole country discharged about 23 million tonnes of sulfur dioxide, 18 million tonnes of nitrogen oxide, 12 million tonnes of smoke dust, and 8 million tonnes of industrial dust (National Bureau of Statistics 2010).

Coal-Burning Pollution

Coal is both the new economy's black gold and the fragile environment's dark cloud. Coal consumption increased 14 percent in both 2009 and 2010, as Chinese industries grew rapidly. China uses more coal than the United States, the European Union, and Japan combined; it is the world's largest coal producer as well as the largest consumer of coal. Seventy-eight percent of the electricity, 60 percent of the civilian commercial energy, and 70 percent of the chemical production in China rely on coal.

The combustion of coal and coal bricks is the primary source of atmospheric gaseous and aerosol fluoride, which can easily enter exposed food products and the human respiratory tract. One study of dental fluorosis in students showed a high level of urinary fluoride concentration and an accompanying increase in bone density. Reducing emissions of fluoride from coal-burning plants will have a positive effect on the health of the country's citizens (Kun et al. 2002).

Traffic Pollution

Much of the air pollution in urban areas in China is a mixture of coal smog and automobile exhaust. The Ministry of Environmental Protection reported that 39.7 percent of the 522 cities monitored experienced moderate or severe pollution in 2005, and that traffic pollution was a major contributor (Ma 2006). Car ownership in China is growing rapidly and will reach 131 million cars in 2020 (from 31 million in 2005). Since car ownership in small and medium-size cities will increase, urban vehicle emissions in 2020 will be more than twice those of 2000 if vehicle emissions standards and fuel quality are not improved promptly.

In Beijing, for example, in 1990, four out of five residents pedaled to work through one of the world's best systems of bicycle lanes. But the modern passion for cars has made two-wheeled transportation so treacherous, dirty, and unfashionable that barely one-fifth of the population dares to use lanes that are now routinely blocked by parked cars and invaded by vehicles trying to escape from jams on the main roads. Researchers at Peking University have found a close link between air pollution from city traffic and the asthma risk for children and elders who require emergency room visits (Yao 2008). Choosing an appropriate automobile policy will be key to solving air pollution and energy consumption issues in China.

Particulate and Rubbish Pollution

Many Chinese cities are surrounded by garbage dumps. Moreover, a thriving rural industry in recycling global electronic waste exposes workers to cadmium, mercury, and brominated flame retardants. According to the Ecological Society of China (ESC), a nongovernmental organization, the amount of waste produced in China exceeds 500 million tonnes per year, and there is little room for additional disposal (ESC 2004). In 1988, the cumulative amount of waste was 6.5 billion tonnes nationwide, about 6 tonnes per capita. According to statistics, 60 million tonnes of municipal solid waste was produced in 2003, twice the amount of 1993, and at least two-thirds of 380 cities were surrounded by garbage. In Beijing alone, more than 4,500 garbage heaps about 50 meters high are situated between the Third Ring Road and the Fourth Ring Road and cover more than 2,800 hectares.

Large sums of garbage dumps resulted in serious particulate and rubbish pollution as a result of combusting in many Chinese cities. For example, the concentrations of total suspended particles (TSP) and particulate matter (PM$_{10}$) in Lanzhou City have been consistently high since 1990. From November through April, the high alert level for air pollution is reached about eight days out of ten.

Agriculture also contributes to air pollution. Nitrogen fertilizer, for example, accounts for about 8 percent of carbon dioxide emissions. *Cost of Pollution in China: Economic Estimates of Physical Damages*, a report published by the World Bank in 2007, concluded that China's air pollution led to higher mortality rates. Loss of human resources caused by excessive air pollution lowered gross domestic product (GDP) by 2.9 percent annually, a number that includes premature death, illness, and losses in means of production and urban construction. Statistics show that there are 350,000 respiratory-system cases in Chinese cities per year because of the air pollution (Cai 2007).

Soil Deterioration

Sixty-five percent of China's total area of 9.6 million square kilometers is classified as mountainous, hilly, or plateau regions, and is, by definition, vulnerable to erosion. Most of the serious erosion problems in China occur in four regions, namely the Loess Plateau, the Red Soils area, the Northeast China Plain, and the Northwest Grasslands, which together make up 70 percent of China's land area. Commonly used techniques of erosion control, such as terracing, can still allow for significant, long-term soil and fertility losses, and serious economic consequences. In Guangxi Province, for example, officials claim that more than 20 percent of their provincial irrigation systems have been damaged to various degrees by siltation, resulting in large decreases in provincial grain yields.

Furthermore, serious soil pollution jeopardizes ecology, food safety, human health, and the sustainable development of agriculture. It is estimated that nationwide 12 million tonnes of grain are polluted each year by heavy metals that have found their way into the soil (Li 2011). Direct economic losses exceed 20 billion yuan (about $2.5 billion). China has around 1.8 billion mu (120 million hectares) of arable land. But China's first soil pollution survey that analyzed the amount of heavy metals, pesticide residue, and organic pollutants in the soil reported that about 49 million tonnes of industrial solid waste and 40,000 tons of industrial hazardous waste contaminate the soil. Heavy metal pollution amounted to nearly 20 million hectares or 20 percent of the total available farmland. Of these, 2 million hectares were polluted by mineral contamination, 5 million hectares by oil, about 50,000 hectares by solid waste, and 10 million hectares by industrial residue, and sewage contributed 3.3 million hectares. The output of grain has declined by 13 million tonnes nationwide due to soil pollution in 2010. Other enormous economic losses caused by other types of pollution, including pesticides, organic pollution, radioactive contamination, and hazardous bacteria, are difficult to estimate.

One example of soil contamination occurred at a subway construction site in Songjiazhuang, Beijing. On 28 April 2004, three workers were digging an exploratory well at 3 meters below the surface when they were suddenly met by a strong and pungent smell (Liu 2011). Although the three were wearing gas masks, they were overcome by fumes, and one of them began to vomit. All three were sent to a nearby hospital. The construction site was subsequently identified as the location of a now-demolished pesticide plant. There are many other sites of this type throughout China.

The Root Causes of Pollution

With the rapid development of economy and society, the contradiction between the environment and the sustainable development of society and economy is becoming increasingly acute. Throughout the country, air, water, and soil contamination occur at large and small scales. Three main factors—industrialization, population pressure, and globalization—contribute to this widespread problem.

Industrialization

In recent decades, China has achieved rapid economic and industrial growth. Annual increases in GDP of 8 to 9 percent have lifted some 400 million people out of extreme poverty. At the same time, emissions of industrial waste are a primary cause of pollution. Eight industries, including papermaking and textiles, contribute 83 percent of chemical oxygen demand and 73 percent of ammonia-nitrogen emissions. Six industries, including electrical power, heating, and nonmetallic mineral products, contribute 89 percent of sulfur dioxide emissions and 93 percent of nitrogen oxide emissions. All these industries started from a low base and developed quickly in an effort to catch up with developed countries. Industrialization grew with a high capital investment and high consumption of resources, as well as a high cost to the environment. In the process of industrialization in developed countries, pollution peaked when per capita GDP reached $8,000, and then declined. In China, per capita GDP exceeded $3,000 in 2008, but there was still a long way to go to reach the developed countries' peak pollution loads. China will have to take a different route to industrialization than Western countries did if it is to reduce its output of contaminants.

Population Pressure

Despite a population of more than 1.3 billion, China has harnessed its resource base to provide its citizens with sufficient food, clothing, and housing, as well as a number of reasonably priced products for its rapidly growing urban and industrial economy. Although the rapid growth of China's population contributed to its economic development in the short term, this growth has become a huge pressure on the ecological environment and will be the biggest obstacle to China's modernization process. To survive, people have engaged in many unsustainable activities, including deforestation, reclaiming land from lakes, indiscriminate and unauthorized mining, and destruction of vegetation. The results surpassed the output capability and bearing capacity of the ecosystem in many areas. Without some kind of policy intervention, population pressure may continue to degrade air, soil, and water in the long term.

In addition to investing in environmental cleanup efforts, the Chinese government may work to alleviate poverty and slow population growth, which may have a positive, albeit indirect, impact on the quality of the environment.

Globalization

China has become the world's biggest provider of cheap commodities and the dumping ground for garbage from the United States, Britain, and other developed countries. Much of the waste is toxic and is sorted by migrant workers who are not protected from the effects of contamination. In fact, roughly 3 million tonnes of garbage from the United Kingdom ends up in China because it is cheaper to dump waste there than in British landfill sites. This transfer corresponds with the English political economist David Ricardo's economic theory that suggests polluting industries will move from countries with higher environmental standards to those with lower environmental standards because of the lower cost of doing business there (Ricardo 1976). Consumption patterns in wealthier countries, which increase demand for a variety of products, also affect Chinese society. As consumerism becomes a part of contemporary Chinese culture, the demand for goods and associated environmental damage will increase.

Outlook

Rapid economic growth has had some positive environmental impacts but has also created new environmental challenges. The resources that such growth demands and the environmental pressures it brings raise grave concerns about the long-term sustainability and hidden costs of growth. Premier Wen Jiabao announced in early 2011 that, in order to strengthen environment protection, the central government had decided to reduce its economic growth target from 7.5 percent to 7 percent. Obviously, environmental pollution, ecological destruction, and resource depletion have severely restricted the potential of China's economic and social development. As a result, if solving environment and resource challenges is not established as a priority, China will face unprecedented conflicts and challenges, for example, so-called accidental pollution events and accompanying social unrest. The route to environmental sustainability, overcoming the challenges of rapid industrialization, consumerism, and global movement of waste, will have to be addressed in a new, specifically Chinese context.

GONG Xiangqian and CUI Can
Beijing Institute of Technology Law School

See also Activism, Judicial; China; Consumerism; E-Waste; Fisheries (China); Five-Year Plans; Great Green Wall (China); Huang (Yellow) River; Media Coverage of the Environment; Nongovernmental Organizations (NGOs); Outsourcing and Offshoring; Public Health; Rule of Law; Water Security

FURTHER READING

Cai Rupeng. (2007). Huánjìng wūrǎn xià de jiànkāng yīnyǐng [Health harm caused by enviromental pollution]. *Chinese Newsweek, 23*(5), 36–41.

Dong Jiahua. (2011, April 01). Wǒguó shuǐ wūrǎn xiànzhuàng jí fángzhì cuòshī [Current water pollution statement and prevention measures in China]. Retrieved February 1, 2012, from http://news.lanbailan.com/html/2011/04/571301639371_1.shtml

Ecological Society of China (ESC). (2004, November 29). Zhōngguó shēngtài huánjìng zhuàngkuàng [Ecological and environmental conditions in China]. Retrieved November 25, 2011, from http://it.sohu.com/20041129/2232414n03.shtml

Jiang Ying. (2011, June 02). Kòngzhì nóngyè miàn yuán wūrǎn féiliào yě yào lǜsè huánbǎo [Use of environmentally protective fertilizer to control agricultural non-point source pollution]. Retrieved November 2, 2011, from http://www.agri.gov.cn/Ü0/ZX/nyyw/201106/t20110602_2006725.htm

Kun Li, Xu Lirong, Li Ribang, & Xiang Lianhua. (2002). Zhōngguó Huáběi dìqū hé xīběi dìqū dònglì méi fú de páifàng liáng [Emissions of fluorine from coal in north and northwest China]. *Chinese Science Bulletin, 47*(11), 56–58.

Li Yan. (2011, February 22). Nóngtián zhòngjīnshǔ wūrǎn chùmù jīngxīn měinián wūrǎn 1200 wàn dūn liángshi [Heavy metal pollution in soil leads to crop failure of 12 million tonnes annually]. Retrieved December 22, 2012, from http://huanbao.gongyi.ifeng.com/detail_2011_02/22/4787234_0.shtml

Li Yan. (2011, September 16). COPD zhī shāng: Shéi dòng le wǒde fèi? [Dying early from COPD: Who stole our lungs?]. *China Medical Tribune*. Retrieved November 25, 2011, from http://www.cmt.com.cn/detail/28320.html

Li Yang. (2012). Tǔrǎng wūrǎn zhuàngkuàng diàochá yǒuwàng pīlù "páidú" dòngzhé qiānwàn yuán [China's first soil pollution survey reveals the high price paid for soil pollution]. *BanDao News*. Retrieved February 22, 2012, from http://news.bandao.cn/news_html/201202/20120221_news_20120221_1812601.shtml?i|148130:1

Liu Xiaoxin. (2011, March 14) Guīfàn wūrǎn chǎngdì zàikāi fāxíng wéi [Regulation of redevelopment of contaminated sites]. Retrieved December 17, 2011, from http://www.cenews.com.cn/xwzx/fz/qt/201103/t20110313_700161.html

Ma Li. (2006, May 31). Chéngshì kōngqì 39.7% zhōng dù zhòngdù wūrǎn [39.7% of cities suffer from severe air pollution in China]. Retrieved October 11, 2011, from http://www.envir.gov.cn/info/2006/5/531295.htm

Ministry of Environmental Protection of the People's Republic of China. (2008, April 14). Huánghé zhōng shàngyóu liúyù shuǐ wūrǎn fángzhì guīhuà (2006–2010) [Water pollution prevention program of the middle-upper breaches of the Yellow River, Huaihe, and the Haihe River Basin from 2006 to 2010]. Retrieved January 18, 2012, from http://www.zhb.gov.cn/info/bgw/bwj/200804/W020080423440539177717.pdf

National Bureau of Statistics of China. (2010, February 11). Dìyīcì quánguó wūrǎn yuán pǔchá gōngbào [Bulletin of the first official nationwide pollution sources census of China]. Retrieved February 7, 2012, from http://www.stats.gov.cn/tjgb/qttjgb/qgqttjgb/t20100211_402621161.htm

Ricardo, David. (1976). Zhèngzhì jīngjìxué jí fùshuì yuánlǐ [Principles of political economy and taxation] (Guo Daili, Trans.). Beijing: The Commercial Press.

Rozelle, Scott; Huang, Jikun; & Zhang, Linxiu. (1997). Poverty, population and environmental degradation in China. *Food Policy, 22*(3), 229–251.

Tang Li. (2010, June 18). Huánbǎo bù chūtái shuǐyuán dì huánjìng guīhuà jìn 1/5 shuǐyuán wūrǎnwù chāobiāo [A water resource protection plan announced by the Ministry of Environmental Protection]. Retrieved January 25, 2011, from http://www.chinatibetnews.com/huanbao/2010-06/18/content_488562.htm

Watts, Jonathan. (2010a, June 6). China's "cancer villages" reveal dark side of economic boom. *The Guardian*. Retrieved January 5, 2012, from http://www.guardian.co.uk/environment/2010/jun/07/china-cancer-villages-industrial-pollution

Watts, Jonathan. (2010b, August 6). The dark side of the boom. *China Dialogue*. Retrieved February 18, 2012, from http://www.chinadialogue.net/article/show/single/en/3762-The-dark-side-of-the-boom

World Bank & State Environmental Protection Administration, People's Republic of China. (2007). *Cost of pollution in China: Economic estimates of physical damages*. Retrieved March 7, 2012, from http://siteresources.worldbank.org/INTEAPREGTOPENVIRONMENT/Resources/China_Cost_of_Pollution.pdf

Yao Yijiang. (2008, April 4). Wǒguó chéngshì huī mái tiānnián duó mìng 30 wàn jiāotōng wēiqì wūrǎn zhàn shǒuwèi [Automobile emissions contribute to haze resulting in great loss of life]. Retrieved December 20, 2011, from http://news.enorth.com.cn/system/2008/04/03/003081906.shtml

Nongovernmental Organizations (NGOs)

Asian nongovernmental organizations (NGOs) exhibit a wide range of forms and scale. Present in almost every country in the region, NGOs have contributed significantly to the rise of environmental consciousness. In spite of substantial social and political differences between India, China, and other countries, NGOs have found ways to accomplish their objectives. As Asia's environmental crisis intensifies, the role and importance of NGOs will increase.

The rise of nongovernmental membership associations, relief and development agencies, and political advocacy groups—collectively known as nongovernmental organizations, or NGOs—has been a characteristic feature of Asian societies since at least the 1980s. The term *nongovernmental organization* has become commonly accepted despite the fact that it defines a type of social organization only by what it is not. Even more confusing, many NGOs are not strictly nongovernmental at all. Most register with domestic regulatory agencies that, depending on the regime, may exert control over the organization's fund-raising, political activities, and/or project scope. Some NGOs receive funding or contracts from their own national or local governments to carry out social services. Others apply for grants, usually short-term and project-based, from foreign governments, foundations, and corporations. In some countries, the state itself has created "government-organized NGOs" or GONGOs. Filipinos, who have acronyms for just about everything, have coined additional neologisms for business-organized NGOs (BONGOs), quasi-state organizations (QUANGOs), and fly-by-night rent-seekers (COME'NGOs), among others (Constantino-David 1998).

An initial distinction is often made between international NGOs, usually based in the global North, and local or domestic NGOs in developing countries. The best-known Northern aid and environmental organizations, such as CARE and the World Wide Fund for Nature (WWF), typically—but not always—have longer histories, bureaucratic structures, and larger budgets. This often results in moderate, engagement-based approaches to governments and corporations, though there are exceptions, such as the campaigning direct action done by Greenpeace. Local NGOs, by contrast, are frequently smaller and newer, comprising both informal service delivery groups and political activists. But again, this is not always the case: the world's largest NGO, BRAC, was founded as the Bangladesh Rehabilitation Assistance Committee in 1972 and now serves more than 110 million people worldwide through 120,000 staff and volunteers. Perhaps more useful than a local/international division is a grouping of NGOs into grassroots organizations (GROs) with membership constituencies and grassroots support organizations (GRSOs) that are professional intermediary groups (Fisher 1998).

The legal status of NGOs varies widely across Asia. The US law professor Mark Sidel characterizes Asian political systems, broadly speaking, in two categories: those that recognize freedom for NGOs to operate and those that seek to control their growth. In neither case have NGOs unambiguously led to democratic politics. Some of the Asian countries with the largest NGO sectors, such as Bangladesh and Thailand, have highly imperfect democracies. In others, including Indonesia and the Philippines, NGOs have contributed to the overthrow of dictators and opening of political spaces, yet they have also been linked to corruption and ethnic and religious violence. A measured conclusion is that the growth of NGOs can result in increased political space but is not sufficient to bring about democratic transitions, which are contingent on many factors outside of the control of NGOs (Alagappa 2004). Yet both the "basic freedom" and "controlled growth" models have been conducive to the growth of environmental NGOs, as a comparison between the region's two largest countries makes clear.

India: Freedom without Influence?

The modern history of environmental sustainability in India is closely linked to the legacy of Mohandas Gandhi (1869–1948). Gandhian impulses of self-reliance and nonviolence underpin many of India's 1.2 million nonprofit organizations and an additional twenty to thirty thousand movements and informal groups. On paper at least, the Indian state is open and encouraging to NGOs, and funds many of their local activities. Over time, particularly since the 1980s, Indian NGOs have become more professionalized (Chandhoke 2011). Recent decades have also witnessed the emergence of numerous NGOs connected to the Hindu right wing. This plural and diverse NGO sector has contributed to India's economic growth and democratic politics, but at the same time, massive challenges remain to improve the lives of the poorest and most marginalized (Behar and Prakash 2004).

One of the many notable Indian NGOs contributing to environmental sustainability is Ekta Parishad (Unity Forum), based in Madhya Pradesh State with a membership of more than 200,000 people, especially those in poor, tribal, and forest areas. It began, according to its website, as "a loose grouping of NGO training institutes" that formed into a people's organization in 1991 (Ekta Parishad 2010). Drawing on Gandhian roots, Ekta Parishad promotes "people-centered development," specifically, the idea that resources should be controlled by local communities. On this participatory democratic basis, the organization has advocated for land redistribution, access to forest resources, improved social legislation, and women's involvement in leadership and policy formation. Its achievements include a logging ban in Bastar District and the preservation of local fishing and cultural rights for villagers in Madhya Pradesh (Behar and Prakash 2004, 207–208). In recent years, Ekta Parishad has expanded its activities nationwide through the tactic of mass nonviolent marches for environmental rights.

Indian NGOs have been involved in environmental campaigns since the 1970s, including the Chipko movement against deforestation of the western Himalaya, the Chilika campaign against commercial shrimp farming, and the Kaiga antinuclear campaign (Tandon and Mohanty 2003). The best-known of these campaigns outside India has been the Narmada dam movement (Narmada Bachao Andolan) to protest construction of the gargantuan Sardar Sarovar dam in Gujarat in western India. The movement's advocacy succeeded in pressuring the World Bank to retract its support for the project in 1995. Despite the participation of numerous NGOs, tribal groups, farmers, and even Bollywood film stars, however, the movement has been unable to prevent either the construction or the subsequent expansion of the dam, which has been reaffirmed by judicial rulings. The Indian state has opened democratic spaces that allow environmental movements to rise, yet has often resisted adoption of their demands.

China: Influence without Freedom?

Environmental organizations in China have formed since the mid-1990s, a response both to elements of opening in Chinese society and to rising environmental problems, particularly water and air pollution. The environmental NGO sector includes state-backed GONGOs such as the All-China Environment Federation, registered grassroots and professional NGOs, and many unregistered student and citizen associations across the country. China's NGOs are restricted in their operations by a series of legal and extralegal barriers: for instance, NGOs must register with both a host government agency and an administrative "mother-in-law," and annual renewals may be declined for unclear reasons. In China's bureaucratic hierarchy, only one organization is permitted to operate in one subject area in a particular location, making legal recognition impossible for many grassroots NGOs. In spite of these obstacles, dynamic individuals and organizations have found many ways to maneuver within and around these structures (Howell 2011).

Such creative maneuvering is evident in the experiences of Green Watershed (Luse Liuyu), an NGO formed in Kunming in 2002 among researchers at the

Yunnan provincial Academy of Social Sciences. Green Watershed's small core staff includes scientists and activists who advocate for social and environmental preservation of river valleys affected by dam construction. The group's strategies include engagement with the media through environmental "journalists' salons" and, more controversially, organizing local villagers to counter hydropower plans. Green Watershed has also cooperated actively with other environmental NGOs, serving as the first coordinator of the China Rivers Network in 2004–2005 and more recently as chair of a green banking network (Wells-Dang 2012). The organization's efforts are appreciated by allies in the Ministry of Environmental Protection, but not by local dam proponents. In 2005, in retaliation for Green Watershed's anti-dam activism, provincial authorities restricted travel to river communities, seized the director's passport, and threatened to close the organization (Mertha 2008). Yet the NGO has remained open and diversified its activities. Green Watershed has supported local poverty alleviation projects along the Nu (Salween) and upper Yangzi (Chang) rivers, contributed to NGO relief efforts after the 2008 Sichuan earthquake, and developed a specialty in independent research on the effects of hydropower.

A Beijing-based NGO, Global Village (GVB), has focused its campaigning instead on individual behavior change through "Green Community" efforts to reduce the use of plastic bags, set air conditioners at 26°C, and promote low-energy lightbulbs. A nonmembership organization founded in 1996, GVB is registered as a business enterprise. Through innovative use of communication strategies and what GVB terms "years of outdoor, community, media, government and enterprise outreach," the so-called 26 Degree Campaign succeeded in convincing not only urban residents, but eventually the Chinese government as well. In 2006, central authorities mandated that the thermostats in all government offices be set no lower than 26°C in summer and no higher than 18°C in winter, resulting in immense energy savings. The contributions of Global Village, Green Watershed, and thousands of other Chinese environmental organizations have demonstrated that influence on policy makers is possible, even in a context of limited political space.

Crossing Borders: Transnational NGOs

Both local GROs and intermediary GRSOs form networks among themselves, with each other, and with government and other partners for information sharing, project cooperation, and policy advocacy. In Asia, although there is no single environmental network of NGOs, organizations participate in many overlapping subregional and topical networks, most formed in the 1990s. The International Union for Conservation of Nature (IUCN) hosts forums on wildlife, water resources, and related issues. A South Asian Network for Development and Environmental Economics (SANDEE) links NGOs and researchers in seven South Asian countries. The Asian NGO Coalition for Agrarian Reform and Rural Development (ANGOC) dates to 1979 and includes sixteen regional and national organizations working on land use and the rights of indigenous communities. ANGOC is one of the few networks to include both Indian and Chinese members.

The most dynamic transnational networks go beyond dialogue, conferences, and information sharing to engage in joint advocacy campaigns on cross-border issues. Rivers and anti-dam campaigns are a prime example, since many major Asian rivers extend across national borders, and a project in one country may have significant downstream effects. In 2009, as Laos and Cambodia prepared proposals for up to eleven dams on the Mekong River, a network of activists and environmental NGOs launched the Save the Mekong Coalition. The twenty-six coalition members gathered more than twenty-three thousand individual signatures on a petition to the prime ministers of Cambodia, Laos, Thailand, and Vietnam, calling for a moratorium on dam construction. Save the Mekong's efforts contributed to the 2011 suspension of the Xayaburi dam in Laos and have also influenced NGOs in Myanmar (Burma) to successfully campaign against the Chinese-funded Myitsone dam on the Irrawaddy River.

Future Directions for Asian NGOs

Amid diversity, nongovernmental organizations have contributed substantially to the development of environmental consciousness and sustainable policies across Asia. The Indian and Chinese experiences show a clear contrast between a state-guided growth model for NGOs on one hand and a freer political context on the other. Most Chinese NGOs are either professional and elite-based or local and fragmented. A large-scale, movement-based organization like India's Ekta Parishad, for instance, would not find space to develop in China. Yet the differences in legal and political frameworks do not necessarily determine the results of NGO efforts. Some Indian campaigns have failed to change unsustainable practices of the state, while certain campaigns in China and other restrictive contexts have succeeded. NGOs in controlled-growth settings may have less autonomy from government authorities, but at the same time benefit from more points of connection with parts of the state that they wish to influence.

Using a wide variety of organizational forms and strategies, Asian NGOs have accommodated themselves to differing social and political circumstances. Local and/or international NGOs are present on the ground in every Asian country, even to a limited extent in North Korea. The scope and activities of NGOs around environmental issues may be expected to increase in all parts of Asia, as the combined effects of climate change, pollution, and unsustainable megaprojects take a larger toll. If funding from donors in the global North is reduced, however, domestic NGOs will have to turn to other sources of operating funds, including local private philanthropy, social enterprises, and government contracts. Where these resources are not easily available, the focus of civil society may shift away from professional NGOs toward informal networks and people's movements that operate on a volunteer, self-sustaining basis. Both types of organizations are necessary to help address Asia's growing crises in sustainability and governance.

Andrew WELLS-DANG

Independent scholar, Hoi An, Vietnam

See also Activism, Judicial; China; Education, Environmental (*several articles*); Gandhism; India; Media Coverage of the Environment; Mekong-Lancang River; National Pollution Survey (China); Public-Private Partnerships; Rule of Law; Southeast Asia; Transboundary Water Issues; Yangzi (Chang) River

FURTHER READING

Alagappa, Muthiah. (Ed.). (2004). *Civil society and political change in Asia: Expanding and contracting democratic space.* Menlo Park, CA: Stanford University Press.

Behar, Amitabh, & Prakash, Aseem. (2004). India: Expanding and contracting democratic space. In Muthiah Alagappa (Ed.), *Civil society and political change in Asia: Expanding and contracting democratic space* (pp. 191–222). Menlo Park, CA: Stanford University Press.

Chandhoke, Neera. (2011). Civil society in India. In Michael Edwards (Ed.), *The Oxford handbook of civil society* (pp. 171–182). Oxford, UK: Oxford University Press.

Constantino-David, Karina. (1998). From the present looking back: A history of Philippine NGOs. In G. Sidney Silliman & Lela Garner Noble (Eds.), *Organizing for democracy: NGOs, civil society, and the Philippine State* (pp. 26–48). Honolulu: University of Hawai'i Press.

Economy, Elizabeth. (2010). *The river runs black: The environmental challenge to China's future* (2nd ed.). Ithaca, NY: Cornell University Press.

Ekta Parishad. (2010). Our history. Retrieved November 27, 2011, from http://www.ektaparishad.com/about-us/our-history

Fisher, Julie. (1998). *Nongovernments.* Bloomfield, CT: Kumarian Press.

Hirsch, Philip, & Warren, Carol. (Eds.). (1998). *The politics of environment in Southeast Asia.* London: Routledge.

Howell, Jude. (2011). Civil society in China. In Michael Edwards (Ed.), *The Oxford handbook of civil society* (pp. 159–170). Oxford, UK: Oxford University Press.

Kalland, Arne, & Persoon, Gerard. (Eds.). (1998). *Environmental movements in Asia.* Surrey, UK: Curzon.

Lee, Yok-shiu, & So, Alvin. (Eds.). (1999). *Asia's environmental movements: Comparative perspectives.* Armonk, NY: M. E. Sharpe.

Mertha, Andrew. (2008). *China's water warriors.* Ithaca, NY: Cornell University Press.

Save the Mekong: Our River Feeds Millions. (2009). Key issues: About saving the Mekong Coalition. Retrieved July 17, 2011, from http://www.savethemekong.org/issue_detail.php?sid=13

Tandon, Rajesh, & Mohanty, Ranjita. (Eds.). (2003). *Does civil society matter? Governance in contemporary India.* New Delhi: Sage.

Wells-Dang, Andrew. (2012). *Civil society networks in China and Vietnam: Informal pathbreakers in health and the environment.* Basingstoke, UK: Palgrave Macmillan.

O

One-Child Policy

China's one-child policy discourages couples from having more than one child. Introduced in 1979, it became a national law in 2001. Its application varies, being stricter in urban areas and more flexible for rural areas and ethnic minorities. Despite it being considered by the Chinese government effective in reducing population growth, many questions about its sustainability implications are raised by demographers, environmentalists, and human rights activists.

China's one-child policy is a family planning strategy that aims to discourage couples from having more than one child. Demographers classify this as an active, explicit, and direct policy to control population size through the lowering of birth rates.

The one-child policy was initiated in China in 1979 by the Chinese government in order to slow population growth and allow for more favorable economic and social development. In the 1970s, the country already had witnessed a significant reduction in fertility rates following the "late, long, few" policy—encouragement for later childbearing, longer spacing between children, and fewer children—but the government wanted to take further action to deal with the population problem within the context of national development. Since 1949 when the People's Republic of China was established, the country's population had been growing rapidly and by 1979 had reached 975 million, an 80 percent increase (Liu 2010). Implementation of the one-child policy included providing a large range of contraceptives and services free of charge and available to the entire population, in both urban and rural areas, through employment- and community-based medical clinics. Its goal has been to drastically reduce the number of births in China and, along with economic reforms, improve the country's economic development and the quality of life of its people.

It is seen as a necessary short-term measure by the government to break the vicious cycle of poverty in which poor people have more children to provide caretaking and security in old age and thus inadvertently contribute further to poverty. Children from poor families have less access to education, health services, and other opportunities that could allow them to lead a better life. Consequently getting out of poverty remains as difficult for them as it was for their parents.

As stated in its name, the main aim of the policy is to restrict to one the number of children born to a married couple. In a country where being a single mother or giving birth out of wedlock is still not socially accepted, this policy aimed at married couples immediately controls population numbers. (In many Western societies, a policy that restricted the number of births for couples would not be as effective because a large percentage of children are born to single mothers.) There are regional, demographic, and cultural differences in the way the policy is applied, however. Urban couples are covered by the firm one-child policy, which states that only one child per couple is allowed, unless it is a second marriage with one partner having no child of his/her own or the only child possesses an abnormality. These firm requirements also apply to government workers in the countryside. For some minority ethic groups (regulated individually for each province or autonomous region) and couples in rural areas, the policy is more relaxed. Its application varies between provinces; for example, a second child may be allowed if the first one is a girl or if there is a four-year interval between the two children.

The different rules and exceptions that apply to the various provinces are clearly stipulated on the government's family planning website. According to Feng Wang (2005), a US professor of sociology and demography, these rules are divided among three broad categories.

First are the six provinces or municipal regions directly under the central government's jurisdiction, namely Chongqing, Jiangsu, Sichuan, Beijing, Shanghai, and Tianjin; people there are covered by the one-child policy unless they belong to an ethnic minority or live in a very impoverished area. This involves around 35 percent of China's population. Secondly, in areas populated by ethnic minorities, such as the Xinjiang Uygur, Inner Mongolian, Ningxia Hui, and Guangxi Zhuang autonomous regions, couples can have a second or even a third child. This involves about 11 percent of the population. Thirdly, in the remainder of the country couples in rural areas are allowed to have a second child if the first one is a girl. These areas account for 54 percent of the population.

Wang (2005) also claims that this in effect translates to an overall policy of 1.47 children per couple across China's entire population. Despite these drastic restrictions on reproduction, China's population is continuing to grow (though at a much slower rate than previously) because of its relatively large young population, with many people being of childbearing age. This is a historically built-in growth momentum as a result of the high fertility levels in the past.

In 2001 China passed a range of regulations that made this family planning policy a national law, and an extensive system was created to keep track of contraceptive use and pregnancy status. More recently, parents without any siblings have been allowed to have a second child.

According to Wang (2005, 2), China's one-child policy "is the largest and most extreme social experiment in population growth control via government intervention in human reproduction in world history." Another country that has used similar intrusive government intervention in policies aimed at population reduction in the past is Singapore. It employed a combination of open persuasive publicity and advertising as well as tangible material incentives and disincentives. Following the success of these interventions, the sharply declining fertility rates in the 1960s and 1970s caused the Singaporean government to reconsider the economic and demographic implications for the country amid concerns about its overall survival as a nation. Consequently it revamped its population policies in the 1980s from "Stop at Two" to "Have Three or More, if You Can Afford It" (Yap 2003). Despite the many new government incentives to encourage couples to have more children, Singapore's total fertility rate continues to be very low and has been steadily dropping from 1.6 children per woman in 2000 to 1.2 in 2011 (Prime Minister's Office Singapore 2012).

China's one-child policy has been highly debated and criticized worldwide in relation to the fines imposed on families to cover the social costs for raising another child, work-based administrative penalties for noncompliance, as well as the push for women to abort second and subsequent pregnancies. In urban areas, couples subject to the firm one-child policy risk losing employment and access to housing and other state-controlled resources, if they become parents to an unauthorized child. The application, monitoring, and administering of the policy have created a massive bureaucracy, and many institutions, including local governments, now have vested interest in collecting fines and maintaining public jobs. The nature of the policy and its implications have drawn considerable attention from demographers, environmentalists, and civil rights activists.

Impacts on Sustainability

The one-child policy has important social and economic impacts as well as implications for environmental sustainability in China. The dramatic fall in fertility between the late 1960s and 1979, combined with the further fertility decrease triggered by the policy, undoubtedly contributed to improvements in people's standards of living at a time when the Chinese economy was developing at phenomenally high rates. Between 1979 and 2011 the country's gross domestic product (GDP) grew at 9.7 percent per annum, and the slow population growth allowed for resources to be invested in priority areas of the Chinese economy, such as industrialization, health, and education (NBS 2012). The reduced family sizes helped improve the educational levels of children, and much-needed prenatal and postnatal care has been provided to mothers through the wide network of governmental health clinics.

The first generation of one-child-policy single children have now grown to adulthood, and they have been called "Little Emperors" because of the care and attention they have received from their parents and grandparents in the family home. Some psychological effects of being an only child have already been identified (Hesketh and Zhu 1997).

Another impact of the policy derives from the fact that it overtly restricts people's choices about the number of children they can have. In some cases this has prompted citizens to emigrate from China to other countries such as Australia, New Zealand, and the United States. Families with more than the allowed number of children received refugee status in the early 1990s.

The one-child policy slowed China's population growth rate in the three decades between the 1980s and 2010s. The tough policy helped China achieve a rapid decline in its average annual population growth rate from 1.2 percent in 1978 (Central People's Government of the People's Republic of China 2012) to 0.5 percent in 2011 (US Census Bureau 2012) and its total fertility rate from almost 4 children per woman in the 1970s (UN 2010) to 1.5 births per woman in 2011 (US Census Bureau 2012). China has now achieved a modern shift in population growth from a pattern of high fertility, low mortality, and high natural growth rate to a pattern of low fertility, low mortality, and low natural growth rate. The overall standards of living and health have improved, and as a consequence, life expectancy at birth in China has reached seventy-five years in 2011 (US Census Bureau 2012).

There is evidence that Chinese women already prefer smaller families, with one or two children, both in urban and rural areas (Wang 2005), and the country's economic development remains strong. Thus there is not a pressing need for the one-child policy to remain in place. The push to phase out the policy is substantiated with the high negative social costs that have come from its implementation.

Effects of the one-child policy include potentially problematic changes to the Chinese demographic. One concern is the country's serious newborn sex-ratio imbalance (120 boys to 100 girls in 2009, 118 to 100 in 2010), which has been proliferated by gender discrimination and preference for boys when families are allowed to have only one child (Xinhuanet 2010 and UPI 2011). (Because sex-screening technologies and abortions are available, families can act on this preference.) Particularly in rural areas parents traditionally prefer boys, who can best look after them in old age and offer social security. What this means is that when these babies become adults, there will be consistently not enough young women for almost a fifth of the young male population. This is likely to have potentially unprecedented destabilizing social effects. The Chinese government now limits sex screening during pregnancies and has introduced punishments for sex-selective abortions. Rewards (such as retirement pensions) for parents who have girls are also being considered.

Fertility rates are far below the replacement level (of around 2.1 children per woman), and this makes the country unable to replace its working-age population cohorts. It is also contributing to a dramatically older average age of the population (*Economist* 2011). The Chinese government thus faces an aging crisis triggered by the country's nonaction prior to the 1970s and the firm family planning policy implemented afterward. The rapid decline in mortality and fertility rates means that people now live longer and there are fewer children. This has significantly reduced the proportion of young and working-age people. China's aging process has been faster than in any other industrialized country, and the traditional burden of responsibility for old dependents will rest on a relatively small number of young people. China's social security system has yet to implement solutions to meet this challenge.

The country's fast industrialization, on the other hand, has triggered serious pollution and environmental problems, which are felt not only at the local level but also globally. For example, China as of 2008 was the world's largest greenhouse gas emitter, and the 2012 environmental performance index issued by Yale University (2012) ranks it 116th out of 132 countries. In response to these problems, the Chinese government has announced its commitment to the reduction of carbon dioxide per GDP and a plan for transitioning toward a low-carbon economy. The task and responsibility for a change toward decarbonizing the country's economy and maintaining ecological health rest with that same shrinking workforce.

Future of the Policy

The Chinese government has actively attempted to control the country's population growth with its long lasting family planning program since the 1970s. Despite the negative demographic, social, psychological, and human rights effects the one-child policy has brought about, China's efforts have contributed to reduction in the country's population growth and have improved its citizens' living standards, including higher educational levels and better health. Effects of the policy are considered to have been helpful also from an environmental and economic point of view (Liu 2010). China's population of 1.34 billion is still growing due to its relatively young composition (NBS 2012), and this growth, accompanied by fast economic development, continues to put pressure on the country's natural resources and to influence the quality of people's lives.

At the time of the one-child policy's inception, its architects, namely the Central Committee of the Chinese Communist Party, did not expect for it to last longer than thirty years. There are numerous calls now from within academia and civil society that it is time for the policy to be revised. Assuming current trends continue, demographers project China's population growth rate to drop to 0 percent and its population size to stabilize by 2025 (US Census Bureau 2012). Despite claims that other countries around the globe have achieved comparable fertility reductions without draconian measures imposed on families and individuals, the Chinese government remains cautious about changing its current population policy.

Dora MARINOVA and Xiumei GUO
Curtin University

See also China; Consumerism; Education, Environmental (China); Education, Female; Five-Year Plans; Gender Equality; Indigenous Peoples; Labor; Microfinance; Nongovernmental Organizations (NGOs); Outsourcing and Offshoring; Public Health; Religions; Rural Development; Rural Livelihoods; Singapore; Traditional Knowledge (China)

FURTHER READING

The Central People's Government of the People's Republic of China. (2012). *Rénkǒu zēngzhǎng yú jìhuà shēngyù* [Population growth and family planning]. Retrieved March 13, 2012, from http://www.gov.cn/test/2005-07/26/content_17364.htm

Economist. (2011). China's population: The most surprising demographic crisis, a new census raises questions about the future of China's one-child policy. Retrieved March 13, 2012, from http://www.economist.com/node/18651512

Ehrlich, Paul R. (1968). *The population bomb*. New York: Ballantine Books.

Fong, Vanessa L. (2004). *Only hope: Coming of age under China's one-child policy*. Palo Alto, CA: Stanford University Press.

Guo, Xiumei; Marinova, Dora; & Hong, Jin. (2012). China's shifting policies towards sustainability: A low-carbon economy and environmental protection. *Journal of Contemporary China* (forthcoming, acceptance date February 28, 2012).

Guo, Xiumei; Marinova, Dora; & Jia, Ruiyue. (2011). Population ageing and the ecology in China: Towards a balanced developmental strategy model (MODSIM 2011 International Congress on Modelling and Simulation). Perth, Australia: Modelling and Simulation Society of Australia and New Zealand. Retrieved March 13, 2012, from www.mssanz.org.au/modsim2011/D12/guo2.pdf

Hemminki, Elina; Wu, Zhuochun; Cao, Guiying; & Viisainen, Kirsi. (2005). Illegal births and legal abortions: The case of China. *Productive Health*, 2(5). Retrieved March 13, 2012, from http://www.ncbi.nlm.nih.gov/pmc/articles/PMC1215519/

Hesketh, Therese, & Zhu, Wei Xing. (1997). Health in China: The one child family policy: The good, the bad and the ugly. *British Medical Journal, 314*(7095), 1685. doi: 10.1136/bmj.314.7095.1685

Hesketh, Therese; Li, Lu; & Zhu, Xing Wei. (2005). The effect of China's one-child family policy after 25 years. *The New England Journal of Medicine, 353*, 1171–1176.

Jackson, Richard. (2011). Can an aging China be a rising China? *The China Business Review*. Retrieved March 13, 2012, from https://www.chinabusinessreview.com/public/1104/jackson.html

Liu, Jianguo. (2010). China's road to sustainability. *Science, 328*(5974), 50.

National Bureau of Statistics of China (NBS). (2012). Statistical data. Retrieved April 3, 2012, from www.stats.gov.cn/english

National Population and Family Planning Commission of People's Republic of China. (2001). *Zhōnghuá rénmín gònghéguó rénkǒu yú jìhuà shēngyù fǎ* [Population and family planning law of the People's Republic of China]. Retrieved March 13, 2012, from http://www.chinapop.gov.cn/xxgk/zcfg/flfg/200403/t20040326_87200.html

Prime Minister's Office Singapore. (2012). Prime Minister's 2012 Chinese New Year message. Retrieved March 13, 2012, from http://www.pmo.gov.sg/content/pmosite/mediacentre/speechesinterviews/primeminister/2012/January/prime_minister_2012_chinesenewyearmessage.html

United Nations (UN). (2010). *World population ageing 2009*. New York: Economic and Social Affairs Population Division.

United Press International (UPI). (2011). China reports latest sex ratio figures. Retrieved January 8, 2012, from http://www.upi.com/Top_News/World-News/2011/08/16/China-reports-latest-sex-ratio-figures/UPI-94121313495480/

United States Census Bureau. (2012). International data base. Retrieved March 13, 2012, from http://www.census.gov/population/international/data/idb/country.php

Wang, Feng. (2005). Can China afford to continue its one-child policy? *Asia Pacific Issues: Analysis from the East-West Center, No. 77*. Retrieved March 13, 2012, from http://scholarspace.manoa.hawaii.edu/bitstream/handle/10125/3796/api077.pdf?sequence=1

Xie, Zhenming. (2000). Population policy and the family-planning programme. In Xizhe Peng & Zhigang Guo (Eds.), *The changing population of China* (pp. 51–63). Oxford, UK: Blackwell.

Xinhuanet. (2010). Experts: Gender discrimination creates China's sex ratio imbalance. Retrieved March 13, 2012, from http://news.xinhuanet.com/english2010/indepth/2010-04/03/c_13236130.htm

Yale University. (2012). Environmental Performance Index. Retrieved April 3, 2012, from http://epi.yale.edu/epi2012/rankings

Yap, Mui Teng. (2003). Fertility and population policy: The Singapore experience. *Journal of Population and Social Security: Population Study*, Supplement to Volume 1, 643–658. Retrieved March 13, 2012, from http://www.ipss.go.jp/webj-ad/webjournal.files/population/2003_6/24.yap.pdf

Zhao, Zhongwei, & Guo, Fei. (Eds.). (2007). *Transition and challenge: China's population at the beginning of the 21st century*. Oxford, UK: Oxford University Press.

Zhu, Wei Xing. (2003). The one child family policy. *Archives of Disease in Childhood, 88*(6), 463–464.

Outsourcing and Offshoring

Outsourcing occurs when one firm contracts out part of its production process to another firm, rather than producing the entire value chain internally. Outsourcing does not necessarily have an international dimension, although the term is often used informally to describe the movement of jobs overseas. Offshoring describes the shifting of production across borders. Although the economics of both of these practices are well understood, many questions remain about their implications for environmental sustainability.

Outsourcing happens any time a firm acquires inputs from an outside source rather than producing them internally. When the Indian firm Wipro designs the satellite navigation system for automaker Fiat's Alfa Romeo cars, that process is called outsourcing. Although there does not have to be an international component—it would still be outsourcing if an Italian-based firm designed Fiat's navigation system—the media and others use the term *outsourcing* to describe firms that source internationally.

Economists describe the shifting of production across borders as *offshoring*. Offshoring occurs when a firm acquires inputs from abroad, regardless of whether or not it owns the supplier. If US-based computer company Dell opens a call center in India, for example, economists would refer to it as offshoring as long as Dell owns the center in India. When General Motors contracts some of its back-office services to the Indian company Wipro in Bangalore, that is both offshoring and outsourcing.

Another closely related concept is foreign direct investment (FDI). FDI occurs when a firm based in one country opens an affiliate or branch in another country. FDI is offshoring without outsourcing. FDI takes place, for example, in the above example in which Dell opens up its own call center in India.

Outsourcing and offshoring refer to sourcing of both goods and services. The focus in the twenty-first century has been on services because technological developments have led to rapid increases in the tradability of certain services. Companies can now geographically separate activities such as data entry, call center support, accounting, and other information technology (IT) and back-office services from the rest of the firm. According to World Bank data, from 1994 to 2009 the total volume of global trade in services more than tripled, from about $1 trillion to $3.4 trillion (World Bank 2011). Data on total global offshoring is more difficult to collect given the wide variety of activities that can be classified as offshoring. Measures of various individual types of offshoring have shown tremendous increases in recent years. US firms' imports from their affiliates in other countries increased by about 70 percent from 1999 to 2005.

Size and Growth

The management consulting firm A. T. Kearney (2010) produces an annual Global Services Location Index (GSLI), which ranks the most attractive offshoring destinations for activities such as IT services and support, contact centers, and back-office support. Each country's score is based on approximately forty measurements, which are grouped into three categories: financial attractiveness, people and skills availability, and business environment. From 2004, the first year that Kearney produced the index, through 2010, India ranked number one, China number two, and Malaysia number three. Countries outside of the top three have changed quite a bit over the life of the index; Southeast Asia and the

Middle East have gained at the expense of Eastern Europe and Latin America. The top three destinations have remained stable over time, however.

The A. T. Kearney index is based on characteristics of countries that are likely to make them desirable locations for offshoring. Data on actual flows of offshoring and outsourcing are difficult to collect, however, because data collection agencies generally do not observe whether an imported good or service is an input to a larger production process or whether it is a finished product sold directly to a private consumer. It thus is often not possible to separate offshoring from other types of imports. Because offshoring is one subset of total imports, an examination of aggregate data gives a general sense of the trend.

Despite the attention given to China, India, and other emerging markets as potential offshoring destinations, their shares in global trade are still relatively small. Only 3.75 percent of global exports of services and about 1.4 percent of global exports of goods originated in India in 2009. China was responsible for 9.6 percent of global goods exports, but less than 2.7 percent of global service exports. Although these numbers (with the exception of China's manufacturing exports) are small relative to the economic activity of more developed countries, in the context of the local economies they are very large, especially for India. In 2009, service exports accounted for 6.5 percent of India's gross domestic product (GDP), slightly above the world average of about 5.8 percent. China's service exports were only 2.6 percent of GDP (UNCTAD 2012).

What explains the difference in offshoring experiences between China and India, specifically in terms of their focus on goods versus services? Offshoring is a form of international trade and thus follows the same principles as any other type of trade. One of the most important of these principles is the concept of *comparative advantage*. Countries specialize in the production of goods and services based on what they are relatively good at producing compared to other countries. China has a comparative advantage relative to India in the production of manufactured goods, and India has a comparative advantage in services. Comparative advantage can stem from a number of different sources, but in this case the abundance of low-wage laborers contributes to China's comparative advantage in labor-intensive manufacturing sectors. A number of factors, such as the relatively higher population of college-educated English-speaking workers, contribute to India's advantage in services.

Will these offshoring trends continue? The current data show no signs of a slowdown in offshoring work in China and India. As greater exports lead to economic growth, however, wages will also increase in these countries, changing their relative positions as sources of low-skilled workers. According to the international business scholar John Dunning (1988), the flow of foreign direct investment into or out of a country is directly related to that country's level of economic development, as defined by GDP per capita. He identifies four stages of FDI development. In the first stage, the country receives little investment and makes no outward investments. In stage two, inward FDI begins to increase. The country starts to make some outward investments, but inward investment far outweighs outward investment. In stage three, inward FDI still outweighs outward investment, but the gap is narrowing. In stage four, the country is finally a net investor, rather than a recipient of investment. China and India are both somewhere between stages two and three of this development process. If their GDP growth continues as it has for the first decade of the twenty-first century, averaging about 7 percent annually for India and 10 percent annually for China, their offshoring strategies will likely change as well. As wages increase along with overall economic development, these countries will have to increase production efficiency to compensate for rising wages and place a greater emphasis in innovation. In addition to performing work that more-developed countries have offshored, both China and India are beginning to offshore more of their own production to other parts of Southeast Asia and Africa as they move up the value chain.

Impacts

Most of the research done on offshoring is from the perspective of the firms doing the offshoring. Much less work has been done on its effects on the countries that receive the investment. Most evidence that does exist suggests that the overall economic effects are positive in terms of employment, GDP growth, and poverty reduction (see Bottini, Ernst, and Luebker 2007 for a survey of this literature). Even if offshoring benefits China and India in aggregate economic terms, however, it does not affect everyone equally. There are likely to be both negative and positive impacts at a more disaggregate level. Regional differences in offshoring intensity within countries are well documented. According to India's National Association of Software and Services Companies, seven Indian cities account for 95 percent of export revenues (Panagariya 2008). China's economic growth has been concentrated in coastal regions. In 2005, the southeast, lower Yangzi (Chang) River, and northeast regions accounted for 36, 38, and 19 percent of exports, respectively. The rest of

China was responsible for only 7 percent of the country's total exports (Naughton 2007, 397). Differential impacts on economic versus environmental outcomes are another potential source of the unequal effects of offshoring.

Environmental and Sustainability Issues

One open question is whether or not international trade allows developed areas such as the United States and the European Union to enjoy cleaner environments at home by offshoring the production of goods whose manufacturing processes produce high levels of pollution abroad. Just as firms headquartered in countries with relatively high corporate tax rates can evade taxation by locating key production processes in tax havens, so-called pollution havens may allow them to get around strict environmental regulations in their home countries. Evidence on whether offshoring of polluting activities has actually occurred in the United States is mixed, however. Most studies find either no evidence of a correlation between US imports and pollution intensity of an industry, or their results suggest that US imports have become less pollution intensive over time (see Levinson 2010a for a survey of this literature). Most of these studies rely on measures of pollution intensity of industries in the United States. They thus say very little about how the goods are actually produced in developing countries such as China and India.

A related concept is *carbon leakage*. The Kyoto Protocol requires only some countries to reduce their carbon emissions. The export of high-emission products from countries without emissions caps to countries that are subject to these caps constitutes a "leakage." The exact extent of carbon emissions is difficult to measure for total trade volumes, and it is even more difficult to isolate the share due to offshoring. The Chinese government claims that demand on the part of industrialized countries for cheap, high-emission exports from China drives much of the country's emissions and has used this claim as an argument against adopting strict emission caps (Wang and Watson 2008). A number of studies have attempted to quantify the share of Chinese carbon emissions that exports embody. These estimates range from 7 to 14 percent (Shui and Harriss 2006) to 34 percent (International Energy Agency 2007). Other studies have found shares ranging from 15 to 32 percent (Ahmad and Wyckoff 2003; Peters and Hertwich 2008; Wang and Watson 2008). When these studies control for imports, estimates of the share of emissions due to net exports from these same sources range from –2 to 23 percent. The wide range of these estimates is due to a number of data and estimation challenges. First, there is a lack of reliable data on Chinese production technologies. Second, trade data are measured as gross flows rather than as value added, making it difficult to isolate exactly how much of the production of a single good was done in China. Third, there may be differences in emissions between domestic Chinese producers and multinational companies offshoring in China.

One possible response to the issue of carbon leakage is to move to a consumption-based measure of emissions, rather than one based on production. This move would shift some of the responsibility for high-emission goods produced in China to the countries that consume them. One drawback of this approach is the difficulty of measuring the carbon content of imports. In addition, if countries responsible for production do not directly bear the cost of emissions, they may have less of an incentive to invest in clean technologies. Any attempt to share the emissions responsibility between producers and consumers brings up complex questions about the appropriate division of responsibility. Even moving to a pure consumption-based system would complicate the process because a country attempting to reduce the emissions of its imports would have to engage in bilateral or multilateral negotiations, rather than acting under its own sovereign power. In spite of these issues, understanding the extent of carbon leakage is still useful for understanding and informing the debate on the sources of global emissions.

There is also evidence that service trade pollutes less than goods trade (Levinson 2010b). That finding does not imply that there are no sustainability issues associated with services offshoring. Many IT service activities, such as data centers, use a large amount of electricity. Offshoring also involves a high volume of international air travel by consultants and managers. Researchers have done very little work on this topic. One recent study does attempt to quantify the sustainability efforts made by global IT outsourcers (Babin and Nicholson 2011). They divide a group of nineteen global IT outsourcing firms into three categories based on their adoption of or intent to adopt global sustainability standards such as the Global Reporting Initiative, the Carbon Disclosure Project, the International Organization for Standardization's ISO 26000, and the United Nations Global Compact. The highest category of sustainability includes three of the largest Indian outsourcing firms: Tata Consultancy Services, Wipro, and Infosys. The study also finds that large IT outsourcing firms are much more likely than small firms to adopt global sustainability standards due to the high costs of adoption.

Although China's total energy demand has risen sharply over time, the country's energy efficiency has greatly improved. Chinese economic activity in 2007 required two-thirds less energy per unit of output relative to the start of economic reforms in 1978 (Bergsten et al. 2009, 139). The presence of foreign firms contributed greatly to this reduction, both because they represented a shift away from energy-intensive heavy industries toward labor-intensive light manufacturing and because foreign firms used more advanced energy-efficient technology, which also pollutes less. Most of the gains occurred prior to 2000, however. Since 2000, individual firms have continued to become more energy efficient, but the composition of the Chinese economy has started to shift back toward energy-intensive heavy industries such as steel, cement, glass, and aluminum. If China continues to subsidize and otherwise encourage investment in these industries, it would have continued negative effects on their energy situation. One dollar of economic output from light industries such as apparel, electronics, or services requires less than one-tenth of the energy required for one dollar's worth of steel or cement production (Bergsten et al. 2009, 158). In India, offshoring growth has been concentrated in services, which are much more energy efficient.

Another issue associated with global fragmentation of production is the carbon use required to ship goods across borders. Consider a laptop computer designed in Silicon Valley, assembled in Taiwan using parts produced in China and Malaysia, and sold to a customer in Europe. How is the purchaser of the computer to think about the carbon footprint of that laptop, especially when he or she may have no way of knowing where the various components were produced? In this sense, economists would expect offshoring manufactured goods to have a much larger impact than offshoring services. No studies have attempted to quantify this effect, however.

As China and India move from being recipients to being providers of direct investment, the question arises as to what sustainability issues surround their outward investment. While the United States, Japan, and other rich countries are outsourcing manufacturing, and to a lesser extent services, production to China, China is meanwhile sourcing many basic commodities from Africa. This moves energy-intensive commodity production out of China. These products are generally very heavy, however, and require a large amount of energy to transport.

Outlook

The relationship between offshoring and environmental sustainability is generally unclear. There has not been enough research on the topic to definitively identify either a positive or a negative relationship. The composition of offshoring matters with respect to sustainability of development, however. The offshoring of heavy industries such as steel and cement, for example, requires much more energy use than light industry and services. If foreign firms invest in industries with more advanced energy efficiency and less polluting technology, the effects will be positive.

Lindsay OLDENSKI
Georgetown University

See also Automobiles and Personal Transportation; Chennai, India; China; Consumerism; Corporate Accountability (China); Energy Industries (*several articles*); India; Information and Communication Technologies (ICT); Kuala Lumpur, Malaysia; Labor; Microfinance; Nanotechnology; Pearl River Delta; Rural Development; Rural Livelihoods; Southeast Asia; Steel Industry; Utilities Regulation and Energy Efficiency; Yangzi (Chang) River

Further Reading

Ahmad, Nadim, & Wyckoff, Andrew. (2003). *Carbon dioxide emissions embodied in international trade of goods* (DSTI/DOC[2003]15). Paris: Organisation for Economic Cooperation and Development (OECD).

A. T. Kearney. (2010). A. T. Kearney's Global Services Location Index. Retrieved August 15, 2011, from http://www.atkearney.com/index.php/Publications/at-kearneys-global-services-location-index-volume-xiii-number-2-2010.html

Babin, Ron, & Nicholson, Brian. (2011). How green is my outsourcer? Measuring sustainability in global IT outsourcing. *Strategic Outsourcing: An International Journal, 4*(1), 47–66.

Bergsten, C. Fred; Freeman, Charles; Lardy, Nicholas R.; & Mitchell, Derek J. (2009). *China's rise: Challenges and opportunities.* Washington, DC: Peterson Institute for International Economics.

Bottini, Novella; Ernst, Christoph; & Luebker, Malte. (2007). Offshoring and the labour market: What are the issues? (Economic and Labour Market Paper). Geneva: International Labour Office, Employment Analysis and Research Unit, & Economic and Labour Market Analysis Department.

Dunning, John H. (1988). *Explaining international production.* London: Unwin Hyman.

International Energy Agency (IEA). (2007). *World energy outlook 2007.* Paris: IEA.

Larcon, Jean-Paul. (Ed.). (2009). *Chinese multinationals.* Singapore: World Scientific Publishing.

Levinson, Arik. (2010a). Offshoring pollution: Is the U.S. increasingly importing polluting goods? *Review of Environmental Economics and Policy, 4*(1), 63–83.

Levinson, Arik. (2010b). Pollution and international trade in services. *International Environmental Agreements: Politics, Law and Economics, 10*(2), 93–105.

Moran, Theodore H. (2011). *Foreign direct investment and development: Launching a second generation of policy research.* Washington, DC: Peterson Institute for International Economics.

Naughton, Barry. (2007). *The Chinese economy: Transitions and growth.* Cambridge, MA: MIT Press.

Panagariya, Arvind. (2008). *India: The emerging giant.* Oxford, UK: Oxford University Press.

Peters, Glen P., & Hertwich, Edgar G. (2008). CO_2 embodied in international trade with implications for global climate policy. *Environmental Science and Technology, 42*(5), 1401–1407.

Shui, Bin, & Harriss, Robert C. (2006). The role of CO_2 embodiment in US-China trade. *Energy Policy, 34*(18), 4063–4068.

United Nations Conference on Trade and Development (UNCTAD). (2012). UNCTADstat. Retrieved March 6, 2012, from http://unctadstat.unctad.org

Wang, Tao, & Watson, Jim. (2008). China's carbon emissions and international trade: Implications for post-2012 policy. *Climate Policy, 8*(6), 577–587.

World Bank. (2011). World development indicators. Retrieved July 5, 2011, from http://data.worldbank.org/

Share the *Encyclopedia of Sustainability*: Teachers are welcome to make up to ten (10) copies of no more than two (2) articles for distribution in a single course or program. For further permissions, please visit www.copyright.com or contact: info@berkshirepublishing.com

P

Parks and Preserves

Parks and preserves are areas dedicated to the protection and maintenance of forests, wildlife, and cultural resources. Environmental conservation in the developing nations of South and Southeast Asia, including India and China, anchors on these parks and preserves. These nature reserves are also focal areas of human–nature conflicts because of limitations placed on human activities within and outside the preserves.

India and China, among other countries in South and Southeast Asia, are considered megabiodiversity countries. Both countries have established protected area networks in their attempts to preserve natural resources. Although their efforts began centuries ago, the number and size of protected areas in both countries have been on a rise since the 1970s. India plays a pivotal role in global tiger conservation effort as one of the thirteen tiger-range countries. Two of China's nature reserves—Qiangtang (298,000 square kilometers) and Sanjianqyuan (152,300 square kilometers)—are included in the United Nations' 2005 list of the world's ten largest protected areas. Both countries face park–people conflicts, however. The number of protected areas and levels of protection have increased, affecting the livelihoods of local people in many of these areas. The intensity of conflicts ranges from noncooperation to active hostilities in different locations.

History and Development

The epitome of the US conservation movement was the Yellowstone National Park, established by the US Congress in 1872. Conservation history in Asia dates back to as early as 500 BCE, however, although most of these efforts were private.

India

The history of protected areas in India has come a long way from the royal reserves of ancient times to today's national parks and community conserved areas. Indian kings and royal families established reserve forest areas at least as early as 500 BCE. Rulers and elites maintained most of these earliest reserves for hunting and trophy collecting. In addition, earlier emperors also maintained reserves to protect areas that harbored elephants, which were essential to warfare for the expanding empire. Emperor Ashoka of central India pioneered the protection of forests and wildlife. He issued the first known government decree for protected areas in 252 BCE. Shortly after this, King Devanampiyatissa of Sri Lanka set up some of the oldest wildlife sanctuaries. Religious beliefs and cultural practices from a range of religions including Hinduism, Buddhism, and Jainism as well as native animist practices have supported conservation and protection of forests and wildlife throughout Indian history.

During the British rule in India (1757–1947), the empire focused on forests primarily for hunting and commercial resource extraction. The British introduced forest categories such as reserved forest (RF) and protected forest (PF) during their rule. The postindependence government of India (post-1947) retained these categories. RFs presently enjoy a higher degree of protection than PFs because no hunting or grazing is allowed in the former except under specific orders. Many of these RFs later provided the basis for the modern protected area networks.

The government established Corbett National Park, India's first modern conservation-oriented national park, in 1936. Both the number and size of protected areas rapidly expanded during the 1960s and 1970s. Parks expanded not only in India, but also in other South Asian countries, including the Sundarbans South Wildlife Reserve in Bangladesh (1960), the Ras Koh Wildlife Sanctuary in Pakistan (1962), the Manas Wildlife Sanctuary in Bhutan (1966), and the Chitwan National Park in Nepal (1973). India's Wildlife (Protection) Act of 1972 laid the legal framework for establishing protected areas. Since then the Indian protected-area network has expanded significantly from 6 national parks and 59 wildlife sanctuaries in 1970 to 89 national parks and 489 wildlife sanctuaries in 2002. According to the World Database on Protected Areas, however, only about 153,825 square kilometers in India (5.03 percent of the total land area) were under protection in 2010, which means protected-area coverage in India falls far behind that of Bhutan (28 percent), Cambodia (26 percent), Sri Lanka (21 percent), Malaysia (18 percent), Nepal (17 percent), China (17 percent), Japan (16 percent), and Indonesia (14 percent) (WDPA 2011).

Most Indian parks are owned and managed by Indian state and central governments without any participation by local people. Some of these protected areas are designated as tiger reserves (thirty-five in 2009). Many of the parks and sanctuaries consist of only core forest (a supposedly undisturbed area, with no human settlements, farming, or tourism), with high human activities right outside the preserves. Multiple Indian parks and sanctuaries (such as Tadoba-Andhari Tiger Reserve) still host forest villages within the core forest, however. Many of these villages face challenges of relocation after the notification of the park. To minimize the human pressure on the core reserves, buffer zones now surround some of the protected areas. These buffer zones act as a transition area for both human and wildlife and play an important role in minimizing human–wildlife conflicts. The Indian government added two new protected area categories—community reserves and conservation reserves—in 2002, allowing local people greater participation. The Forest Rights Act (FRA) of 2006 originated in the idea that indigenous communities can protect, regenerate, conserve, and sustainably use forest resources. The legislature empowered these communities with the rights to protect trees, biodiversity, wildlife, and other natural resources. The FRA recognizes and assigns forest rights to traditional forest-dwelling communities and aims to integrate conservation with sustainable livelihoods.

China

Throughout the history of eastern Asia, religion has played an important role in the protection of the environment. Sacred forests and holy mountains were some of the first protected areas, such as those areas the Qín dynasty (221–206 BCE) protected. Although some countries in eastern Asia declared protected areas earlier than others, such as Mongolia (1778) and Japan (1934), China established Dinghushan in Guangdong Province, its first official nature reserve, in 1956. Four distinct phases mark protected area development in China: initiation, stagnation and devastation, restoration with the slow addition of new protected areas, and rapid growth in the late 1970s. Shortly after the State Forestry Department established the first reserve, the Great Leap Forward in 1958 drastically changed the political scenario in China. Further political chaos during the Cultural Revolution (1966–1976) led to extensive environmental degradation. This was accelerated by ill-conceived industrial and agricultural projects, suppression of traditional ethnic cultures and religious institutions, and damaged human–ecosystem relationships. The government showed a growing concern over environmental sustainability in the decades following the Cultural Revolution. As a result, protected area coverage in China has increased from 1,267,366 square kilometers in 1990 to 1,557,431 square kilometers in 2010, currently covering approximately 16.64 percent of the total land area (WDPA 2011).

Protected areas in China fall under three categories: natural ecosystems protection, wildlife protection, and natural relics protection. China considers national scenic landscapes and historic sites, along with national and local forest parks, protected areas. According to the Bylaw of Protected Areas of the People's Republic of China, central and local administrative agencies respectively supervise national and local preserves. Nature reserves (NRs), which are the most common type of protected area in China, can fall under any of the four administrative categories (national, provincial, prefecture, and district). Two agencies, however, primarily manage nature reserves in mainland China: the State Environmental Protection Administration (SEPA) and the State Forestry Administration (SFA). The reserves have three management zones: the core area with no human activity except limited scientific research, the buffer zone with limited activities including some collection, measurements, management, and scientific research, and the experimental zone with activities such as tourism, public education, scientific investigation, and endangered wildlife conservation and management.

Toward Sustainability: Challenges and Threats

Protected area management faces numerous challenges worldwide, many of which are sourced from conflicts between parks and people in human-dominated landscapes. To better understand the challenges and threats park managers experience, it is imperative to understand the legacy of forest management activities in a particular socioeconomic context and the complexity of the resulting human-nature dynamics.

India

Forest management practices in postindependence India continued to reflect the colonial legacy of commercial extraction, which is still practiced in most nonreserve forests. Postindependence priority changes introduced need-based forest management; commercial enterprises cleared and selectively cut vast areas of forest to supply timber for farm building construction, industry, and hydroelectric projects. These activities resulted in alarming forest loss, especially in regions with limited protection. Other factors, such as frequent relocation of forest villages outside the protected areas, national-level emphasis on agricultural expansion, and industrial activities including mining, and road network development, also contributed to postindependence forest degradation. The government implemented various remedial measures nationwide mostly during the 1970s and 1980s to restrict deforestation and degradation. These measures included a complete ban on tree felling within any national park, plantation programs in the surrounding areas, and the launch of Project Tiger in 1973–1974 to protect tigers and their habitats. India has banned resource collection, grazing, and hunting in the core reserves. Such exclusionary conservation measures have led to pockets of RFs (often upgraded to national parks and wildlife sanctuary) embedded within a PF matrix; rapidly changing land uses in the surroundings along with additional threats from tourism activities have isolated many reserves.

Given the proximity of human-dominated landscapes, park managers often find it difficult to maintain a balance between biodiversity conservation and the sustainable livelihood of local people. Forest-fringe communities have been resource dependent for centuries. Protected area notification often results in relocation of these communities outside the preserves, and restricts or bans resource extraction. The animosity the relocated communities feel toward park management often results in wildlife poaching, deliberate fires, and illegal tree felling. The World Bank–supported India Ecodevelopment Project (1996–2004) aimed to decrease communities' forest dependence through livelihood-support activities. Although this project was designed to increase opportunities for local participation in protected area management, critics have accused it of never being a participatory project.

Given these flaws in the project's implementation, many conservationists are skeptical about its impact on decreasing human pressure on the preserves. The FRA and its provisions for community forest management provide significant scope for local communities to become involved in forest management in protected areas. Proponents of the fence-and-fine conservation approach, however, believe it is not possible to secure both tribal rights and conservation. They believe the FRA poses threats to endangered species such as the tiger.

China

Unlike other countries in South and Southeast Asia, China has a formalized land tenure system, which started during collectivization and communization. This land tenure system has resulted in collective forests, the management regime of which is complex and has changed frequently in the past. During the postrevolution period in China (post-1949), many of the private, communal, and state-owned forests changed to elementary cooperative-managed forests to promote sustainable forestry. China witnessed large-scale deforestation as a consequence of further amalgamation of these cooperative lands into communes and associated corruption, however. Government-promoted iron- and steel-production programs also contributed to massive forest loss.

China has rapidly increased the number of protected areas since the late 1970s, in an effort to restrict the forest and biodiversity loss. Conflicts between parks and people have consequently increased, as conservation restrictions affect traditional forest management practices. In addition, growing tourism activities, lack of well-delineated park management strategies, and overlaps of management responsibilities of different institutions have worsened the scenario. More than ten different ministries manage nature reserves in mainland China, including the two primary agencies—SEPA and SFA. SEPA is the national authority for environmental management and biodiversity protection. SFA is the national agency for forest, wetland, and biodiversity conservation and manages over 70 percent of China's NRs (Simonov and Dahmer 2008). The management under SFA is further subdivided between the Forest Industry Bureau and the provincial forest bureaus that report to the provincial governments. Protected areas suffer from this confusing regime because these agencies have different planning and management strategies and communicate poorly with one another. Scholars have suggested that protected areas are more effective under traditional community management rather than constantly changing institutional regimes (Xu and Melick 2007). The command-and-control management system has rarely engaged local communities who might have centuries of traditional knowledge of sustainable forestry. Recent efforts to implement integrated conservation and development projects and community-based conservation have brought the communities direct and tangible economic benefits from the reserves.

China's growing pressure on park agencies to generate part of their revenue from tourism also affects the balance between threats from increased recreation and parks' effectiveness as clean air, water, and forest landscape providers. Many of the park agencies perceive invasive species' encroachment and loss of native plant diversity associated with increasing tourism pressure to be the single most significant pressure on natural resources. In addition, parks in proximity to neighboring cities and highways face imminent threats from air, water, and solid waste pollution and a heavy tourist flow. These challenges raise a dilemma for the park agencies, which must decide whether to accept an increase in internal environmental threats from tourism in order to raise funds to counter external political, economic, and environmental threats.

The Future

Protected areas have increased in area by 500 percent since the 1980s. Skepticism about the effectiveness of parks as management regimes reflects current controversies over strict protectionism versus community conservation. The strictly exclusionary fence-and-fine conservation approach has played a crucial role in conservation efforts and has succeeded in many places across the globe. Yet there are also several "paper parks" that remain only as administrative boundaries on a paper map. These parks are not economically and socially sustainable in the long term. Conservationists supporting community involvement in protected area management also consider strict protection to be the wrong approach for human-dominated landscapes because the chances of alienating local people are high.

In an early response to the challenge of protected area effectiveness and sustainability, the United Nations Educational, Scientific, and Cultural Organization (UNESCO) launched the Man and the Biosphere (MAB) Programme in the early 1970s. The program's key concept was to allow human use in a network of areas with varying degrees of environmental protection. Biosphere reserves ideally contain a core protected area surrounded by a series of buffer zones. These reserves can also be a cluster of core areas surrounded by transition and buffer zones embedded within a larger matrix of areas with lower levels of protection against human use. Several Asian countries including Cambodia, China, India, Indonesia, Malaysia, Mongolia, Pakistan, Sri Lanka, Thailand, and Vietnam have built on and modified the MAB concept in various ways. UNESCO's 2010 list of World Network of Biosphere Reserves includes seven and twenty-eight reserves from India and China, respectively. Achieving the three interconnected functions—conservation, development, and logistic support (as identified by the MAB program)—warrants regional strategies in South and Southeast Asian developing countries. The landscape surrounding parks and preserves in these countries supports increasing human populations. Land tenure systems also differ from one country to the other. It thus might not be feasible to propose a single solution applicable to all scenarios.

Biodiversity conservation and social sustainability both can claim to be the primary axes for evaluation of park effectiveness. It is, however, the responsibility of the park management to recommend and implement a strategy to balance these two components, depending on the unique environmental and socioeconomic setting of the preserve.

Pinki MONDAL
Columbia University

Harini NAGENDRA
Ashoka Trust for Research in Ecology and the Environment

See also Biodiversity Conservation Legislation (China); Biosafety Legislation (China); China; Ecotourism; Endangered Species; Five-Year Plans; Genetic Resources; India; Indigenous Peoples; Japan; Korean Peninsula; Property Rights (China); Southeast Asia; Reforestation and Afforestation (Southeast Asia); Traditional Knowledge (China); Traditional Knowledge (India)

Further Reading

Bose, Indranil. (2010). How did the Indian Forest Rights Act, 2006, emerge? Retrieved February 11, 2012, from http://www.ippg.org.uk/publications.html

Karanth, Krithi K., & DeFries, Ruth. (2010). Nature-based tourism in Indian protected areas: New challenges for park management. *Conservation Letters, 4*(2), 137–149.

Liu, Jianguo, et al. (2003). Protecting China's biodiversity. *Science, 300*(5623), 1240–1241.

Loucks, Colby J., et al. (2001). Giant pandas in a changing landscape. *Science, 294*(5546), 1465.

Shahabuddin, Ghazala. (2010). *Conservation at the crossroads*. Uttaranchal, India: Permanent Black.

Shahabuddin, Ghazala, & Rangarajan, Mahesh. (2007). *Making conservation work*. Uttaranchal, India: Permanent Black.

Simonov, Eugene A., & Dahmer, Thomas D. (Eds.). (2008). *Amur-Heilong River Basin reader*. Hong Kong: Ecosystems Ltd. Retrieved February 11, 2012, from http://amur-heilong.net/other/00_intro/AHRBR.pdf

United National Educational, Scientific and Cultural Organization (UNESCO). (2011). Ecological sciences for sustainable development: Man and the Biosphere Programme. Retrieved February 11, 2012, from http://www.unesco.org/new/en/natural-sciences/environment/ecological-sciences/man-and-biosphere-programme/

Wang, Chao-Hui, & Buckley, Ralf. (2010). Shengtai anquan: Managing tourism and environment in China's forest parks. *Ambio, 39*, 451–453.

World Database on Protected Areas (WDPA). (2011). National stats for 1990–2010 from the 2011 MDG analysis. Retrieved February 11, 2012, from http://www.wdpa.org/Statistics.aspx

Xu, Jianchu, & Melick, David R. (2007). Rethinking the effectiveness of public protected areas in southwestern China. *Conservation Biology, 21*(2), 318–328.

Berkshire's authors and editors welcome questions, comments, and corrections. Send your emails about the *Berkshire Encyclopedia of Sustainability* in general or this volume in particular to: sustainability.updates@berkshirepublishing.com

Pearl River Delta

China's highly developed Pearl River Delta region has been one of the most economically dynamic regions in the country, benefiting from a strategically and environmentally advantageous location. Industrial and population growth, however, have had harmful environmental impacts, which central and local governments are trying to mitigate.

The Pearl River Delta (PRD), in south China's Guangdong Province, has played a fundamental role in a key global trade route—the Maritime Silk Route—and attracted the attention of foreign traders since the sixteenth century. From the start of China's economic reform in 1978, the PRD has been at the forefront of an unprecedented economic growth story. The impact on the region's environment is now receiving increased political attention as well.

The Pearl River basin is located in southern China and covers an area of about 450,000 square kilometers, roughly the size of the state of California, in the United States. The annual flow of the Pearl River amounts to approximately 341 billion cubic meters, which represents the second largest river flow in China after the Yangzi (Chang) River. The Pearl River consists of a drainage system formed by the West River, the North River, and the East River, which converge into a common delta with eight outlets to the South China Sea. The river basin encompasses six provinces (Yunnan, Guizhou, Guangxi, Guangdong, Jiangxi, and Hunan) as well as the two special administrative regions (SARs) of Hong Kong and Macao located in the delta. The Pearl River Delta occupies around 4,170 square kilometers—roughly the size of the United States' smallest state, Rhode Island—and was home to 48 million people in 2008. For comparison, Rhode Island, the second most densely populated US state, has just over 1 million residents (US CIA 2012).

The PRD has been one of the most economically dynamic regions in mainland China since the launch of the country's economic reform program in 1979. At the outset of reform, the central government designated four special economic zones nationally, including Shenzhen and Zhuhai, as well as the neighboring cities of Hong Kong and Macao. Being adjacent to international trade centers, both cities have received enormous foreign investment, have experienced unprecedented growth, and have passed on their experience to other regional governments. A PRD economic zone, comprising the nine municipalities of Guangzhou, Shenzhen, Zhuhai, Foshan, Jiangmen, Dongguan, Zhongshan, Huizhou, and Zhaoqing, was established by the provincial government of Guangdong in 1985. From 1980 to 2005, the gross domestic product (GDP) in the PRD economic zone grew by 16 percent annually, well above the national average of 9.8 percent. According to the 2010–2011 UN-Habitat biannual report *State of World Cities*, the Hong Kong-Shenzhen-Dongguan-Guangzhou urban conglomerate is considered to be the world's largest "mega-region," with an estimated 120 million residents in 2011 (UN-Habitat 2011, 30). Such rapid development would hardly have been possible without the enormous amounts of water readily available in the river system; the PRD accounts for 0.48 percent of China's landmass, but 13 percent of the nation's water drains through it.

The PRD transformed itself from a predominantly agricultural area to a massive international manufacturing hub, where textiles, printing and dyeing, tannery, food and beverage, electroplating, and paper industries prevail. This change was largely due to the preferential fiscal policies enjoyed by foreign companies in the region. From January 2008, a regulation provided tax exemptions and other fiscal privileges to nonpolluting production activities, such as the high-tech, energy efficiency, and renewable energy sectors and other environment-friendly industries. Many of the original PRD manufacturing industries relocated upstream, to other parts of China, in search of cheaper labor and more preferential policies from local governments. Provincial incentives currently play a greater role than national ones.

In 2004, the Greater PRD (Guangdong's PRD economic zone plus Hong Kong and Macao) had an estimated GDP of $270 billion, equivalent to the sixteenth largest economy or the tenth biggest export base worldwide. In 2008, this region accounted for 9.9 percent of China's GDP and 25.6 percent of the nation's total trade (Yeh et al. 2006; Enright et al. 2010).

Infrastructure development in the Greater PRD has been equally breathtaking. The region has more than 27,000 kilometers of highways, six airports (with Guangzhou, Hong Kong, and Macao having international airports) and sixty-seven harbors. The construction of a 47-kilometer bridge linking Hong Kong and Shenzhen in the eastern side of the Delta to Zhuhai and Macao on the western side is due to be finalized by 2016. While construction work on the mainland's share of the project has been under way, work on the Hong Kong side was halted in April 2011 following a judicial review of the project's environmental impact assessment, which had been approved by Hong Kong's Environmental Protection Department. Concerns over air quality in residential areas near construction sites and an incomplete environmental impact assessment report prompted the Hong Kong Special Administrative Region's Court of First Instance to rule against the department's approval and in favor of the litigant, an elderly resident living near the future construction site. Work resumed in December 2011, and the original schedule has been kept. The transportation link, however, is seen as fundamental to consolidate the economic expansion of the PRD and reaffirm its role in southwestern China. A Pan–Pearl River Delta economic cooperation agreement was initiated in June 2004.

Environmental Change: Drivers, Pressures, and Impacts

Rapid urbanization, massive industrialization, intense population growth, deforestation, construction of dams, sand dredging, agriculture, and shipping together provide a challenging mix of drivers liable to cause serious environmental impacts on the ecological system of the Delta.

Exponential population growth presents serious challenges to drinking water supply and wastewater treatment. Water availability per person in the province of Guangdong is on average 1,927 cubic meters, well below the world average of 8,210 cubic meters (Sadhwani et al. 2009). Water shortages have been aggravated by pollution. In 2009, the provincial water resources department reported that 24.7 percent of monitored river sections were unfit for any human use. Petroleum, ammonia, and nitrates were the main pollutants. In 2007, provincial authorities reported that untreated wastewater was the main source of pollution in the province, with 7.5 billion metric tons of wastewater generated by the PRD.

Land-use restructuring caused a 20 percent decrease in arable land during the 1980s, while overall demand for agricultural production kept rising (Leung 2007). Traditionally, the mulberry dyke–fishpond system was an important part of land use in the delta. This system combined fish with silk production and enabled nutrient recycling among aquaculture, sericulture, fruit tree, and flower and vegetable plantations. The use of organic waste in agriculture has declined, however, in favor of modern agricultural practices. Application of chemical fertilizers increased by almost 500 percent in the period from 1950 to 1995, according to official data for Guangdong Province, while the amount of chlorinated pesticides in the Pearl River was found to be the highest in Chinese rivers, with about 863 metric tons per year (Fu et al. 2003, 2).

The high input of pollutants has had serious impacts on the environment, including eutrophication, algal blooms, oxygen depletion, and loss of resources. The western waters of Hong Kong have often suffered the occurrence of red tides, which in 1998 resulted in a massive fish kill and economic losses of some $80 million. Bioaccumulation of persistent organic pollutants has a serious impact on the food chain and thus on human health.

The impacts of these pressures on biodiversity and the ecosystem balance have been severe. Among a total of 296 freshwater fish species identified in the Pearl River, the Pearl River Water Resources Commission has estimated that the survival of 92 species was threatened, including the Reeves shad and the Chinese sturgeon, which live in the South China Sea and return to the rivers to reproduce (Leung 2007). The near total collapse of these fish populations has been attributed to overfishing, interruption of migratory routes by dams, and destruction of habitats by river channelization. In some rivers, fish are caught using explosives or electrical shocks, causing devastation to the entire ecosystem. A dwindling population of Chinese white dolphins in the estuary is increasingly threatened directly by the high level of pollutants present in the water (chemicals and heavy metals) and indirectly by the high sediment load, which has an impact on the smaller fish and bottom-feeding organisms on which they feed.

Specific concerns surround the impact of the new Hong Kong-Zhuhai-Macao Bridge not only on the delta and estuary ecological system but also on public health, related to expected air quality deterioration in residential areas near the bridge and its access roads. The project is also expected to generate pollution related to dredging and reclamation works, which affect the riverbed and stir up contaminated sediments. In addition, the hydrodynamic regime of the estuary may be changed, effecting sensitive habitats nearby such as mangrove and brackish marsh areas.

The impacts on human well-being are also quite significant. Access to safe drinking water is not fully guaranteed in the region. Pollution affects drinking water sources in both urban and rural areas. In Guangdong Province, Chinese authorities reported in 2007 that about 40 percent of the province's rivers were too polluted to be used as sources of drinking water. Consequently, about 14 percent of the population, equivalent to some 16 million residents, faced water shortages on account of pollution in that year (Yeung 2007). Drought episodes have further compounded the region's difficulties.

The western side of the delta, mostly in Zhuhai and Macao, has faced drinking water shortages since the start of the twenty-first century due to periods of high salinity in the dry season (October to April) as a consequence of seawater intrusion. In 2004, a 25 percent reduction in the low flow of the river resulted in the sodium content in the western part of the delta increasing to 800 milligrams per liter, well above the 250-milligram level permissible for drinking water (Macao Water Company 2004 and 2005). Water use forecasts expect a 50 percent increase in demand from 2002 to 2020, well above the river's supply capacity even if a new program of infrastructure development is carried out.

According to research conducted at Sun Yat-sen University in Guangzhou, seawater intrusion derives from a combination of factors, including climate change, higher water level variability, reduced river flows, and drought and sea level rise, as well as human factors such as the construction of numerous dams, lack of intergovernmental coordination in respect to their operation, and unregulated sand dredging. Sand dredging has, in fact, affected sediments in the delta river networks in such a way that the channel bed has been lowered between 3 and 14 meters in some sections. This seriously alters flow velocity and facilitates seawater intrusion (Zhang and Deng 2010).

Responding to Environmental Change

In order to improve ecosystem status and human health, the Guangdong government is determined to reduce sulfur dioxide (SO_2) emissions by 21 percent and chemical oxygen demand (COD) by 24 percent by 2020, relative to 2006 levels. In order to attain these objectives, the government has earmarked $20.6 billion for investment in six sectors: ecological protection, wastewater treatment, desulfurization of electricity plants, solid waste disposal and treatment, radioactive waste disposal, and emergency systems. The Guangdong authorities aimed to increase their investment in environmental protection from about 2.5 percent of GDP in 2002 to 3 percent by 2010 (Sadhwani et al. 2009). According to the Chinese Investment Advisory Network, Guangdong's investment in environmental protection during the period of the eleventh Five-Year Plan (2006–2010) was the highest among the Chinese provinces, representing just above 2.5 percent of its GDP.

Efforts to respond to environmental change in the PRD at the scale of the entire ecological system are benefiting from increased investment and enhanced political engagement from the central government, provincial authorities, municipal authorities, and special administrative regions. A plan for the reform and development of the PRD for the period 2008–2020, released by the central government's National Development and Reform Commission (NDRC), provides longer-term objectives guiding investments set out in the eleventh (2006–2010), twelfth (2011–2015), and thirteenth (2016–2020) Five-Year Plans. The new national plan aims to promote the PRD as an international center for modern service industries, while promoting synergies among the various jurisdictions in the PRD in a number of areas, including environmental protection and pollution prevention. The plan envisages that by 2012, domestic wastewater treatment will reach 80 percent, and by 2020, 90 percent, while the industrial wastewaters discharge compliance rate will reach 90 percent in 2012 and 100 percent in 2020 (Sadhwani et al. 2009). Serious obstacles remain, however, in the treatment of wastewater and disposal of sludge at county level, and in the treatment of industrial discharges of small companies.

Faced with the difficulties of maintaining drinking water supply, the Pearl River Water Resources Commission devised a program to operate upstream reservoirs in the dry season so as to flush saltwater tides out of the delta. This involves releasing water upstream so that it reaches the delta at low tide and raises the freshwater levels, a procedure that is viewed only as a short-term solution. The construction of China's second-largest dam in Datengxia, Guangxi Province, is advocated in order to enable satisfactory minimum flow regulation with the use of a single infrastructure. In order to address a sharp decline in the fish population, provincial authorities agreed in 2007 to joint enforcement of a fishing moratorium every April and May, and fish-stock recovery programs for the Chinese sturgeon and other commercially important species have been set up in the West River.

André F. Reynolds Castel-Branco da SILVEIRA
University of Cambridge

See also Agriculture (China and Southeast Asia); Beijing, China; Cities—Overview; Education, Environmental (China); Endangered Species; Fisheries (China); Five-Year Plans; Guangzhou, China; Huang (Yellow) River; Mekong-Lancang River; National Pollution Survey (China); Shanghai, China; Steel Industry; Water Security; Yangzi (Chang) River

FURTHER READING

Bosselmann, Peter C., et al. (2010). The future of a Chinese village: Alternative design practices aimed to provide new life for traditional water villages in the Pearl River Delta. *Journal of Urban Design, 15*(2), 243–267.

Enright, Michael J.; Scott, Edith E.; Petty, Richard; Enright, Scott; & associates. (2010). *The Greater Pearl River Delta*. Hong Kong: InvestHongKong.

Fu, Jiamo, et al. (2003). Persistent organic pollutants in environment of the Pearl River Delta, China: An overview. *Chemosphere, 52*(9), 1411–1422.

Leung Sze-lun, Alan. (2007). *Epson Pearl River Delta scoping study*. Hong Kong: World Wide Fund for Nature.

Ma Jun. (2004). *China's water crisis*. Norwalk, CT: International River Networks.

Macao Water Company. (2004). Annual report, 2004. Retrieved April 6, 2012, from http://www.macaowater.com/index.php?option=com_content&view=article&id=116&Itemid=234&lang=en

Macao Water Company. (2005). Annual report, 2005. Retrieved April 6, 2012, from http://www.macaowater.com/index.php?option=com_content&view=article&id=116&Itemid=234&lang=en

Sadhwani, Dinesh; Chau, Jonas; Loh, Christine; Kilburn, Mike; & Lawson, Andrew. (2009). *Liquid assets: Water security and management in the Pearl River Basin and Hong Kong*. Hong Kong: CivicExchange.

United Nations Human Settlement Programme (UN-Habitat). (2011). *State of the world's cities 2010/2011: Bridging the urban divide*. London: Earthscan. Retrieved April 10, 2012, from http://www.unhabitat.org/pmss/listItemDetails.aspx?publicationID=2917

United States Central Intelligence Agency (US CIA). (2012). World fact book. Retrieved March 28, 2012, from https://www.cia.gov/library/publications/the-world-factbook/index.html

Yeh, Anthony Gar-on; Sit, Fung-shuen; Chen, Guanghang; & Zhou, Yunyuan. (2006). *Developing a competitive Pearl River Delta in South China under One Country Two Systems*. Hong Kong: Hong Kong University Press.

Yeung, Jonathan. (2007, July 19). Guangdong gives rural population water pledge. Retrieved April 6, 2012, from http://www.chinadaily.com.cn/cndy/2007-07/19/content_5439018.htm

Zhang, Xinfeng, & Deng, Jiaquan. (2010). *Affecting factor of salinity intrusion in the Pearl River Estuary and sustainable utilization of water resources in the Pearl River Delta*. In Kensuke Fukushi, Mahbub Hassan, Ryo Honda and Akimasa Sumi (Eds.), Sustainability in food and water: An Asian perspective. Dordrecht, The Netherlands: Springer Science + Business Media B.V.

Property Rights (China)

After the founding of the People's Republic of China in 1949, land was nationalized and regarded as a means of production, following the doctrine of Marxism. Economic reforms launched in 1978 have restored land as assets and created urban land leaseholds. Property rights over rural land, however, are more ambiguous, since the land is owned collectively by agricultural communities.

Property rights are primarily a bundle of rights associated with ownership that consist of the right to use an asset, the right to derive income from it, the right to change its form and substance, and the right to transfer these rights to another party at a price mutually agreed upon (Pejovich 1990). They are defined by prevailing legal opinions (Bazelon 1963) and are concerned with economic efficiency and distributive justice, which places limits on the actions of individuals and governments (Becker 1977). On an individual level, property rights affect peoples' freedom and well-being (Denman 1978). Sustainability is fundamentally built upon efficiency and equity in the utilization of scarce resources. The regimes of property rights structure the relationships between users and resources, which will affect, directly or indirectly, how resources should be utilized efficiently and equitably.

Land is a specific kind of property with several characteristics. Parcels of land are very different from each other, and each is suitable for only certain uses; the costs of buying and selling property are high; and land cannot be moved (unlike so many other products). Institutions are crucial to the understanding of the property rights over land in any country, and property rights in China evolved in the context of its specific history and culture. From the perspective of political economics in China today, there are two distinct types of ownership over land: common and private.

The Era of Central Control

Before the 1949 revolution, private landownership was the norm. In the countryside, most agricultural land was owned by landlords who either hired peasants to work it or leased it to tenant farmers. In 1950, well-to-do farmers and landlords accounted for only 9.4 percent of the rural population, but their land holdings represented 51.9 percent of the total land stock. Poor farmers and peasants made up 52.4 percent of the total, but the land they owned accounted for only 14.3 percent of the land stock (Du 1996). Soon after 1949, land was confiscated from owners and redistributed to landless peasants. After the socialist agrarian land reforms, the share of land held by well-off farmers was reduced to 8.6 percent, and the poor farmers' share increased to 47.1 percent (Du 1996).

In 1953, the cooperative movement completely abolished the private ownership of farmland and replaced it with collective ownership. The subsequent people's commune movement in the countryside and ownership transformation in the city virtually eliminated private ownership of land. According to China's 1982 constitution, urban land is owned by the state, and rural land is collectively owned by rural communities. A survey of land resources in 1996 found that 53 percent of China's territory was owned by the state and 46 percent by the collective. The ownership of the remaining 1 percent was unclear (Ho and Lin 2003).

Under the planned economy, property rights over natural resources and the means of production were nationalized soon after the Chinese Communist Party came into power in 1949, although the nationalization of urban land was not officially finalized until the promulgation of the constitution. Urban land has been entrusted to and is controlled by the state, which is accountable to the public. The ownership is officially termed *shehui zhuyi quanmin suoyouzi* (socialist people's ownership). As the representative of "all the people," the state, in theory, has full ownership, enabling it to handle resources and assets in the interests of the public. Following Marxist doctrine and the socialist principle of public land ownership, land was excluded from economic transactions in China in the era of central control.

The central planning system allocated land plots to users (agents of the state) through administrative channels. There was no charge to users to occupy the land, and users had no rights to transfer land. Urban land was virtually a free good. Once land had been allocated to state-owned enterprises and "the people," however, it was very difficult in practice for the state to repossess the land, because the state-owned enterprises were basic units of the socialist state economy and the people were the "masters" of the socialist society. Tenants' entitlement to land-use rights was a unique socialist institution incorporated into the formation of cities. As a result, the structures of socialist cities are dramatically different from their capitalist counterparts (French and Hamilton 1979).

Following Clause 4, Article 10 of the 1982 constitution, land was excluded from market transactions: "No organizations or individuals may appropriate, buy, sell, or lease land, or unlawfully transfer it in any way." Land users were unable to exchange land use rights for other benefits if they moved. As there were no incentives to relinquish occupied land because there was no compensation, users held firmly onto their land plots. In spite of the official prohibition on buying and selling land, an active informal market in exchanging state-owned housing did develop. There seemed to be an explicit value for housing use rights. For example, a unit in a desirable location could be traded for a larger one in a less desirable location. This informal trading mechanism was very firmly rooted in residents' minds. Even before urban housing was formally privatized much later, residents openly traded their public housing (with use rights only) in the market. Buyers' willingness to pay clearly showed their confidence in the security of housing with use rights attached, while the government's tacit approval of transactions verified this faith.

Economic Reforms

In 1988, after a ten-year trial period in the Shenzhen Special Economic Zone, an amendment to the constitution formally replaced the free allocation of land with commoditization (making it an asset) and marketization: "the right of land use can be transferred in accordance with the law." In cities, public land leasing allows developers or other users to lease land for a fixed period after a payment of a lump sum to the state. Land leaseholds can be acquired through tender, auction, or negotiation. This new institution of land leasing complements the emerging market economy. After thirty years of free allocation as a socialist means of production, urban land again became an economic asset.

Land leasing and the resulting ability to transfer land and buildings have generated a new organization—the market-driven property development industry—and have provided a powerful land development incentive to local governments. When building construction was tightly controlled by centralized government, there was a shortage of urban buildings. Since restrictions were eased, property developers have benefited from a robust demand for new buildings. Urban areas, especially coastal cities, are experiencing building booms.

The Pressure of Urbanization

In the countryside, China's rural property is managed by a three-tiered governance system composed of the commune, the brigade, and the production team. The system is the cornerstone for rural collective land ownership. The household production responsibility system, introduced by economic reforms in 1978, gives the use rights of agricultural land to individual farm households for an initial period of thirty years (Putterman 1993). This system replaced the collective farming system; farm households replaced the People's Commune as the production units making decisions about what to grow and what to sell at market prices after fulfilling the required planned output quotas. Collective land ownership remains vested in the three entities, whose names have been changed: communes, brigades, and teams are known as townships (*xiang/zhen*), administrative villages (*xingzhengcun*), and natural villages (*zirancun*) respectively (Ho 2001).

In practice, how much land each of these levels is entitled to is ambiguous (Zhu and Hu 2009). One saying describes owners of the collective assets: *sanji suoyou, dui wei jichu* (collective ownership belonging to three entities, with the team being the primary holder). A nationwide investigation of 271 villages in the late 1990s revealed the perception of the collective ownership among the stakeholders (i.e., those people who have a stake in an enterprise). Forty-five percent of respondents believed that natural villages should be the primary owners; 40 percent reckoned that administrative villages should be the owners; and 15 percent thought that natural villages and administrative villages should own the land jointly (Cai 2003). Regardless of who holds the land, the holder does not have the right to develop it by changing from agricultural to nonagricultural use unless the urban governments grant the right to the collective.

Urbanization and urban expansion are creating a strong demand for the conversion of agricultural land to nonagricultural and urban uses. According to the constitution, only the state has the right to expropriate collectively owned rural land and allocate it to urban users. Villagers who lose such land are to be properly compensated and offered resettlement. The Land Administration Law (1986) centralized the management of rural land in the hands of the state. The collective has neither the right to derive income from land by letting it out, nor the right to change its form and substance by developing it for nonagricultural activities without approval from the government at the county level or above. The members of the rural collectives are explicitly entitled to (1) the use right over farm land allocated to them under the household production responsibility system, and the right to the residual farming income; (2) the use right over a small plot of land to build housing for the household; and (3) the right to benefit from land held under the three-tier hierarchy of management of the rural communities.

The state has been the dominant actor in the conversion of rural land to urban land in the progressive economic reform. Local governments have become the decision makers, placing highest priorities on economic development, productivity, and national competitiveness (Zhu 2005). Advancing development strategies to stimulate local growth and to raise revenue are two essential goals of local governments (Wong 1987). At the same time, however, the rural collective also seeks local development and revenues of its own. The rural collective and the local governments are thus in competition for revenue and control. Incomplete and ambiguously delineated collective land rights result in disordered competition for land rents. In the transition zone between urbanized areas and agricultural regions, mixed land uses incorporate both agricultural and nonagricultural activities (Zhu and Hu 2009).

Outlook

The changes in property rights over land in China since 1949 have been drastic. The revolution led by the Communist Party abolished private land ownership, nationalizing urban land and collectivizing rural land. Economic reforms since 1978 have developed a private urban land leasehold system based upon public land ownership, intended to rationalize usage of land as economic assets. Collective land ownership in rural areas is still in the process of transformation. Land used for agricultural production has been leased to farming households, but property rights over collective land used for nonagricultural activities remain unclear and ambiguous, resulting in unproductive utilization of land.

Jieming ZHU
National University of Singapore;
Tongji University

See also Agriculture (China and Southeast Asia); China; Education, Environmental (China); Five-Year Plans; Labor; Rule of Law; Rural Development; Rural Livelihoods; Three Gorges Dam

FURTHER READING

Bazelon, David T. (1963). *The paper economy*. New York: Random House.

Becker, Lawrence C. (1977). *Property rights: Philosophic foundations*. London: Routledge & Kegan Paul.

Cai, Yongshun. (2003). Collective ownership or cadres' ownership? The non-agricultural use of farmland in China. *The China Quarterly, 175,* 662–680.

Denman, Donald R. (1978). *The place of property: A new recognition of the function and form of property rights in land*. Berkhamsted, UK: Geographical Publications.

Du, R. S. (Ed.). (1996). *Zhōng guó de tǔ dì gǎi gé* [Land reforms in China]. Beijing: Contemporary China Press.

Fischel, William A. (1985). *The economics of zoning laws: A property rights approach to American land use controls*. Baltimore, MD: Johns Hopkins University Press.

French, Richard Anthony, & Hamilton, F. E. Ian. (Eds.). (1979). *The socialist city: Spatial structure and urban policy*. Chichester, UK: John Wiley & Sons.

Ho, Peter. (2001). Who owns China's Land? Property rights and deliberate institutional ambiguity. *The China Quarterly, 166,* 394–421.

Ho, Samuel P. S., & Lin, George C. S. (2003). Emerging land markets in rural and urban China: Policies and practices. *The China Quarterly, 175,* 681–707.

Pejovich, Svetozar. (1990). *The economics of property rights: Towards a theory of comparative systems*. Dordrecht, The Netherlands: Kluwer Academic Publishers.

Putterman, Louis G. (1993). *Continuity and change in China's rural development: Collective and reform eras in perspective*. New York: Oxford University Press.

Wong, Christine P. W. (1987). Between plan and market: The role of the local sector in post-Mao China. *Journal of Comparative Economics, 11,* 385–398.

Zhu, Jieming. (2005). A transitional institution for the emerging land market in urban China. *Urban Studies, 42,* 1369–1390.

Zhu, Jieming, & Hu, Tingting. (2009). Disordered land rent competition in China's peri-urbanization: Case study of Beiqijia township, Beijing. *Environment & Planning A, 41,* 1639–1646.

Public Health

Human health is a fundamental component of sustainable development and intrinsically linked to the environment. Population growth, urbanization, and rapid economic and industrial development throughout India and China are damaging the natural environment and negatively affecting population health. A multisector approach must ensure that development does not come at the expense of the environment, consequences that will be passed on to the health of future generations.

We have known since the time of Hippocrates that health and environment are intrinsically linked: the air we breathe, the food we eat, the toxins, pollutants, and viruses we are exposed to all affect our health and well-being. Indeed, the World Health Organization (WHO) estimates that one-quarter of all preventable diseases are caused by environmental factors.

WHO defines health not just as the presence or absence of disease or illness. Health is a state of complete mental, physical, and social well-being and relates to an individual's ability to respond or adapt to life's challenges and changes. Seeing health as a resource or capacity, rather than just a physical state, allows policy makers to consider more fully the broader societal and environmental influences on the capacity of humans to maintain positive health. This disease ecology approach to health recognizes that public health—the means to ensure that humans achieve positive health—operates at the intersection of biological (biomedical model) and social and environmental determinants (socio-ecological model) of health. Public health is dominated by approaches emphasizing a biomedical definition of health that focuses primarily on the medical control of disease and illness. It is now increasingly clear, however, that improving the capacity of individuals to achieve positive health requires a population health perspective, whereby the health of the entire population is improved through a holistic and integrated approach, tackling broader social, biological, and environmental causes.

Environment can be defined broadly. It is the socio-economic, cultural, physical, and natural elements of the world around us. This environment includes many features—physical and environmental conditions (such as landscape, climate, natural hazards, pollution), socioeconomic factors (such as access to services, education, employment opportunities), and infrastructure (such as the built environment). The environment influences our health in many ways, through direct exposure to risk factors, such as chemicals or viruses, through influences on our behavior and our responses to risk factors, and through our access to goods, services, and resources. For individuals to achieve their full potential and maintain positive health they require adequate housing, safe drinking water, sanitation, clean air, a nutritious diet, and equitable access to health care, education, and employment. These factors are themselves intrinsically intertwined with the natural and physical environment.

Health and Sustainability

Sustainable development enables individuals to lead a positive life while safeguarding the human experience for future generations. Health and well-being is the central tenet of a positive human experience. Sustainability is therefore fundamentally about ensuring equitable positive health for all, now and in the future.

Given the clear role the environment plays in human health, policy makers cannot disconnect issues in sustainable development from human health concerns. It is crucial that all development policies and practices consider their wider health impacts. The prospects for population health in China and India are, like elsewhere, intimately linked with their prospects for sustainable development and the conditions in their built and natural environments.

Health in China and India

Since 1960 China's population has doubled while India's has tripled. During this period these vast countries made significant progress in improving their populations' health. By 1965 China's death rate was 9.5 per 1,000, although India's was considerably higher at 45 per 1,000 (Dummer and Cook 2008). In 2011 India had reduced its death rate to a more favorable 7.5 per 1,000, just slightly higher than the equivalent rate of 6.9 in China (US CIA 2010). Infant mortality also halved in India during this time period, although the current rate of 49.5 deaths per 1,000 births remains unacceptably high and considerably higher than China's rate of 16.5, which is fast approaching the levels seen in developed Western areas such as the United States (6.1) and the United Kingdom (4.7) (US CIA 2010). China's life expectancy is currently approaching Western levels at 73 years; by contrast, in India life expectancy is 66 years.

Despite major health improvements throughout both countries, the processes of development and urbanization have had many negative impacts, including increasing poverty and widespread environmental degradation, with secondary adverse effects on health. For many of the poorest in each country, infectious and parasitic diseases, linked to poor water quality, lack of sanitation, inadequate housing, and environmental conditions, dominate the health landscape. For many areas of both countries, however, the major population health improvements since the 1960s may be significantly eroded if the forces of development and globalization continue unchecked and without full recourse to their social, environmental, and health costs.

Changing Environmental Impacts on Disease

The classical epidemiological transition model (Omran 1971) states that in undeveloped countries mortality commonly results from famine and infectious diseases—the diseases of poverty. As societies develop, public and environmental health improvements and medical developments cause infectious diseases to decline. Mortality and morbidity caused by lifestyle factors and chronic illnesses increase, linked to increasing life expectancy—the diseases of affluence. China, and to a lesser extent India, has moved through this epidemiological transition into what can be defined as a late-stage epidemiological transition phase characterized by health changes associated with the current era of rapid development and globalization (Cook and Dummer 2004). Improvements in health in this new phase occur as a result of medical developments and socioeconomic changes. Health problems associated with diseases of poverty (infectious diseases) coupled with environmental health concerns result from uneven development, however.

The rapid population growth and associated social and economic transition since the 1960s in India and China has resulted in a complex picture of emerging (including HIV/AIDS, severe acute respiratory syndrome, avian influenza) and reemerging infectious disease (such as tuberculosis, schistosomiasis). The infectious diseases of poverty, which public health improvements were expected to curtail, have combined with emerging chronic diseases (diabetes, cardiovascular disease, cancer) that are associated with increased longevity and lifestyle changes.

Whoever wishes to investigate medicine properly, should proceed thus: in the first place to consider the seasons of the year, and what effects each of them produces for they are not at all alike, but differ much from themselves in regard to their changes. Then the winds, the hot and the cold, especially such as are common to all countries, and then such as are peculiar to each locality. We must also consider the qualities of the waters, for as they differ from one another in taste and weight, so also do they differ much in their qualities.

Hippocrates,
On Airs, Waters, and Places, 400 BCE

The Persistence of Infectious Diseases

It is estimated that around 60 million rural Chinese still suffer from endemic parasitic diseases that have an environmental basis, including malaria, Japanese encephalitis, and schistosomiasis, with the last reappearing after decades of attempts to eradicate the snails that cause this serious disease. Tuberculosis (TB) is also a major health concern in China and has reappeared following a significant decline, becoming the tenth major killer in rural areas in 2003; current estimates suggest 2 million TB cases (Dummer and Cook 2008). TB is a disease of poverty and a disease associated with bad environmental living conditions. Waterborne and food-related infectious diseases, including bacterial diarrhea, hepatitis A, and typhoid are also common throughout China. Newly emerging infectious diseases in China include HIV/AIDS, severe acute respiratory syndrome (SARS), and avian influenza A. The latter two are significantly related to environmental conditions, especially in rural and farming areas, whereas the former is an outcome of a complex interplay between cultural, lifestyle, and risk-exposure changes linked to globalization, development, and urbanization.

India also has serious problems with mosquito-vectored diseases, such as malaria and dengue fever, which are closely related to environmental conditions. Indeed, dengue fever continues to cause significant health impacts across metropolitan areas such as Delhi and rural states such as Haryana and Maharashtra despite major attempts to control the disease. The common waterborne and food-related diseases prevalent in China are also rampant in India, particularly in the burgeoning urban slums and impoverished and environmentally damaged rural areas. Across much of India, from the vast rural areas to the overcrowded urban slums, infectious and parasitic diseases still dominate the health landscape, where basic environmental improvements in sanitation, drinking water, and living conditions have bypassed many. Similar to China, TB is also a major health concern in India.

Environmental Pollution as a Growing Risk

The rapid industrialization and urbanization occurring in India and China relies on the increasing use of fossil fuels to power the expanding megacities, the proliferation of automobiles, and the rapidly burgeoning manufacturing industries. Burning fossil fuels produces sulfur dioxide, particulates, ozone, and nitrogen dioxide. These environmental pollutants contribute to not only global warming, with clear long-term implications for health and sustainability, but also directly affect respiratory and cardiovascular health. Air pollution has also been implicated in certain cancers. Of the nine most polluted cities in the world, seven are in India and China. The rapid increase in the use of fossil fuels throughout the major cities in India and China means that respiratory and cardiovascular diseases are leading causes of death in urban areas.

Burning coal and charcoal in homes for heating and cooking, common throughout India and China and especially in rural areas, produces indoor air pollutants that are extremely hazardous to health. In rural China respiratory disease is the leading cause of death, and in rural India it is the second leading cause of death. These diseases are linked firmly to indoor air pollution. WHO estimates that indoor and outdoor air pollution causes a staggering 656,000 deaths annually in China and 527,700 deaths annually in India (Holden Platt 2007).

Pollution of drinking water from natural and human sources is a significant environmental health problem throughout the region. Arsenic is a naturally occurring toxin that causes bladder, kidney, skin, and lung cancers. It contaminates well-water sources obtained from arsenic-containing bedrock and is a major issue in specific areas of China and India, especially rural areas where untreated well water is commonplace. Pollution from human activity, including chemical contamination from industrial facilities, nitrates, and other hazards from farming practices and discharge of untreated sewage into water sources, is also common, creating serious environmental health issues.

Global Change and Natural Disasters

Historically environmental events in the region, such as floods, famines, earthquakes, and typhoons (in China) and cyclones (in India), have hugely affected health. In the twentieth century the largest single loss of life in China was during the 1930s. A range of natural disasters including a series of floods killed somewhere between 2 and 4 million people. In India the Bengal famine of 1943 killed up to 2 million across the Bengal delta. Recently, the 2008 Sichuan earthquake killed 85,712 in China, and the Asian tsunami of 2008 resulted in nearly 300,000 deaths throughout the Asia Pacific region, including 16,389 in India. Overall between 1971 and 2000, natural disasters claimed around 120,000 lives in India and 310,000 lives in China (UNEP 2002).

Human-induced global climate change is having, and will continue to have, wide-ranging environmental impacts with concomitant impacts on human health. Natural disasters and extreme events, including heat waves, floods, and cyclones, have major effects on population health in India and China. Such events will undoubtedly increase over the next millennia. Infectious diseases—such as malaria and dengue fever—are related to climatic and environmental conditions and will continue to surge with the advent of climate change; for example, increasing air temperatures allow the parasites that cause these two diseases to migrate to new areas. Other infectious diseases, such as cholera, are commonly associated with major floods that damage water and sanitation and cause massive population displacement and contamination of drinking water in overcrowded and inadequate refugee camps. Famines will continue to affect the region and will likely be more frequent, with clear implications for diet, nutrition, and population health. As always, the poor will suffer the most.

Some health effects will be indirect. For example, climate change and related adverse events will likely affect the poor disproportionately, reducing the livelihoods of many of the most economically vulnerable. Many of the worst affected will be rural dwellers, who will be forced to migrate to cities to search for jobs. In the megacities of India and China, these people will live in overcrowded and unsanitary conditions and may be forced, through economic hardship, into hazardous industries, such as the sex industry with its related health risks such as HIV/AIDS. This cycle will continue as the poor attempt to cope with the economic, social, and environmental pressures associated with global environmental change.

The Urban Environment and Health

India and China are both rapidly urbanizing countries. Currently, 43 percent of China's population and 29 percent of India's population live in cities. These rates are expected to soar to 64 percent and 38 percent for China and India respectively by 2025 (Dobbs and Sankhe 2010). It is estimated that China and India will experience 40 percent of the global urban population growth between 2005 and 2025. This huge urban growth will exert significant pressures on the sustainability of the natural and built environment, and ultimately on human health.

The urban environment impacts upon health through three major pathways: social changes that alter health-related behaviors; physical environment risk factors, including pollution and poor sanitation; and disruption of natural ecosystems through the physical growth of cities (McMichael, Smith, and Corvalán 2000). Migration to urban centers is often associated with changing social and cultural behavioral norms and sexual activity, and economic hardship often forces migrants into the sex industry, with clear implications for the rise of infectious diseases such as HIV/AIDS. Indeed, the rise of HIV/AIDS in India and China has already been associated with population migratory patterns and rapid unplanned urbanization. Urban centers provide easy access to high-fat and high-calorie junk foods and are often associated with a decrease in physical activity, both factors fueling the global obesity epidemic. As the populations in the urban centers in China and India adopt lifestyles and habits from the West, obesity is increasing, with clear implications for a range of health issues, including cardiovascular disease, diabetes, and cancer.

Cities have always been associated with environmental risks related to housing quality, availability of clean drinking water, and sanitation. In the megacities of China and India the provision of these essential services is usually socially polarized. It is the urban poor who often live in overcrowded and substandard housing lacking sanitation and clean drinking water. Such environments inevitably impact negatively on human health. Furthermore, very poor air quality and environmental pollution in many of the cities in the region make these urban environments hazardous to human health.

As the megacities of India and China continue to expand, the negative impact on the natural environment of this sheer physical growth and population movement will continue to increase. Urban centers infringe on farming areas and natural spaces, destroying ecosystems as they advance farther into the countryside while draining rural areas of their populations. These processes lead inevitably to further environmental degradation of natural habitats, increasing poverty and negative health.

Population Growth, Environmental Degradation, and Human Health

The environment is fundamental to human health and well-being. The immense population growth in India and China, coupled with rapid economic development, exerts extreme pressure on the natural environment and depletes resources for future generations. Water shortages and species loss, as well as the effects of climate change and human-induced and natural disasters, are closely aligned with this population growth and development. All of these problems have serious implications for the sustainability of human health in China and India, and mirror many of the problems faced in both the developed and developing world. The health gains experienced by both countries since the 1960s are acutely vulnerable to the environmental effects of their recent rapid social and economic development and population growth.

The Future: Health and Global Environmental Change

China and India are the two most populated countries in the world and are at the forefront of globalization in the twenty-first century. China is set to become the world's largest economy, and India will soon be ranked third. Both countries' global profiles will only increase as the century unfolds. This growth and development, however, is coming at a severe cost to long-term environmental sustainability and, by definition, population health and well-being. Widening inequalities in health in both countries are developing hand in hand with widening social and economic inequalities and environmental degradation. Globalization and development are not simply promoting wealth and opportunity for China and India; they are failing to eradicate the diseases of poverty, contributing to the emergence of diseases of affluence, and fueling the unchecked growth that is seriously impacting the environment.

Human activity is damaging the natural environment. Population growth, urbanization, and rapid economic and industrial development throughout India and China are negatively affecting population health and reducing the opportunity for future generations to achieve positive health. Given the size of these huge nations the health and environmental impacts of this development will be experienced far beyond the borders of each country: in every sense the prospects for sustainability and health worldwide are intrinsically linked to India and China.

Health and environmental sustainability are intertwined and require a multisector approach, encompassing partnerships across a range of policy sectors, including environment, development, energy, transport, housing, education, and health. It is only through partnerships and the pursuit of a holistic approach to development, incorporating health and environment considerations throughout, that the goals of sustainable development will be attained. It is imperative that both China and India seek to encapsulate health within all development policies. There must be an acknowledgment that health is a fundamental aspect of sustainable development, coupled with a commitment to ensure that social and economic development does not come at the expense of the environment, consequences that will be passed on to future generations. Only through such commitment will the long-term prospects for sustainable health and development in the two largest nations on Earth be assured.

Trevor J. B. DUMMER
Dalhousie University

See also China; Cities—Overview; Climate Change Migration (India); Climate Change Mitigation Initiatives (China); Consumerism; Education, Environmental (*several articles*); India; National Pollution Survey (China); One-Child Policy; Rural Development; Rural Livelihoods; Traditional Chinese Medicine (TCM); Water Security; Water Use and Rights (India)

FURTHER READING

Castree, Noel; Demeritt, David; Liverman, Diana; & Rhoads, Bruce. (Eds.). (2009). *A companion to environmental geography*. Chichester, UK: Wiley-Blackwell.

Cook, Ian G., & Dummer, Trevor J. B. (2004). Changing health in China: Re-evaluating the epidemiological transition model. *Health Policy, 67*(3), 329–343.

Corvalán, Carlos F.; Kjellström, Tord; & Smith, Kirk R. (1999). Health, environment and sustainable development: Identifying links and indicators to promote action. *Epidemiology, 10*(5), 656–660.

Day, Kristen A. (Ed.). (2005). *China's environment and the challenge of sustainable development*. New York: M. E. Sharpe, Inc.

Dobbs, Richard, & Sankhe, Shirish. (2010, July). Comparing urbanization in China and India. *McKinsey Quarterly*. Retrieved March 3, 2012, from http://www.asia.udp.cl/Informes/2010/china_india.pdf

Dummer, Trevor J. B., & Cook, Ian G. (2008). Health in China and India: A cross-country comparison in a context of rapid globalisation. *Social Science & Medicine, 67*(4), 590–605.

Feachem, Richard G. A. (2001). Globalisation is good for your health, mostly. *British Medical Journal, 323*(7311), 504–506.

Holden Platt, Kevin. (2007, July 9). Chinese air pollution deadliest in world, report says. *National Geographic News*. Retrieved March 3, 2012, from http://news.nationalgeographic.com/news/2007/07/070709-china-pollution.html

Landon, Megan. (2006). *Environment, health and sustainable development*. Maidenhead, UK: Open University Press, McGraw-Hill Educational.

Licari, Lucianne; Nemer, Leda; & Tamburlini, Giorgio. (2005). *Children's health and environment: Developing action plans*. Copenhagen, Denmark: WHO Regional Office for Europe.

McMichael, Anthony J.; Smith, Kirk R.; & Corvalán, Carlos F. (2000). The sustainability transition: A new challenge. *Bulletin of the World Health Organization, 78*(9), 1067–1067.

Meade, Melinda S., & Emch, Michael. (2010). *Medical geography* (3rd ed.). New York: Guilford Press.

Misra, Kamal K. (2001). *Peoples and environment in India*. New Delhi: Discovery Publishing House.

Omran, Abdel R. (1971). The epidemiologic transition: A theory of the epidemiology of population change. *The Milbank Memorial Fund Quarterly, 49*(4), 509–538.

Shaw, Mary; Dorling, Daniel; & Mitchell, Richard. (2002). *Health, place and society*. London: Prentice Hall.

United Nations Environment Programme (UNEP), GRID-Arendal. (2002). Global environment outlook 3 (GEO 3). Retrieved November 25, 2010, from http://www.grida.no/publications/other/geo3/?src=/geo/geo3/english/458.htm

United States Central Intelligence Agency (US CIA). (2010). The world factbook. Retrieved November 29, 2010, from https://www.cia.gov/library/publications/the-world-factbook/

World Health Organization (WHO). (2000). Obesity: Preventing and managing the global epidemic. Report of a WHO consultation. *World Health Organization Technical Report Series, 894*, i–xii, 1–253.

World Health Organization (WHO). (2009a). Gender, climate change and health. Retrieved November 25, 2010, from http://www.who.int/globalchange/publications/reports/gender_climate_change/en/index.html

World Health Organization (WHO). (2009b). Protecting health from climate change. Retrieved November 25, 2010, from http://www.who.int/globalchange/publications/reports/9789241598880/en/index.html

Public-Private Partnerships

There is a growing worldwide trend of public entities joining with private groups to develop projects that make significant improvements to environmental infrastructure, address climate change, or otherwise contribute sustainable solutions. These public-private partnerships and their accomplishments are highly visible in East Asian countries, proving effective in such areas as power generation, clean water supplies, reforestation, and ecosystem rehabilitation.

The Asian Development Bank (ADB) defines a public-private partnership (PPP) as a contractual arrangement between public (national, state/provincial, or local) and private entities through which the skills, assets, and/or financial resources of each are allocated in a complementary manner, thereby distributing the risks and rewards and providing optimal service delivery and good value to citizens.

The revolutionary approach of PPPs in sustainable development and as an economic framework is a global trend that offers opportunities for industrial upgrading and state-society ties in the East Asian region. The demand for roads, bridges, railroads, water and sanitation facilities, climate change mitigation projects, and energy generation grow as individual economies prosper. The Association of Southeast Asian Nations (ASEAN) is working toward a tariff-free market among their member countries by 2015, and this prospect fuels further demand for transportation and environmental infrastructure projects across borders (ASEAN 2009). ASEAN connectivity would increase the efficiency of such networks for both production and consumption since most of the countries in the region have experienced a rapid economic expansion since the 1980s (McNamara 2011). Several countries across the ASEAN, including the Philippines, Laos, Thailand, Malaysia, and Indonesia, are promoting PPPs. Projects include the installation of sewage systems, telecommunications systems, highways, and airports, among others.

The Philippines has been the pioneer in private sector participation and has the most developed PPP framework in the region. In the 1970s, reforestation projects were implemented with a public-private approach called the People's Forest Project, which dealt with the management, protection, and conservation of the country's forest. The Philippines' PPP programs formally started in 1990 with the approval of the Build-Operate-Transfer (BOT) Law (NEDA 1994). In response to a power crisis at that time, PPP arrangements made possible the building and operation of thirty-eight power plants, which ended the power problems by 1995. The privatization of the Manila Water and Sewerage System (MWSS) is one of the largest PPPs of public water utilities in the developing world. Other successful PPP projects in the Philippines include the North Luzon Expressway (NLEX), the Civil Registry System Information Technology Project (CRS-ITP), and the Mandaluyong City Marketplace.

In 1993 the governments of Laos and Thailand entered into a memorandum of understanding for the development of a 3,300-megawatt hydroelectric power plant in Laos. Under a twenty-five-year purchase agreement, the Lao government supplies power, which is purchased by the government of Thailand. The Asian Development Bank extended loans to the government of Laos after it issued a sovereign guarantee to the project funding.

Since 1983 the government of Malaysia has implemented five hundred PPP projects, with an estimated capital value of 161 billion Malaysian ringgit, equivalent to almost US$52.5 billion. These projects include the construction and installation of a light rail transit system, the installation of the telecommunications company

Telecom Malaysia Berhad, and the development and construction of the Kuala Lumpur International Airport.

Indonesia's first PPP arrangements came in the 1990s, when it awarded two concession contracts for water supply in Jakarta. While there were water treatment facilities already established under the PPP program, the immediate focus of Indonesia is still getting supplies of freshwater to its people. The government has yet to seriously address issues of sanitation; of seventy-nine PPP projects proposed in 2011, only one involves the construction of a wastewater treatment plant (Global Water Intelligence 2011).

Features of PPPs

The process of developing effective PPPs involves many stakeholders (i.e., those people who have a stake in an enterprise), government agencies, and financing institutions. Political commitment and a strong leadership are required to implement PPP projects.

A successful PPP project must be feasible and bankable, with demonstration of the need for the project, estimation of broad-level project costs, and indication of commercial viability. The assessment of affordability is the cornerstone for all PPP projects, for both the government and the general public. As financiers will be reluctant to commit funding when a project entails high participation costs, unreasonable risk transfer, or lengthy and complex contract negotiations, projects will remain attractive to the private sector through cost recovery pricing policy.

PPP projects are evaluated for economic and social benefits rather than a focus on financial considerations. The underlying principle of the PPP approach is that the public authority remains responsible for services provided to the public, without necessarily being responsible for corresponding investment. Through PPPs, the public authority is relieved of investment-related obligations and is able to concentrate on service quality control, while the private operator focuses on finances and seeks to optimize its capital outlay (Agra and Perez-Alabanza 2010).

Toward Sustainable Development

Public-private collaboration has made significant contributions to climate change mitigation. The approach is considered a means of climate technology transfer and of investment that can benefit both local concerns and international climate change policy. Waste-to-energy (WTE) technology is one example of partnerships between investors and citizens. Investors may be large or small transnational corporations, which may or may not specialize in waste treatment or renewable energies, or domestic companies. Investment in WTE offers partnerships of various forms between companies and communities, with or without the facilitation of state or bilateral aid agencies (Forsyth 2005).

In 2000 a Thai-owned company, AT Biopower, built six 16-megawatt WTE power plants fueled by rice husks in the central plains of Thailand. The investor used a variety of techniques to ensure that the supply of rice husks would be secured and sustainable: the investor contracted with twenty to thirty rice millers per power plant and used only 10 to 15 percent of their total rice husk production; millers contracted to produce a guaranteed quantity of husks and to be fined if they fail to deliver but rewarded with a yearly bonus if they achieve their target. All of these mechanisms are intended to ensure that partnerships between companies succeed, and they have ensured the successful embedding of new energy technologies (Forsyth 2005).

The Cebu City (Philippines) Landfill Gas and Waste-to-Energy Project is registered with the United Nations Framework Convention on Climate Change as a Clean Development Mechanism (UNFCCC-CDM). It was begun in 2005 by Greenergy Solutions. Under a twenty-five-year PPP agreement, the project will process the 2 million tons of residual waste at the 17-hectare Inayawan Landfill and the daily generated municipal solid waste of the city. Employing waste conversion technologies known as anaerobic digestion and refuse-derived fuel (RDF), the project will generate 20 megawatts per hour of renewable energy that will be sold to the national grid under a renewable energy purchase agreement. Additional income of the WTE facility will come from the sale of carbon credits and the tipping fees being paid for every ton of waste delivered. A special purpose corporation composed of the developers, technology providers, and equity investors was created for the development and operation of the Cebu project.

In eastern Indonesia, the development agency Winrock has established new forms of decentralized electrification using wind turbines imported from the United States, with local nongovernmental organizations and community-based organizations administering the projects by creating new institutions for financial and technical management (Forsyth 1999).

The sewerage collection and treatment system in the town of Sabang, Puerto Galera, in Oriental Mindoro, Philippines, is a wastewater treatment project of the local government of Puerto Galera, along with the Partnerships in Environmental Management for the Seas of East Asia (PEMSEA) and the Development Bank of the Philippines (DBP). The DBP extended a loan facility of 100 million Philippine pesos, equivalent to about US $2.3 million, payable in fifteen years. The project provides lessons for national agencies and donors who are providing technical assistance to local governments for the development and implementation of environmental infrastructure improvements. The experience has shown that environmental programs must involve more than just constructing new facilities; there must also be efforts to build institutional capacity, ensure ongoing funding for operation and maintenance and engagement of political leaders and stakeholders in the various stages of development and implementation of the project (PEMSEA 2009).

PEMSEA is involved in projects of environmental rehabilitation of coastal areas of Thailand. A project to rehabilitate the declining crab population through a "crab condominium" has been implemented in the municipalities of Sriracha, Laem Chabang, and Bangphra. The crab condominium is an artificial shelter for spawning crabs until they release their eggs. The project, which has increased the crab catch along the coasts by at least two-fold, relies on the active participation of fisherfolk and community members. These stakeholders bring spawning crabs caught in the wild to the concerned caretakers for protection and nurturing in the crab condos, which now contain around two thousand crabs.

In the Thai municipalities of Chonburi, Angsila, and Saensuk, a series of community mangrove reforestation activities has resulted in thriving mangrove areas that serve as habitats to marine life, coastline protection, and learning areas for local students. In Sattahip municipality, demonstration areas for community-based waste management activities involving recycling and organic composting, which aim to reduce the burden on local landfill sites, have been set up in three communities with the participation of individual households (PEMSEA 2009). This project and the others in East Asian countries described herein represent only a small number of the many endeavors worldwide that are using public-private collaboration to address needed change for sustainable development.

Ruth P. BRIONES
Greenergy Solutions Inc., Quezon City, The Philippines

See also Association of Southeast Asian Nations (ASEAN); Corporate Accountability (China); Energy Industries (*several articles*); Energy Security (East Asia); Five-Year Plans; Green Collar Jobs; Information and Communication Technologies (ICT); Microfinance; Outsourcing and Offshoring; Public Health; Public Transportation; Reforestation and Afforestation (Southeast Asia); Rural Development; Rural Livelihoods; Utilities Regulation and Energy Efficiency

FURTHER READING

Agra, Alberto, & Perez-Alabanza, L. F. Cynthia D. (2010). Institutionalizing the Swiss challenge method of bidding. Retrieved April 9, 2012, from http://www.forensicsolutions.info/page5.html

Asian Development Bank (ADB). (2008). Public-private partnership (PPP) handbook. Retrieved April 2, 2012, from http://www.adb.org/documents/public-private-partnership-ppp-handbook

Association of Southeast Asian Nations (ASEAN). (2009). Roadmap for an ASEAN community 2009–2015. Retrieved April 3, 2012, from http://www.aseansec.org/publications/RoadmapASEANCommunity.pdf

Forsyth, Tim. (1999). International investment and climate change: Energy technologies for developing countries. London: Earthscan.

Forsyth, Tim. (2005). Enhancing climate technology transfer through greater public-private cooperation: Lessons from Thailand and the Philippines. *Natural Resources Forum, 29*(2), 165–176.

Global Water Intelligence. (2011, August). Indonesia's innovation in infrastructure. Retrieved April 3, 2012, from http://www.globalwaterintel.com/archive/12/8/market-profile/indonesias-innovation-infrastructure.html

McNamara, Dennis. (2011). Directions for sustainable development: Public-private partnerships for infrastructure investment. Washington, DC: Georgetown University.

National Economic and Development Authority, Republic of the Philippines (NEDA). (1994). Republic Act No. 6957, Philippine Law on Build-Operate-Transfer. Retrieved April 2, 2012, from http://www.neda.gov.ph/references/RAs/RAs%207718%20or%20the%20BOT%20Law.pdf

Partnerships in Environmental Management for the Seas of East Asia (PEMSEA). (2009, November). Public-private partnership in sustainable development: The case of Puerto Galera. Retrieved April 2, 2012, from http://beta.pemsea.org/publications/public-private-partnership-sustainable-development-case-puerto-galera

Public Transportation

Rapid population growth and economic development in Asian countries have escalated the demand for urban transport. Policy makers in most Asian cities are working to implement improved public transportation systems, which will contribute to sustainable development by reducing pollution, fuel consumption, and vehicle congestion, and providing affordable services to the population.

The term *public transportation* is defined as a form of transport available to any person who pays a prescribed fare. Public transport, also known as *mass transport*, is designed to carry large numbers of people every day along designated routes and is usually local in nature. Public transportation can be broadly divided into rail and road-based transport. It includes buses, bus rapid transit systems, metro rail, light rail, trams, and suburban trains. Systems may be owned and operated by either public or private agencies. Public transport, properly administrated, can be the cheapest, safest, and most sustainable mode of transportation.

In Asia, the vast majority of people use public transport as their main mode of transportation, and in some areas, walking or biking is the predominant mode. The role of intracity public transport has become all the more important in any country, given that the world urbanization level crossed 50 percent in the year 2009, meaning that more than 50 percent of the world's total population now lives in urban areas. A 2010 study by the United Nations predicts that the number of megacities (with 10 million or more people) will be increasing, especially in Asia, with the worldwide count rising from eleven to sixteen by the year 2025 (UN 2010). This article provides an overview of public transport in Asia with specific reference to rail and road-based transport.

Evolution in Asian Countries

Most Asian cities have had similar kinds of public transportation. Beginning in the mid-nineteenth century, rail-based systems came to be used to move goods and passengers from one city to another, and tramways and buses were used for intracity commuting. This was especially the case in countries where British influences were felt, such as India, Pakistan, Sri Lanka, and Bangladesh.

India

The first passenger train in India operated between Bombay (now Mumbai) and Thane for a distance of about 35 kilometers and carried four hundred passengers in 1853. The first passenger train that operated in southern India, which went from Royapuram/Veyasarapady (Madras) to Wallajah Road (Arcot) for a distance of about 100 kilometers, was initiated by the Madras Railway Company in 1856. By 1870, India had close to 6,400 kilometers of tracks.

About forty railway companies operated in India by the time of independence from British rule in 1947; all of them were merged shortly thereafter to become Indian Railways, a public sector undertaking entirely owned by the government of India. Indian railways have the second largest network in Asia with more than 63,000 route kilometers of track. Indian railways employ one of the world's largest workforces, 1.54 million workers, to run the lifeline of Indian transport. In terms of cost of transport, the Indian railway still remains the cheapest mode of transport within India. It is one of the largest railway systems under government control in the world (Ministry of Railways 2011). In India, the rail system is mostly used for intercity travel except in megacities like Mumbai, Chennai (Madras), Delhi, and Kolkata (Calcutta), where it is also used for travel within cities. Mumbai Suburban Railway is one of the largest systems in the world, carrying nearly 6.9 million passengers daily.

Public road transport in India began in the nineteenth century. As the share of road transport increased, so also did the competition among operators of privately owned systems. After independence, the government was forced to nationalize the road transport services through enactment of the Road Transport Corporation Act of 1950. Participation of state governments in road transport commenced at that time, and since then road transport undertakings have been formed in all of the twenty-eight states of India. At present, there are about fifty-eight State Road Transport Corporations (SRTCs) in the country rendering the most essential transport service to the traveling public, particularly the poor in both rural and urban areas. These corporations operate far and wide with a fleet of over 115,000 buses employing more than 800,000 people (ASRTU 2012).

People's Republic of China

Rail-based systems are the major mode of public transport in the People's Republic of China. Railroads are the principal means of travel for long distances, and subways are used within cities for frequent travel and faster transport. Some cities also provide buses and trolley buses for intracity travel. The first railway line in China was constructed between Shanghai and Woosung in 1876; three more lines were built from Beijing to other major cities from 1897 to 1912. By 1940 China had about 27,000 kilometers of railway lines; however, most of the tracks were destroyed in the civil war (1945–1949). After the formation of the People's Republic of China, service was first resumed in 1952 between Beijing and Lanzhou. In 2010 China's railway network covered approximately 92,000 kilometers (Ministry of Railways 2011).

The first subway line was introduced in China in 1969, running between Beijing railway station and the army barracks at Fushouling for a distance of about 21 kilometers with sixteen stations. A second line was established in 1984 from Fuxingmen to Jianguomen for a distance of 16 kilometers, and few more stations were added to the network later. Tianjin initiated the construction of its subway system in 1970 and was soon followed by Beijing. In the early 1980s, cities such as Shanghai and Guangzhou (Canton) developed subway systems to meet the demand of the local commuters, and as of 2012 other cities, including Chongqing, Shenzhen, Chengdu, and Nanjing, are in various stages of developing subway systems.

Other Asian Countries

Similar to India and China, Thailand also had railway lines for long-distance travel in the nineteenth century. The first line was started in 1893 between Bangkok and Samut Prakarn. A second line was started from Bangkok to Ayutthaya by the end of the nineteenth century. Tramways were introduced in 1891 for transport within cities. Road-based public transport was introduced in Bangkok in 1902.

In Pakistan (part of British India until independence in 1949) the first railway line was introduced between Karachi and Kotri in 1861. Later, a railway line from Pakistan was extended to the Afghanistan border and to Iran, in 1878 and 1918, respectively. Pakistan had about 13,000 kilometers of rail network in 1944. For intracity travel in Pakistan, the first tramway was introduced in Karachi in 1885 (Imran 2009). Rail-based transport was not introduced to Karachi until the early 1940s. Both tramways and suburban rail systems were discontinued, however, due to poor service and patronage, and buses have become the predominant mode of transport for intracity travel in Pakistan.

In Sri Lanka, buses are the major form of public transportation. The first bus service was introduced in 1907 between Colombo and Chilaw by the Ceylon Motor Transit Company. Ruthless competition and rivalry among private operators forced the government to nationalize the bus transport in 1958. As in India and Pakistan, rail infrastructures were constructed during the British period mostly for moving goods. The first railway line was constructed between Colombo and Ambepussa in 1864/1865, with a length of about 55 kilometers (Sri Lanka Railways 2011). After independence (1948), railways were constructed from Colombo to other major cities, such as Kandy, Badulla, and Matara.

Current Trends in Asia

Asian cities are compact and dense, with mixed land-use development. This enables extensive use of public transport and nonmotorized transport (walking and biking) for daily commuting, compared to more expansive cities in North America and Europe. Public transport provides mobility to a large percentage of people in many cities, especially the poor who often do not have other alternatives. Different forms of public transportation are operated across different cities in Asia, including buses (defined as motorized vehicles designed to carry passengers and driver), trolley buses (electric buses that draw power from overhead electric lines via trolley), bus rapid transit (combines the quality of rail and the flexibility of bus transport; see the sidebar on page 302), mass rapid transit (operates on a grade-separated right of way and has lower frequency of stops compared to subways), subways (fully segregated urban rail systems, mostly underground), suburban trains (fully segregated urban rail systems, mostly above ground), and trams (urban rail-based systems operating along streets in mixed traffic). (See table 1 below). Public transportation systems are changing rapidly. Cities such as Shanghai, Kolkata, and Chennai have more than one form of transit. Small and medium-size cities, however, such as Patna and Varanasi in India, do not have any public transport; intermediate public transport, or paratransit, such as three-wheelers, jeeps, cycle-rickshaws, and jitneys serve as the less formal means of meeting the travel demand in such cities.

TABLE 1. Forms of Public Transportation in Asian Cities

City	Bus[1]	Trolley Bus[2]	Bus Rapid Transit[3]	Mass Rapid Transit[4]	Subway[5]	Suburban Train[6]	Tram[7]
Mumbai, India	✓					✓	
Delhi, India	✓			✓			
Bangalore, India	✓						
Chennai, India	✓			✓		✓	
Kolkata, India	✓			✓			✓
Ahmedabad, India	✓		✓				
Hyderabad, India	✓						
Shanghai, China	✓	✓			✓		
Beijing, China	✓		✓		✓		
Guangzhou, China	✓	✓	✓		✓		
Chongqing, China	✓	✓	✓		✓		
Xi'an, China	✓	✓					
Wuhan, China	✓	✓			✓		
Jinan, China	✓	✓	✓				
Zhengzhou, China	✓	✓	✓				
Dhaka, Bangladesh	✓						
Colombo, Sri Lanka	✓					✓	
Karachi, Pakistan	✓						
Lahore, Pakistan	✓						
Manila, Philippines	✓			✓	✓	✓	

Source: author.
1. A motorized vehicle designed to carry passengers including driver.
2. An electric bus that draws power from an overhead electric line via trolley.
3. A rapid transit system that combines the quality of a railway and the flexibility of a bus.
4. A grade-separated right-of-way system with less frequency of stops compared to subways.
5. A fully segregated urban rail mostly underground.
6. A fully segregated urban rail mostly on the surface.
7. An urban rail-based system operating along streets in mixed traffic.

Private ownership of vehicles has increased substantially in most Asian cities in the early twenty-first century, though the share of travel that is by public transport is still relatively high compared to Western countries. In cities such as Hong Kong, Colombo, Bangkok, Mumbai, and Delhi, more than 40 percent of commuters take public transportation, which clearly indicates the importance of public transport. Although the share of public transportation use is low in most Chinese cities, it is rapidly increasing. In China, biking and walking are still the predominant modes of transport. (See figure 1 below.)

Provision of public transportation is lagging far behind demand in most cities in spite of its importance. Travel demand increases exponentially with the expansion of cities and consequent increase in trip lengths. Improvements in public transport often are offset by the increase in travel demand. A further complication is the inability of the people to pay for the cost of the service; the general perception is that public transportation is a service that government must provide for the sake of the urban poor. In most Asian cities public transport is subsidized; there is no private backing, as operation is not profitable. Public transportation is not given due importance in most cities in Asia even though the declared policies of governments are to promote it. There also is a lack of coordination among different agencies at national and local levels. Due to these factors, many people are shifting toward private modes of transportation, such as personal cars and motorized two-wheelers.

Urban sprawls have made cities car dependent. This, coupled with the buying power of the upper middle classes and the social status the car ownership has conferred, increased car sales in most Asian cities during the early twenty-first century. This has worsened the traffic congestion and consequent pollution. In China, for example, per capita income has doubled, and car use has tripled. Increase in per capita income has also increased the number of trips. Bus commuters shifting to private vehicles are the accepted trend in Asia, and this has accentuated the traffic congestion and decreased the

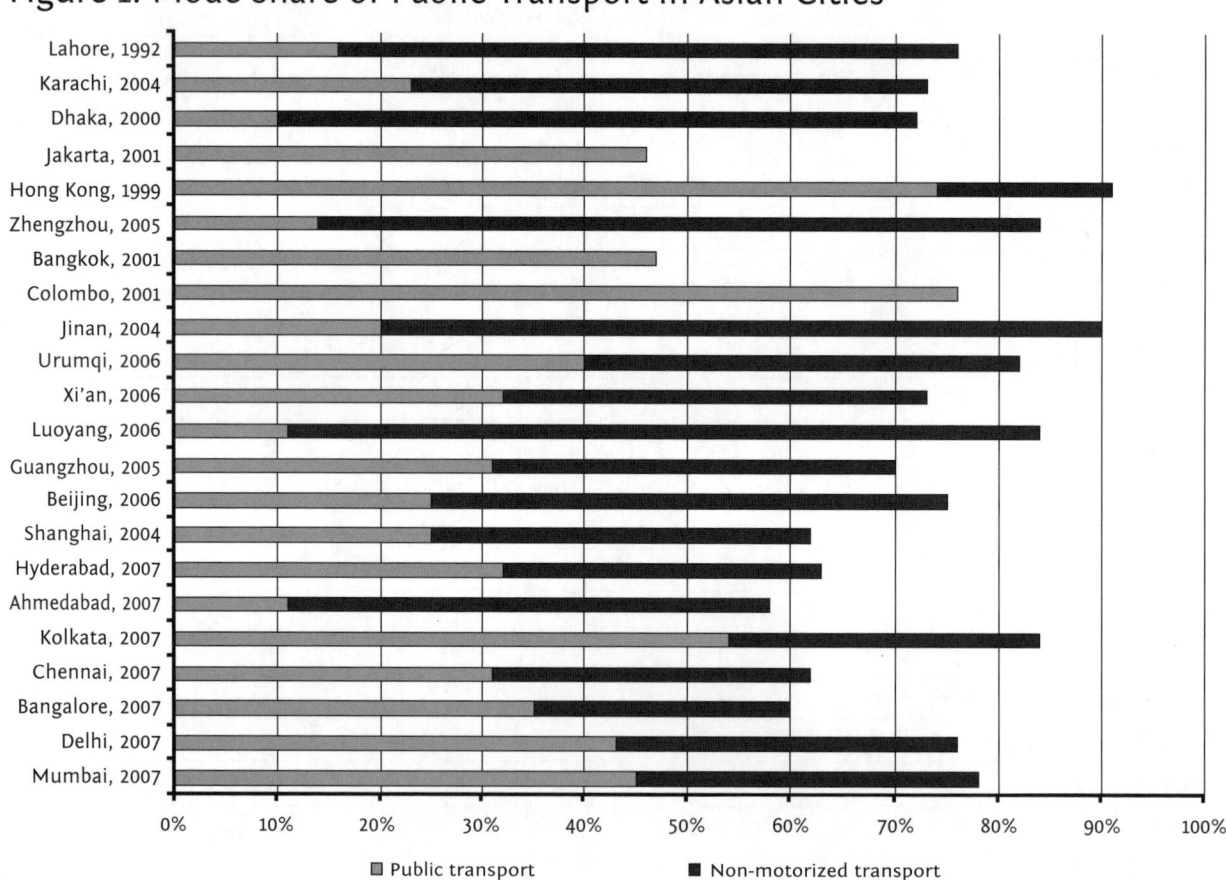

Figure 1. Mode Share of Public Transport in Asian Cities

Source: Compiled by the Institute for Transportation Policy and Development with inputs from WRI/EMBARQ and CAI-Asia; Darido, Torres-Montoya, and Mehndiratta (2009).

Although private ownership of vehicles has increased greatly in most Asian cities since the 1990s, the use of public transport is still relatively high compared to that in Western countries. The share of public transport use is low in most Chinese cities, where biking and walking predominate.

Bus Rapid Transit in Asia

Bus rapid transit (BRT) system has become the latest buzzword in discussions of public transport in Asia. Most cities in Asia are moving toward BRT—a modern public transport that combines the comfort of rail systems and the flexibility of buses. It is seen as an innovative, high-capacity, low-cost public transport solution that can significantly improve urban mobility (IEA 2002). In Asia, as of 2012, more than twenty cities have BRT in operation and more than fifty have BRT under consideration or at some stage of implementation.

The concept of BRT is not a recent development. It has been discussed and been evolving since the 1930s. The first such system was established in Curitiba, Brazil, in 1974, and its success there has inspired other cities to develop similar systems. It is portrayed as the most cost-effective means of transport in urban environments. The vehicles operate in exclusive bus lanes and can also go on mixed traffic lanes. A multidoor system enables people to board and alight quickly, and a simple and easy fare collection system reduces waiting time at stations. Success of BRT depends in part on integration with other modes such as existing public transport and nonmotorized transport.

efficiency of buses. This has become a vicious cycle and further induced more people to shift to private vehicles. This tendency has significantly increased both the energy consumption and emissions and eventually exerts pressure on governments to increase the investment in transport infrastructure.

Public Transportation and Sustainable Development

Sustainable development and sustainable transport are two sides of the same coin. The soaring population and economic growth in most Asian cities creates enormous difficulties for sustainable development. Rapid increase in motor vehicle use causes adverse impacts such as traffic congestion and deteriorating air quality. According to the Asian Development Bank, the share of carbon dioxide from the transportation sector in Asia was 19 percent of the worldwide total in 2006; it is predicted to increase to 31 percent by the year 2030 (ADB 2006). The reality is that, in developing transport policies, environmental concerns are overshadowed by economic and political issues in most Asian cities.

Public transport systems are environmentally friendly in terms of energy consumption and emissions rate per passenger. Increasing the share of public transport reduces congestion on roads and thereby brings down the carbon dioxide emissions and criteria pollutants that are the primary cause of global climate change. Public transport is one of the safest modes of transport, which means fewer accidents. Further, public transportation helps to alleviate poverty by providing an affordable means of transport to most people.

Moving Forward

Most Asian cities have begun to realize that providing enough road space and parking facilities for personal vehicles may not be possible. Therefore, action is being taken to improve the public transport systems in Asian cities. Both India and China are moving toward sustainable modes of transport. In China, for example, there are plans to add one metro line each year to the existing system. Similarly in India, numerous cities are considering various forms of rail systems.

Many Asian cities are integrating land use and transit, focusing development along transit corridors; Hong Kong, Taipei (Taiwan), and several cities in China are at various stages of implementing such transit-oriented development. Similarly in India, Chennai Metropolitan Development Authority is planning to intensify the development along mass transit corridors through increasing the floor space index (ratio of total floor area of a building to plot size, i.e., measuring the intensity of use of land and resources) and by relaxing parking regulations. Public transportation holds the key for rapid, safe, and convenient movement of people.

K. S. NESAMANI
Ford Foundation International Fellowship Program

See also Automobiles and Personal Transportation; Beijing, China; Chennai, India; Cities—Overview; Consumerism; Delhi, India; Dhaka, Bangladesh; Ecotourism; Energy Security; Five-Year Plans; Green Collar Jobs; Guangzhou, China; Information and Communication Technologies (ICT); Jakarta, Indonesia; Kuala Lumpur, Malaysia; Mumbai, India; Public-Private Partnerships; Shanghai, China; Singapore; Tokyo, Japan; Utilities Regulation and Energy Efficiency

FURTHER READING

Asian Development Bank (ADB). (2006). Energy efficiency and climate change considerations for on-road transport in Asia. Retrieved on November 29, 2011, from http://www2.adb.org/Documents/Reports/Energy-Efficiency-Transport/

Association of State Road Transport Undertakings (ASRTU). (2012). About us. Retrieved March 18, 2012, from http://www.asrtu.org/aboutus.htm

Darido, Georges; Torres-Montoya, Mariana; & Mehndiratta, Shomik. (2009). Urban transport and CO_2 emissions: Some evidence from Chinese cities (Working paper: 55773). Washington, DC: The World Bank.

Dimitriou, Harry T., & Gakenheimer, Ralph. (2010). *Urban transport in the developing world*. Gloucestershire, UK: Edward Elgar Publishing Limited.

International Energy Agency (IEA). (2002). Bus systems for the future: Achieving sustainable transport worldwide. Paris: IEA Publications.

Gilbert, Richard, & Perl, Anthony. (2010). *Transport revolutions: Moving people and freight without oil*. British Columbia, Canada: New Society Publisher.

Iles, Richard. (2005). *Public transport in developing countries*. Amsterdam, The Netherlands: Elsevier.

Hu, Xiaojun; Chang, Shiyan; Li, Jingjie; & Qin, Yining. (2010). Energy for sustainable road transportation in China: Challenges, initiatives and policy implications. *Energy, 35*(11), 4289–4301.

Imran, Muhammad. (2009). Public transport in Pakistan: A critical overview. *Journal of Public Transportation, 12*(2), 53–83.

Jönson, Gunilla, & Tengström, Emin. (2005). *Urban transport development: A complex issue*. Berlin: Springer-Verlag.

Leather, James, et al. (2011). Walkability and pedestrian facilities in Asian cities: State and issues (Working paper Series No. 17). Manila, Philippines: Asian Development Bank (ADB).

Ministry of Railways. (2011). About Indian railways: Lifeline to the nation. Retrieved November 14, 2011, from http://www.indianrailways.gov.in/

Ponnalurai, V. Raj. (2011). Sustainable bus rapid transit initiatives in India: The role of decisive leadership and strong institutions. *Transport Policy, 18*(1), 269–275.

Pucher, John; Korattyswaropam, Nisha; Mittal, Neha; & Neenu, Ittyerah. (2005). Urban transport crisis. *Transport Policy, 12*(3), 185–198.

Ramanathan, R. (2004). *Indian transport towards the new millennium*. New Delhi, India: Concept Publishing Company.

Sri Lanka Railways. (2011). History. Retrieved March 26, 2012, from http://www.railway.gov.lk/index.php?option=com_content&view=article&id=137&Itemid=181&lang=en

United Nations. (2010). World urbanization prospects: The 2009 revision. New York: Department of Economic and Social Affairs/Population Division. Retrieved March 26, 2012, from http://esa.un.org/unpd/wup/Documents/WUP2009_Highlights_Final.pdf

Zhang, Guohua; Li, Ming; & Wang, Jingxia. (2007). Application of the advanced public transport system in cities of China and the prospect of its future development. *Journal of Transportation Systems Engineering & Information Technology, 7*(5), 24–30.

Share the *Encyclopedia of Sustainability*: Teachers are welcome to make up to ten (10) copies of no more than two (2) articles for distribution in a single course or program. For further permissions, please visit www.copyright.com or contact: info@berkshirepublishing.com

R

Reforestation and Afforestation (Southeast Asia)

Reforestation and afforestation efforts in Southeast Asia have relied on the use of a small number of non-native tree species, often planted as monocultures, with little participation by local communities. The situation is changing, however, as regional institutions have developed more ecologically and socially sustainable approaches to restore forest cover, and market-based funding mechanisms are beginning to finance these efforts in the region.

Most countries in Southeast Asia have experienced widespread deforestation and forest degradation over the last century due to unsustainable forestry practices, conversion to agriculture, mining, urbanization, infrastructure development, and fire. This dramatic transformation in the region's vegetative cover has impacted not only the availability of timber and non-timber forest products, but has also had a correspondingly large effect on the ecosystem's ability to sequester carbon, maintain the hydrological cycle, minimize soil erosion, and preserve biodiversity. Most countries in the region now have large areas of degraded land, which governments are targeting for return to productivity through reforestation and afforestation.

While the exact definitions of reforestation and afforestation vary from source to source, both processes can generally be understood as the practice of planting trees in areas that are considered degraded or otherwise of low productivity. Reforestation is typically differentiated from afforestation by virtue of the fact that it involves returning tree cover to land that was formerly forested. Afforestation, on the other hand, involves planting trees on land that either never was forested, or that has been deforested or under an alternative land use for a long period of time. Successful reforestation and afforestation are marked by reestablished tree cover, without consideration given to the type of tree cover, or the diversity of reestablished trees. Forest restoration is a related term that often connotes an attempt to return the forest's original structure, function, and composition to the degraded land. Forest restoration is also sometimes used as a general term that includes tree planting, as well as less active methods to speed up natural succession (like assisted natural regeneration; see below).

Conventional Approaches

Reforestation and afforestation has a long history in Southeast Asia, having been initiated by colonial and, in some cases, precolonial governments. Usually these early programs were small in scale and aimed at restoring denuded areas and increasing supplies of premium timber species. Since the 1950s and 1960s, reforestation and afforestation have taken on much greater importance as the high levels of forest exploitation have resulted in huge areas of degraded lands. Government forestry departments and large industrial corporations have typically taken the lead in these efforts. Throughout the region, these reforestation and afforestation programs have tended to rely on the large-scale planting of a small number of species, including *Acacia mangium*, *Gmelina arborea* (beechwood), *Eucalyptus* spp., *Swietenia macrophylla* (mahogany), and *Tectona grandis* (teak), which are non-native in part, if not all, of the region and are planted as monocultures (i.e., as the sole crop). These species are favored by foresters, because they have well-established markets, good survivorship in open areas, and because they are easy to propagate and manage. Local community members, if involved at all in these reforestation and afforestation efforts, have often been employed as hired laborers with little stake in the program. Funds available through government initiatives have generally been allocated to meeting the goal of planting large numbers of trees, but little effort has been put on maintaining those trees, with the result that few survive. The exact impact of these programs remains largely unknown due to the lack of any long-term, systematic monitoring.

New Approaches

There are currently a number of programs underway working to restore forest cover that are both more ecologically and more socially sustainable than previous approaches. The United Nations Food and Agricultural Organization, for example, is promoting an approach known as assisted natural regeneration (ANR) in the Philippines, Indonesia, Cambodia, Laos, and Thailand. ANR consists of a series of techniques to reduce the labor and cost associated with nursery establishment and tree planting by facilitating the growth of the small, woody seedlings that are typically found even on extremely degraded sites. ANR techniques revolve around working with local communities to protect these seedlings from disturbances, such as animal grazing and fire, to reduce competition from weeds, and to promote their growth through fertilizing and mulching. The resulting forest, which is usually dominated by fast-growing, pioneer species, can be planted with shade-demanding tree species, if there are no nearby forest patches that can provide seedlings through natural dispersion methods (e.g., dispersal by wind, birds, or bats).

The Forest Research Restoration Unit (FORRU) at Chiang Mai University in Thailand is promoting a technique known as the framework species method (FSM). This approach, which was initially developed in Australia, has been successfully adapted to the ecological conditions of northern Thailand. FSM relies on the planting of moderately high densities of thirty or so native species of trees that have been chosen for their high survivorship, ability to shade out grasses by quickly achieving canopy closure, and attractiveness to wildlife, which, in turn, brings in seeds of additional tree species. This influential approach, which is being disseminated to southern Thailand, Cambodia, Indonesia, the Philippines, and elsewhere, is particularly relevant in national parks and other areas where there are nearby remnant patches of forest and where restoration for biodiversity conservation is the primary objective.

In the Philippines, a reforestation approach, known as rainforestation or rainforestation farming (RF), was developed by Visayas State University and the German Agency for International Cooperation (GTZ) as an agroforestry system that integrates the use of annual crops, fruit trees, and native timber trees. The mixing of economically and ecologically important species was considered necessary in the Philippines, where the rural population density is very high, as a way for local communities to gain multiple economic benefits while restoring forest cover to the land. A number of organizations in the Philippines have adopted RF, leading to a diversification of approaches aimed at using native species to address an array of management objectives, including timber production, biodiversity conservation, watershed rehabilitation, slope stabilization, urban beautification, and others. RF is now being widely promoted in the Philippines and is also being disseminated to Cambodia, Vietnam, Sri Lanka, and southern China.

ANR, FSM, and RF are some of the best-known alternative approaches to reforestation and afforestation in Southeast Asia because information about them is widely disseminated through publications and trainings. There are many similarities between these approaches: all three involve collaboration with local communities and rely on natural succession to develop more diverse forests that provide a greater variety of environmental services and are more resilient to disturbance than are the conventional methods. There are also other approaches to reforestation and afforestation being used in Southeast Asia that have not been institutionalized in the same kind of way. The Borneo Orangutan Survival Foundation, for example, conducted significant experimentation on forest restoration at the 1,800-hectare Samboja Lestari site in East Kalimantan, Indonesia, for which it has received significant international attention, even if it did not develop its own "brand" of reforestation. This project was particularly noteworthy because it involved the planting of large numbers of indigenous plants.

Local Communities

The meaningful involvement of local communities in reforestation and afforestation efforts in Southeast Asia is being facilitated by a broad paradigm shift away from centralized government control of forestlands (which are often highly degraded and in need of reforestation) to one in which rural communities are given a direct stake in how those lands are managed. This trend toward decentralization has occurred due to the recognition that state agencies are not able to adequately control access to the huge areas of forestland that they claim authority over, while rural and indigenous communities have a greater stake and ability to see that those resources are managed sustainably. Decentralization or cooperative management agreements have also become more appealing to government forestry departments since most of the valuable timber resources have often already been extracted. While the nature and extent of decentralization varies from country to country, reforestation and afforestation projects typically require that institutional arrangements be established between the different stakeholders (i.e., those people who have a stake in an enterprise) to determine who will contribute labor to the project, how benefits will be divided, and how conflicts can be managed. Community members are then often involved in all stages of reforestation and afforestation programs including planning, species selection, seed collection, nursery establishment, planting (or assisted natural regeneration), maintenance, and monitoring.

New Sources of Funding

Reforestation and afforestation programs in the past have been largely financed through government budgetary allocations, reforestation funds collected from concessionaires, corporate investment, and bilateral and multilateral grants and loans. In recent years, however, new funding mechanisms, known broadly as payments for ecosystem services (PES), have been developed that financially link the people who protect and/or restore forests with various stakeholders who receive direct economic benefits from the forested areas. These PES programs hold the potential to significantly increase the amount of regional, national, and international funds available for reforestation and afforestation initiatives.

The most developed of the PES programs revolve around the role of forests in sequestering carbon as a way to mitigate climate change. There are currently two different types of carbon markets through which carbon credits from reforestation and afforestation projects can be traded. The Kyoto Protocol's clean development mechanism (CDM), which is part of the so-called regulatory market, includes afforestation and reforestation as a way for developed countries with greenhouse gas emissions targets to offset their emissions by paying for projects in countries of the developing world, which have no such targets. To date, most reforestation and afforestation projects in the region have been developed in China and India, but there is one such project in Vietnam as well. Reforestation and afforestation also constitute a significant part of the voluntary carbon market, with projects currently in the Philippines, Indonesia, and Cambodia. The voluntary carbon market differs from the CDM in that it is not tied to any regulations, but rather is primarily driven by peoples' and companies' desires to offset their own emissions, and by corporate social responsibility campaigns. Under these two programs, as well as the Reducing Emissions from Deforestation and Forest Degradation (REDD+) mechanism, which is still under development, reforestation and afforestation project proponents are required to put in place stringent carbon accounting, monitoring, reporting, and verification systems, which help insure that reforestation projects achieve their greenhouse gas reduction goals. Many of reforestation and afforestation projects also seek validation under the Climate, Community, and Biodiversity Alliance (CCBA) standards, which are designed to ensure that carbon projects also have significant community and biodiversity benefits.

PES programs are also being developed to provide funding for the pursuit of other environmental advantages resulting from the presence of forests, including a greater abundance of water and increased biodiversity. Payments for watershed-related services focus on the role played by forests in mitigating the severity of flooding and drought, and in ensuring the quantity and quality of water resources. In various locations throughout Southeast Asia, for example, upland farmers are paid to protect and restore forestlands in order to secure water supply for the downstream production of hydroelectric and geothermal power, for irrigation, and for direct human consumption. Biodiversity markets are also now being looked at as vehicles for companies or individuals to fund the protection and restoration of important wildlife habitat areas, sometimes as required by regulations to mitigate habitat loss elsewhere.

Future Outlook

Conservation initiatives in Southeast Asia continue to be dominated by efforts to protect large tracts of primary forest, but reforestation and afforestation of degraded land are gaining increasing attention as the natural forests of the region continue to dwindle in scale and the demand for the goods and services provided by the forests increase. Climate change in particular has added a new impetus for governments to restore their forests. While conventional patterns of government-led reforestation, which prioritize the usage of non-native species in relatively homogenous plantings and allow for a minimal role by local communities, remain the dominant approach throughout much of the region, the situation is changing, as nongovernmental organizations, scientists, and concerned citizens have begun to question why such approaches are used, especially when more socially and ecologically sustainable practices are available. Capacity building and training are being used to disseminate these new approaches to a variety of practitioners in the field while networks are being developed to help address the other constraints to field implementation. It is imperative that these efforts continue to be scaled up, though, because as things currently stand, deforestation is still outpacing reforestation and afforestation efforts in most countries of the region.

J. David NEIDEL
National University of Singapore

See also Agriculture (China and Southeast Asia); Agriculture (South Asia); Biodiversity Conservation Legislation (China); Endangered Species; Great Green Wall (China); Nongovernmental Organizations (NGOs); Public-Private Partnerships; Rural Development; Southeast Asia

FURTHER READING

Alexander, Sasha, et al. (2011). Opportunities and challenges for ecological restoration within REDD+. *Restoration Ecology, 19*(6), 683–689.

Corlett, Richard T. (2009). *The ecology of tropical East Asia.* London: Oxford University Press.

Diaz, David; Hamilton, Katherine; & Johnson, Evan. (2011). *State of the forest carbon markets 2011: From canopy to currency.* Washington, DC: Ecosystem Marketplace.

Forest Restoration Research Unit. (2005). *How to plant a forest: Principles and practice of restoring tropical forests.* Thailand: Chiang Mai University. Retrieved April 3, 2012, from http://www.forru.org/PDF_Files/htpafbook/htpafbook.pdf

Friday, Kathleen S.; Drilling, M. Elmo; & Garrity, Dennis, P. (1999). *Imperata grassland rehabilitation using agroforestry and assisted natural regeneration.* Bogor, Indonesia: International Centre for Research in Agroforestry, Southeast Asian Regional Research Programme.

Lamb, David. (2011). *Regreening the barren hills: Tropical forest restoration in the Asia-Pacific region.* Dordrecht, The Netherlands: Springer.

Madsen, Becca; Carroll, Nathaniel; Kandy, Daniel; & Bennett, Genevieve. (2010). *State of biodiversity markets: Offsets and compensation programs worldwide.* Washington, DC: Ecosystem Marketplace.

Milan, Pacencia. (2009). *Rainforestation farming: A farmer's guide to sustainable forest biodiversity management* (2nd ed.). Baybay, Leyte, Philippines: Visayas State University. Retrieved April 3, 2012, from http://www.rainforestation.ph/resources/pdf/howto/Milan_2009_Rainforestation_Farming.pdf

Schulte, Andreas. (2002). *Rainforestation farming: Option for rural development and biodiversity conservation in the humid tropics of Southeast Asia.* Aachen, Germany: Shaker Verlag, GmbH.

Stanton, Tracy; Echavarria, Marta; Hamilton, Katherine; & Ott Caroline. (2010). *State of watershed payments: An emerging marketplace.* Washington, DC: Ecosystem Marketplace.

TED: Ideas worth spreading. (2009). TED talks: Willie Smits restores a rainforest. Retrieved April 3, 2012, from http://www.ted.com/talks/lang/en/willie_smits_restores_a_rainforest.html

Religions

The religious and philosophical traditions of Asia value balance and connections between the human body and spirit and the natural world. Hindu, Buddhist, Confucian, Daoist, and other Asian worldviews offer distinct sensibilities that support a sensitivity to sustainable practices. As the countries of Asia experience rapid economic development, these traditional values form a variety of conceptual resources for resisting a degradation of the environment and traditional social fabrics.

Sustainability requires a rethinking of the very premises upon which civilizations have been built. Traditional worldviews attempted to sort out the place of the human being in relationship with the cosmos. In India, a continuity was seen between the parts of the human body and the great powers of the universe, with correlations noted of the eyes with the sun and the moon, the feet with the soil of the Earth, the breath and lungs with the movement of the wind. By seeing the core of human experience (*atman*) as inseparable from the vastness of space (*cidakasha*) and hence from consciousness itself (*brahman*), Hindu ideas and sensibilities lend themselves to valuing the foundational elements of nature. Hinduism, Buddhism, Jainism, and Sikhism all adhere to the doctrine of reincarnation or rebirth. This establishes a kinship link with the myriad array of nonhuman species, each of which is said to have been inhabited at one time or another by individuals who now find themselves blessed with human birth. Due to this belief, many Asians practice vegetarianism, which is reputed to be a far less resource-intensive diet than carnivorism.

Confucianism extols the basic dignity of the human person; its ethical system requires the cultivation of human heartedness (*ren*) and proper living (*li*) in order to create harmony. Both Daoism and Confucianism advocate finding the path (*dao*) through which all things may be brought into balance. This emphasis on human dignity defies suppression in East Asia, as seen in the many protests against harmful environmental policies and practices. Sustainability in South, Southeast, and East Asia is developing its own idiom, employing notions of societal order (*dharma*) in Hinduism and Buddhism and propriety (*li*) in Confucianism as organizing concepts for positive change.

India and China

India and China are home to several of the world's most ancient philosophical and religious traditions, each of which holds enduring relevance as these great civilizations anticipate the changes and challenges of the twenty-first century. Both nations are renowned for their recent economic growth and emergence onto the world stage politically. Both nations face looming threats due to pollution and scarcity of resources sufficient for the modernization of their burgeoning populations.

India gave birth to many religious traditions. In ancient times these were grouped into two major categories. The Brahmanical traditions rely upon the authority of sacred texts such as the Vedas and the Upanishads and include detailed rituals that include veneration of the five great elements (earth, water, fire, air, space). The Sramanical traditions require renunciation of worldly involvement and emphasize meditation rather than ritual. The Brahmanical traditions gave rise to what today is referred to as Hinduism in its various forms, including Vaishnavism, Saivism, and various local devotional or Bhakti movements. The Sramanical traditions evolved into Buddhism, Jainism, and various styles of Yoga practice. In the sixteenth century, an amalgam of Brahmanical, Sramanical, and monotheistic ideas and practices gave birth to Sikhism, which now has over 26 million adherents. These traditions deal with the basic issues of human fulfillment and survival, anchoring their practice to connections with a sense of the transcendent.

China likewise gave birth to many philosophies that also include what appear to be religious practices. China's early text, the *I Ching* (*Yijing*), sets forth a worldview predicated on the complementarity of opposites known as yin (the feminine, the valley, the dark) and yang (the masculine, the mountain, the bright). Confucianism drew from this imagery to create a way of life that gives honor to one's ancestors, articulates the centrality of moral behavior, and seeks harmony through regulation of self, family, community, and nation. Daoism contrasts with Confucianism in that it emphasizes nonaction rather than action, surrendering rather than striving, flowing rather than exerting. For instance, a Confucian would meticulously reflect on ethics before acting, while a Daoist might be more spontaneous. Both traditions developed shrines and rituals; in imitation of the Buddhists, the Daoists also developed monastic orders. Two thousand years ago, the teachings of the Buddha spread from India to China, and those teachings melded with the sensibilities of Confucianism and Daoism to create a largely harmonious blend of faiths and philosophies.

Hindu Traditions

The Hindu traditions are in close accord with the goals of sustainable development as they ground themselves in a sense of antiquity and an abiding reverence for place. The Himalaya, poised above the Gangetic Plain and the lower peninsula of India, serve as inspiration for forest and water conservation. In India, Hindu women, empowered by the idea that nature (*prakrti*) is an expression of the power of the goddess (*devi-sakti*), have encircled trees with their bodies to prevent the trees being felled. Social movements such as Chipko, which grew especially in the 1970s in response to deforestation, have successfully protected forests from excessive logging. The Tehri Dam resistance movement of Sunderlal Bahuguna, a leading Gandhian, though only partially successful, has brought into question the wisdom of massive re-engineering of India's watersheds. The physicist and educator Vandana Shiva, drawing from the folk wisdom of local farmers, has become a champion against corporatization of agriculture and a leading advocate of preserving indigenous seeds and applying organic methods. M. C. Mehta, an environmental advocate at India's Supreme Court, has achieved legislative success in forcing the abandonment of dirty technologies such as kerosene-burning autorickshaws in several cities including New Delhi, Ahmedabad, and Varanasi. (In Agra, the site of the Taj Mahal, polluting vehicles are banned from a 1,500 meter radius surrounding the mausoleum to protect the monument's marble.) Medha Patkar helped convince the World Bank to withdraw financial support from the Narmada River damming project that has displaced thousands of farms. Religious leaders in Vrindaban on the banks of the Yamnua River and in Varanasi on the Ganges River had organized various campaigns to encourage the cleanup of severe pollution problems.

All these advocates have been steeped in the Gandhian tradition of taking local action in order to effect broad change, grounded in the religious precepts of nonviolence (*ahimsa*) and holding to truth (*satyagraha*). With its vast population and largely decentralized governmental structures, India boasts hundreds of nongovernmental organizations (NGOs) dedicated to environmental causes.

Japan, Korea, and Singapore

Japan, Korea, and Singapore have utilized the communitarian sensibility of Confucianism to modernize rapidly. Japan adopted the Western industrial model in the latter part of the nineteenth century; South Korea undertook an Americanization of its economy in the 1960s; and Singapore became a self-appointed successor to the British business systems upon the end of colonial rule in 1959. Each country has made great strides in enhancing the material well-being of its citizens, while remaining grounded in Asian sensibilities. Each country struggles in its own way, however, with the pressing problems of pollution, the diminishment of sound agricultural practices, and the feelings of malaise and alienation that tend to plague the modern world.

Religious identities in East Asia are complex. Shifts in religious practices in the first decades of the twenty-first century reflect the struggles between modernity and tradition. South Korea is now 26 percent Christian and 23 percent Buddhist, while Singapore's multicultural community is reflected in the diversity of its major religions with a population that is 33 percent Buddhist, 18 percent Christian, 15 percent Muslim, and 11 percent Daoist. In addition, Confucian ethics dominate the society in Singapore. Whereas the advent of Christianity has changed South Korean society, and Singapore includes both Christians and Muslims, Japan has a long tradition of multifaith practice. Many professed Buddhists also practice Shinto, while many who profess to practice Shinto also practice a form of Buddhism, and we can also find large numbers who claim no religious beliefs but may still participate in major ceremonies marking births, deaths, and marriages. China, officially atheist since the accession of Mao Zedong in 1949, recognizes Buddhism, Daoism, Islam, and Protestant and Catholic Christianity but only allows government-approved forms of these faiths to congregate. Confucianism, with its emphasis on respect for family and "keeping face" in society, so firmly underlies East Asian thought that, despite the Maoists' best efforts, it can still be found in China.

In South Korea, Buddhist monks and nuns have lobbied and protested against deforestation and increasing urbanization. In Thailand, Buddhist monks have draped trees in monks' robes to stave off logging. Japan is questioning its reliance on nuclear energy in the wake of the 2011 Tohoku earthquake and multiple nuclear power plant meltdowns. China faces more than ninety-thousand annual demonstrations, often in protest of severe pollution.

In order for the nations of East Asia to sustain their economies and political systems, further work must be done by government and nongovernmental organizations to address pressing issues of resource allocation. This may include a rethinking of the wholesale adoption of the Western consumer-driven lifestyle and perhaps a return to the abstemious ideas of Confucianism and Daoism.

Readings Related to Sustainability

Resources for learning about sustainability in Asian traditions include the multivolume series called Religions of the World and Ecology (1997–2002), published at Harvard University through the Forum on Religion and Ecology and edited by Mary Evelyn Tucker and John Grim. *The Encyclopedia of Religion and Nature,* edited by Bron Taylor (2005), provides key summary entries on the major traditions of Asia in light of ecology, including Buddhism, Hinduism, Confucianism, Daoism, Jainism, Sikhism, Yoga, Shinto, and other traditions. *The Oxford Handbook of Religion and Ecology,* edited by Roger Gottlieb (2006) includes longer articles on Asian traditions, including extensive studies of Jainism, Hinduism, Buddhism, Daoism, and Confucianism. These articles build on and draw from primary sources in original languages and give contemporary examples of activism in Asia.

The Academy of Korean Studies in 2009 published an anthology with all articles appearing both in English and Korean on religion and ecology in an Asian context, titled *Civilization and Peace* and edited by Kim Jung-Bae. A French language resource, *Crise écologique, crise des valeurs? Défis pur l'anthropologie et la spiritualité,* edited by Dominique Bourg and Philippe Roch, includes many articles on Asian religions and ecology, both in response to the US professor of medieval history Lynn White Jr.'s seminal article, "The Historical Roots of Our Ecologic Crisis" (1967), and dealing with the broader issues surrounding the discourse of sustainability.

Four significant case studies on religion and ecology in India have been published. *Belief, Bounty, and Beauty: Rituals around Sacred Trees in India* by Albertina Nugteren (2005) draws upon traditional literature from the Vedas, the Dharma Shastras, and the literature of Buddhism Tantra to explain the significance of tree worship in India. It cites the contemporary examples of the harvesting of sacred trees for worship in Puri during the time of the Jagannath festival and the ongoing influence of the Chipko tree protection movement. *Plant Lives: Borderline Beings in Indian Traditions* by Ellison Banks Findly (2008) similarly deals with plants, addressing such topics as plant sentience, stability, and karma. It includes a survey of traditional literature from Hinduism, Buddhism, and Jainism and cites numerous examples of religiously inspired environmental activism, as found in Auroville, the Ashram of Ammachi, the work on behalf of seed preservation by Vandana Shiva, and other contemporary examples. It also discusses the Thai Buddhist tradition of forest protection. *River of Love in an Age of Pollution* by David Haberman (2006) documents the ravaging of one of Asia's great rivers through industrial pollution and neglect. Drawing from traditional lore, science, and his own experience, Haberman describes the flow of this river from the Himalaya through the megalopolis of Delhi down into the sacred region of Braj, narrating its decline and the attempts at its revitalization. He includes original translations of religious songs and poems in praise of the river. Pankaj Jain's *Dharma and Ecology of Hindu Communities: Sustenance and Sustainability* (2011) describes three Indian ecological movements: the tree-planting initiatives of the Svadhyayis, the tree and animal protection actions taken by the Bishnois, and the simple lifestyle of the tribal Bhils.

Voices from within the Indian tradition include many books written by Vandana Shiva, including *Earth Democracy* (2005), *Staying Alive* (1989), and *Violence of the Green Revolution* (1988). She exposes numerous ways in which traditional life patterns are being interrupted in Asia. With vibrant language, including a critique of "food fascism," Shiva advocates the honoring of local village lifestyles as an antidote to creeping global consumerism as the only solution to the looming environmental challenges in Asia. Ramachandra Guha documents the interruption of local forestry practices by British colonial policy in *This Fissured Land* (Gadgil and Guha 1992) and in *How Much Should a Person Consume? Environmentalism in India and the United States* (2006), which makes a convincing case for localized social ecology and subsistence farming as the best alternatives to scientific industrialism. As in earlier critiques, he decries the notion that

North American deep ecology, which criticizes the conveniences of modern life while still indulging in them, bears relevance for India, which must meet the needs and demands of a huge population clamoring for middle-class urban amenities. Meera Nand presents a critique of the tendency to romanticize the traditional insights of the Hindu faith or overstate their relevance to contemporary life in *The Wrongs of the Religious Right: Reflections on Science, Secularism, and Hindutva* (2005).

The Yoga tradition has become a globalized voice for Asian religious traditions. Three recent books have highlighted the potential for ecological values of Yoga as expressed in the Hindu, Buddhist, Jaina, and Gandhian practice of nonviolence (*ahimsa*). David Frawley, a popular writer and advocate of the Hindu view of life, suggests in his book *Yoga and the Sacred Fire: Self-Realization and Planetary Transformation* (2004) that the experiences of meditation and ritual can help people reconnect with the bare essentials needed for human flourishing. Georg and Brenda Feuerstein give practical advice in their books *Green Yoga* (2007) and *Green Dharma* (2008), supported with traditional practices and textual resources in light of what the authors regard to be a new ethical imperative. *Yoga and Ecology: Dharma for the Earth*, edited by Christopher Key Chapple (2009), examines the Atharva Veda, the "Earth-friendly" aspects of Patanjali's *Yoga Sutra*, the influence of the *Bhagavad Gita* on Arne Naess's theory of deep ecology, and the world-affirming aspects of Tantra through an ecological prism.

Three additional books place the overall field of religious environmentalism in a context that by necessity includes Asian worldviews. Thomas Berry's *The Sacred Universe* (2009) speaks of the pan-Asian image of the relationship between microphase and macrophase as essential for the development of a feeling of sensitivity to the Earth. Berry identifies this with key terms in Sanskrit and Chinese: *Brahman, maya, nirvana, karma, dharma, li, tao, t'ien, jen*. Bron Taylor's *Dark Green Religion: Nature Spirituality and the Planetary Future* (2010), although seeking a postmodern, nontheistic response to the problems foisted upon the globe by rapacious human activity, draws heavily from Asian religious traditions. *Ecology and the Environment: Perspectives from the Humanities*, edited by Donald Swearer (2009), includes essays on nature in East Asia and extensive discussion in the introduction of Thai Buddhist environmental activism.

Christopher Key CHAPPLE
Loyola Marymount University

See also Activism, Judicial; China; Climate Change Mitigation Initiatives (China); Consumerism; Corporate Accountability (China); Gandhism; India; Indigenous Peoples; Japan; Korean Peninsula; Nongovernmental Organizations (NGOs); Singapore; Southeast Asia; Traditional Knowledge (China); Traditional Knowledge (India)

FURTHER READING

Berry, Thomas. (2009). *The sacred universe: Earth, spirituality, and religion in the twenty-first century*. West Sussex, UK: Columbia University Press.

Bourg, Dominique, & Roch, Philippe. (Eds.). (2010). *Crise écologique, crise des valeurs? Défis pur l'anthropologie et la spiritualité*. Geneva: Labor et Fides.

Chapple, Christopher Key. (Ed.). (2009). *Yoga and ecology: Dharma for the Earth*. Hampton, VA: A. Deepak Publishing.

Feuerstein, Georg, & Feuerstein, Brenda. (2007). *Green Yoga*. Eastend, Canada: Traditional Yoga Studies.

Feuerstein, Georg, & Feuerstein, Brenda. (2008). *Green Dharma*. Eastend, Canada: Traditional Yoga Studies.

Findly, Ellison Banks. (2008). *Plant lives: Borderline beings in Indian traditions*. New Delhi: Moltilal Banarsidass Publishers.

Frawley, David. (2004). *Yoga and the sacred fire: Self-realization and planetary transformation*. Detroit, MI: Lotus Press.

Gadgil, Madhav, & Guha, Ramachandra. (1992). *This fissured land: An ecological history of India*. Berkeley: University of California Press.

Gottlieb, Roger S. (Ed.). (2006). *The Oxford handbook of religion and ecology*. New York: Oxford University Press.

Guha, Ramachandra. (2006). *How much should a person consume? Environmentalism in India and the United States*. Berkeley: University of California Press.

Haberman, David L. (2006). *River of love in an age of pollution*. Berkeley: University of California Press.

Jain, Pankaj. (2011). *Dharma and ecology of Hindu communities: Sustenance and sustainability*. Surrey, UK: Ashgate.

Kim Jung-Bae. (Ed.). (2009). *Civilization and peace*. Seongnam-si, Korea: Academy of Korean Studies.

Nand, Meera. (2005). *The wrongs of the religious right: Reflections on science, secularism, and hindutva*. Palam Vihar, Gurgaon, India: Three Essays Collective.

Nugteren, Albertina. (2005). *Belief, bounty, and beauty: Rituals around sacred trees in India*. Leiden, The Netherlands: Brill.

Shiva, Vandana. (1988). *Violence of the Green Revolution: Third world agriculture, ecology and politics*. London: Zed Books.

Shiva, Vandana. (1989). *Staying alive: Women, ecology and development*. London: Zed Books.

Shiva, Vandana. (2005). *Earth democracy: Justice, sustainability, and peace*. Cambridge, MA: South End Press.

Swearer, Donald K. (Ed.). (2009). *Ecology and the environment: Perspectives from the humanities*. Cambridge, MA: Harvard University Press, Center for the Study of World Religions.

Taylor, Bron. (2010). *Dark green religion: Nature spirituality and the planetary future*. Berkeley: University of California Press.

Taylor, Bron. (Ed.). (2005). *The encyclopedia of religion and nature*. New York: Continuum International Publishers.

Tucker, Mary Evelyn, & Grim, John. (Eds.). (1997–2002). Religions of the world and ecology (series). Cambridge, MA: Harvard University Press, Center for the Study of World Religions.

White, Lynn, Jr. (1967, March 10). The historical roots of our ecologic crisis. *Science, 155*(3767), 1203–1207. Retrieved January 27, 2012, from http://www.sciencemag.org/content/155/3767/1203.citation

Rule of Law

Formally established laws, regulations, and procedures serve as only the "thin" part of rule of law; also required for its full, "thick" realization are institutional capacity, judicial neutrality, informational transparency, and social space for civic engagement. In the context of rapid, large-scale industrialization in China, India, and neighboring countries, rule of law for sustainability is an area in urgent need of further development.

Rule of law is an important but complex and often controversial concept for sustainability in South and East Asia, as elsewhere. It may be defined in the first instance as (environmental) governance on the basis of formal and transparent rules, institutions, and procedures for environmental ends, rather than by individuals and institutions interested in more narrow, short-term (especially economic) gain. How, and by whom, is it determined whether and where a development project—for example a new hydroelectric dam, industrial park, urban development, or waste incinerator—may proceed, and what the anticipated social and environmental impacts and possible long-term consequences are? And after the fact, who will bear, if needed, the associated burdens and expenses of relocation, environmental cleanup, restoration, and compensation to victims of pollution and unbridled resource exploitation, and how will this be determined?

As major players in today's global markets for goods and services, China, India, and their neighbors increasingly are expected—by local citizens and communities, nongovernmental organizations (NGOs), consumers both domestic and global, foreign governments, and others—to heed growing global social and environmental norms with respect to human rights (e.g., limits on use of child, prison, and slave labor; recognition of indigenous rights) and environmental sustainability (e.g., use of lead-free solder in electronics). Movements in this direction come in many forms, including green supply-chain management, product certification programs and ecolabels, international environmental directives, environmentally preferred purchasing agreements, environmental and human rights advocacy campaigns, consumer boycotts and "buycotts," and more.

Though constructed on the basis of diverse traditions and institutions, legal codes and regulatory structures in most South and East Asian nations today (Myanmar [Burma] and North Korea are notable exceptions) incorporate provisions for pollution control, environmental impact assessment, and resource conservation. Some nations in the region recognize traditional resource rights and other rights of indigenous peoples and communities; front-runners in formal recognition of indigenous land rights include the Philippines, India, and, in some respects, Indonesia. Citizens across the region, emboldened by and in some cases subsidized through domestic and international support, have for decades sought legitimate channels to redress environmental and other grievances against public and private sector actors and institutions. In response, governments have strengthened environmental laws, institutions, and procedures for greater legitimacy, if not also improved sustainability. Though not always followed, regulations in many countries in the region now formally require, for example, environmental impact assessments for major new development projects, including infrastructural projects. Even when not utilized for a particular project, such provisions provide a basis for legal challenges and appeals to news media and high officials. Considerable work remains to be done, however.

Western and Eastern Traditions

In Western contexts, rule of law has long been closely associated with liberal democracy; legal principles and practices protecting human rights and individual liberties were well established, if incomplete and still developing, prior to the rise and institutionalization of contemporary environmental concern. In the United States, the National Environmental Policy Act (1970) established formal procedures for environmental impact assessment; it was followed by the Clean Air Act (1970), Clean Water Act (1972), Endangered Species Act (1973), and other landmark statutes. These acts established legal standing for local citizens, NGOs, and others on environmental matters. Four decades of legal and political struggles, advances, and retreats, have ensued, with rule of law protecting individuals and corporations (as fictitious individuals) alike.

By contrast, in East and Southeast Asia imperial traditions, a hierarchical "rule by man" dominated for centuries, with citizen-subjects having little say or input into environmental or other decision making. Four centuries of European colonization brought various legal traditions to the region, alongside ruthless colonial violence, bloody wars, and rebellions. The twentieth century was nothing short of tumultuous, variously bringing national liberation, democracy, communism, military takeovers, and ultimately marketization. In the newly industrialized East and South Asia of the latter decades of the twentieth century, governments (including those under authoritarian and/or military rule) adopted foundational environmental laws and regulations, with technical assistance from Japan, the United States, Germany, and other nations. Even today, however, many of the governments lack the legal and institutional capacity for effective implementation of environmental regulations. This is perhaps especially true in the region's most expansive, most populous, and most rapidly developing economies, including China, India, Indonesia, and Bangladesh; however, even wealthier, more advanced countries in the region, such as Singapore and Malaysia, can improve in this area. Procedural innovation has lagged, encumbered by administrative fragmentation, corruption, and other conflicts of interest, including with state-owned enterprises, lack of political will, and the weak or nonexistent development of civil society and institutions. Such difficulties are arguably most acute in China, Vietnam, and other "transitional" countries that maintain strong, centralized, one-party states functioning in close cooperation with economic elites.

Variations in Sectors

In rapidly developing China, India, and neighboring countries, rule of law today is most clearly established in commercial sectors—a condition of participation in global markets. In the economic sphere, rule of law protects and encourages investors to commit financial, organizational, and other resources in exchange for promises of future revenue. When efforts have been made to extend rule of law in the region to noneconomic spheres, including with respect to the environment and natural resources, results have been mixed.

The early decades of the twenty-first century have seen increasing environmental concern among citizens, news media, government officials, and others in most countries across the region. Some countries, including China, have progressed significantly in making environmental information more transparent and publicly available, an important foundation for rule of law in the environmental arena. This has empowered citizens and raised pressure on underperforming local officials and enterprises.

Gradually, social and institutional capacities in environmental law, as well as regulatory infrastructures, are being established. This has for the most part gone hand in hand with economic development and internationalization, with Singapore, for example, being an early leader, although today's booming economies—China and India—are rapidly catching up. Big strides have been taken since the beginning of the new millennium: environmental officials have growing support at the highest levels; more and more environmental lawyers have been trained and are working in the region; environmental NGOs operate in most countries; new information and communication technologies strengthen citizen education and mobilization around environmental issues; and space is opening up for civic action. As just one example of the latter, in China the not-for-profit Center for Legal Assistance to Pollution Victims (CLAPV) has patiently and successfully represented local citizens in pollution and related health compensation claims before administrative and legal officials since 2001.

Obstacles and Issues

Through good economic times and bad, however, economic and political initiatives have largely remained prioritized in the region, to the detriment of long-term environmental sustainability. Sustained, large-scale, and rapid economic growth in China, India, and some of their neighbors brings with it pressing concerns with respect to rule of (environmental) law—domestically, across the region, and globally. In East and South Asia, key stumbling blocks for rule of law in the environmental arena include ambiguous rights to use and exploit natural resources; uncertain rights of citizenship for millions; weak or nonexistent protection of human rights for individuals and communities; lack of independent and impartial judiciaries or arbitration systems; growing inequalities in affluence, power, and access to institutions; and in many cases (though arguably not for India) weakly developed civil societies. Resource rights throughout the region often are claimed, in the first instance, by central governments, even in situations of long-term customary use by local residents.

Millions of people in remote and upland areas, such as in northeast India, Thailand, and Myanmar, lack basic citizenship rights. Being historically migratory and thus crossing district, provincial, and national boundaries, without regular contact with or recognition by central governments, they have few or no legitimate avenues for influencing or participating in decisions involving the natural environments in which they live. National priorities, reflecting elite interests, in many cases hold sway over interests of local residents, communities, and environments. Judges or administrative hearing officers, if there are any, may be closely aligned with authorities against whom complaints have been made. Media platforms and citizens' organizations in support of environmental education, communication, and advocacy may be absent, tightly controlled, or heavily monitored. It may be suggested that today, through widespread diffusion and adoption of environmental laws and regulations, East and South Asian countries have many aspects of formal (thin) rule of law in the environmental arena, but, for reasons outlined above, for most countries this has yet to develop into a more full and robust (thick) realization of the same.

Alleviating the persistent, acute poverty of hundreds of millions of people, both rural and urban, is perhaps the primary issue that rule of law in East Asia must face. Immediate human conditions threaten political stability as well as environmental sustainability; examples include reports of rural unrest in some regions of China, food and fuel price riots in Indonesia, and the displacement of thousands by flooding in Bangladesh, the Philippines, and elsewhere. A closely related debate in the region and globally is over the extent to which a basic level of economic development is prerequisite for rule of (environmental) law. Yet increasing environmental risks in China, India, and neighboring countries—from acute air and water pollution, energy and resource shortages and competition, desertification, and, not least, effects of global climate change, for example—greatly raise the stakes for all social sectors, including public, private, and civil.

Future Prospects

Further development of rule of law with respect to sustainability in China, India, and neighboring countries—as in many places in the world today—is part of a long-term, multilevel institutionalization of rule of law in general, plus the strengthening of particular provisions with respect to the environment and natural resources. Environmental rules, regulations, and procedures were the first to be established—thin rule of law. Now comes the hard part: building scientific, administrative, and legal capacity; developing independent judicial and arbitration systems; recognizing traditional resource rights; gathering and disseminating environmental information; engaging in environmental education; and strengthening popular participation in environmental decision making—thick rule of law. Pressed by continuing major social and environmental challenges, rule of law for sustainability in East and Southeast Asia will continue to evolve, taking a variety of forms based on the region's richly diverse cultural and legal traditions.

David A. SONNENFELD
State University of New York
College of Environmental Science and Forestry

See also Activism, Judicial; Biodiversity Conservation Legislation (China); Biosafety Legislation (China); Consumerism; Education, Environmental (*several articles*); Indigenous Peoples; Labor; Media Coverage of the

Environment; National Pollution Survey (China); Nongovernmental Organizations (NGOs); Outsourcing and Offshoring; Property Rights (China); Public-Private Partnerships; Water Use and Rights (India)

Further Reading

Chang, Shenglin; Chiu, Hua-mei; & Tu, Wen-ling. (2006). Breaking the silicon silence: Voicing health and environmental impacts within Taiwan's Hsinchu Science Park. In Ted Smith, David A. Sonnenfeld & David Naguib Pellow (Eds.), *Challenging the chip: Labor rights and environmental justice in the global electronics industry* (pp. 170–180). Philadelphia: Temple University Press.

Cohen, Jerome A. (2008). China's reform era legal odyssey. *Far Eastern Economic Review, 171*(10), 34–38. Retrieved June 29, 2011, from: http://www.usasialaw.org/wp-content/uploads/2009/03/200812-feer-chinas-reform-era-legal-odyssey.pdf

Mol, Arthur P. J. (2008). *Environmental reform in the information age: The contours of informational governance*. New York: Cambridge University Press.

Ocko, Jonathan K., & Gilmartin, David. (2009). State, sovereignty, and the people: A comparison of the "rule of law" in China and India. *Journal of Asian Studies, 68*(1), 55–133.

Peerenboom, Randall. (2002). *China's long march toward rule of law*. Cambridge, UK: Cambridge University Press.

Peerenboom, Randall. (Ed.). (2004). *Asian discourses of rule of law: Theories and implementation of rule of law in twelve Asian countries, France and the U.S.* New York: RoutledgeCurzon.

Rock, Michael T. (2009). Integrating environmental and economic policy making in China and Taiwan. In Arthur P. J. Mol, David A. Sonnenfeld & Gert Spaargaren (Eds.), *The ecological modernisation reader: Environmental reform in theory and practice* (pp. 418–437). London and New York: Routledge.

Scott, James C. (2010). *The art of not being governed: An anarchist history of upland Southeast Asia*. New Haven, CT: Yale University Press.

Sonnenfeld, David A., & Mol, Arthur P. J. (2006). Environmental reform in Asia: Comparisons, challenges, next steps. *Journal of Environment and Development, 15*(2), 112–137.

Stern, Rachel E. (2010). On the frontlines: Making decisions in Chinese civil environmental lawsuits. *Law & Policy, 32*(1), 79–103.

Sundar, Nandini. (2011). The rule of law and citizenship in central India: Postcolonial dilemmas. *Citizenship Studies, 15*(3–4), 419–432.

Tamanaha, Brian Z. (2004). *On the rule of law: History, politics, theory*. Cambridge, UK: Cambridge University Press.

Wang, Alex. (2007). The role of law in environmental protection in China: Recent developments. *Vermont Journal of Environmental Law, 8*, 195–233. Retrieved July 13, 2011, from http://www.vjel.org/journal/VJEL10057.html

Wang Canfa. (2007). Chinese environmental law enforcement: Current deficiencies and suggested reforms. *Vermont Journal of Environmental Law, 8*, 159–193. Retrieved July 11, 2011, from http://www.vjel.org/journal/VJEL10058.html

Berkshire's authors and editors welcome questions, comments, and corrections. Send your emails about the *Berkshire Encyclopedia of Sustainability* in general or this volume in particular to: sustainability.updates@berkshirepublishing.com

Rural Development

China and India both have taken different approaches to rural development in an effort to reverse the exploitation that is often pervasive among poor populations whose livelihoods depend on natural resources. While challenges to China involve uneven development over vast territories and India struggles with sufficient productivity, both countries need to adapt to agricultural modernization and new technologies to continue to develop a sustainable rural sector.

The human population depends on natural resources. The base of natural resources is often fragile, however. The fragility makes for the classic *tragedy of the commons*, when many rural poor people turn to natural resources around them to make a living in a way that exploits the resources and reduces their availability, a problem of sustainability.

Rural development as an intervention is a systematic attempt to reverse the story. Many of the interventions in the field of rural development add to the sustainability problems rather than solve them, however. Intensive agriculture or cattle breeding severely impacts the environment, for instance, although the small farmers engaged in such production do not realize the effects. The huge number of such small farmers in countries like India and China unwittingly brings pressure on the environment.

A historical approach to rural development in India and China shows how the interventions have changed in different time periods and how these interventions have impacted sustainability.

China

The People's Republic of China was founded in 1949. Although China has 22 percent of the world's population, it has only 9 percent of the planet's cultivable land. Rural development in China has undergone huge changes, which can be categorized in three stages.

Collective Stage: 1958–1982

The people's commune dominated the Chinese countryside. Individual households pooled their property, including land, animals, farm equipment, and savings. They worked and lived in common; farmers in the same unit, regardless of their age or gender, worked the same schedule and ate together in the public dining hall. The government increased its investment in agriculture and pursued agricultural sustainability through modernization and technology. It mobilized rural labor forces and funded large-scale projects, such as hydropower stations and farmland improvement. The number of small hydropower stations in rural areas increased from 544 in 1957 to 83,224 in 1979. The percentage of irrigated land increased from 24.4 percent of the total cultivated areas in 1957 to 45.2 percent in 1979. Tractor-plowed land area reached 42.4 percent in 1979, compared to 2.4 percent in 1957. The central government set up 40,000 agricultural technological expansion offices in rural China. These offices extended multiple cropping and intercropping to most rural areas, which increased the number of crops planted. During this stage, agricultural production increased significantly. Grain production reached 259 million tonnes in 1977, compared to 164 million tonnes in 1952 (National Bureau of Statistics of China 1983).

Decline: 1983–2004

The people's commune system collapsed and the household responsibility system (HRS) rose to take its place. A remarkable step in the history of land reform, HRS was a land-lease system with the features of collective ownership and individual use rights. The government distributed collective farmland to individual households and gave them full rights to agricultural production and labor allocation.

The government invested more and more in industrialization and urbanization during this stage; they conversely reduced their investment in agriculture. Most of the agricultural development from the collective stage came to a halt. China invested less in agricultural infrastructure and production and failed to maintain existing projects, including irrigation and drainage systems and hydropower stations. Farms de-mechanized; because households become the basic unit of agricultural production under the HRS, the farmland area of every household was less than 0.2 hectares. It was hardly worthwhile for households to buy expensive machinery (such as tractors) for such limited plots.

China also lost farmland to industrial use, tourism, residential and commercial housing, and desertification. It increased its use of chemical fertilizer instead of organic fertilizer, creating pollution. Water shortages, caused by increasing industrial production and numbers of urban residents, affected agricultural production.

Despite the decline in agriculture, rural development was still booming in this stage. The government located township and village enterprises (TVEs) in the countryside and employed farmers. Between the 1980s and 1990s, the number of TVEs went from 6.1 million in 1984 to 23.4 million in 1996; their gross output increased from 169.8 billion yuan in 1984 to 6,834.3 billion yuan in 1996. TVEs made a vast contribution to rural economic development, making up 77 percent of the total output in the countryside in 1995 (Fujita and Hu 2001).

Overall Development: 2005 Onward

The Chinese central government realized the decline of agricultural development and proposed new socialist countryside construction in 2005 in order to reach overall rural development. China launched or enhanced a series of preferential policies during this stage to spur agricultural production. It subsidized grain producers, farm machinery, and land conversion to grassland and extended microcredit. China created policies for rural infrastructure and natural resource management, including road construction, broadcast and television policies, power grid reconstruction, a land contract system, a basic farmland protection policy, a compensation system for resettlement, and forestry and forest protection. It implemented rural education and health policies, including nine years' compulsory education, student loans, training programs for rural migrant workers, distance education for farmers, a minimum living allowance, a rural pension system, and health insurance. The gross output of agricultural products increased from 766 billion yuan in 1990 to 6,036 billion yuan in 2009. Meanwhile, farmers' per capita net annual income rose to 5,153 yuan in 2009, compared to 686 yuan in 1990 (National Bureau of Statistics of China 2009).

Farmers' rural-to-urban migration became a common social phenomenon. Migrant workers moved from less developed regions to employment in prosperous coastal regions. By 2010, the number of migrant workers reached 242 million. They were mostly young people with relatively good educations. Their salaries, which made up two-thirds of the household income, most obviously and directly affected their families. The money promoted rural households' consumption, which helped the rural economy.

Aside from the economic contribution to rural areas, migrant workers played an important role in the countryside's transformation. After a few years of living in cities, migrant workers' ideas and behaviors changed, including their knowledge of health issues and their consumption habits. These changes brought diverse elements to homogeneous traditional rural society. With their increased skills and the money they had saved, many returned migrants chose to start their own businesses. This entrepreneurialism benefited not only themselves, but also promoted regional economic development and offered employment opportunities to the local labor force.

India

Similarly to China, rural development in India has undergone three distinct phases but the issues, interventions, and achievements in each phase are different.

Before Independence

Many scholars have shown that during colonial rule, colonists extracted resources from rural areas and took them to urban areas and finally back to Europe. Although Indians during this period were generally impoverished, it had not always been this way. In his report titled *The World Economy: A Millennial Perspective*, Angus Maddison (2001), a British economic historian who studied ancient world economy, reports that India had the world's largest economy from the first to the eighteenth centuries, with a 32.9 percent share of world's gross domestic product in the first century to 28.9 percent in 1000 CE and 24.4 percent in 1700 CE. In 1952, following colonial administration, this share of world income was reduced to 3.2 percent.

Sustainability problems surfaced during the colonial period. Colonists extracted resources through the creation of cash crop plantations such as tea, cotton, oil, forest goods, and spices. They created new cash crops and, with them, related technology and fertilizers. Because cash crops required huge areas of land, landlords took over large parts of rural areas. Small landholders, often indebted to their landlords, were forced to relinquish their lands. By the time of independence, 15 percent of Indians were landless laborers, a number that has been increasing ever since. Tensions between the landowning classes and laborers became a permanent feature of rural life. Although some historians view these developments in the colonial era as the cause of rural underdevelopment, others argue that labor exploitation in developing countries had existed even prior to colonial times (Stein and Subrahmanyam 1996).

Until Liberalization

Counties throughout the world undertook intervention in rural development primarily after World War II and in India after independence in 1947. The government of India attempted to redistribute the land and reduce the inequality created by the colonial administration. Because the landowning class was the dominant political class, however, this strategy achieved little success.

The government's early attempts at rural development included programs to improve agriculture through reclamation of wastelands. The government constructed irrigation canals, tube wells, and lift irrigation from rivers by pumps or other mechanical means. They brought electrification to rural areas, constructed roads, and met needs jointly prioritized by communities and the state. The government developed the High Yielding Varieties Programme and the Intensive Cattle Development Programme to produce more food. Extension workers trained at agricultural universities traveled to villages to train farmers in these methods. During the White Revolution of the 1970s, India became the biggest milk-producing country in the world. Between 1951 and 2000 India's food production increased fourfold, from 51 million tonnes to 200 million tonnes, primarily because of the expansion of irrigation. Wells and tube wells provided water for about 75 percent of irrigated land. This unregulated exploitation of groundwater would have long-term implications for availability of clean water in India. Other sustainability issues included the mechanization and commercialization of agriculture, dam construction for irrigation and electricity generation, and fertilizer and pesticide use.

Although production increased tremendously, these programs did little to improve rural poverty. The government instituted the Integrated Rural Development Programme (IRDP) in 1978–1979 to address the needs of marginal farmers and people who possessed limited assets. Common pool resources (CPRs) were one focus of the program. People with limited assets depended on CPRs for food, fuel, wood, fodder, and similar basic needs. Lack of access to CPRs was one reason for rural poverty, and commercial exploitation only added to the problem. The program aimed to rejuvenate and replenish CPRs through technological and managerial intervention. India has nearly 100 million hectares of common pool land and about 30 million hectares of common pool forests. The bulk of its water and fisheries resources are also common pool resources (Singh 2001). The government initiated a range of programs and policies to conserve water and forest resources. The Forest Policy of 2006 affirmed traditional rights of communities to forest resources.

After Liberalization

The third phase of rural development begins with the liberalization of the Indian economy since 1991. India has allowed market forces to determine the development path in this phase. The market logic changed the production systems drastically. One of the key aims of government in the postliberalization era is to move large numbers of agricultural workers to other sectors such as industry or service. In the second decade of the twenty-first century, approximately 60 percent of the labor force works in the agricultural sector, although the share of agriculture in India's gross domestic product in only approximately 15 percent. The government encourages agricultural workers to develop micro-enterprises that bring better returns to rural products.

Liberalization has opened the economy to foreign investment. Foreign investment needs resources for production. Land and water are the central rural resources. As industry expands, it transforms agricultural land to industrial land. Land records follow the colonial system developed in the nineteenth century, making the system for buying property extremely outdated. Because property titles are unclear, the system has prevented industry from buying land. Rural people, frightened about losing their land-based livelihoods, also resist the government's acquisition of land for infrastructural development such as highways. The government is considering new legislation regarding land acquisition, including having rural workers share the industry's profit or find jobs with the new industries.

Liberalization and foreign investment have changed the rural development path through the development of genetically modified seeds. Traditional seeds provided limited output. New seeds have brought new challenges, however, such as greater fertilizer requirements (local seeds have more resistance capacity), farmers' dependency on the seed provider, and the need for large-scale plantations. Bt cotton, a variety introduced to Indian farms in the late 1990s, expanded to 90 percent of Indian cotton production in less than five years. This development has been linked to a large number of farmer suicides. When Bt genes were engineered for cotton, use of pesticides to combat new pests increased the cost of production over 13 fold and, often unable to pay back the debt, farmers resorted to suicide. This relationship has been denied by biotech firms (Barker 2011). Imported animals have replaced indigenous milk animals. From a sustainability point of view, such homogenization brings huge challenges. One key challenge is loss of interdependency between species because of the introduction of monoculture. Indigenous milk animals had been used for variety of purposes, rather than for milking alone. Livelihoods of the farmers also change since the focus becomes solely on one aspect of the imported animals.

Challenges

The processes and outcomes in the arena of rural development command strong attention both in China and India. The sustainability challenges that both countries face are different but contrasting. China faces the challenges of regional imbalanced development, whereas India faces productivity challenges.

Rural-urban disparities in China are increasing: urbanites typically make roughly three times what their rural counterparts do. India, on the other hand, has managed to reduce urban-rural inequality to a great extent. Inequality between rural areas in China also presents a worrisome scenario because there is a significant income gap between well-off regions and less-developed regions. Rural poverty is still a serious problem in the less-developed regions.

India's rural agrarian sector is in crisis because of increasingly falling productivity. Income from farming is much lower than that of any other profession in the country. Between 2002 and 2006 about 17,500 Indian farmers committed suicide. Productivity is also a challenge in rural China because technology innovation is still behind, and farmers still use traditional methods.

Transitional issues present a second set of problems that affect both China and India. Desertification and soil erosion have reduced the availability of water and land in China. The per capita water share is 2,700 cubic meters annually, only one-quarter of the world average. Desertification affects 27.3 percent of China's land, and it is expanding at a rate of 2,460 square kilometers each year. China loses 4 billion tonnes of soil through erosion every year, costing around 20 billion yuan annually. Industry in India makes similar demands on water and land, making appropriate pricing that does not neglect farmers' interests difficult.

Outlook

Although China and India are among the fastest-growing economies in the world, both countries face a dilemma in the sustainability of rural development. On the one hand, they need to meet the increasing demand for agricultural consumption by the growing population. (In 2011, the populations of China and India were 1.33 billion and 1.15 billon, respectively.) On the other hand, they need to protect limited natural resources to achieve long-term sustainability. Agricultural resources such as land and water have been overextended in both countries. The challenge for both countries is how to maintain rural development at least at current levels. Scholars argue that agricultural modernization and technologies should be the priority for sustainable rural development (Ching 2008).

Sony PELLISSERY
Institute of Rural Management, Anand

Li SUN
Bielefeld University

See also Agriculture (China and Southeast Asia); Agriculture (South Asia); China; India; Five-Year Plans; Green Collar Jobs; Indigenous Peoples; Labor; Microfinance; Nongovernmental Organizations (NGOs); One-Child Policy; Outsourcing and Offshoring; Public Transportation; Rural Livelihoods; Traditional Knowledge (China); Traditional Knowledge (India); White Revolution of India

FURTHER READING

Barker, Debbie. (2011). *The wheel of life*. Washington, DC: The Center for Food Safety.

Ching, Pao-yu. (2008). How sustainable is China's agriculture? A closer look at China's agriculture and Chinese peasants. Retrieved July 5, 2011, from http://www.foodsov.org/resources/resources_000009.pdf

Chun Oi, Jean. (1999). *Rural China takes off: Institutional foundations of economic reform*. Berkeley and Los Angeles: University of California Press.

Fan, Jie; Heberer, Thomas; & Taubmann, Wolfgang. (2006). *Rural China: Economic and social change in the late twentieth century*. Armonk, NY: M. E. Sharpe.

Fujita, Masahisa, & Hu, Dapeng (2001). Regional disparity in China 1985–1994: The effects of globalization and economic liberalization. *The Annals of Regional Science, 35*(1), 3–37.

Maddison, Angus. (2001). *The world economy: A millennial perspective*. Development Centre Studies, Development Centre of the Organisation for Economic Co–operation and Development. Retrieved March 7, 2012, from http://www.nkeconwatch.com/nk-uploads/theworldeconomy.pdf

National Bureau of Statistics of China (NBS). (1983). *China statistical yearbook 1983*. Beijing: China Statistics Press.

National Bureau of Statistics of China (NBS). (2009). *China statistical yearbook 2009*. Beijing: China Statistics Press.

Singh, Katar. (1986). *Rural development: Principles, policies and management*. New Delhi: Sage Publications.

Stein, Burton, & Subrahmanyam, Sanjay. (1996). *Institutions and economic change in South Asia*. Delhi: Oxford University Press.

Tilt, Bryan. (2010). *The struggle for sustainability in rural China: Environmental values and civil society*. New York: Columbia University Press.

Rural Livelihoods

Researchers have been studying rural livelihoods, including agriculture and other rural employment, with the aim of developing both intervention models and a conceptual model to guide rural societies in sustainable development. With the intervention model, goals are to reduce poverty and increase economic sustainability. As a concept, the approach ranges from consideration of broad development issues to household-level strategies.

Rural livelihoods are the means and practices by which rural peoples provide for themselves. Development of sustainable approaches to rural livelihoods is a pressing problem in many countries. The approach to rural livelihoods has two different aspects. Scholars tend to treat the examination of livelihoods as a concept distinct from development, while practitioners treat the livelihood approach as an intervention framework that keeps people at the center of sustainable development. Livelihood as a concept helps us to understand sustainability beyond aggregate indicators at national and regional levels (such as gross domestic product). The focus on livelihood as an intervention is useful to make the linkage between macro-level indicators (e.g., food self-sufficiency) and actual day-to-day lives of the people. This article is divided according to these two aspects.

The discussion below deals with the livelihoods approach as it is relevant in developmental contexts of China and India, contexts that may have similarities with many other low-income and transitional countries. A conceptual grounding of the livelihood approach will help to transcend country specificities and to make clear its practical significance for a variety of sustainability challenges.

As a Concept

The term *rural livelihoods* has come to refer to an approach toward sustainable development in which state government or nongovernmental organizations (NGOs) plan for growth and development taking household-level strategies of rural living into consideration. The term *sustainable livelihood* similarly refers to a "people-centered" concern in approaches to development. Traditionally, growth and development approaches have dealt with issues separately as economic or environmental interventions; the sustainable livelihood approach, however, requires that the intervention happens in dynamic fashion through economic, environmental, social, and institutional sectors all at the same time. This holistic but complex approach emphasized local solutions for macro problems. Adding the designation "rural" adds an indication of locale, which could be contrasted with urban livelihoods. In a similar way, occupational (e.g., farming or fishing livelihoods) or socially differentiated (gendered or age-specific livelihoods) classifications are possible.

Consideration of rural livelihoods has a long history, with its roots extending to the beginning of the twentieth century. Soviet planners of the 1920s (such as Alexander V. Chayanov and Nikolai Ivanovich Bukharin) noticed that the peasant way of living was essentially opposed to capitalism, since peasant labor was utilized primarily for living (subsistence) rather than for profit making. The challenge was to incorporate such household-level behavior with national-level planning. In the 1960s a wide range of farm management studies and microeconomic theories shaped the approaches to how peasants could improve their lives.

These ideas received conceptual backing through the Indian Nobel Prize–winning economist Amartya Sen's theories of functioning and capabilities: rather than emphasizing the providing of resources for the poor, Sen said, income opportunities and market access could reduce poverty (Sen 1985). Simultaneously, a variety of developments and intervention tools emerged in the 1980s and 1990s. Some of them focused on gender analyses, participatory appraisals, sustainability (especially in response to the Brundtland Commission's 1987 *Report of the World Commission on Environment and Development*, also known as *Our Common Future*) and resilience studies, which study ecosystems' abilities to bounce back from disturbance. All these perspectives and analytical tools have shaped the rural livelihoods approach.

The interworking of these different perspectives as put together by the British development scholars Robert Chambers and Gordon Conway has been considered the key work in the development of scholarship on livelihoods approaches. They originally defined livelihood as "the capabilities, assets (including both material and social resources), and activities required for a means of living" (Chambers and Conway 1992). In addition, they defined sustainability criteria for the livelihood saying: "a livelihood is sustainable when it can cope with and recover from stresses and shocks and maintain or enhance its capabilities and assets both now and in the future while not undermining the natural resource base." In the second half of the 1990s, the Department for International Development of the United Kingdom (DFID) adopted this sustainable livelihood framework as the official condition for international aid. This was crucial in the development of the concept (Scoones 2009).

The strength of the concept of livelihood is its ability to incorporate diversity that is present among rural people and to synchronize different preferences held by rural people that may look contradictory to an outsider (Ellis 2000). For the purpose of conceptual clarity, this diversity is represented by working with five types of capitals: natural (resources based on physical environment, such as land and water), physical (human-produced goods, including infrastructure), social (relation-based arrangements, such as reciprocity in a community), human (capacity of human beings to transform resources into other forms, such as education or skill level improving income), and financial (transaction ability, such as availability of credit facilities). In addition to these five dimensions, some scholars add other dimensions of political, spiritual, and/or cultural capital. Those who make livelihood interventions, typically NGOs, make efforts to enhance all different capitals simultaneously, rather than in segregated fashion.

As an Approach for Development Intervention

In the post–World War II era, as modernization theories captured the imagination, development intervention became the active agenda of developing countries and international agencies such as the United Nations and the World Bank. At that time, development intervention was primarily carried out in a monodisciplinary manner. For instance, an economist or agronomist would frame what is best for a community to reduce poverty. This approach tended to neglect the people for whom development was designed and planned. There was denial of local knowledge, of the priorities of the people themselves, and of sustainability. The following oft-quoted anecdote illustrates this:

> A landless widow was delighted to receive a cow from a nongovernmental organization promoting livelihoods. The promoters were pleased because milk enjoyed great local demand, and the return earned from the sale of milk clearly was an addition to her income. When the NGO representatives returned later to see how she was getting on, they were surprised to be greeted with wrath. She said, "Earlier we moved to where the work was. Now you have tied this millstone around my neck. How can I look after this wretched animal? I have to come back to feed it every day. It stops me from going out to earn my daily wages." (Datta et al. 2004)

The livelihoods approach emerged as a solution to this paradox. If a solution is to be sustainable, it needs to be adaptable to the local economy. NGOs and development practitioners involved in livelihood intervention achieve such adaptation and sustainability in three stages. In the first stage, a sincere attempt is made to learn about the local economy and the people operating there. Specifically, products and services and how local demand conditions operate are studied through the eyes of local people. In the second stage, livelihood activities suitable for the impoverished people are selected using the information from the first stage. In the third stage, mediating institutions, which may also manage these activities, are developed. Some of these institutions could be already existing but dormant in the social traditions of the people, in which case the task of interventionists is to identify such institutions rather than replacing them with new institutions. A good example is provided by a common property resource (CPR), such as a river bed, grazing land, or forest resources; the livelihood approach neither proposes appropriation of such CPRs as individual property nor allows them to be degraded as open-access resources. Rather, livelihood strategy requires sustainable use of such CPRs through creation of appropriate user rules by the communities living around CPRs. Often, these resource protection rules have been practiced for many generations, for example when indigenous communities limit themselves to picking up dried leaves and twigs from the forests, rather than cutting trees.

On some occasions, however, such institutions and rules do not exist. When it is necessary to create new institutions, attention is paid to four aspects: ecological, techno-economic, distribution, and income and expenditure patterns. These four aspects are considered in relation to each other, with the goal of positive livelihood outcome—namely, increased income, decreased expenditure (cost, time, energy), increased employment and opportunities, and decreased or diversified risk(s).

Two Examples

In China, livelihoods promotion occurred in two different models in two time periods. First, during the period 1983–2004, the People's Republic of China introduced a system combining a household responsibility system (HRS) and township and village enterprises (TVEs). HRS is regarded as a land-lease system: collective farmland was distributed to individual households, with full rights to agricultural production and labor allocation but not ownership of the land, which is owned by village committees. TVEs functioned as a system in which the community's produced goods were subjected to value addition and marketing, and later the profit was distributed among the producers. This had a huge impact and resulted in an increase in agricultural production many times over.

Since 2005, the Chinese government has taken a new approach to rural livelihoods, focusing on improvement of natural resource use and infrastructure in rural areas. Also important to the new approach is the encouragement of rural families to diversify their income sources, adding to their livelihood by having some household members working in cities, and contributing in that way as well to national production and growth. Remittances in cash by these workers have increased. Evaluation of this approach has shown that, beyond remittances, benefits for ecology and human beings are evident (Qin 2010). For instance, engagement in nonagricultural production by some members of a household has allowed families to continue sustainable agricultural production and usage of the lands, which otherwise would have been abandoned and completely uncultivated.

The government of India initiated a massive program called National Rural Livelihood Mission (NRLM) in 2011. One of the central aims of the program is to encourage entrepreneurship and to connect entrepreneurs with banks for loans or to assist in initial investment. Presently in India about 25 million impoverished people are organized into self-help groups of ten to fifteen members. NRLM envisages organizing another 45 million poor households into self-help groups (social capital). These groups would be encouraged to initiate small enterprises through bank loans and subsidies provided to them (financial capital). Wherever required, the members of groups would be provided with skills required to undertake income generation (human capital). This approach would improve rural livelihoods by increasing rural productivity and market linkages for the produced goods.

Sony PELLISSERY
Institute of Rural Management, Anand, India

See also Agriculture (China and Southeast Asia); Agriculture (South Asia); Consumerism; Education, Environmental (*several articles*); Education, Female; Fisheries (China); Gender Equality; Indigenous Peoples; Labor; Microfinance; Nongovernmental Organizations (NGOs); Property Rights (China); Rural Development; Traditional Knowledge (China); Traditional Knowledge (India); White Revolution of India

FURTHER READING

Carney, Diana. (Ed). (1998). *Sustainable rural livelihoods.* London: Department for International Development.

Chambers, Robert, & Conway, Gordon R. (1992). *Sustainable rural livelihoods: Practical concepts for the 21st century* (IDS Discussion Paper 276). Brighton, UK: Institute of Development Studies, University of Sussex.

Datta, Sankar; Mahajan, Vijay; Thakur, Gitali; Livelihood School; & Ford Foundation. (2004). *A resource book for livelihood promotion.* Hyderabad, India: BASIX and New Economic Foundation.

Ellis, Frank. (2000). *Rural livelihoods and diversity in developing countries.* Oxford, UK: Oxford University Press.

Qin, Hua. (2010). Rural to urban migration, household livelihoods, and the rural environment in Chongqing Municipality, southwest China. *Human Ecology, 38*(5), 675–690.

Scoones, Ian. (2009). Livelihoods perspectives and rural development. *Journal of Peasant Studies, 36*(1), 12–27.

Sen, Amartya K. (1985). *Commodities and capabilities.* Oxford, UK: Oxford University Press.

S

Shanghai, China

23 million est. pop. 2010. (including 9 million migrant workers)

Shanghai is China's center of industrial, financial, and commercial activities, boasting the country's highest economic productivity, largest urban population, and busiest seaport. Shanghai faces challenges similar to urban centers worldwide: housing conditions, water and air quality, solid waste management, transportation, and land use planning. Shanghai has committed itself to confronting myriad issues head-on, recognizing the need to implement sustainability strategies to maintain economic prosperity and its attractiveness to Chinese and foreigners alike.

Shanghai, China's most populous city and largest seaport, is China's center of industrial, financial, and commercial activities. The city generates about 8.3 percent of China's gross industrial output value and 12.5 percent of the total revenue of China due to its major industries: chemicals, textiles, electronics, ship building, metallurgy, and machine building. Commerce, banking, and ocean shipping play crucial roles in the city's vibrant economy. This vibrancy comes with a price: population pressures, water and air pollution problems, and resource management issues. Sustainability, therefore, is crucial to Shanghai's future development.

One of four province-level municipalities controlled directly by the Chinese central government, Shanghai, also known in China as Hù, comprises eighteen districts, one county (Chongming) and three islands—Chongming, Changxing, and Hengsha. The central part of the city lies on the Yangzi (Chang) River delta where the river spills into the East China Sea on the country's eastern coastline. Shanghai's total land area covers 6,340.5 square kilometers, about twice the size of the US state of Rhode Island and almost three times the size of Tokyo. Rivers and lakes cover nearly 11 percent of the city's total territory, providing abundant water resources for Shanghai's sustained agricultural production and industrial sector. The Suzhou Creek, Chuanyang River, and Dianpu River are tributaries of the Huangou River, which meanders through the city's downtown. Enjoying an average annual temperature of 17.5°C, Shanghai's subtropical climate includes significant monsoons, which produce 70 percent of the precipitation during flood season.

According to China's 2010 national census, Shanghai's population of 23 million (14 million permanent residents and 9 million migrant workers along with families) increased by more than 3 million people since the last census in 2005, an average annual growth rate of 660,000 people per year, creating a population density of 6,400 people per square kilometer (CNNGo 2011). Urban dwellers constitute nearly 90 percent of the population while a fraction above 10 percent lives in the rural areas. Life expectancy stands at 82.5 years, a national record and the sixth-longest life expectancy in the world, but that high life expectancy rate, combined with a low fertility rate, has produced an aging populace with 23 percent over the age of sixty (Wenjun 2011, 2012).

Shanghai's mayor, Han Zheng, predicts an 8 percent increase in the city's 2012 gross domestic product (GDP). In 2011, the real estate market dipped slightly but retail sales, imports, and foreign direct investment all increased by double digits. Shanghai's unemployment rate fell to below 4.5 percent (Shasha 2012; Lina 2012). Buffeted by the European debt crisis and softening exports, Shanghai's industrial output declined in 2011 as Shanghai prepares to phase out traditional manufacturing, pushing most of its current production to rural areas outside the city, and replace it with high-tech manufacturing and R&D

(Collier's International 2012, 1). As of 2012, Shanghai's industrial base relies primarily on pillar industries such as electronics, information technology products, automobile manufacturing, biomedicine, chemicals, and steel processing. The city has recently begun a shift toward business park development, which increases professional job opportunities and city tax revenues.

Shanghai's geographical location has proven advantageous to its agricultural sector. Moderate temperatures, fertile soil, and plentiful rain and sunshine provide Shanghai sufficient conditions for high agricultural output despite its limited arable land. Generally Shanghai is able to produce sufficient levels of grains, meats, dairy products, fruits, and vegetables to meet urban and rural consumer demands along with a level of excess for regional and international export.

Buses, subways, taxis, light rail, river ferries, and a maglev (derived from the words *magnetic levitation*) train line form the basis of Shanghai's mass transportation infrastructure. Known for its speed, low cost, and convenience, Shanghai's public transport system serves over 7 million people daily. The system connects the urban districts to the neighboring suburban areas. The twelve metro lines, 273 stations, and 420 kilometers of track make the city's rail system the largest in the world. Shanghai also boasts the world's largest bus system with a thousand separate lines. Shanghai's road network is part of an integrated system encompassing all of eastern China. Within the city proper, elevated expressways experience overcrowding and traffic jams during the rush hours. The bicycle laws that do exist are restricted to normal roads, while the elevated expressways and the city's main streets disallow bicycle and motorcycle traffic.

Car ownership is severely restricted and comes at a high price. The city holds monthly auctions for new car permits but limits the number issued to eight thousand and charges a fee to acquire the permit. The auction system is designed to address the congestion problem. Nevertheless, the number of registered vehicles rose 10 percent in 2011 to 2.5 million vehicles (Minjie 2012). Increased air pollution, greater congestion, and insufficient parking exacerbate Shanghai's rising exhaust emissions. Along with creating more parking spaces, the city government has pledged to spend 10.3 billion yuan ($1.6 billion) to alleviate air pollution problems (Hang'e 2012).

Sustainability

According to Jeffrey Sachs, director of the Earth Institute at Columbia University, Shanghai confronts the same two challenges as other growing urban areas: the ability "to achieve a high and sustainable quality of life, and a high economic productivity" (Sachs 2008, A6). Sachs details the characteristics of a twenty-first-century sustainable city: "low-carbon energy, public health for an aging population and an obesity epidemic, sustainable clean water, reduced air and water pollution, effective waste management, and resilience to global climate change" (Sachs 2008, A6). Additional challenges for Shanghai's sustainable future include issues that affect the inhabitants' general quality of life: public health, transport, clean water, sustainable food, clean energy, and distributive population policies (Sachs 2008, A6).

To meet those future requirements, city leaders embarked on two particularly ambitious development projects in recent years that have met with mixed results. The earliest project was the creation of the world's first large-scale eco-city: Dongtan. Located on the eastern end of Chongming Island, Dongtan was intended to display all the characteristics of sustainable living: zero-carbon footprint, renewable power sources, carbon neutral buildings, car-free transportation models, green-building materials, recycled waste water for irrigation, and even an eco-farm. Nearly 500,000 residents were expected by 2030; the first 25,000 by 2010. The project was launched in 2005 when the Shanghai Industrial Investment Corporation hired Arup, a British-based engineering firm, to design the master plan. By 2010, the project had ground to a halt with a bridge-tunnel and wind turbines the only constructed features. Funding issues between Arup and the Shanghai Corporation, the arrest and imprisonment of Chen Liangyu (former Communist Party chief and Dongtan's primary political patron) on corruption charges, and the lack of local input in the design and implementation stages jeopardized the project's completion. The practical realities associated with the project included its consuming a vital green space around Shanghai as well as being connected to one of the world's largest non-eco urban centers (Brenhouse 2010). Further concerns involve the project's encroachment on a sensitive wetlands area and disruption of a migratory route for birds.

When Shanghai was named as the site for World Expo 2010, city leaders proposed various solutions to transform Shanghai into a sustainable city, but its startling growth resulted in crowded skyscrapers consuming enormous amounts of energy, increased congestion, and higher levels of air pollution. World Expo 2010 Shanghai was designed "to explore the full potential of urban life in the 21st century and a significant period in urban evolution." At the time, given that 55 percent of the world was expected to live in cities by the year 2010, the expo focused on the theme "Better City, Better Life." The expo billed itself as an opportunity for exhibitors to demonstrate "urban civilization to the full extent, exchange their experiences of urban development, disseminate advanced notions on cities and explore new approaches to human habitat, lifestyle and working conditions in the new century. [Exhibitors] will learn how to create an eco-friendly society and maintain the sustainable development of human beings" (Expo 2010 Shanghai China 2008). The expo put on display various demonstrations of best practices that addressed the growing issues of modern urbanization while promoting "future urban development to focus on environmental sustainability, efficiency and diversity."

Shanghai's leaders, in the aftermath of World Expo 2010, pledged that sustainability would be the central guiding philosophy of the city's future development. Shanghai's initial attempt revolved around the expo site, a former industrial area with over two-hundred pollution-belching factories. City officials have offered a future vision of the site as "an eco-friendly zone of parks, conference and convention centers and pedestrian-friendly retail and commercial space" (Powell 2011). Wind and solar energy sources will provide power while recycled and eco-friendly materials, much of which will come from the demolished expo buildings, would form the basis of future construction. The city gained some immediate advantages from the expo: increased city revenues, enhanced international image, newer transport infrastructure, updated LED lighting, the world's largest solar panel on the roof of the performing arts center (the former Chinese pavilion) and over a thousand "renewable energy" cars designed for taxi services (Knowledge@Wharton 2010; Scarlatelli 2010).

A number of ongoing projects, large and small in scope, aim to improve Shanghai's sustainability. For example, Shanghai Tower (China's tallest skyscraper under construction as of 2012 and scheduled for completion in 2014), will offer tradition amenities with office space, a hotel, and cultural venues; the building's sustainable features include wind-load resistant construction methods to save materials and cost, a rainwater collection system for heating and cooling, and wind turbines to generate power (Facilities Society n.d.; D'Alterio 2012). On the financial front, the Shanghai Stock Exchange, the world's fifth largest, established a sustainable stock index comprising forty stocks and will emphasize companies trading in three broad areas: low carbon economy, cyclic economy, and education services and publishing. (Kropp 2011). Although the concept of "balcony farming" is not new for city planners concerned with global climate change, improving air quality, and reducing waste and the city-island heat effects, urban farming in the form of rooftop gardens, community plots, hydroponics, and aeroponics offer a possible solution for sustainable ways to feed increasingly growing urban populations—and by 2035, 70 percent of China's population is expected to live in urban areas. The high cost of organics and concerns over food safety have convinced thousands of Shanghai's residents to explore and invest in urban farming (Pandora 2011). In another effort to improve air quality, Xuhui District's Tourism Bureau launched a bike-share program in April 2010 to provide transit riders a low-carbon solution from the train station; the program mimics similar programs begun the previous year in Minhang, Baoshan, and Pudong districts.

Future Challenges

Shanghai was one of China's first cities to open to Western contact when it became a treaty port at the end of First Opium War in 1842. The city served as the birthplace of the Chinese Communist party and the location of its First National Congress in 1921, and it played an instrumental role by establishing a model commune during the Cultural Revolution (1966–1976). The 1972 Shanghai Communiqué established formal relations between the People's Republic of China and the United States after US president Richard Nixon's visit to China. Like much of China, Shanghai drifted into stagnation until the end of the 1990s after the period of national reform and revitalization. Shanghai now serves as China's largest city and its most dynamic economy. The Australian economist Peter Abelson has noted that Shanghai remains intimately connected to the rest of China particularly as more and more people flood into Shanghai in search of stability and prosperity. As Abelson rightly identifies, however, Shanghai's expanding population stresses the city's resources to create ever greater levels of "overcrowding, slums, traffic congestion, air pollution, waste disposal and other environmental problems that especially afflict most large cities" (Abelson 1999). Shanghai's problem is how to manage economic growth with environmental sustainability in the face of ever-increasing population.

Shanghai has many strengths lacking in other developing world urban centers: "its outstanding domestic and international location, its huge store of human capital and skills, and the breadth and depth of its industrial base" (Abelson 1999). Five major weaknesses, however, confront Shanghai's future: the city's "economic success attracts large numbers of workers into the city; the increasing city population places ongoing stress on the environment—on housing, transportation systems, air and water quality, solid waste disposal, land uses and so on; economic performance is sensitive to international conditions and to foreign investment; much of Shanghai's industry in not internationally competitive; and the [city's] economy is still highly reliant on the public sector" (Abelson 1999). Shanghai's challenges are not unlike urban centers throughout the world (although magnified due to its population size): housing conditions, water and air quality, solid waste management, transportation, and land use planning (Abelson 1999). But in ways both large and small and in starts and stops, Shanghai, as the rest of China, has committed itself to confronting its myriad issues head-on. At the forefront of the city's future planning is both the recognition and desire to implement sustainability strategies to maintain its economic prosperity and its attractiveness to foreigners and Chinese alike.

John C. HORGAN
Concordia University–Wisconsin

See also Automobiles and Personal Transportation; Beijing, China; China; Cities—Overview; Consumerism; Green Collar Jobs; Guangzhou, China; Media Coverage of the Environment; Nongovernmental Organizations (NGOs); Pearl River Delta; Public Transportation; Yangzi (Chang) River

Further Reading

Abelson, Peter. (1999). Economic and environmental sustainability in Shanghai. Retrieved April 2, 2012, from http://www.appliedeconomics.com.au/pubs/papers/pa99_shanghai.htm

Brenhouse, Hillary. (2010, June 24). Plans shrivel for Chinese eco-city. Retrieved April 2, 2012, from http://www.nytimes.com/2010/06/25/business/energy-environment/25iht-rbogdong.html

Cheng, Hefa, & Hu, Yuanan. (2010). Planning for sustainability in China's urban development: Status and challenges for Dongtan eco-city project. *Journal of Environmental Monitoring, 12*(1), 119–126.

City Government of Shanghai. (2010). Shanghai basic facts 2011. Retrieved April 4, 2012, from http://en.shio.gov.cn/facts.html

CNNGo. (2011). Shanghai officially just got a bit more crowded. Retrieved April 2, 2012, from http://www.cnngo.com/shanghai/life/shanghai-just-officially-got-bit-more-crowded-096925

Collier's International. (2012). Shanghai industrial property market research report and forecast 2011 4Q. Retrieved April 2, 2012 from http://rightsite.asia/en/article/shanghai-industrial-property-market-research-report-and-forecast-2011-4q

D'Alterio, Emily. (2012). China's tallest skyscraper is green. Retrieved April 11, 2012, from http://designbuildsource.com.au/china-tallest-skyscraper-green

Expo 2010 Shanghai China. (2008, January 26). Brief introduction of World Expo Shanghai. Retrieved April 2, 2012, from http://en.expo2010.cn/a/20081116/000004.htm

Facilities Society. (n.d.). Shanghai sustainability. Retrieved April 2, 2012, from http://www.facilities.ac.uk/j/news/39-features/96-shanghai-sustainability

Hong'e, Mo. (Ed.). (2012). Shanghai to spend 10 bln yuan to curb air pollution. Retrieved April 2, 2012, from http://news.xinhuanet.com/english/china/2012-02/29/c_131437961.htm

Kanthor, Rebecca. (2010). Cycle city: Shanghai ramps up its bike-share schemes. Retrieved April 2, 2012, from http://www.cnngo.com/shanghai/play/shanghai-gets-its-ride-shanghai-rideshare-307485.

Knowledge@Wharton. (2010). Expo 2010's legacy: What did Shanghai gain? Retrieved April 2, 2012, from http://www.knowledgeatwharton.com.cn/index.cfm?fa=viewArticle&articleID=2336&languageid=1

Kovac, Matt. (2006). China's green issues set to burst bubble. *ICIS Chemical Business, 1*(40), 13.

Kropp, Robert. (2011). Shanghai stock exchange to launch index for low-carbon companies. Retrieved April 2, 2012, from http://www.greenbiz.com/news/2011/08/02/shanghai-stock-exchange-launch-index-low-carbon-companies

Lee, Leo Ou-Fan. (1999). Shanghai modern. Cambridge, MA: Harvard University Press.

Li, Junxiang, et al. (2011). Impacts of landscape structure on surface urban heat islands: A case study of Shanghai, China. *Remote Sensing of Environment, 115*(12), 3249–3263.

Lina, Yang. (2012). Shanghai's GDP grows 8.2% in 2011. Retrieved April 2, 2012, from http://news.xinhuanet.com/english/china/2012-01/20/c_131371288.htm

Minjie, Zha. (2012). Number of vehicles in city zooms past 2.5 million. Retrieved April 2, 2012, from http://english.eastday.com/e/120301/u1a6395330.html

Pandora, Neeno. (2011). Balcony farms sprout in city: Urban farming in Shanghai. Retrieved April 2, 2012, from http://www.theurbn.com/2011/05/balcony-farmers-sprout-city-urban-farming-shanghai/

Powell, Bill. (2011). Taming Shanghai's sprawl. Retrieved April 2, 2012, from http://www.time.com/time/specials/packages/article/0,28804,2026474_2026675_2046073,00.html

Rowe, Peter G. (2004). *Shanghai: Architecture and urbanism for modern China*. New York: Prestel Publishing.

Sachs, Jeffrey. (2008). Better city, better life: Challenges for Shanghai. Retrieved April 2, 2012, from http://www.earth.columbia.edu/sitefiles/file/about/director/pubs/Shanghai%20Daily_12November08.pdf

Scarlatelli, Andrea. (2010). Shanghai's gains (and losses) from the World Expo. Retrieved April 2, 2012, from http://www.echinacities.com/expat-corner/shanghai-s-gains-and-losses-from-the-world-expo.html

Shasha, Deng. (2012). Shanghai sets 2012 GDP growth at 8 pct. Retrieved April 2, 2012, from http://news.xinhuanet.com/english/china/2012-01/11/c_131354762.htm

Shi, C. (2004). Evaluation of coastal zone sustainability: An integrated approach applied in Shanghai Municipality and Chong Ming Island. *Journal of Environmental Management, 71*(4), 335–344.

Wagner, Cynthia G. (2008). China's eco-city: Model for urban sustainability. *Futurist, 42*(3), 68.

Wenjun, Cai. (2012). Shanghai life expectancy rises to 82.51 years. Retrieved April 2, 2012, from http://www.shanghaidaily.com/nsp/Metro/2012/02/20/Shanghai%2Blife%2Bexpectancy%2Brises%2Bto%2B8251%2Byears/

Wenjun, Cai. (2011). Shanghai's population reaches 22m. Retrieved April 2, 2012, from http://www.shanghaidaily.com/nsp/Metro/2011/04/07/Shanghais%2Bpopulation%2Breaches%2B22m/

Winter, Tim. (Ed.). (2012). *Shanghai Expo: An international forum on the future of cities*. New York: Routledge.

Xueqin, Jiang. (2011). How Shanghai schools beat them all. Retrieved April 2, 2012, from http://globalpublicsquare.blogs.cnn.com/2011/08/01/how-shanghai-schools-beat-them-all/

Yiyao, Wu. (2011). Car-sharing will ease Shanghai's traffic problems. Retrieved April 2, 2012, from http://www.chinadaily.com.cn/cndy/2011-01/08/content_11812146.htm

Zhao, Shuqing, et al. (2006). Ecological consequences of rapid urban expansion: Shanghai, China. *Frontiers in Ecology and the Environment, 4*(7), 341–346.

Zoninsein, Manuela. (2012). Sustainable in Shanghai. Retrieved April 2, 2012, from http://www.zesterdaily.com/environment/1300-shanghai-chefs-adopt-sustainable-practices.

Singapore

5.1 million est. pop. 2010, including 1.8 million foreign workers/residents

The island city-state of Singapore is an economic powerhouse, located in a geographically strategic location on key trade routes. Planning is constrained by the island's small size, limited resources, and growing population. Environmental awareness (and stresses on its water and other natural resources) has put Singapore in the forefront of water technologies and green urban planning.

Located in the center of Southeast Asia, between China and India, Singapore is a small city-state with a 2010 population of 5.1 million people (1.8 million are foreign workers/residents) living within a 712.4 square kilometer land area. It was established by Sir Stamford Raffles, a British official (and founder of the London Zoo), in 1819, and in 1824 the island became a British colony. Singapore became part of the Federation of Malaysia from 1963 to 1965 before it gained independence in 1965. In 1967 it became one of the five founding members of the Association of Southeast Asian Nations (ASEAN). Singapore has been ruled by one political party, the People's Action Party (PAP), since 1959. The city-state is built around fifteen "towns," each with their respective town councils.

Singapore had a per capita gross national product (GNP) of S$59,813 in 2010 (S$1.25 = US$1), and the median income per month was S$2,400. In 2008, the World Bank and International Monetary Fund (IMF) placed Singapore as the fourth-highest per capita (PPP) earning country globally. In 2011 Singapore ranked third in the global competitiveness rankings. Despite its modern foundations, Singapore has remained a multiethnic (Chinese, Malays, Indians), multireligious (Daoism, Buddhism, Islam, Christianity, Hinduism), and multilingual (there are currently four official languages: Malay, Chinese, Tamil, and English) society.

Economy

Singapore's economy is based on four pillars: transportation and communication, finance, high-tech industry, and tourism. The city-state controls 2 percent of global trade. Singapore has always been an important global shipping hub. In 2010 the port handled a gross of 48 million tons of goods, placing it among the top-ten ship registries in the world. In 2010 the port was ranked the second-busiest container port in the world after Shanghai.

Besides being a port city, Singapore has also become a major air hub since the development of Changi International Airport. In 2010, Changi Airport serviced 100 airlines flying to over 200 cities in 60 countries and handled more than 42 million passengers. The airport remains the regional air hub for both British Airways and Qantas.

Since the mid-1960s, Singapore has gradually been building its role as a financial hub in Asia and the world. In 2010, it had 2,880 financial institutions that managed over US$1.1 trillion. In 2011, the Chinese government decided to make Singapore the second offshore hub for trading the yuan.

Like most developing countries, Singapore was a processing center for raw materials based on cottage industries during its colonial period. Since independence, Singapore rapidly industrialized. As Singapore developed over the decades, many labor-intensive industries were replaced with higher-level industries requiring skilled labor. In modern times, Singapore is an industrial base for microchips, airplane industrial parts, pharmaceuticals, biotechnology, environmental technologies, ships and oil rigs, a prominent research and development

(R&D) center, and the second-largest oil refining center (Exxon-Mobil and Shell) globally.

Tourism remains a key industry in Singapore, contributing 10 percent of the city-state's GNP and attracting 11.6 million tourists in 2010, and the city-state's educational institutions also attract many foreign students. Singapore's tourism industry is founded on cultural attractions, such as zoological gardens and ethnic districts of Chinatown and Little India. In 2010, two major integrated resort casinos were opened: the US-based Marina Bay Sands (MBS) and the Malaysian-developed Resorts World Sentosa (RWS). RWS includes the family attraction of Universal Studios. In their first year of operation, both casinos reaped record returns.

Environment

Singapore was one of the first countries to establish a Ministry of the Environment (ENV), in 1972. Since renamed the Ministry of Water Resources and the Environment (MEWR), the agency handles mainly the "brown" issues (clean water, pollution, sewage, waste disposal, energy, public health) while the Ministry of National Development (MND) oversees the "green" issues (parks and gardens, tree planting, biodiversity). Singapore's main environmental nongovernmental organizations (NGOs) are the Nature Society, Singapore (NSS), and the government-assisted Singapore Environment Council (SEC). Broadly speaking, the NSS concentrates on green issues such as biodiversity and nature reserves while the SEC handles a lot of the brown issues and provides environmental awards for green companies and organizations.

As a city-state, Singapore has major sustainability handicaps since all its major essential needs are imported—water, food, natural resources, and energy. Its ecological footprint is thus large, with food imports coming from as far as Brazil and the United States. Its large food imports leave a large virtual or embedded water footprint. (Virtual water is the water used to produce a good or service.) The state's oil comes from the Middle East countries, and gas from Indonesia and Malaysia.

Water Technologies

Despite an annual rainfall of 2,400 millimeters, Singapore is classified as a water-stressed (less than 1,000 cubic meters of water per capita) country. Singapore has been dependent on Malaysian water since the early twentieth century. The rocky political relationships between former prime ministers Mahathir Mohamed of Malaysia and Lee Kuan Yew of Singapore was a blessing in disguise for Singapore, as it compelled the city-state to begin to explore ways to become water independent. Besides importing Malaysian water (which will cease in 2061), Singapore relies on three domestic water sources: developing reservoirs from all its rivers, recycling water, and desalinization.

Singapore remains one of the world's leaders in water technology, both by government agencies (Public Utilities Board) and private sector companies (Hyflux, Black and Veatch, Siemens Water). It exports its water technologies to North Africa, the Middle East, China, Vietnam, and Australia. The water industries contributed S$1.25 billion of gross domestic product (GDP) in 2010, and the target is S$1.7 billion by 2015.

Urban Planning

Singapore's successful intra-urban environmental programs are the foundation for accumulated eco-city expertise, which is exported to China and other countries. Despite its oil refining, industrial activities, incineration plants, and transportation activities, Singapore's air quality is relatively good. Given its concern with air pollution and traffic congestion, Singapore has introduced innovative ways of limiting vehicle transportation into the city during peak periods by the electronic road pricing (ERP) system. It has introduced a novel way of restricting car population by a monthly tender system, the certificate of entitlement (COE). It has invested heavily on a public transportation system based on an integration of the mass rapid transit (MRT) with public buses. The city-state is currently building a bicycle route around the island to promote a green and healthy lifestyle. It also is providing green corridors (trees, parks) around the island to encourage bird life and other organic life forms.

Given its small finite space, Singapore is expanding its livable space in three ways: through land reclamation, which has increased land area by over 22 percent over the last forty years; vertical space; and underground space. Singapore's spatial and land-use limitations make planning essential and necessary for the city-state's development programs. The government aims to increase population to 6.5 million, which will mean more compact urban planning and development. As with other cities, Singapore faces increasing challenges with the impending environmental impacts from climate change, such as intense precipitation that causes major urban floods, heat waves, and higher sea-level rises. These are likely to affect both tourism and domestic residential patterns.

Victor R. SAVAGE
National University of Singapore

See also Association of Southeast Asian Nations (ASEAN); Automobiles and Personal Transportation;

Cities—Overview; Jakarta, Indonesia; Information and Communication Technologies (ICT); Kuala Lumpur, Malaysia; Labor; Outsourcing and Offshoring; Public Transportation; Rule of Law; Utilities Regulation and Energy Efficiency; Water Security

FURTHER READING

Ban, Kah Choon; Pakir, Anne; & Tong, Chee Kiong (Eds.) (2004). *Imagining Singapore*. Singapore: Eastern Universities Press by Marshall Cavendish.

Briffett, Clive, & Ho, Hua Chew. (2002). *State of the natural environment in Singapore*. Singapore: Nature Society.

Chong, Terence. (Ed.) (2010). *Management of success: Singapore revisited*. Singapore: Institute of Southeast Asian Studies.

Chua Beng Huat. (2011). Singapore as model: Planning innovations, knowledge, experts. In Ananya Roy & Aihwa Ong (Eds.), *Worlding cities: Asian experiments and the art of being global* (pp. 29–54). Oxford, UK: Wiley-Blackwell.

Frost, Mark Ravinder, & Yu-Mei, Balasingamchow. (2009). *Singapore: A biography*. Singapore: EDM & National Museum of Singapore.

Jayakumar, S. (2011). *Diplomacy: A Singapore experience*. Singapore: Straits Times Press.

Lee Kuan Yew. (2000). *From third world to first: The Singapore story, 1965–2000*. New York: Harper Collins.

Lee Kuan Yew. (2000). *The Singapore story: Memoirs of Lee Kuan Yew*. Singapore: Singapore Press Holdings.

Ng, Peter K. L.; Corlett, R. T.; & Tan, Hugh, T. W. (2011). *Singapore biodiversity: An encyclopedia of the natural environment and sustainable development*. Singapore: Didier Miller.

Lee, Poh Oon. (2010). The four taps: Water self-sufficiency in Singapore. In Terence Chong (Ed.), *Management of success: Singapore revisited* (pp. 417–439). Singapore: Institute of Southeast Asian Studies.

Ministry of the Environment, Singapore. (1993). *The Singapore green plan: Action programmes*. Singapore: The Ministry of the Environment.

Neo, Boon Siong, & Chen, Geraldine. (2007). *Dynamic governance: Embedding culture, capabilities and change in Singapore*. Singapore: World Scientific Co.

Savage, Victor R. (2004). Singapore's environmental ideology. In Kah Choon Ban, Anne Pakir & Chee Kiong Tong (Eds.), *Imagining Singapore* (pp. 210–239). Singapore: Eastern Universities Press by Marshall Cavendish.

Tan, Yong Soon; Lee, Tung Jean; & Tan, Karen. (2009). *Clean, green and blue: Singapore's journey towards environmental and water sustainability*. Singapore: Institute of Southeast Asian Studies.

South–North Water Diversion

Water shortages in northern China have become increasingly acute as pressures from agriculture, industry, and population have grown. The government has undertaken a massive engineering project that aims to transfer nearly 45 billion cubic meters of water annually from the water-rich Yangzi (Chang) River watershed in southern China to the dry north. The South–North Water Diversion project presents numerous challenges in engineering, social and ecological impacts, and administrative oversight.

China's South–North Water Diversion (SNWD; *nánshuǐ běidiào* in Chinese) aims to resolve water shortages in northern China with one of the largest, most technically challenging, and most expensive engineering projects the world has ever seen. The project features three massive conduits—eastern, central, and western—that will transfer approximately 44.8 cubic kilometers (44.8 billion cubic meters) of water hundreds of kilometers from the water-rich Yangzi (Chang) River in southern China to drier areas in the Huang (Yellow) River basin in the north. Aside from inherent engineering difficulties—pumping 14 billion cubic meters per year of water uphill along the eastern route or traversing towering ridges at the edge of the Tibetan Plateau—the project presents numerous challenges for social, ecological, and institutional sustainability.

Background and Overview

China is not water poor, but the geographic and temporal distribution of freshwater resources across the continent-size country is quite uneven. Southern China receives the lion's share of precipitation, due primarily to the summer monsoons. These rains, coupled with the tropical and subtropical climate, make possible double and even triple cropping of wet rice in some southern provinces. They also bring flood conditions that threatened some 3 million people in the southern city of Wuhan in 1998 and tested the flood-control limits of the Three Gorges Dam in 2010.

The 6,300-kilometer-long Yangzi River drains much of southern China, channeling some 951.3 billion cubic meters per year of runoff to the sea—fourteen times as much as the Huang River in the north (National Bureau of Statistics 2010). Faced with what he saw as an overabundance of water in China's south, Chairman Mao Zedong, in the early days of the People's Republic of China, suggested that the drought-prone north simply borrow water from the south. Mao's musings are today materializing in the form of the SNWD (State Council Office of the SNWD Construction Committee 2003). Agricultural, industrial, and municipal users' ever-increasing demands for freshwater have brought greater stresses to north China's water resources, lending urgency to what once seemed a far-flung idea.

Project Details

The SNWD project aims to channel water along three routes: eastern, central, and western. Each presents its own challenges. Work officially began in 2002, and plans originally called for the eastern route to be completed in time for the 2008 Beijing Olympics. A number of problems have delayed the project and pushed the target date for completion of that route to 2013 or later, and the final (western) route, if it is built at all, should be finished after 2030. (See figure 1 on the next page.)

Figure 1

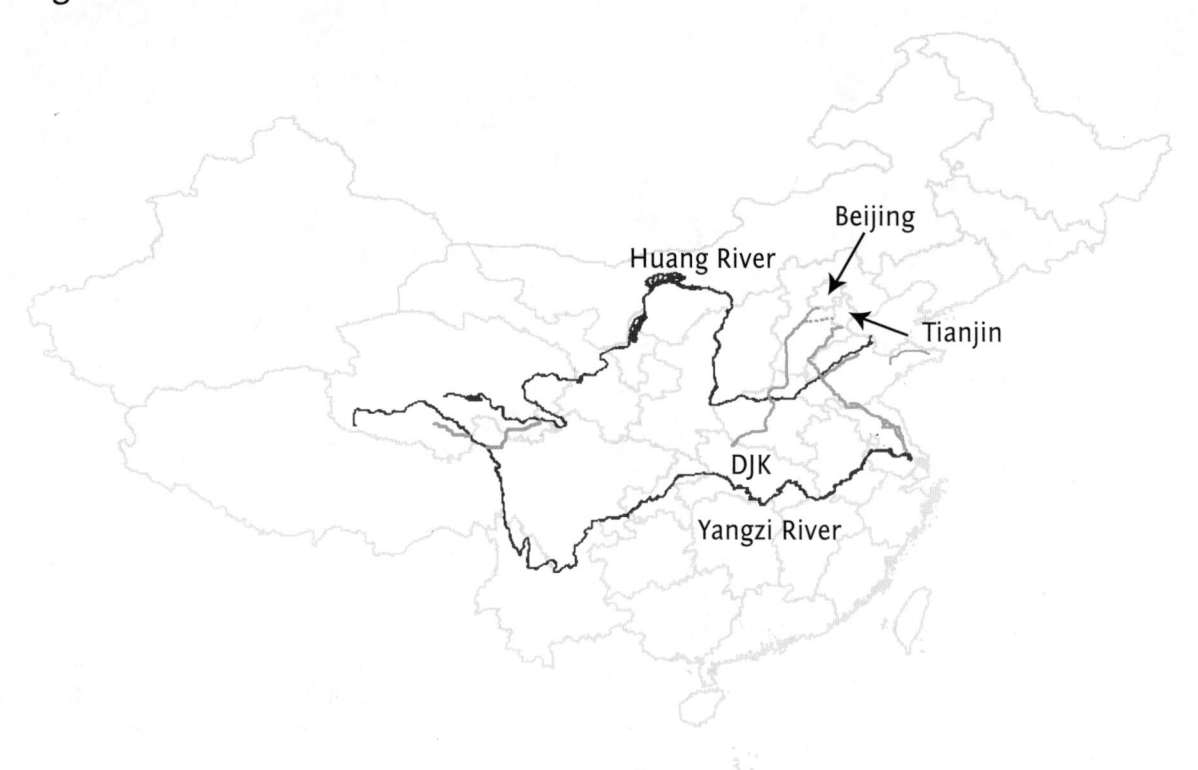

Source: Magee (2011a, 1501). Printed with kind permission from Springer, 10 April 2012. The original publication is available at www.springerlink.com.

An overview of China's South–North Water Diversion project. Eastern, central, and western conduits will carry more than 48 cubic kilometers of water from the water-rich south to the drought-prone north when the project is complete.

The Eastern Route

The channel for the eastern route is essentially complete, consisting of interconnected waterways that constitute the ancient Grand Canal that has linked southern and northern China for more than a thousand years. The route is 1,150 kilometers long and is expected to transfer 14.8 billion cubic meters of water annually. It suffers from one vexing fact, however: the highest point in the channel bed is just a few hundred kilometers from its output. Pumps must lift the water originating in the south past that high point before it will finally flow downhill to its destination. According to the office of the SNWD Construction Committee, this task requires nearly seventy pumping stations along the first two-thirds of the route, making the SNWD not only a water project but also an energy project. To lift some 15 trillion kilograms of water per year, those pumps would require more than 1,600 terawatt-hours (equal to 1 trillion watts) of electricity each year. Coal-fired power plants would generate some 70 percent of this electricity. The eastern route traverses numerous heavily industrialized and densely populated areas, many contributing runoff polluted with industrial, agricultural, and municipal waste. The success of the eastern route at bringing "fresh" water northward, therefore, depends on improving waste-water treatment capabilities in over a hundred cities and counties along the route, a capital- and energy-intensive undertaking.

The Central Route

The central route is somewhat simpler from a technical standpoint since it requires no pumping. It does, however, feature a tunnel under the Huang River and requires raising the height of the existing dam at Danjiangkou, whose reservoir provides the input for the central route, nearly 15 meters. This will enable water to flow by gravity northward along the 1,380-kilometer channel. The central route is eventually expected to transfer 14 billion cubic meters of water annually to northern China, but according to a prominent Chinese water industry source, that is unlikely to happen before 2030 (Zhou, Yang, and Shi 2011).

The state has set interim goals on the order of moving 9–10 billion cubic meters of water per year, but technical and political challenges on both the eastern and central routes have already caused some delays and may well further postpone development. If the project develops the central route to its full capacity, it will transfer an expected 9 billion cubic meters of its annual volume directly to the Huang River. It will send the remaining 5 billion cubic meters to Beijing and its neighboring metropolis to the east, Tianjin—megacities that collectively housed roughly 30 million people in 2011. The central route, like its eastern counterpart, traverses populous and developed areas, creating similar demands for water treatment infrastructure along the way. Because the central route requires construction of a new channel, it will displace more people than will the other two routes. Population displacement, of course, is a key concern in a country with high population densities in central and eastern regions and limited arable land per person. In principle, compensation for evacuated residents should accompany all displacement (from SNWD, dams, or other projects), but outcomes are often far from ideal because of the social dislocation involved in large-scale resettlement efforts.

The Western Route

The western route is by far the most ambitious from a technical and engineering standpoint. If constructed, it will supplement upper Huang tributaries with water from the headwaters of upper Yangzi tributaries (and perhaps others), at elevations ranging from 3,000 to 4,500 meters above sea level. The multistage diversion will require pumping stations, siphons, and dozens of kilometers of tunnels in some of the country's most challenging terrain and climate conditions. Parts of the western route infrastructure will intersect areas of extreme cultural and biological diversity, creating a different set of social and environmental challenges than the central and eastern routes. The mountainous region of southwestern China (encompassing parts of Tibet [Xinzang] Autonomous Region and Yunnan and Sichuan provinces) already boasts a number of national- and international-level biodiversity hotspots and United Nations Economic, Social and Cultural Organization (UNESCO)–designated areas of cultural and biological diversity. Geopolitical instability is a threat if the western route dips into the Yarlung Tsangpo, an upper tributary of the Brahmaputra and Ganges rivers, which could cause controversy in India and Bangladesh, both downstream countries.

Outlook

China's history is rich with ambitious water management projects, and the future looks to be no different. Although some engineering fixes like the SNWD, which see increased water supply as the solution to regional water shortages, are inevitable, aggressive water conservation efforts accompanied by sound ecological and cultural preservation policies and practices, along with robust and transparent administrative oversight mechanisms, should supplement those solutions. Failing that, the long-term social and ecological sustainability of mega-engineering projects like the SNWD is questionable.

Darrin MAGEE
Hobart and William Smith Colleges

See also Agriculture (China and Southeast Asia); Beijing, China; China; Great Green Wall (China); The Himalaya; Huang (Yellow) River; Three Gorges Dam; Tibetan Plateau; Transboundary Water Issues; Utilities Regulation and Energy Efficiency; Water Security; Yangzi (Chang) River

FURTHER READING

Conservation International. (n.d.). Biodiversity hotspots: Mountains of southwest China. Retrieved March 15, 2012, from http://www.biodiversityhotspots.org/xp/hotspots/china/Pages/default.aspx

Liu, Changming. (1998). Environmental issues and the South–North Water transfer scheme. *The China Quarterly, 156* (Special Issue: China's Environment), 899–910.

Magee, Darrin. (2011a). Moving the river? China's South-North Water transfer project. In Stanley D. Brunn (Ed.), *Engineering Earth: The impacts of megaengineering projects* (pp. 1499–1514). Dordrecht, The Netherlands: Springer.

Magee, Darrin. (2011b). Polluted water challenges China's engineering efforts. Retrieved December 6, 2011, from http://www.asiapacificmemo.ca/polluted-water-challenges-china-engineering-efforts

National Bureau of Statistics. (Ed.). (2010). *China statistical yearbook.* Beijing: China Statistics Press.

State Council Office of the SNWD Construction Committee. (n.d.). South-to-North Water Diversion. Retrieved December 28, 2011 from http://www.nsbd.gov.cn/zx/english/

State Council Office of the SNWD Construction Committee. (2003, August 29). SNWD major events timeline of 1952. Retrieved April 24, 2009, from http://www.nsbd.gov.cn/zx/dsj/20030829/200308290015.htm [in Chinese]

United Nations Education, Scientific and Educational Organization (UNESCO). (n.d.). World Heritage list. Retrieved March 15, 2012, from http://whc.unesco.org/en/list

Zhou Tao, Yang Zhaohan, & Shi Fuquan. (2011, January 21). *Nán shuǐ běi diào dōng xiàn tōngshuǐ hòu Hàihé liúyù shuǐ zīyuán pèizhì fēnxī* [Analysis of Hai River watershed configuration following completion of South–North Water Diversion]. Retrieved March 21, 2012, from http://www.hwcc.gov.cn/pub/hwcc/ztxx/hhslw/12345/12346/201101/t20110121_327622.html [in Chinese]

Share the *Encyclopedia of Sustainability*: Teachers are welcome to make up to ten (10) copies of no more than two (2) articles for distribution in a single course or program. For further permissions, please visit www.copyright.com or contact: info@berkshirepublishing.com

Southeast Asia

622 million combined est. pop. 2012.

Southeast Asia consists of eleven countries and is an area that is historically significant as well as culturally rich. The region has a large and often very crowded population (over 622 million people as of 2012) and has seen much social and political change in the past few decades, which has caused major environmental problems, including pollution, deforestation, and increasing carbon dioxide emissions. Environmental protection has been slow to occur in recent years.

Southeast Asia is made up of eleven countries: Laos, Cambodia, Vietnam, Thailand, Malaysia, Indonesia, Singapore, Myanmar (Burma), Brunei, the Philippines, and East Timor. It has a subtropical climate and is hot and humid all year; the temperature rarely drops below 20°C. Over 622 million people live in the region, with roughly 40 percent (248.2 million) living in Indonesia, the world's fourth most populous nation, and the world's most populous Muslim nation. Other populous countries include the Philippines (103.7 million); Vietnam (91.5 million); Thailand (67 million); Myanmar (Burma) (54.5 million); and Malaysia (29.1 million) (US CIA 2012). Southeast Asia is a resource-rich region with a long history of colonial exploitation. Burma and Thailand were exploited for their rice, teak, and minerals; Java (part of Indonesia) for coffee and sugar; the Philippines for sugar, abaca, and coconuts; and Malaysia for palm oil and rubber. Deforestation has been a major factor in environmental change in the region, as has industrialization (Parnwell and Bryant 1996, 4–5).

Some of the world's greatest rivers—the Irrawaddy, Red, and Mekong-Lancang—all flow through the region, which gives it good accessibility (both historically and in the twenty-first century). The regions with the most significance are the lowlands surrounding these great rivers; today these areas are densely populated. Geographically, the region is made up of mountains as well as rivers and lowland areas. The mountains are the remains of once-great ranges and have gentle rolling slopes interspersed with areas of younger mountains that are characterized by steeper slopes, mostly consisting of active or extinct volcanoes. These younger mountains provide the spine of Indonesia and the Philippines, which link to the older mountains on the edge of the western Pacific Ocean (Karan 2004, 243–244). Tropical Southeast Asia, with its rain forests, is one of the Earth's most diverse ecosystems. From a worldwide total of 250,000 flowering plant species, a massive 170,000 are tropical; of these, 40,000 are in Asia and 25,000 alone live in Malaysia and Indonesia (Weightman 2006, 34).

Ancient History and the Middle Ages

About 3000 BCE, the two major populations of people in Asia were concentrated in the east and south of the continent (notably China and the Indus River valley region of northern India and Pakistan). These regions had agricultural systems that were advanced enough to encourage growth and allow expansion (Weightman 2006, 49). People began moving en masse into maritime Southeast Asia from south China between 2500 and 1500 BCE. Early bronze working occurred in 2000 BCE, probably with techniques imported from China. Iron was worked as early as 500 BCE and was used for practical purposes—making farming implements, weapons, and jewelry (Lockard 2009, 7, 10). The ability to create agricultural ecosystems, as communities settled down and began to farm, led to landscape changes, notably the cultivation of wet rice that could sustain large numbers of people (Barnard 2010, 173).

Indian traders dominated the region until 1500 CE. There was also Indian expansion in the early Common Era into southern Thailand, Burma, and Cambodia (Karan 2004, 245; Jameson 2008, 4). As pressure from the Chinese intensified, various people of the Yunnan area (the southern tip of China), including the Lao, Shan, and Thai, were forced southward and established a new state of Siam (now called Thailand) (Karan 2004, 246).

Soil erosion can be seen as early as 1000 BCE in the Khao Wong Pra Chan valley in Thailand, a direct result of deforestation to meet fuel requirements needed for smelting. Evidence of salt extraction has been discovered in central Thailand, and evidence of moated settlements has been found. Wood was one of the principal items traded with neighbors China and India and further afield (Chew 2001, 100–103).

By the eleventh century, maritime trade had become an important aspect of life in the region. Both the Chinese and Arabs were actively trading in Southeast Asia. This area of trading became much larger when Indian Ocean routes became central to Southeast Asia and the Middle East in the course of the century (Lockard 2009, 63). By 1500, Southeast Asia was united by its environment and by increasing commerce, but divided by war, religion, and cultural differences.

At the beginning of the sixteenth century, Europeans began to arrive (Lockard 2009, 74). The Portuguese arrived in 1511, and sometime afterward, the Dutch landed in Java and established settlements at Bantam (1600) and Batavia (now Jakarta, 1619). At a similar time the Spanish appeared and invaded the Philippines (Karan 2004, 246).

Seventeenth and Eighteenth Centuries

In the 1600s, the Spanish and Portuguese were faced with a new player in the region—the Dutch. They already had colonies in South Africa and Sri Lanka and were now looking further east. During the following centuries, the Dutch established a power hold on much of Indonesia, with the exception of the Portuguese half of the island of Timor. Eventually the Dutch focused on Java as a place of importance in their growing empire (Lockard 2009, 85–86). The British and French came to the region in the seventeenth and eighteenth centuries. Most of the Malay Peninsula had not been colonized, except for Portuguese and Dutch Melaka, before the late 1700s. Penang Island, in the Malay Peninsula, was taken by the British in 1786, and Singapore was taken in 1819, giving the British access to the South China Sea (Karan 2004, 245; Lockard 2009, 98).

Nineteenth and Twentieth Centuries

In the nineteenth century, the Netherlands controlled Indonesia (the Dutch East Indies); the French, Indochina (Vietnam, Cambodia, and Laos); the British, Hong Kong, Burma, Borneo, and Malaysia; and the United States (by 1900), the Philippines. These colonial powers also exploited the landscape of Southeast Asia. Burma was viewed by Britain as an extension of its Indian Empire, and as such its economy and resources were developed. Rubber was planted over much of Sumatra, Malaysia, and Indonesia, radically changing the environment. Tin was also extracted in Malaysia, Indonesia, and Thailand. Many of the workers growing rubber and mining tin were foreign; they needed their own quarters and living areas. Cities had to be accessed, so there was a rapid increase in transportation links (Weightman 2006, 335–336). Colonial powers expanded and adapted indigenous ideas of resource use so much so that by the end of colonial rule, commercial resource exploitation was prevalent throughout the region (Bryant 1998, 30–31).

Colonial ideas of science and technology were also used in the Southeast Asian setting. Transport was expanded to allow for large-scale resource extraction. Railways and steamboats, the primary forms of transporting these resources, were also used to transport laborers to sites of exploitation to ensure the maximum amounts of products were produced. Advances in drilling in mines also allowed previously unobtainable products to be excavated (Bryant 1998, 37–44).

At the start of the twentieth century, all countries in Southeast Asia except Thailand were controlled by the British, Dutch, French, and the United States. Thailand is the only country in the region never to have been colonized.

In terms of industrialization, the region entered the "modern period" (i.e., experiencing a rapid growth in industrialization) around the 1970s. High-rise buildings were rapidly built and became as common as they were in the West, with large numbers of people inhabiting them. They were full of air-conditioning units, and with this period of development and industrialization came the growth of consumerism—televisions, personal computers, cars, radios, dishwashers, washing machines, and so on. Consumerism grew exponentially in Southeast Asian households (Boomgaard 2007, 273–275).

As with any period of industrialization, this caused serious environmental issues. In big cities, such as Jakarta (capital of Indonesia) and Bangkok (capital of Thailand), the increased road transport, precipitated by more people owning cars, led to major road congestion. This also caused high levels of air pollution to become prevalent in big cities, and a thin haze of pollutants still hangs in the lower atmosphere immediately above these big industrial areas. Deforestation and soil erosion is also a major problem, particularly in coastal and forested areas, as is water pollution—not only from waste from growing towns and cities but also from fertilizers and chemicals running into lakes and rivers (Boomgaard 2007, 274–275). This pollution of land, air, and water, which have been familiar features of the industrial landscape of the West for more than a century, have now reached Southeast Asia (Boomgaard 2007, 275).

Contemporary Environmental Issues

By far the largest and worst environmental problem that currently plagues the region is deforestation; the major cause is commercial logging. Southeast Asian forests hold high value, and much of the wood imported to the West today originates from these forests; however, most of these forests are logged illegally. As a result of this unlawful logging, animal species extinction is a major issue, especially with the depletion of rainforest cover in areas like Borneo and Sumatra. Two endangered examples include the Sumatran rhino and the Sumatran tiger. In addition to loss of habitat, these animals have also been affected by the use of traditional Asian medicines, which hold that rhino horns and tiger bones have medicinal properties (IUCN 2012; WWF n.d.a and n.d.b). Perhaps the most well-known animal of the region, the orangutan, is also endangered due to the continuing destruction of its home—the Indonesian rain forest.

A major health threat hit Southeast Asia in 2006—bird flu (H5N1). The region was more at risk than other areas owing to the fact that humans and birds, especially chickens, live in closer proximity to each other than they might elsewhere in the world (Boomgaard 2007, 281). Rivers and seas are increasingly polluted with untreated human waste, pesticides, herbicides, mercury from mining operations, and artificial fertilizers. All of this pollution ends up entering the food chain through animals eating seafood, plants, or other contaminated food products (Boomgaard 2007, 281).

Pollution was a problem prior to 1960, but since then, with rapid industrialization and the emergence of a more modern state, it has grown exponentially and is now a major environmental issue. Before the 1960s pollution was mainly localized; today, however, it is national and even international. Air pollution is an especially big problem in the region. It results from high population growth, high rates of urbanization, increasing industrialization, and a growing use of fossil fuels per capita. Forest fires have added to this problem, such as those of Sumatra and Borneo in 1997–1998, which affected the air as far away as in Singapore (Boomgaard 2007, 314).

The rapid increase in large-scale exploitation of the forests of Southeast Asia since the 1960s has been disastrous. A huge decrease in forest populations has occurred in recent years. Thailand has witnessed a decrease in mature forest cover from approximately 55 percent in 1960 to 20 percent in 2000 (see below for activism in Thailand relating to deforestation). In the same period, the Philippines has seen its mature forest cover drop from 45 percent to 20 percent; in Indonesia those figures are from 70 percent to 50 percent respectively; and in Cambodia and Laos the figure today hovers around 50 percent mature forest cover (Boomgaard 2007, 303–305). Deforestation brings with it problems such as increased production of carbon dioxide, which causes more carbon dioxide to enter the atmosphere. Soil erosion also is prolific with deforestation, which causes further problems such as desertification.

Much damage has also been done to forests during the many military engagements in the region; during the Vietnam War, Agent Orange was used to deforest huge areas so the North Vietnamese army could not use the jungle for survival and fighting. Greenhouse gases—notably carbon dioxide, methane, and nitrous oxide—have increased sharply in the region over the last few decades. Carbon dioxide has been produced from forest fires and industrial processes; methane has come from land and agriculture, especially wet land used in rice cultivation; and nitrous oxide has been produced mainly from fertilizers and animal manure (Boomgaard 2007, 304). Large-scale expansion of biofuels is also a concern; palm-oil production has greatly increased in the region with rain forest destruction in Sumatra and in Borneo, and it has also created a local "haze" from burning the land in preparation for clearing. Wet rice cultivation results in the release of the greenhouse gas methane, and projections show a fourfold increase in total carbon dioxide emissions in the region between 2002 and 2030 (Symon 2007).

Water pollution is an equally serious problem. Again, although this was not new in the 1960s, it has increased significantly since then. Huge amounts of pollutants now enter rivers and estuaries (Boomgaard 2007, 315–316). In 2000 a navigation agreement passed between China, Thailand, Laos, and Myanmar, in which they promised to develop their ports so ships from the others countries could dock there. Many of the plans were scaled down, not only because of cost but also because of the environmental damage these ports would cause. Farmers, who plant crops along riverbanks and rely on natural flood waters to irrigate the soil, were concerned that the seasonal flow of water would be disrupted, and also that large ships would disturb the flow of waves, which would drown their plants. On the Mekong, fishermen already complain that fast rapids caused by large ships are adversely affecting fish supply and that these rapids cause smaller ships to overturn (Weightman 2006, 327).

Local Environmentalism

Southeast Asia has a number of environmental movements that have emerged since the 1970s. Geographically spread out, they have also campaigned on area-specific issues. For example, in the Philippines during the 1970s and 1980s, the movement engaged in struggles against nuclear power; in Thailand, the Philippines, and Indonesia, against hydroelectric projects; and in Thailand and the Philippines, against deforestation and marine pollution. These were not small-scale events; many resulted in epic battles, like the struggle against the Chico River Dam in the northern Philippines and the fight against the Pak Mun Dam in northeastern Thailand, which forced the World Bank to withdraw its planned support for hydroelectric projects. In this region, protest was done by the masses—not just middle-class activists. In the Chico struggle, the opposition was made up of indigenous people, while in the fight against the Pak Mun Dam, it was smallholders and fisherfolk who fought (Bello 2007).

The demand for pulp has resulted in an alliance between state and business groups that have been attempting to evict poor people from their lands under the guise that they are preserving the forests. Local resistance has occurred. The idea of "forest monks" in Thailand and the communal management of village forests predate modern environmentalism and the rise of "modern" environmental management systems (Rigg 2003, 56–57, 63). In Thailand, the Land Redistribution Programme for the Poor Living in Forest Reserves was imposed controversially in 1990. It was set up to rehouse 250,000 families who lived illegally on 2.25 million hectares of forest reserve land and 800,000 hectares of degraded forest land, but land allocated for resettlement was smaller and poorer in quality than the land the families had left. A Buddhist monk, Phra Prajak Khuttajitto, who lived in the forest in northeastern Thailand, stayed with the people who were threatened with eviction. At first Prajak had to convince the people of the importance of forest management and ecosystems. He outlined how the local families could help and promoted sustainable community forestry (Rigg 2003, 65–66).

Out of the carnage of Thailand's (and specifically Bangkok's) economic growth and environmental destruction, especially through large-scale logging, local Buddhist monks have been "ordaining" trees, tying orange robes—usually worn by the monks themselves—around the tree trunks. Through this method, and by working with small villages and local communities, they are slowly saving Thailand's disappearing forests. The monks value the forests as a close connection to the teachings of the Buddha; seeing the forests as important to both the physical and spiritual well-being of locals, the brave monks have gone into areas where illegal logging has occurred and ordained the trees. The ceremonies are large, and the monks hope this will dispel loggers from cutting down trees for fear they will experience bad karma. In provinces across Thailand, the monks have been very successful (Kornfield 2007).

Unlike government environmental and agricultural policies, which are nationally oriented, the monks' focus is on the local communities and their quality of life. "In utilizing sustainable practices in the villages, the engaged Buddhists teach that the whole country will thrive when all of the individual parts are healthy" (Kornfield 2007). The monks have also founded the Independent Development Monks' Movement, which since the 1980s has rallied against consumerism and government policy that has negatively affected local farmers by moving them from subsistence to market farming, meaning farmers became dependent on outside markets.

Following the monks' examples, more environmental groups have sprung up across the country in recent years. One estimate, in 1999, was that thirty-nine community forests and one hundred fish sanctuaries existed across the country. Buddhist principles are being applied at every step of the journey. Buddhism teaches that suffering is caused by the grasping of material objects, and while poverty is not a blessing, wealth accumulation goes against Buddhist teaching (Kornfield 2007).

In 2009 there were over one hundred local environmental groups in Vietnam, most under three years old. Environmental activism also has a high level of interest among young people. Various groups offer different things. For example, the Raising Awareness on Environmental and Climate Change Program (RAECP) provides education in environmental issues and sustainable development. This organization was only established in

2008. The political situation in Vietnam (it is a socialist republic) makes it difficult for young people to speak to officials in government. RAECP is organized by professional and enthusiastic young activists who are eager to spread the message of sustainable development and green issues more widely to Vietnamese youth. Although difficult, they are persevering (Year of No Flying 2009; Chương trình Nâng 2012). There are also examples of wildlife protection from environmental activists in Vietnam, such as Nguyen Dinh Xuan, a legislator, National Assembly member, and director of the Lo Go-Xa Mat National Park. On visits to farms in May 2009 in Ha Long City and Quang Ninh, he found evidence of bears being bred for the bile they produced, which was sold to South Korean tourists. He sent letters to South Korean agencies making them aware of the situation and advising them not to buy any bile (Nhung 2010). Bear bile is used in traditional Chinese medicine, believed to reduce fever, protect the liver, improve eye sight, and act as an anti-inflammatory (Bear Necessity Korea 2009). The Budget Committee of the National Assembly of Korea has recently begun to discuss the topic of bear protection; however, work remains. It was revealed that at least three bear farms in Vietnam received South Korean tourists between August and December 2011 (Bear Necessity Korea 2012a and 2012b).

In Indonesia, the environmental activist Prigi Arisandi fights against water pollution. Surabaya, Indonesia's second largest city, is heavily industrialized, with much of the industry lying along the banks of its main waterway, the 41-kilometer Surabaya River. Since 1980, industry has regularly released thousands of tons of toxic effluent into the river, and much of the population remains unaware of the levels of toxins in the river. As much as 96 percent of the city's drinking water comes from the river, and high levels of mercury have been found in the water and in the blood of local people. Being educated and scientifically trained (he studied biology at university), Arisandi was aware of the dangers of the river water. He felt he had a commitment to the communities living along the river, and so he founded Ecological Observation and Wetlands Conservation (Ecoton) while still at university. The organization set out to protect the water resources and wetlands ecosystems of Indonesia. Arisandi won the Goldman Environmental Prize (which honors grassroots environmentalists) in 2011 for his pioneering activism. He has inspired many people to protect the river and has created experimental environmental education programs for the region. In 2007 he and his company sued the governor of East Java, as well as the area's environmental management agency, for failing to control water pollution. In 2008, the court issued a decision, telling the governor to introduce regulations relating to water quality for industries operating along the river bank, and establishing a maximum daily limit for release of chemicals into the river. This was the first time in the region a governor had been taken to court to change policy. Arisandi has also spoken directly to industry; a Surabaya sugar factory invested US$220,000 in a water treatment plant, meaning that it is now one of the most environmentally responsible companies based along the river bank (Goldman 2011).

In June 2011, Greenpeace ran a campaign against the toy company Mattel, manufacturer of the Barbie doll, for their association with Asia Pulp and Paper (APP), which Greenpeace claimed was responsible for deforestation of the Indonesian rain forest. Greenpeace said that by "analyzing the fibers in Barbie packaging and digging into the commercial links between various companies, we've been able to link the carbon-rich forests and peat-lands of Indonesia with the packaging of toys on sale in shops around the world. The trail leads directly from Mattel to APP and its suppliers in a chain of destruction that spans the globe" (Greenpeace 2011). They did stress that it is not just Mattel who uses the deforested trees in their packaging, but also Disney, Lego, and Hasbro. Nevertheless, Greenpeace ran a campaign in which Ken, Barbie's boyfriend, "dumped" her. By October, *New Internationalist* magazine ran a short piece saying that it had worked—at Mattel at least. Mattel had decided to suspend their contract for paper and packaging with APP and said they would convert to up to 70 percent recycled or sustainable fiber paper packaging by the end of 2011 (Healey and Powell 2011, 57).

The Future

Southeast Asia is one of the most vulnerable areas susceptible to climate change—many of its huge population live in low-lying areas close to rivers or on islands that could flood if water levels rise. Eight countries in the region have signed the Kyoto Protocol, but a 2011 report stated that, owing to the number of natural disasters in recent years, the region is already being disproportionately affected (AsiaOne 2011). What these stories all show is that in areas where climate change and environmental problems are major issues—such as Southeast Asia—which in the future will only get worse, there is still room for optimism and hope. There are people fighting for the rights of ordinary citizens, often inspiring them to fight themselves.

Mark WILSON
Northumbria University

See also Agriculture (China and Southeast Asia); Association of Southeast Asian Nations (ASEAN); Consumerism; Ecotourism; Endangered Species;

Indigenous Peoples; Jakarta, Indonesia; Kuala Lumpur, Malaysia; Mekong-Lancang River; Nongovernmental Organizations (NGOs); Public-Private Partnerships; Reforestation and Afforestation (Southeast Asia); Religions; Rule of Law; Rural Livelihoods; Rural Development; Singapore; Traditional Chinese Medicine (TCM)

FURTHER READING

AsiaOne. (2011, January 23). Climate change fastest in S-E Asia. Retrieved January 10, 2010, from http://www.asiaone.com/News/Latest+News/Asia/Story/A1Story20110123-259721.html

Barnard, Timothy P. (2010, February). Review of "Southeast Asia: An environmental history." *Journal of Southeast Asian Studies, 41*(1), 173–175.

Bear Necessity Korea. (2009, October 3). An "unbearable trade" and a dying wild population. Retrieved March 17, 2012, from http://bearnecessitykorea.com/

Bear Necessity Korea. (2012a). 2012 commitment. Retrieved March 17, 2012, from http://bearnecessitykorea.com/2012-commitment/

Bear Necessity Korea. (2012b). 2012: VN black markets and Korea: Dialogue. Retrieved March 17, 2012, from http://bearnecessitykorea.com/news/2012-vn-black-markets-and-korea-dialogue/

Bello, Walden. (2007, October). The environmental movement in the global South. Retrieved February 17, 2012, from http://www.tni.org/archives/act/17458

Boomgaard, Peter. (2007). *Southeast Asia: An environmental history*. Oxford, UK: ABC-CLIO.

Bryant, Raymond L. (1998). Resource politics in colonial South-East Asia: A conceptual analysis. In Victor T. King (Ed.), *Environmental challenges in South-East Asia* (pp. 29–52). Richmond, UK: Curzon Press.

Chew, Sing C. (2001). World ecological degradation: Accumulation, urbanization and deforestation 3000 BC–AD 2000. Oxford, UK: AltaMira.

Chương trình Nâng cao nhận thức về Môi trường và Biến đổi khí hậu (RAECP) [Awareness Programme on Environment and Climate Change]. (2012). *Giới thiệu tổ chức* [About the organization]. Retrieved February 17, 2012, from http://www.raecp.org/about-our-organization [in Vietnamese]

CTV News. (2008, February 13). Development pressures threaten Angkor Wat ruins. Retrieved January 9, 2012, from http://www.ctv.ca/CTVNews/SciTech/20080213/angkor_wat_080213/

Dove, Michael R., & Carpenter, Carol. (Eds.). (2008). *Environmental anthropology: A historical reader*. Oxford, UK: Blackwell Publishing.

Goldman Environmental Prize. (2011). Prigi Arisandi. Retrieved February 17, 2012, from http://www.goldmanprize.org/2011/islands

Greenpeace. (2011, June). Ken dumps Barbie! He doesn't date girls who are into deforestation. Retrieved January 6, 2012, from http://www.greenpeace.org.uk/blog/forests/ken-dumps-barbie-he-doesnt-date-girls-who-are-deforestation-20110607

Healey, Hazel, & Powell, Libby. (2011, December). Barbie sends deforesters packing. *New Internationalist, 448*, 57.

Hirsch, Philip, & Warren, Carol. (Eds.). (1998). *The politics of environment in Southeast Asia: Resources and resistance*. London: Routledge.

Hughes, J. Donald. (2009). *An environmental history of the world: Humankind's changing role in the community of life* (2nd ed.). Oxford, UK: Routledge.

International Union for the Conservation of Nature (IUCN). (2012). EAZA-IUCN SSC Southeast Asia campaign launched. Retrieved January 12, 2012, from http://www.iucnredlist.org/news/eaza-iucn-ssc-southeast-asia-campaign-launched

Jameson, Antony. (2008). A short history of South East Asia. Retrieved January 6, 2012, from http://aero-comlab.stanford.edu/jameson/world_history/A_Short_History_of_South_East_Asia1.pdf

Karan, Pradyumna P. (2004). *The non-Western world: Environment, development, and human rights*. Oxford, UK: Routledge.

King, Victor T. (Ed.). (1998). *Environmental challenges in South-East Asia*. Richmond, UK: Curzon Press.

Kornfield, Caroline. (2007, Fall). Ordaining trees in Thailand: Engaged Buddhists come together to save the forest. *PeacePower, 3*(2). Retrieved February 17, 2012, from http://calpeacepower.org/0302/ordainingtrees.htm

Lockard, Craig A. (2009). *Southeast Asia in world history*. Oxford, UK: Oxford University Press.

Nhung, Le. (2010, November 18). Nguyen Dinh Xuan: A legislator & environmental activist. Retrieved February 17, 2012, from http://english.vietnamnet.vn/en/special-report/1678/nguyen-dinh-xuan---a-legislator---environmental-activist.html

Parnwell, Michael J. G., & Bryant, Raymond L. (1996). *Environmental change in South-East Asia: People, politics and sustainable development*. London: Routledge.

Peet, Richard; Robbins, Paul; & Watts, Michael J. (Eds.). (2011). *Global political ecology*. Oxford, UK: Routledge.

Rigg, Jonathan. (2003). *Southeast Asia: The human landscape of modernisation and development* (2nd ed.). London: Routledge.

Stott, Philip. (2001, January). Review of "Nature and the orient: The environmental history of South and Southeast Asia." *Journal of Historical Geography, 27*(1), 119–122.

Sun Star Manila. (2012, January 15). Asian nations urged to work together for climate change adaption. Retrieved January 15, 2012, from http://www.sunstar.com.ph/manila/local-news/2012/01/15/asian-nations-urged-work-together-climate-change-adaptation-200670

Symon, Andrew. (2007, May 26). Southeast Asia's climate-change challenge. *Asia Times*. Retrieved January 10, 2010, from http://www.atimes.com/atimes/Southeast_Asia/IE26Ae01.html

Thomas, Gareth. (2008, May 5). The cleanest city in the world. Retrieved February 17, 2012, from http://www.cbn.com/cbnnews/world/2008/May/The-Cleanest-City-in-the-World-/

United States Central Intelligence Agency (US CIA). (2012). The world factbook: East and Southeast Asia. Retrieved April 5, 2012, from https://www.cia.gov/library/publications/the-world-factbook/wfbExt/region_eas.html

Weightman, Barbara A. (2006). *Dragons and tigers: A geography of South, East and Southeast Asia* (2nd ed.). New York: Wiley.

World Wide Fund for Nature (WWF). (n.d.a). Asian rhinos. Retrieved January 12, 2012, from http://www.wwf.org.uk/what_we_do/safeguarding_the_natural_world/wildlife/asian_rhinos/

World Wide Fund for Nature (WWF). (n.d.b). Tigers. Retrieved January 12, 2012, from http://www.wwf.org.uk/what_we_do/safeguarding_the_natural_world/wildlife/tigers/

Year of No Flying. (2009, December 6). Young green activists rise up in Vietnam. Retrieved February 17, 2012, from http://www.yearofnoflying.com/2009/12/vietnam-young-green-activists.html

Steel Industry

As one of the primary sectors of economy, the steel industry has been growing rapidly in China and India, consuming large amounts of energy and producing much pollution. The industry is faced with increasing environmental concerns, raw material scarcity, and other issues. To become sustainable, the sector needs to consolidate and adopt more advanced technology, including long-term strategies for energy conservation and reduction of polluting emissions.

Steel is an essential component of both China's and India's efforts to modernize their industrial and economic infrastructure. Steel production in both of these newly industrialized countries, however, is energy intensive and highly polluting. As industrial output continues to rise rapidly, the steel sector will be faced with making decisions that can spur economic development without incurring the high cost of environmental degradation.

Environmental Impact

The Chinese and Indian steel industries have recently experienced a period of tremendous growth. Since 1978, in step with overall economic development, the Chinese steel industry has been growing at an average rate of 9 percent annually. Between 1983 and 1996, Chinese steel production rose from 38 million tons to 101 million tons, making China the largest steel producer in the world. After 2000, driven by large-scale industrialization and rapid urbanization, China's steel industry grew exponentially at an average annual rate of 20 percent. By 2010, China's crude steel production reached 626 million tons, which amounted to 43 percent of the world's steel production (World Steel Association 2010). At the same time, India's steel industry grew about 7 percent annually, and India ranked as the world's fifth largest steel producer, with an annual production of 66 million tons, in 2010 (World Steel Association 2010). Benefiting from its soaring economic growth since 2006, India expects to continue to experience annual double-digit increase in steel demand going forward (Business Monitor International 2011b).

China's and India's steel industries are among the highest energy consumers and pollution producers in the world. The Chinese steel industry accounts for 16 percent of the country's total energy consumption. (Energy consumption per unit of steel averages about 20 percent higher than it does in developed countries such as the United States, South Korea, and Japan.) The industry generates 14 percent of the country's total wastewater and 6 percent of solid waste materials (Guo and Fu 2010), and its carbon dioxide emissions account for nearly 50 percent of the industry's worldwide total. The situation is similar in India, where the steel industry accounts for 13 percent of the fuel consumed in the manufacturing sector. India's carbon dioxide emissions are among the highest in the world (World Steel Association 2008, 9). In short, rapid growth of the steel industry in China and India has been achieved at the price of severe environmental damage including deforestation, widespread acid rain, and deteriorating air quality.

Energy-Efficient Technology and Industry Consolidation

Adopting energy-efficient and clean technologies is the key to reducing the industry's environmental footprint and balancing economic, environmental, and social goals. Although technological innovations require massive and continuous investment, major companies have recognized the importance of the issue, and have been moving toward improving energy efficiency and reducing emissions. For example, the Shagang Steel Group, a top producer in China, has gained access to the advanced Finex iron-making process through its joint venture with the Pohang Iron and Steel Company (POSCO) of South Korea, one of the world's most efficient steel producers. The Finex technology, noted for its innovation by POSCO as a new chapter in world steel production, can lower raw material operation costs by 85 percent, and reduce the emission of sulfur oxides by 19 percent and nitrogen oxides by 10 percent. In India, Tata Steel, the country's largest steel producer, has adopted the Baosteel short slag treatment technology (BSSF), which has been identified by the World Steel Association (WSA) as a promising new technology in reducing carbon dioxide emissions. Major steel companies in both India and China have participated actively in various exploratory projects launched by the WSA that aim to reduce energy consumption and emissions. If successfully implemented, technological advancement will allow major steel producers to turn their plants into environmentally friendly operations. Unfortunately, a large number of small steel plants in China and India will not be able to take advantage of the new technologies because they lack capital.

At the same time, government intervention and tightening of environmental regulations are crucial in mitigating the acute environmental problems generated by high-polluting steel plants. Since 2000, the Chinese government has forced industry-wide mergers, acquisitions, and mandatory shutdowns of inefficient and outdated steel plants. These actions reduced excessive emissions from high-polluting small plants and increased the economies of scale in the industry. About six hundred high-polluting small steel plants in eighteen provinces were forced to shut down between 2008 and 2010, and seventeen large mergers and acquisitions in 2008 reshaped the industry with a higher level of centralization by establishing four national steel production bases. In addition, more steel mills are planning to relocate to coastal and interior waterways where they will be able to use seawater for steelmaking and to save on transportation costs. The Chinese government's environmental target for 2015 is to reduce energy consumption per unit of gross domestic product (GDP) by 16 percent and emissions by 17 percent. This target exerts significant pressure on the steel industry.

In contrast with the governmental intervention in China, India's steel industry consolidation has been self-initiated, and restructuring plans often have to undergo a lengthy approval process by government agencies. India's National Action Plan on Climate Change aims to save 5 percent of energy consumption by 2015, and to reduce carbon intensity from the 2005 level by 20–25 percent by 2020 (Prime Minister of India 2008). To do this, the Indian government may have to adopt a more aggressive approach in formulating environmental regulations and technical standards for its fast-growing steel industry.

Raw Material Issues

In the long run, both China and India will face challenges in obtaining raw materials. In brief, steel can be made in one of two ways: from iron ore and coke in a blast furnace / basic oxygen furnace (BOF) or from steel scrap in an electronic arc furnace (EAF). The EAF has significant advantages over the BOF, including consuming less energy, creating less waste material, and using recycled raw material rather than iron ore, which is becoming more expensive and more difficult to obtain. The price of iron ore increased for eight consecutive years after 2003, and rose 72 percent in 2006 alone (Lan 2008). China depends heavily on imported iron ore, since nearly 90 percent of its crude steel production is made by the BOF process and its domestic iron ore supply is very limited. The rising price of iron ore significantly reduced the industry's profit margin, and as a consequence, China has been investing heavily in global foreign energy and mining assets to secure supplies of raw material. For example, in 2009, Chinese firms accounted for nearly 40 percent of all mining deals with foreign investors in Australia, the origin of more than half the world's supply of iron ore. China is also actively investing in South Africa, Canada, South Korea, and Latin America. India, on the other hand, is the world's fourth largest iron ore producer, and it provides 16 percent of the iron ore China imports. One way that India intends to conserve its iron ore deposits is by adding an export tax (Siddesh 2011).

Iron ore is a nonrenewable resource, and research shows that the world's identified iron ore reserves of 230 billion tons will last for only about fifty years at current levels of production (Yellishetty, Ranjith, and Tharumarajah 2010). Using scrap metal, on the other hand, is sustainable in the long term because steel can be recycled indefinitely without loss of structural properties. The trend toward using the EAF process caused the price of scrap to rise substantially after 2000. Since that time, the consumption of steel scrap has reached an all-time high due to strong demand for iron and steel internationally (Yellishetty et al. 2011, 653). In 2010, China produced 9 percent of its steel using EAF, while India produced 63 percent of its steel using that method. In fact, India produces more recycled steel on a percentage basis than does either Japan or the United States (World Steel Association 2010). China and India both import scrap for steelmaking because the quantity and quality of domestic recycled steel are limited. Steel recycling chains from major scrap sources such as automobiles are in the early stages compared to those in developed countries. As China's and India's steel recycling markets mature, an increasing supply of high-quality scrap may cause more steel producers to switch to scrap from iron ore in their production processes. Although both China and India have promoted metal recycling, neither government has enacted legislation to support the use of recycled metals. The World Steel Association estimates that 459 million tons of steel scrap were recycled in 2006, which saved an equivalent of 868 million tons of iron ore and 827 million tons of carbon dioxide emissions (World Steel Association 2008, 16). Continuing to move toward using the EAF process has huge potential in sustainable steelmaking in both China and India.

Future Challenges and Opportunities

The growth potential in the steel industry in Asia has attracted many global players. In the case of South Asia, steel giants from Japan, South Korea, and Europe have all launched expansion plans in India. As one of the biggest recipients of foreign direct investment, India attracted $36 billion of investment in 2008, a 60 percent increase from the previous year (Business Monitor International 2011b). The abundance of an inexpensive and skilled English-speaking labor force contributes to the competitiveness of India's steel industry. Challenges to growth, such as power shortages, inferior infrastructure, and outdated transportation systems, could be improved through massive domestic and international investment and government initiatives. Other controversial issues such as nontariff barriers to trade, subsidies, and discriminatory customs duties on exports and imports have to be addressed by the government. Looking forward, India aims to become the second largest steel producing nation with a targeted production capacity of 120 million tons by 2012 and 293 million tons by 2020 (Business Monitor International 2011b). The steel industry will grow sustainably if the Indian government tackles environmental challenges and metal recycling issues through careful planning, policies, funding, and, more importantly, legal initiatives.

Facing mounting challenges in steelmaking, China adjusted its steel import and export tariffs and removed the steel export rebate in 2010 to cool trade disputes with other countries. To limit overcapacity and oversupply, about 68 million tons of excess capacity will be eliminated by 2015 (Business Monitor International 2011a; KPMG China 2011). China's steel industry is improving its productivity and increasing its profit margin through more technology upgrades and further industry consolidation. Under the pressure of tightening policies to reduce energy consumption and emissions, China's steel producers will continue to pursue sustainable development instead of rampant expansion and growth.

The steel industry in both China and India will continue to grow in tandem with their overall economic growth. As they do, a strong commitment to sustainable development may include a shift to recycled steel as principal raw material, and new technologies to improve productivity and quality.

Jinong SUN
Fayetteville State University

Wenxian ZHANG
Rollins College

See also Automobiles and Personal Transportation; Climate Change Mitigation Initiatives (China); Corporate Accountability (China); Energy Industries—Renewables (China); Energy Industries—Renewables (India); Five-Year Plans; National Pollution Survey (China); Outsourcing and Offshoring; Public Transportation

FURTHER READING

Business Monitor International Ltd (BMI). (2011a). China metals report Q2 2011. *Business Monitor International, 3*(2), 6–69. [Available through an institution with access to EBSCOhost]

Business Monitor International Ltd (BMI). (2011b). India metals report Q2 2011. *Business Monitor International, 3*(2), 5–61. [Available through an institution with access to EBSCOhost]

Costa, Anthony. (1999). *The global restructuring of the steel industry: Innovations, institutions and industrial change.* New York: Routledge.

Guo, Zhan-cheng, & Fu, Z. X. (2010). Current situation of energy consumption and measures taken for energy saving in the iron and steel industry in China. *Energy, 35*(11), 4356–4360.

Hogan, William. (1999). *The steel industry of China: Its present status and future potential.* New York: Lexington Books.

Hu, Yue. (2009). Market watch. *Beijing Review, 52*(4), 4–36.

Huang, Xueli; Schroder, Bill; & Steffens, Paul. (1999). The Chinese steel industry in transition: Industry perspective on innovation policy. *R&D Management, 29*(1), 17–25.

KPMG China. (2011). China's 12th five-year plan: Iron and steel. Retrieved May 26, 2011, from http://www.kpmg.com/CN/en/IssuesAndInsights/ArticlesPublications/Documents/China-12th-Five-Year-Plan-Iron-Steel-201105-2.pdf

Lan, Xinzhen. (2008). Streamlining iron and steel production. *Beijing Review, 51*(4), 36–37.

Lin, Boqiang; Wu, Ya; & Zhang, Li. (2011). Estimates of the potential for energy conservation in the Chinese steel industry. *Energy Policy, 39*(6), 3680–3689.

Ma, Jinlong; Evans, David G.; Fuller, Robert J.; & Stewart, Donald F. (2000). Technical efficiency and productivity change of China's iron and steel industry. *International Journal of Production Economics, 76*(3), 293–312.

Matthew, Robert Guy. (2011, May 5). Steelmakers pump up volume. *Wall Street Journal.* Retrieved July 16, 2011, from http://online.wsj.com/article/SB10001424052748703992704576305351560300260.html

Matthew, Robert Guy. (2011, May 24). For global steel industry, China poses guessing game. *Wall Street Journal.* Retrieved July 16, 2011, from http://online.wsj.com/article/SB10001424052748704083904576335630184298602.html

Moritsugu, Ken. (2007, May 1). India rising: Is India ready to become a world power. *CQ Global Researcher, 1,* 101–124. Retrieved July 24, 2011, from http://library.cqpress.com/globalresearcher/document.php?id=cqrglobal2007050000

Prime Minister of India. (2008). National action plan on climate change. Retrieved November 1, 2011, from http://pmindia.nic.in/climate_change.htm

Schumacher, Katja, & Sathaye, Jayant. (1998). *India's iron and steel industry: Productivity, energy efficiency and carbon emissions.* Berkeley, CA: Lawrence Berkeley National Laboratory. Retrieved July 16, 2011, from http://ies.lbl.gov/iespubs/41844.pdf

Siddesh, Mayenkar. (2011). RPT-UPDATE 3-India ups iron ore export duty, China hardest hit. Retrieved from http://www.reuters.com/article/2011/03/01/india-ironore-idUSSGE72001120110301

Stephen, Cooney. (2007). *CRS report for Congress: Steel price and policy issues.* Washington, DC: Congressional Research Service. Retrieved July 16, 2011, from http://opencrs.com/document/RL32333/2007-10-31/download/1005/

Tang, Rachel. (2010). *China's steel industry and its impact on the United States: Issues for Congress.* Washington, DC: Congressional Research Service. Retrieved July 16, 2011, from http://www.fas.org/sgp/crs/row/R41421.pdf

World Steel Association (WSA). (2005). Crude steel statistics total 2005. Retrieved July 3, 2011, from http://www.worldsteel.org/?action=stats&type=steel&period=latest&month=13&year=2005

World Steel Association (WSA). (2008). *2008 sustainability report of the world steel industry.* Retrieved November 8, 2011, from http://www.szs.ch/user_content/editor/files/FAQ/worldsteel_sustainability_report_2008_english.pdf

World Steel Association (WSA). (2010). *Steel statistical yearbook 2010.* Retrieved July 16, 2011, from http://www.worldsteel.org/pictures/publicationfiles/SSY%202010.pdf

Worrell, Ernst. (1995). Advanced technologies and energy efficiency in the iron and steel industry in China. *Energy for Sustainable Development, 2*(4), 27–30.

Wu, Yanrui. (2000). The Chinese steel industry: Recent developments and prospects. *Resource Policy, 26*(3), 171–178.

Yap, Chuin-Wei. (2011, February 23). China plans overseas iron ore asset spree. *Wall Street Journal.* Retrieved July 16, 2011, from http://online.wsj.com/article/SB10001424052748703775704576161382499336732.html

Yellishetty, Mohan; Mudd, Gavin M.; Ranjith, Pathegama Gamage; & Tharumarajah, Ambalavanar (Rajah). (2011). Environmental life-cycle comparisons of steel production and recycling: Sustainability issues, problems and prospects. *Environmental Science & Policy, 14*(6), 650–663.

Yellishetty, Mohan; Ranjith, Pathegama Gamage; & Tharumarajah, Ambalavanar (Rajah). (2010). Iron ore and steel production trends and material flows in the world: Is this really sustainable? *Resources, Conservation, and Recycling, 54*(12), 1084–1094.

Berkshire's authors and editors welcome questions, comments, and corrections. Send your emails about the *Berkshire Encyclopedia of Sustainability* in general or this volume in particular to: sustainability.updates@berkshirepublishing.com

T

Three Gorges Dam

The Three Gorges Dam has been the focus of world attention since the project was approved in 1992. Although it has given the Chinese people a sense of national pride, the project has been highly criticized inside and outside of China because of the many issues it raises. The dam was conceived as part of an ambitious plan to redirect needed water from the Yangzi (Chang) River. For the first time in the history of the People's Republic of China, some delegates of the Politburo Standing Committee voted against the project in April of 1992.

The Three Gorges Dam is the latest of a long list of dams built in China. Chinese engineers have an extensive history of building dams, but this one is unique because of the spatial and temporal dimension of the work and because of the number of people who have been displaced.

The Three Gorges Dam is located along the Yangzi (Chang) River, at Sandouping, close to one of its narrowest points at the three gorges (Qutang, Wu, and Xiling). The dam itself is 2,335 meters long, with twenty-six turbines that can provide 18,200 megawatts of electricity, or 80 terawatt-hours per year. It is the largest generator of electricity of any kind on Earth: the controversial dam generates twenty times the electricity-generating power of the Hoover Dam in the United States (Handwerk 2006). Additional dams are planned upstream and on tributaries to slow sedimentation; once they are in place, electricity production from the Three Gorges Dam could be doubled. A boat lift and two bidirectional locks facilitate boat passage. It is a gravity dam, the world's largest in this category at 185 meters high (Delin 2000). The dam itself is built in Hubei Province, close to Yichang, but the area affected by the rising water is in the municipality of Chongqing. This territory (82,400 square kilometers with a population of 32 million), although officially a municipality, has the administrative rank of a province and is under the direct supervision of the central government (Chongqing Municipal Government 2011). Chongqing was carved out of Sichuan Province in 1997 in order to handle the ecological, economic, and social challenges of the construction of the dam. In order to fulfill this mission, the Chongqing authorities gained some economic advantages similar to those in special economic zones (which are more free-market oriented). Chongqing is now a strategic point linking the western part of China to the more developed coastal areas. A national plan is in place to integrate inner remote areas to the Yangzi development zone. The river is imagined as a dragon, with Shanghai at the mouth, Wuhan in the middle, and Chongqing at the tail. The Three Gorges Dam is intended to integrate the different parts of the dragon.

History and Construction

The People's Republic of China (PRC) has undertaken many hydrologic projects since its founding in 1949. Seventy thousand dams (22,104 large ones) and about 83,387 reservoirs have been built. Until the 1980s, their main purposes were irrigation and flood prevention. At the end of the 1970s, only 3 percent of the dams were producing electricity (Pan and He 2000). China is rich in oil and coal resources, and as a result, there was no push for the development of hydropower until the 1980s. The change in strategy then was due to the need to diversify energy sources and the acknowledgment that cleaner sources of energy had to be found. Nonetheless, in the decade after 2000, fossil fuel was still responsible for about 80 percent of electricity output. Renewable energy, including hydroelectricity, was just 18.5 percent of electricity output in 2012 (US CIA 2012).

The Three Gorges Dam has a long history, starting with President Sun Yat-sen. The first suggestion for it can be traced back to Sun Yat-sen's 1919 paper "Plan to Develop Industry." Later, Chairman Mao Zedong expressed his interest in the idea, around 1949, but other urgent needs diverted him from it. During the 1980s, the idea sprang up again under the leadership of Vice Premier Deng Xiaoping. In 1985, the leadership team for the assessment of the Three Gorges Dam Project (TGDP) was established under the Ministry of Water Resources and Electric Power. Li Peng, as of that year a member of the Standing Committee of the Chinese Communist Party (CCP) Politburo, directed this group, which was composed of 412 experts. Li, who had been trained in hydrology in the Soviet Union, was the most vocal leader in favor of the dam. Like those built during the Maoist era, the Three Gorges Dam symbolizes modernity and the power of a nation-state that is able to control nature. Prior to 1989, there was some discussion of the feasibility of the dam project inside China—mainly among scientists and political authorities—and some voices were raised in opposition (Qing 1998). After 4 June 1989, however, no more criticism was allowed, and the project was pushed forward. In 1991, after the examination committee for the TGDP had completed its investigation, the state council gave the green light. In February 1992, the Politburo Standing Committee agreed, and in April, during the Fifth Plenum of the Seventh National People's Congress, the Resolution on the Construction of the Yangzi River Three Gorges Project was adopted. For the first time in the history of the PRC, some delegates voted against the project (177), and there were 644 abstentions. In 1994, work officially started, and three years later, the Yangzi was diverted. In 2003, the structure of the dam was finished in time for the National People's Congress, and the first increase in water level (to 135 meters) took place in June. Electricity generation started soon thereafter.

In August 2003, an official technical study advocated filling the reservoir to 139 meters. This suggestion was adopted by the state council representative of the TGDP on 5 September, and by 5 November, the water level was at 139 meters. Even though this was not a big technical issue, it was a big challenge for resettlement. A difference of 5 meters affected four districts and more than one thousand people, who had to be relocated on a tight schedule. Construction was projected to be completed in 2009, and the water level would be raised to 175 meters in 2013. This official schedule, however, had to be moved up to allow for the safe passage of large shipping vessels. In 2009, the dam was officially completed, and it was inaugurated for the sixtieth anniversary of the founding of the People's Republic of China.

There are three main public reasons, and a more hidden one, for this dam. The Chinese central government listed three points: to regulate water flow and prevent floods in the central part of the river (in the 1980s, 1990, and 1991, huge floods affected the flatlands along the Yangzi), to accelerate electricity production for the development of Chinese industries (the aim is that 10 percent of overall electricity production will come from the Three Gorges Dam), and to improve navigation for large boats carrying up to 10,000 tons so that they can reach Chongqing. The fourth point, which was not made public at first, was the need for a reservoir as part of a bigger project diverting water from the Yangzi to the northern part of the country through a canal (known as the South-North Water Diversion, or SNWD, Project).

Challenges

The Three Gorges Dam has been criticized both inside and outside China by intellectuals, scientists, and environmental activists. The Chinese activist and journalist Dai Qing was one of the most vocal opponents of the project, both writing and editing books in Chinese and English in an attempt to stop construction. There are four main critiques: the impact on the natural environment (climate change, pollution, dolphin disappearance, landslides, etc.); the loss of historical artifacts (archaeologists and historians were not given enough funding or time to study the ancient civilization of Ba, and its remains were not protected); the resettlement of nearly 2 million people affected by the rising water; and finally, the dam itself for various reasons (siltation problems, site in an area of seismic activity, loss of beneficial sediments for agriculture downstream, and the real risk of salinization of the water in the Yangzi delta) (Qing 1998; International Rivers n.d.).

Only India, which has almost as many dams as China, is linking dams with development policy and, in affecting so many people, faces a comparable challenge. Although the number of displaced people is similar, the primary difference between the two situations is civil society, which is very active in India but not in China (Duflo and Pande 2005).

Like other dams and reservoirs in the world, the main impact on population is not felt at the dam site, but upstream in the newly flooded reservoir. Many affected people live hundreds of kilometers from the dam. The Yangzi River has five main tributaries in the Three Gorges area plus a myriad of smaller ones that are also affected by the rise in water level. The consequences of the flooding of the reservoir (632 square kilometers) are felt even in areas far from the Yangzi itself. All the activities linked with the river that have been very important for local families from generation to generation are also disturbed. Fishing and boat transportation had been traditional income sources (Hessler 2001). It is estimated that in Chongqing, 23,800 hectares of cropland and more than 4,900 hectares of citrus groves were submerged. It was not possible to compensate farmers for losses from these rich alluvial fields that had been double cropped. They were resettled on less-fertile land. In any case, people who were displaced were expected to learn new ways to earn their living (Padovani 2006).

The large numbers of displaced people are also applying more pressure on the hilly slopes in the area. Peasants did not want to move away from their ancestral lands, but the available land cannot support more people. Either willingly or by force, people were displaced in three phases following the rising water: 1993–1997, 1998–2003, and 2004–2009. People who could not stay in their native districts were sent to one of twelve provinces and/or municipalities (the provinces of Hubei, Sichuan, Anhui, Jiangsu, Zhejiang, Shandong, Hainan, Hunan, Jiangxi, Fujian, and Guangdong; and the municipality of Shanghai). Local cadres in these provinces were responsible for finding land to accommodate the people being relocated. Some places, like Hainan, were completely unable to accommodate the arrivals, and all the displaced people soon moved on (International Rivers Network n.d.).

As is often the case in the building of hydropower dams, most of the people displaced by the construction live in rural areas and are poorly educated. While the majority of those resettled were farmers, a significant proportion was relocated in urban areas. Official figures indicate that 1.3 million people have been affected, but opponents contest these figures and argue that as many as 2 million have been displaced (International Rivers n.d.). The success of the relocation was closely linked with the ability of the national economy to absorb the surplus labor force. This proved difficult because the resettlement occurred just as the planned economy came to an end in the 1990s. In the new, more competitive job market, the waves of peasants who moved to big cities to earn a living made it even more difficult for those displaced by the Three Gorges Dam. The city of Chongqing was unable to absorb them.

The Chinese government passed new legislation and changed the way it dealt with resettlement as problems arose. In May 1982, the State Council issued the Regulations of Land Requisition for National Development Projects. This was followed by the Specifications of Reservoir Inundation Disposal Design for Water Resources and Hydropower Projects issued by the Ministry of Water Resources in December 1984. Even later, in August 1993, a specific statement came from the State Council, the Resettlement Guidelines for the Three Gorges Dam Project. In response to problems, the State Council issued further regulations in May 1999, the Two Regulations for Resettlement Policies.

A large-scale project like this dam is conceptualized by the central government but left to lower levels of the hierarchy to implement. This decentralized implementation partly explains why there are great differences among the affected districts. They have more powers than they once did, but at the same time, they have more responsibilities in a more complex economic environment. Part of the allocated resettlement fund is used to develop the local economy, building new roads, hospitals, schools, and townships, for example. The aim is to develop the local economy to guarantee sustainability. One drawback to this policy is that less-developed areas with limited or no experience in running factories or developing business activities are especially disadvantaged and risk growing even poorer than before. Another problem is the way the money is sometimes used, for example, on grandiose buildings that will not benefit the local economy. Corruption is also a recurrent problem. Misuse of public funds is one of the major complaints of the Chinese.

For the Chinese government, the Three Gorges Dam is the symbol of a triumphant China. Its engineers were able to build the biggest dam on Earth; its administration was able to resettle most of the displaced; and Chongqing is a booming economic center. Although the Chinese government is open to modifying some of its practices (developing a legal and regulatory framework for its actions), it still relies on traditional beliefs when it comes to mastering nature. Displaced people are also playing a part in maintaining national pride; they do not criticize the government for the project itself but for the inefficiency of local leaders. Many of those who were relocated believe that the dam project is good for China, and as a result, they do not directly question it. At the same time, they believe that the state has a responsibility to take care of them. Finally, the disintegration of social networks due to resettlement means that the "domestic order" (local and personal ties), "civic order" (equality and solidarity), and "market order" (economic performance) have all been put under pressure and will take many years to stabilize.

Florence PADOVANI

Paris 1 Sorbonne University

See also Activism, Judicial; Energy Industries—Renewables (China); Five-Year Plans; The Himalaya; Indigenous Peoples; Media Coverage of the Environment; Property Rights (China); Rule of Law; Rural Development; South–North Water Diversion; Tibetan Plateau; Water Security; Yangzi (Chang) River

FURTHER READING

Chetham, Deirdre. (2002). *Before the deluge: The vanishing world of the Yangtze's Three Gorges.* New York: Palgrave Macmillan.

Chongqing Municipal Government. (2011). About Chongqing. Retrieved March 6, 2012, from http://en.cq.gov.cn/AboutChongqing/

Delin, Huang. (2000). *Atlas of China Yangtze Three Gorges reservoir area.* Beijing: China Geographic Maps Publishing House.

Duflo, Esther, & Pande, Rohini. (2005). Dams (National Bureau of Economic Research Working Paper Series, Working Paper 11711). Retrieved February 3, 2012, from http://www.nber.org/papers/w11711.pdf

Handwerk, Brian. (2006, June 9). China's Three Gorges Dam, by the numbers. Retrieved April 18, 2012, from http://news.nationalgeographic.com/news/2006/06/060609-gorges-dam.html

Hessler, Peter. (2001). *River town: Two years on the Yangtze.* London: John Murray.

International Rivers. (n.d.). Three Gorges Dam. Retrieved January 6, 2012, from http://www.internationalrivers.org/china/three-gorges-dam

International Rivers Network. (n.d.). Major problems found in Three Gorges Dam resettlement program. Retrieved March 6, 2012, from http://www.internationalrivers.org/china/three-gorges-dam

Liu Jian; Feng, Xiating; & Ding, Xiu-Li. (2003). Stability assessment of the Three Gorges Dam foundation, China, using physical and numerical modeling. *International Journal of Rocks Mechanics & Mining Sciences, 40,* 609–631.

Padovani, Florence. (2006, July–August). Displacement from the Three Gorges region. *China Perspectives, 66.* Retrieved January 6, 2012, from http://chinaperspectives.revues.org/1034

Pan, Jiazheng, & He, Jing. (2000). *Large dams in China: A fifty-year review.* Beijing: China Water Power Press.

Qing, Dai. (1998). *The river dragon has come! The Three Gorges Dam and the fate of China's Yangtze River and its people.* New York: M. E. Sharpe.

Tan, Yan. (2008). *Resettlement in the Three Gorges project.* Hong Kong: Hong Kong University Press.

United States Central Intelligence Agency (US CIA). (2012). The world-fact book: Electricity: Production by source. Retrieved March 14, 2012, from https://www.cia.gov/library/publications/the-world-factbook/fields/2045.html

Share the *Encyclopedia of Sustainability*: Teachers are welcome to make up to ten (10) copies of no more than two (2) articles for distribution in a single course or program. For further permissions, please visit www.copyright.com or contact: info@berkshirepublishing.com

Tibetan Plateau

The sustainability of the Tibetan Plateau is a dynamic topic involving overlapping and often contradictory ideas about the management and preservation of its environment and people. As Chinese economic development and international conservation investments continue to expand in the region, it will be critical to continuously weigh and reevaluate the trade-offs of various approaches to biodiversity conservation and rangeland management policies.

The Tibetan Plateau, located in Central Asia, is the highest raised landmass in the world. Eighty-five percent of its total 2.5 million square kilometer area (it is approximately four times the size of the US state of Texas) rises above 3,000 meters elevation, and 50 percent of its landmass lies above 4,500 meters elevation (Schaller 1998). Mountains rim the raised plateau on all sides, an artifact of past and persistent collisions between the northern-moving Indian tectonic plate and the relatively stationary Asian tectonic plate that began 40 to 50 million years ago. The Himalaya form the southern boundary of the plateau; the Karakoram Range, the western boundary; the Kunlun Mountains lie to the north; the Qilian Mountains, to the northeast; and the Hengduan Mountains form the eastern boundary. Administratively, the Tibetan Plateau encompasses the Tibet (Xizang) Autonomous Region (TAR) and Qinghai, western Sichuan, southwestern Gansu, and northwestern Yunnan provinces.

Rangeland Environments and Livelihoods

The Tibetan Plateau is dominated by rangelands with variable elevation, precipitation, and temperature across east-to-west and south-to-north gradients. Generally, the freezing winter months span from September to April, and warmer spring and summer months span from May to August. Summer Indian monsoons bring most of the plateau's annual precipitation during July and August, falling most heavily in the southeast plateau (approximately 500 mm per year) and dissipating toward the north and west (50–400 mm per year), rendering most of the plateau characteristically arid and frigid (Schaller 1998).

Because of the dry rangeland environment and the high variability in interannual precipitation, the Tibetan Plateau is defined as a nonequilibrium rangeland system. In nonequilibrium rangelands, high variation in abiotic factors (such as temperature, precipitation, and wind) strongly influences rangeland condition, while, in equilibrium rangelands (e.g., temperate North American rangelands) biotic factors (such as the disturbances caused by livestock grazing) have the greatest influence on rangeland condition. Ecologists commonly describe rangeland condition using the following metrics: percent vegetation cover (how much foliar cover there is per unit area), vegetation biomass (weight, in grams, of clipped material per unit area), species abundance (how many individuals of a given species there are per unit area), and species richness (how many different species there are per unit area).

While both biotic and abiotic factors can simultaneously influence rangeland condition, the designation of a rangeland as either nonequilibrium or equilibrium becomes meaningful in the context of rangeland management and policies. Equilibrium rangeland management approaches, such as fencing grazing plots, providing water sources, adjusting stocking rates, and determining carrying capacities (ideal number of grazing animals per unit area) are designed to balance disturbance (grazing) with vegetation regeneration, based on the rationale that decreasing the disturbance will allow for increased vegetation regeneration and will result in an increase in standing vegetation stocks. Nonequilibrium rangeland management approaches (policies that enable pastoralism and mobile [not fenced] livestock herds) are designed to opportunistically capitalize on patchy resource availability, based on the rationale that abiotic factors predominantly limit vegetation regrowth.

Because the Tibetan Plateau rangeland is a nonequilibrium system, management policies that are likely to be most successful there are ones that foster mobile pastoralism. These policies, however, must not only be based on environmental variability, but must also take into consideration the social and political transitions taking place across the region.

Policies and Tibetan Livelihoods

Tibetans comprise the largest ethnic group of the Tibetan Plateau, constituting nearly 90 percent of the plateau's population—approximately 3 million people; the other 10 percent is comprised of Hui, Han, Bai, Yi, and several other ethnic groups (Ma 2010). The Tibetan population is distributed across four geographically and linguistically distinct areas: Amdo is located in the northeast, which is administratively part of Qinghai, Gansu, and Sichuan provinces; Kham lies in the east and southeast, encompassing parts of western Sichuan, northwestern Yunnan, and southern Qinghai provinces and eastern parts of the TAR; Tsang refers to the central and central-west regions of TAR; and Ngari is located in the far west of the TAR.

Tibetan livelihoods across the plateau are intimately attuned to the variable environmental, climatic, and political conditions of the region. Tibetan pastoralists have been using the plateau's rangelands, characterized by low-lying vegetation and dominant cover of perennial sedges *Kobresia pygmaea* (Shimono et al. 2010), as suitable forage for their grazing yak herds for hundreds of years.

The Tibetan Plateau is currently undergoing a wave of social and economic transitions that are part of China's "Develop the West" campaign, which seeks to equilibrate the economic conditions of "the West" (economic hinterlands) with China's eastern seaboard (a longstanding site of industry and economic development, and home to China's rising middle class). The campaign has spurred administrative expansion into the economically recessed areas of China's western regions, investment in urban areas, and infrastructural development projects, such as the construction of roads and the Qinghai-Tibetan railroad. As a consequence of these development projects, there has been a notable influx of Han migrants into the growing townships of the plateau. These migrants either migrate involuntarily (they are sent by the Chinese government to serve as government officials and technical experts) or migrate for economic reasons (they come to work as farmers, miners, builders, restaurant owners, business operators, or shopkeepers). The incentives for both groups are higher wages, tax amnesties, allowances, and better housing. Total migrant populations are difficult to quantify because their movement is not reflected in census data, but the "floating population" of migrants is evident across the region through their use of social services, administration services, and through the volume of business they bring.

The consequences of these development initiatives are mixed; some result in benefits and others in disadvantages. On the beneficial side, health and education services have improved in some areas; tax burdens on poor, semi-pastoral Tibetans have been alleviated; and roads and transportation services have made travel possible and easier in new areas. At the same time, environmental destruction has expanded in some areas due to increased construction and local resource use; income disparity has grown within and between villages as some families have had access to new jobs while others have not; there has been an increase in the migration of younger generations from villages to cities; employment opportunities in the construction sector have been more available to migrants than to local residents; and ethnic conflicts have increased in some areas. In fact, many scholars are skeptical that state investments in the region will ever benefit the local "western" residents: as of 2005, the amount spent on capital construction was four times greater than the amount spent on education in the TAR (Fischer 2005). Infrastructural construction continues to be a major outcome of the "Develop the West" campaign.

For Tibetan pastoralists, development in the region is most manifest through "settlement" policies. These policies, set in motion during the land reforms of the 1980s—initiated by then Party General Secretary Hu Yaobang, who led a high-level group to survey conditions in the TAR (Bauer 2005)—give pastoralists an incentive to "settle" in villages and peri-urban villages where they can engage in livestock production practices similar to those used in North American rangelands. Unlike pastoralist practices, however, which use rangeland resources collectively and nomadically, settlement policies privatize rangeland use and assign individual parcels of land to households for household-level livestock production. These policies are promoted by the Chinese state as a way of increasing livestock production rates and mitigating rangeland degradation; they are also used to locate pastoralists closer to medical care facilities, schools, and alternative labor opportunities so that they can more readily avail of development benefits. Subsidized fencing and housing, the imposition of carrying capacities, and technical improvements to shelters and forage production often go hand-in-hand with these settlement processes (Yeh and Gaerrang 2011).

The settlement policies, however, are highly contested. In nonarable and variable rangelands like the Tibetan Plateau, resources vary from one grazing plot to another, leading to an array of tensions across households and regions. Fencing costs are generally prohibitive, too, unless they are highly subsidized by the government, and water access is restricted and a source of strain for some families who have to travel long distances to obtain water. Many conflicts have already occurred due to poor allocation of pastures and to widening gender gaps (after fences were constructed around rangeland, men—who traditionally were responsible for overseeing herds—suddenly had more leisure time at their disposal).

Some ecologists contend, however, that pastoral grazing practices do not degrade the rangelands as has been claimed (Dorji et al. 2010), making the state's claim that settlement mitigates degradation a moot point. Indeed, while human and livestock populations have essentially tripled over the past thirty-five years (Fox, Dhondup, and Dorji 2009) and there have been instances of pasture degradation and associated increases in toxic plants in Gertse County, Ngari Prefecture, TAR (Dorji et al 2010), there exists no large-scale documentation of the negative impacts of pastoralism on rangeland condition.

There are, however, some benefits of settlement. In Sichuan, for example, individual grazing areas can reduce the overall labor demand for households; herds can better survive heavy winters; and market access is generally improved due to holding pens and feedlots (Richard, Yan, and Du 2006).

Allocation of private pasture plots appears to be more successful in areas, such as the southeastern regions of the plateau, where water is not limited and where hay cultivation is possible. In these areas, government subsidies should be available to ensure that the ability to fence is not precluded by poverty. In the more arid northern and western reaches of the plateau, rangeland settlement policies should allow for flexible interpretation and implementation of the household-level grazing rights. In many areas like Gansu and Qinghai provinces, individuals have chosen to combine their household pastures to allow for shared, mobile livestock access to patchy resources and have developed local rules to ensure all households have equal access to water resources and fodder (Richard, Yan, and Du 2006).

Such benefit-sharing arrangements should be enhanced through multilevel governance arrangements where township and natural village officials coordinate to reinforce such efforts to equilibrate access and benefits across households.

Multiple Scales of Interest

Tibetan Plateau rangeland policies are not only subject to local and national interests but are also implicated in international ideas regarding which resources should be controlled and maintained. The Tibetan Plateau's glacial history, persistent permafrost layer, and its abundance of high-altitude wetlands (HAWs) give rise to all of the major rivers in Southeast Asia: the Ganges, Indus, Brahmaputra, Irrawaddy, Salween, Mekong-Lancang, Amu, Darya, Hilmand, Yangzi (Chang), and Huang (Yellow) rivers.

As of 2012, the connection between climate change and local land-use practices, and their potential influence on HAWs and international water resources, are poorly understood. As a consequence, political organization is growing around water research and management.

The World Wide Fund for Nature (WWF) is one of several interested conservation organizations trying to formulate sustainable watershed management to ensure freshwater provision for local residents as well as for much of Asia and the world. In 2010, the WWF designated Longbaotan Wetland—situated at the source of the Yangzi River in southern Qinghai Province—a research exemplar, because of the organization's success in protecting black-necked crane *Grus nigricollis* habitats by convincing Tibetan pastoralists (who had settled on the significant wetland meadows during the 1990s and had been using it for year-long livestock grazing ever since) to alter the grazing habits of their herds during the summer nesting seasons. The potentially negative impacts of grazing in and around wetland meadows like Longbaotan, along with the combined effects of climate change and other rangeland use patterns (agriculture and tourism development, for example) are just some of the reasons why additional research is needed and why the region is likely to face policy tensions in the years to come.

International wildlife and plant biodiversity conservation interests in the plateau also play a role in decisions about local and national resource use. The northwestern Tibetan Plateau is home to populations of chiru, or Tibetan antelope *Pantholops hodgsonii*, categorized as Endangered on the IUCN Red List (the world's most comprehensive inventory of the conservation status of species, prepared by the International Union for Conservation of Nature). It is also home to other sparse populations of high steppe and montane ungulates, wild yak *Bos grunniens,* Near Threatened Tibetan argali *Ovis ammon hodgsoni,* Near Threatened Tibetan gazelle *Procapra picticaudata,* and Tibetan wild ass or kiang *Equus kiang* (Schaller 1998). These wildlife populations are increasingly impacted by livestock development and nomadic settlement policies because grazing fences interrupt ungulate migration patterns, prevent predator and hunter evasion, and can physically kill animals that become entangled in them. Development projects also have effects on wildlife population: the railroad-highway corridor from Qinghai to Lhasa has already interrupted the migratory passage of the Tibetan antelope population through the Hoh-Xil National Nature Reserve (Fox, Dhondup, and Dorji 2009). Hunting, which also poses a significant threat to wildlife conservation, is claimed to be secondary to fencing-related impacts on wildlife.

Plant biodiversity across the Tibetan Plateau is also remarkable. So far, more than 1,500 genera and 12,000 species of vascular plants have been identified, including 3,500 endemic species (Shimono et al. 2010). Recent research suggests that plant species richness for the plateau is high across all elevation gradients from 3,000 to 5,000 meter elevation. For this reason, additional sampling is necessary across the region to document the current biodiversity register and to understand how grazing, development projects, and climate change are influencing this important biological reservoir.

One growing sustainability issue for Tibetan livelihoods, rangeland management, and conservation biologists, is the burgeoning economy centered around the caterpillar fungus *Ophiocordyceps sinensis*. The caterpillar fungus is a rare parasitic fungus endemic to the Tibetan Plateau and highly valued in traditional Chinese medicine. It is also highly valued by international pharmaceutical industries, the Chinese gift economy, and, increasingly, by biologists who value its genetic diversity. Most semi-pastoral and pastoral Tibetans across the plateau earn 40 to 80 percent of their annual household cash income by harvesting the lucrative resource, making it the cornerstone of the rural Tibetan economy amid the wave of Chinese economic development across the region. As of 2012, it remains unclear how harvesting (a practice that takes place in high alpine meadows, at elevations of 3,500 to 5,000 meters, during the fruit bearing season in May and June) impacts fungal viability. This lack of understanding is directly tied to a limited biological and ecological understanding of the fungus. Market demand for the fungus is high and steady, causing more and more harvesters to travel to harvesting areas to access the lucrative resource. Resource access and tenure are contested topics in many locations as villages define or reinforce their ownership rights of harvesting areas; conflicts have occurred across some regions that have resulted in fatalities. Management of the caterpillar fungus will be an important sustainability issue in the years ahead.

Looking Ahead

The sustainability of the Tibetan Plateau is defined and negotiated at the intersections of rangeland management policies, biodiversity conservation priorities, economic development initiatives, and human livelihood security. China's current and future economic development and environmental conservation policies will have to carefully consider and attend to the local, national, and transnational interests at stake across the region. Multilevel, multistakeholder governance will be an important approach going forward.

Michelle O. STEWART
University of Colorado at Boulder

See also Biodiversity Conservation Legislation (China); China; Ecotourism; Endangered Species; Ganges River; Genetic Resources; Great Green Wall (China); The Himalaya; Huang (Yellow) River; India; Indigenous Peoples; Mekong-Lancang River; One-Child Policy; Property Rights (China); Rural Development; Rural Livelihoods; South–North Water Diversion; Three Gorges Dam; Traditional Chinese Medicine (TCM); Transboundary Water Issues; Yangzi (Chang) River

FURTHER READING

Bauer, Kenneth. (2005). Pastoral development and the enclosure movement in the Tibet Autonomous Region since the 1980s. *Nomadic Peoples, 9*, 85–115.

Chatterjee, Archna, et al. (2010). WWF initiatives to study the impact of climate change on Himalayan high-altitude wetlands (HAWs). *Mountain Research and Development, 30*(1), 42–52. doi: 10.1659/MRD-JOURNAL-D-09-00091.1

Dorji, Tsechoe; Fox, Joseph L.; Richard, Camille; & Dondrup, Kelsang. (2010). An assessment of nonequilibrium dynamics in rangelands of the Aru Basin, northwest Tibet, China. *Rangeland Ecology and Management, 63*(4), 426–434.

Fischer, Andrew Martin. (2005). *State growth and social exclusion in Tibet: Challenges of recent economic growth.* Copenhagen: NIAS Press.

Fox, Joseph L.; Dhondup, Kelsang; & Dorji, Tsechoe. (2009). Tibetan antelope *Pantholops Hodgsonii* conservation and new rangeland management policies in the western Chang Tang Nature Reserve, Tibet: Is fencing creating an impasse? *Oryx, 43*(2), 183–190.

Goodman, David. (2004). China's campaign to "open up the west": National, provincial and local perspectives. *The China Quarterly, 178*, 1–18.

Ma Rong. (2010). *Population and society in contemporary Tibet.* Hong Kong: Hong Kong University Press.

Richard, Camille; Yan Zhaoli; & Du Guozhen. (2006). The paradox of the individual household responsibility system in the grasslands of the Tibetan Plateau, China. In Donald J. Bedunah (Ed.), *Rangelands of Central Asia: Proceedings of the Conference on Transformations, Issues, and Future Challenges* (USDA Forest Service Proceedings RMRS-P-39, pp. 81–91). Fort Collins, CO: USDA Forest Service.

Schaller, George B. (1998). *Wildlife of the Tibetan steppe.* Chicago: University of Chicago Press.

Shimono, Ayako, et al. (2010). Patterns of plant diversity at high altitudes on the Qinghai-Tibetan Plateau. *Journal of Plant Ecology, 3*(1), 1–7.

Stewart, Michelle O. (2009). The "Himalayan gold" rush: Prospectors' practices and implications for management. In Brandon Dotson, Kalsang Norbu Gurung, Georgios Halkias, & Tim Myatt (Eds.), *Contemporary visions in Tibetan studies: Proceedings of the First International Seminar of Young Tibetologists* (pp. 69–91). Chicago: Serindia Publications.

Yeh, Emily T. (2007). Tropes of indolence and the cultural politics of development in Lhasa, Tibet. *Annals of the Association of American Geographers, 97*(3), 593–612.

Yeh, Emily T., & Gaerrang. (2011). Tibetan pastoralism in neoliberalising China: Continuity and change in Gouli. *Area, 43*(2), 165–172.

Berkshire's authors and editors welcome questions, comments, and corrections. Send your emails about the *Berkshire Encyclopedia of Sustainability* in general or this volume in particular to: sustainability.updates@berkshirepublishing.com

Tokyo, Japan

35 million est. pop. 2010 (metropolitan area)

Tokyo is arguably the largest city in the world and one of the leading hubs of the global economy. It is known for excessive crowding and a high cost of living, but it is also remarkably well organized and livable. Construction is a major part of the economy, and everywhere there are new tall buildings replacing those from the past. The city is at great risk from earthquakes; as a result, Tokyo is in the forefront of earthquake-proof building technology.

Tokyo is the capital of Japan and, by most definitions, the largest city in the world. It is located on the Pacific Coast of Honshu, Japan's largest island, at the head of Tokyo Bay, and is the focus of an enormous metropolitan region that comprises all of Tokyo Prefecture (population approximately 13 million) and the neighboring prefectures of Kanagawa, Chiba, and Saitama. With some 35 million inhabitants according to the Japanese census, the Tokyo metropolitan area (defined as the four above-named prefectures) is far and away the world's largest (Cox 2011). The region is also called Kantō, after Japan's largest plain. There is technically no city of Tokyo, as that designation was abolished in an administrative reform in 1943, and what we call Tokyo today is actually an eccentric special administrative unit made of the old city plus suburban towns and cities immediately to the west of the center, an area of mountains and forests beyond that, and chains of small islands in the Pacific far to the south of the urban core. The boundaries of the old city are referred to as the twenty-three wards or the special wards and total a little more than 8 million residents.

Before 1868 the city was named Edo and was the seat of power of Japan's shoguns. Imperial rule was restored in 1868, and the emperor's capital was moved that year from Kyoto to Tokyo, which means "Eastern Capital." A drive for modernization and Western learning commenced thereafter. It was strategically centered in Tokyo and resulted in Japan's rise as a global military and industrial power. Imperial ambitions ended with defeat in World War II, but Japan and Tokyo specifically emerged from the ashes to become one of the world's leading economic powers based on exports of automobiles, electronics goods, and other high-quality and technologically innovative products.

Tokyo Today

In addition to its role as the government center of Japan, Tokyo is a major business and financial hub of global significance and the headquarters for many of Japan's largest corporations, including manufacturing companies, investment banks, advertising agencies, the Tokyo Stock Exchange, insurance companies, and newspapers, television, and other media. It is also a major port and an important center of higher education, tourism, and world-class arts and entertainment. Manufacturing is an important industry, although it has been declining as much factory production has relocated to sites where land or labor costs are cheaper. The downtown of Tokyo is an enormous commuter magnet, with more than 2 million workers and students arriving every working day by train and subway from surrounding areas. The business district is very crowded as a result, and land costs are among the highest in the world. The commute itself is very long and crowded, and is recognized as a major inconvenience of Tokyo life. It is also costly to the national economy because of time and energy lost, and for the same reasons it is an added impediment for workers to spending quality time with their families. To remedy the situation, there have been significant efforts in recent decades by city planners and private developers alike to decentralize the economy to outlying commercial centers and to develop new housing in the city's innermost wards.

Despite crowding and expensive costs of living there, Tokyo is generally thought of as a very livable city. It is remarkably clean for a city of it size and is safe from crime. Its public services are generally excellent, including transportation, utilities, communications, education, recreation, and emergency assistance. It lags behind other cities in wealthy countries in park space per capita, but the parks that it does have are typically clean, safe, and well equipped. At peak times, such as when cherry blossoms are in bloom, the parks are thronged with people. In some of Tokyo's oldest residential neighborhoods, where there are fewer parks and not much room for trees, and where much of the population is elderly, potted plants placed in front of private homes green the narrow streets, beautifying the streetscape and ameliorating a microclimate at least a little.

Most of the city terrain is quite flat and conducive to riding bicycles. The challenges, however, are that bikes are confined to sidewalks in crowded urban neighborhoods, where they compete for space with pedestrians, and that popular destinations such as subway and commuter rail stations or busy retail centers often lack sufficient room for bicycle parking. Sometimes municipal authorities haul away illegally parked bikes by the hundreds from crowded commercial centers, making it seem that they wage war against a bike-riding public. Bicycle lanes are mostly in outlying districts, as city streets are far too crowded.

Redevelopment

In recent years large parts of the waterfront have been developed with recreation and open space as primary goals, including the establishment of new sand beaches for public enjoyment. Indeed, much of Tokyo's growth since the 1980s has been on land reclaimed from Tokyo Bay. In addition to the recreation facilities on the new islands, there are new shopping and other commercial centers, entertainment and amusement parks, and warehousing and industrial districts, as well as fast-developing residential districts, such as Toyosu, that offer fresh and clean surroundings only minutes away by bridge or subway from the center of the city. A parallel trend has been the redevelopment of old industrial land near the waterfront and along rail corridors into office districts and high-rise residential developments. Not only has such construction resulted in the greening of old brownfields but it has also helped to populate parts of the metropolis that, like much of the land reclaimed recently from Tokyo Bay, are not far from the downtown center. Many of the new apartments are quite small, reflecting demands generated by Tokyo's many one-person households and childless couples.

The face of Tokyo is continually changing, as construction is one of the city's biggest businesses, even in the face of the long economic slump of the early twenty-first century. Indeed, almost the entire city is quite new, as most historic structures were destroyed in a giant earthquake and fire in 1923 and by Allied firebombing in 1945 near the end of World War II. Most of the few pockets of traditional Tokyo that remain have since been redeveloped by private-sector construction firms. The result is a city of ever taller high-rises and a history that is remembered mostly by old place names, new historical markers, and occasional reconstructions of famous temples and shrines. Prominent new developments include Roppongi Hills and Tokyo Midtown at the edge of Tokyo's central business district, new construction near Tokyo Station, and Odaiba in Tokyo Bay. It is said that Tokyo expands in every direction possible: outward to the far reaches of the Kantō Plain and beyond, onto new land taken from a shrinking bay, upward to new heights of skyscrapers, and downward where new subway lines and highways are being constructed below ground, and where shopping concourses and other business are built beneath the expensive land above.

Environmental Issues

Increasingly the new developments include green spaces and sustainable architectural design, but as a whole Tokyo is a world of end-to-end buildings and concrete, streets and highways congested with automobiles and other vehicles, and millions of heat-producing air-conditioning and heating units. It is one of the world's prime examples of an urban heat island, and it is especially muggy and uncomfortably hot in summer. The city produces enormous quantities of waste each day, presenting great challenges for disposal. The amount of waste that has gone to landfill operations has declined recently because of Japan's economic slump and because of increased intermediate treatment for Tokyo's waste. There are twenty-one incineration plants for the twenty-three central wards of the city alone, and newer ones are equipped with state-of-the-art ash-processing technology. Tokyo Metropolitan Government aggressively promotes large-scale waste reduction and recycling programs with catchy names such as "Tokyo Slim," which was introduced in 1989. The "My Bag Campaign," announced in 1991, is designed to cut back on excessive packaging. These and other measures have heightened the public's awareness about environmental issues and resulted in measurable declines per household in waste produced.

Tokyo is at significant risk from earthquakes. It sits at the boundary of three major tectonic plates and was severely damaged by quakes in 1703, 1782, 1812, 1855, and 1923. The 1923 disaster, known as the Great Kantō Earthquake, had an estimated magnitude of 8.3 and took approximately 142,000 lives. Japan is a world leader in earthquake-proof building technology, but recent tragic experiences in other parts of the country (e.g., Kobe in 1995 and Tōhoku on 11 March 2011) highlight that great dangers exist in concentrating so many people and so much of a nation's economy in one highly vulnerable place. The extensive damage that was caused by the Tōhoku quake and the ensuing tsunami to the Fukushima Daiichi nuclear power plant north of Tokyo continues to have the city and much of the rest of Japan on alert to increases in radiation levels, and they are even more aware than before about the need to conserve electrical energy. For the time being at least, Tokyo has been reducing energy consumption in response to the closing of the Fukushima power-generating facility by rolling blackouts, stepped-up voluntary conservation, and the darkening of some of its iconic bright lights.

Roman Adrian CYBRIWSKY
Temple University

See also Cities—Overview; E-Waste; Education, Environmental (Japan); Energy Industries—Nuclear; Japan; Parks and Preserves; Public Transportation; Utilities Regulation and Energy Efficiency

FURTHER READING

Ashihara, Yoshinobu. (1989). The hidden order: Tokyo through the twentieth century. Tokyo: Kodansha.

Cox, Wendell. (10 May 2011). Japan's 2010 Census: Moving to Tokyo. *New Geography*. Retrieved April 5, 2012, from http://www.newgeography.com/content/002227-japan%E2%80%99s-2010-census-moving-tokyo

Cybriwsky, Roman Adrian. (2011). Roppongi crossing: The demise of a Tokyo nightclub district and the reshaping of a global city. Athens: University of Georgia Press.

Cybriwsky, Roman Adrian. (1998). Tokyo: The shogun's city at the twenty-first century. New York: Wiley.

Okata, Junichiro, & Murayama, Akito. (2011). Tokyo's urban growth: Urban form and sustainability. In André Sorensen & Junichiro Okata (Eds.), *Megacities: Urban form, governance, and sustainability* (pp. 15–41). Tokyo: Springer.

Seidensticker, Edward; Richie, Donald; & Waley, Paul. (2010). *Tokyo from Edo to Showa 1867–1989: The emergence of the world's greatest city*. North Clarendon, VT: Charles E. Tuttle.

Sorensen, André, & Funck, Carolin. (2007). Living cities in Japan: Citizens' movements, machizukuri and local environments. New York: Routledge.

Worrall, Julian, & Solomon, Erez Golani. (2010). *21st century Tokyo: A guide to contemporary architecture*. Tokyo: Kodansha.

Share the *Encyclopedia of Sustainability*: Teachers are welcome to make up to ten (10) copies of no more than two (2) articles for distribution in a single course or program. For further permissions, please visit www.copyright.com or contact: info@berkshirepublishing.com

Traditional Chinese Medicine (TCM)

Traditional Chinese Medicine (TCM) is a holistic approach to treating illness through the use of herbal, mineral, and sometimes animal ingredients. TCM was practiced for thousands of years before the introduction of Western medicine to China. The controversy surrounding traditional medicine focuses on the resultant environmental impact of the need for certain ingredients and, by extension, the scientific validity of TCM.

In this article, traditional Chinese medicine (TCM) is used in the general sense, including all of its historical and modern practices. TCM has a long history; its medical theory and practical usage existed before any written or oral history. Surviving at least four thousand years in Chinese civilization, it is one of the oldest medical systems in the world, with some of the earliest written documentation.

Today there are nearly 1.5 billion people worldwide using TCM. Outside of China, the Joseon physicians in North Korea, Korean physicians in South Korea, Eastern physicians in Vietnam, and Han physicians in Japan have evidently accepted, and are influenced by, TCM theories and practices. In addition, TCM is used by people in Europe, the Americas, and Oceania as well as Asia. The influence of TCM has clearly spread beyond the boundaries of China (Hsiao 2007).

At present, TCM has two modes of transmission: the teacher-disciple faction, and the so-called institution faction. The Chinese government actively intervenes in the medical field, including its instruction, licensing examinations, and services, and a large proportion of physicians trained in these medical education institutions (the institution faction) currently work in many medical schools, hospitals, and TCM clinics. Since the mid-twentieth century, the institution faction has become an official, licensed, and regulated medical field; it is mainstream in China today. This form of Traditional Chinese Medicine—capitalized—has absorbed many Western medical practices (e.g., electronic acupuncture and chemical analyses of herbal drugs). The older traditional Chinese medicine, which is uncapitalized, usually indicates the teacher-disciple faction, which was common before 1950 but is rare now.

Traditional medicine theories are not entirely systematic and regulated, however. Some practitioners, especially those not trained in institutions and who promise immortality and/or employ witchcraft, follow practices that can result in disease or death of the patient, and even of the practitioner. This obviously results in a negative impression of TCM, and the practitioners who pursue these misconceptualized methods call into question the scientific validity of TCM. These unjustified wellness theories may have a major impact on the environment as well; their practice often demands rare ingredients.

Skilled traditional physicians can make a strong impact on society and are crucial to its stability and sustainability. Environmentally speaking, most traditional physicians pursue harmony with their surroundings and will rarely destroy them in order to develop treatment methods. Most common herbal products are already in cultivation, and in some areas they are important economic sources, as ginseng is in Jilin Province and *Lycium chinense* (wolfberry or goji berry) in Ningxia Hui Autonomous Region. The main problem arising from herbal agriculture is the overuse of pesticides, fertilizers, and preservatives. There is also an economic impact on cultivation areas due to the fluctuation in prices, and a variation in efficacy of herbal products due to the difference in cultivation methods and genetic resource quality (which is decreasing). Herbal plants that have not undergone cultivation and are collected mainly from the wild are rapidly being exhausted, which affects other countries as well. For example, since the *Paris polyphylla* supply within Chinese borders has been depleted, demand for the same species turned to Vietnam, Myanmar (Burma), Nepal, and India, and these supplies will undoubtedly also be affected. In fact, wild rare herbal plants have even become highly valuable. The collection of certain plants has resulted in environmental destruction; harvesting of *Cistanche deserticola,* which grows in desert regions of China, has led to extreme land degradation. Due to its market price, ginseng is also nearing extinction in the wild. Wild medicinal herbs and animals are considered to have more "magical" power and to be more genuine (*dao di* in Chinese) than the cultivated ones, which has caused the overharvesting of wild resources. Many species of medicinal herbs in their wild forms are at risk. The Chinese government has made many attempts to prevent this consumption of wild medicines, but often too late to save the resource. Few nongovernmental or international organizations are involved in such matters.

Aside from species endangerment, another concern arising from medicine collected from animals is the ethics. Demand for deer horn (nascent horn of *Cervus nippon* Temminck [sika deer] and other species), seal oil (taken from lipids of seals), bear's gall, rhinoceros (*Rhinoceros* spp.) horn, and tiger (*Panthera tigris*) bone not only causes a large negative impact on these animal species, but due to ruthless collection methods (such as repeatedly collecting bile from live bears), it also raises treatment issues. Many animals are endangered largely because of their medicinal value, resulting in the depletion of resources; this causes inflation in their value, which again negatively impacts the reserve of medicinal animals in- and outside China. A portion of animal medicines has been replaced by human-made components, such as synthetic gallstones of cattle (*Bos taurus domesticus* Gmelin), but on the whole, human-made medicines haven't noticeably reduced the environmental impact of TCM.

Due to distrust for traditional medicine theories, as well as recognition for modern science, there have been arguments on the efficacy of traditional medicines and herbs since the early twentieth century, and disputes are gradually heating up. Those who support traditional medicine use its effectiveness as their basis of defense, whereas the opposition argues that traditional medicine cannot be accurately explained using modern scientific theories.

Because traditional medicines receive huge national support, especially by their inclusion in China's national medical insurance program, the traditional medicine market in China is continuously developing. There are difficulties in passing on the heritage of traditional medical theories and in training personnel, however, in addition to problems such as the short supply of traditional medicine herbs. Similarly, the impact of traditional medicine on the environment's sustainability is complex. What can be expected within the next five to ten years is that the market for traditional medicine will widen and gain greater influence, but it also will continue to deplete various types of rare herbs and animals. As traditional medicine gains popularity around the world, issues of cultivation and sustainable herbal agriculture, as well as ethical replacements for animal medicine, need to be addressed, before many species are harvested to extinction.

Gong CHENG
Minzu University of China

See also Biodiversity Conservation Legislation (China); Consumerism; Ecotourism; Endangered Species; Genetic Resources; Indigenous Peoples; Religions; Rural Livelihoods; Traditional Knowledge (China); Traditional Knowledge (India)

FURTHER READING

Hsiao, Jerry I. H. (2007). Patent protection for Chinese herbal medicine product invention in Taiwan. *The Journal of World Intellectual Property, 10,* 1–21.

Normile, Dennis. (2003). The new face of traditional Chinese medicine. *Science, 299,* 188–190

Qiu, Jane. (2007). Traditional medicine: A culture in the balance. *Nature, 448,* 126–128.

Richard, Stone. (2008). Lifting the veil on traditional Chinese medicine. *Science, 319,* 709–710.

Tang, Jinling. (2006). Research priorities in traditional Chinese medicine. *British Medical Journal, 333,* 391–394.

Wang, Jing-Fang; Wei, Dong-Qing; & Chou, Kuo-Chen. (2008). Drug candidates from traditional Chinese medicines. *Current Topics in Medicinal Chemistry, 8*(18), 1656–1665.

Wang, Lan, et al. (2008). Dissection of mechanisms of Chinese medicinal formula realgar-*Indigo naturalis* as an effective treatment for promyelocytic leukemia. *Proceedings of the National Academy of Sciences of the United States of America (PNAS), 105*(12), 4826–4831.

Yuan, Robert, & Lin, Yuan. (2000). Traditional Chinese Medicine: An approach to scientific proof and clinical validation. *Pharmacology and Therapeutics, 86*(2), 191–198.

Xu, Judy, & Yang, Yue. (2009). Traditional Chinese medicine in the Chinese health care system. *Health Policy, 90,* 133–139.

Xue, Tianhan, & Roy, Rustum. (2003). Studying traditional Chinese medicine. *Science, 300,* 740–741.

Zhang, Grant G.; Bausell, Barker; Lao, Lixing X.; Handwerger, Barry; & Berman, Brian M. (2003). Assessing the consistency of traditional Chinese medical diagnosis: An integrative approach. *Alternative Therapies in Health and Medicine, 9*(1), 66–71.

Berkshire's authors and editors welcome questions, comments, and corrections. Send your emails about the *Berkshire Encyclopedia of Sustainability* in general or this volume in particular to: sustainability.updates@berkshirepublishing.com

Traditional Knowledge (China)

Concern for sustainability informed traditional Chinese thought from the eleventh century BCE. At first it arose from a desire for dynastic longevity, but later it flowed from the wish for continuity in family and social institutions, frugality and conservation of resources, and harmony with nature via noninterference and letting be. An emphasis on court and imperial power eventually overrode the ideal of sustainability, which ironically led to instability.

Sustainability was a deep undercurrent in ancient Chinese thought in a variety of senses. Zhou dynasty (1045–256 BCE) texts from the eleventh century BCE stressed the continuity of humanity and nature, proclaiming that the Mandate of Heaven instructed commoner and courtier alike to respect others and nature, fulfill his or her life role, and stay attuned to the pulse of nature and in step with the cycle of the seasons (Chan 1963, 5–8). Later, the *Classic of Changes*—the *I Ching* (*Yijing*)—suggested that there is a seamless continuity between humanity and nature, and recommended that human actions should be in accord with the ebb and flow of events to maintain human and natural well-being (Chan 1963, 264–270).

Confucianism

Confucius (551–479 BCE) sought to stabilize human relationships and institutions by reminding people of their relationship to each other and the values that accompany this connection. Inspired by the Zhou founders' Way, Confucius's core virtue of humanity charged people with doing their utmost for family and fellows, as reflected in his saying that humanity was rooted in the practices of filial obedience and fraternity (Chan 1963, 20 ch./verse 1.2). He tried to better humanity with the virtues of righteousness, ritual conduct, and wisdom. Righteousness showed one's sensitivity regarding "what to do when" in interpersonal situations. Ritual propriety embodied the traditional, standard ways of exhibiting dignity and paying respect. Wisdom was how the practical fruits of one's learning, experience, and practices were expressed in dealing with novel or unusual situations.

Confucius focused on human relations, but his virtues were holistic, interactive, and in step with the flow of nature. Hence, his Way incorporated nature and dictated humility toward a nature that flows ceaselessly and a Heaven that keeps vigil. Among subsequent works of Confucianism, the *Mencius* asserted the continuity between the humanity of human upbringing and the care of natural resources (Lau 1970, 164–165 ch./verse 6A.8), while the *Mean* proclaimed that those who diligently cultivate themselves are able to develop things fully and "assist in the transforming and nurturing process of nature" and thus "can form a trinity with Heaven and Earth" (Chan 1963, 108).

Mozi and Xunzi

The philosopher Mozi (fl. 479–438 BCE) believed that the Confucian rituals diverted resources needed by society as a whole and were wasteful. His principle of "impartial regard" stressed fairness, and preached economy in expenditures and conservation in the use of natural resources (Chan 1963, 213–215, 227–229). His pragmatic approach, however, was so human-centered that it justified exploitation of nature for human uses. In this he influenced the Confucian Xunzi (c. 300–230 BCE), who discounted the traditional veneration of nature. Xunzi reasoned that people should heed the benefits to be derived from nature and that it was all right to exploit nature fully. In the essay "Nature" he counseled adapting production to local and seasonal conditions, but he regarded nature's bounty as inexhaustible and did not advocate conservation of resources (Chan 1963, 116–124).

Laozi and Zhuang Zi

The Daoism of Laozi (fifth century BCE?) and Zhuang Zi (369–286 BCE) invoked the idea of sustainability through their teaching and cultivating of attunement with *dao* (the path, or the Way), the world, nature, and things—and thus nonintentional action, noninterference, and letting things be. They did not eschew technology or production per se, but preferred keeping them at a basic level, regarding people's demands for goods and self-aggrandizement as something deviant and pathological that was the source of crime and violence. Their teachings were a form of self-cultivation to make their followers more mindful of humanity's union with the world. In their view, as individuals identified with the world more deeply, selfish pursuits would vanish, and the awareness and insight that followed would lead to a sense of being at one with one's situation, the flow of events, and the world. This sensitivity necessarily would involve a belief in and practice of sustainability, for an unsustainable way of life would harm oneself as it would harm the world (Chan 1963, 175).

The *Lushi Chunqiu*

The *Lushi Chunqiu* is a compendium of practical knowledge from the twilight of the Warring States period (475–221 BCE), edited by Lu Buwei (d. 235 BCE). Chapters 3–6 of section 3, book 26 discuss agriculture and focus on geography, soil, and climate (Knoblock and Riegel 2000). Chapter 3 ("The Supreme Importance of Agriculture") underscores the paramount value of agricultural production and handicrafts and the stability and virtues of rural people. It makes the point that since the entire economy is tied to agriculture, it is imperative to respect the farmer's proper seasons of labor (Knoblock and Riegel 2000, 650–654). Chapter 4 ("Requirements of the Land") discusses the proper techniques for plowing, tilling, planting, irrigating, cultivating, and harvesting in order to obtain the highest yields in different terrains (Knoblock and Riegel 2000, 655–658). Chapter 5 ("Discriminating Types of Soil") gives detailed instructions for working various types of soils—thick, thin, hard, sticky, soft, etc.—under differing water and weather conditions. Great attention is paid to the frequency of tilling during the four seasons, and the timing, density, and direction of seeding—the key being to direct tillage toward the removal or killing of weeds (Knoblock and Riegel 2000, 658–662). Finally, chapter 6 ("Examining the Season") applies the early Daoist idea of attuning oneself with nature and with the course of events. It discusses "the Way of farming," including the proper seasons for cutting timber, sowing, cultivating and harvesting wheat, etc., and warns of the risks of doing things too early or too late. Similar instructions are given for growing Setaria millet, panicled millet, rice, hemp, soybeans, and barley. While strategies for maintaining soil fertility are not given (the text breaks off at this point), the instructions given for cultivating grains are assured to yield bountiful crops, with nutritious grains that will be fragrant and tasty—and importantly, make the peoples' senses acute, their wits sharp, their limbs strong, and their bodies resistant to internal maladies (Knoblock and Riegel 2000, 662–667).

Sustainable States

Legalist thinkers, such as Hanfeizi (d. 233 BCE), believed that sustainable states required strong authorities and stressed techniques for governing that were centered on the two levers of power: reward and punishment. Rulers were advised to wield them using (1) the authority of their power, (2) a clear-cut, uniform code of law, and (3) their assessment of the "legality" of people's and ministers' conduct. Several states that instituted this military-style governance became powers and vied against each other in the early third century BCE. Finally, the Qín state unified China in 221 BCE—remaining unified under the first emperor, but (ironically) collapsing in 206 BCE soon after he died.

During the Western Hàn dynasty (206 BCE–24 CE), the scholar Dong Zhongshu (c. 195–105 BCE) observed that the two levers of power used to control the masses had to be concealed beneath a veneer of Confucian civilization and devised a sort of despotism with Confucianism as its ideology (Chan 1963, 272). This Legalist-Confucian hybrid was sustainable in that it was deployed by subsequent dynasties for nearly two millennia; however, as each of these dynasties went through an identical cycle of a golden age followed by a collapse, the model did not provide for sustainability of individual dynasties.

Modern day environmental pollution and other challenges have the Chinese government and its people researching past cultural methods to ensure a sustainable future. China's rich heritage of philosophy and scholarship undoubtedly will provide abundant inspiration.

Kirill Ole THOMPSON
National Taiwan University

See also Agriculture (China and Southeast Asia); China; Consumerism; Indigenous Peoples; Religions; Traditional Chinese Medicine (TCM); Traditional Knowledge (India)

FURTHER READING

Ames, Roger, & Hall, David. (2001). *Focusing the familiar.* Honolulu: University of Hawaii Press.

Ames, Roger, & Hall, David. (2003). *Dao de jing: Making life significant.* New York: Ballantine Books.

Ames, Roger, & Rosemont, Henry. (1998). *The analects of Confucius.* New York: Ballantine Books.

Chan Wing-tsit. (1963). *A source book in Chinese philosophy.* Princeton, NJ: Princeton University Press.

Chang Chung-yuan. (1975). *Tao: A new way of thinking.* New York: Harper Torchbook.

Girardot, Norman J.; Miller, James; & Liu Xiaogan. (Eds.). (2001). *Daoism and ecology: Ways within a cosmic landscape.* Cambridge, MA: Harvard University Press.

Graham, Angus. (1981). *Chuang-tzu: The inner chapters.* London: George Allen & Unwin.

Graham, Angus. (1989). *Disputers of the tao.* LaSalle, IL: Open Court.

Knoblock, John. (1988, 1990, 1994). *Xunzi: A translation and study of the complete works* (3 vols.). Stanford, CA: Stanford University Press.

Knoblock, John, & Riegel, Jeffrey. (2000). *The annals of Lu Buwei.* Stanford, CA: Stanford University Press.

Legge, James. (1960). *The Confucian classics* (5 vols.). Hong Kong: Hong Kong University Press. (Original work published 1862–1872)

Lau, D. C. (1970). *Mencius.* Harmondsworth, UK: Penguin Books.

Lau, D. C. (1979). *Confucius: The analects.* Harmondsworth, UK: Penguin Books.

Rowe, Sharon, & Sellmann, James. (2003). An uncommon alliance: Ecofeminism and classical Daoist philosophy. *Environmental Ethics, 25*(2), 129–148.

Sellmann, James. (2002). *Timing and rulership in Master Lu's spring and autumn annals: Lushi Chunqiu.* Albany: State University of New York Press.

Tucker, Mary Evelyn, & Berthrong, John. (1998). *Confucianism and ecology: The interrelation of heaven, Earth, and humans.* Cambridge, MA: Harvard University Press.

Watson, Burton. (1967). *Basic writings of Mo Tzu, Hsun Tzu, and Han Fei Tzu.* New York: Columbia University Press.

Watson, Burton. (1968). *The complete works of Chuang Tzu.* New York: Columbia University Press.

Traditional Knowledge (India)

Traditional knowledge in India has been passed down through generations in local communities. It is now under threat of overexploitation and unauthorized use by third parties outside the traditional circle. Legal protections for traditional knowledge include the concept of sharing of benefits arising from its use with the indigenous community. Further, the Indian government has launched an online Traditional Knowledge Digital Library to protect against its unlawful patenting.

The term *traditional knowledge* refers to the knowledge systems belonging to indigenous and local communities, comprising wisdom and practices developed over several generations. It includes traditional ways of utilizing land, natural resources, and the environment to achieve sustainable development. One important part of Indian traditional knowledge is traditional systems of medicine such as Ayurveda, Siddha, and Unani, which often make use of the healing properties of certain herbs and other plants.

Traditional knowledge is usually passed down from generation to generation by word of mouth, and it is rarely documented by the indigenous communities who hold the knowledge. Because the knowledge has not been written down, the communities are facing several challenges to retaining and making use of it. On the one hand, factors such as modernization of lifestyles and the dominance of the Western biochemical model of medicine pose a risk to the very language that gives voice to such knowledge traditions and the spiritual worldview that sustains them. On the other hand, the value of traditional knowledge, especially medicinal, is gradually being recognized, accompanied by exponential growth in the use of products based on it. The greatest threat to traditional knowledge is overexploitation and unauthorized use of this knowledge by third parties outside the traditional circle, especially where this is done by commercial entities that disregard the rights and interests of the traditional communities.

Global Protections

Traditional knowledge is protected by several international initiatives. The United Nations Declaration on Indigenous Peoples, endorsed by the United Nations Human Rights Council (UNHRC) in June 2006, recognizes that "respect for indigenous knowledge, cultures and traditional practices contributes to sustainable and equitable development and proper management of the environment" (United Nations 2008, 2). Other international legal provisions for protection of traditional knowledge are found in the Convention on Biological Diversity; the Protection, Conservation and Effective Management of Traditional Knowledge Relating to Biological Diversity Rules; the International Undertaking on Plant Genetic Resources for Food and Agriculture; the Agreement on Trade Related Aspects of Intellectual Property Rights; and the World Intellectual Property Organization (WIPO) Draft Document on Intellectual Property and Genetic Resources, Traditional Knowledge and Folklore.

A concept integral to the protection of traditional knowledge in light of its use in commercial activity is *benefit sharing*. The 1994 United Nations Convention to Combat Desertification, which provided for the protection of traditional knowledge in the ecological environments as well as the sharing of benefits arising from any commercial utilization of traditional knowledge, explicitly promoted benefit sharing. The Convention on

Biological Diversity established that benefit sharing requires the consent of the holders of traditional knowledge for its use and the fair and equitable sharing of benefits arising from such use. India became a signatory to the Convention on Biological Diversity in 1992, and enacted the Biological Diversity Act in 2002 in order to implement the obligations under the convention.

Other Indian legislation, such as the Geographical Indication of Goods (Registration and Protection) Act (1999) and the Plant Variety Protection and Farmers Rights Act (2001), also contain provisions that protect traditional knowledge.

One example of benefit sharing relates to the Kani tribe, living primarily in the Western Ghats of India. This tribe shared its unique traditional knowledge of the antifatigue properties of the plant *Trichopus zeylanicus* ssp. *Travancoricus* with a team of scientists visiting the area. The Tropical Botanical Gardens Research Institute then used the plant to develop a scientifically validated and standardized herbal drug named Jeevani. The research institute transferred the production technology to the pharmaceutical firm Arya Vaidya Pharmacy, and it agreed to share the license fee and royalty equally with the tribal community.

At the same time, the wide implementation of benefit-sharing arrangements remains problematic. Systems for benefit sharing are incomplete without the recognition of rights to self-determination, to territories and resources, and to prior informed consent.

Traditional Knowledge as Intellectual Property

Traditional knowledge is a form of intellectual property belonging to the indigenous community. In some cases, traditional knowledge has been misappropriated by third parties and then patented—a phenomenon known as biopiracy. In theory, patents that misappropriate traditional knowledge can be invalidated by showing that they lack novelty and inventiveness. In practice, however, the prior existence of the traditional knowledge is almost impossible to prove without written documentation. Certain systems have been put into place to protect the interests of traditional communities in the face of the global patenting process, through which large, powerful corporations might be given exclusive patent rights. The Indian Patents Act (1970), for example, by legal fiction and for the purposes of the act, makes inventions derived from traditional knowledge "not inventions" and hence ineligible for patent protection in India. Outside India, it is imperative that traditional knowledge be made available in the public domain, so that foreign patent offices are able to detect the prior existence of the knowledge and reject patent applications misappropriating such knowledge on the grounds of lack of novelty and inventiveness.

Some patents, including the turmeric and basmati patents granted by the United States Patent and Trademark Office and the neem patent granted by the European Patent Office, have been successfully revoked in the past, based on proof of the ancient traditional knowledge and use of the healing properties of these products in India. These successes led to the establishment of an online Traditional Knowledge Digital Library, first suggested by the Department of Ayurveda, Yoga & Naturopathy, Unani, Siddha and Homoeopathy (AYUSH), and initiated in 2001 as a collaborative project of the Council of Scientific and Industrial Research (CSIR), the Ministry of Science and Technology, and the Department of AYUSH in the Ministry of Health and Family Welfare.

This library acts as a safeguard against the granting of unoriginal patents throughout the world by providing information on Indian traditional systems of medicine in languages and formats understandable by patent examiners at international patent offices.

While documentation is undoubtedly important, another school of thought claims that only the holders of the traditional knowledge themselves can develop that knowledge because it is integrally connected to their way of life and makes sense only in situ. This point of view is often disregarded in the modern rush to commercialize and exploit discoveries.

Vaneesha JAIN
Luthra and Luthra Law Offices

The opinions in this article are solely those of the author and not the firm.

See also Activism, Judicial; Consumerism; Education, Environmental (India); India; Indigenous Peoples;

Information and Communication Technologies (ICT); Religions; Rule of Law; Traditional Chinese Medicine (TCM); Traditional Knowledge (China)

FURTHER READING

Agarwal, D. P. (n.d.) The Jeevani elixir of the Kani tribes of Kerala and their intellectual property (IP) rights. Retrieved October 24, 2011, from http://www.infinityfoundation.com/mandala/t_es/t_es_agraw_jeevani_frameset.htm

Chhibber, Bharti. (2008, June 7). Indian cultural heritage and environmental conservation through traditional knowledge. *Mainstream, 46*(25). Retrieved October 29, 2011, from http://www.mainstreamweekly.net/article746.html

Commission on Intellectual Property Rights. (2002). Traditional knowledge and geographical indications. In *Integrating intellectual property rights and development policy* (Chap. 4, pp. 73–94). Retrieved October 24, 2011, from http://www.iprcommission.org/papers/pdfs/final_report/Ch4final.pdf

Convention on Biological Diversity. (1992). Homepage. Retrieved September 30, 2011, from http://www.cbd.int/

United Nations University. (2007, December 19). Developing benefit sharing guidelines in India. Retrieved October 15, 2011, from http://www.ias.unu.edu/sub_page.aspx?catID=35&ddlID=625

Cullet, Phillippe, & Koluru, Radhika. (2002). Plant variety protection and farmers' rights—towards a broader understanding. Retrieved October 24, 2011, from http://www.ielrc.org/content/a0304.pdf

Indian Journal of Traditional Knowledge. (2011). Homepage. Retrieved December 6, 2011, from http://www.niscair.res.in/sciencecommunication/researchjournals/rejour/ijtk/ijtk0.asp

Kothari, Ashish. (2007, September). Traditional knowledge and sustainable development. Retrieved October 24, 2011, from http://www.iisd.org/pdf/2007/igsd_traditional_knowledge.pdf

Saxena, Achintya Nath. (2010). Protection of traditional knowledge as geographical indications: Policy issues. Retrieved October 15, 2011, from http://www.slideshare.net/achintyanath/protection-of-traditional-knowledge-as-geographical-indications

Traditional Knowledge Digital Library. (2011). Homepage. Retrieved October 2, 2011, from http://www.tkdl.res.in/tkdl/langdefault/common/Home.asp?GL=Eng

Traditional Knowledge Online: Mall University of New Hampshire School of Law. (2011). Homepage. Retrieved October 30, 2011, from http://www.traditionalknowledge.info/

United Nations. (2008). United Nations declaration on the rights of indigenous people. New York: United Nations. Retrieved December 6, 2011, from http://www.un.org/esa/socdev/unpfii/documents/DRIPS_en.pdf

Verkey, Elizabeth. (n.d.) Legal protection of traditional knowledge. Retrieved October 15, 2011, from www.iimk.ac.in/wto/seminar/ElizabethVerkey.doc

Berkshire's authors and editors welcome questions, comments, and corrections. Send your emails about the *Berkshire Encyclopedia of Sustainability* in general or this volume in particular to: sustainability.updates@berkshirepublishing.com

Transboundary Water Issues

In the absence of an internationally accredited global regulatory framework to address transboundary water rights, unilateral approaches and fragmented bilateral cooperation make overexploited water resources more vulnerable than ever. Transboundary water issues must consider the hydrological cycle as well as geological, geographical, geopolitical, ecological, and climatic impacts, as well as a user's legal right to water. Multilateral regulatory and integrated institutional management planning by riparian states is necessary to make the water in Asia and elsewhere secure and environmentally sound.

The term used to refer to the surface and/or groundwater of a watercourse that crosses (or is located on) boundaries between two or more countries, states, or regions as it moves directly or indirectly to the ocean is *transboundary water*. This designation deals primarily with freshwater resources and includes rivers, lakes, and aquifers. All of these resources are natural assets of immense value to the economic and social well-being, ecosystem management, and standard of living of the various countries, states, or regions of which they are a part.

Transboundary water is no less an essential component of the biosphere, affecting and affected by the hydrological water cycle that supports the biodiversity of the Earth's ecosystem. In 1997, five years after the Rio Earth Summit (United Nations Conference on Environmental Development), the Commission on Sustainable Development (CSD) of the United Nations prepared a comprehensive assessment of the world's water resources. The report stated: "Freshwater is a fundamental resource for development, used in agriculture, industry and households. It is a resource for which there is no substitute, whether as drinking water for people and animals, for hygiene, for crops and industrial processes or for fish and aquatic life" (UNDSD 1997). Therefore, the sustainable development, conservation, protection, management, and equitable utilization of all nonintegrated and vulnerable transboundary water resources is an urgent need, and must be addressed by multilateral and integrated management planning conducted by riparian countries, regions, and states.

Water Crises

Transboundary freshwater resources are considered limited, finite, vulnerable, and vital natural resources. Overall, global freshwater resources have been (and are being) exploited to meet increasing demands worldwide. The absence of an internationally accredited global regulatory framework, the fragmented bilateral cooperation among the riparian regions (referred to hereafter in this article, as they are in various UN reports, as "states"), as well as the lack of political will, the overexploitation of water, the priority of unilateral management planning to fulfill national water demands, and the impacts of climate change on water are impending crises that make transboundary water resources ever more vulnerable.

These crises are more critical in the Asian region. The availability of water in South and Southeast Asia is mainly dependent on glacier or snowmelt and rainwater. Numerous external factors and challenges, such as population growth, impacts of pollution, increased economic activity, improved standards of living, changes in consumption and production patterns, climate variance, and nonintegrated water governance, are actually decreasing the per capita water availability in Asia every year, particularly across central, southern, southwestern, and western Asia as well as in many parts of India and China. Jan Eliasson, the former president of the UN General Assembly (2005–2006), warned at a UN Water seminar in 2009 that in most cases the central struggle point between conflict and cooperation is the scarcity of water resources, which makes distribution a problem among sharers. He argued that there is a strong need for long-lasting, sustainable methods of cooperation that foster a win-win arrangement between interdependent actors (World Water Week 2010).

In Asia, the shortage and misuses of freshwater as a resource change important hydrological cycles. The current overwhelming and severe water stress in Asia will create future consequences on the Earth's surface and in its atmosphere. It affects climate conditions, sustainable socioeconomic and human development, environmental protection, and global health issues, all of which lead to (and in many cases derive from) conflicts over water sharing.

Hydrological Cycles

The hydrological cycle, simply defined, is the movement of water in its various forms—vapor, liquid, and solid—through the Earth's broad biophysical environment (atmospheric, marine, terrestrial, aquatic, and subterranean) (CBD 2008). This process includes the evaporation of water into the atmosphere, mainly from oceans and seas, as well the precipitation and condensation through which it returns to Earth. Water vapor also enters the atmosphere from other water surfaces such as lakes, rivers, aquifers, and reservoirs, as well as from vegetation.

The hydrological cycle of a transboundary water resource is thus an integral part of this overall water cycle, moving from its source, such as a glacier or an aquifer, to be used in various ways to support flora and fauna, and through transpiration (when the water absorbed through the roots of a plant is carried to small pores on the underside of it leaves and then turns to vapor), evaporation, precipitation, and eventual flow into the ocean. Water movement in the hydrological cycle is not confined within a place or time but is in constant motion, from the ocean to the atmosphere, or, in the case of water sourcing from a glacier, from the mountains to the ocean and back to the atmosphere. As an integral part of a regional ecosystem, transboundary water flow should not be restrained within an area. Any attempt to do so, such as diverting water by dams or barrages, can have a tremendous and often devastating impact on biodiversity and the ecosystems that support it.

Geology and Geography

The geological and geographic characteristics of transboundary water play an important role in the integrated management planning for the sustainability of a resource. For instance, a large percentage of the world's population depends on groundwater for various purposes when surface water is not available or fit for use or consumption. The surface water from a transboundary resource may appear alternately as groundwater on its way toward the ocean. The deterioration of groundwater quality in one state may affect not only groundwater but also surface water in another state, and it may restrict the usability of the resource for riparian state stakeholders (i.e., those people who have a stake in an enterprise) as the water moves closer to the ocean. Groundwater thus requires as much attention as surface water in cooperative and integrated management planning of a transboundary water resource.

The Geopolitical Perspective

In the absence of an internationally accredited global treaty to adhere to the international norms and standards in the management and utilization of a transboundary water resource, riparian states in different regions deliberately apply their own geopolitical theories and issues, at their own choice and discretion, to non-multilateral and cooperative movements. By failing politically to prioritize efforts toward reaching consensus, good faith, and trust, many riparian states further stymie progress toward multilateral management. The geographic position (see the section on management approaches below) and the economic power of riparian states are thus determining factors in the integrated management of a transboundary water resource.

Riparian states were once able to exercise principles and theories to justify their claims over the waters of a transboundary water resource by invoking "absolute and exclusive territorial sovereignty," "absolute territorial integrity," and "limited territorial sovereignty." At about the turn of the twenty-first century, however, numerous riparian stakeholder states of transboundary water resources, such as the Mekong (also known as the Mekong-Lancang), Nile, Rhine, Danube, and Niger rivers, adopted the doctrines of "equitable and reasonable utilization" and "joint management planning."

Management Approaches and Consequences

Uncontrolled unilateral management planning and/or fragmented and limited bilateral cooperation among individual states remain the two most common techniques for managing transboundary water resources in Asia. As a result, riparian states are suffering from the huge shortage of water in quantity and quality, experiencing socioeconomic and environmental problems, and engaging in conflicts over equitable and reasonable sharing of water from the common water resource. A number of upper riparian states conduct unilateral actions on the flow of a transboundary water system—storing, diverting, or withdrawing water by constructing large dams and reservoirs to protect their national interests and needs. They take an absolute unilateral approach, believing it will secure their interests and needs more effectively. The inadequacy of the water supply remains unchanged, however. None of these unilateral initiatives support the protection of vital ecosystems or the safeguards, sustainability, and vulnerability of the resource; none alleviate the environmental threats or prevent the disruption of water rights and equal sharing for the lower riparian state communities.

The World Commission on Dams (WCD) observed that large dams and diversion projects can lead to the loss of forests, wildlife habitat, and aquatic biodiversity, and can affect lower riparian flood plains and wetlands as well as riverine, estuarine, and adjacent marine ecosystems. With this possibility in mind, unilateral management planning must address ways to assess and identify the legitimate claims and entitlement of riparian stakeholders. (Based on the dispute between Hungary and Slovakia that halted progress of the Gabcikovo-Nagymaros Waterworks project, a large barrage project on the Danube intended to reduce catastrophic floods, the International Court of Justice in 1997 unequivocally condemned national unilateral action on a shared water resource.) In general, the limited scope of bilateral cooperation between riparian states has proved inadequate as water demands continue to increase. Uncontrolled national unilateral actions and so-called bilateral cooperation have proved to be unviable and unsustainable because methods of the upper riparian states tend to fulfill needs temporarily but do not address long-term implications and problems. In most cases, these methods actually deprive the lower riparian states and endanger the environment. They also violate the rules and norms of the customary international water law and contradict the proposition of equitable and reasonable sharing, as well as the sustainable development and management of natural resources of common use.

The following major problems that face Asia stem from such unilateral management approaches and the very limited scope of bilateral cooperation:

- *Inadequacy of available water.* Existing methods and uncoordinated development in management planning have resulted in the cumulative decrease of lower riparian flows and the degradation of water quality to the point at which activities in these areas must be compromised. The lack of proper initiative to maintain the resource and mandate the excess use of water make the resource even more vulnerable and exacerbate the severe scarcity of available water.
- *Socioeconomic and environmental problems.* These problems include the reduction in water supply for irrigation and industrial purposes; deteriorating water quality; arsenic contamination and other health hazards; groundwater abstraction (removing water from a ground source temporarily or permanently); substantial morphological changes such as increases in land degradation, silting, river erosion, and salinity due to reduced flow in the resource; floods and droughts; a decrease in river fishery; and displacement of populations.
- *Conflicts over equitable and reasonable sharing of transboundary water.* The equitable water sharing among the basin states is a historical problem that causes conflict between riparian states. In Asia, many riparian states have brought the matter of equitable water sharing before the International Court of Justice (ICJ), or an international arbitral tribunal, or into their national court. Disputes regarding sharing typically involve dam construction, water pollution, and allocation of water resources.

In many cases current management approaches regarding the uses of the transboundary water resources disregard international commitments to the protection of water and environment. In several situations, international legal philosophy has acknowledged the obligation to share the shared natural resources equitably and refrain from causing damage to other states. A 1996 advisory opinion of the ICJ concerning the legality of the threat to use nuclear weapons stated that the "existence of the general obligation of States to ensure that activities within their jurisdiction or control respect the environment of other States is now part of the corpus of international law relating to the environment" (ICJ 1996). In 1941, in the *Trail Smelter* dispute between the United States and Canada (a dispute arising over the air pollution generated by a Canadian smelter that wafted into the United States), the arbitral tribunal affirmed that, "under the principles of international law . . . no state has the right to use or permit the use of its territory in such a manner . . . as to cause injury to other States" (UN ESCAP 2003). In the *Corfu Channel* case (*United Kingdom of Great Britain and Northern Ireland v. People's Republic of Albania*), in which the United Kingdom sued Albania after two of its ships hit mines in Albanian waters, the ICJ affirmed every state's obligation not to knowingly allow its territory to be used for acts contrary to the rights of other states (ICJ 1949). The *Lake Lanoux* arbitration between Spain and France in 1957 (in which Spain and France argued over a proposed hydroelectric dam on the lake, because the lake's waters flowed out of the French lake and into Spain) applied the principles established by the *Corfu*

Channel case relating to the navigation of international watercourses.

The only global convention, the United Nations Convention on the Non-navigational Uses of International Watercourses 1997 (not yet entered into force as of April 2012) emphasizes the need for the sustainable use of the international watercourses and their adequate protection in a number of articles (Articles 5–7). This convention addresses the protection from (and the reduction and control of) pollution, as well as the preservation and management of the ecosystems of the international watercourses, taking into account generally accepted international rules and standards. It also urges states to take preventive measures and to mitigate harmful conditions related to international watercourses that may have an adverse impact on riparian states. Such conditions include severe environmental impacts from natural causes or from human conduct (see the section on the impacts of climate change).

Priorities and Initiatives

The issues and factors discussed so far involving hydrological cycles, geopolitical perspectives, existing management approaches and consequences, and international instruments and case law references about transboundary water resources suggest several initiatives that need to be prioritized by riparian states to protect their shared natural resources and the environment as a whole. These include the following:

- Cooperation in the sustainable development, conservation, protection, management and optimal utilization of a transboundary water resource in an equitable and reasonable manner through multilateral regulatory and integrated institutional management planning
- Commitment not to cause damage to the natural systems and the environment of other states and regions or in areas beyond the limits of national jurisdiction
- Monitoring, timely intervention, and facilitation for conservation policies and methods
- Recognizing the importance of protecting natural systems and introducing appropriate laws and policies in the interests of present and future generations

Water Rights for Riparian States

The right to water is a basic need and fundamental human right relating to life and liberty. "Water rights" and "water as a human right" have been receiving increasing attention in terms of access, diversion, and scarcity. The UN Committee on Economic, Cultural and Social Rights (UNCECSR) has agreed to designate water availability as a human right. It has been formally stated and declared in a broad range of international documents, including declarations, treaties, international agreements, and practices. In these documents, the principle of equitable and reasonable sharing of transboundary water resources were not mentioned explicitly, but water is a basic requirement in every case because the right to food, health, and development cannot be attained or ensured without securing availability to basic clean water. To ensure the human right to water and equitable and reasonable sharing of water for riparian states, many international instruments on the environment and natural resources argue for multilateral and integrated transboundary water resources management (ITWRM) by the riparian states.

Impacts from Climate Change

Climate change affects water resources directly and through its impact on ecosystems indirectly. Water-related climate-change impacts include severe and frequent droughts, floods, salinity, and water quality. Higher water temperatures, changes in precipitation, temperature extremes, and reduced stream flows adversely affect water quality, which in turn affect human uses of water. Climate change also affects the availability of water resources through changes in rainfall distribution, soil moisture, glacier and snow melt, and river and groundwater flows. Many regions of the world are experiencing these impacts on their national and transboundary water resources, and escalating conflicts in different parts of the world concentrate on water quantity and quality issues. Poor states are likely to be affected more because they are often incapable of adopting or mitigating the impacts. Climate change is expected to have broad and extensive impacts on the land and water systems in many states in the Asian region. The threat of climate change will become the major regional environmental concern in water disputes in the coming years.

Water Secure Asia: A Possible Option

Achieving the sustainable management and optimal utilization of a transboundary water resource in an equitable and reasonable manner, taking into consideration environmental, hydrological, geological, geographical, geopolitical, climatic factors, requires an approach that integrates regional and national cooperation. Integrated water resources management (IWRM) is a field devoted to the coordinated development and management of water, land, and related resources to achieve maximum economic and social welfare in an equitable manner without compromising the sustainability of vital ecosystems. In the twenty-first century many states of the world are turning to IWRM planning within their territories as they recognize the need for a sustainable approach to water resource development and management. In some cases multilateral regulatory and integrated institutional frameworks do not exist, however, to support the development and management of large transboundary river basins (shared by two or more states). In these cases, the success of IWRM programs is relatively low.

According to the UN Water (2008) Status Report, "Integrated Water Resources Management and Water Efficiency Plans 2008," implementation of such plans can be rated according to their progress as follows: 25 percent as good, 25 percent as some, and 50 percent as limited or none. In 2009, the UNGA Economic and Financial Committee meeting on the topic "Enhancing Governance on Water" argued that the absence of effective financial support to create new and restructure existing land- and water-related institutions further exacerbates the challenges of water resources management. Developed states are in a better position to implement IWRM planning than developing or less-developed states. Since the hydrological cycle and other important factors of transboundary water resources require integrated management planning, the unilateral or fragmented bilateral cooperation within a territory, or segmented or isolated IWRM planning, cannot sustainably manage the natural resource of common use. Transboundary water resources, therefore, need to be managed from source to mouth through multilateral regulatory and integrated institutional management planning by all stakeholder riparian states.

In Southeast Asia, the transboundary water resources of the Mekong-Lancang River have been successfully managed and utilized jointly by Cambodia, Laos, Thailand, and Vietnam. In 1996, China and Myanmar (Burma) became dialogue partners in the management of the river and now work together within a cooperative framework. The multilateral regulatory framework—the Agreement on the Cooperation for the Sustainable Development of the Mekong River Basin 1995 (the Mekong Agreement)—applies to the water and related resources of the Mekong River basin (MRB). It provides a broad approach to defining the legal parameters of the treaty and establishes an integrated management institution, the Mekong River Commission (MRC), to manage the river. This agreement is one of the best examples of the multilateral regulatory regime that integrates the efforts of riparian states for the sustainable development, management, and optimal utilization of a transboundary water resource. The state parties of the commission adopted IWRM planning in the development and management of the MRB. The commission addresses all interrelated factors to manage collectively and peacefully (MRC 1995, articles 1, 4, and 30) and has produced a very effective hierarchy of institutional management structures (MRC 1995, Chapter IV, articles 33–41). The riparian states of the transboundary rivers, the Nile, Sava, Rhine, Danube, Niger, Lake Chad, Congo, and Senegal rivers are also applying the multilateral regulatory and integrated institutional management planning among their riparian states. Many of these regional regulatory arrangements have been established in line with the broad guidance offered under the 1997 UN Watercourses Convention and have established integrated management institutions to manage transboundary water resources.

Outlook

Managing transboundary water resources remains crucial to overall global sustainable development. Although freshwater is the Earth's most valuable and vital resource, it is also the most exploited due to overuse, pollution, and climate change, as well as to changes in the hydrological water cycle that stem from diverting water sources for seemingly beneficial uses such as flood control and irrigation. All of these factors contribute to the loss of biodiversity on Earth, and are further exacerbated by the lack of an internationally accredited regulatory framework for utilizing transboundary water resources.

None of these problems and effects can be addressed by unilateral or noncooperative water resource management practices that privilege one riparian state over another; instead, riparian states must adopt multilateral and cooperative management and regulatory methods and develop institutions that address water use and respect equitable water rights for users. One example of an institution moving toward such methods in Asia is the Mekong River Commission, which includes member states Cambodia, Laos, Vietnam, and Thailand, with China and Myanmar as dialogue partners in management. Riparian states must recognize the importance of IWRM or ITWRM planning as they refrain from using management scenarios that protect their national or geopolitical interests to the detriment of others.

Jakerul ABEDIN
Macquarie University

See also Fisheries (China); Ganges River; The Himalaya; Huang (Yellow) River; Mekong-Lancang River; Pearl River Delta; South-North Water Diversion; Three Gorges Dam; Tibetan Plateau; Water Security; Water Use and Rights (India); Yangzi (Chang) River

FURTHER READING

Ahmed, Murshed. (2007). Regional co-operation on transboundary water resources management: Opportunities and challenges (paper, Bangladesh Economic Association Conference). Dhaka, Bangladesh.

Burleson, Elizabeth. (2005). Equitable and reasonable use of water within the Euphrates-Tigris River basin. *Environmental Law Reporter, 35,* 10041–10054.

Chellaney, Brahma. (2012). Asia's worsening water crisis: Survival. *Global Politics and Strategy, 54*(2), 143–156.

Convention on Biological Diversity (CBD). (2008). Transboundary water resources management: The role of international watercourse agreements in implementation of the CBD. Retrieved April 16, 2012, from http://www.cbd.int/doc/publications/cbd-ts-40-en.pdf

Fearnside, Philip M. (1995). Hydroelectric dams in the Brazilian Amazon as sources of "greenhouse" gases. *Environmental Conservation, 22*(1), 7–19.

Gleick, Peter. (1999). The human right to water. *Water Policy, 1*(5), 487–503.

Global Water Partnership Technical Advisory Committee. (2000). Integrated water resources management. Retrieved from December 14, 2011, from http://www.gwptoolbox.org/images/stories/gwplibrary/background/tac_4_english.pdf

Houghton, Richard A. (1991). Tropical deforestation and atmospheric carbon dioxide. *Climate Change, 19*(1–2), 99–118.

HSBC Group (2005). Freshwater infrastructure sector guideline. Retrieved September 27, 2011, from http://www.hsbc.ca/1/PA_1_083Q9FJ08A002FBP5S00000000/content/canada2/assets/pdf/sustainability/freshwater_infrastructure_guideline.pdf

Human Rights Education Associates. (2002). Food and water. Retrieved October 3, 2011, from http://www.hrea.org/index.php?doc_id=404

International Court of Justice (ICJ). (1949). Corfu Channel (*United Kingdom of Great Britain and Northern Ireland v. Albania*). Retrieved October 3, 2011, from http://www.icj-cij.org/docket/files/1/1645.pdf

International Court of Justice (ICJ). (1996). Advisory opinion on the legality of the threat or use of nuclear weapons. Retrieved on September 17, 2011, from http://www.icj-cij.org/docket/files/95/7495.pdf (para. 29).

Laurance, William F.; Laurance, Susan G.; & Delamonica, Patricia. (1998). Tropical forest fragmentation and greenhouse gas emissions. *Forest Ecology and Management, 110*(1–3), 173–180.

McCaffrey, Stephen C. (2003). *The law of international watercourses non-navigational uses.* Oxford, UK: Oxford University Press.

Mekong River Commission (MRC). (n.d.). Homepage. Retrieved October 1, 2011, from http://www.mrcmekong.org/

Mekong River Commission (MRC). (1995). Agreement on the cooperation for the sustainable development of the Mekong River Basin. Retrieved April 18, 2012, from http://ns1.mrcmekong.org/agreement_95/agreement_95.htm

United Nations (UN). (2005). The law of the non-navigational uses of international watercourses (study prepared for the use of the ILC, Office of Legal Affairs, UN). Retrieved August 13, 2011, from http://untreaty.un.org/ilc/summaries/8_3.htm

United Nations Economic and Social Commission for Asia and the Pacific (UN ESCAP) Virtual Conference. (2003). International watercourse and rights to use: Trail Smelter arbitration. Retrieved April 16, 2012, from http://www.unescap.org/drpad/vc/document/compendium/int7.htm

United Nations Division for Sustainable Development (UNDSD). (1997, June 23–27). Earth Summit +5: Special session of the General Assembly to review and appraise the implementation of Agenda 21; UN assessment of freshwater resources. Retrieved September 28, 2011, from http://www.un.org/ecosocdev/geninfo/sustdev/waterrep.htm

United Nations Educational, Scientific and Cultural Organization (UNESCO). (2009). Climate change and water: An overview from the world water development report 3: Water in a changing world. Retrieved September 17, 2011, from http://unesdoc.unesco.org/images/0018/001863/186318e.pdf

UN-Water. (2008). Status report on integrated water resources management and water efficiency plans. Retrieved October 10, 2011, from http://www.unwater.org/downloads/UNW_Status_Report_IWRM.pdf

UN-Water. (2009a). Climate change adaptation is mainly about water. Retrieved October 13, 2011, from http://www.unwater.org/downloads/UNWclimatechange_EN.pdf

UN-Water. (2009b). Background note on the special event of the economic and financial committee of the United Nations General Assembly: Enhancing governance on water. Retrieved September 17, 2011, from http://www.unwater.org/downloads/BackgroundNote2ndCommittee.pdf

World Commission on Dams. (2000). *Dams and development: A new framework for decision-making.* London: Earthscan Publications.

World Water Week. (2010). The UN Water seminar [2009]: Managing water in times of global crises: How can the UN system step up its efforts? UN Water. Retrieved November 5, 2011, from http://www.worldwaterweek.org/sa/node.asp?node=471&sa_content_url=%2Fplugins%2FEventFinder%2Fevent.asp&sa_title=Managing+Water+in+Times+of+Global+Crises+%96+How+can+the+UN+System+Step+up+its+Efforts%3F&id=1&event=84

Wouters, Patricia, & Ziganshina, Dinara. (2011). Tackling the global water crisis. In R. Quentin Grafton & Karen Hussey (Eds.), *Water resources planning and management* (pp. 175–183). Cambridge, UK: Cambridge University Press.

U

Utilities Regulation and Energy Efficiency

China, India, and Thailand have all set ambitious national targets for energy efficiency. Efficiency programs managed through electric utilities will likely be an important part of efforts to meet these targets. Thailand was the first to set up a comprehensive utility energy efficiency program, and its experience highlights the importance of having a strong regulatory framework that integrates energy efficiency into utility investment planning.

Across developing Asia, rapid energy demand growth since the early 1990s—with annual growth often in the double digits—has been a major source of economic and environmental stress. By reducing demand growth and the need for new infrastructure (e.g., power plants, pipelines) and its environmental impacts, energy efficiency has emerged as an increasingly practical energy supply option.

New approaches to energy efficiency policy are taking shape throughout Asia, including in the electric utility sector. Internationally, utility-based energy efficiency programs have ranged from simple appliance rebate programs to more comprehensive integrated resource planning, where utility regulation is designed to put demand- and supply-side investments on equal footing. In most Asian countries, utility-based energy efficiency programs are still in the development stage. This paper examines and compares the experiences, plans, and challenges of existing and nascent utility-based energy efficiency programs in China, India, and Thailand.

China

The energy crises of the 1970s spurred more than a decade of aggressive investment in energy efficiency in China. During that time, design and implementation of energy efficiency policies reflected the Chinese government's continued tendency toward central planning. Policies and programs were administered top-down from the central government through the state-owned and operated industrial system. The approach ranged from hands-on, such as the imposition of company energy quotas and the closure of factories, to hands-off, such as the provision of grants and information services, but the scale was unprecedented. By the early 1980s, energy efficiency investment reached an estimated 10 percent of total investment in energy supply (Lin 2007).

Over time, this level of political attention and investment proved unsustainable. As China moved from energy shortage to surplus at the end of the 1990s, interest in energy efficiency waned. Rapid growth in energy demand after 2002—at more than 15 percent per year between 2002 and 2004—led to renewed interest in energy efficiency as a means to rein in energy consumption, and government agencies announced an extensive array of energy efficiency targets, key projects, and enterprise programs in 2006. However, by this time China's energy consumption was much larger, end uses of energy were more diverse, and the central government's control over local governments and the industrial system was much weaker than during the 1980s and early 1990s. The difficulties encountered during this more recent round of energy efficiency policies has led to calls for new approaches, among which is an energy efficiency requirement (EE/DSM Rule) imposed on electric utilities.

Integration of Energy Efficiency into Utility Planning

For more than forty years beginning in the 1950s, China's electricity sector was a state-owned and state-operated, vertically integrated monopoly. In the late 1990s, the sector was corporatized, separating government and business functions, and later was "unbundled," separating the generation and transmission and distribution businesses and creating two national grid companies to oversee provincial grid companies. In 2003 a national, independent regulator, the State Electricity Regulatory Commission (SERC), was established for the sector.

China's utility EE/DSM Rule, adopted in November 2010, is targeted at the country's two national grid companies, the State Grid Corporation of China and the China Southern Power Company. The rule stipulates that the grid companies must obtain at least 0.3 percent of their annual kilowatt and kilowatt-hour sales from energy efficiency. Although a few grid companies in high growth provinces have run their own peak load management programs in the past, the EE/DSM Rule marks the first time that utilities are being required to incorporate energy efficiency as a supply option. The rule, though not particularly ambitious, will allow grid companies and regulators to work through the challenges of integrating energy efficiency into utility planning, providing an essential foundation for scaling up the target.

Challenges of Energy Efficiency Integration

How the EE/DSM Rule will be implemented, and who will be allowed to profit from it, are still open questions. Two widely discussed options are fostering a market for third-party energy service companies and allowing the national grid companies to implement the rule themselves. The grid companies are reportedly establishing regional energy efficiency offices, which seems to indicate that they plan to take charge of implementation.

The most important challenges to China's EE/DSM Rule are electricity pricing and regulation. As yet, there is no dedicated mechanism for raising investment capital for projects that contribute to the 0.3 percent target. The grid companies are reportedly expecting to be able to recoup their investment costs through a small increase in their average wholesale price. Although this might be a viable option for a small target, scaling up the rule to a more meaningful level would require rethinking how prices are set for the grid companies.

Because their wholesale prices are not set on a cost basis, it is, in fact, difficult to sort out what incentives China's grid companies face. Rationalizing their prices, and later decoupling revenues from sales, are important steps to providing the grid companies with incentives for energy efficiency. Both steps are currently under discussion. Another issue to be considered is how to determine the appropriate future target for the EE/DSM Rule. The 0.3 percent target did not have an analytical basis, and scaling up the rule will require some analysis of its avoided cost, or how much the rule saves or costs the electricity system and its ratepayers.

All these considerations imply the need for strong and effective regulatory oversight of the grid companies, which China does not yet have. In addition to restructuring incentives for the grid companies and determining appropriate targets for the EE/DSM Rule, a regulator would need to set rules about the kinds of energy efficiency that would qualify to meet the target, and would have to oversee monitoring and verification of energy efficiency programs and savings. SERC is capable of fulfilling this role, but currently lacks sufficient pricing authority and the capacity to design and oversee energy efficiency programs.

India

The potential for cost-effective energy efficiency in India and its accompanying environmental benefits are well documented, yet utility energy efficiency programs across India have been limited historically. Against a backdrop of unprecedented growth in GDP and demand, increasing energy and capacity shortages, and concerns over climate change, significant efforts have been made since 2000 to promote energy efficiency, especially at the national level.

The Energy Conservation Act (2001) established the Bureau of Energy Efficiency (BEE), a national-level bureau that is responsible for establishing energy efficiency labeling and standards for appliances and for establishing energy conservation standards in building codes. The Electricity Act (2003) promotes power sector reform legislation, and, while not explicitly addressing it, has been interpreted by some state regulators as justifying utility energy efficiency. In 2009, the National Mission on Enhanced Energy Efficiency (NMEEE) established a goal to reduce energy use by 10,000 megawatts by the year 2020. The NMEEE includes four initiatives: tradable energy savings certificates, market transformation, creation of a financing platform to facilitate energy service company (ESCO) activity, and development of a broader economic framework to support energy efficiency (e.g., tax incentives). India's effort to accelerate energy efficiency through national programs recognizes the inherent challenges and supports utility energy efficiency.

Integration of Energy Efficiency into Utility Planning

There is no formal utility-level integrated resource planning (IRP) in India. National-level IRP is conducted primarily by the central government. The state electricity regulatory commissions (SERCs) regulate distribution utilities and, in Maharashtra, Delhi, Karnataka,

Haryana, Punjab and Gujarat, have begun to support utility energy efficiency.

Maharashtra is the first state with regulations that support state-level energy efficiency implementation using an avoided cost framework—one that explicitly takes into consideration the cost the utility avoids by not having to generate or purchase electricity. Currently, pilot programs are underway in the city of Mumbai that target lighting and cooling end uses by providing incentives to reduce the high first costs of the most efficient products (as rated by the BEE). During 2004–2006, Karnataka, with technical assistance from the United States Agency for International Development, initiated a compact fluorescent lamp promotion program that uses on-bill financing. On-bill financing allows customers to finance the upfront costs of the lamps and pay for them over time through their utility bills.

The national government is complementing utility energy efficiency by initiating the Super-Efficient Equipment Program that will provide incentives to manufacturers to develop and sell products that are substantially more efficient than the highest BEE-rated products (e.g., brushless direct current technology for ceiling fans). BEE has also implemented the National Bachat Lamp Yojana compact fluorescent light (CFL) promotion program that uses funds from the clean development mechanism (CDM) to reduce the relatively higher first costs of CFLs as compared with incandescent lamps. BEE is assisting state government agencies to support local municipalities in the promotion of energy efficient building codes. Unlike in China and Thailand, in India the agriculture sector is an important target for energy efficiency programs because of its heavily subsidized nature. Several different energy efficiency delivery models are currently being tested.

Challenges of Energy Efficiency Integration

To date, there has been little coordination between the states and the BEE in their pursuit of energy efficiency. Moving forward, however, discussions are occurring to expand utility energy efficiency to all Indian states with the creation, by the Forum of Regulators, of the DSM Working Group, a statutory body consisting of chairpersons of all SERCs and the Central Electricity Regulatory Commission. BEE is an invited member of the Working Group.

Deep penetration of energy efficiency in India is hampered by typical market barriers, such as lack of awareness, split incentives, lack of leadership among the private sector players who promote energy efficiency, and high up-front costs. Some barriers are accentuated in India, such as lack of access to technology (particularly in rural areas), and inability to assess efficient technology. Furthermore, the lack of a formal legal mandate and the necessary regulatory/institutional framework present primary barriers for scaling up utility energy efficiency to all states. Given that most utilities are state-owned, and that there are political differences between the central government and the states, the central government's ability to encourage utilities to support energy efficiency is further limited.

In practice, the SERCs' authority is still evolving, as they were reorganized only a decade ago. Most utilities are operating at a massive deficit and are unable to raise tariffs that cover existing costs, let alone new costs of energy efficiency programs, primarily because of political considerations. Indian utilities are not held to strict reliability requirements through an obligation-to-serve, as utilities in many other countries are, which in turn limits the possibility of full exploitation of energy efficiency potential in a formal IRP framework.

Thailand

In the late 1980s and early 1990s, Thailand's economy was one of the fastest growing in Asia, with GDP increasing over 10 percent per year. To fuel such growth, Thailand's power usage went through a phase of rapid expansion, growing 14 percent per year and leading to a substantial investment requirement for the power sector. In response, the Thai government set up the Energy Conservation Promotion Fund in 1992 to support energy conservation programs.

In 1993, the government established the Demand Side Management Office (DSMO) within the state-owned Electricity Generating Authority of Thailand (EGAT), the utility in charge of the national grid and sourcing generation, to implement energy efficiency programs for the power sector. The DSMO focused on market transformation, awareness campaigns, and facilitation of energy efficiency and load management technologies. The office grew rapidly and enjoyed a high-profile success in delivering savings that exceeded targets.

In 1997, Thailand's financial crisis not only reduced economic growth to a standstill, but also led to an abrupt change from growth to decline in demand for electricity for the first time in Thailand's history. The Thai power sector was suddenly in a capacity surplus situation, with many more committed projects in the pipeline. Feeling the pinch from having to cut down projects and renegotiate contracts, EGAT singled out the success of DSMO's program as being responsible for the demand shortfalls. While DSMO survived the storm, its growth was stunted. Even long after the crisis, the power sector repeatedly found itself in a cycle of over-optimistic demand forecasts and excess capacity from over-investments. Energy efficiency and demand-side management had to take a back seat and took on more of a green image role so as not to undermine EGAT's financial standing, or the government's other high-priority policy objectives, such as stimulating investment from independent power producers.

Integration of Energy Efficiency into Utility Planning

Despite being a part of EGAT, the DSMO's programs have not been integrated into the utility planning process, known in Thailand as the Power Development Plan (PDP). The need to integrate energy efficiency in the PDP was only recognized and mentioned in the 1995 PDP. The idea did not develop further and was dropped altogether after the 1997 financial crisis and subsequent capacity surpluses. Despite the government's vow and civil society's demand to promote energy conservation, and despite its low cost, energy efficiency only received token treatment in the PDP process. The 2010 PDP is the latest example. The only energy efficiency measure included in the twenty-year plan was a thin tube light replacement program, which would deliver a saving of only 0.3 percent of total load by 2030.

Challenges of Energy Efficiency Integration

The main challenge to the integration of energy efficiency in the PDP process is that it is severely misaligned with the incentive structure faced by EGAT. DSMO's budget is funded by power tariffs but is treated internally (within EGAT) as an expense, not as capital investment on which EGAT can earn a return. Furthermore, EGAT is subject to a fixed, guaranteed rate-of-return, which provides a handsome return on capital investment. As a result, EGAT faces several simultaneous disincentives to investing in energy efficiency. First, energy efficiency leads to a reduction in the amount of electricity sold, which reduces EGAT's revenues. Second, investment in energy efficiency is not considered an "investment" and is therefore not eligible to earn the fixed return on invested capital that determines EGAT's profits and the incentives of its employees. It is not surprising, therefore, that only large-expenditure projects such as coal-fired, gas-fired, and nuclear and large hydroelectric power plants are considered in the PDP, and that energy efficiency is conspicuously absent.

Since the latest PDP was adopted in 2010, the government announced a twenty-year energy efficiency plan in 2011 that calls for a 25 percent reduction in energy intensity (energy use per unit GDP). This goal, which was driven by concerns over Thailand's high energy intensity, was reaffirmed by the newly elected government in August 2011. To achieve this goal, consumption of electricity and other forms of energy must be reduced by 20 percent from the "business as usual," or PDP 2010, baseline consumption. It remains to be seen how this energy intensity target will be integrated into the next PDP.

The key to achieving this goal is to restructure the utilities' incentives. First, energy efficiency measures need to be treated as investments, not expenses. Second, in order to break the over-investment cycles, it is necessary to move away from guaranteed rate-of-return-regulation, which rewards over-investment rather than operational and investment efficiency. And last, the planning process needs to consider energy efficiency as a supply option to meet growing power demand.

Comparison of Experiences and Key Challenges

In response to rapid growth in energy demand and environmental concerns, energy efficiency is enjoying a resurgence across Asia. National governments in China, India, and Thailand have set ambitious, longer-term targets for energy efficiency. To meet those targets, planning and regulatory agencies are now designing and experimenting with new energy efficiency policies and programs, including those managed through electric utilities. Despite differences in national contexts, several themes emerge from a comparison of energy efficiency policy and practice across China, India, and Thailand, offering insights to guide future efforts.

In both China and Thailand, the Asian financial crisis of the late 1990s had a severe impact on commitment to, and funding for, energy efficiency, as surplus production capacity led governments to scale back energy efficiency programs. Cyclical support is perhaps intrinsic to energy efficiency programs that are motivated by high energy demand growth, which makes them politically difficult to sustain when demand growth slows. Integrating energy efficiency into longer-term investment planning processes, such as through electric utility resource planning, could make energy efficiency policies more sustainable through economic growth cycles, but requires political commitment, and an institutional infrastructure to support it.

Thailand was the first country in Asia to set up utility-based energy efficiency programs, whereas this approach is just beginning to take shape in China and India. Difficulties in sustaining commitment to utility-based energy efficiency in Thailand provide a useful point of reference for China and India. The critical weakness of Thailand's Demand Side Management Office continues to be the lack of an institutionalized mechanism that links energy efficiency with utility investment, an avoided cost framework, electricity prices, a system to monitor and verify efficiency savings, and utility profits. Without this more integrated approach to resource planning, high levels of investment in energy efficiency have proven difficult to sustain.

For China, Thailand's experience suggests that, without the support of a strong regulatory framework, its EE/DSM Rule is unlikely to be effective. A strong regulatory framework would require empowering China's electricity regulator, which has historically had little real authority. China has a nationally regulated electricity sector, and providing enough flexibility in the design of national regulation across diverse provinces, several of which are comparable in size to Thailand, will be a challenge. For India, the challenge instead is how to harness the power of local initiatives, by strengthening state-level electricity regulatory commissions, clarifying and improving state-level incentives for energy efficiency, and scaling up local regulatory innovation.

Over the coming decades, utility-based energy efficiency could be an important complement to other sector-based policies and incentives as a means to meet national energy efficiency targets. China, India, and Thailand will all need to develop the institutions and capacity to support more sustained inclusion of energy efficiency in utility planning, which will provide ample opportunities for exchange and shared learning.

Fredrich KAHRL
Energy and Environmental Economics, Inc.

Ranjit BHARVIRKAR
Itron Inc.

Chris GREACEN
Palang Thai

Chuenchom Sangarasri GREACEN
Palang Thai

Mahesh PATANKAR
Customized Energy Solutions

Priya SREEDHARAN
Energy and Environmental Economics, Inc.

James H. WILLIAMS
Monterey Institute of International Studies

See also Cities—Overview; Energy Industries—Nuclear; Energy Industries—Renewables (China); Energy Industries—Renewables (India); Energy Security (East Asia); Five-Year Plans; Green Collar Jobs; Information and Communication Technologies (ICT); Microfinance; Public Transportation; Public-Private Partnerships; Rule of Law; Steel Industry

FURTHER READING

Andrews-Speed, Philip. (2009). China's ongoing energy efficiency drive: Origins, progress and prospects. *Energy Policy, 37*(4), 1331–1344.

Hu Zhaoguang; Moskovitz, David; & Zhao Jianping. (2005). Demand-side management in China's restructured power industry: How regulation and policy can deliver demand-side management benefits to a growing economy and a changing power system. Washington, DC: World Bank.

Lin Jiang. (2007). Energy conservation investments: A comparison between China and the US. *Energy Policy, 35*(2), 916–924.

Sathaye, Jayant, & Gupta, Arjun, P. (2010). Eliminating electricity deficit through energy efficiency in India: An evaluation of aggregate economic and carbon benefits. Lawrence Berkeley National Laboratory Report LBNL-3381E.

Singh, Daljit; Bharvirkar, Ranjit; Kumar, Saurabh; Sant, Girish; & Phadke, Amol. (2011). Using national energy efficiency programs with upstream incentives to accelerate market transformation for super-efficient appliances in India. European Council for an Energy Efficient Economy 2011 Summer Study. Retrieved April 4, 2012, from http://proceedings.eceee.org/docs/eceee_2011_toc.pdf

Singh, Jas, & Mulholland, Carol. (2000). DSM in Thailand: A case study. UNDP/World Bank Energy Sector Management Programme Report. Retrieved September 13, 2011, from http://www.egat.co.th/en/images/stories/pdf/dsm_in_thailand_2.pdf

Sulyma, Iris M., et al. (2000). Taking the pulse of Thailand's DSM market transformation programs. American Council for an Energy-Efficient Economy Summer Study Proceedings Paper. Retrieved September 13, 2011, from http://www.aceee.org/proceedings-paper/ss00/panel08/paper31

Zhou, Nan; Levine, Mark; & Price, Lynn. (2010). Overview of current energy efficiency policies in China. *Energy Policy, 38*(11), 6439–6452.

W

Water Security

Water security is the term used to describe the availability of adequate water to meet the needs of social-ecological systems. Water security varies widely across India, China, and East and Southeast Asia. Key challenges stem from the demands of huge, industrializing populations and climate-related stress. These countries must navigate trade-offs between different social and ecological demands on water if they are to ensure sustained and sustainable development.

Water security refers to protection afforded the biosphere from water-related hazards as well as reliable access to enough water to meet the needs of both humans and the environment. *Water availability* and *water security* are distinct terms. Regions with low levels of water do not necessarily suffer from water insecurity, unless demands outstrip supply. Although the western, arid region of China receives less water than the east, experts consider it relatively secure because of its dramatically lower population and limited economic activity (Vörösmarty et al. 2010).

Water insecurity is a global problem. The journal *Nature* published an analysis of global water threats showing that as of the year 2000, some 80 percent of the world's population was vulnerable to water insecurity and that freshwater ecosystems around the world are in crisis (Vörösmarty et al. 2010). The study also showed how threats to water security overlap significantly with human presence and actions, thus underlining the urgent need for improved water management.

India, East Asia, and Southeast Asia

India, East Asia, and Southeast Asia encompass diverse biomes (ecological communities), from deserts to tropical rain forests; water availability differentiates each one. People practice diverse forms of land-based livelihoods within these landscapes. Water-related challenges affect the livelihoods on which people depend for income and subsistence. Traditional methods of water management as well as modern water-related infrastructure have enabled countries in the region to face the challenges of dryland conditions and the seasonality of the monsoons. Challenges remain, however. With the exception of pockets of water security, people and ecosystems within the entire region are vulnerable to water scarcity. Population growth, industrialization, and urbanization exacerbate existing challenges that come from the seasonality of the monsoons, periodic droughts, floods, and uneven spatial distribution of water. These challenges place heavy demands on existing resources and involve trade-offs between different uses of water that are often skewed in favor of the economically or politically powerful stakeholders (people who have a stake in an enterprise). Mismanagement and the effects of climate change further constrain water security.

Access to safe drinking water has traditionally been a concern throughout the region, especially in rural areas (with some exceptions where drinking water standards are high and strictly enforced, such as in Singapore). Differences between regions and difficulties in compiling accurate data make comparisons between places and across time problematic. United Nations data provide a general picture on progress toward meeting the Millennium Development Goal to "halve, by 2015, the proportion of the population without sustainable access to safe drinking water and basic sanitation" (UN 2010). In 2012, the United Nations announced that the world had met the target to halve the number of the proportion of population without sustainable access to safe drinking water (WHO 2012). Despite gains, however, millions in the region still lack safe and sustainable access to water for drinking and sanitation. For instance, China and India combined are home to some 216 million people without access to improved water supplies (UNICEF and WHO 2012).

The United Nations reports that East Asia has made the most progress toward improvements in access to drinking water. Access to drinking water improved by about 23 percent from 1990 to 2010 (UNICEF and WHO 2012). There has been less progress in improving access to sanitation facilities, especially in rural areas, and especially in India and the countries of Southeast Asia (UNICEF and WHO 2012). Lack of access to drinking water and lack of sanitation are closely tied to waterborne disease and gender inequality in the region, both of which impose a tremendous human and economic cost on those societies.

Freshwater biodiversity is a key element of water security and a very significant conservation priority. The Hong Kong ecologist and biodiversity expert David Dudgeon and his colleagues (2006) list five interacting factors that threaten freshwater biodiversity: overexploitation, pollution, flow modifications, invasive species, and habitat degradation. Each of these factors is ubiquitous within the freshwater systems of Asia. A pervasive knowledge gap within Asia on the status of freshwater biodiversity further challenges conservation (Dudgeon et al. 2006).

Hotspots for freshwater biodiversity in the region include India's Western Ghats region, the world's most heavily populated biodiversity hotspot. Damming, mining, and quarrying modify natural flows, pollute water, and pose a significant and urgent conservation challenge for many endemic species. Another hotspot is Lake Biwa in Japan, which hosts over two thousand species (both terrestrial and aquatic). Climate change, pollution, and the introduction of exotic species challenge species conservation. The Greater Mekong-Lancang River basin in Southeast Asia is one of the most biodiverse places on Earth, hosting many rare, endemic, or endangered species. (Note: the portion of the river that flows in China is called the Lancang; the river, upon entering Cambodia, is called the Mekong). Habitat destruction, overfishing, wildlife trade, and the pressures induced by dams, road building, mining, and the effects of climate change threaten biodiversity here (WWF 2009).

East Asia

East Asia (including China with Macao and Hong Kong) is one of the most densely populated areas in the world, hosting some 22 percent of the global population. The region is one of great contrasts between desert and coast, drought and flood, and livelihoods ranging from subsistence agriculture to the industrial production of high-technology items for the global market. The needs and challenges of water management in the region are correspondingly diverse. In the arid zones of Mongolia, the spread of mining operations imposes heavy demands upon a relatively water-scarce region; in Japan, seasonal deluges of heavy rain and typhoons have serious human and economic costs.

With the globalization of food systems and global markets for other products, the state of water security in other countries affects individual nations if they are net water importers and affects other countries' demands by if they are net water exporters. Japan and South Korea are among the world's largest importers of virtual water (the water used to produce a good or service). Importing water-intensive goods helps Japan save some 134 billion cubic meters per year of its domestic water (Mekonnen and Hoekstra 2011). Market demands correspondingly challenge water-stressed regions. For example, virtual water flows from the relatively water-scarce north of China to the relatively water-secure south (Water Footprint Network 2012) in order to meet the demands originating from the latter region.

Large areas of East Asia, notably in Mongolia and China, are classed as drylands. Water is a primary limiting factor to biological processes in these regions. Climatic factors or mismanagement of land and water resources in drylands leads to desertification, manifested by soil erosion, declining groundwater stocks, and vegetation loss. Desertified areas closely overlap with areas of high poverty. People suffer from low availability of drinking water, lack of water for sanitation, and an inability to farm productively. Northern China suffers from particularly severe desertification (FAO 2011).

The environmental researcher Jungfeng Zhang and his colleagues describe how in China "[t]he heavily populated northern river basins contain 44 percent of the population and 65 percent of its cultivated land, but have less than 13 percent of the water supply . . . substantially less than the amount commonly defined as water scarcity" (Zhang et al. 2010, 1114). These regions provide a good example of how patterns of use, rather than purely climatic factors, determine water security. The Huang (Yellow) River basin, for example, contains only 2 percent of China's water resources but it supports some fifty cities and between 120 and 200 million people. It generated 16 percent of China's grain and 12 percent of its gross domestic product in 2000. In addition it was the site of water-intensive cotton cultivation, expanding mining operations, population growth, and industrialization (Cenacchi et al. 2011).

Heavy pollution threatens water security in the arid zones of eastern Asia. The 2003 Mongolian water census report prepared by the Mongolian Ministry of Nature and Environment implicates unsustainable gold mining operation in the contamination, diminishment, or total drying up of over three thousand freshwater bodies in the country (Centre for Human Rights and Development 2006). Aside from heavy water use, mining effluents significantly pollute the area (Byambaa and Todo 2011). Water pollution also poses an extremely severe and widespread challenge in China, affecting 40 percent of rural residents (more than 200 million people) and 6.2 percent of urban residents (46 million people), putting them at risk for problems related to unsafe drinking water and inadequate sanitation. Industrial pollution has caused some 11 percent of digestive system cancers (Zhang et al. 2010).

Southeast Asia

Although this region has relatively more abundant fresh water than parts of eastern Asia, rapid population growth and industrialization challenge water security. The Mekong Basin, for instance, doubled its population over the past forty years and industrialization is proceeding rapidly. The Mekong floods annually, which impacts Cambodia, Vietnam, Thailand, and Laos. Flooding has been unusually severe over the first decade of the twenty-first century. Flooding in 2011 damaged hundreds of thousands of homes, affecting some 700,000 residents in Vietnam (UNICEF 2011) and submerging some 63,000 homes and 170,000 hectares of rice in Cambodia (AlertNet 2011).

Periodic floods also affect Japan and the Philippines. Scientists expect that as the climate changes, the rates and intensity of flooding will change. Although experts have traditionally considered Japan a world leader in the development and use of disaster management plans to predict and manage floods, they are concerned about flood management. The Organisation for Economic Co-operation and Development (OECD) reviewed the risk management practices and policies of large-scale floods in Japan (OECD 2009). They expect Japan's vulnerability to flooding to grow because of its aging population, increasing population density in affected urban areas, and changes government decentralization, privatization, and regulatory reform bring to conventional flood management practices and policies.

India

India's water resources are in a state of deepening crisis. Population growth, urbanization, agricultural transitions involving more water-intensive crops, and industrial development raise water demand. Water pollution is a widespread challenge. A 2008 review by WaterAid describes how waterborne diseases annually affect an estimated 37.7 million people, kill 1.5 million children by diarrhea alone, and cause the loss of 73 million working days. The review estimates the economic burden to be $600 million a year (India Water Portal 2008).

These concerns have implications for food security, economic growth, and human and ecological well-being. India provides a particularly urgent example of the links between food and water security. Investment in irrigation and land and water management resulted in a tripling of food production between the 1960s and the 1990s (FAO 2011), but the country is still home to the largest number of hungry people in the world (FAO 2008).

The picture for hunger and food security therefore remains grave. Ensuring adequate water availability for food production is an ever-present and urgent priority. Although irrigated areas have provided previous increases in production, dryland, which constitutes the bulk of India's cropland areas, will need to supply further increases. Approximately 90 percent of India's cropland is located within the "water-limited tropics" (Milesi et al. 2010), and most of the country's agricultural land is cultivated under rainfed conditions. In these areas, people try to improve water security through soil and water conservation programs and the use of private wells, although the expansion of private wells has seen a drop in groundwater levels in some parts of India, which further exacerbates water insecurity in the region. The government has also promoted and spread water-harvesting and water-conserving technologies such as farm ponds and drip irrigation. Efforts to improve water security in the drylands have not always been sustainable. The Indian Planning Commission estimated aquifer abstraction in 2010 to be 210 billion cubic meters per year—the highest in the world and greatly in excess of recharge (India Water Portal 2010).

India is one of the world's largest net exporters of virtual water, but significant amounts of virtual water also move within the country through domestic trade or the state-run public distribution system. Like China, Indian states demonstrate a paradoxical pattern of virtual water trade, wherein relatively water-scarce states produce food or materials exported to relatively water-abundant states. This pattern maintains or exacerbates water insecurity in exporting states. "Nonwater factors" such as the food procurement patterns of the Food Corporation of India keep the system in place (Water Footprint Network 2012).

Managing Resources

Water management determines water security. East Asia, Southeast Asia, and India have a wealth of diverse traditional practices for water management. Some of these are still functional, others are being revived, and newer structures and policies meant to cater to more intensive water use have replaced some older ones. Traditional systems provide an excellent example of how water security can be managed relatively sustainably over a long period, but many have fallen into disrepair due to the collapse of the community-based institutions and the collective effort required to maintain and run them. India's Centre for Science and Environment documented traditional Indian systems in its seminal report *Dying Wisdom: The Rise, Fall and Potential of India's Traditional Water Harvesting Systems* (Agarwal and Narain 1997). The report triggered a nationwide interest in reviving traditional structures and implementing community-based water management in India.

India is increasingly recognizing integrated and community-based management strategies as key to ensuring water security in the region. From the early 1990s onward, the country has recognized that water security depends on both "integrated" land and water management as well as on the active and sustained involvement of communities themselves. Community involvement in programs tailored appropriately to the local context can yield significant impact. For example, a partnership between WaterAid, a local Indian nongovernmental organization, and local communities on a project to develop local water security plans ensures reliable access to some 13,000 people across fourteen villages (The Institution of Civil Engineers, Oxfam GB, and WaterAid 2011).

Alongside local, community-based initiatives, the entire region—especially India and China—also has huge centralized mechanisms such as large dam and canal projects for storing and allocating water. India, for example, had some four thousand large dams by the year 2000. China hosts almost half the world's large dams. Dam building—especially the construction of huge dams such as India's Sardar Sarovar Dam or China's Three Gorges Dam—is the subject of much controversy. Countries construct dams to cater to the intensive demands of commercial agriculture and a growing and industrializing population. They often have unequal impacts, however, and exacerbate water-related conflict across borders—an important challenge for managing water security in an increasingly water-constrained world. Dams also accentuate tensions between different uses of water. China built the Three Gorges project to generate hydropower. Damming the Yangzi (Chang) River has resulted in shortages for agriculture, however. The Yangzi Basin suffered a major drought in 2011, and the role of the Three Gorges Dam has been the subject of much debate. Scientists allege that water diverted toward hydropower generation compromises water availability for drinking, farming, and ecosystems. The following points summarize the impact of the dam (International Rivers 2009)

- Submergence and displacement: The dam submerges some 13 cities, 140 towns, and 1,350 villages and has displaced over 1.2 million people.
- Ecological factors: The Yangzi is Asia's longest river, and disrupting its natural flow and the pollution caused by submergence of settlements and factories has profoundly altered its ecology, especially in conjunction with existing challenges such as overfishing and pollution.
- Geological impacts: Massive impoundment of water has been implicated in the destabilization of the slopes of the Yangzi Valley and associated landslides and reservoir-induced seismicity.
- Downstream impacts: Deprives downstream regions of the silt carried by the river, with implications for agriculture, fisheries, and the integrity of the delta.

Transboundary water sharing arrangements are an important—and potentially contentious—instrument for ensuring countries' water security. Water from international rivers flowing through India and the countries of eastern and southeastern Asia has been the source of significant international conflict. Treaties and agreements between nations are designed to mitigate this conflict or arrange for transboundary water management. Important treaties in the region include the 1960 Indus Waters Agreement between India and Pakistan and the 1995 Mekong Agreement between Cambodia, Laos, Thailand, and Vietnam (for a full listing see Oregon State University [n.d.]).

Outlook

Investment in water security yields multiple benefits. A report on the status of water resources in Asia describes how "$1 invested in the water sector turns into $6" (Asian Development Bank 2006, 2). A range of government bodies, aid agencies, and nongovernmental organizations made considerable investments in the various dimensions of water management throughout the region. The area needs considerable further investment to ensure sustainable water security into the future. Given the centrality of water to all dimensions of ecological and human well-being, such investment will yield multiple benefits for wider sustainable development and for continued human well-being.

Zareen Pervez BHARUCHA
University of Essex

See also Agriculture (China and Southeast Asia); Agriculture (South Asia); Climate Change Migration (India); Education, Environmental (*several articles*); Fisheries (China); Five-Year Plans; Ganges River; Huang (Yellow) River; Mekong-Lancang River; Public Health; South–North Water Diversion; Three Gorges Dam; Transboundary Water Issues; Utilities Regulation and Energy Efficiency; Water Use and Rights (India); Yangzi (Chang) River

Further Reading

Agarwal, Anil, & Narain, Sunita. (1997). *Dying wisdom: The rise, fall and potential of India's traditional water harvesting systems.* New Delhi: Centre for Science and Environment.

AlertNet. (2011). Floods kill 158 in Thailand, 61 in Cambodia. Retrieved January 2, 2012, from http://www.trust.org/alertnet/news/floods-kill-158-in-thailand-61-in-cambodia/

Asian Development Bank. (2006). Asia water watch 2015: Are countries in Asia on track to meet Target 10 of the Millennium Development Goals? Retrieved January 2, 2012, from http://www.adb.org/documents/books/asia-water-watch/asia-water-watch.pdf

Byambaa, Bayarlkham, & Todo, Yasuyuki. (2011). Technological impact of Placer Gold Mine on water quality: Case of Tuul River Valley in the Zamaar Goldfield, Mongolia. *World Academy of Science, Engineering and Technology, 75,* 167–171.

Cenacchi Nicola; Xu, Zongxue; Yu, Wang; Ringler, Claudia; & Zhu, Tingju. (2011). Impact of global change on large river basins: Example of the Yellow River Basin (International Food Policy Research Institute discussion paper 01055). Washington, DC: IFPRI.

Centre for Human Rights and Development. (2006). Discussion paper for the national dialogue: Mining and human rights in Mongolia. Retrieved April 4, 2012, from http://www.rimmrights.org/Documents/final%20discussion%20paper%20amended%20CHRD%20(i).pdf

Dudgeon, David, et al. (2006). Freshwater biodiversity: Importance, threats, status and conservation challenges. *Biological Reviews of the Cambridge Philosophical Society, 81,* 163–182.

Food and Agriculture Organization (FAO). (2008). *The state of food insecurity in the world: High food prices and food security: Threats and opportunities.* Rome: FAO.

Food and Agriculture Organization (FAO). (2011). *The state of the world's land and water resources for food and agriculture: Managing systems at risk.* Rome: FAO.

India Water Portal. (2008). Drinking water quality in rural India: Issues and approaches: A background paper by WaterAid. Retrieved January 2, 2012, from http://www.indiawaterportal.org/node/798

India Water Portal. (2010). Water resources: Mid-term appraisal of the eleventh Five Year Plan: Report by the Planning Commission. Retrieved January 2, 2012, from http://www.indiawaterportal.org/node/12733

Institution of Civil Engineers, Oxfam GB, & WaterAid. (2011). *Managing water locally. An essential dimension of community water development.* Retrieved January 2, 2012, from http://www.wateraid.org/documents/managing_water_locally.pdf

International Rivers. (2009). China's Three Gorges Dam: A model of the past. Retrieved January 2, 2012, from http://www.internationalrivers.org/files/ThreeGorgesFactsheet.pdf

Mekonnen, Mesfin M., & Hoekstra, Arjen Y. (2011). National water footprint accounts: The green, blue and grey water footprint of production and consumption. (Value of water research report series no. 50, UNESCO-IHE). Delft, The Netherlands: Water Footprint Network. Retrieved January 2, 2012, from http://www.waterfootprint.org/?page=files/Publications

Milesi, Cristina, et al. (2010). Decadal variations in NDVI and food production in India. *Remote Sensing, 2*(3), 758–776.

Oregon State University, The Program in Water Conflict Management and Transformation. (n.d.). The transboundary freshwater dispute database. Retrieved April 1, 2012, from www.transboundarywaters.orst.edu

Organisation for Economic Cooperation and Development (OECD). (2009). OECD reviews of risk management policies: Japan, large-scale floods and earthquakes. Paris: OECD.

Pacific Institute. (2009). MDG progress on access to safe drinking water by region. Retrieved January 2, 2012, from http://www.worldwater.org/data20082009/Table5.pdf

United Nations (UN). (2010). The Millennium Development Goals Report, 2010. Goal 7: Ensure environmental sustainability. Retrieved April 3, 2012, from http://www.un.org/millenniumgoals/environ.shtml

United Nations Children's Fund (UNICEF). (2011). Mekong flooding causes widespread damage in Viet Nam. Retrieved January 2, 2012, from http://www.unicef.org/infobycountry/vietnam_60261.html

United Nations Children's Fund (UNICEF), & World Health Organization (WHO). (2012). Progress on drinking water and sanitation 2012 update. Retrieved April 6, 2012, from http://www.unicef.org/media/files/JMPreport2012.pdf

Vörösmarty, Charles J., et al. (2010). Global threats to human water security and river biodiversity. *Nature, 467,* 555–561.

Water Footprint Network. (2012). The water footprint of India. Retrieved January 2, 2012, from http://www.waterfootprint.org/?page=files/India

World Health Organization (WHO). (2012). Millennium Development Goal drinking water target met. Retrieved April 6, 2012, from http://www.who.int/mediacentre/news/releases/2012/drinking_water_20120306/en/

World Wide Fund for Nature (WWF). (2009). The Greater Mekong and climate change: Biodiversity, ecosystem services and development at risk. Retrieved January 2, 2012, from http://www.worldwildlife.org/climate/Publications/WWFBinaryitem15238.pdf

Zhang, Jungfeng, et al. (2010, March 27). Environmental health in China: Progress towards clean air and safe water. *The Lancet, 375*(9720), 1100–1119.

Water Use and Rights (India)

Water use is regulated by a number of laws, rules, and principles in India. These include rights of control asserted by the government and individual usufructuary (i.e., use rather than ownership) rights. Water use is also regulated through much broader pronouncements, such as the fundamental right to water. In recent years, water law reforms have introduced significant changes, including the establishment of water regulatory authorities and water user associations.

Water rights in India are complex, and laws and practices involving them have been fast evolving since the late twentieth century. These include a series of different, and sometimes contradictory, concepts and perspectives ranging from sovereign and individual appropriation of water to a prohibition of the ownership of water and the existence of a fundamental human right to water. The different rules and principles governing water use are found in a variety of contexts, including national law and laws specific to any of the states or union territories, high court and Supreme Court judgments, common law, and customary rules. Additionally, water is for the most part a state subject, and a significant part of the legal framework governing water use is thus developed by each individual state. The complexity of the system is accentuated by the fact that water law has developed for the most part in a sectoral manner. As a result, partly contradictory principles can coexist in different parts of the legal framework despite attempts by the Supreme Court to foster a sense of unity in water law by setting on paper some principles that are applicable everywhere for every water use. The lack of an overall single framework for water rights can also be attributed to the absence of a framework water law. In practice, this leads to a situation where there are still different rights concerning, for instance, groundwater and surface water in the same locality.

The discussion below briefly examines the different forms of control over water use in India and points out some of the ongoing reforms that are impacting rights related to water use.

State and Individual Control

The development of water use rights over time has been marked in India, as in a number of other countries, by two contradictory tendencies. On the one hand, in recognition of the special nature of water as a source of life, it has often been suggested that water cannot be owned. On the other hand, administrators understanding the importance of water have often tried to assert as much control as they could over its use. The dichotomy between these two opposed perspectives has also allowed the development of a series of individual rights over water, mostly of a usufructuary nature (i.e., use rights rather than ownership rights).

India's current framework for access to and control over water has been largely influenced by its colonial history, which had a significant impact in shaping various laws and principles that are still applied today. Two of the main forms of control that have been recognized in modern times are state control and individual rights.

State Control

Since at least the second half of the nineteenth century, the government has sought to justify its control over water as an extension of its sovereign control over all resources under its jurisdiction. This led to the assertion of control in the public interest in the late nineteenth century with the Canal and Drainage Act of 1873, which declared in its preamble the right of the government to "use and control for public purposes the water of all rivers and streams flowing in natural channels, and of all lakes." This later culminated in the assertion of full control, as for instance in the Madhya Pradesh Irrigation Act of 1931, which stated that "all rights in the water of any river, natural stream or natural drainage channel, natural lake or other natural collection of water shall vest in the Government" (section 26). Such absolute assertion of control can still be identified in the much more recent Bihar Irrigation Act of 1997, which restates word for word the provision of the 1931 act.

The case law also provides a continued reassertion of the controlling interest of the state over water. A relatively early decision of 1936 specifically indicated that the state had the sovereign right to regulate the supply of water in public streams (*Secretary of State v. PS Nageswara Iyer*, AIR 1936 Mad 923, Madras High Court, 1936). Much more recently, the Supreme Court has reaffirmed that "undoubtedly the state is the sovereign dominant owner" of water (*Tekaba AO v. Sakumeren AO* (2004) 5 SCC 672, Supreme Court of India, 2004). In the latter decision judges understand the power of the state as extending even where there are acknowledged customary norms that govern control over water.

Since the last decades of the twentieth century, challenges to the state's assertion of complete power over water have been raised. The most significant development in legal terms has been the assertion by the Supreme Court that all surface waters fall under the doctrine of public trust. Underlying the concept of public trust is the idea that the state holds certain resources in trust for the public because they are intrinsically valuable to the public and cannot be owned by any person. It also implies that the trustee has a fiduciary duty of care and responsibility to the general public. In the words of the Supreme Court, "the State is the trustee of all natural resources which are by nature meant for public use and enjoyment. Public at large is the beneficiary of the sea-shore, running waters, airs, forests and ecologically fragile lands. The State as a trustee is under a legal duty to protect the natural resources. These resources meant for public use cannot be converted into private ownership" (*MC Mehta v. Kamal Nath* (1997) 1 SCC 388, Supreme Court of India, 1996). The Supreme Court has since then extended in principle the scope of the application of the public trust to groundwater (*State of West Bengal v. Kesoram Industries* (2004) 10 SCC 201, Supreme Court of India, 2004).

The introduction of the doctrine of public trust to water is a significant step forward in curtailing the power of the state over water. Yet this has had no impact in practice beyond the specific decisions where courts have used this principle. Indeed, neither have individual states amended legislation that recognizes state ownership of water, nor have any of the many legislative enactments concerning water adopted since 1997 taken notice of this principle.

Individual Control

Individual entitlements over water include a variety of rights of access to water, rights to use water, or rights to use water-based resources such as fish. Most of these rights are linked to control over land, and as a result access to land has until recently been the main precondition for asserting water rights.

In certain cases landowners have been granted entitlements to appropriate water flowing past their land. This amounts to a usufructuary right to use a portion of the flow of a watercourse. Another type of individual entitlement concerns rights to use a specific quantity of water. This can take the form of a water license for designated uses, such as irrigation. These entitlements are usually linked to property rights in land. There is no right to the water itself but rather a right to a certain allocation of water, which may be conditioned by such factors as actual availability in a given year.

A different set of entitlements obtains in the case of groundwater. The distinction is due to the fact that groundwater has usually been considered separately from surface water. Since groundwater has a direct link to the land above, a link was established between ownership of the land and control, if not outright ownership, of the water found underneath the plot. While no specific groundwater legislation arose until the late 1990s, basic principles of access and control can be derived from the Indian Easements Act of 1882. Under these principles, landowners have easementary rights to collect and dispose of all water found under their land. There is thus an indissociable link between land ownership and control over groundwater.

In recent years, several states have adopted groundwater laws in response to the increasing depletion of groundwater. These laws reflect a model first proposed by the central government in 1970. From a water rights perspective, the main feature of these acts is that they do not address the crucial issue of groundwater rights. They keep the status quo intact and do nothing to ensure that groundwater regulation progresses toward twenty-first century concerns about the environmental sustainability of use and the inequitable access to groundwater resulting from the link with access to land, a resource that is controlled by a minority of people.

Fundamental Right to Water

The intrinsic link between water and survival makes water a central part of any catalog of fundamental human rights. Yet in practice, in India as in various other countries, the fundamental right to water remained unstated until the late twentieth century. While the Indian constitution still does not specifically recognize a fundamental right to water, courts have repeatedly affirmed and progressively delineated the broad contours of the right in three essential ways.

Firstly, the Supreme Court has repeatedly derived a human right to water from the right to life recognized at Article 21 of the Constitution (e.g., *Subhash Kumar v. State of Bihar*, AIR 1991 SC 420, Supreme Court of India, 1991).

Secondly, courts have also derived the human right to water from Article 47 of the Constitution (Duty of the state to raise the level of nutrition and the standard of living and to improve public health). In the Hamid Khan case of 1996, the complaint focused on the health consequences of the supply of water with excessive fluoride content. The Madhya Pradesh High Court found that under Article 47 the state has a duty "towards every citizen of India to provide pure drinking water" (*Hamid Khan v. State of Madhya Pradesh*, AIR 1997 MP 191, Madhya Pradesh High Court, 1996, para 6).

Thirdly, courts have found on repeated occasions that the human right to water includes a duty on the part of the state to provide water. This was, for instance, the case in the Hamid Khan decision. The same position has been restated in strong terms in *Vishala Kochi Kudivella Samarkshana Samithi v. State of Kerala* ((2006)(1), KLT 919, High Court of Kerala, 2006), where the High Court of Kerala stated that "we have no hesitation to hold that failure of the State to provide safe drinking water to the citizens in adequate quantities would amount to a violation of the fundamental right to life enshrined in Article 21 of the Constitution of India and would be a violation of human rights. Therefore, every Government, which has its priorities right, should give foremost importance to providing safe drinking water even at the cost of other development programmes" (para 3).

Overall in India at a broad level, the fundamental right to water is well structured and partly delineated in the case law. The actual entitlements that ensue from the recognition of this right are, however, not well determined in Indian law. This is mainly due to the absence of a broad-based drinking water legislation that would take forward the fundamental rights mandated at the legislative level.

Water Rights and Law Reforms

Since the beginning of the twenty-first century, there has been significant legislative activity related to water. Numerous new water laws have been adopted in various states of India. Most of these new laws, such as those providing for establishment of water user associations for irrigation, affect the water use rights of water users even though they may not address the issue of water rights directly.

Some laws, such as those providing for establishment of water regulatory authorities, have much more direct impact on water use rights. In the case of the Maharashtra Water Resources Regulatory Authority Act of 2005, the regulatory authority is thus specifically called upon to issue water entitlements and to set up criteria for trading these entitlements. This constituted a complete departure from the existing legal framework, which did not specifically provide for any trading of water rights independently of land rights.

Water law reforms are ongoing in most sectors of Indian law. Further important changes to the structure of water use rights in India can thus be expected in years to come. The rationale for nearly all the reforms taking place is a broad concern for the environment. Yet this concern about the environment is first narrowly focused on issues of water scarcity. Further, the actual laws that have been adopted in recent years do not integrate environmental concerns.

Philippe CULLET
University of London

See also Activism, Judicial; Agriculture (South Asia); Five-Year Plans; Gandhism; Ganges River; The Himalaya; Public Health; Rule of Law; Tibetan Plateau; Utilities Regulation and Energy Efficiency; Water Security

Further Reading

Briscoe, John, & Malik, R. P. S. (Eds.). (2007). *Handbook of water resources in India: Development, management and strategies.* New Delhi: The World Bank and Oxford University Press.

Cullet, Philippe. (2009). *Water law, poverty and development: Water sector reforms in India.* Oxford, UK: Oxford University Press.

Cullet, Philippe; Gowlland-Gualtieri, Alix; Madhav, Roopa; & Ramanthan, Usha. (Eds.). (2010a). *Water governance in motion: Towards socially and environmentally sustainable water laws.* New Delhi: Cambridge University Press.

Cullet, Philippe; Gowlland-Gualtieri, Alix; Madhav, Roopa; & Ramanthan, Usha. (Eds.). (2010b). *Water law for the twenty-first century: National and international aspects of water law reforms in India.* Abingdon, UK: Routledge.

Gulati, Ashok; Meinzen-Dick, Ruth; & Raju, K. V. (2005). *Institutional reforms in Indian irrigation.* New Delhi: Sage Publications.

International Environmental Law Research Centre. (IELRC). (n.d.). Water law documents: India documents. Retrieved February 26, 2012, from http://ielrc.org/water/docs.htm

Iyer, Ramaswamy R. (Ed.). (2009). *Water and the laws in India.* New Delhi: Sage Publications.

Joy, K. J.; Gujja, Biksham; Paranjape, Suhas; Goud, Vinod; & Vispute, Shruti. (Eds). (2007). *Water conflicts in India: A million revolts in the making.* New Delhi: Routledge.

Muralidhar, S. (2006). The right to water: An overview of the Indian legal regime. In Eibe Riedel & Peter Rothen (Eds.), *The human right to water* (pp. 65–81). Berlin: Berliner Wissenschafts-Verlag.

Pant, Niranjan. (2008). Some issues in participatory irrigation management. *Economic & Political Weekly, 43*(1), 30–36.

Planning Commission of India. (2007). Report of the expert group on groundwater management and ownership. New Delhi: Government of India Planning Commission.

Shah, Tushar. (2009). *Taming the anarchy: Groundwater governance in south Asia.* New Delhi: Routledge.

Singh, Chhatrapati. (1991). *Water rights and principles of water resources management.* Bombay, India: N. M. Tripathi.

Wagle, Subodh M., & Warghade, Sachin. (2010). New laws establishing independent regulatory agencies in the Indian water sector: Long-term implications for governance. *South Asian Water Studies, 2*(1), 49.

White Revolution of India

Dairy development programs in India have led the country to become the world's largest milk producer, provided sustainable livelihoods to more than 70 million smallholder dairy farmers, and evolved designs of farmers' institutions to manage resources. Called the White Revolution of India, these programs have increased milk production from about 22 million tonnes in 1970 to 121 million tonnes in 2010.

The White Revolution of India refers to the development programs and policy interventions that transformed India's dairy sector. In particular, it refers to Operation Flood, one of the first programs in the world to use food aid for development. Characterized by shortages and significant imports in the 1950s and 1960s, the dairy sector has transformed itself to a model of sustained growth and self-sufficiency. India's National Dairy Development Board developed the program in 1970 to provide a stimulus to milk production and enhance the livelihoods of millions of smallholder dairy farmers. Operation Flood has provided them assured access to urban markets through a cooperative institutional structure managed and controlled by farmers.

India's average dairy farmer owns one or two milk animals, cows or buffalo. The animals subsist on fodder derived primarily from common pool resources, such as pastures and irrigation systems that everyone uses but nobody owns, that is supplemented by crop residues and irrigated fodder. The farmers sell the surplus milk and use the dung as precious farm manure, a critical input to agriculture. The residues from one system become crucial inputs for the other. This system neither warrants a major shift in land use nor generates significant additional waste. Operation Flood is built on such sustainable low-external-input practices. Its institutional structure continues to evolve, which is a key for sustainability.

Farmer-managed cooperatives collect milk at the village level. District and state-level cooperatives pool, process, and market the milk. The cooperatives plow back valuable cash incomes on a daily basis. They also provide the farmers with services that improve the animals' productivity and enhance the quality and the mix of feed and fodder. These improvements, added to efficient and timely veterinary care, have increased production without placing additional demands on land resources or displacing other livestock population.

Of the 121 million tonnes of milk produced in the country every year, buffalo account for about 55 percent and cows, about 42 percent. Dairy cooperatives procure on an average 26 million kilograms of milk every day from about 15 million dairy farmers. They pay farmers an average daily cash income of about US$1.50, significant in a country where about 400 million live on less than a dollar a day (Government of India 2011). Whereas India has achieved near self-sufficiency in milk production and evolved an institutional model of farmer-managed institutions other countries could replicate, neighboring countries such as China, Pakistan, and Sri Lanka continue to import increasing quantities of dairy commodities to meet their milk demands.

The Design

The institutional model of the economic enterprise of dairying is nested within the social fabric of village life, which in turn is embedded within the threshold limits of the local ecosystems. The institutions have woven together the economic, social, and ecological domains of village life and energized collective action. Although built on the platform of dairying, the institutions are a model for other domains of village life.

Operation Flood designed principles of cooperation in the economic enterprise of dairying. It built a generation of rural entrepreneurs in millions of rural households in more than 140,000 villages. The process cut across caste, sex, and class barriers. The gradual and successful spread of the White Revolution through such institutions shaped dairying in India as "production by the masses" rather than "mass production." The White Revolution spread to about 20 percent of India's villages, although it did better in some parts of the country than others. It also built a sound and powerful alternative to government-controlled institutions. (See figure 1 below.)

By improving the quality of life for smallholder dairy farmers, the White Revolution has emerged as more than just a dairy development program. Because more than 75 percent of the 70 million milk producers are landless or have small and marginal landholdings (less than one hectare), dairying is an important source of livelihood for the poorest in the country (Shukla and Brahmankar 1999). Given that much of dairying is a household activity, women play an important role. Besides giving women the space for participation in decision making, it also provides them a direct access to cash incomes.

A Challenge and an Opportunity

The institutional design of dairy cooperatives and the rich experience of the White Revolution in India lend support to the strong case that has been made in academic literature in recent years that people are capable of regulating themselves and creating norms for governance that are most suited to local contexts. The political economist and 2009 Nobel laureate Elinor Ostrom argues that rational individuals forge social contracts in the form of institutions that, in turn, facilitate collective action and reduce transaction costs. Ostrom (2010) argues that there are no panaceas; market, state, and community must work in a synergetic arrangement appropriate to each particular society.

Figure 1. From a Drop to a Flood

Source: National Dairy Development Board archives.

This photograph shows the pooling of milk in a village cooperative.

This argument is especially relevant in light of the changed policy context that is today challenging India's dairy sector to innovate. The White Revolution came into being in a protected environment and one where the national demand for milk far exceeded supply. Since the 1990s government has withdrawn these protections, and the cooperatives face competition from private domestic and international players. The extent of freedom that governments have given farmers' institutions varies across locations. The political force of peoples' institutions created under the White Revolution helped engender the emergence of parallel legislation as well as new laws that allow member-controlled institutions to work with greater autonomy. In a country as vast as India, the White Revolution must reach many more smallholders to enable them to earn a livelihood from milk.

Outlook

Farmers need a plurality of institutions that evolve from an interplay between the ecological, social, and economic life of rural areas and help in judicious and economic use of resources. This interplay must emerge as the dominant vision to govern national and global landscapes and societies. A holistic approach to sustainability is vital. It is in interconnectedness, to the extent that people can fathom and comprehend, that humankind may find answers.

Amrita PATEL
National Dairy Development Board, India

See also Activism, Judicial; Agriculture (South Asia); Microfinance; Nongovernmental Organizations (NGOs); Public-Private Partnerships; Rural Development; Rural Livelihoods

FURTHER READING

Banerjee, Animesh. (1994). Dairying systems in India. *World Animal Review, 79*(2), 8–15.

Candler, Wilfred, & Kumar, Nalini. (1998). India: The dairy revolution; The impact of dairy development in India and the contribution of the World Bank. Washington, DC: The World Bank.

Government of India, Ministry of Finance. (2011). *Economic survey 2010–11*. New Delhi: Oxford University Press.

Ostrom, Elinor. (2010). Beyond markets and states: Polycentric governance of complex economic systems. *American Economic Review, 100*(3), 641–672.

Patel, Amrita. (2003). Smallholder dairying in India: Challenges ahead. Retrieved October 18, 2011, from http://www.fao.org/ag/againfo/programmes/en/pplpi/docarc/LL03.pdf

Rajendran, K., & Mohanty, Samarendu. (2004). Dairy co-operatives and milk marketing in India: Constraints and opportunities. *Journal of Food Distribution, 35*(2), 34–41.

Sharma, Vijay Paul, et al. (2003). Annex III: Livestock industrialization project: Phase II—Policy, technical, and environmental determinants and implications of the scaling-up of milk production in India. In Christopher L. Delgado, Clare A. Narrod & Marites M. Tiongco (Eds.), *Policy, technical, and environmental determinants and implications of the scaling-up of livestock production in four fast-growing developing countries: A synthesis*. Rome: FAO Corporate Document Repository.

Shukla, Rajesh K. & Brahmankar, S. D. (1999). *Impact evaluation of Operation Flood on rural dairy sector*. New Delhi: National Council of Applied Economic Research.

Uotila, M., & Dhanapala, S. B. (1994). Dairy development through cooperative structure. *World Animal Review, 79*(2), 16–22.

World Bank. (1997a). Implementation completion report: India Second National Dairy Project (Cr 1859-IN/Ln. 2893-IN, Report No. 16218, Agriculture and Water Operations Divisions, Country Department II, South Asia Region). Washington, DC: The World Bank.

World Bank. (1997b). The impact of dairying development in India: The Bank's contribution (Report No. 16848-IN, Operation Evaluation Department). Washington, DC: World Bank.

y

Yangzi (Chang) River

The Yangzi (Chang) River is the longest river in China. Approximately one-third of the population of China lives within the Yangzi River valley. The river floods, on average, every ten years. Almost half of the industrial sewage produced in China flows into the Yangzi, much of it untreated, polluting the river and leading to the apparent extinction of the Baiji dolphin and risking extinction of the Chinese river sturgeon.

The Yangzi (Chang) River is the longest river in China and one of the country's most important waterways. From its headwaters in the Tibetan Plateau, the Yangzi stretches eastward more than 6,276 kilometers before emptying into the Pacific Ocean near the industrial port city of Shanghai. Three thousand smaller tributaries feed the river, which covers a watershed of almost 1.8 million square kilometers. In its upper reaches the river flows through mountainous terrain marked by numerous rapids and gorges. After crossing through the Yangzi Gorges region (also known as the Three Gorges region), about 1,000 kilometers inland from the coast, the Yangzi becomes much wider and gentler for the remainder of its length.

More than 350 million people, around one-third of China's population, live within the boundaries of the Yangzi River valley. The river runs through many of China's largest cities, including Chongqing, Wuhan, and Nanjing. The Yangzi has been an important trade route for thousands of years. Oceangoing vessels can navigate it up to the Three Gorges region. An average of 170 cargo ships use the river each day (Chinese Embassy 2007). It also flows through many of China's most fertile and highly developed agricultural areas and provides irrigation for thousands of square kilometers of farmland. The floodplains in Jiangsu Province at the mouth of the Yangzi are an especially important center of rice production.

The Yangzi River valley has been prone to extensive flooding throughout China's recorded history. Major floods occur once every ten years on average. Devastating floods occurred in 1931 and 1954, both of which killed tens of thousands of people. China's recent economic development has compounded the problem. Not only has deforestation in the hinterland created significantly higher erosion levels, but many of China's new industrial centers have sprung up within the flood zone along the river's lower reaches. Despite government flood control efforts, the river flooded again in 1991 and 1998, causing significant property damage.

Three Gorges Dam

In an effort to solve the flooding problem and promote industrial development in the region, the Chinese government launched a mammoth hydroelectric dam project at the Three Gorges site. The Three Gorges Dam, completed in 2006 (but not officially opened until 2009), is the largest hydroelectric dam in the world. It has a total generating capacity of 18,200 megawatts of electricity and a 650-kilometer-long reservoir (Sample 2007).

The dam has a controversial history, however. Its construction relocated more than 1 million people and destroyed more than a thousand towns and villages, which disappeared under rising water levels. The dam has caused great environmental damage, as China's premier Wen Jiabao acknowledged in early 2011 (Watts 2011b). The dam has negatively impacted the downstream part of the river. Increased algae and pollution, both of which would otherwise have been flushed away, have formed downstream because of the dam. Two-thirds of the upstream sediment is prevented from going downstream by the dam each year. As a result of this, serious erosion problems are occurring downstream, and the river's delta is actually shrinking. The dam is blamed for increased seismic activity and landslides. Drought in the middle sections of the river, caused by the dam, has affected the drinking water of about 300,000 people (Sample 2007; Three Gorges Dam shrinking Yangtze delta 2007).

Environmental Issues

Industrial development along the Yangzi's banks has raised pollution levels. The river receives almost half of China's industrial sewage, much of which is untreated. Although the government announced a series of environmental protection measures in the 1980s and 1990s, more than 21 billion metric tons of industrial waste and sewage were discharged into the Yangzi in 2000. In addition to causing serious health problems for the region's inhabitants, the increased pollution levels also threatened several of the river's indigenous species, including the Baiji dolphin and the Chinese river sturgeon. In 2007, the Baiji dolphin, also called the Yangzi River dolphin, became officially extinct (Sample 2007).

China is building two more megadams, at Xiangjiaba and Xiluodu, on the Yangzi. The construction of these dams has further affected animal life, including fish, which were moved into a protected zone in the early 1990s in response to the Three Gorges Dam's construction. River traffic, damming, and overfishing have drastically reduced the number of fish downstream (Watts 2011a).

The Future

With the unknown effects of climate change on major rivers still leaving scientists questioning long-term problems, it is difficult to assess what the future holds for the river, especially in light of China's rapid industrial development (WWF 2009). Thirteen cities; 140 towns; 4,000 villages; and 100,000 acres of farmland were lost when the Three Gorges Dam was built. Yet some locals, who were relocated, have stated they were pleased to move. They were not happy at first, they said, but "we received generous compensation. And the government sent around representatives, who convinced us we would be better off. We would not go back to our old lives now" (Cole 2011). The area, for better or worse, is passing through a period of social transition, toward a vision of the future, and the dam is the star of the show (Cole 2011). The river and its delta is a major manufacturing center in China, and cities close to the river are booming. Intercity railways connect the cities, which have formed close ties with one another. The biggest city on the delta, which is also one of the biggest cities in the world, is Shanghai. A major expo was held there in 2010, promoting the city and region to the world (Wang 2009).

James H. LIDE
History Associates Incorporated

See also China; Climate Change Mitigation Initiatives (China); Education, Environmental (China); Energy Industries—Renewables (China); Fisheries (China); Huang (Yellow) River; Mekong-Lancang River; National Pollution Survey (China); Pearl River Delta; Property Rights (China); Public Health; Reforestation and Afforestation (Southeast Asia); Rural Development; Shanghai, China; South-North Water Diversion; Three Gorges Dam; Tibetan Plateau; Water Use and Rights (China)

This article was adapted by the editors from James H. Lide's article "Chang River" in Shepard Krech III, J. R. McNeill, and Carolyn Merchant (Eds.), the *Encyclopedia of World Environmental History*, pp. 208–209. Great Barrington, MA: Berkshire Publishing (2003).

FURTHER READING

Cannon, Terry, & Jenkins, Alan. (Eds.). (1990). *The geography of contemporary China: The impact of Deng Xioping's decade*. New York: Routledge.

Chao, Songqiao. (1994). *Geography of China: Environment, resources, population, and development*. New York: John Wiley.

Chinese Embassy, United States of America. (2007, December 6). Three Gorges Dam unleashes water to ensure shipping. Retrieved November 11, 2011, from http://www.china-embassy.org/eng/zt/sxgc/t387590.htm

Cole, Teresa Levonian. (2011, May 29). China's Yangtze cruise is a journey towards a vision of the future. *The Daily Telegraph*. Retrieved January 7, 2012, from http://www.telegraph.co.uk/travel/destinations/asia/china/8541827/Chinas-Yangtze-cruise-is-a-journey-towards-a-vision-of-the-future.html

Edmonds, Richard L. (1994). *Patterns of China's lost harmony: A survey of the country's environmental degradation and protection*. New York: Routledge.

Geping, Qu, & Jinchang, Li. (1994). *Population and the environment in China*. Boulder, CO: Lynne Rienner.

Leeming, Frank. (1993). *The changing geography of China*. Cambridge, MA: Blackwell.

Sample, Ian. (2007, August 8). Yangtze River dolphin driven to extinction. *The Guardian*, p. 13. Retrieved November 11, 2011, from http://www.guardian.co.uk/environment/2007/aug/08/endangeredspecies.conservation

Three Gorges Dam shrinking Yangtze delta. (2007, May 21). Retrieved January 7, 2012 from http://www.physorg.com/news98971115.html

Wang Zhenghua. (2009, October 9). A brighter future within reach for Yangtze River Delta. *China Daily*. Retrieved January 7, 2012, from http://www.chinadaily.com.cn/cndy/2009-10/09/content_8768458.htm

Watts, Jonathan. (2011a, January 18). Last refuge of rare fish threatened by Yangtze dam plans. *The Guardian*. Retrieved November 11, 2011, from http://www.guardian.co.uk/environment/2011/jan/18/fish-reserve-yangtze-dam

Watts, Jonathan. (2011b, May 20). China warns of "urgent problems" facing Three Gorges Dam. *The Guardian*, p. 24. Retrieved November 11, 2011 from http://www.guardian.co.uk/world/2011/may/20/three-gorges-dam-china-warning

World Wide Fund for Nature (WWF). (2009). What the Yangtze needs: The future of China's longest river. Retrieved January 7, 2012, from http://www.wwfchina.org/english/loca.php?loca=593

Index

A

Activism, Judicial, 2–7
China and, 3–4
Guangzhou Municipality Haizhu District Procuratorate v. Zhongmin Chen (2008), 4
Hongming Liu v. Shanghai Songjiang District Environmental Protection Bureau (2008), 3
India and, 4–5
Juan Antonio Oposa and Others v. the Honorable Fulgencio S. Factoran and another (1993), 5
M. C. Mehta v. Union of India (1984), 4
Metropolitan Manila Development Authority v. Concerned Residents of Manila Bay (2008), 5, 6
Philippines and, 5
Two Lakes and One Reservoir Administration v. Tianfeng Chemical Plant (2002), 3, 6
Vellore Citizen Welfare Forum v. Union of India (1996), 5
Agenda 21, 98
Agriculture (China and Southeast Asia), 8–12
China and, 9–10, 330
Indonesia and, 10–11
Malaysia, Vietnam, and Myanmar (Burma) and, 11–12
rice cultivation, 8–10, 11, 50, 244, 345
Agriculture (South Asia), 13–16, 167
air quality
particulate matter (PM), 30, 265
aquaculture, 152–153
Arisandi, Prigi, 347
Ecological Observation and Wetlands Conservation (Ecoton), 347
Association of Southeast Asian Nations (ASEAN), 18–21, 302
ASEAN Wildlife Enforcement Network (ASEAN-WEN), 19

Automobiles and Personal Transportation, 22–26
alternative fuels, 22
China and, 24
electric vehicles, 25, 26
India and, 23

B

Bamako Convention, 1991, 89
Basel Action Network (BAN), 88
Basel Ban Amendment, 1995, 89
Basel Convention of 1989, 88–89
Beijing, China, 28–33, 50, 266
2008 Olympic Games, 29, 30, 32, 75
Bhopal tragedy, 243
Bhutan
forest conservation in, 189
Biodiversity Conservation Legislation (China), 34–37
conservation and biodiversity management laws, 34–35
Biological Diversity Act (BDA), India, 2002, 172, 373
Biosafety Legislation (China), 38–40
quarantine of biological specimens, 35–36
Brundtland Report. See *Our Common Future*
Burma. See *Myanmar (Burma)*
bus rapid transit (BRT) systems. *See* **Public Transportation**

C

carbon dioxide (CO_2), 8, 19, 309
China and, 53, 65, 76, 276
emissions, xxiv, 24, 125, 309
See also greenhouse gasses (GHGs)

403

Central Electricity Regulatory Commission (CERC), India, 139, 140
    renewable energy certificates (RECs), 139
Chennai, India, 42–45
    flooding in, 44
China, 46–54
    1949 revolution of, 71, 286, 293, 295
    air quality, 30, 265
    cancer rates in, 264
    child labor, 75
    Chinese forest frog as pest management, 10
    displacement and resettlement in, 341
    flooding in, 49
    forest management in, 48, 158, 190, 285, 286–287
    Great Leap Forward of 1958–1961, 48, 156
    hydropower in, 131, 149, 354
    integrated pest management (IPM) in, 10
    Ministry of Agriculture, 38
    no-tillage farming in, 10
    population statistics of, 297
    See also specific subjects/headwords
China's Water Crisis. See Ma Jun
Chipko movement, India, xxvi, 165, 169, 243
Cities—Overview, 55–60
    pollution in, 58
    poverty issues, 56
    urbanization rates, 55
    See also individual cities
Climate Change Migration (India), 61–64
Climate Change Mitigation Initiatives (China), 65–69
common property resources/common pool resources (CPRs), 326, 329–330
Confucianism, 316, 317, 318, 369
    Confucian virtues *yi* and *li*, 74
    the *Mean*, 369
    the *Mencius*, 369
    See also Daoism; Mozi (philosopher); Xunzi (philosopher)
Confucius, 369
    See also Daoism; Mozi (philosopher); Xunzi (philosopher)
consumer product quality, 76
Consumerism, 70–73
Convention on Biological Diversity (CBD), 171
    biodiversity (definition of), 34
    megadiversity countries, 171–172
The Convention on International Trade in Endangered Species (CITES), 120
Corporate Accountability (China), 74–78

Bold entries and page numbers denote encyclopedia articles.

D

Dai Qing, 241, 355
Daoism, 316, 317, 370
    Laozi and Zhuang Zi, 370
    the Way, 370
Decade of Education (2005–2014), 109, 112, 113
deep ecology movement, 163
Delhi, India, 80–81
    clean water plumbing/pipes, 80
    the master plan, 80–81
    pollution of the Yamuna river, 80, 81
desertification, 72, 175, 327, 389
Dhaka, Bangladesh, 82–84

E

E-Waste, 86–91, 213–214
Ecotourism, 92–96
Education, Environmental (China), 97–103
Education, Environmental (India), 104–108
    historical water conservation, 104–105
Education, Environmental (Japan), 109–114
    Council for Outdoor and Nature Experiences (CONE), 112
    integrated study, 112–113
    Minamata City, 113
    nature experiences for children, 112
    nature schools, 112
Education, Female, 115–117
    China and, 116–117
    India and, 115–116
    National Policy for the Empowerment of Women (2001), India, 115–116
    Right to Education Act, 2010, India, 116
education for sustainable development (ESD), 98, 111, 112, 113
    See also Decade of Education (2005–2014)
Elvin, Mark. See *The Retreat of the Elephants: An Environmental History of China*
Endangered Species, 118–121
    Arabian oryx, 120
    critically endangered classification, 119
    extinct classification, 118
    extinct in the wild classification, 118
    extinction issues, 93, 118, 189, 345
    giant panda, 93, 120–121
    Père David's deer, 118–119
    Steller's sea cow, 119–120
energy efficiency. *See* **Utilities Regulation and Energy Efficiency**
Energy Industries—Nuclear, 122–129
    breeder reactors, 122, 125, 127–128
    China and, 125–126

India and, 125, 196
Japan and, 123–125, 143
levelized electricity cost (LEC), 123–124, 126
Pakistan and, 125
South Korea and, 123–125
Taiwan and, 123–125
See also Fukushima Daiichi Nuclear Power Plant
Energy Industries—Renewables (China), 53, 68, **130–137**
    Certified Emissions Reductions (CERs) credits, 134
    National Development and Reform Commission (NDRC), 132, 133, 134, 149, 157
    Renewable Energy Law (REL), 2005, 68, 132–133
Energy Industries—Renewables (India), **138–142**, 253
    electricity tariffs, 139
    energy policies, 139–140
    renewable energy certificates (RECs), 139
    renewable purchase obligations (RPOs), 139
Energy Security (East Asia), **143–150**
    demand-side management (DSM), 145–146
    natural disasters and, 145
    Nautilus Institute's Pacific Asia Regional Energy Security (PARES) project, 143
environmental rights
    nomadic people and, 322
environmental sustainability index (ESI), 226
European Enlightenment period, 8
European Union's Waste Electrical and Electronic Equipment (WEEE) Directive (2009), 88, 89
extended producer responsibility (EPR), 89, 212–213

F

feed-in-tariff (FIT) policies, 68, 133, 134, 140, 178, 179
Feynman, Richard P., 260
Fisheries (China), **152–155**
Five-Year Plans, **156–160**
    China and, 66–68, 98, 131, 133, 135, 150, 156–157
    India and, 157–158
Flavin, Christopher, 97
flooding. *See* **Public Health**; **Water Security**; *individual river, city, and country/region articles*
forest-fringe communities, 286
Forest Rights Act (FRA) of 2006, India, 285
Fukushima Daiichi Nuclear Power Plant, 53, 143, 146, 149, 225–226, 365

G

Gandhi, Indira (former prime minister of India), 105
Gandhi, Mohandas (Mahatma), 115, 162, 163, 198, 270
Gandhism, **162–163**, 270
Ganges River, **164–165**

Gender Equality, **166–170**
    natural disasters and, 169
Genetic Resources, **171–173**
    biopiracy, 36, 171, 373
    bioprospecting, 171, 173
    Nimura Genetic Solutions (NGS) (company), 172–173
    Nagoya Protocol, 171, 173
genetically modified (GM) crops, 244–245
    See also **Biosafety Legislation (China)**
genetically modified organisms (GMOs). *See* **Biosafety Legislation (China)**
Grain for Green program, China, 48
Great Green Wall (China), **174–176**
    State Forestry Administration (SFA), 174, 287
Green Collar Jobs, **177–180**
Green Revolution, 8–9, 12, 13–14, 15
green school movement, 99
greenhouse gas (GHG) emissions, 19, 24, 44, 53, 65, 130, 345
    compressed natural gas (CNG), 4–5, 81
    methane, 345
    nitrous oxide, 345
    See also carbon dioxide (CO_2)
Guangdong Province
    environmental legislation in, 4
    polluted rivers in, 291
Guangzhou, China, **181–186**
    Guangzhou Agenda 21, 181

H

haze pollution, 19–20
    Agreement on Transboundary Haze Pollution (ATHP), 20
heavy metal poisoning and pollution, 51, 164, 264, 266
The Himalaya, 94, 165, 196, 198, **188–192**
Hippocrates, 297
Huang (Yellow) River, **193–194**
    flooding and, 193–194
    reforestation and, 194

I

illiteracy rates of women, 116, 117, 168
Independent Development Monks' Movement, 346
India, **196–200**
    air quality, 4, 23
    forest management in, 199, 286
    population statistics of, 197, 297
    political participation of women in, 167
    See also specific subjects/headwords
Indian Patents Act (1970), 373
Indian Supreme Court, 4, 5, 81

Indigenous Peoples, 201–205
    conflicts in agriculture (southeast Asia), 203
    definition of, 201
    ethnic minorities (China), 202–203
    International Fund for Agricultural Development (IFAD), 1976, 203–204
    Muthanga incident, 202
    Sawit Watch, 203
    Scheduled Tribes (India), 202
Indonesia
    integrated pest management (IPM) in, 11
    See also **Southeast Asia**
Information and Communication Technologies (ICT), 206–216, 233
    Moore's law, 206, 212
    rural education and healthcare, 211
    rural manufacturing outsourcing, 210–211
International Organization for Standardization (ISO)
    ISO 14001, 113
International Union for Conservation of Nature (IUCN)
    IUCN Red List, 118–119, 361

J

Jakarta, Indonesia, 218–221
    air quality, 219–220
    bus rapid transit (BRT), 219–220
    Dutch settlers in, 218–219
    electronic road pricing (ERP) system, 220
    flooding in, 219
    Green Radio 89.2 FM, 220
    Mass Rapid Transit (MRT) Jakarta, 220
    Monsoon Vermont (company), 220
Japan, 222–226
    agriculture in, 222–223, 224
    e-waste recycling in, 88, 89
    Fukushima Daiichi Nuclear Power Plant, 123, 143, 225, 365
    Industrialism, 224
    pollution (industrial) in, 225
    reforestation in, 225
    See also specific subjects/headwords

K

Kani tribe of India, 373
Korean Peninsula, 228–231
    demilitarized zone (DMZ)
    e-waste in, 89–90
    Kim Dae Jung (president), 229
    See also specific subjects/headwords

Bold entries and page numbers denote encyclopedia articles.

Kuala Lumpur, Malaysia, 232–234
    Kuala Lumpur City Centre (KLCC), 232, 233
    Kuala Lumpur Plan 2020, 234
    Verandaways, 233
    See also **Malaysia**
Kyoto Protocol, 20, 280
    clean development mechanism (CDM), 134, 314

L

Labor, 236–240
    poor labor practices in China, 75–76
Laos
    hydroelectricity in, 19, 302
    See also **Southeast Asia**
Li Peng, 335

M

Ma Jun (environmental activist), 245
Maddison, Angus
    The World Economy: A Millennial Perspective, 325
Mahatma Gandhi National Rural Employment Guarantee Act, 2005, India, 63
Malaysia
    biodiversity and bioresources, 172
    public–private partnerships in, 302–303
    soil depletion and erosion, 11–12
    See also **Kuala Lumpur, Malaysia; Southeast Asia**
Malthus, T. Robert, 11
the Manchus, 46
Mao Zedong, xxv, 8, 71, 75, 156, 339
    Maoist era, 70, 174
mass rapid transit (MRT). *See* **Public Transportation**
Media Coverage of the Environment, 242–246
    26 Degree Campaign, 271
Mehta, M. C., 106, 165, 317
Mekong-Lancang River, 247–250, 379
    flood patterns and, 248–249, 390
    Mekong River Commission (MRC), 379
    river basin organizations (RBOs), 249
    Save the Mekong Coalition, 271
    Tonle Sap Lake, 248
Microfinance, 251–254
    Andhra Pradesh, 253
    Yunus, Muhammad, 251, 253
Millennium Development Goals
    safe drinking water, 388

Monsanto Company
    soy bean patents and biopiracy, 36
Mozi (philosopher), 369–370
    See also Confucianism
Mumbai, India, 57, **255–258**
    flooding and, 257
    Parinee I building, 257
Myanmar (Burma)
    soil quality in, 12
    See also **Southeast Asia**

N

Nanotechnology, 260–263
    China and, 261, 262
    India and, 261, 262
    Taiwan and, 261, 262
National Pollution Survey (China), 234–268
    air pollution, 265–266
    soil pollution, 266–267
    water pollution, 264–265
Nguyen Dinh Xuan (legislator), 347
Nongovernmental Organizations (NGOs), 269–272
    China and, 77, 100, 270–271
    Friends of Nature, 6, 100, 242
    Green Watershed (Luse Liuyu) (China), 270–271
    India and, 270
    Narmada dam movement (Narmada Bachao Andolan) (India), 270
non-profit organizations
    Center for Legal Assistance to Pollution Victims (CLAPV), China, 322
nuclear energy. *See* **Energy Industries—Nuclear**

O

One-Child Policy, 49, 166, **274–277**
Operation Flood. *See* **White Revolution of India**
Ostrom, Elinor (Nobel laureate), 397
Outsourcing and Offshoring, 208, **278–282**
    A.T. Kearney index, 278–279
    China and, 208, 210
    foreign direct investment (FDI), 278, 279
    India and, 208, 209
    rural outsourcing, 210, 211
Our Common Future, 98, 329

P

Pakistan. *See under* **Energy Industries—Nuclear; Public Transportation**
Parks and Preserves, 284–288
    China and, 285, 286–287

    India and, 284–285, 286
    protected forest (PF), 284
    reserved forest (RF), 284
payments for ecosystem services (PES), 314
Pearl River Delta, 289–292
    fish population decline, 290, 291
    fishing moratorium, 291
    salinization of, 291
People's Republic of China (PRC). *See* China
Philippines. *See under* **Activism, Judicial**
pollution. *See* haze pollution; heavy metal poisoning and pollution; **National Pollution Survey (China)**
    See also specific subjects/headwords
Phra Prajak Khuttajitto (Buddhist monk), 346
Property Rights (China), 293–295
Public Health, 296–301
    flooding and, 299
    natural disasters and, 299
    pollution, 298
    respiratory diseases, 298
    tuberculosis (TB), 298
Public-Private Partnerships, 302–304
    AT Biopower, 303
    crab condominiums, 304
    Landfill Gas and Waste-to-Energy Project, 303
Public Transportation, 305–310
    bus rapid transit (BRT), 309
    China and, 306
    India and, 305–306
    Pakistan and, 306
    Sri Lanka, 306
    Thailand and, 306
    See also individual city articles

R

red tides, 50, 290
Reforestation and Afforestation (Southeast Asia), 312–315
    assisted natural regeneration (ANR), 313
    community involvement in, 313–314
    framework species method (FSM), Thailand, 313
    rainforestation farming (RF), the Philippines, 313
    reducing emissions from deforestation and forest degradation (REDD+), 314
Religions, 316–319
    See also Confucianism; Daoism
The Retreat of the Elephants: An Environmental History of China, 101
Rio Earth Summit (1992), 99–100, 111
rubber plantations, 11, 249, 344
Rule of Law, 320–323

Rural Development, 324–327
 China and, 324–325
 common pool/property resources (CPRs), 326, 329–330, 396
 India and, 325–327
 township and village enterprises (TVEs), 52, 325, 330
 tragedy of the commons, 324
Rural Livelihoods, 328–330
 development intervention, 329
 National Rural Livelihood Mission (NRLM), 2011, India, 330

S

Sardar Sarovar dam, India, 119, 244, 270
 A Narmada Diary, 244
 See also **Three Gorges Dam**
Sen, Amartya (economist), 329
Shanghai, China, 332–335
 Dongtan eco-city, 333
 World Expo 2010, 59, 333–334
Singapore, 336–338
 electronic road pricing (ERP) system, 337
 water industry, 337
State Environmental Protection Agency (SEPA), China, 98, 287
slash-and-burn agriculture, 20, 203, 243
South China Sea, 153
South–North Water Diversion, 339–342, 355
Southeast Asia, 343–348
 dam construction in, 346
 flooding in, 390
 greenhouse gases (GHGs) in, 345
 Mattel's impact on, 347
 tree ordaining by monks, 346
Sri Lanka. *See under* **Public Transportation**
State Electricity Regulatory Commissions (SERCs)
 China and, 132, 133
 India and, 139, 383
The State of World Fisheries and Aquaculture, 152
Steel Industry, 349–352
 Baosteel short slag treatment technology (BSSF), 350
 Finex technology, 350
 World Steel Association (WSA), 350
sulfur dioxide (SO_2)
 desulfurization, 52, 53, 145
 See also greenhouse gas (GHG) emissions
Sundarbans delta, India, 62
swidden agriculture. *See* slash-and-burn agriculture

Bold entries and page numbers denote encyclopedia articles.

T

Taiwan. *See under* **Energy Industries—Nuclear; Nanotechnology**
Thailand. *See under* **Public Transportation; Utilities Regulation and Energy Efficiency**
 See also **Southeast Asia**
Three Gorges Dam, 354–357, 391, 400–401
 flooding and, 355
 See also Sardar Sarovar dam, India
Tibetan Plateau, 358–362
Tokyo, Japan, 363–365
Traditional Chinese Medicine (TCM), 366–368
 bear bile harvesting, 347, 367
 species management, 35
Traditional Knowledge (China), 369–371
 I Ching (*Yijing*), xxv, 317, 369
 the *Lushi Chunqiu*, 370
 Mandate of Heaven, 369
 See also Confucianism; Daoism
Traditional Knowledge (India), 372–374
 Traditional Knowledge Digital Library, 373
Transboundary Water Issues, 375–380
 climate change impacts and, 378
 integrated water resources management (IWRM), 378–379
 the hydrological cycle and, 376

U

United Nations Conference on Environment and Development, 1992. *See* Rio Earth Summit
United Nations Conference on the Human Environment in Stockholm, 1972, 105, 158
United Nations Decade of Education for Sustainable Development (2005–2014). *See* Decade of Education
United Nations Declaration on Indigenous Peoples, 372
United Nations Environment Programme (UNEP), 88
 Recycling: From E-waste to Resources, 88
United Nations Framework Convention on Climate Change (UNFCCC), 61
United States
 environmental policies in, 321
 National Environmental Policy Act, 1970, 321
Utilities Regulation and Energy Efficiency, 382–386
 Bureau of Energy Efficiency (BEE), 383, 384
 China and, 382–383
 energy efficiency requirement (EE/DSM Rule), 382–383, 386
 India and, 383–384

Power Development Plan (PDP), 385
Thailand and, 384–385
Top 1,000 Enterprises Program, 66, 67, 157

V

Vietnam
    integrated pest management (IPM) in, 12
    rice cultivation in, 11–12
    See also **Southeast Asia**
virtual water, 337, 389, 391
Vision 2020, 18, 20

W

Water Security, 388–392
    East Asia and, 389–390
    flooding and, 390
    freshwater biodiversity, 389
    India and, 390–391
    Southeast Asia and, 390

Water Use and Rights (India), 393–395
    individual control, 393, 394
    legal rights, 394–395
    state control, 393–394
White Revolution of India, 396–398
World Health Organization (WHO), 296
    air quality standards, 23, 30, 159, 298
World Trade Organization (WTO), 177–178, 230
World Wide Fund for Nature (WWF), 99, 361
    See also **Nongovernmental Organizations (NGOs)**

Y

Yangzi (Chang) River, 10, 339, 391 **400–402**
    Baiji dolphin (extinction of), 119, 401
    flooding and, 50, 356, 400
    pollution of, 50
Yangtze! Yangtze! See Dai Qing

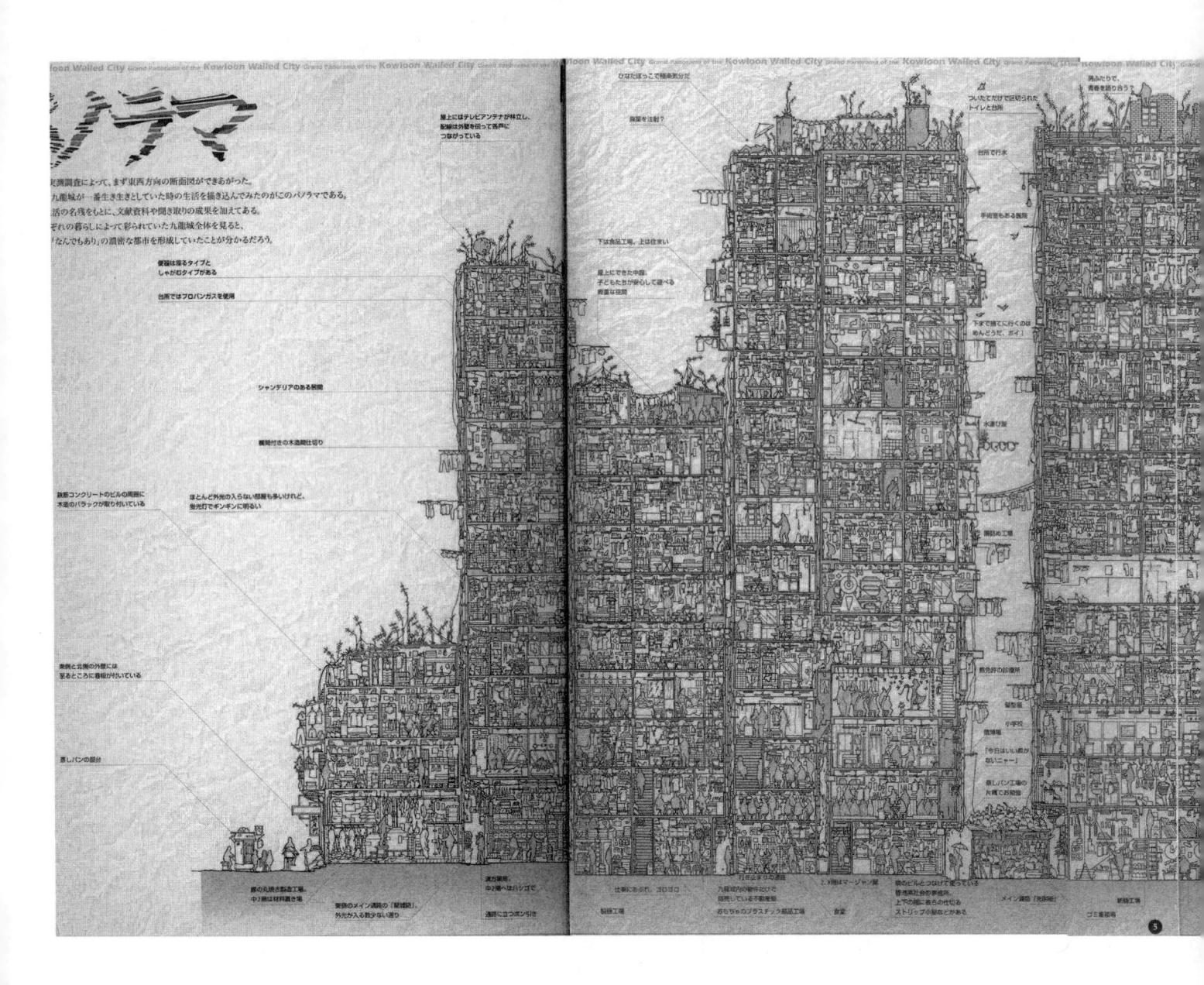

This image, titled "Grand Panorama of the Kowloon Walled City," is a schematic diagram of the Kowloon section of Hong Kong, as recorded by a Japanese team shortly before the demolition of the walled city. Retrieved from the Zoohaus website at http://zoohaus.net/WP/?p=4872.

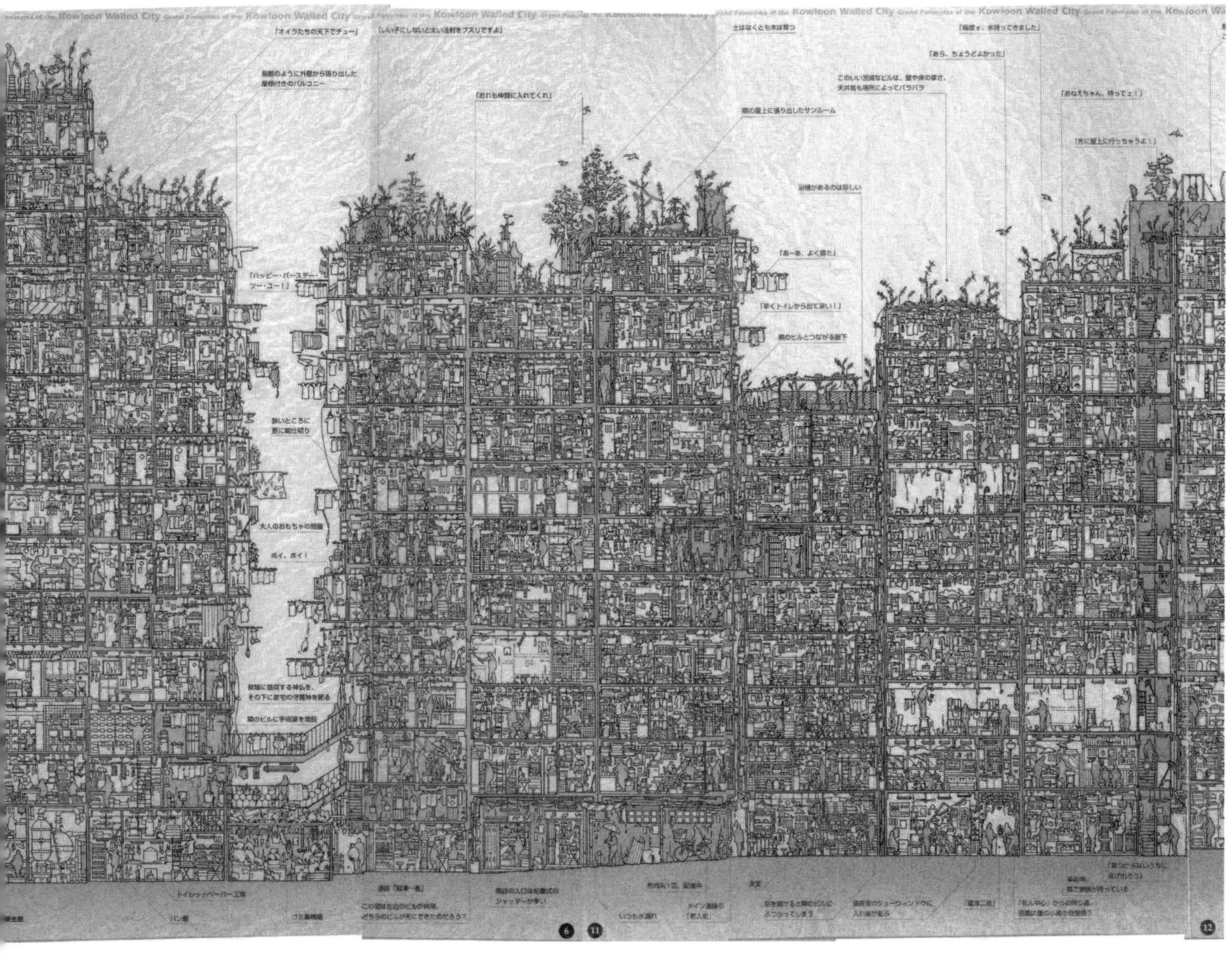
Grand Panorama of the Kowloon Walled City
「オイラたちの天下でチュー」
鳥籠のように外壁から張り出した
屋根付きのバルコニー
「ハッピー・バースデー・
ツー・ユー！」
狭いところに
更に間仕切り
大人のおもちゃの問屋
ポイ、ポイ！
隣のビルに手術室を増設
「いい子にしないと太い注射をブスリですよ」
「おれも仲間に入れてくれ」
土はなくとも木は育つ
隣の屋上に張り出したサンルーム
浴槽があるのは珍しい
「あ～あ、よく寝た」
「早くトイレから出て来い！」
隣のビルとつながる廊下
このいい加減なビルは、壁や床の厚さ、
天井高も場所によってバラバラ
「あら、ちょうどよかった」
「おねえちゃん、待ってェ！」
「先に屋上に行っちゃうよ！」
トイレットペーパー工場
パン屋
ゴミ集積場
この壁は左右のビルが共用。
どちらのビルが先にできたのだろう？
商店の入口は蛇腹式の
シャッターが多い
いつも水漏れ
メイン通路の
「老人街」
窓を開けると隣のビルに
ぶつかってしまう
「見つからないうちに
逃げ出そう」
「老人中心」からの帰り道、
話題は誰の小鳥の自慢話？